JOURNAL OF MONEY, CREDIT AND BANKING

February 1990

ARTICLES

Inflation and Taxation with Optimizing Governments
James M. Poterba and Julio J. Rotemberg

Optimal Advice for Monetary Policy
Susanto Basu, Miles S. Kimball, N. Gregory Mankiw, and David N. Weil

The Influence of the Federal Advisory Council on Monetary Policy
Thomas Havrilesky

The Value of Time and the Transactions Demand for Money *Kevin Dowd*

Economic Forecasts, Rationality, and the Processing of New Information over Time *Steve Swidler and David Ketcher*

A Multicountry Characterization of the Nonstationarity of Aggregate Output *Roger C. Kormendi and Philip Meguire*

Returns to Scale and Input Substitution for Large U.S. Banks
Athanasios G. Noulas, Subhash C. Ray, and Stephen M. Miller

NOTES, COMMENTS, REPLIES

The Forerunners of "New Monetary Economics" Proposals to Stabilize the Unit of Account *A Note by Scott Sumner*

Market Discipline and Bank Subordinated Debt
A Note by Gary Gorton and Anthony M. Santomero

(continued on back cover)

Manuscripts should be submitted in triplicate to the Editors, *Journal of Money, Credit, and Banking*, Department of Economics, Ohio State University, 1945 North High Street, Columbus, Ohio 43210–1172. Carolyn South, Secretary to the Editors. Submission fee: individual subscribers U.S. $30; nonsubscribers U.S. $40. Checks are to be made payable to The Ohio State University –JMCB and enclosed with submitted manuscripts. Instructions for preparing text and illustrations appear in the February issue.

JOURNAL
OF MONEY, CREDIT
AND BANKING

VOLUME 22 NUMBER 1 FEBRUARY 1990

ARTICLES

Inflation and Taxation with Optimizing Governments
James M. Poterba and Julio J. Rotemberg 1

Optimal Advice for Monetary Policy
Susanto Basu, Miles S. Kimball, N. Gregory Mankiw, and David N. Weil 19

The Influence of the Federal Advisory Council on Monetary Policy
Thomas Havrilesky 37

The Value of Time and the Transactions Demand for Money *Kevin Dowd* 51

Economic Forecasts, Rationality, and the Processing of New Information over Time *Steve Swidler and David Ketcher* 65

A Multicountry Characterization of the Nonstationarity of Aggregate Output *Roger C. Kormendi and Philip Meguire* 77

Returns to Scale and Input Substitution for Large U.S. Banks
Athanasios G. Noulas, Subhash C. Ray, and Stephen M. Miller 94

NOTES, COMMENTS, REPLIES

The Forerunners of "New Monetary Economics" Proposals to Stabilize the Unit of Account *A Note by Scott Sumner* 109

Market Discipline and Bank Subordinated Debt
A Note by Gary Gorton and Anthony M. Santomero 119

BOOK REVIEWS

Toward of World of Economic Stability: Optimal Monetary Framework and Policy, edited by Yoshio Suzuki and Mitsuaki Okabe
Reviewed by Michael M. Hutchison 129

Money, Interest, and Banking in Economic Development by Maxwell Fry *Reviewed by Wassim Shahin* 131

JOURNAL OF MONEY, CREDIT, AND BANKING (ISSN 0022-2879). Published quarterly in February, May, August, and November by the Ohio State University Press, 1070 Carmack Road, Columbus, Ohio 43210. Margaret Starbuck, Managing Editor; Peg Carr, Production Editor; Tom Kangas, Subscriptions Manager. Second-class postage paid at Columbus, Ohio, and at additional mailing offices. *Postmaster:* Send address to: *Journal of Money, Credit, and Banking*, Ohio State University Press, 1070 Carmack Road, Columbus, Ohio 43210.

SUBSCRIPTIONS. Individual: U.S. $27.50 per year; library: U.S. $45; student: U.S. $20.00; additional subscriptions to the same address: U.S. $20.00 per subscription. Postage outside the United States: add $5.00 per year. Sponsoring Subscriptions: U.S. $1000 per year. Sustaining Subscriptions: U.S. $500 per year. Supporting Subscriptions: U.S. $100 per year. Claims for missing issues must be made within four months of the date of publication. Allow six weeks for address change. Checks should be made payable to the Ohio State University Press, 1070 Carmack Road, Columbus, Ohio 43210.

BACK ISSUES, REPRINTS, AND MICROFILM. Most back issues from 1983 to the present are available from the Ohio State University press. Microfilms of back volumes and reprints of articles may be obtained from University Microfilms International, 300 North Zeeb Road, Ann Arbor, Michigan 48106. Back volumes from 1969 through 1982 in reprint edition may be obtained from Schmidt Periodicals GmbH, Dettendorf, D-8201 Bad Feilnbach 2, West Germany.

first consider the case where commitment is possible, then examine how the absence of commitment affects the results.

The government's objective is to minimize the expected total cost of raising revenue, given by

$$W(t) = E_t \sum_{j=0}^{\infty} \rho^j k \left[h(\theta_{t+j}) - v\left(\frac{P_{t+j-1}}{P_{t+j}}\right)\right] \quad (1)$$

where ρ is a discount factor, θ_t *equals the ratio of taxes to income (a tax rate)* in period t, and P_t is the price level. We assume that $k(\ )$ is a monotone increasing function while $h(\ )$, the tax distortion, is increasing and convex.

The increasing and concave function $v(\ )$ gives the benefits from deflation so that the costs of inflation are $-v(\ )$. This function is not just intended to capture the distortionary effects of inflation on the demand for money, as in Drazen (1979), Phelps (1973), Kimbrough (1986), and Lucas (1986). Instead, it reflects the many possible consequences of inflation enumerated by Fischer and Modigliani (1978).[4] In particular, the government might be concerned with the distributional consequences of inflation as well as with the difficulties inflation introduces in a world with pervasive nominal contracts.

The government's budget constraint is described by the evolution of real government debt, b_t:

$$\mathrm{b}_t = [b_{t-1}(1+i_{t-1}) + m_{t-1}]\frac{P_{t-1}}{P_t} + g_t - \theta_t y_t - m_t \quad (2)$$

where m_t, g_t, and y_t denote real money balances, real government spending, and real income, respectively. The nominal interest rate is i_t. We treat government spending as exogenous, but allow real income to depend on the tax rate. Real money balances and the nominal interest rate at t depend on anticipated inflation between t and t+1.[5]

The Commitment Case

Suppose the government chooses a tax schedule which specifies payments as a function only of past actions. Absent reputational effects, such a government will regard all taxes as nondistortionary. While there are distortions from *anticipation* of these taxes, they do not influence the government's ex post actions. A rather different situation arises when the government chooses taxes which specify payments as functions of current or future decisions. Such a government's choice of tax instruments may be guided by considerations of excess burden. At

[4]Because we consider relatively many effects of inflation, there is no presumption, as in the more narrow models of Kimbrough (1986) or Faig (1987), that the optimal tax rate on money is given by the Friedman rule. This presumption actually disappears as soon as money services are not viewed as perfect substitutes for other arguments in the utility function (see Romer 1987).

[5]Real money balances could also depend on income and taxes without altering our substantive conclusions, although for simplicity we ignore these effects through most of our analysis.

least in the United States, we routinely take government commitment regarding tax rates for granted. Income tax schedules are often legislated several years in advance. This commitment is in part the result of time lags in the legislative process.

Monetary policy differs from fiscal policy in several important ways. First, the Federal Reserve can react quickly to changed circumstances: time lags are shorter. Second, the Fed announces its intentions about future policy only in very broad terms. There is no counterpart to the publication of future tax tables. Verifying breaches of commitment by the central bank is therefore much more difficult than identifying similar breaches by the tax authority. These considerations do not imply that commitment by the monetary authorities is impossible. Reputational forces might be strong enough to ensure that the money supply always remains on the agreed-upon path. Whether central banks can commit to future actions is therefore an emprical matter.

Optimal policies with commitment can be modeled by allowing the government, which maximizes (1) subject to (2) at time t, to pick a contingency plan for tax rates and, by choosing future money supplies, for prices at $t+1$. This plan, which allows taxes and inflation to depend on the realizations of all $t+1$ variables including g_{t+1} and y_{t+1}, is chosen before households choose their money holdings. Thus, real money demand and interest rates are determined after the government chooses the next period's taxes and inflation. The government choosing taxes and inflation for period $t+1$ takes as given the end-of-period stock of government liabilities, $b_t + m_t$. The stock of liabilities is the only state variable for the government's problem, the sole channel through which policy choices in period t affect future values of money demand, prices, and output. The division of these liabilities between money and bonds, however, depends on the government's decisions in period t.

Holding constant the end-of-period stock of liabilities $b_t + m_t$, altering inflation between periods t and $t+1$ and taxes in period $t+1$ only affects interest rates and real money demand in period t and output in period $t+1$.[6] These shifts leave the path of government revenue unchanged, so at the optimum they cannot affect the government's welfare. Formally, equation (2) implies that the differential change in the tax rate θ_{t+1} that raises enough revenue to offset a change in (P_t/P_{t+1}) holding constant the level of government liabilities at the end of period $t+1$ is

$$y_{t+1}(1+\epsilon_\theta)d\theta_{t+1} = \left[-m_t + (R - P_t/P_{t+1})\frac{dm_t}{d(P_t/P_{t+1})}\right]d\left(\frac{P_t}{P_{t+1}}\right) = -m_t(1+\eta)d\left(\frac{P_t}{P_{t+1}}\right) \quad (3)$$

[6]Inflation in period $t+1$ is defined as the change in the price level between t and $t+1$.

2. THE EMPIRICAL RELATIONSHIP BETWEEN INFLATION AND TAXES

This section evalutes the model of the previous section by examining the relationship between taxes and inflation in several nations and over several time periods.[9] We first consider the empirical counterpart of equation (4), which is valid with commitment.[10] Mankiw (1987) estimates an equation similar to this on postwar U.S. data. We also estimate the empirical counterpart of (6), the first-order condition that holds without commitment.

To estimate the first-order condition implied by government optimization, we must specify functional forms for $h(\ )$ and $v(\ )$, the deadweight losses due to taxation and inflation respectively. We assume constant elasticity functions so that our objective function is a generalization of the CES welfare function: $h(\theta_t) = \kappa_1 \theta_t^{\alpha+1}$ and $v(P_{t-1}/P_t) = \kappa_2 (P_{t-1}/P_t)^{1-\beta}$, for κ_1, κ_2, α and β positive constants. This implies that (4) can be written as

$$\ln(P_t/P_{t-1}) = \gamma_0 + \gamma_1 \ln(\theta_t) + \gamma_2 \ln(m_{t-1}/y_t) \qquad (7)$$

where $\gamma_1 = \alpha/\beta$ and $\gamma_2 = 1/\beta$. This specification relaxes Mankiw's (1987) assumption that the ratio of m_{t-1} to y_t is constant.

If the functions $h(\ )$ and $v(\ )$ were literally time-invariant and correctly specified, equation (7) would hold without error. This literal version of our model is easy to reject. We are not, however, interested in testing the proposition that the theory can explain the exact relationship between taxes and inflation, but in exploring whether the theory can explain a substantial fraction of the movements in these series. We therefore test the prediction that higher taxes tend to be associated with higher inflation by simply adding an error term, ϵ_t, to (7) and estimating the resulting equation for several countries.

Our estimation employs annual data for five countries: the United States, Britain, France, Germany, and Japan. Our analysis is confined to taxes levied by the central government, since this is the level of government choosing monetary policy. Price indices, measured using consumer prices in each country, are annual average values. The stocks of money and debt are measured as midyear values or yearly averages. Since both inflation and the tax rate are highly persistent, ordinary-least-squares estimation of (7) would recover the trends in the two series. We therefore add a time trend to (7) and estimate the resulting equation allowing for residual autocorrelation, or we difference (7) and estimate the resulting specification by ordinary least squares.[11]

We begin by analyzing the time series evidence for the United States, using two measures of the tax rate θ_t. The first is the ratio of federal government tax receipts

[9]Under our assumption that the Fisher hypothesis holds, the empirical results do not depend on whether inflation or the nominal interest rate is used as the dependent variable. Mankiw (1987) found similar results in the United States time series using both dependent variables.

[10]It is also valid in a world without commitment if the government has access to taxes on bonds.

[11]Table 5 also reports instrumental variables estimates.

to GNP, each measured as flows during the calendar year. If the government chooses its mix of tax instruments optimally, then the ratio of taxes to GNP is a summary statistic for the degree of tax distortion. This is a crude tax *rate*, and it is available for a long time period. The second measure of the tax burden is the weighted average marginal tax rate on labor income computed by Barro and Sahasakul (1986). Their tax measure, including both federal income and Social Security taxes, is available for the 1916–1985 period. Data limitations restricted our sample period to begin in 1890, even when we use T/GNP for our tax measure.[12]

The results of estimating equation (7) for a variety of different sample periods are shown in Table 1. The tax rate is positively correlated with the inflation rate for all the sample periods, but the strength of this correlation is strongest for the post–World War II period. For the entire 1891–1986 period, a ten-percentage-point increase in the share of taxes in GNP predicts a one-half of one-percentage-point increase in the inflation rate. The tax rate and trend, however, explain less than 6 percent of the variation in inflation rates. The estimates in the AR(1) with trend and the differenced equations are similar, with slightly larger effects of the tax rate on inflation in the latter equations. For the period since 1919 but excluding World War II, the coefficient estimates are close to those for the full sample, although now the null hypothesis of no tax effect on inflation cannot be rejected at standard levels.

This conclusion is reversed when the sample is restricted to the postwar period. A 10 percent of GNP increase in taxes now raises the inflation rate by approximately 3.4 percent, and the impact coefficient is estimated much more precisely than for the longer sample periods. When the Barro-Sahasakul marginal tax rate series is used in place of the tax-to-GNP ratio, the estimated inflation effect of a tax increase is smaller. A ten-percentage-point rise in the marginal tax rate raises the inflation rate by just under two percentage points.

The coefficient on $\log(m_{t-1}/y_t)$ in the full sample equations in Table 1 is negative, although the null hypothesis that it is zero cannot be rejected at standard confidence levels. Since the coefficient on this variable is $1/\beta$, the negative estimate is inconsistent with the theory underlying equation (7). The negative parameter estimates are apparently due to the prewar sample since the estimates for the post–World War II period suggest a positive effect of the money-to-income ratio on the inflation rate. The same coefficient pattern, negative in longer samples and positive for the postwar period, emerges in both the AR(1) and the differenced esimates.[13]

[12]The Consumer Price Index for the United States is reported in *Historical Statistics of the United States*, and was updated using the *Economic Report of the President*. The money stock is the stock of high-powered money, reported in Friedman and Schwartz (1982, Table 4.8). The interest rate is the nominal call money rate, again as reported in Friedman and Schwartz with updates by the authors. Government debt is measured as the publicly held stock of government debt on July 1 of each year, as reported in Federal Reserve Board, *Banking and Monetary Statistics*.

[13]Mankiw (1987) excludes the m_{t-1}/y_t variable, assuming both that the quantity equation holds, so that m_t/y_t is constant, and that observations are sufficiently close together (as they are in his continuous-time theoretical model) so that the difference between m_t and m_{t-1} can be ignored. To

TABLE 1

U.S. TIME SERIES EVIDENCE ON INFLATION AND TAX RATES

Sample/Tax Rate	Level Specification Constant	Tax Rate	M/Y	Trend	AR(1)	R^2	Difference Specification Constant	Tax Rate	M/Y	R^2
1891–1985/TGNP	.093	.051	−.050	−.0011	.579	.052	−.001	.062	−.072	.031
	(.088)	(.024)	(.031)	(.0008)	(.084)		(.004)	(.032)	(.059)	
1919–40, 1946–1985/TGNP	.039	.039	−.022	.0002	.411	.157	−.003	.063	−.078	−.002
	(.113)	(.034)	(.034)	(.0012)	(.118)		(.006)	(.057)	(.078)	
1919–40, 1946–1985/MTR	.043	.030	−.017	−.0001	.409	.163	−.003	.059	−.082	.013
	(.105)	(.023)	(.030)	(.0012)	(.118)		(.006)	(.041)	(.078)	
1946–1986/TGNP	.572	.320	.205	.007	.543	.452	.009	.334	.294	.464
	(.145)	(.074)	(.056)	(.002)	(.148)		(.004)	(.069)	(.064)	
1946–1986/MTR	.382	.177	.170	.004	.542	.334	.0007	.184	.271	.090
	(.145)	(.059)	(.062)	(.002)	(.141)		(.0041)	(.059)	(.072)	

Estimates correspond to equation (14) in the text. Standard errors are reported in parentheses. All equations are estimated by ordinary least squares. TGNP denotes equations where the tax rate is measured as the ratio of taxes to GNP, while MTR denotes equations using estimated marginal tax rates on labor income.

Institutional changes during the postwar period, notably the shift from fixed to flexible exchange rates in 1973, could affect the stability of the coefficients linking taxes to inflation rates. We test this possibility by allowing the coefficients in (7) to differ before and after 1973. The hypothesis of constant coefficients is not rejected in any of the equations estimated over long sample periods, either 1891–1985 or 1919–1985.[14] For the postwar period, however, the AR(1) equations fail the test of subsample stability while the differenced equations do not. We examine the source of this failure by constraining γ_1 and γ_2 to be constant, while allowing the intercept and trend coefficients to differ before and after 1973. The null hypothesis of constancy for this subset of coefficients is not rejected; the $\chi^2(2)$ statistics are 1.96 when the tax rate variable is *T*/ *GNP*, and 3.66 with the Barro-Sahasakul marginal tax rate series (the .05 critical value for a $\chi^2(2)$ random variable is 5.99).

Our findings for the United States strengthen Mankiw's (1987) conclusions based on the postwar period. To evaluate the robustness of the positive relationship between inflation and tax rates, however, we now consider data from four additional countries. For France, Germany, and Japan, we draw data from the International Monetary Fund *International Financial Statistics* for the postwar period to construct tax-to-GNP ratios and inflation rates.[15] More extensive data are available for Britain. For the period 1872–1985, we constructed a tax-to-GNP ratio using data from *British Historical Statistics* and various issues of the *Annual Abstract of Statistics*. The annual price index was measured using the Retail Price Index (post-1948) and the *Statist* price index.[16]

Table 2 reports estimates of (7) for these four countries. The positive association between inflation and taxes that appears in U.S. data does not generalize. The French and British data show a statistically significant and *negative* relationship between tax levels and the inflation rate. In Germany the relation is again negative although the standard error of the estimated coefficient is too large to reject the null hypothesis of no tax effect. Only the Japanese data confirm the

verify that our results are not due to our inclusion of log (m_{t-1}/y_t), we also estimated a modified version of (7) excluding this variable. The estimated coefficients on the tax rate variable decline slightly, and the standard errors increase. The overall conclusions about the links between tax rates and inflation are not affected by this change in specification.

[14]The likelihood ratio test statistic for the constant-coefficient hypothesis when (7) is estimated in levels with an AR(1) correction is 4.26 for the 1891–1985 sample, and 5.92 for the 1919–40, 1946–85 sample. Both tests have four degrees of freedom (the constant and time trend coefficient are also allowed to vary). The .05 level of the $\chi^2(4)$ distribution is 9.50.

[15]Data on annual averages of consumer price indexes, as well as reserve money, government debt outstanding, gross domestic product, and call money interest rates, were drawn from the IFS. In some cases these series were spliced together using values from several different IFS publications and domestic statistical sources. The tax receipts of the central government are reported in the UN National Accounts.

[16]Interest rates and the stock of high-powered money are drawn from Friedman and Schwartz (1982, Table 4.9). The stock of government debt is drawn from *British Historical Statistics*, updated using the *Annual Abstract of Statistics*. Implicit in our use of data from the gold standard is the notion that seigniorage is available even when pounds are measured in terms of a commodity. Seigniorage is possible as long as the gold stock held by the government bears no relation to government currency.

U.S. finding of a positive relationship between inflation and taxes. A 10 percent of GNP increase in the tax burden is estimated to increase the inflation rate by 3.1 percent in the AR(1) specification, and by 4.7 percent in the differenced model. The estimated effects of the money-to-income ratio are positive in each equation in Table 2, in contrast to the often negative coefficients for the United States.[17]

We repeated our analysis of subsample stability for the equations reported in Table 2. Constancy of γ_1 and γ_2 is not rejected for the United Kingdom, Germany, or Japan. In France, however, there is evidence of parameter instability. In equation (7) with all coefficients free to change in 1974, the pre-1974 estimate of γ_1 is −.56 (.10), with an estimated change for the period after 1974 of .79 (.63). Most of the evidence against parameter constancy arises from the change in the coefficient on the money-to-income ratio, however. The pre-1974 estimate is .53 (.08), while the change is −.51 (.13).

The first four rows of Table 2 report country-by-country estimates of equation (4). These estimates ignore the information about inflation rates in one country that may be contained in the coincident experience of other nations. To remedy this problem, we also estimated the equations for the postwar period in all countries using the seemingly unrelated regression technique. The resulting estimates are shown in Table 3, and are quite similar to the country-by-country findings in Table 2. The last row of Table 3 reports estimates which constrain γ_1 and γ_2 to be constant across countries. The levels equation yields a small and statistically insignificant coefficient linking tax rates and inflation rates. In the differenced specification, even though three of the five countries show negative coefficients when estimated alone, the constrained estimate of γ_1 is .11 (.03). In both specifications, however, the hypothesis of constant (γ_1, γ_2) across countries is clearly rejected.[18] We therefore focus primarily on the unconstrained results, which yield a negative correlation between inflation and tax rates in three of the five countries.

Our failure to find a positive association between tax rates and inflation might be due to an incorrect specification. We have assumed that governments can either precommit or that they can tax outstanding government debt without resorting to inflation. If these assumptions are incorrect, the first-order condition linking taxes and inflation rates is equation (6) which includes the government's outstanding interest-bearing debt. Under the same parametric assumptions used to derive (7) from (4), the version of (6) that we estimate is

[17]As in the United States data set, excluding $\log(m_{t-1}/y_t)$ does not affect the broad character of the findings. France and Britain continue to show statistically significant negative coefficients on the tax variable. For Japan, the tax variable has an even stronger positive association with inflation when we exclude the money-to-income ratio. Finally, the coefficient on the tax share for Germany moves from negative in the equation with $\ln(m_{t-1}/y_t)$ to positive without this variable, but the coefficient is never statistically significant.

[18]The likelihood ratio tests (which are distributed as $\chi^2(8)$ under the null) are 52.6 in the level specification, and 64.1 in differences.

TABLE 2

INTERNATIONAL EVIDENCE ON INFLATION AND TAX RATES

	Level Specification						Difference Specification			
Sample	Constant	Tax Rate	M/Y	Trend	AR(1)	R^2	Constant	Tax Rate	M/Y	R^2
France	−.332	−.681	.252	.013	.805	.647	.011	−.589	.302	.598
1948–1985	(.250)	(.123)	(.076)	(.003)	(.095)		(.008)	(.129)	(.075)	
Germany	.175	−.041	.088	.0014	.595	.121	.0014	−.084	.076	.077
1954–1984	(.130)	(.107)	(.038)	(.0011)	(.159)		(.0022)	(.112)	(.039)	
Japan	1.264	.313	.228	−.008	.796	.349	−.011	.472	.187	.440
1955–1984	(.337)	(.226)	(.103)	(.004)	(.121)		(.007)	(.230)	(.101)	
U.K.	.734	−.243	.778	.010	.957	.755	.011	−.236	.789	.765
1872–1984	(.235)	(.051)	(.044)	(.002)	(.026)		(.005)	(.050)	(.044)	
U.K.	−.501	−.094	.425	.015	.772	.502	.015	−.130	.468	.527
1947–1984	(.170)	(.081)	(.076)	(.003)	(.103)		(.005)	(.085)	(.076)	

Estimates correspond to equation (7) in the text. Standard errors are shown in parentheses. Equations are estimated using OLS country-by-country with no cross-equation constraints or allowance for contemporaneous residual correlation.

$$\ln(P_t/P_{t-1}) = \gamma_0 + \gamma_1 \ln(\theta_t) + \gamma_2 \ln[(b_{t-1}(1+i_{t-1}) + m_{t-1})/y_t] + \epsilon_t . \tag{8}$$

Since the earlier results suggest that differencing and autoregressive corrections with time trends yield similar results, we present only the latter.

Table 4 reports estimates of (8) for all five countries in our sample. The inclusion of the broad government liabilities variable does not substantively alter our estimates of the association between taxes and inflation. In particular, the coefficient on the tax rate remains negative and statistically significant for Britain and France, positive and significant for Japan and the United States, and statistically insignificant for Germany. The broad liability measure is less correlated with inflation than $\ln(m_{t-1}/y_{t-1})$. The point estimates for the total liability variable are negative (that is, incorrectly signed) for Germany and Japan, whereas the money-to-GNP ratio had the sign predicted by the foregoing theory.

The superiority of models including only the ratio of money to GNP, relative to models with total government liabilities as a share of GNP, can be demonstrated by estimating regression equations which include *both* variables. This is equivalent to the nonnested hypothesis test of the null hypothesis that one variable affects the inflation rate against the alternative that the other variable affects it. For the United States, Germany, and Japan, including both variables yields a negative coefficient on the liability variable but a positive and usually statistically significant coefficient on the money variable. For France both variables have positive and statistically insignificant coefficients, while for Britain both are positive and statistically significant, but the coefficient on money is roughly three times as large as that on the broader liability measure. Overall, the results are more supportive of a specification including the ratio of lagged money to GNP than the total level of government liabilities.[19]

A referee argued that inflation and the tax-to-GNP ratio are affected by many common factors, and that a more appropriate test of the theory would focus on the variation in each due to changes in government outlays. We performed such tests, estimating (7) by instrumental variables (IV) with T/GNP treated as endogenous and using the ratio of government consumption to GNP as an instrument. (See Table 5.) For the United States, the IV results are similar to the OLS findings, but for the other nations, γ_1 changes erratically and the standard errors rise substantially, making it impossible to draw any firm conclusions. The null hypothesis that $\gamma_1 = 0$ is not rejected by the IV results for any nation except the United States.

[19]According to the standard theory of optimal taxation, tax rate changes should not be predictable using any lagged information such as past inflation rates. An earlier version of this paper explored the links between *changes* in tax rates and the level of inflation, yielding substantial evidence that inflation rates predict future changes in tax rates in the United States, Britain, and France. These findings are related to Sahasakul's (1986) finding that tax rates respond strongly to transitory changes in spending, which is evidence against the standard theory.

TABLE 3

INTERNATIONAL EVIDENCE ON INFLATION AND TAX RATES: SUR RESULTS

Sample	Level Specification					Difference Specification		
	Constant	Tax Rate	M/Y	Trend	AR(1)	Constant	Tax Rate	M/Y
France	−.506	−.575	.221	.0078	.899	.0080	−.541	.222
1948–1985	(.349)	(.109)	(.067)	(.0018)	(.072)	(.0071)	(.110)	(.064)
Germany	.095	−.073	.097	.0014	.557	.0013	−.100	.087
1954–1984	(.147)	(.086)	(.032)	(.0008)	(.152)	(.0018)	(.084)	(.028)
Japan	2.106	.544	.181	−.0113	.969	−.0096	.519	.152
1955–1984	(.360)	(.162)	(.074)	(.0029)	(.048)	(.0047)	(.158)	(.071)
U.S.	.312	.172	.074	.0029	.493	.0066	.213	.224
1948–1985	(.130)	(.057)	(.062)	(.0018)	(.104)	(.0043)	(.054)	(.071)
U.K.	.025	−.017	.265	.0098	.601	.0130	−.018	.410
1948–1984	(.104)	(.060)	(.060)	(.0021)	(.088)	(.0050)	(.060)	(.058)
Constrained		.0029	.123				.106	.142
		(.0337)	(.025)				(.033)	(.024)

Estimates correspond to equation (7) in the text. Standard errors are shown in parentheses. Equations are estimated by seemingly unrelated regressions. The likelihood values for the systems allowing free parameters for c_1 and c_2 in each equation are 489.63 in the levels system, 486.25 in differences. The likelihood values for the constrained systems, allowing free intercepts and (in the first system) time trend and autocorrelation coefficients, are 463.63 and 454.18 respectively.

TABLE 4

INFLATION NOMINAL LIABILITIES, AND TAX RATES: INTERNATIONAL EVIDENCE

Country/ Sample	Tax Rate Measure	Constant	Tax Rate	Government Liabilities	Trend	ρ	R^2
France	T/GNP	−.778	−.770	.259	.0185	.709	.643
1948–85		(.180)	(.119)	(.099)	(.0043)	(.119)	
Germany	T/GNP	−.0024	.037	−.029	.0012	.530	.043
1954–84		(.1410)	(.108)	(.028)	(.0013)	(.167)	
Japan	T/GNP	1.178	.841	−.167	−.063	.477	.352
1957–83		(.346)	(.222)	(.043)	(.003)	(.185)	
U.K.	T/GNP	−1.335	−.479	.693	.0085	.976	.669
1872–1984		(.317)	(.060)	(.049)	(.0034)	(.016)	
U.K.	T/GNP	−2.733	−.241	.594	.025	.900	.539
1947–1984		(0.535)	(.087)	(.098)	(.005)	(.062)	
U.S.	T/GNP	.201	.074	−.055	−.0001	.513	.115
1891–1985		(.082)	(.024)	(.019)	(.0007)	(.089)	
U.S.	MTR	.311	.184	.063	−.0003	.678	.228
1946–85		(.186)	(.062)	(.043)	(.0020)	(.121)	
U.S.	T/GNP	.414	.288	.071	.0022	.700	.301
1946–1985		(.184)	(.079)	(.042)	(.0017)	(.119)	

Estimates correspond to equation (8) in the text. Values in parentheses are standard errors. All equations are estimated by ordinary least squares.

3. CONCLUSIONS

The view that governments use both taxes and inflation to raise revenue while attempting to minimize total deadweight loss cannot explain our finding that higher taxes are just as often associated with lower as with higher inflation. The positive association between inflation and tax rates in U.S. time series data which has been cited as support for the optimizing government model of monetary and fiscal policy does not recur in other nations.

Several explanations may be advanced to account for our results. One is that governments are unable to adjust the structure of taxes frequently enough to enforce the first-order conditions implied by optimizing models. This view is implicit in the work of Feldstein (1983) and others who view the effects of inflation on tax burdens as largely accidental and unanticipated. Even when tax rules are costly to change, however, policymakers could implement the links between taxes and inflation described above. An unindexed tax system which raises corporate tax burdens during inflationary periods because depreciation is based on historic cost, for example, generates a positive association between tax rates and inflation.

A second possibility, which we regard as more promising, is that the government's objective function which guides inflation and tax policy varies over time. The perceived costs of inflation and taxes may change with the political party in power, shifts in voter preferences, or changes in the transactions or tax-collecting technology.[20] Models of "political business cycles," which predict variation in the

[20]Barro's (1987) analysis allows preferences to shift in this way since the government's preferred interest rate changes over time. Rogoff and Sibert's (1988) model of budget cycles could generate time-varying government preferences as the politician's desire to signal his type depends on the time until the next election.

TABLE 5

INFLATION AND TAX RATES: INSTRUMENTAL VARIABLES ESTIMATES

Sample	Level Specification					Difference Specification		
	Constant	Tax Rate	M/Y	Trend	AR(1)	Constant	Tax Rate	M/Y
France	.038	−.021	.011	.0016	.530	−.0110	1.320	.210
1950–1985	(.465)	(.340)	(.076)	(.0040)	(.150)	(.3601)	(3.570)	(1.130)
Germany	.238	.005	.092	.0009	.580	.0001	.081	.066
1954–1984	(.148)	(.130)	(.045)	(.0013)	(.160)	(.0040)	(.510)	(.050)
Japan	.871	−.047	.325	−.0025	.570	−.124	7.440	−1.820
1957–1983	(.369)	(.236)	(.109)	(.0040)	(.170)	(.435)	(26.570)	(7.670)
U.K.	−.440	−.066	.473	.016	.780	.018	−.003	.505
1947–1985	(.213)	(.116)	(.107)	(.004)	(.100)	(.006)	(.200)	(.082)
U.S.	.612	.340	.190	.0060	.540	.015	1.077	.497
1946–1985	(.163)	(.083)	(.060)	(.0020)	(.150)	(.012)	(.889)	(.303)

Estimates correspond to equation (7) in the text. The tax rate is treated as endogenous and the equations are estimated by instrumental variables using the logarithm of the ratio of government consumption to GDP as the instrument for log(T/GNP). Standard errors are shown in parentheses.

policy preferences of given political actors, or models of multiparty government with intertemporal variation in the identity of political actors, could explain our findings. Alesina and Sachs (1988) provide some support for the view that different political parties in the United States have different macroeconomic preferences, and Hibbs (1982) documents intertemporal variation in the inflation-unemployment preferences of the U.S. electorate. If governments that are willing to tolerate inflation also like expansionary policies in general, then total revenues will decline in periods of high inflation, reinforcing the negative inflation-tax correlation.[21]

The view that negative inflation-tax correlations are due to unstable government tastes is mildly supported by the fact that countries with more stable governments and less diverse political parties, such as postwar Japan and the United States, exhibit positive tax-inflation correlations. Countries with more political instability, such as Britain and France, tend to exhibit negative correlations. Roubini and Sachs (1988) present intriguing evidence on other links between political structure and the nature of fiscal policy. Further work could usefully explore how political institutions or other aspects of social structure are related to the inflation-tax correlation.

LITERATURE CITED

Alesina, Alberto, and Jeffrey Sachs. "Political Parties and the Business Cycle in the United States, 1948–1984." *Journal of Money, Credit, and Banking* 20 (February 1988), 63–82.

Alesina, Alberto, and Guido Tabellini. "Rules and Discretion with Noncoordinated Monetary and Fiscal Policy." *Economic Inquiry* 25 (1987), 619–30.

Barro, Robert J. "On the Determination of Public Debt." *Journal of Political Economy* 87 (October 1979), 940–71.

______. "Interest Rate Smoothing." National Bureau of Economic Research Working Paper 2581, May 1988, Cambridge, Mass.

Barro, Robert J., and David Gordon. "A Positive Theory of Monetary Policy in a Natural Rate Model." *Journal of Political Economy* 91 (August 1983), 589–610.

Barro, Robert J., and Chaipat Sahasakul. "Average Marginal Tax Rates from Social Security and the Individual Income Tax." *Journal of Business* 59 (October 1986), 555–66.

Bohn, Henning. "Why Do We Have Nominal Government Debt?" *Journal of Monetary Economics* 21 (January 1988), 127–40.

[21]The possibility that monetary policy is set based on stabilization objectives, rather than deadweight loss minimization, cannot explain our findings. Traditional Keynesian policy would call for coincident reductions in tax burdens and increases in the money stock. The observed correlation between taxes and inflation is nevertheless likely to remain positive since stabilization policy responds to shocks. When exogenous factors cause a business slowdown, both inflation and the share of taxes in GNP are likely to decline. If the government responds with a monetary expansion accompanied by a tax cut, the ratio of taxes to GNP will be unambiguously lower than without the shock and associated stabilization. Inflation will also be lower unless the stabilization policy more than offsets the disturbance it was designed to correct.

Calvo, Guillermo. "On the Time Consistency of Optimal Policy in a Monetary Economy." *Econometrica* 46 (November 1978), 1411–28.

Drazen, Allan. "The Optimal Rate of Inflation Revisited." *Journal of Monetary Economics* 5 (April 1979), 231–48.

Faig, Miguel. "Characterization of the Optimal Tax on Money When It Functions as a Medium of Exchance." *Journal of Monetary Economics* 22 (1987), 137–48.

Feldstein, Martin S. *Inflation, Tax Rules, and Capital Formation.* Chicago: University of Chicago Press, 1983.

Fischer, Stanley, and Franco Modigliani. "Towards an Understanding of the Real Effects and Costs of Inflation." *Weltwirtschaftliches Archiv* 114 (1978), 810–33.

Friedman, Milton, and Anna J. Schwartz. *Monetary Trends in the United States and the United Kingdom: Their Relation to Income, Prices, and Interest Rates, 1867–*1975. Chicago: University of Chicago Press, 1982.

Helpman, Elhanan, and Efraim Sadka. "Optimal Financing of the Government's Budget: Taxes, Bonds, or Money?" *American Economic Review* 69 (March 1979), 1952–60.

Hibbs, Douglas. "On the Demand for Economic Outcomes: Macroeconomic Performance and Mass Political Support in the U.S., Great Britain, and Germany." *Journal of Politics* 44 (1982), 426–61.

Kimbrough, Kent P. "The Optimum Quantity of Money Rule in Public Finance." *Journal of Monetary Economics* 18 (November 1986), 277–84.

Lucas, Robert E., Jr. "Principles of Fiscal and Monetary Policy." *Journal of Monetary Economics* 17 (January 1986), 117–34.

Mankiw, N. Gregory. "The Optimal Collection of Seigniorage: Theory and Evidence." *Journal of Monetary Economics* 20 (September 1987), 327–42.

Phelps, Edmund S. "Inflation in the Theory of Public Finance." *Swedish Journal of Economics* 75 (March 1973), 67–82.

Rogoff, Kenneth. "Reputational Constraints on Monetary Policy." *Carnegie-Rochester Conference Series on Public Policy* 26 (1987), 141–82.

Rogoff, Kenneth, and Anne Sibert. "Macroeconomic Policy Cycles." *Review of Economic Studies* 55 (1988), 1–16.

Romer, David. "Why Should Governments Issue Bonds." Princeton University, mimeo, 1987.

Rotemberg, Julio J. "Constituencies with Finite Lives and the Valuation of Government Bonds." Massachusetts Institute of Technology, mimeo, 1987.

Roubini, Nouriel, and Jeffrey Sachs. "Political and Economic Determinants of Budget Deficits in Industrial Democracies." National Bureau of Economic Research Working Paper 2682, August 1988, Cambridge, Mass.

Sahasakul, Chaipat. "The U.S. Evidence on Optimal Taxation over Time." *Journal of Monetary Economics* 18 (November 1986), 251–75.

SUSANTO BASU
MILES S. KIMBALL
N. GREGORY MANKIW
DAVID N. WEIL

Optimal Advice for Monetary Policy

MACROECONOMISTS GIVING POLICY ADVICE know that their advice is followed only intermittently. In contrast, academic analysis of optimal monetary policy usually assumes that the monetary authority chooses a policy rule that is followed thereafter without interruption.[1] This paper takes a step toward bridging this gap. It addresses the issue of how to give optimal advice about monetary policy when the advisor knows that the advice might be ignored.

The possibility that advice might be ignored introduces at least two new considerations into the advisor's problem. First, the advisor may try to increase the likelihood that his advice will be heeded. Second, the possibility that the advice will not be heeded may alter the optimal advice.

The problem of getting policymakers to do what one wishes is the more obvious consideration. It finds various expressions in common wisdom. For example, an advisor may moderate his views in order to gain favor. Alternatively, an advisor may exaggerate his views knowing that actual policy will be a watered down version of what he recommends—and thus equivalent to what he actually thinks should be done. Or an advisor may take into account how the advice he gives today affects his probability of being listened to in the future: he might take

The authors are grateful to Kenneth Kuttner, David Romer, Lawrence Summers, and the referees for helpful comments. Mankiw is grateful to the National Science Foundation for financial support.

[1]See, for example, the discussions of optimal policy in Fischer (1977), Blinder and Mankiw (1984), and Aizenman and Frenkel (1986).

SUSANTO BASU *and* DAVID N. WEIL *are graduate students, Harvard University.* MILES S. KIMBALL *is assistant professor, University of Michigan, and faculty research fellow, National Bureau of Economic Research.* N. GREGORY MANKIW *is professor of economics, Harvard University, and research associate, National Bureau of Economic Research.*

Journal of Money, Credit, and Banking, Vol. 22, No. 1 (February 1990)

an unpopular stand, for example, with the knowledge that he will not be heeded today, but will ultimately be proven right and thus gain credibility.

The second consideration is more subtle: the fact that policy advice may or may not be heeded changes its impact on the economy, both when the advice is taken and when it is ignored. Advice has an effect even when it is ignored because the possibility that it might have been followed was incorporated into the expectations of agents in the economy, and these expectations in turn affect outcomes.

In this paper we choose to focus only on the second of these issues. We assume that there is some fixed probability that the advisor will be listened to, and that this probability is known to all the agents in the economy. We assume further that this probability cannot be affected by the advisor's actions.[2] Finally, we assume that the advisor is disinterested—that is, he cares about outcomes both when he is listened to and when he is not.[3] It might seem that these simplifications would make the advisor's problem trivial, but this turns out to be far from true. The decision problem facing our advisor is much more subtle than one might anticipate.

The purpose of this paper is thus to solve for the optimal rule for policy advice and compare it to the optimal policy rule. The notion of policy rules is often criticized on the grounds that, in practice, policy is made not by rule but by discretion.[4] Yet economists are often asked for their advice on monetary policy, and there is no reason that they cannot follow a rule in providing advice. Unless such advice is always sought and followed, however, the optimal rule for policy advice is generally not the same as the optimal policy rule.

We examine a simple macroeconomic model in which monetary policy has the ability to stabilize output by offsetting exogenous shocks to aggregate demand. The optimal policy rule, when the policymaker's objective is to stabilize output, is a common one: offset the demand shocks to the extent possible. In other words, optimal policy attempts to stabilize nominal GNP. If economists' advice were always followed, this optimal policy rule would also be the optimal rule for policy advice. Yet if economists' advice is followed only with some probability, the optimal rule for policy advice can differ substantially from the optimal policy rule.

The difference between optimal policy and optimal advice arises because the advisor has two conflicting goals. First, he would like to offset exogenous shocks to aggregate demand, which motivates him to advise an activist monetary policy.

[2]Making these simplifications does indeed rule out many of the circumstances in which advice is given, but by no means all of them. Consider, for example, the case of a presidential election in which each candidate has a trusted economic "guru" to whom he listens. The candidates' attachment to their gurus may not depend on the gurus' view of monetary policy, and the candidates' chances of getting elected are almost certainly not strongly dependent on their positions on monetary policy. The problem facing such a guru exactly conforms to the way in which we have set up the advice problem in this paper.

[3]Thus, the policy advisor depicted in our model has objectives different from those found in models of bureaucratic self-interest. In such a model, an advisor would be concerned only with outcomes that take place "on his watch," that is, when his advice is listened to.

[4]See, for example, the arguments of Sims (1982).

Second, he would like to make monetary policy more predictable, which motivates him to mimic the alternative policy followed when his advice is ignored. Optimal advice entails trading off these two objectives.

This problem is in some ways analogous to those studied by Friedman (1953) and Brainard (1967). These authors show that uncertainty about the economy makes optimal policy less activist. In our model, the uncertainty is not about the economy but about whether the advice will be followed. We show that this advisor's uncertainty also makes the advisor less activist, in the sense that he recommends a policy that deviates less from what will be done if he is not heeded.

There are, however, important differences between the advisor's uncertainty we examine and the uncertainty of Friedman and Brainard. As uncertainty increases in the Friedman/Brainard framework, policy loses none of its power to affect the state of the economy, while in the model presented here, as his chance of being heeded falls, the policy advisor has reduced power to do good or harm. The two kinds of uncertainty also affect optimal behavior differently. As the policymaker in the Friedman/Brainard framework is less and less certain about the economy, his optimal policy approaches full passivity; in our model, as the chance of an advisor being heeded goes to zero, his optimal advice remains partially activist.

Our analysis proceeds as follows. In section 1, we present a simple model of the economy and solve for the optimal policy rule where the objective of the monetary authority is to minimize the variance of output. In section 2, we consider the problem of an advisor who knows that his advice will only be followed with a certain probability, the alternative being a passive monetary policy. We show that the smaller is the probability that the advice will be followed, the less activist the advice should be, that is, the smaller the recommended offset of aggregate demand shocks. Even if the probability of the advice being followed is close to zero, however, some non-negligible offset of demand shocks should be recommended.

The optimal advice problem considered in section 2 is constrained in several ways to simplify the exposition and to provide intuition. Specifically, we restrict the optimal advice rule to have the same functional form as the optimal policy rule derived in section 1. In section 3 we show that the fully optimal advice is qualitatively different from the constrained advice found in section 2. In particular, optimal advice depends on the lagged "money surprise," the difference between actual and anticipated money, which was caused by the uncertainty as to whether the advice would be followed. In section 4 we allow for a very general specification of the alternative monetary policy and once again solve for the unconstrained optimal advice.

In section 5, we return to the simple model of section 2 to explore the value of compromise. We consider an economy with two advisors who have different objective functions. After deriving the advice that the advisors would give in a noncooperative game, we show that there exists a set of compromise policies that both advisors would prefer. Giving optimal advice is thus no substitute for compromising. In many situations, however, we would not expect the compromise solution to be the outcome of a one-shot game.

We conclude in section 6.

1. THE SETUP: THE ECONOMY AND THE OPTIMAL POLICY RULE

In this section we first present a standard model of the role of monetary policy in stabilizing output, and then solve the model in the traditional fashion for the optimal monetary policy rule. Following Fischer (1977) and Taylor (1980), we examine a model in which aggregate demand has real effects because of nominal stickiness which takes the form of overlapping wage contracts. All variables are in logarithms, and constants have been omitted.

$$m_t + v_t = p_t + y_t \,. \tag{1}$$

$$y_t = p_t - w_t \,. \tag{2}$$

$$w_t = 1/2\,({}_{t-1}p_t + {}_{t-2}p_t) \,. \tag{3}$$

$$v_t = v_{t-1} + \epsilon_t \,. \tag{4}$$

Equation (1) is aggregate demand and equation (2) is aggregate supply. The wage is fixed, and firms are able to hire as much labor as they want; an increase in the price level lowers the real wage, increases the quantity of labor demanded, and thus increases output. The money supply in period t, m_t, is set by the monetary policy authority at the end of period $t-1$.

Equation (3) represents the wage-setting process. Contracts are two periods long. Hence, in period t, half of the work force is governed by contracts written in period $t-1$ and half by contracts written in period $t-2$. The expectation of prices in period t formed in period $t-i$, which is denoted ${}_{t-i}p_t$, is based on the observation of shocks that take place in $t-i$ and on a complete knowledge of the rule governing monetary policy. Equation (4) determines the evolution of velocity, which is assumed to follow an exogenous random walk.

We can solve equations (1)–(4) to get output as a function of monetary policy, expectations of monetary policy, and the realization of the shock to velocity:

$$y_t = 1/6\,(m_t - {}_{t-1}m_t) + 1/3\,(m_t - {}_{t-2}m_t) + 1/2\,\epsilon_t + 1/3\,\epsilon_{t-1} \,. \tag{5}$$

We assume that the goal of the monetary policy authority is to minimize the variance of output around its natural level of $y=0$. The standard result for this model is that an optimal policy is to set $m_t = -v_{t-1}$ or, equivalently, $m_t - m_{t-1} = -\epsilon_{t-1}$. In doing this, the policy authority is able to undo the effect of the shock in period $t-1$ on contracts written in period $t-2$, thus allowing workers covered by those contracts to receive a wage closer to the equilibrium real wage. Workers who write contracts in period $t-1$ (that is, contracts that cover periods t and $t+1$) are not affected by the policy in period t because they observe ϵ_{t-1} before they write their contracts. Since they know the policy rule, they know the value of m_t. By engaging in such a policy, the monetary authority is able to reduce the variance of output to the level that would prevail in a model with one-period contracts. Hence the monetary authority can eliminate at least part of the adverse effects of the nominal wage rigidity.

2. OPTIMAL ADVICE WHEN THE ALTERNATIVE POLICY IS PASSIVE

We now consider the problem of an advisor asked to suggest a policy when that advisor knows that there is a chance his advice may not be heeded. As in all of the models below, we assume that the probability that the advisor's advice will be followed is exogenous: with probability λ the monetary policy authority will set m_t at the level suggested by the advisor and with probability $(1-\lambda)$ the authority will engage in no policy at all, setting $m_t = m_{t-1}$.[5] We consider policy advice rules of the form $m_t = m_{t-1} + \psi\epsilon_{t-1}$; this set of rules includes the optimal policy rule derived above as the special case $\psi = -1$ and the completely passive policy as the special case $\psi = 0$. We show that the optimal advice is not the same as the optimal policy. The variance of output under the optimal advice rule that we consider here is lower than that which would obtain if the advisor were to recommend the optimal policy rule derived above. We show in section 3, however, that the rule for advice derived in this section is not the unconstrained optimum.

To solve equation (5) for the variance of output, we must first solve for expected money. At time $t - 1$, when workers are signing wage contracts, the shock ϵ_{t-1} has been observed, and the expected value of monetary policy is

$$_{t-1}m_t = \lambda(m_{t-1} + \psi\epsilon_{t-1}) + (1-\lambda)m_{t-1} = m_{t-1} + \lambda\psi\epsilon_{t-1} \,. \tag{6}$$

The two-period-ahead expectation of monetary policy in this case is $_{t-2}m_t = {}_{t-2}m_{t-1} = m_{t-2} + \lambda\psi\epsilon_{t-2}$. From equation (5), it is clear that current output y_t depends on velocity shocks and the setting of monetary policy in both the current and immediately preceding period. To obtain the unconditional variance of output we must consider four possible permutations: advice heeded in both periods, advice heeded only in period t, advice heeded only in period $t-1$, and advice heeded in neither period. Taking the square of output in each case (since its mean is zero) and multiplying by the corresponding probabilities (for example, λ^2 for the case where advice is followed in both periods) yields

$$\begin{aligned} \operatorname{var}(y) = \Big(&1/4 + \lambda([1/3 + 1/3\,\psi - 1/6(\lambda-1)\psi]^2 + [1/3(\lambda-1)\psi]^2) \\ &+ (1-\lambda)([1/3 - 1/6\,\lambda\psi]^2 + [1/3\,\lambda\psi]^2)\Big)\,\sigma_\epsilon^2 \,. \end{aligned} \tag{7}$$

[5]In section 5 we motivate this policy as the advice of a "monetarist" whose objective is to minimize the variance of money growth.

We can minimize the variance of output with respect to ψ to find the optimal policy advice rule:

$$\psi^* = \frac{-4}{13 - 9\lambda} . \quad (8)$$

When $\lambda=1$ the advisor is certain that his advice will be followed and this rule returns the optimal policy derived in section 1. As the probability of being heeded declines, the strength of the advice given falls. That is, the smaller is the probability that the advisor is listened to, the less activist is his advice.

What is perhaps surprising is that as the probability of being heeded goes to zero, the strength of advice given remains non-negligible. The intuition for this result is as follows. In early analyses of optimal policy, such as the work of Friedman and Brainard, monetary policy that becomes unpredictable nonetheless loses none of its power. As the uncertainty of policy in these models increases, activist policy becomes a rogue elephant—powerful, but doing far more harm than good. Under such circumstances, the optimal policy is a completely passive one. But in our model, the harm of activist advice comes through the rational expectations effect of distorting people's expectations about the future. The assumption of rational expectations, however, guarantees that the harm of the advice falls as λ goes to zero, since people know that the chance of the advisor being listened to is small and thus do not modify their expectations significantly. Thus, in our model, the harm caused by activist advice falls as its probability of being heeded declines. Of course, the power of the advice to do good falls in the same proportion. In the limit as λ shrinks, the desirability of activist advice must be calculated by weighing two effects that are similar in magnitude but of opposite sign. Thus, there is no general presumption that advice should become completely passive as the probability it will be heeded goes to zero.[6]

3. THE GENERAL SOLUTION WHEN THE ALTERNATIVE POLICY IS PASSIVE

This section generalizes the previous results by allowing the optimal advice function to take a more general form. In particular, we allow the advice rule to accept arguments in addition to the one that appears in the optimal policy rule. We show that the constrained advice rule studied in section 2 does not achieve the smallest possible variance of output. For now we retain the assumption that the alternative policy is passive.

The most interesting conclusion that we can draw from allowing for a more general specification is that the optimal advice will depend not only on past veloc-

[6]When $\lambda=0$, that is, when there is no chance that the advice will be heeded, then the variance of output is not affected by the choice of ψ. This can be seen in equation (7), where setting λ to zero eliminates ψ from the equation. In such a case, it obviously makes no sense to talk about optimal advice, and so equation (8) should only be seen as applying to values of λ greater than zero.

where we have assumed that real returns, $R = (1+i_t)P_t/P_{t+1}$, are constant. In our notation, ϵ_θ is the elasticity of income with respect to taxes and η is the elasticity of money demand with respect to the nominal interest rate. A government minimizing social losses in (1) subject to this revenue constraint will choose tax rates and inflation rates satisfying the first-order condition:

$$\frac{P_t}{P_{t+1}} = \phi\left(\frac{h'(\theta_{t+1})m_t(1+\eta)}{y_{t+1}(1+\epsilon_\theta)}\right) \tag{4}$$

where $\phi = (-v')^{-1}$, $\phi' < 0$. This expression equates the excess burden per unit revenue for each revenue source.

Equation (4) implies that positive shocks to government spending that raise taxes and their associated excess burden should be accompanied by increases in inflation that raise the marginal excess burden from seigniorage. It also states that inflation between t and $t+1$ should be an increasing function of m_t/y_{t+1}. When this ratio is large, the revenue from a given inflation rate is high since, with commitment, revenue from inflation is obtained at $t+1$ as people replenish the money that has been depleted by inflation. When more money is carried over, these replenishments are larger and the relative cost of inflation is lower.

The No-Commitment Case

When commitment about inflation is impossible, the government in period t can only choose the tax rate and the price level at t. The government recognizes that it can cause unexpected inflation at t. Of course, if there were no exogenous uncertainty, the government's problem at t would be known at $t-1$ so there would be no unexpected inflation in equilibrium. The equilibrium inflation rate is just that rate at which the government will not choose to induce any unexpected inflation.[7] Inflation will only be finite without commitment if it is nonetheless costly so that the function $v(\ )$ does not become degenerate.

Some might argue that the costs of inflation are much lower for a government that cannot precommit. One of the costs of expected inflation, the increase in transaction costs due to economizing on money holdings at $t-1$, is immaterial for such governments since the government that picks the price level at t cannot alter the choice of money holdings at $t-1$. Many other costs nevertheless remain even when inflation is unanticipated. For example, the government may be averse to redistributing wealth between debtors and creditors. Reestablishing the original distribution of wealth may require the use of distortionary taxes and subsidies. Alternatively, even unanticipated inflation may distort subsequent behavior by households and firms in ways the government finds undesirable. For example, workers may press for premature renegotiation of their contracts, firms may incur additional costs of changing prices, and individuals may be forced to en-

[7]The structure of this model resembles that of Barro and Gordon (1983), although they do not consider the revenue created by inflation.

gage in additional financial transactions to restore their liquidity. Indeed, insofar as the costs of inflation are due to its deleterious effects on nominal contracts, unexpected inflation may be more costly than anticipated inflation because it has not been reflected in contracts.

In the absence of commitment, the only state variable when taxes and the price level at t are chosen is the total beginning of period level of liabilities, $\ell_t = b_{t-1}(1+i_{t-1}) + m_{t-1}$. The government at t then chooses both the tax rate and nominal money balances at t. These choices determine interest rates and the price level.

At the policy optimum without commitment, the government must be indifferent to small perturbations in the policy mix which leave b_t, next period's *beginning* of period stock of government liabilities, unchanged. Feasible perturbations thus satisfy

$$y_t(1+\epsilon_\theta)d\theta_t = - \ell_t \, d(P_{t-1}/P_t) \, . \tag{5}$$

This expression differs from the trade-off in the commitment case because it excludes the response of money demand and nominal interest rates to expected inflation. Maximizing (1) subject to (5) gives a first-order condition for the no-commitment case:

$$\frac{P_{t-1}}{P_t} = \phi \left(\frac{h'(\theta_t)[m_{t-1} + b_{t-1}(1+i_{t-1})]}{y_t(1+\epsilon_\theta)} \right) \tag{6}$$

Inflation is a positive function of both taxes and total government liabilities as a share of GNP. As in the commitment case, when high deadweight burdens are being imposed with the tax instrument, higher inflation taxes will also be appropriate. The positive effect of outstanding liabilities obtains because governments with large nominal obligations will find inflation more attractive than those with less heavy debt burdens, since inflation erodes the value of these obligations.[8]

The inflationary erosion of government liabilities is totally anticipated, at least in models without stochastic disturbances. It is nevertheless possible for governments to accumulate stocks of such obligations, provided they are willing to pay sufficiently high nominal yields. It is even possible for inflaton to raise no revenue: the revenue raised ex post from reducing the value of bonds and money may be more than offset ex ante by increases in nominal interest rates and reductions in the demand for real money balances.

[8]If the government has access to a tax levied solely on the income from government bonds, then it is again the level of money and not the stock of nominal liabilities outstanding that affects the inflation rate. The reason is that there is now another instrument for taxing bonds, so there is no need to make inflation depend on their stock. These issues are explored in more detail in an earlier version of this paper, available from the authors on request.

tries.[2] This means that other considerations must be important determinants of inflation rates. One possibility is that governments choose inflation and tax rates based on stabilization objectives. Alternatively, the government's dislike for inflation may vary over time for political or other reasons. We discuss these issues in the conclusion.

Models with and without commitment imply a positive relationship between the inflation rate and tax rates. In both cases, the marginal social cost of raising additional revenue with the inflation tax is an increasing function of the inflation rate. The marginal deadweight burden of tax finance also rises with the tax rate. An optimizing government which equates the marginal social costs of obtaining revenue from inflation and taxation will therefore raise both the inflation rate and tax rates in response to higher revenue demands.

Readers who pay serious attention to the actual pronouncements of policymakers may believe that revenue considerations have no place in a positive theory of monetary policy. Central bankers rarely, if ever, mention the seigniorage that results from alternative monetary policies. While we view this as evidence against the class of optimizing models studied below, it might nevertheless be possible to reconcile the speeches of policymakers with the optimizing government models. When government spending is high, governments tend to raise taxes and also to increase debt finance. Central bankers who react by purchasing government bonds with newly minted money, thereby raising seigniorage revenues, may rationalize this behavior with fear of high interest rates generated by large government debt stocks.[3] Their behavior may, however, be consistent with the predictions of positive models of government based on deadweight burden minimization.

Our analysis of inflation and taxation is divided into three sections. The first summarizes the links between inflation and tax policy, first when the government is able to commit, and then when it is not. Section 2 studies the empirical relationship between taxes and inflation in the United States, the United Kingdom, Japan, West Germany, and France. We show that a positive association between inflation and the level of tax burdens obtains only in the U.S. and Japanese data. The conclusion discusses why simple positive models of government behavior such as those analyzed here may be incapable of explaining monetary and fiscal policy.

1. INFLATION AND TAXATION

This section models an optimizing government's choice of inflation and tax rates when these policies are chosen only with regard to their revenue effects. We

[2]Roubini and Sachs (1988) have independently tested the predictions of the optimizing government models with respect to inflation and tax rates. They study a sample of fifteen OECD countries for the period since 1960 and find virtually no support for these models outside the United States.

[3]Our analysis only applies if the central government and the central bank are actually cooperating. Alesina and Tabellini (1988) present a model in which these arms of government behave noncooperatively.

JAMES M. POTERBA
JULIO J. ROTEMBERG

Inflation and Taxation with Optimizing Governments

A GOVERNMENT CAN SATISFY ITS BUDGET CONSTRAINT either by printing money or by levying taxes. Each method of finance has efficiency costs. Higher inflation rates may adversely affect the economy's transaction mechanism and lead to inefficiencies in contracting. Higher taxes may distort labor supply, saving, and investment decisions. Numerous authors have examined the optimal inflation rate in the presence of tax finance, describing the behavior of governments concerned only with minimizing the deadweight burden of raising a given revenue.[1] Whether these prescriptions are consistent with actual government behavior is an unresolved and relatively unstudied issue. Mankiw (1987) reports a striking positive correlation between tax burdens and inflation rates in the postwar United States, a finding consistent with the predictions of these optimizing government models.

This paper extends previous work on the interaction between taxes and inflation. We present new empirical evidence on the correlation between inflation and tax rates in a sample of OECD countries, and conclude that optimizing models with time-invariant tastes cannot explain the observed correlations in most coun-

The authors are grateful to Barry Perlstein for research assistance, to Gregory Mankiw, Lawrence Summers, members of the NBER Taxation Group, the editor, three referees, and especially David Romer, for helpful comments. This research was supported by the National Science Foundation and the Alfred P. Sloan Foundation. A data appendix for this project has been deposited with the ICPSR in Ann Arbor, Michigan.

[1]Previous studies include Phelps (1973), Calvo (1978), Drazen (1979), Helpman and Sadka (1979), Kimbrough (1986), Lucas (1986), and Romer (1987).

JAMES M. POTERBA *is professor of economics, Massachusetts Institute of Technology.*
JULIO J. ROTEMBERG *is professor of applied economics, MIT School of Management.*

Journal of Money, Credit, and Banking, Vol. 22, No. 1 (February 1990)

ity shocks, but also on past "money surprises"—that is, the difference between actual policy and policy expected one period earlier. In the standard optimal policy problem there are, of course, no such money surprises. Their existence in the advice problem is attributable to the uncertainty about whether advice will be followed. Money surprises in period $t-1$ are random shocks that affect the money supply in period t in ways that could not have been anticipated by workers signing contracts in period $t-2$. In this sense they are analogous to the velocity shocks, ϵ, and thus a natural determinant for output-stabilizing policy. We thus derive the interesting result that the unconstrained optimal advice in a setting where the advice is not always heeded is different qualitatively as well as quantitatively from the certainty case.

To anticipate the result, Figure 1 plots the variance of output as a function of the probability of being listened to for four advice rules: (1) passive advice, (2) advice recommending the optimal policy derived in section one, (3) the constrained optimal advice derived in section two, and (4) the unconstrained optimal advice derived in this section. Perhaps the most surprising implication of Figure 1 is that, if the probability of being heeded is small (low λ), the "optimal policy rule" is the worst advice; it produces the highest variance of output.

We now proceed with the derivation of the unconstrained optimal advice. For

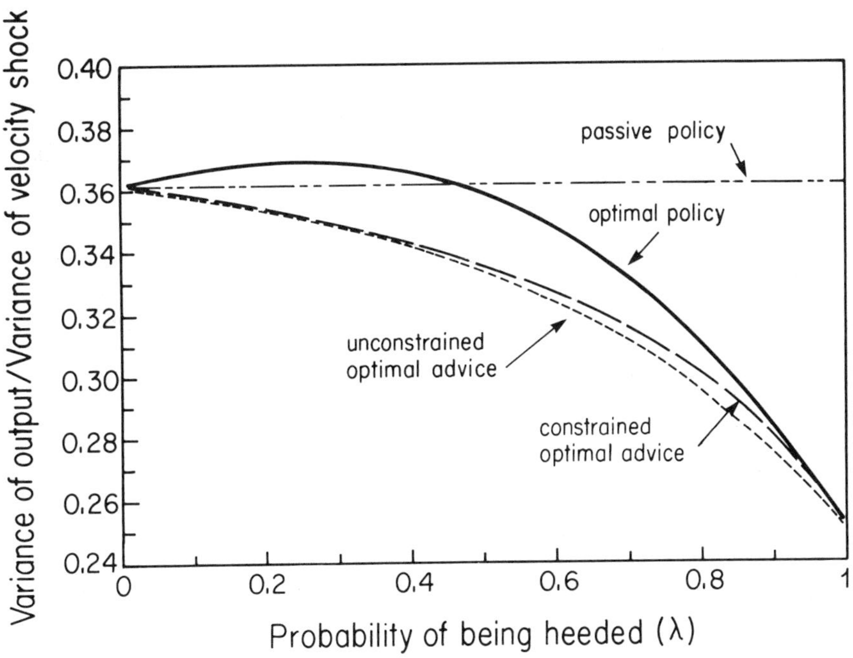

FIG. 1. Variance of Output under Alternative Advice Rules

convenience, let $z_t = m_t - m_{t-1}$ be the change in the money stock. The equation for output can be written as

$$y_t = 1/2\,(z_t - {}_{t-1}z_t) + 1/3\,(z_{t-1} - {}_{t-2}z_{t-1}) + 1/3({}_{t-1}z_t - {}_{t-2}z_t) + 1/2\,\epsilon_t + 1/3\,\epsilon_{t-1}\,. \tag{9}$$

Output is thus determined by the current and lagged money surprises, the revision at time $t-1$ of the expectation of time t money growth that had been formed at $t-2$, and the current and lagged velocity shocks. If the monetary authority followed any single feedback rule with certainty, the first and second terms would be identically zero. In our problem, however, these terms play a crucial role. Let π_t be an i.i.d. binomial random variable that takes on the value one if the advisor is heeded and zero if the alternative passive policy is followed. The expected value of π_t is λ. Also define the zero mean random variable $\eta_t = \pi_t - \lambda$ as the surprise as to which advice was followed in period t. We now write the optimum advice rule as

$$x_{t-1} = \phi\eta_{t-1}x_{t-2} + \psi\epsilon_{t-1}\,, \tag{10}$$

where x_{t-1} is the advice regarding the optimal setting of z_t.[7] In section 2, where we derived a constrained advice rule, we set ϕ equal to zero. In section 4, we will show that when the alternative policy is passive, the optimal advice takes the form of (10), that is, the arguments given are the only ones that appear in the unconstrained advice rule. Since the advice x_{t-1} is followed if π_t equals one and the alternative policy z_t=0 is followed if π_t equals zero, the actual change in the money stock is given by

$$z_t = \pi_t x_{t-1}\,, \tag{11}$$

while the anticipated change in money is

$${}_{t-1}z_t = \lambda\, x_{t-1}\,. \tag{12}$$

Using this notation, the money surprise is simply

$$z_t - {}_{t-1}z_t = (\pi_t - \lambda)x_{t-1} = \eta_t x_{t-1}\,. \tag{13}$$

From equations (9), (12), and (13), we can express output as follows:

[7]Throughout the paper we use the convention that a variable is dated in the period in which it is first known. Thus the advice about how to set money in period t is dated x_{t-1} because it is based on information available at time $t-1$.

$$y_t = 1/2\, \eta_t x_{t-1} + 1/3\, \eta_{t-1} x_{t-2} + 1/3\, [\lambda(x_{t-1} - {}_{t-2}x_{t-1})] + 1/2\, \epsilon_t + 1/3\, \epsilon_{t-1}\,. \tag{14}$$

Substituting (10) for x_{t-1} where it appears in the third term of (14) and eliminating ${}_{t-2}x_{t-1}$, which is zero, gives

$$y_t = 1/2\, \eta_t x_{t-1} + 1/3(1+\lambda\phi)\eta_{t-1} x_{t-2} + 1/3(1+\lambda\psi)\epsilon_{t-1} + 1/2\, \epsilon_t\,. \tag{15}$$

We have arranged matters so that each of the terms in (15) is orthogonal to all of the others. By assumption, η_t and ϵ_t are independent of each other and are both i.i.d. random variables. Even though x_{t-1} is correlated with both ϵ_{t-1} and x_{t-2}, the first term will not be correlated with either the second or third terms because η_t has a mean of zero conditional on everything known at time $t-1$.[8]

Again we minimize the variance of output, which is

$$\text{var}(y) = [1/4\, \lambda(1-\lambda)\, E(x_{t-1}^2) + 1/9\, (1+\lambda\phi)^2\, \lambda(1-\lambda)\, E(x_{t-2}^2)] + [1/4 + 1/9(1+\lambda\psi)^2]\sigma_\epsilon^2\,. \tag{16}$$

The variance of x can be found from equation (10). All of the terms on the right-hand side of that equation are mutually orthogonal, allowing us to write

$$E(x_{t-1}^2) = \phi^2\lambda(1-\lambda)\, E(x_{t-2}^2) + \psi^2\sigma_\epsilon^2\,. \tag{17}$$

As long as ϕ is not too large, x is stationary and $E(x_{t-1}^2) = E(x_{t-2}^2) = \sigma_x^2$, where

$$\sigma_x^2 = \frac{\psi^2\sigma_\epsilon^2}{1-\lambda(1-\lambda)\phi^2}. \tag{18}$$

Substituting this expression[9] into (16),

$$\text{var}(y) = \frac{[1/4 + 1/9\,(1+\lambda\phi)^2]\lambda(1-\lambda)(\psi^2\sigma_\epsilon^2)}{1-\lambda(1-\lambda)\phi^2} + [1/4 + 1/9(1+\lambda\psi)^2]\sigma_\epsilon^2\,. \tag{19}$$

Minimizing this expression for var(y) yields the optimal settings of the two policy parameters:

[8]If f_{t-1} is anything known at time $t-1$, cov $(\eta_t, f_{t-1}) = E\,(\eta_t f_{t-1}) = E\,(E_{t-1}(\eta_t f_{t-1})) = E\,(f_{t-1} E_{t-1}(\eta_t)) = 0$.

[9]When the denominator is negative or zero, the variance of x becomes infinite. Minimizing the variance of y with respect to ϕ guarantees that the variance of x is finite.

$$\phi^* = \psi^* = \frac{9\lambda - 13 + \sqrt{169 - 298\lambda + 145\lambda^2}}{8\lambda(1-\lambda)} \tag{20}$$

Figure 2 plots the optimal value of the policy parameter ψ obtained in this case and in the constrained case treated in section 2, both as functions of λ, the probability of being heeded. Note that the extent to which velocity shocks are offset is always smaller in the constrained case ($\phi = 0$) than in the case of unconstrained policy advice. The reason for this result provides insight into the general advice problem: a large ψ has a directly beneficial effect in that it reduces the variance of output due to velocity shocks, but it indirectly increases the variance of output to the extent that it increases uncertainty about the level of the money supply. In the case of the unconstrained advice, however, the effects of monetary surprises are somewhat mitigated because the advisor partially offsets lagged money surprises. Thus, in his advice with respect to velocity shocks, the advisor can afford to be more activist. When λ is very low, the probability that a money surprise will be offset is reduced, and so the gap between the unconstrained and constrained offsets to velocity shocks is small.

The fact that the optimal values of ϕ and ψ are the same when the alternative policy is passive can be explained as follows: from the point of view of a person signing contracts in period $t-2$, a velocity shock in $t-1$ and a policy surprise have the same effect on nominal GNP ($m+v$). This result is not robust to different specifications of the alternative policy, however, as will be seen in section four.

As λ approaches one, ϕ^* and ψ^* approach negative one. As the likelihood of being listened to approaches certainty, the optimal advice approaches the optimal policy: both policy shocks and velocity shocks are fully offset. Of course, when λ actually equals one, ϕ is irrelevant since there are no policy surprises. As λ approaches zero, ϕ^* and ψ^* approach $-4/13$, which is the same limiting value as we obtained in section 2. The fact that these parameters do not tend toward zero confirms the result obtained in the restricted model above: the deviation from the alternative policy does not vanish even as the likelihood of being listened to declines to zero. Of course, as in section 2, ϕ^* and ψ^* are not defined when $\lambda=0$. In such a case, advice has no ability to affect the variance of output and so it does not make sense to talk about any particular value of the advice parameter being optimal.

4. OPTIMAL ADVICE FOR A GENERAL ALTERNATIVE POLICY

We can generalize the previous results along yet another dimension by allowing the alternative policy to take a more general form. The general form we consider can readily incorporate an alternative policy that is itself the result of an optimization problem for another advisor with a different objective function. An example of such an alternative advisor is provided in section 5. The derivation of

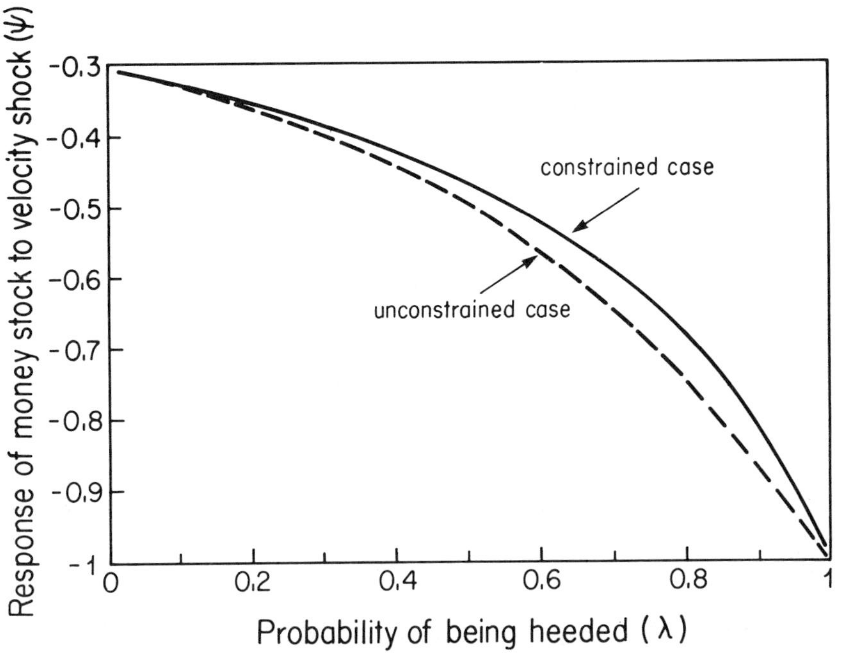

FIG. 2. Advised Offset to Velocity Shocks

optimal advice in this case is tedious, and we defer it to an Appendix. In this section we simply set up the problem and state some of our results.

We specify a very general alternative policy as follows:

$$z_t^{alt} = a(z_{t-1} - {}_{t-2}z_{t-1}) + b\epsilon_{t-1} + s_{t-1} + q_{t-2}\ , \tag{21}$$

where q_{t-2} can be anything known at time t–2, and s_{t-1} is a random variable known at t–1 but orthogonal to everything known at time t–2 and to the lagged money surprise $z_{t-1} - {}_{t-2}z_{t-1}$. The only restrictions that we impose on the alternative policy are that the parameters a and b be constant and that s be covariance stationary. The previous section considered the special case in which $a = b = s_{t-1} = q_{t-2} = 0$.

The alternative policy, z^{alt}, has been given a general linear form that nests a number of interesting economic phenomena. For example, s_{t-1} may be viewed as a "sunspot," a variable which is not inherently significant. We show in the Appendix that the optimal advice will react to sunspots that affect the alternative policy. The parameter a dictates the response of the alternative policy to money stock surprises. These surprises might appear in the alternative policy rule for the same reason that they appear in the optimal advice rule. The term q_{t-2} can include any deterministic factors in the alternative policy rule; for example, if the alternative rule were a "k percent growth rule," then k would appear as part of

q_{t-2}. In the Appendix we show that the optimal advice exactly matches the alternative policy in its responses to q_{t-2}. For example, if the alternative policy is inflationary (high q_{t-2}) in certain periods like election years, the optimal advice tends to be inflationary then as well. Finally, since the general optimal policy has three reaction parameters, we show in the Appendix that it is possible for the advisors to agree completely on some elements of policy advice and still disagree on others.

5. THE VIRTUE OF COMPROMISE

In this section we show that optimal advice is not a substitute for compromise. We show that two advisors with different objective functions can be made better off by compromising with each other over what advice to give than by noncooperatively giving "optimal advice."

For purposes of simplicity, we once again restrict the advisor's reaction functions to have a single parameter. That is, our advisor is the one considered in section 2, who gives advice of the form $m_t = m_{t-1} + \psi \epsilon_{t-1}$. To explore the set of possible compromises, we also endow the "alternative advisor" of section 2 with a simple objective function that justifies the alternative policy considered in that section. Specifically, we posit that the alternative advisor is a "monetarist" in the sense that he wants to minimize the variance of growth in the money stock. Such an advisor always advises $\Delta m = 0$, regardless of the advice of his competitor. Thus the optimal advice that we derived in section 2 is also the Nash equilibrium of a game between these two advisors.

Our goal here is to find a set of "compromise" values of the advice parameter ψ that, if adhered to all of the time, would make both advisors better off. That is, if both advisors were to advise this compromise value (so that it was applied all of the time), both the variance of output and the variance of money growth would be lower than if the advisors played the Nash equilibrium.

We begin by finding $\underline{\psi}$, defined as the smallest absolute value of the reaction parameter that, if applied all of the time, would produce the same level of the variance of output as the Nash equilibrium. Any value of ψ between $\underline{\psi}$ and negative one, if agreed to by both advisors, would make the output-stabilizing advisor better off than he would be under the Nash equilibrium. Substituting the equation for the optimal advice (8) into the expression for the variance of output (7) yields an expression for the variance of output under the Nash solution, as a function of λ. We define this expression as $K(\lambda)\sigma_\epsilon^2$. The variance of output when both advisors agree on policy ψ is:

$$\text{var}(y) = (1/4 + [1/3 + 1/3\,\underline{\psi}]^2)\,\sigma_\epsilon^2. \tag{22}$$

Setting these two expressions equal yields an expression for $\underline{\psi}$

$$\underline{\psi} = -1 \pm 3\sqrt{1/4 + K(\lambda)}. \tag{23}$$

Only the larger solution of this equation is between zero (the value that the monetarist advisor would choose) and negative one (the value that the output stabilizer would choose if he were sure of being listened to), and so there is no ambiguity regarding the value of $\underline{\psi}$.

We define $\bar{\psi}$ analogously to $\underline{\psi}$. That is, $\bar{\psi}$ is the highest absolute value of ψ that, if applied all of the time, would produce the same variance of money growth as the Nash equilibrium. The monetarist advisor would be happy to agree to any value of ψ between $\bar{\psi}$ and zero. To find $\bar{\psi}$, note that under the Nash equilibrium ($\psi = \psi^*$), the variance of changes in the money stock is $\lambda\psi^{*2}\sigma_\epsilon^2$. When both advisors agree on a policy $\bar{\psi}$, the variance is $\bar{\psi}\sigma_\epsilon^2$. Setting these two equal yields an expression for $\bar{\psi}$:

$$\bar{\psi} = \psi^*\sqrt{\lambda}\,.$$

Figure 3 graphs $\underline{\psi}$ and $\bar{\psi}$ as functions of λ. Also included in the figure is the value of ψ^*, the optimal advice of the output stabilizing advisor under Nash equilibrium. As can be seen, for any value of λ, there is always a set of compromise values of ψ that will make both advisors better off. For any value of λ strictly between zero and one, there is a multiplicity of values of ψ that satisfy both advisors: the exact value of ψ chosen would presumably be the outcome of some bargaining process between the two.

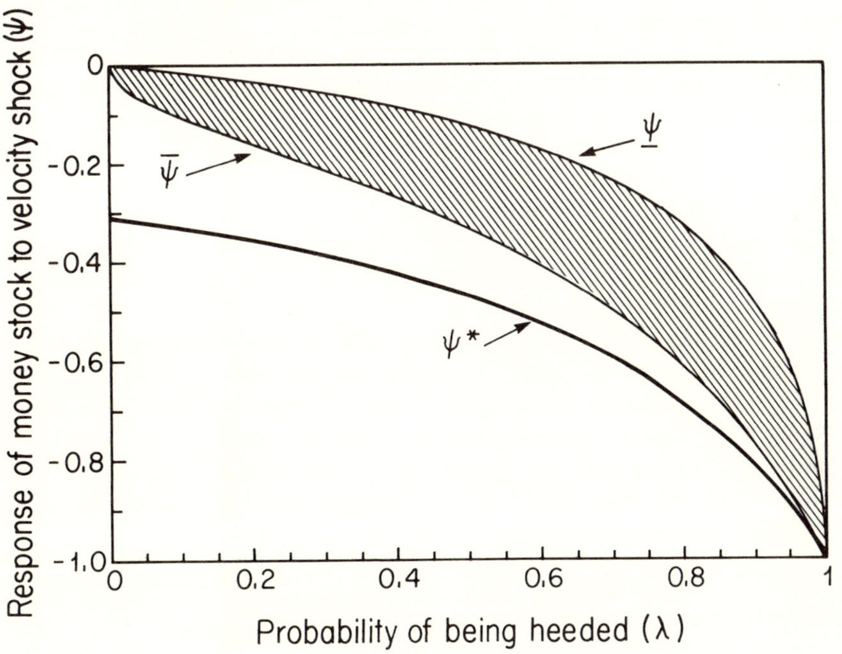

FIG. 3. Optimal Advice versus Compromise

It should also be noted that any of the "compromise" values of ψ derived above could be viewed as the subgame perfect equilibrium of an infinitely repeated game with sufficiently little discounting (see Fudenberg and Maskin 1986).[10] To the extent that giving advice is better characterized as a one-shot game, however, it may be the case that compromise cannot be achieved, and thus we would expect the advisors to arrive at the Nash solution of the one-shot game.

6. CONCLUSION

In this paper we have explored the problems facing an economist asked to give prescriptions for monetary policy who knows that his advice might not be heeded. We have shown that the optimal advice rule generally differs from the conventionally derived optimal policy rule. Specifically, optimal advice tends to resemble the alternative policy that will be followed if the advice is ignored. This is because giving advice that is very different from the alternative policy raises the variance of unanticipated money and thus of output. The advisor faces a dilemma: his optimal advice reflects a compromise between his desire to make monetary policy predictable by copying the alternative policy and his desire to offset exogenous shocks to aggregate demand.

The rule that we have derived is clearly sensitive to the choice of model. The model that we have chosen is representative of a class of models in which systematic monetary policy can be used to stabilize output because of the existence of nominal stickiness. The informational advantage of the monetary authority in these models comes from its ability to set the money supply after some prices have been set in nominal terms. The tension between recommending the optimal monetary policy and mimicking the alternative policy disappears if the monetary authority has no such informational advantage. In such a model (for example, Lucas's 1973 misperceptions model), unanticipated money can only raise the variance of output, and the optimal advice exactly copies the alternative policy.

Various extensions of this work are possible. One step toward realism is to imagine that there are many different advisors. It is easy to show that if there are n advisors, all of whom have the same objective function and each with probability of being heeded λ_i, then they will all give the same advice, and this advice will be the same as the advice given by a single advisor with a probability of being heeded of $\sum_i \lambda_i$. Thus the "advisor" in our model could be reinterpreted as a particular school of thought comprised of many like-minded individuals. This result follows immediately from the fact that all n advisors are maximizing the same function. Another type of extension of our model is to deal explicitly with the

[10]Note that in previous sections we have implicitly assumed zero discounting by taking the variance of output, rather than the discounted sum of squares of future deviations of output from its mean, as the argument in the advisor's objective function. Note also that the complete set of equilibria of the long-run game is larger than the set of "compromise" equilibria that we identify, because reversion to the Nash equilibrium is not the worst possible punishment that can be imposed upon a player who deviates.

issue, raised in the introduction, of how the probability that advice will be followed is determined. In the notation of the model, we would like to make λ endogenous. Future work on this problem might thus combine the framework for optimal advice developed here with a richer model of the political decision-making process.

APPENDIX

In this appendix we present the derivation of optimal advice when the "alternative policy" is of a very general form. It is convenient to specify the optimal advice as a deviation from the alternative policy. Let x_{t-1} represent this deviation. Above we used x_{t-1} to represent the advice itself rather than its deviation from the alternative policy; since the alternative was passive, however, these came to the same thing.

Using the notation developed above, the change in the money stock is given by

$$z_t = a(z_{t-1} - {}_{t-2}z_{t-1}) + b\epsilon_{t-1} + s_{t-1} + q_{t-2} + \pi_t x_{t-1} . \tag{13'}$$

Proceeding as in the last section, we can express output as follows:

$$y_t = 1/2\, \eta_t x_{t-1} + 1/3\, \eta_{t-1} x_{t-2} + 1/3\, [a\eta_{t-1} x_{t-2} + b\epsilon_{t-1} + s_{t-1} + \lambda(x_{t-1} - {}_{t-2}x_{t-1})] + 1/2\, \epsilon_t + 1/3\, \epsilon_{t-1} . \tag{14'}$$

We now specify x in a manner that allows us to separate the elements that are essential to reaching an optimum from those that are extraneous:

$$x_{t-1} = \phi\eta_{t-1} x_{t-2} + \psi\epsilon_{t-1} + \omega s_{t-1} + g_{t-1} + h_{t-2} , \tag{10'}$$

where h_{t-2} can be anything known at time $t-2$ and g_{t-1} is orthogonal to all information at time $t-2$ and to $\eta_{t-1}x_{t-2}$, ϵ_{t-1}, and s_{t-1}. We will prove below that for the optimal advice g and h are always zero. This will allow us to exclude some variables that do not appear explicitly in (10′) that one might expect would appear in the optimal advice rule. For example, we can establish that the value of π_{t-1}, which indicates which advisor was heeded in period $t-1$, does not enter the advice rule since it is potentially part of g_{t-1}.

Substituting (10′) into (14′) gives

$$y_t = 1/2\, \eta_t x_{t-1} + 1/3(1+a+\lambda\phi)\eta_{t-1} x_{t-2} + 1/2\, \epsilon_t + 1/3(1+b+\lambda\psi)\epsilon_{t-1} + 1/3(1+\lambda\omega)s_{t-1} + 1/3\, \lambda g_{t-1} . \tag{15'}$$

Again we have arranged matters so that each of the terms in (15′) is orthogonal to all of the others. By assumption, η_t and ϵ_t are independent of each other and with everything known at time $t-1$; therefore, the first and third terms are orthogonal to each other and to all other terms. For the same reason, the second and fourth terms are uncorrelated. They are orthogonal to the last two terms by construction. Finally, g_{t-1} is constructed to be orthogonal to s_{t-1}.

We minimize the variance of output, which is

$$\begin{aligned}\mathrm{var}(y) = {} & [1/4\,\lambda(1-\lambda)\,E(x_{t-1}^2) + 1/9\,(1+a+\lambda\phi)^2\,\lambda(1-\lambda)\,E(x_{t-2}^2)] \\ & + [1/4 + 1/9(1+b+\lambda\psi)^2]\sigma_\epsilon^2 + 1/9(1+\lambda\omega)^2\sigma_s^2 \\ & + 1/9\,\lambda^2\sigma_g^2\,. \qquad (16')\end{aligned}$$

The variances of the policy deviations can be found from equation (10′). All of the terms on the right-hand side of that equation are mutually orthogonal, allowing us to write

$$\begin{aligned}E(x_{t-1}^2) = {} & \phi^2\lambda(1-\lambda)\,E(x_{t-2}^2) + \psi^2\sigma_\epsilon^2 + \omega^2\sigma_s + E(g_{t-1}^2) \\ & + E(h_{t-2}^2)\,. \qquad (17')\end{aligned}$$

It is clear from (16′) and (17′) that g and h can only add to the variance of output. Thus the optimal advice will always set them equal to zero. Once g and h are set to zero, x is covariance stationary and

$$\sigma_x^2 = \frac{\psi^2\sigma_\epsilon^2 + \omega^2\sigma_s^2}{1-\lambda(1-\lambda)\phi^2}\,. \qquad (18')$$

Substituting this expression into (17′),

$$\begin{aligned}\mathrm{var}(y) = {} & \frac{[1/4 + 1/9\,(1+a+\lambda\phi)^2]\lambda(1-\lambda)(\psi^2\sigma_\epsilon^2 + \omega^2\sigma_s^2)}{1-\lambda(1-\lambda)\phi^2} \\ & + [1/4 + 1/9(1+b+\lambda\psi)^2]\sigma_\epsilon^2 + 1/9(1+\lambda\omega)^2\sigma_s^2\,. \qquad (19')\end{aligned}$$

The minimization of variance with respect to ϕ is separable from the rest of the problem. By minimizing

$$F(\phi) = \frac{1/4 + 1/9\,(1+a+\lambda\phi)^2}{1-\lambda(1-\lambda)\phi^2} \qquad (24)$$

with respect to ϕ, we minimize the variance of y with respect to ϕ. Taking the derivative of F with respect to ϕ and setting it equal to zero yields the following quadratic equation for the optimal ϕ:

$$4\lambda(1-\lambda)(1+a)\phi^2 + [4(1-\lambda)(1+a)^2 + 9 - 5\lambda]\phi + 4(1+a) = 0 . \quad (25)$$

For the denominator of F to be positive, ϕ must fall in the range $(-\ 1/\sqrt{\lambda(-\lambda)},\ 1/\sqrt{\lambda(1-\lambda)}\ )$. This criterion eliminates one of the roots of (25) for the following reason: the quadratic in ϕ is always negative when $\phi = -1/\sqrt{\lambda(1-\lambda)}$ and positive when $\phi = 1/\sqrt{\lambda(1-\lambda)}$; therefore the quadratic must cross the axis an odd number of times in this range. Since the quadratic can cross the axis two times in all, it must cross it exactly once in this range.

Note that if $a = -1$ (that is, the alternative policy involves fully offsetting the money surprise), then the optimal ϕ is zero, which implies agreement with this element of the alternative policy. There could still be disagreement about other elements of monetary policy, such as the response to ϵ_{t-1}, so that there may still be money surprises. Once we have found the minimized value of F, it is straightforward to solve for the optimal ψ and ω. These are:

$$\psi^* = -(1+b)\ /\ [9(1-\lambda)\ F(\phi^*) + \lambda] \text{ and} \quad (26)$$

$$\omega^* = -1\ /\ [9(1-\lambda)\ F(\phi^*) + \lambda]\ . \quad (27)$$

The equivalence of ϕ^* and ψ^* which held in section 3 breaks down if either a or b does not equal zero. From (26) it is clear that if the alternative policy completely offsets velocity shocks (if $b = -1$), then the optimal advice is in agreement with the alternative policy's response to these shocks ($\psi^* = 0$). The similarity of form in the expressions for ψ^* and ω^* can be explained as follows. The part of the velocity shock that is left uncancelled by the alternative policy is $(1+b)\epsilon_{t-1}$. In terms of the optimal advice, the part of the velocity shock that is not offset by the alternative policy is just like any other extraneous action of the alternative policy that is a surprise dated $t-1$ (which is exactly what s_{t-1} represents).

Since $F \geq 1/4$,

$$1\ /\ [9(1-\lambda)\ F(\psi^*)+ \lambda] \leq 1.$$

Therefore ψ^* and ω^* bring the optimal advice only part of the way from the alternative policy toward the first best policy.

As λ approaches one, ϕ^* approaches $-(1+a)$, so that the policy parameter $\phi^* + a$ approaches negative one. The reaction to the sunspot s_{t-1}, which is $\omega^* + 1$, approaches zero. As λ approaches zero,

$$\phi^* \text{ approaches } -4(1+a)/\ [4(1+a)^2 + 9]$$

$$\text{and } \omega^* \text{ approaches } -1\ /\ [(9/4) + (1+a+\phi^*)^2].$$

The fact that neither of these quantities tends toward zero confirms the result obtained in the restricted models above: the deviation from the alternative policy does not vanish even as the likelihood of being listened to declines to zero.

LITERATURE CITED

Aizenman, Joshua, and Jacob A. Frenkel. "Supply Shocks, Wage Indexation, and Monetary Accommodation." *Journal of Money, Credit, and Banking* 18 (August 1986), 304–22.

Blinder, Alan S., and N. Gregory Mankiw. "Aggregation and Stabilization Policy in a Multi-Contract Economy." *Journal of Monetary Economics* 13 (January 1984), 67–86.

Brainard, William C. "Uncertainty and the Effectiveness of Policy." *American Economic Review* (May 1967).

Fischer, Stanley. "Long-Term Contracts, Rational Expectations, and the Optimal Money Supply Rule." *Journal of Political Economy* 85 (February 1977), 191–205.

Friedman, Milton. "The Effects of a Full-Employment Policy on Economic Stability: A Formal Analysis." In *Essays in Positive Economics*. Chicago, University of Chicago Press, 1953.

Fudenberg, Drew, and Eric Maskin. "The Folk Theorem in Repeated Games with Discounting or with Incomplete Information." *Econometrica* 54 (May 1986), 533–54.

Lucas, Robert E., Jr. "Some International Evidence on Output-Inflation Tradeoffs." *American Economic Review* 63 (June 1973), 326–34.

Sims, Christopher A. "Policy Analysis with Econometric Models." *Brookings Papers on Economic Activity* 1 (1982), 107–52.

Taylor, John. "Aggregate Dynamics and Staggered Contracts." *Journal of Political Economy* 88 (February 1980), 1–23.

THOMAS HAVRILESKY

The Influence of the Federal Advisory Council on Monetary Policy

SCHOLARLY INTEREST IN THE POLITICAL AND INTEREST GROUP INFLUENCES on Federal Reserve policy-making has grown rapidly in recent years. This awareness is motivated by the literature on the new political business cycle (the electoral/partisanship cycle) and the public choice theory of monetary policy as well as the growing consensus regarding the nature of the symbiosis between the Federal Reserve System and the executive and legislative branches of government. Researchers agree on the existence of political influences but disagree as to their importance. The traditional notion of Congressional influence on Federal Reserve policy has fairly weak empirical support (Beck 1990). There is, however, somewhat stronger evidence of systematic Administration influence on monetary policy decisions (Havrilesky 1988a).

Considerably less work has been done on private interest group influence on monetary policy. Three significant questions need to be answered. First, do private interest groups attempt to influence Federal Reserve policy-making systematically over time? The impact of fiscal and other shocks on interest rates, exchange rates, and output may be so variable over time (for example, because of changes in the tax and financial regulatory structures) and the political clout of certain interest groups may be so variable over time (for example, because of demographic changes) as to militate against persistent pressures from specific

The author thanks John Gildea, Dek Terrell, and Charles Wickliffe for their assistance with this paper, and Henry Chappel, Robert Eisenbeis, William Kaempfer, Allan Meltzer, Woo Sik Jung, Dudley Wallace, and two referees for their helpful comments. Participants in the seminars at the University of South Carolina and at the Center for the Study of Public Choice at George Mason University were also helpful. Allan Meltzer kindly provided the Shadow Open Market Committee *Policy Statements*.

THOMAS HAVRILESKY *is professor of economics at Duke University.*

Journal of Money, Credit, and Banking, Vol. 22, No. 1 (February 1990)

private groups.[1] Second, if systematic attempts are made to influence monetary policy, what are the channels of communication? Do private interest groups try to affect monetary policy directly through formal institutions within the Federal Reserve System, such as the Bank directorates, where they are represented (Havrilesky 1986), the Federal Advisory Council or the Consumer Advisory Council, does their influence work indirectly through lobbying pressure on the executive and legislative branches which, in turn, may periodically transmit related signals to the Federal Reserve, or does their influence work because Federal Reserve officials pay attention to the opinions of spokespersons and analysts employed by private interest groups?[2] Third, whatever the interest groups and their communications channels, can the signals be measured? If policy directives within formal institutions are not made public and if analysts, spokespersons, and lobbyists do not regularly receive public media exposure, evidence of signaling will be difficult to uncover.

Among the constellation of private interests that are strongly affected by monetary policy perhaps the most directly and persistently impacted is the financial services sector. Bankers bear the initial impact of open market policy and Federal Reserve officials have long been concerned with their adjustment to and opinion of monetary policy actions. Within the financial services sector the banking industry is probably the most affected. However, the relationship between the Federal Reserve and the banking industry is not one-sided. In order to protect its regulatory and budgetary powers the Federal Reserve frequently relies on the political support of the banking industry. Banking's traditional concern with regulatory and monetary policy and the Federal Reserve's desire to sustain the industry's political support help to account for the presence of formal communications structures within the Federal Reserve System. For example, there are three bankers and three banker-elected nonbankers among the nine directors of each Federal Reserve Bank. In addition, Federal Reserve Bank Presidents and Board of Governors appointees often are selected because they have a background in the banking industry (Havrilesky and Schweitzer 1990).

Despite its symbiotic ties with the Federal Reserve and the fact that it is the source of the best articulated private opinions on the state of the economy, the banking industry, unlike other groups that may be concerned about interest rates, exchange rates, etc., rarely allows its monetary policy preferences to be

[1]As an example of variable political clout, in the 1960s and 1970s before financial deregulation, first-time homebuyers and the attendant home construction industry (debtor clientele of depository intermediaries) were vocal and powerful opponents of interest rate increases. After deregulation and with the growth of the creditor–senior citizens lobby, debtor clientele became less vocal and less important sources of private pressure on monetary policy. As an example of the variable impact of shocks, after 1982 the liberalization of Japanese foreign exchange laws and the elimination of the withholding tax on interest paid to foreigners may have caused fiscal shocks to impact more powerfully on exchange rates, rather than interest rates, and raised the ire of export-oriented and import-sensitive sectors (Havrilesky 1988b).

[2]The published commentary of banking industry analysts is carefully studied by Federal Reserve officials. Perhaps these opinions constitute signals which propel monetary policy actions. To identify the analysts and to develop a historical record of their opinions would constitute a valuable research undertaking (see footnote 15).

publicized. Banking lobbying groups never publicly reproach Fed officials, hardly ever openly signal their policy desires, and are seldom terribly vocal about prospective Board of Governors appointments. In fact, neither the American Bankers Association nor the Association of Reserve City Bankers appear to even bother to monitor monetary policy (Wooley 1984). The lack of measurable signaling is remarkable given the regular interchanges that occur between private and central banking personnel, and their mutual interests, critical insights, and forecasts regarding the effects of monetary policy.[3]

Given the absence of overt monetary policy signaling, the most important systematic and measurable communications between the banking industry and the Federal Reserve System would appear to emanate from the Federal Advisory Council. Thus, even though banking's influence on monetary policy may primarily occur through direct communication with the legislative and executive branches and with Fed leadership (other than through the Federal Advisory Council), evidence of such signaling is difficult to uncover. This leaves the directives of the Federal Advisory Council as the best measure of the banking sector's monetary policy preferences.

Created by the Federal Reserve Act of 1913, when the original plan for creating a bank-governed System was abandoned (Lindley 1977), the Council is composed of twelve bankers, almost always from larger banks, each elected for a one-year term by the directorates of each of the Federal Reserve Banks.[4] The Council meets with the Board of Governors four times a year in a formal advisory role.

There are two distinct views of the importance of the Federal Advisory Council (FAC) directives. The conventional view, found in many textbooks and monographs (for example, Bach 1971), is that the Council's opinions are relatively unimportant. This view is supported by the lack of significant publicity regarding the FAC opinions, except when it is convenient to the Board, for example, in 1974 when the Council urged caution in bank lending practices. Although quite active and openly vocal in the thirties, the FAC has been virtually invisible in recent decades [Wooley 1984]. The conventional view is consistent with the aforementioned low profile of banking lobbying groups in discussing monetary policy and may be exacerbated by the fact that FAC deliberations and directives have long been kept secret. In short, the conventional view seems to be that since there is little hard evidence of banking's influence, there is scant reason to suspect

[3]There are two plausible explanations for the banking industry's suppressing its opinions regarding monetary policy. First the public atmosphere is usually hostile toward banking's involvement in politics. The American populist tradition has never held political activity by bankers in high regard. Moreover, there is often palpable public resentment whenever banks raise the prime rate. Finally, recent controversy over the campaign contributions of big bank Political Action Committees (Havrilesky 1989) has increased the public's wariness. Second, as discussed later, private and central bankers enjoy a comfortable symbiosis. Central bankers regularly side with their private banking clientele in regulatory matters and private bankers are usually prepared to protect the Federal Reserve from proposed legislation which would reduce its powers. Given this mutually supportive behavior in such a (latently) hostile political environment, it is probably wise that banks sustain a low profile with regard to monetary policy.

[4]This lends support to the notion that large banks (not small banks, other depository or financial services institutions) influence monetary policy.

that such influence exists. The alternative to the conventional view, which we call the symbiotic view, is less sanguine.

The growing consensus in the scholarly literature is that a symbiosis has evolved between Congress, the executive branch, the Federal Reserve, and the financial community. Every Congress, with the blessing of the Administration, continues to grant the Federal Reserve autonomy, budgetary authority, and regulatory hegemony. The financial community has long been supportive of this arrangement. On many occasions the Federal Reserve has enlisted the support of private bankers to lobby against bills which would reduce its autonomy [Auerbach 1985]. In exchange, the Federal Reserve serves as every Administration's whipping boy (for economic misfortune) and sound money oracle, pledging anti-inflationary vigilance at every opportunity. Further, in exchanges at Congressional hearings, its officials tend to support the regulatory policies favored by the most important financial services' interest groups.

Autonomy permits the Fed to operate under a cloak of obscure and esoteric operating procedures. This together with its sound money homage may set the stage for politically favorable monetary surprises. Most importantly, autonomy may allow the executive branch and private sector interest groups periodically to signal covertly, rather than to direct publicly, the monetary policy they desire.[5] The purpose of this paper is to discover whether the banking industry is one of those interest groups.

Occasionally, the symbiotic view takes on traditional populist overtones (for example, Greider 1987) that call forth images of a banker-controlled monetary policy and harken back to an earlier era when Representative Wright Patman headed the House Banking and Currency Committee (U.S. Congress 1964). The populist variant can border on a capture theory of monetary and financial regulatory policy. The FAC would figure prominently in this theory since it is part of a unique institutional arrangement, a regulated industry holding secret meetings with its regulators.

The purpose of this paper is to test the hypothesis that monetary policy is responsive to signals from the banking industry as reflected in the directives issued quarterly by the Federal Advisory Council. The existence of an influence would not necessarily support a capture theory since the FAC could, indeed, be acting in the public interest rather than in the interest of the banking industry. Moreover, the existence of influence would not necessarily even support the view that the FAC is an important means of the industry signaling the Fed. As pointed out earlier, FAC directives may simply be a proxy for signaling that is occurring

[5]According to the public choice theory of monetary policy, monetary surprises generally occur in response to dissonance from economic interest groups over the impact of an Administration's income redistribution program on interest rates and exchange rates (Havrilesky 1988b). (Despite persuasive theoretical arguments aligned against the idea, "the divine right of interest rate selection" is still ceremoniously conveyed on a dutiful Federal Reserve by elected leaders and the nation's financial community still gives its blessing.) Given the enormous amount of noisy signaling from so many quarters, public and private, and the secret nature of FAC directives, there could exist considerable latitude for monetary surprises to affect interest rates in response to select banking sector signals.

by way of the under-publicized activity of analysts, spokespersons, and lobbyists (see footnote 3). Nevertheless, the presence of such influence, however it is motivated, should serve to repudiate the conventional view that the directives of the Council are insignificant.

TESTS

In the following tests the posture of monetary policy is first measured by the Federal funds rate because it was the primary intermediate target of monetary policy over most of the entire 1973–1985 period[6] and because it is of paramount concern to the banking industry. Inasmuch as banking profits are widely believed to have been sensitive to changes in the level and term structure of interest rates during the sample period, interest volatility is viewed as being "costly" to the banking industry (Lombra and Karamouzis 1990).[7]

The FAC directives were obtained from the Board of Governors for the thirteen-year period from 1973 to 1985 by invoking the Freedom of Information Act. Of the fifty-two meetings over that span, the Council failed to issue a directive on one occasion and the Board did not relinquish two other directives. Until this paper FAC directives have never been published.

While the structure of the directives has changed over the years, they were always worded as responses to questions from the Board about the appropriate posture of monetary policy. The Council's answers indicate either agreement with current monetary policy or provide fairly explicit requests for a desired change in the direction of ease or tightness. Each directive that explicitly calls for ease was rated +1; each directive that explicitly calls for tightness was rated −1. Many directives contain qualified agreement with the monetary policy current at the time they were issued. Those that qualified on the side of ease were rated +1/2; those that qualified on the side of tightness were rated −1/2. Directives that gave unqualified support for the current thrust of monetary policy were assigned a value of zero. Excerpts from each directive and the index value assigned to it are reported in the Appendix.

As a test for consistency, the author's assigned values were compared to those assigned by a senior undergraduate economics major. Disagreements occured in only five of forty-nine cases. Four of these emanated from FAC concerns for "policy volatility" to which the student assigned a rating of zero. The author, having lived through the period, assigned a value of −1/2 to these directives (see footnote 9). As another test, the author's assigned values were compared to those

[6]A number of reaction function studies have employed the Federal funds rate as a measure of monetary policy over this time span.

[7]In order for banking sector signaling to be plausible, it is not necessary to make the extreme assumption that certain banks position their balance sheets to take advantage of the subsequent interest rate changes which they direct through the FAC; it is sufficient that the banking industry, in general, simply favors interest rate smoothing and that the FAC is aware of this sentiment (see footnote 5).

assigned strictly independently by an economics professor at another university. In this case there were no disagreements across the entire sample of directives.

The log of the Federal funds rate was regressed by ordinary least squares on its lagged value and the index of FAC directives. Three-month averages of weekly Fed funds rates were used. The value of the index for each period was derived from the directive issued at the very beginning of the period. Directives were issued at the beginning of February, May, September, and November. Logs were employed in order to collapse the tremendous range of Federal funds rate levels that prevailed over the 1973–1985 period. The result was[8]

$$\ln FedFundsRate_t = \underset{(2.575)}{0.375} + \underset{(15.723)}{0.852} \ln FedFundsRate_{t-1} - \underset{(-4.972)}{0.185}\, FAC\ index_t . \quad (1)$$

$\bar{R}^2 = .86$ DF $= 47$ D-W $= 2.04$

Comparing this result to the same regression without the FAC index,

$$\ln FedFundsRate_t = \underset{(2.051)}{0.299} + \underset{(13.076)}{0.865} \ln FedFundsRate_{t-1} . \quad (2)$$

$\bar{R}^2 = .78$ DF $= 48$ D-W $= 1.80$

Specifying the dependent variable as a first difference, the result was

$$\Delta \ln FedFundsRate_t = \underset{(-0.345)}{0.007} + \underset{(-4.666)}{0.178}\ FAC\ index_t . \quad (3)$$

$\bar{R}^2 = .31$ DF $= 47$ D-W $= 2.02$

The t-statistics are in parentheses. The estimated coefficients for the index are highly significant and the fit improves considerably from equation (2) to equation (1).[9]

While the FAC directives were couched in terms of both monetary aggregates and interest rates, movements in the latter have a greater impact on bank profits and are of considerably greater concern to all financial market participants (see footnote 7). Therefore, it was felt that the Federal funds rate would be a more appropriate measure of policy. However, when the monetary aggregates were

[8]I did not estimate a reaction function using three-month averages of Fed funds rates as the dependent variable and three-month averages of state-of-the-economy measures as the explanatory variables because Fed funds rates are generally thought to be responsive to conditions over a shorter time span, such as a month. Unfortunately, the employment of monthly data would have disallowed the use of the FAC index which is only observed every three months.

[9]When the student's index was employed as the explanatory variable the regression results were very similar to those reported in equations (1), (2), and (3) below. For example,

employed as dependent variables the estimated coefficient for the FAC index was not statistically significant.

These OLS results are, at a minimum, an indication of how close the Fed's perspective is to that of the larger commercial banks. But do they indicate FAC influence on policy? In other words, there is a likelihood that both the monetary policy control variable and the FAC index were responding to the same information set over the sample period. After all, the FOMC is widely believed to have adjusted the Federal funds rate in response to contemporaneous data on the state of the economy. The FAC could simply have been responding to the same data, especially since FAC meetings over the sample period typically included Federal Reserve staff briefings on the stance of monetary policy and the contemporaneous state of the economy, especially the state of the regional economies of the FAC members.[10]

These conditions could result in the spurious inference of causality from equation (1). However, when the FAC index was regressed, as a dependent variable, on the Federal funds rate, as an explanatory variable, the estimated coefficient was statistically insignificant. In order to further corroborate the predictive power of the FAC index, a test for Granger causality was performed. Two basic regressions were run with the current Federal funds rate as the dependent variable, one with lagged values of the dependent variable and lagged values of the FAC index as arguments. Distributed lags of three, four, and six quarters were tried. In all cases the test statistic exceeded the critical value of the F-distribution at the 0.01 level. The results indicate that the FAC index of directives to the

---

$$\ln FedFundsRate_t = \underset{(2.056)}{0.280} + \underset{(13.931)}{0.868} \ln FedFundsRate_{t-1} - \underset{(-3.574)}{0.141}\ Student's\ FAC\ index_t \qquad (2')$$

$\bar{R}^2 = .83$ DF = 47 D-W = 2.07

When the Fed funds rate was not transformed into logs the results were similar to equations (1), (2), and (3) in terms of the signs and significance of the estimates, except that the $\bar{R}^2$s each fell by approximately 10 percentage points.

When the FAC index is broken up into two variables, $FACE$ for all ease directives and $FACT$ for all tightness directives, the result was

$$\ln FedFundsRate_t = \underset{(2.527)}{0.300} + \underset{(15.591)}{0.844} \ln Fed\ FundsRate_{t-1} - \underset{(-1.477)}{0.108}\ FACE_t - \underset{(-4.228)}{0.238}\ FACT_t$$

$\bar{R}^2 = .85$ DF = 46 D-W = 1.94

Compared to (1), the fit improves but only the tightness directives $FACT$ have a statistically significant coefficient. This suggests that the Federal Open Market Committee responds to FAC requests for tightness but is motivated by other information in its moves toward ease.

[10]FAC members are often said to be sources of information to the FOMC regarding their regional economies. The Federal Reserve Staff's Beige Book collates information on these economies prepared by the staffs of Federal Reserve District Banks. This Beige Book information is an important input at FOMC meetings. Thereby, FAC directives could simply be a proxy for Beige Book information and thereby have no predictive power.

Board of Governors is econometrically causal over the sample period, containing information that predicts the Federal funds rate. This does not disprove the conjecture that, if it is targeting on the Fed funds rate, the Open Market Committee was responding to the Federal Advisory Council, rather than both the Committee and the Council responding to the same information set.

A problem arises if it is assumed that the Federal Reserve was not targeting the Federal funds rate during the 1973–1985 time period. Alternative measures of monetary policy could be extracted from the directives of the Federal Open Market Committee. Because there are so many directives issued by the FOMC during the entire three-month period following each FAC meeting and because the less proximate directives surely reflect non-FAC influences on policy, only the first change in the FOMC directives after the release of each FAC directive was considered. These changes were the basis of an FOMC index. A value of +1 was assigned for FOMC directive changes which called for an easing of monetary policy during the period following the FAC meeting; a value of −1 was assigned for changes which called for a tightening of monetary policy during the period; a value of zero was assigned for no change in policy over the entire three-month period.

The FOMC index was regressed on the index of FAC directives (issued at the beginning of the period) using ordered probit estimation analysis. The result was

$$\mathit{FOMC\ index}_t = \underset{(4.511)}{1.049} + \underset{(2.809)}{0.958}\ \mathit{FAC\ index}_t\,. \tag{4}$$

Log likelihood = −43.79 Number of observations = 49

Percent correctly predicted = 59.18

The t-statistics are in parentheses. The estimated coefficient is highly significant.[11]

This result further strengthens the conjecture that an advisory panel with strong ties to the Fed, the FAC, influences monetary policy and interest rates through its directives to the FOMC.[12] Of course, there are other advisory panels

[11]As explained in footnote 8, whenever the dependent variable is believed to respond to monthly data, it is inadvisable to estimate reaction functions using data for three-month intervals for the explanatory variables. (FOMC directives, like Federal funds rates, are probably responsive to monthly data.) Nevertheless, when such a reaction function was estimated by ordered probit analysis the result was

$$\mathit{FOMC\ index}_t = \underset{(0.178)}{-0.007} + \underset{(0.967)}{63.763}\ \dot{P}_{t-1} + \underset{(1.782)}{0.668}\ \Delta U_{t-1} + \underset{(1.952)}{0.783}\ \mathit{FAC\ index}_t$$

Log likelihood = −44.25 Number of observations = 49

Percent correctly predicted = 61.22

The coefficients for the lagged change (ΔU) in unemployment and for the FAC index were statistically significant and had the expected signs. The coefficient for the lagged inflation rate ($\dot{P}$) was not statistically significant. This result is consistent with the test for Granger causality reported below.

[12]In an OLS regression, the FOMC index was found to have a statistically significant and negative

that also try to influence the FOMC. One of the more prominent of these is the Shadow Open Market Committee (SOMC). In order to test whether the SOMC influences the FOMC, we obtained the SOMC's biannual *Policy Statements* from 1973 to 1989. We indexed these statements +1, −1, and 0, representing the Committee's desire for easier, tighter, or unchanged monetary policy. We then took the first change in the FOMC directive in the period following the SOMC *Policy Statement* and indexed it in the fashion described earlier.[13] The FOMC index was regressed using ordered probit analysis on the SOMC index, as an explanatory variable. The result was

$$FOMC\ index_t = \underset{(0.450)}{0.126} - \underset{(-1.148)}{0.331}\ SOMC\ index_t\,. \quad (5)$$

Log likelihood = −19.90 Number of observations = 25

Percentage correctly predicted = 14.03

The t-statistics are in parentheses. The SOMC index is not significant at a high level of significance.[14] This suggests that an advisory panel with far less formidable ties to the Federal Reserve than the Federal Advisory Council, the SOMC, has little influence on changes in the FOMC directive.[15]

In order to further corroborate our conjecture that the FAC influences monetary policy, a test for Granger causality was performed. Two basic ordered probit regressions were estimated with the current FOMC index as the dependent vari-

---

effect on the change in the log of the average Federal Funds rate during the subsequent three-month period.

$$\Delta \ln FedFundsRate_t = \underset{(0.499)}{0.012} - \underset{(-2.319)}{0.060}\ FOMC\ index_t$$

$\bar{R}^2 = .09$ DF = 47 D-W = 1.95

Comparing this result to equation (3) indicates that the FAC index explains three times more of the variation in the Federal funds rate than the FOMC index over the same historical period.

[13]When the values assigned to this index were compared to those assigned by another money and banking professor who independently examined the same *Policy Statements*, there was disagreement in three of twenty-five cases. However, using his values for the index did not improve the results reported below.

[14]When "no change" directives were discarded and the remaining observations of the SOMC index were dichotomized into ease and tightness directives, there was no improvement in the results reported in (5).

Because the Shadow Open Market Committee pays so much attention to the money supply, the narrow money growth rate for the period following the *Policy Statement* was regressed on the SOMC index as an explanatory variable. The estimated coefficient was insignificant and the $\bar{R}^2$ was very small.

[15]Other advisory groups which may have influenced monetary policy over this period include the Federal Reserve's Consumer Advisory Council as well as the ever-changing panel of economists who were invited to advise the FOMC four times a year until the scheme was scuttled under Paul Volcker's leadership. Unfortunately, the file containing the essential opinions of this group over time was not available at this writing.

able, one with values of the dependent variable lagged four quarters as arguments, the second with the same lagged values of the dependent variable and with lagged values of the FAC index as arguments. The test statistic exceeded the *F*-statistic at the 0.10 level. The results provide support for the idea that the FAC index of directives to the Board of Governors contains information that predicts changes in the FOMC's directive. They do not disprove the conjecture that the Federal Open Market Committee was responding to the Federal Advisory Council, rather than both the Committee and the Council responding to the same information set.

CONCLUDING COMMENT

The issue of banker influence over monetary policy has a long and controversial history. Established by the Federal Reserve Act, the Federal Advisory Council has for decades lurked in the shadows of the monetary policy stage. From the perspective of the Federal Reserve's protective self-interest and interests within the financial services industry, this backstage role is understandable. From other perspectives, any latitude for private interest groups to have a less-than-open influence on monetary policy is questionable.

The evidence adduced in this paper supports the symbiotic view that Federal Reserve monetary policy responds to the signals from the banking industry as reflected in the directives of the Federal Advisory Council. Symbioses in the political economy, as in nature, are remarkably stable. The public choice theory of monetary policy would predict that such symbioses would persist as long as monetary surprises generate short-run net benefits for interest groups and there are sizable costs of (private groups organizing to demand) monetary restraint.

One way in which effective monetary reform might proceed would be to reduce the net benefits to private interest groups of attempting to influence the central bank and to raise the costs to central bankers who would respond to their messages. Another path to effective reform of our monetary institutions would be to reduce the costs of imposing permanent monetary restraint. The results of this paper suggest that either means would be advanced if the Federal Reserve could be insulated from all private interest group influence, including that of the banking industry.

LITERATURE CITED

Auerbach, Robert D. "Politics and the Federal Reserve." *Contemporary Policy Issues* (Fall 1985).

Bach, George Leland. *Making Monetary and Fiscal Policy.* Washington Brookings Institution, 1971.

Beck, Nathaniel. "Congress and the Fed; Why the Dog Doesn't Bark In the Night." In *The Political Economy of American Monetary Policy,* edited by Thomas Mayer. New York: Cambridge University Press, 1990.

Greider, William. *Secrets of the Temple*. New York: Simon and Schuster, 1987.

Hastings, Delbert C., and Ross M. Robertson. "The Mysterious World of the Fed." *Business Horizons* (Spring 1962).

Havrilesky, Thomas. "The Effects of the Federal Reserve Reform Act on the Economic Affiliations of Directors of Federal Reserve Banks." *Social Science Quarterly* 67 (June 1986), 393-401.

______. "Monetary Policy Signaling from the Administration to the Federal Reserve," *Journal of Money, Credit, and Banking* (February 1988), 83–101. (a)

______. "Electoral Cycles in Economic Policy," *Challenge* (July/August 1988), 14–21. (b)

______. "The Causes and Consequences of Big Bank PAC Contributions." Unpublished, September 1989.

Havrilesky, Thomas, and Robert Schweitzer. "A Theory of FOMC Dissent Voting with Evidence from the Time Series." In *The Political Economy of American Monetary Policy*, edited by Thomas Mayer. New York: Cambridge University Press, 1990.

Lindley, James Thomas. "An Analysis of the Federal Advisory Council of the Federal Reserve System, 1914–1938." Ph.D. dissertation, University of Georgia, 1977.

Lombra, Raymond, and Nicholas Karamouzis. "A Positive Analysis of the Policymaking Process of the Federal Reserve." In *The Political Economy of American Monetary Policy*, edited by Thomas Mayer. New York: Cambridge University Press, 1990.

U.S. Congress, House, Subcommittee on Domestic Finance and Committee on Banking and Currency. *Hearings, The Federal Reserve after Fifty Years*. Washington, Government Printing Office, 1964.

Whittlesey, C. R. "Power and Influence in the Federal Reserve." *Economica* (February 1963).

Wooley, John. *Monetary Politics*. New York: Cambridge University Press, 1984.

APPENDIX

INDEX OF FEDERAL ADVISORY COUNCIL DIRECTIVES, 1973–1985

Date of Directive	Excerpt	Index
Feb. 2, 1973	. . . the Council believes a more moderate rate of growth of the monetary aggregates than we experienced in 1972 is appropriate for the period ahead.	−1
May 4, 1973	Monetary and credit policy should continue in the same general posture of recent months.	0
Sept. 7, 1973	. . . any signs of an early easing of restraint should be avoided.	−1/2
Nov. 2, 1973	. . . monetary and credit policy should continue under restraint until inflation is brought under a greater measure of control	0
Feb. 1, 1974	The members of the Council approve monetary and credit policy . . .	0
May 3, 1974	The members of the Council in general favor present monetary and credit policy under current circumstance.	0
Sept. 6, 1974	. . . the continuation of the current restraint effort involves some serious risks. . . On balance, the Council believes that the time is at hand when a modest easing in monetary and credit policy is appropriate and desirable.	+1
Nov. 1, 1974	The Council believes that current monetary and credit policy should provide for a slow growth in money supply. . . . it probably will be necessary to ease monetary policy somewhat in the first half of 1975.	+1/2

APPENDIX (*Continued*)

INDEX OF FEDERAL ADVISORY COUNCIL DIRECTIVES, 1973–1985

Date of Directive	Excerpt	Index
Feb. 6, 1975	Further deterioration in the economy would indicate that monetary policy should continue to move towards ease at least into the second quarter.	+1
May 1, 1975	The Council believes that significant rates of increase in the monetary aggregates will be necessary over the next several months if meaninful recovery is to occur this year.	+1
Sept. 12, 1975	The Council is in accord with the long-term targets for aggregate growth now being pursued by the Federal Reserve System. However, these targets might be too restrictive . . .	+1/2
Nov. 7, 1975	The members of the Council in general approve of present monetary and credit policy under current circumstances . . .	0
Feb. 6, 1976	. . . the Council believes that the Board's ranges for the growth of the monetary aggregates is satisfactory.	0
May 6, 1976	In our judgment, the recent moderate downward revision in monetary aggregate targets outlined by the Chairman is appropriate in present circumstances.	0
Sept. 10, 1976	The Council believes that the pause is temporary and that it does not justify a move toward credit ease. We are in accord with present monetary and credit policy.	0
Nov. 5, 1976	The Council believes that Federal Reserve monetary and credit policy has been appropriate in current circumstances.	0
Feb. 4, 1977	The Council believes that present monetary and credit policy is appropriate under current circumstances	0
May 6, 1977	. . . the Council believes that the growth of the monetary aggregates must be further slowed if the rate of inflation is to be reduced in the years ahead.	−1
Sept. 9, 1977	. . . the Council is concerned that the growth in the monetary aggregates is exceeding the targets with all the implications this has for inflation in the future.	−1/2
Nov. 4, 1977	The Council is in accord with current monetary and credit policy and believes that no change in the present approach toward restraining the growth of money supply would be appropriate, given prevailing economic and financial conditions.	0
Feb. 3, 1978	. . . growth of the monetary aggregates should be kept well in check — and, indeed, lowered on a trend basis — even if this restraint implies a further upward move in interest rates.	−1
May 5, 1978	. . . policy of moderate restraint is thus called for. . . . Fiscal, monetary and credit policy should give first priority to a reduction in the rate of inflation.	−1
Sept. 1978	[The directive for this meeting was not provided.]	
Nov. 1978	[The directive for this meeting was not provided.]	
Feb. 2, 1979	The Council hopes that a more stimulative policy will not be adopted until substantial progress is made towards reducing inflation.	−1/2
May 4, 1979	. . . sustained 8 percent growth in the base and around 10 percent growth in nominal GNP implies a sustained high rate of inflation — averaging 7-8 percent which is still too high. . . . It is the view of some members of the Council, however, that monetary policy should be directed at reducing the present high rate of inflation notwithstanding the risk of recession and the possibility of a subsequent overreaction.	−1/2
Sept. 7, 1979	. . . the need to slow the rapid growth in monetary aggregates should take priority over concerns about further upward moves in domestic interest rates.	−1
Nov. 2, 1979	The words, however, must be followed by the actions that will impact in the weekly reported numbers; that is, a	−1

APPENDIX (*Continued*)

INDEX OF FEDERAL ADVISORY COUNCIL DIRECTIVES, 1973–1985

Date of Directive	Excerpt	Index
	slowing of the growth rate of the monetary base, bank reserves and the monetary aggregates.	
Feb. 8, 1980	The Council continues to believe that domestic monetary policy cannot be considered in isolation. The need to maintain a strong dollar, combined with the more expansive fiscal policy puts even greater weight on the importance of the Fed's actions to reduce the growth rate of the monetary aggregates over the long term and to pursue this objective with determination	−1
May 2, 1980	Continuing with the policy of meeting the monetary targets (particularly M1-B) announced for the year is the appropriate course of action in the months ahead.	0
Sept. 5, 1980	In short, the Council is pleased with the thrust of monetary policy but hopes that the FOMC will take mesures to improve on the conduct of policy. In the months ahead the FOMC should not swerve from its efforts to control monetary growth.	−1/2
Nov. 7, 1980	The Council suggests that the discount rate be adjusted more closely to levels required by the market. This might help prevent excessively rapid borrowed reserve and aggregate growth. The Council is hopeful that the extreme gyrations in the growth of the aggregates may be modified.	−1/2
Feb. 5, 1981	. . . the general policy prescription must be to continue underscoring the need to stay the anti-inflation course . . . continued emphasis on slowing growth of the aggregates . . . continued bias toward resolving doubts on the side of keeping interest rates high in real terms.	−1/2
April 30, 1981	The Council strongly endorses a continuation of a restrictive monetary policy designed to reduce gradually the growth of the monetary aggregates.	−1
Sept. 11, 1981	(No question/comments on monetary policy at the meetings.)	0
Nov. 6, 1981	Some members of the Council are concerned that non-borrowed reserves have been growing at an excessive rate over the last several months.	−1/2
Feb. 5, 1982	. . . there is a great concern over the growth of the aggregates in recent weeks, particularly in view of the weakness in economic activity. The weakness argues against restraint, . . . the Council urges the Federal Reserve to maintain its restrictive policy with growth preferably in the upper end of the target range.	−1/2
May 21, 1982	The Council believes that recent monetary policy has been generally appropriate . . .	0
Sept. 17, 1982	We concur with the Federal Reserve policy of accepting money supply growth somewhat above the existing fourth quarter to fourth quarter targets.	0
Nov. 5, 1982	The Council believes that current monetary policy has been appropriate.	0
Feb. 4, 1983	We suggest a continuance of current policy until there is strong evidence that a recovery is actually underway.	0
May 6, 1983	Current monetary policy seems appropriate in light of sharply lower inflation and the apparent modest pace of the developing recovery.	0
Sept. 9, 1983	Half of the members of the Council believe that in the administration of monetary policy, lesser restraint may prove desirable in the near future.	+1/2
Nov. 4, 1983	The Council agrees that maintaining the present degree of reserve restraint is appropriate.	0
Feb. 3, 1984	At present, if there is any easing in monetary policy, it should be moderate.	−1/2

APPENDIX (*Continued*)

INDEX OF FEDERAL ADVISORY COUNCIL DIRECTIVES, 1973–1985

Date of Directive	Excerpt	Index
May 4, 1984	The Council concurs with the recent tightening of monetary policy. The ramifications of this change need to be observed and carefully evaluated. Should there be meaningful indications of weakening in the economy, a more accommodative policy would be in order.	+1/2
Sept. 7, 1984	At the present time, monetary policy should not become any more restrictive.	+1/2
Nov. 2, 1984	The Council strongly affirms that it was appropriate for Fed policy to allow the recent decline in interest rates. . . . it was felt that monetary policy should not change.	0
Feb. 8, 1985	No further easing is indicated at this time, inasmuch as economic growth appears to have been resumed at a reasonable level.	0
May 3, 1985	The current monetary policy is appropriate.	0
Sept. 6, 1985	The Council believes that the Federal Reserve has appropriately balanced monetary policy in light of the economic environment.	0
Nov. 1, 1985	Present conditions do not seem to warrant change in current monetary policy but a bias towards an easing of credit conditions might be justified if the economy softens, the dollar rebounds, and/or credit problems intensify domestically or abroad.	+1/2

KEVIN DOWD

The Value of Time and the Transactions Demand for Money

THIS PAPER INVESTIGATES THE IDEA that the wage rate influences the demand for money as a proxy for the value of transactions time. This idea was first suggested by Dutton and Gramm (1973) and Karni (1973, 1974, 1975a), but their work had little impact on the literature despite the relatively favorable empirical results they presented. The argument behind this hypothesis is very simple: If money saves transactions costs, and those costs include the time costs of transacting, then it would seem to follow that the value of time—or some proxy, like the wage rate—should be one of the determinants of the demand for money.

This "value-of-time" hypothesis is worth examining further for several reasons. First, most monetary economists would accept that households' time is constrained and valuable, that transactions take time, and that, at the margin at least, the holding of money saves time. Yet traditional transactions cost models of the demand for money seem to deny this by implicitly ruling out any effective role for the time costs of transacting. There is therefore a tension between what we think money does and how we have traditionally modeled it, and the resolution of this tension requires that we acknowledge the role of the value-of-time hypothesis. It follows, then, that we need a transactions cost model that is broad enough to encompass the time costs of transacting as well as nontime (or "resource") costs such as shoe leather costs from visiting the broker and foregone interest on money holdings. Second, the value-of-time hypothesis is worth ex-

This paper is based on chapter four of Dowd (1987). The author thanks Mike Artis, Dave Chappell, Alec Chrystal, Doug Fisher, Jack Gilbert, David Laidler, Tony Sampson, and several anonymous referees whose comments have improved the paper very substantially.

KEVIN DOWD *is lecturer in economics, University of Nottingham.*

Journal of Money, Credit, and Banking, Vol. 22, No. 1 (February 1990)

ploring because of its empirical implications: it suggests that "standard" transactions models of the demand for money could be seriously misspecified, and this potential misspecification would seem especially worth investigating given the apparently widespread view [reflected, for example, in Laidler (1985)] that the empirical performance of demand-for-money equations leaves something to be desired.[1] Third, as already mentioned, the value-of-time hypothesis arises in the context of transactions cost models, and it is becoming apparent that these models have important implications for optimal policy. Recent work by Kimbrough (1986a, b) and Faig (1986) suggests that Friedman's optimum-quantity-of-money rule (1969) is optimal in these transactions models (with or without a value-of-time component) even though the alternative to inflation might be to levy explicit taxes that distort economic activity. To the extent that the value-of-time hypothesis strengthens confidence in transactions costs models, therefore, it would seem to lend additional support to the optimal-quantity-of-money rule—and weaken the argument [suggested, for example, by Phelps (1973)] that inflationary finance might be optimal when other taxes distort economic activity.

The layout of this paper is as follows: Section 1 reviews the origins of the value-of-time idea in the literature on the foundations of the transactions demand for money, and section 2 examines the empirical evidence to date. Section 3 develops a theoretical framework which allows us to derive value-of-time and non-value-of-time models of the transactions demand for money, and 4 presents empirical results.

1. MONEY, EXCHANGE, AND THE VALUE OF TIME

The idea that people use money because it saves them valuable time is a very old one. It is at least implicit in the discussions of philosophers from Aristotle onwards which attempted to explain the use of money on the grounds of the inconvenience of barter. As Menger (1871, 1892) discussed, individuals benefit from trade but run into coincidence of wants problems if they barter. They therefore look for intermediate commodities to carry out trades more quickly, and the dominant intermediate commodity can be considered as "money." This approach to the use of money was formalized by Saving (1971, 1976) and Niehans (1971) who adapted the well-known inventory-theoretic models of Baumol (1952) and Tobin (1956) to provide analyses of the use of money based on the "transaction time saving aspect of using (it)" (Saving 1971, pp. 419–20).[2] More recently, Kimbrough (1986a, b) has also used the inventory-theoretic approach

[1]While this paper makes an empirical comparison between value-of-time and non-value-of-time models, it does not attempt to measure the improvement made by the value-of-time hypothesis to transactions models or to explain the (puzzling) behavior of velocity in the 1980s.

[2]A money-demand equation with a real wage argument was also presented en passant by Fried (1973) in his analysis of money and growth.

to examine money-holding where money is used to reduce the time costs of transacting.[3]

These analyses provided not only a theory of *why* money is held, but also a model of *how much* is held, that is, a model of the demand for money. They nevertheless failed to have much impact on the empirical literature on the demand for money, perhaps because most writers interested in the empirical demand for money have tended to neglect the role of time once they have settled on some rationale for the use of money, and therefore overlooked the potential importance of the time factor in determining how much money people hold. Dutton and Gramm (1973) was one of the few studies to appreciate the significance of this factor on the demand for money. As they put it:

> Since a unit of leisure may be purchased by decreasing work or by increasing money balances, an increase in the wage rate results therefore in an increase in the relative price of purchasing leisure by decreasing work. It thus follows that an increase in the wage rate will lead to an increased demand for money independent of any increase in transactions (p. 664).

Karni (1973) had a similar logic. His model was

> an attempt to incorporate explicitly the value of time into the demand for money. The main hypothesis proposed here is that, ceteris paribus, the demand for money is positively related to the value of time, reflecting attempts on the part of households and business firms to save on this resource in conducting their transactions (pp. 45–6).

We turn now to review the empirical evidence.

2. EMPIRICAL EVIDENCE ON WAGE RATE ARGUMENTS IN MONEY DEMAND EQUATIONS

Dutton and Gramm (1973) used their model to derive an equation relating the demand for money to real wages, initial assets, and the rate of interest, and they estimated these equations using U.S. annual data for the period 1919–58. Three different interest and four different real wealth variables were used, but only one monetary variable and one real wage rate series. They found that the coefficients on real wages were everywhere positive and significant at the 1 percent level, and estimates of the real wage elasticity of the demand for money varied from 0.76 to 1.27. The coefficients on interest and wealth had the expected signs. Their results were therefore consistent with the predictions of their model, but they are difficult to assess because they did not report any residual diagnostics.

At about the same time, Khan (1973) developed a model of the velocity of money based on the Baumol-Tobin square root formula which interpreted the brokerage fee as varying with the wage rate. This model was estimated using

[3]Jones (1976) gave a related analysis of the use of money based on the expected search costs of different exchange processes, while Brunner and Meltzer (1971) saw money as a means of economizing on the costs of obtaining information about different exchange possibilities. Their approach was echoed by Alchian (1977).

annual U.S. data for 1900–65 and the implied wage elasticities of the demand for money were relatively close to 0.5 and highly significant. The D-W statistics he reported are not strong evidence of residual serial correlation, so his results appear quite reliable.

Karni's approach was to start from the Baumol-Tobin square root formula and derive predictions about the elasticities of money demand with respect to wages, income, hours worked, and interest. His empirical work is presented in his 1974 and 1975a papers. The former used annual data for the period 1919 and 1968. Equations for currency, M1, and M2 were estimated in which the independent variables were wages, interest, and income. Once again, however, only one real wage series was used. He found that the M1 and M2 equations were broadly consistent with the value-of-time hypothesis, but that the currency equation was not, and none of his results was consistent with the permanent income hypothesis applied to the demand for money. His estimates of the real wage elasticity of the demand for money varied from about 0.6 for currency to around 1.0 for M1 and M2. This elasticity was highly significant for M1 and M2, but insignificant for currency. The reliability of his results must be questioned, however, since his D-W statistics indicate the presence of residual serial correlation.[4]

His 1975a paper used annual U.K. data for the periods 1919–39 and 1946–69. Equations were estimated relating money holdings to property income, labor income, and interest. He found a "substantial difference between labor-income and property-income elasticities of the demand for money" (p. 236) which he interpreted as supporting the value-of-time hypothesis but not the inventory model of the demand for money. The statistical significance of this difference is questionable, however, and the D-W figures he reports undermine the assumption of serial independence on which his tests are based.

Several other studies also present evidence on the effect of wages on money demand. Both Diewert (1974) and Phlips (1978) estimated demand for money equations as part of a complete system of household demand equations in which the independent variables were real full wealth, real wages, prices, and interest. Both studies used M1 as the monetary variable and one real wage series. Diewert found a real wage elasticity of 0.54 and Phlips found real wage elasticities of 0.54 in the short run and 0.25 in the long run, but neither study reported any statistics to indicate the significance of these elasticities.[5] Finally, Dotsey (1988, p. 34) provides empirical results which suggest that the real wage rate parameter in a transactions-based demand for money equation is positive and reasonably signif-

[4]Karni's empirical work can also be criticized for his failure to use an estimation procedure that allowed for the endogeneity of income and work time. His work was also the subject of a debate between himself (1975b) and Lenard and Moss (1975).

[5]It is also worth noting that changes in the wage rate in these models reflect the conventional income and substitution effects of a relative price change and *not* a value-of-time effect of the kind discussed by Dutton and Gramm and Karni. This indicates that we can get demand-for-money equations with wage rate arguments for reasons other than the value-of-time hypothesis. We therefore need a model that allows us to distinguish genuine value-of-time effects from other wage rate effects on the demand for money. See footnote 15.

icant.[6] His elasticity estimates vary from 0.57 to 0.87, and are consistent with earlier studies. He uses an instrumental variables estimation procedure with a correction for second-order residual serial correlation, so his results can be taken as reliable.

Thus all the empirical evidence so far suggests that the wage parameter in a demand-for-money equation should be positive, and most studies suggest that that parameter is also relatively significant, and that these results can be taken as evidence in favor of the value-of-time hypothesis.

3. A THEORETICAL FRAMEWORK

We now develop a theoretical framework to investigate the value-of-time hypothesis. Consider a representative household which lives in a market-clearing environment. It maximizes the following utility function at the beginning of the current period:[7]

$$U = U(x,l) \tag{1}$$

where x is (real) expenditures, and l is leisure, both over the current period. Utility is to be maximized subject to the constraint:

$$Y = Px + Wl + rM + TC \tag{2}$$

where Y is current full income (as in Becker 1976), P is the price of x, W the wage rate, r the interest rate, M average money balances, and TC is transactions cost. Each of these variables refers to the current period, and Y, W, M, and TC are in nominal terms. Where convenient, we shall deal with wages (w) and money (m) in "real" terms (that is, $w \equiv W/P$ and $m \equiv M/P$). Money is taken to be the non-interest-bearing transactions medium used by the household, and so rM represents the opportunity cost of holding it.[8]

TC is a function of prices, real expenditures, real money balances, and real wages:

$$TC = P k_0 x^{k1} m^{-k2} w^{A} \tag{3}$$

[6]Dotsey reports three estimated wage coefficients. If we test the null hypothesis that the coefficient is zero against the alternative that it is positive, the null hypothesis can be rejected at the 2.5 percent level in two cases, and at the 5 percent level in the other.

[7]If one likes, one can view this as the second stage of a multistage budgeting problem the first stage of which involves the allocation of total expenditure (Y_t) to each period t. The model is therefore consistent with an intertemporal model provided that the requisite separability conditions hold.

[8]This definition is used only for convenience. "Money" could be made to be interest-bearing, but the opportunity cost would then be $(r-r_m)M$, where r_m is the interest rate on money. One can therefore easily modify the analysis to deal with interest-bearing money, but one then has the comparatively difficult problem of finding an empirical proxy for the own-return on money (see, for example, Startz 1979). Note also that the sign on rM is positive because Y is "full income" (or "full expenditure"), and the right-hand side is composed of the sum of expenditures on goods, leisure, the 'rental cost' of money balances, and transactions costs.

The Cobb-Douglas functional form for the cost function is chosen because it is the most general specification that still yields an empirically tractable demand-for-money equation.[9] Note also that we can reasonably rule out a "corner solution" and postulate an optimum in which x, m, and TC (and therefore k_0 as well) are all positive.[10] It seems reasonable to impose the following conditions on TC:

1. TC should be homogeneous of degree one in nominal magnitudes (that is, no "money illusion"). This condition is satisfied by construction.
2. Transactions costs should rise with expenditures (that is, $TC_x > 0$, where we use a subscript to denote a partial derivative). This condition is satisfied if $k_1 > 0$.
3. The idea that people hold money to reduce transactions costs implies we should have $TC_m < 0$. This condition is satisfied if $k_2 > 0$.
4. We assume appropriate second-derivative conditions for TC. The conditions we impose are $TC_{xx} > 0$ and $TC_{mm} > 0$. The former captures the idea that the marginal costs of transacting (that is, TC_x) rise with x; the latter captures the idea that the marginal benefits of holding money in terms of saved transactions costs (that is, $-TC_m$) *fall* with m. These conditions are satisfied if $k_1 > 1$ and $k_2 > 0$.

Conditions 1–4 are thus satisfied if $k_0, k_2 > 0$, and $k_1 > 1$.

In addition, A is an index parameter which lies in the range (0,1). There are three cases to consider:

Case (a). $A = 1$: In this case, the TC function can be decomposed into the product of W and a "real term" ($k_0 x^{k_1} m^{-k_2}$) which can be interpreted as transactions time. TC can then be interpreted as the cost of transactions time, and there are no resource costs as such. Since there are no resources costs, we shall refer to this as the pure value-of-time (PVT) model.

Case (b). $A = 0$: In this case the wage term disappears from the TC function. Transaction costs are to be interpreted as resource costs, and there are no time costs. This case corresponds to the "standard" transactions model which makes no allowance for a value-of-time effect on the demand for money.[11] We shall refer to it as the non-value-of-time (NVT) model. It is important to consider the NVT

[9] The next most general functional form is the CES and one can easily show that that does not yield a tractable demand-for-money equation. I should like to thank one of the referees to suggesting this precise formulation.

[10] The simplest argument for ruling out corner solutions is that we propose to test the model using a data set from a highly monetized economy in which virtually no household chooses to operate at a boundary (that is corner solutions are of little practical relevance). An alternative argument is to suppose that in an economy with an advanced division of labor the household must conduct some minimum level of transactions to survive, and so $x>0$. This being so, we might expect $TC>0$. If we also assume $w>0$ the structure of our cost function then implies that $m>0$.

[11] It is very difficult to visualize a reasonable scenario where resource costs were important, but time costs were not. To argue that time costs are irrelevant, one seems forced to argue either that there is no time constraint to the problem at hand, or that the value of time is zero, and either is highly implausible. This undermines the plausibility of the NVT model, and lends further support to the value-of-time hypothesis. The fact remains, however, that the literature has concentrated on the NVT model, and that is one reason why we must consider it.

model because we are interested, not in the transactions model per se, but in the extent to which the performance of value-of-time transactions models improves upon that of transactions models that ignore the value-of-time hypothesis. The NVT model thus provides a benchmark against which the value-of-time hypothesis can be assessed.

Case (c). $0 < A < 1$: In this intermediate case, *TC* consists of both time and resource costs, and there is still a role for the value-of-time effect on the demand for money. This can be considered as the general value-of-time (GVT) model.

It should be stressed here that our primitive concept here is transactions time rather than the number of trips to the broker which one finds in conventional "brokerage-fee" transactions models. This allows us to avoid the awkward integer constraint one meets when dealing with trips to the broker. As Barro (1976) has shown, the integer constraint complicates both the optimization analysis and the aggregation procedure from the individual to the market levels. However, the procedure adopted here still allows one to derive brokerage-fee models as special cases if one wants to obtain them.[12]

Substituting (3) into (2), we derive the Lagrangean optimization problem:

$$\text{maximize } L = U(x, l) + \lambda[Y - Px - Wl - rM - Pk_0 x^{k_1} m^{-k_2} w^A] . \quad (4)$$

The first-order conditions for this problem are

$$L_x = U_x - \lambda[P + TC_x] = 0 \quad (5)$$

$$L_l = U_l - \lambda W = 0 \quad (6)$$

$$L_m = -\lambda[r - Pk_0 k_2 x^{k_1} M^{-k_2-1} P^{k_2} w^A] = 0 \quad (7)$$

We now rearrange (7) to get [13,14]

$$m = ((k_0 k_2 x^{k_1} w^A)/r)^{1/(k_2+1)} . \quad (8)$$

[12]To see this, consider (8) below. We can derive a version of the model corresponding to the Baumol-Tobin (BT) model if we set $k_1 = k_2 = 1$. The (8) reduces to

$$m = [(k_0 w^A x) / r]^{1/2} .$$

This looks like the BT model with $2k_0 w^A$ instead of a brokerge fee. When A=0, the model above becomes the exact BT model:

$$m = [(b x)/(2r)]^{1/2}$$

where the brokerage fee b is fixed and equal to $k_0/2$. In this case *TC* reduces to $[bx/2m]$, and $x/2m$ can be interpreted as the number of trips to the broker (see, for example, Laidler 1985, p. 60)

[13]The model outlined here could easily be extended to allow for technical change in the exchange technology. The simplest way to do this would be to add a time variable to (3). This leads to the addition of a time trend to (9). Technical change was dropped from the model in the text because the time trend made no difference to our empirical results.

[14]There is little to be gained from manipulating the other first-order conditions. Suppose that we used them to substitute out λ and assumed that the utility function was Cobb-Douglas. This is the

Taking natural logs:

$$\ln m = \frac{1}{k_2+1} \ln (k_o k_2) + \frac{A}{k_2+1} \ln w + \frac{k_1}{k_2+1} \ln x - \frac{1}{k_2+1} \ln r \, . \tag{9}$$

We could proceed to estimate the nonlinear (in parameters) equation (9), but it is more convenient to work with a linear equation. We therefore let β be the (real) wage coefficient, γ be the (real) expenditure coefficient, δ be the interest coefficient, and φ be the price coefficient, (so $\beta = [A/(k_2+1)]$, etc.) and our model predicts that an estimate of the equation

$$\log m = \alpha + \beta \log w + \gamma \log x + \delta \log r + \varphi \log P + u \tag{10}$$

should satisfy the following conditions (where u follows an appropriate error structure):

$$0 \leqslant \hat{\beta} < 1, 0 < \hat{\gamma} < \infty, -1 < \hat{\delta} < 0, \text{ and } \hat{\varphi} = 0 \, . \tag{11}$$

The predicted ranges of $\hat{\beta}$, $\hat{\gamma}$, and $\hat{\delta}$ follow from the assumed ranges of k_1, k_2, and A, and the expressions relating them to these underlying structural parameters, while the prediction for $\hat{\varphi}$ reflects the condition that the demand for money equation should be free from money illusion. Thus our model preserves the standard predictions of the transactions model that money demand should rise with expenditures and fall with the rate of interest, and it makes the additional prediction that $\hat{\beta}$ lie in the range (0,1(.

In the pure value-of-time case (that is, A=1), the predictions of the model are sharpened:

$$0 < \hat{\beta} = -\hat{\delta} < 1, 0 < \hat{\gamma} < \infty, \hat{\varphi} = 0 \, , \tag{12}$$

that is, $\hat{\beta}$ becomes positive, and should equal minus $\hat{\delta}$. The PVT model thus confirms the Dutton-Gramm-Khan-Karni prediction that an increase in wages should increase money demand, but it restricts the range of $\hat{\beta}$ to (0,1(. The PVT model also restricts the two "time costs" w and r to restrict money demand through their *ratio*, and not independently of one another.

In the NVT case (A=0) the predictions (11) become

---

simplest plausible (?) case, and gives us simple expressions for $U_{\dot{x}}$ and U_l. Suppose then that we derived estimates of k_0, k_1, k_2, and A from our money demand estimates (as we do below). We would still have only one (nonlinear) equation with the Cobb-Douglas parameters as unknowns. Even if we simplified further by imposing homogeneity on the utility function, and took the variables in the equation at their mean values, we would still need data on l even to identify the remaining parameter. When we make more plausible (less restrictive) assumptions, we cannot even get that far.

$$\hat{\beta} = 0, 0 < \hat{\gamma} < \infty, -1 < \hat{\delta} < 0, \text{ and } \hat{\varphi} = 0 \,, \tag{13}$$

that is, $\hat{\beta}$ should now be insignificant. The significance of $\hat{\beta}$ thus provides a direct test of the value-of-time hypothesis.[15]

Finally, in the intermediate case ($0 < A < 1$), (11) becomes

$$0 < \hat{\beta} < 1, 0 < \hat{\gamma} < \infty, -1 < \hat{\delta} < 0, \text{ and } \hat{\varphi} = 0 \,, \tag{14}$$

that is, $\hat{\beta}$ is now positive [unlike (13)], but unlike (12) it is not restricted to equal minus $\hat{\delta}$.

Several points about the money-demand equation (10) are worth noting. First, it is not a money-demand equation in the conventional sense. When one speaks of a money-demand equation one normally means a function which relates money demand to the variables on which it depends, but what we have here is a first-order condition which shows the relation between two choice variables—m and x—which must hold in the household optimum, and neither variable can be said from this actually to *depend* on the other. One therefore has to be careful how one interprets the equation. One also has to be careful how one estimates it. The endogeneity of x in (10) implies that a single-step estimation procedure will be inappropriate because x will generally have errors which will be correlated with those in (10), thereby violating the orthogonality condition necessary for single-stage estimation. The appropriate estimation procedure is therefore an instrumental variables (IV) procedure which allows for the simultaneity of x.

Second, the *TC* function must show either increasing, decreasing, or constant average costs with respect to scale. These correspond respectively to $k_2 > k_1$, $k_2 < k_1$, or $k_2 = k_1$. In terms of the parameters of (10) these correspond to $\gamma > 1, \gamma < 1$, and $\gamma = 1$. Estimates of (10) thus allow us to infer whether there are decreasing, increasing, or constant returns to scale in money holdings.

4. THE EMPIRICAL PERFORMANCE OF THE MODELS

Our demand-for-money equation was estimated with non-seasonally adjusted quarterly data for the United Kingdom. Money was proxied by a series on personal-sector non-interest-bearing checkable deposits. This corresponds fairly closely to our notion of money as households' non-interest-bearing transactions media. This series was more appropriate than more conventional series like M1 because they include business as well as personal-sector deposits, and our theory explicitly refers only to households. The wage rate was proxied by a series on hourly after-tax earnings made available by Martin Robson at Newcastle Uni-

[15]The reader will not that the wage rate does not enter the NVT demand-for-money equation even though we have not excluded any conventional income and substitution effects in that model. That implies that the wage rate enters the value-of-time equations *precisely because* it represents a genuine value-of-time effect. This addresses the concern raised in footnote 5.

versity.[16] The scale variable was consumers' expenditures, and the interest rate was the (quarterly) interest rate on three-month deposits in London, as it prevailed on the last day of the previous quarter. The money, wage, and expenditures series were deflated by a CPI to give the series in 1980 £s. The money and expenditure series were also deflated by working population because the theory refers to individual behavior. The data set covers the period 1975:3 to 1984:4 and is restricted by the monetary series starting at 1975:3 and the wage series ending at 1984:4.[17] Altogether this gives us thirty-eight observations. All the data apart from the hourly earnings series are taken from DATASTREAM.

The estimations were carried out using an instrumental variables estimation routine on Pesaran's DATAFIT and it proved to be necessary to make allowance for up to fourth-order residual serial correlation. The instruments used were the right-hand-side variables, plus up to four lags of both the dependent variable and the right-hand-side variables. Following Fair (1972) these instruments were chosen to ensure that the estimates were consistent. The results did not appear to be sensitive to seasonal dummies or to time trends so these are omitted in the results reported below.

The equation estimated was

$$\ln m = \alpha + \beta \ln w + \gamma \ln x + \delta \ln r + u \tag{15}$$

and our estimates are reported in Table 1. The main features are the following:

—The adjusted residuals pass all the reported tests for normality.

—The wage coefficient is positive and significant at the 2.5 percent level. The prediction of the value-of-time models that $\hat{\beta}$ lie in the range $(0,1($ is therefore confirmed, while that of the NVT model that it be zero is rejected at this level of significance. Note also that our estimate of β is close to most of those reported in the studies reviewed earlier.

—The expenditure coefficient is positive and very significantly less than unity. This would seem strong evidence of economies of scale in money holding. However, the expenditure coefficient is also insignificantly different from zero, and this might suggest that the conventional result that expenditures or income have significant coefficients in money demand equations arises because the scale variable is proxying the value of time, and not because it is a particularly important explanatory variable per se.

—The interest coefficient lies in the predicted $(-1,0($ range and is very significantly different from zero.

[16]Strictly speaking, our theory refers to the household's value of time rather than its wage rate as such, but the experimental results of Deacon and Sonstelie (1985) suggest that this kind of after-tax hourly earnings series is a reasonably good proxy.

[17]A major potential problem with any study on the value of time and the demand for money is the introduction of automatic teller machines (ATMs). Electronic banking would have altered time costs quite considerably. ATMs were only introduced in the United Kingdom at the end of our data period, however, so there is no reason to believe that they would have had a significant effect on our results. One would suppose that studies that use later data will have to tackle the issue.

TABLE 1

IV ESTIMATES OF VALUE-OF-TIME MODEL

$$\ln m = \underset{(.916)}{5.095} + \underset{(.270)}{.566} \ln w + \underset{(.139)}{.071} \ln x - \underset{(.024)}{.071} \ln r$$

$$R^2 = .953 \qquad F_{3,30} = 174.04$$

$$\text{COMFAC } (\sim F_{12,14}) = .82 \quad \text{CHOW } (\sim F_{8,22}) = .94$$

Residual Analysis

$$u = \underset{(.174)}{1.665}\, u(-1) - \underset{(.311)}{1.258}\, u(-2) + \underset{(.308)}{.912}\, u(-3) - \underset{(.173)}{.456}\, u(-4) + \epsilon$$

$$\text{D-W} = 2.20$$

$\chi^2(4)$ test for further serial correlation = 4.08*

$\chi^2(2)$ test for normality = .33**

$\chi^2(2)$ test for homoskedasticity = .19†

NOTES: The instruments used are the right-hand-side variables, plus the first, second, third, and fourth lags of both them and the dependent variable.

The equation is estimated using data for the period 1975:3 to 1984:4. Allowing for the lags there are thirty-four observations.

The figures in parentheses below the coefficient estimates are their estimated standard errors.

COMFAC tests the common-factor restrictions which the estimated equation imposes on the general distributed lag model (16).

CHOW is the Chow prediction error test. It is based on a comparison of results for the periods 1976: 3–1982:4 and 1976:3–1984:4. Note that the 5 percent significance level is 2.40.

*Based on a Lagrange multiplier test.

**Based on the skewness and kurtosis of residuals.

†Based on the regression of squared residuals on fitted squared values.

—The COMFAC statistic tests for the common factor restrictions that must hold if the reported equation is a valid representation of the more general model:

$$\ln m = \alpha + \sum_{i=0}^{4} \beta_i \ln w(-i) + \sum_{i=0}^{4} \gamma_i \ln x(-i) + \sum_{i=0}^{4} \delta_i \ln r(-i) + \sum_{i=1}^{4} \mu_i \ln m(-i) + u\,. \tag{16}$$

The reported test statistic is insignificant indicating that the restrictions are valid. This means that our results can also be interpreted in terms of a "dynamic disequilibrium" model (for examples, see Hendry 1985 or Hendry and Mizon 1978), and if one does this our results suggest that a shock "persists" for four quarters before the system returns to equilibrium.

—The model passes a Chow prediction error test for out-of-sample predictions for 1983–84. This gives us some reason to believe that the model is reasonably stable.

Table 2 reports test statistics for the predictions of the models. It also reports the implied estimates of the structural-form parameters—k_0, k_1, and k_2—based on estimates of (15), as well as estimates of the parameters of the PVT model. Apart from the rejection of the $\hat{\beta} = 0$ prediction of the NVT model which we already discussed, there are several other results:

TABLE 2

TEST RESULTS FOR THE PREDICITONS OF THE VT MODEL

t-test for homogeneity:[a] $t = -.56$

t-test for $\hat{\beta}=-\hat{\delta}$:[b] $t = 1.89$

t-test for the $\hat{\beta}=0$:[c] $t = 2.10$

Restricted Parameter Estimates[d]

$$\hat{\alpha} = \underset{(.956)}{4.883},\ \hat{\beta} = \underset{(.026)}{.059},\ \hat{\gamma} = \underset{(.126)}{.194}$$

Implied Estimates of Structural Parameters[e]

$$\hat{k}_0 = \exp(79.6),\ \hat{k}_1 = 3.270,\ \hat{k}_2 = 15.863$$

NOTES: [a]Obtained by adding $\ln p$ to equation (15).
[b]Obtained by imposing this restriction to equation (15) and adding $\ln r$. Since we have no priors on whether $\hat{\beta}$ should be greater or less than $-\hat{\delta}$ if the hull hypothesis is untrue, the alternative hypothesis is that $\hat{\beta} \neq \hat{\delta}$. The marginal significance level for the null hypothesis is then 6.8 percent.
[c]This is the test statistic for the significance of $\hat{\beta}$ in (15). Since we have a one-sided alternative hypothesis ($\hat{\beta} > 0$), this statistic implies a marginal significance level for the null hypothesis of about 2.2 percent.
[d]Obtained by imposing the restriction $\beta=-\delta$ on (15). The figures in parentheses are the parameters' estimated standard errors.
[e]These are derived from the estimates of α, β, and γ above using the definition of these parameters in terms of k_0, k_1, and k_2.

—The t-test statistic for the homogeneity condition is quite insignificant, so there is no evidence of money illusion for any model.

—The $\hat{\beta}=-\hat{\delta}$ condition for the PVT model cannot be rejected at the 5 percent significance level—the actual probability value is 6.8 percent—so the PVT model cannot easily be rejected.

—The implied estimates of k_0, k_1, and k_2 also fall in the predicted ranges,[18] as do the estimates of β and γ—.059 and .194 respectively—obtained when (15) is restricted to satisfy the conditions imposed by the PVT model.

Taken together, these results suggest that the GVT and PVT models cannot easily be rejected, while the NVT model probably can. The value-of-time hypothesis thus appears to lead to a significant improvement on the empirical performance of conventional transactions cost models.

5. CONCLUSIONS

This paper developed a framework to investigate the empirical importance of the value-of-time hypothesis in the context of the transactions demand for money. We found that the predictions of value-of-time transactions models

[18]The estimate of k_0 seems a bit high. It stems from the relatively low value of $\hat{\beta}$ when the restriction $\beta=-\delta$ is imposed. One might also add that the implicit estimate of A is .566 (1+15.863) = 9.544. This is obviously outside the predicted range, but the $\hat{\beta}=-\hat{\delta}$ test result reported in the text implies that this is not significantly different from unity, although the $\hat{\beta}=0$ test implies that it *is* significantly different from zero.

could not easily be rejected, and that these models performed significantly better than the standard transactions model that ignores the value-of-time effect. Our results are thus consistent with—and lend further support to—earlier studies which also suggested that the value-of-time effect on the demand for money was empirically significant. The value-of-time hypothesis seems to deserve more attention that it has so far received.

LITERATURE CITED

Alchian, Armen A. "Why Money?" *Journal of Money, Credit, and Banking* 9 (February 1977), 133–40.

Barro, Robert J. "Integral Constraints and Aggregation in an Inventory Model of the Demand for Money." *Journal of Finance* 31 (March 1976), 77–87.

Baumol, William J. "The Transactions Demand for Cash: An Inventory Theoretic Approach." *Quarterly Journal of Economics* 66 (November 1952), 545–56.

Becker, Gary S. *The Economic Approach to Human Behavior.* Chicago: Chicago University Press, 1976.

Brunner, Karl, and Allan H. Meltzer. "The Uses of Money: Money in the Theory of an Exchange Economy." *American Economic Review* 61 (December 1971), 784–805.

Deacon, Robert T., and Jon Sonstelie. "Rationing by Waiting and the Value of Time: Results from a Natural Experiment." *Journal of Political Economy* 93 (August 1985), 627–47.

Diewert, W. Erwin. "Intertemporal Consumer Theory and the Demand for Durables." *Econometrica* 42 (May 1974), 497–516.

Dotsey, Michael. "The Demand for Currency in the United States." *Journal of Money, Credit, and Banking* 20 (February 1988), 22–40.

Dowd, Kevin. "Consumption, the Demand for Money, and Real Wages." Ph.D. dissertation, University of Sheffield, England, November 1987.

Dutton, Dean S., and William P. Gramm. "Transactions Costs, the Wage Rate and the Demand for Money." *American Economic Review* 63 (September 1973), 652–65.

Faig, Miguel, "Optimal Taxation of Money Balances." Ph.D. dissertation, Stanford University, Stanford, Cal. 1986.

Fair, Ray C. "Efficient Estimation of Simultaneous Equations with Auto-Regressive Errors by Instrumental Variables." *Review of Economics and Statistics* 54 (November 1972), 444–49.

Fried, Joel. "Money, Exchange and Growth." *Western Economic Journal* 11 (September 1973), 285–301.

Friedman, Milton. "The Optimal Quantity of Money." In *The Optimal Quantity of Money and Other Essays*, pp. 1–50. Chicago: Aldine, 1969.

Hendry, David F. "Monetary Economic Myth and Econometric Reality." *Oxford Review of Economic Policy* 1 (Spring 1985), 72–84.

Hendry, David F., and Grayham E. Mizon. "Serial Correlation as a Convenient Simplification, Not a Nuisance: A Comment on a Study of the Demand for Money by the Bank of England." *Economic Journal* 88 (September 1978), 549–73.

Jones, Robert A. "The Origin and Development of Media of Exchange." *Journal of Political Economy* 84 (August 1976), 757–76.

Karni, Edi. "The Transactions Demand for Cash: Incorporation of the Value of Time into the Inventory Approach." *Journal of Political Economy* 81 (September 1973), 1216–25.

______. "The Value of Time and the Demand for Money." *Journal of Money, Credit, and Banking* 6 (February 1974), 45–64.

______. "The Value of Time and the Demand for Money: Evidence from UK Time Series Data." *Australian Economic Papers* 14 (December 1975), 231–39. (a)

______. "The Value of Time and the Demand for Money: A Rejoinder." *Journal of Monetary Economics* 1 (October 1975), 497–99. (b)

Khan, Mohsin S. "A Note on the Secular Behaviour of Velocity within the Context of the Inventory Theoretic Model of the Demand for Money." *Manchester School* 51 (June 1973), 207–13.

Kimbrough, Kent P. "Inflation, Employment, and Welfare in the Presence of Transaction Costs." *Journal of Money, Credit, and Banking* 18 (May 1986), 127–40. (a)

______. "The Optimum Quantity of Money Rule in the Theory of Public Finance." *Journal of Monetary Economics* 18 (May 1986), 277–84. (b)

Laidler, D. *The Demand for Money: Theories, Evidence, and Problems,* 3rd ed. New York: Harper and Row, 1985.

Lenard, Thomas M, and William G. Moss. "A Comment on the Value of Time and the Demand for Money." *Journal of Monetary Economics* 1 (October 1975), 489–96.

Menger, Carl. *Principles of Economics*, translated by James Dingwall and Bert F. Hoselitz. New York: New York University Press, 1981. Reprint of 1871 edition.

______. "On the Origin of Money." *Economic Journal* 2 (June 1892), 239–55.

Niehans, Jürg. "Money and Barter in General Equilibrium with Transactions Costs." *American Economic Review* 61 (December 1971), 773–83.

Phelps, Edmund S. "Inflation in the Theory of Public Finance." *Swedish Journal of Economics* 75 (March 1973), 67–82.

Phlips, Louis. "The Demand for Leisure and Money." *Econometrica* 46 (September 1978), 1025–43.

Saving, Thomas R. "Transactions Costs and the Demand for Money." *American Economic Review* 61 (June 1971), 407–20.

______. "Transactions Cost Functions and the Inventory-Theoretic Approach to Money Demand." *Journal of Money, Credit, and Banking* 8 (August 1976), 339–45.

Startz, Richard. "Implicit Interest on Demand Deposits." *Journal of Monetary Economics* 5 (October 1979), 515–34.

Tobin, James. "The Interest Elasticity of Transactions Demand for Cash." *Review of Economics and Statistics* 38 (August 1956), 241–47.

STEVE SWIDLER
DAVID KETCHER

Economic Forecasts, Rationality, and the Processing of New Information over Time

ECONOMIC EXPECTATIONS PLAY A CENTRAL ROLE in explaining the dynamics of any equilibrium market. Because of their importance, the properties of economists' expectations of key price and income variables have been the focus of several earlier studies. Papers by Pesando (1975), Carlson (1977), and Pearce (1979) used the Livingston survey data and found that the consensus inflation forecasts were not rational. Figlewski and Wachtel (1981) and Pearce (1984) analyzed individual responses and concluded, respectively, that the inflation and stock price forecasts violated the rationality assumption. In contrast, Mullineaux (1978) found that the mean inflation forecasts appeared to be rational, and Brown and Maital (1981) concluded that the Livingston forecasts for several economic variables were unbiased, although information was underutilized. More recently, Schroeter and Smith (1986) made adjustments to the Livingston data and corrected for previous statistical errors only to find mixed results concerning the rationality of the Consumer Price Index and Producer Price Index.

An earlier version of the paper was presented at the Federal Reserve Bank of Cleveland and the Western Economic Association meetings. The authors are indebted to Walt Elliott for his helpful discussion of the generalized method of moments technique used in the analysis. The revised paper benefitted from comments by Huston McCulloch and two anonymous referees. The authors also thank Sol Shalit, Tom McCaleb, Larry Lockwood, and Bruce Bender for their useful comments, and Jerry Lieberthal, Dave Diltz, Tom Woodward, Michelle Mok, and Elaine Kornitzky for their computational assistance.

Partial funding for this research was provided by the Management Research Center, University of Wisconsin-Milwaukee.

STEVE SWIDLER *is assistant professor of finance and real estate, University of Texas at Arlington.* DAVID KETCHER *is a graduate student of finance, University of Missouri*

Journal of Money, Credit, and Banking, Vol. 22, No. 1 (February 1990)

This study probes the unbiasedness of economic forecasts which is a necessary condition for rationality. However, the present analysis uses a different data set than in previous studies, and examines, in detail, the process by which new information is incorporated into updated forecasts of an economic variable. Two important variables, real GNP growth and the inflation rate as measured by the Consumer Price Index, are the focus of this study.

The Blue Chip Economic Indicators provide the real GNP and inflation forecasts used in this paper. In contrast to previous studies of rationality, the anlaysis in this paper makes no assumptions about the relevant information set used by economists. Instead, the monthly revisions of the Blue Chip forecasts make it possible to directly analyze the value of new information. Using regression analysis, the empirical results suggest that revised forecasts provide more accurate estimates of the variable's actual value and that Blue Chip respondents process new information in a rational manner.

1. DATA

Since 1976, the Blue Chip Economic Indicators has surveyed prominent economists in universities and private industry, asking for their forecasts of several business variables. The number of economists has varied over the years; however, in recent surveys, approximately forty-five to fifty responses have been reported for each variable. While the forecasts are for annual values, the economists are polled monthly. Their forecasts are gathered by phone during the first three business days of each month, thus ensuring a timely reporting of the data in a newsletter published one week later.

Before 1980, the first forecast for each variable was given in June of the previous year, and a new forecast followed in the succeeding eleven months. Starting in 1980, the June figures became the last Blue Chip forecasts for a given year. Thus in more recent years, the first forecast for each variable was made in the beginning of July, eighteen months prior to the realization of the actual value on December 31st of the following year. The final forecast, produced in the beginning of June, was made seven months prior to the realization date.[1] This polling procedure from July to June makes it possible to infer the value of new information as it occurs over time and to see if economists use this information in a rational manner.

The two variables analyzed in this study are the real GNP growth rate and the rate of inflation measured by the Consumer Price Index (CPI). The economic importance of examining these two key variables is clear, and not surprisingly, they have been the central focus of several of the papers cited above. Both rates are determined from annual index values as year over year percentage changes.

[1]In 1984, the policy was again changed, and the survey began running two sets of projections with each issue, one for the current year all the way through December and one representing forecasts for the next year.

Blue Chip forecasts for the real GNP growth rate began in July 1976, while the first CPI inflation forecasts started in February 1979.

Although the actual value of each ratio's numerator is realized on December 31st, the reporting of each value occurs later. For the CPI, the Bureau of Labor Statistics publishes the annual index number in their *CPI Detailed Report*, printed in January of the following year. The Department of Commerce also releases the first estimate for real GNP in their *January Survey of Current Business*. This value is subject to a July revision and subsequently to several annual and benchmark revisions. The actual real GNP figures used in this study are the first estimates released in January, which are assumed to be the real GNP figures forecast by the Blue Chip participants.[2]

Even though annual figures for both variables are released after the actual values are realized on December 31st, information about real GNP and inflation occurs on a more frequent and timely basis. Every month, the Bureau of Labor Statistics releases the CPI index for the previous month. With one exception, the CPI series has not been revised since 1979, the year Blue Chip inflation forecasts began.[3]

In contrast, revision of the GNP index is the norm rather than the exception. The Department of Commerce calculates real GNP on a quarterly basis. An initial or "flash" estimate is released during the final month of a quarter, relying on data from the quarter's first month.[4] A preliminary estimate follows in one month, and the first and second revisions follow one and two months later. Beyond this, the GNP figures are subject to adjustment in each of the next three years, typically in July, and to further revisions every five years. Results of a Department of Commerce study show that revisions in the GNP estimates are far from insignificant.[5]

The frequent release of relevant information and the monthly Blue Chip forecasts make it possible to test the properties of rationality. In particular, the next section discusses the methodology used to examine the change in forecasts over time as new information occurs.

[2]It seems reasonable that when January real GNP estimates are released, Blue Chip participants move on to forecasting real GNP one and two years ahead and do not measure their performance against subsequent revisions. In any event, it seems unlikely that forecasters are trying to predict benchmark figures which are released with a five-year lag and sometimes include definitional changes.

[3]The Bureau of Labor Statistics changed the expenditure weights in its market basket of goods in January 1987, effectively creating a second index. The two indexes were linked in December 1986 to provide one continuous series. A description of the revision appears in *CPI Detailed Report, January 1987*, U.S. Department of Labor, page 3.

The fact that the CPI is infrequently revised makes it a desirable index to be used by the Coffee, Sugar, and Cocoa Exchange in its inflation futures contract. The GNP deflator, also used to measure inflation, is subject to several revisions like the GNP index, and it would be difficult to settle futures contracts on the expiration date. It should be noted that the inflation futures contract is traded on the CPI for Urban Wage Earners and Clerical Workers, whereas the index used in this study is the CPI for All Urban Consumers. However, the two indices are highly correlated.

[4]Recently, the BEA stopped publishing "flash" GNP estimates.

[5]A complete report of the ten-year study appears in the *United States Department of Commerce News*, January 22, 1985.

2. THEORETICAL CONSIDERATIONS

Basic Concepts and Estimation

The methodology used in this paper is similar to the analysis first suggested by Bigman, Goldfarb, and Schectman (1983) in a study of futures prices as predictors of commodity spot prices. A necessary condition for rationality is that a variable's forecast is an unbiased estimate of the realized value. This relation can be written as

$$E_t(A_T - F_{t,T} | I_t) = 0 , \tag{1}$$

where A_T is the variable's actual value determined at time T, $F_{t,T}$ equals the consensus (mean) forecast of A_T in period t, I_t is the information set available at time t, and E_t is the expectation operator which is conditional on the information set available as of period t.

Over time, new information is added that is relevant in determining A_T, and it follows that the information set at time t is contained in all subsequent periods:

$$I_{t+j} \supseteq I_t \text{ for } j > 0 . \tag{2}$$

Now consider a series of forecasts of A_T made at different times. The forecast $F_{t+1,T}$ should also be an unbiased estimate of A_T, and conditional on the information set at time t+1, this can be written as

$$E_{t+1}(A_T - F_{t+1,T} | I_{t+1}) = 0 . \tag{3}$$

If forecasts are rational, one more statement can be made about the relation between $F_{t+1,T}$ and $F_{t,T}$. Since $I_{t+1,T}$ contains all the information in set $I_{t,T}$, $F_{t+1,T}$ should provide a better forecast of A_T than does $F_{t,T}$.

Operationally, the tests for rationality can be performed using regression analysis. If $F_{t,T}$ is an unbiased estimate of A_T, then estimating the regression,

$$A_T = a + bF_{t,T} + u_{t,T}, \tag{4}$$

across T will satisfy the null hypothesis that a=0 and b=1. Rejection of the joint hypothesis, a=0 and b=1, leads to a rejection of unbiasedness and, thus, the rationality hypothesis.

The Blue Chip survey provides several monthly revisions of consensus forecasts for the value of a variable realized at time T. If we consider only those forecasts made j months prior to the realization of the variable's actual values, it is possible to estimate the linear relation,

$$A_T = a_j + b_j F_{T-j,T} + u_{T-j,T}, \tag{5}$$

across all T. Separate regressions may then be estimated for each set of forecasts made j months before the realization of A_T, where $j=m, m+1, \ldots, T-t$.[6] If the forecasts are rational, then unbiasedness implies the joint hypothesis that $a_j=0$ and $b_j=1$ for each regression. Moreover, from the previous discussion of rationality, more recent forecasts should provide better estimates of A_T as new information becomes available. Since the R^2 value in equation (5) measures the forecasts's predictive power of A_T, it follows that each regression's R^2 should get larger the closer the forecast is to time T. Thus, a second test of rationality is that the R^2 statistic monotonically increases as j approaches m.

While estimation of equation (5) tests for the rationality of consensus economic forecasts, it is also instructive to examine the forecasts of real GNP growth and inflation made by the individual survey participants. Let ${}_iF_{T-j,T}$ equal individual i's forecast of A_T made j months prior to the realization date, T. If the Blue Chip economists are jointly rational, then for each j ($j=m, m+1, \ldots, T-t$), the regression,

$$A_T = a_j + b_j({}_iF_{T-j,T}) + {}_iu_{T-j,T} \tag{6}$$

estimated over all individuals i and time T, should yield estimates of a_j and b_j that do not differ significantly from 0 and 1 respectively. Once more, rationality suggests that as new information becomes available over time, individual forecasts become better estimates of A_T, and the R^2 values should monotonically increase as j approaches m. Consequently, rationality implies that as forecasts by individuals are updated, the dispersion of these forecasts should tighten around the actual value A_T.

An Econometric Problem

Before turning to the next section, a few comments about the estimation of regression equations (5) and (6) are in order. Hansen and Hodrick (1980), Brown and Maital (1981), and Hansen (1982) first showed that tests of rationality based upon the usual ordinary-least-squares technique may not be appropriate due to serial correlation of the error terms. The reason to expect serial correlation is that economists will not have knowledge of all previous prediction errors when making their next forecast if there are overlapping forecasting intervals. If the forecast errors for more recent periods are not part of the available information set, it is likely that the covariances of these error terms will be nonzero, thus violating one of the OLS assumptions. While the OLS coefficients will be unbiased, the covariance estimates are inconsistent.

In this case, generalized least squares is usually not an effective solution to the serial correlation problem. As Brown and Maital (1981) point out, the regressors in equations (5) and (6) are not strictly exogenous, and the use of GLS will prob-

[6]The subscript $T-m$ allows for the possibility that the last forecast occurs m months prior to the realization of A_T.

ably produce inconsistent estimators. Following their suggestion, the analysis tests for rationality of consensus forecasts by estimating equation (5) using OLS, but corrects the covariance matrix by employing the generalized method of moments (GMM) technique first proposed by Hansen (1979, 1982). In addition to Brown and Maital (1981), the GMM procedure has previously been applied to the Livingston data by Schroeter and Smith (1986), Bryan and Gavin (1986), and Batchelor and Dua (1989).

Theoretically, it is also appropriate to adjust the covariance matrix for the problem of overlapping forecasting intervals when estimating equation (6). However, since the respondents have changed over time, it is not possible to track each individual's forecast errors during the entire period. Consequently, correcting the covariance matrix is also impossible. Fortunately, the OLS estimators in the individual forecast equations are unbiased, although the error statistics may be biased, and hypothesis testing must proceed with caution.

3. EMPIRICAL RESULTS

The first test of rationality requires that the real GNP forecast be an unbiased estimate of the actual value. Panel A of Table 1 exhibits results that use Hansen's generalized method of moments technique, where the asymptotically appropriate test statistic for the joint hypothesis $a_j=0$ and $b_j=1$ is distributed $\chi^2(2)$. The results show that the null hypothesis cannot be rejected. Nevertheless, for August and all subsequent revisions, the estimated line is steep relative to the unbiased 45-degree line, $A_T=F_{t,T}$. Starting with February forecasts, the estimated lines suggest that for high (low) levels of real GNP, predictions tend to systematically understate (overstate) the actual value.

The result that $a_j<0$ and $b_j>1$ is similar to Brown and Maitals' finding for real GNP which used six-month and twelve-month Livingston forecasts. Although unbiasedness cannot be rejected, it is troubling that after January, the slope continues to increase. For the latest revisions in May, the slope equals 1.14. One possible explanation for this puzzling result is that forecasters find it difficult to predict real GNP when the actual values are continually being revised by the Department of Commerce.

A second test of rationality requires that as new information becomes available, forecasts for a given variable should become "better" estimates. As discussed in the previous section, one implication is that the R^2 statistic should increase as the forecasts are revised every month. The R^2 statistic for July equals .3948 and monotonically increases over time. By May, consensus forecasts explain almost 93 percent of the variation of real GNP.

The fact that the R^2 of equation (5) rises as the forecasting horizon gets shorter should not necessarily be interpreted as an increase in forecasting accuracy when the estimated coefficients do not converge to their rational expectations values. One alternative is to look at changes in the mean squared forecast error (MSE) over time. The mean squared forecast error weights large errors more heavily

TABLE 1

ACTUAL PERCENTAGE CHANGE OF REAL GNP REGRESSED ON THE FORECASTED CHANGE OF REAL GNP

Panel A: Consensus Forecasts
(Annual Forecasts from July 1976 to May 1988; Revised Monthly)

$$A_T = a_j + b_j F_{T-j,T} + u_{T-j,T}$$

Month, j	$\hat{a}_j$	$\hat{b}_j$	R^2	$\chi^2(2)$	MSE	n
July, 18	−.21 (−.23)	.95 (−.16)	.3948	1.41	3.24	12
August, 17	−.45 (−.53)	1.03 (.13)	.4715	1.48	2.82	12
September, 16	−.66 (−.83)	1.11 (.43)	.5349	1.67	2.50	12
October, 15	−.51 (−.71)	1.11 (.46)	.5801	.77	2.25	12
November, 14	−.01 (−.01)	1.01 (.07)	.6614	.02	1.82	12
December, 13	.17 (.34)	1.01 (.08)	.7391	.57	1.39	12
January, 12	.19 (.42)	1.01 (.06)	.7476	.76	1.35	12
February, 11	−.10 (−.19)	1.08 (.45)	.7645	.31	1.25	12
March, 10	−.35 (−.69)	1.12 (.77)	.8113	.59	1.01	12
April, 9	−.39 (−1.03)	1.13 (1.15)	.8910	1.33	.58	12
May, 8	−.37 (−1.26)	1.14 (1.50)	.9281	2.25	.38	12

Panel B: Individual Forecasts
(Annual Forecasts from August 1976 to May 1988; Revised Monthly)

$$A_T = a_j + b_j({}_iF_{T-j,T}) + {}_iu_{T-j,T}$$

Month, j	$\hat{a}_j$	$\hat{b}_j$	R^2	$F(2,n\text{-}2)$	MSE	n
July, 18	.87 (4.92)**	.59 (−7.77)**	.2042	39.03**	3.99	488
August, 17	.68 (4.21)**	.67 (−7.20)**	.2882	34.79**	3.52	519
September, 16	.51 (3.33)**	.72 (−6.04)**	.3348	26.85**	3.21	526
October, 15	.47 (3.31)**	.77 (−5.45)**	.3920	18.87**	2.85	526
November, 14	.67 (5.98)**	.77 (−6.54)**	.4886	22.39**	2.42	522
December, 13	.67 (6.88)**	.81 (−6.00)**	.5741	24.18**	2.05	525
January, 12	.67 (7.17)**	.82 (−5.90)**	.5919	25.85**	1.94	532
February, 11	.38 (3.92)**	.90 (−3.40)**	.6258	7.73**	1.69	539
March, 10	.17 (1.84)†	.94 (−2.10)*	.6680	2.30	1.46	539
April, 9	.06 (.74)	.98 (− .78)	.7670	.31	1.02	541
May, 8	−.10 (−1.64)	1.05 (2.35)*	.8421	3.04*	.70	541

NOTES: j = number of months before realization of variable's actual value.
t-ratios in parentheses test the null hypothesis that $a_j = 0$ or $b_j = 1$; t-tests are two-tailed tests with (n-2) degrees of freedom.
** = significant at the.01 level.
* = significant at the .05 level.
† = significant at the .10 level.
χ^2 and F-statistics test the joint hypothesis that $a_j = 0$ and $b_j = 1$.
n = number of observations in the regression.

relative to small ones and is frequently used as a measure of forecasting accuracy [see, for example, McNees (1988) and Dua (1988)]. The monotonic decline of the mean squared errors in panel A provides further evidence that later consensus forecasts are more accurate.

Real GNP regression estimates for equation (6) appear in panel B of Table 1. For distant forecasts, the estimated line is flat relative to the unbiased 45-degree line. Initially, the joint hypothesis, $a_j=0$ and $b_j=1$, can be rejected at the .01 significance level. Over time, the estimated line becomes steeper, and for April forecasts, the null hypothesis of unbiasedness cannot be rejected at even the .1 level. However, similar to the results for the consensus forecasts in panel A, the slope continues to increase. For May forecasts, the estimated line is steep relative to the unbiased line, and unbiasedness can be rejected at the .05 significance level.

The monthly Blue Chip revisions again suggest a rigorous test of changes in forecast accuracy over time. The R^2 statistic in July equals .2042 and monotonically increases to .8421 in May. This implies that during the forecast period, individuals continually assimilate new information and their expectations converge. The mean squared error criterion provides futher support of the hypothesis that revised forecasts are more accurate. The mean squared forecast error declines with revisions of real GNP forecasts.

While expectations converge over time, the dispersion of economists' forecasts in a given month provides information about the group's agreement (or lack of agreement) at that point. An interesting question is whether a small dispersion of forecasts implies that the monthly consensus forecast is a relatively accurate one. To answer that question, individual real GNP forecasts were partitioned by months. For each year, the standard deviation of individual forecasts and the absolute error between the consensus forecast and actual value were calculated. Table 2 lists the Spearman rank correlation coefficients for each month between these two variables. No sign pattern of the rank correlation coefficients emerges and only one month, December, is even marginally significant. The results indicate that a relatively small dispersion of individual forecasts does not necessarily imply a good consensus forecast for that month.

Table 3 presents regression results for the inflation rate as measured by the Consumer Price Index. The July consensus forecast equation in panel A is a relatively steep line with a slope of 1.49. This suggests that 3 percent change in the actual inflation rate corresponds to slightly more than a 2 percent change in the expected inflation rate. In years where actual inflation turns out to be relatively high (greater than 7.14 percent), July forecasts tend to underpredict the inflation rate. July forecasts tend to overpredict the inflation rate when consumer prices are relatively stable.

As forecasts are revised, the estimated line becomes less steep and the intercept larger. Each revision appears to provide a better forecast of the actual inflation rate. By May, the point estimates for a_j and b_j are little different from 0 and 1, and statistically, the regression and unbiased 45-degree line are one and the same. In contrast to real GNP, the CPI is not revised, and the results suggest that the information from monthly changes in the actual index is efficiently utilized by economists.

The changes in the R^2 statistic over time provides further evidence of informational efficiency. With the exception of February, the coefficient of determination monotonically increases as forecasts are revised. The February result is a consequence of including CPI forecasts for 1979 for the months of February through May only. Blue Chip forecasts of the CPI began in February 1979 and are included in Table 3 to conserve the degrees of freedom in the regressions. If CPI forecasts for 1979 are exluded, the R^2 statistic in February increases to .9242 and is equal to .9633, .9924, and .9956 in successive months. If mean squared error is used to measure changes in forecast accuracy, support for informational efficiency also obtains as errors generally decline over time.

Regression estimates for equation (6) using individual inflation forecasts appear in panel B of Table 3. In the early months, the estimated lines are steep

TABLE 2

SPEARMAN RANK CORRELATION BETWEEN DISPERSION OF ANALYSTS' REAL GNP FORECASTS AND ERROR OF CONSENSUS FORECASTS

Month, j	Spearman Rank Correlation
July, 18	−.37
August, 17	−.08
September, 16	−.17
October, 15	.02
November, 14	.31
December, 13	.61*
January, 12	.41
February, 11	.27
March, 10	.08
April, 9	.06
May, 8	−.03

NOTES: j = number of months before realization of variable's actual value.
* = significant at the .05 level, two-tailed test.
The formula for the Spearman rank correlation coefficient may be found in Conover (1980, p. 252).
Critical regions for the Spearman rank correlation coefficient appear in Conover (1980, p. 456).

TABLE 3

ACTUAL INFLATION RATE REGRESSED ON THE FORECASTED INFLATION RATE

Panel A: Consensus Forecasts
(Annual Forecasts from February 1979 to May 1988; Revised Monthly)

$$A_T = a_j + b_j F_{T-j,T} + u_{T-j,T}$$

Month, j	$\hat{a}_j$	$\hat{b}_j$	R^2	$\chi^2(2)$	MSE	n
July, 18	−3.50 (−1.60)	1.49 (1.45)	.7261	2.60	4.81	9
August, 17	−3.42 (−1.63)	1.50 (1.53)	.7409	2.67	4.59	9
September, 16	−3.07 (−1.59)	1.43 (1.45)	.7631	2.56	4.17	9
October, 15	−2.97 (−1.66)	1.42 (1.54)	.7765	2.77	3.95	9
November, 14	−2.14 (−1.54)	1.27 (1.32)	.8410	2.41	2.78	9
December, 13	−1.90 (−1.64)	1.23 (1.34)	.8695	2.82	2.33	9
January, 12	−1.44 (−1.52)	1.15 (1.13)	.8893	2.61	1.88	9
February, 11	−1.17 (−1.25)	1.17 (1.29)	.8841	1.71	1.97	10
March, 10	−.63 (− .91)	1.09 (.92)	.9258	.89	1.18	10
April, 9	−.20 (− .42)	1.02 (.31)	.9606	.18	.58	10
May, 8	−.14 (− .41)	1.03 (.54)	.9777	.30	.33	10

Panel B: Individual Forecasts
(Annual Forecasts from February 1979 to May 1988; Revised Monthly)

$$A_T = a_j + b_j({}_iF_{T-j,T}) + {}_iu_{T-j,T}$$

Month, j	$\hat{a}_j$	$\hat{b}_j$	R^2	$F(2,n\text{-}2)$	MSE	n
July, 18	−2.05 (−6.60)**	1.25 (5.14)**	.6143	26.50**	5.29	414
August, 17	−2.09 (−7.10)**	1.27 (5.83)**	.6454	27.78**	4.90	412
September, 16	−2.02 (−7.42)**	1.26 (5.98)**	.6755	30.75**	4.56	416
October, 15	−2.05 (−8.30)**	1.27 (6.82)**	.7209	36.99**	4.03	416
November, 14	−1.45 (−7.20)**	1.16 (5.29)**	.7772	30.60**	3.18	411
December, 13	−1.32 (−7.43)**	1.14 (5.11)**	.8099	35.38**	2.73	415
January, 12	−1.01 (−6.48)**	1.09 (3.71)**	.8362	32.14**	2.30	418
February, 11	− .84 (−5.70)**	1.11 (5.18)**	.8527	16.33**	2.16	459
March, 10	− .38 (−3.17)**	1.04 (2.59)*	.8889	5.13**	1.57	467
April, 9	.02 (.27)	.98 (−1.58)	.9302	3.16	.97	467
May, 8	.00 (0)	1.00 (0)	.9526	.01	.66	466

NOTES: See notes to Table 1.

relative to the unbiased 45-degree line, and we can strongly reject the null hypothesis of unbiasedness. The fact that the null hypothesis is rejected in the early months of panel 3B but not 3A may be due to both positive correlation of individual forecasts and autocorrelated disturbance terms. If all Blue Chip participants tend to make similar forecasts each month and commit similar prediction errors, Johnston (1984, pp. 311–12) shows that the OLS sampling variances will be biased downward. This would cause t statistics to be overestimated, and therefore, would cause unwarranted rejection of the null hypothesis of unbiasedness.[7]

As expectations are revised, a_j and b_j approach 0 and 1 respectively and are not significantly different from these values by April. Moreover, the R^2 values continually increase over time and the mean squared forecast errors decline. The individual forecast results parallel those found using consensus forecasts and suggest that economists efficiently use new information about inflation.

Table 4 displays the Spearman rank correlation coefficients between the dispersion of analysts' inflation rate forecasts and consensus forecast errors. In general, it appears that for early forecasts, there is no relation between the dispersion of expected inflation and forecast errors. For later forecasts, the evidence suggests that the more economists agree about expected inflation, the lower is the ex post error of the consensus forecast. However, in May, the latest revision, this relationship breaks down and the correlation between the dispersion of expected inflation and forecast errors is statistically insignificant. One possible explanation is that the extremely small May forecast errors make the dispersion of expected inflation and forecast error relationship unstable.

4. CONCLUSION

This paper tests two hypotheses on whether economists' forecasts of real GNP growth and the inflation rate are rational. The first test concerns unbiasedness of economic forecasts, and the second, the improvement of revised estimates as new information becomes available. Unlike previous studies that employ the semiannual Livingston data, the monthly revisions of the Blue Chip Economic Indicators enable more rigorous tests of rationality.

Regression analysis of real GNP growth suggests that consensus forecasts are unbiased. However, for May, the regression line tends to be steep relative to the unbiased 45-degree line. The same result holds for real GNP regressions using individual forecasts in May, and the joint hypothesis of unbiasedness can be rejected at the .05 significance level. Nevertheless, the R^2 statistic and mean squared forecast error measure the predictive power of the economic forecasts, and it appears that changes in both measures over time imply that later forecasts

[7]Unfortunately, the change in the number of Blue Chip participants each month makes it impossible to specify an autoregressive process for either the forecasts or error terms, and therefore, it is not possible to correct for this bias. This serial correlation problem, which is independent of the overlapping forecasting problem, may also affect the OLS test statistics found in Table 1B.

TABLE 4

Spearman Rank Correlation between Dispersion of Analysts' Inflation Rate Forecasts and Error of Consensus Forecasts

Month, *j*	Spearman Rank Correlation
July, 18	−.15
August, 17	.10
September, 16	−.13
October, 15	.08
November, 14	−.17
December, 13	.23
January, 12	.43
February, 11	.61†
March, 10	.67*
April, 9	.59†
May, 8	−.12

Notes: See notes to Table 2.
† = significant at the .10 level, two-tailed test.

are more accurate. One possible explanation for these apparently contradictory results is that continual revisions by the Department of Commerce make it difficult for economists to accurately forecast real GNP.

Unlike real GNP figures, the Consumer Price Index is not revised. When a new index level for the previous month is announced, economists can use this information without fear that the number will be changed. The empirical analysis suggests that the revised inflation forecasts incorporate this information in a rational manner. Later inflation forecasts are found to be unbiased, and they provide better estimates than early expectations using both the R^2 and mean squared error criteria.

Data for this paper are available from the JMCB *editorial office.*

LITERATURE CITED

Batchelor, Roy, and Pami Dua. "Household versus Economist Forecasts of Inflation: A Reassesment." *Journal of Money, Credit, and Banking* 21 (May 1989), 252–57.

Bigman, David, David Goldfarb, and Edna Schectman. "Futures Market Efficiency and the Time Content of the Information Sets." *The Journal of Futures Markets* 3 (1983), 321–34.

Brown, Bryan, and Shlomo Maital. "What Do Economists Know? An Empirical Study of Experts' Expectations." *Econometrica* 49 (March 1981), 491–504.

Bryan, Michael, and William Gavin. "Models of Inflation Expectations Formation: A Comparison of Household and Economist Forecasts." *Journal of Money, Credit, and Banking* 18 (November 1986), 539–44.

Carlson, John. "A Study of Price Forecasts." *Annals of Economic and Social Measurement* 6 (Winter 1977), 27–56.

Conover, W. J. *Practical Nonparametric Statistics*. New York: John Wiley & Sons, 1980.

Dua, Pami. "Multiperiod Forecasts of Interest Rates." *Journal of Business and Economic Statistics* 6 (July 1988), 381–84.

Figlewski, Stephen, and Paul Wachtel. "The Formation of Inflationary Expectations." *Review of Economics and Statistics* 63 (February 1981), 1–10.

Hansen, Lars-Peter. "The Asymptotic Distribution of Least Squares Estimators with Endogenous Regressors and Dependent Residuals." Graduate School of Industrial Administration, Carnegie-Mellon University, March 1979.

______. "Large Sample Properties of Generalized Method of Moments Estimators." *Econometrica* 50 (July 1982), 1029–54.

Hansen, Lars-Peter, and Robert Hodrick. "Forward Exchange Rates as Optimal Predictors of Future Spot Rates: An Economic Analysis." *Journal of Political Economy* 88 (October 1980), 829–53.

Johnson, J. *Econometric Methods*. New York: McGraw-Hill, Inc., 1984.

McNees, Stephen. "How Accurate Are Macroeconomic Forecasts?" *New England Economic Review* (July/August 1988), 15–35.

Mullineaux, Donald. "On Testing for Rationality: Another Look at the Livingston Price Data." *Journal of Political Economy* 86 (April 1978), 329–36.

Pearce, Douglas. "Comparing Survey and Rational Measures of Expected Inflation: Forecast Performance and Interest Rate Effect." *Journal of Money, Credit, and Banking* 11 (November 1979), 447–56.

______. "An Empirical Analysis of Expected Stock Price Movements." *Journal of Money, Credit, and Banking* 16 (August 1984), 317–27.

Pesando, James. "A Note on the Rationality of the Livingston Price Expectations." *Journal of Political Economy* 83 (August 1975), 849–58.

Schroeter, John, and Scott Smith. "A Reexamination of the Rationality of the Livingston Price Expectations." *Journal of Money, Credit, and Banking* 18 (May 1986), 239–46.

ROGER C. KORMENDI
PHILIP MEGUIRE

A Multicountry Characterization of the Nonstationarity of Aggregate Output

WHETHER THE UNIVARIATE TIME SERIES REPRESENTATION of real GNP contains a unit root or a deterministic linear trend has been much debated of late. The straightforward application of Box-Jenkins identification techniques strongly suggests the presence of a unit root, in that the autocorrelations of the first differences of the log of annual real GNP are all smaller than two (asymptotic) standard errors after the second lag or so, and the $Q(k)$ statistic for low-order ARIMA models is small for large k. The tests derived by Dickey and Fuller concur in this conclusion.[1] The classic reference is Nelson and Plosser (1982), who find that a unit root dominates a linear trend in nearly every long U.S. macroeconomic series they examine. Schwert (1987) reached similar conclusions. Using varying methods, Harvey (1985), Rose (1986), Stock and Watson (1986), and Campbell and Mankiw (1987) report similar results for quarterly U.S. GNP.[2]

The authors' interest in this topic was stimulated by Coleman Kendall and Victor Bernard. They also thank John Cochrane and Noel Cressie for helpful comments.

[1]See Dickey, Bell, and Miller (1986) for a discussion and review of these tests, with references and applications.

[2]While not formally testing for unit roots, Kormendi and Meguire's (1984) analysis of post war real GDP and M1 from forty-seven countries found evidence of unit roots in these series.

ROGER C. KORMENDI *is professor of business economics and public policy in the School of Business Administration, University of Michigan, and director of the Mid America Institute for Public Policy Research.* PHILIP MEGUIRE *is research investigator in the School of Business Administration, University of Michigan, and fellow of the Mid America Institute for Public Policy Research.*

Journal of Money, Credit, and Banking, Vol. 22, No. 1 (February 1990)

In a paper that focuses on the "long" U.S. GNP data, Cochrane (1988) reached a contrary conclusion. He found that less than 20 percent of the variance of the growth rate of the log of annual real per capita U.S. GNP (henceforth simply GNP) over the period 1869–1986 could be attributed to the presence of a unit root.[3] Cochrane contended that previous evidence in favor of a unit root in GNP is misleading, because nonrandomness in the high-order autocorrelations was overlooked. Although small, these autocorrelations are mostly negative, which is consistent with overdifferencing. He concluded that a stationary AR(2) model about a linear trend fits the data better in-sample than did parsimonious unit root models.

The question of whether or not GNP contains a unit root arises frequently in macroeconomics.[4] For example, Mankiw and Shapiro (1985) show that when income has a unit root, findings that consumption is "too sensitive" to innovations in income (for example, Flavin 1981) may be an artifact of assuming trend stationarity. In fact, using differenced specifications, Deaton (1986), Campbell and Deaton (1987), and West (1988a) (all for the United States) and Kormendi and LaHaye (1987) (for a panel of thirty countries) found that consumption appears to be *undersensitive* to income. A properly specified consumption function is also needed to analyze aspects of fiscal policy such as the substitutability between public and private consumption, the possibility of Ricardian equivalence and the effects of transfer payments on savings.[5] Whether or not income and money have unit roots is also important when estimating the demand for money and the effects of monetary policy under rational expectations.[6] Finally, recent theories of endogenous growth by P. Romer (1986), Lucas (1988), and King and Rebelo (1986) have implications for the nonstationarity of aggregate output.

Because the literature to date yields conflicting results for U.S. GNP, particularly for the long data, we examine the data from many countries, using the longest time series possible. In this paper, we draw on Cochrane (1988), Campbell and Mankiw (1987), and Cressie (1987) to develop the *scaled variogram*, $R(k)$. We compute $R(k)$ for the century-long data on annual real output for twelve countries, and for thirty-two countries over the postwar era. Campbell

[3]Watson (1986) and Clark (1987), applying an unobserved components decomposition to the postwar U.S. data, reached a similar conclusion.

[4]Independently of any particular economic hypothesis, the failure to account for possible unit roots by differencing may have serious statistical consequences. Regressions estimated from levels data with unit roots can have nonstationary residuals, leading to the "spurious regression" phenomenon; cf. Granger and Newbold (1974), and Plosser and Schwert (1978). Series with unit roots reveal spurious periodicities when detrended (Nelson and Kang 1981). OLS estimators computed from data with unit roots may not possess standard asymptotic sampling distributions (Phillips 1986). Stock (1984), Engle and Granger (1987), and Stock and West (1988) argue that economic time series with unit roots may be cointegrated, and that regressions relating cointegrated variables and estimated in levels can be well-specified under certain conditions. In future work, we plan to extend the methods of this paper to allow for cointegration. See Kormendi and Meguire (1990) for an application.

[5]In particular, as Brunner (1986) has emphasized, tests of fiscal policy using time series data should be done using differenced specifications. See also Kormendi (1983) and Kormendi and Meguire (1986, 1990).

[6]Cf. Fama (1982), Kormendi and Meguire (1984), Mankiw and Summers (1986), and Rush (1986).

and Mankiw (1989) also compare results computed from the postwar quarterly time series for seven countries, and find results similar to our own.[7]

In section I, we briefly discuss the scaled variogram and its simulated sampling distribution. In section 2, we estimate the scaled variograms for the century-long series from twelve countries and the postwar series from thirty-two countries. In section 3, we present a new simulation method for determining whether these series are more properly characterized as parsimonious trend stationary (TS) or difference stationary (DS) processes. The results reveal that parsimonious DS models are almost always more probable than TS models over our data. Section 4 presents concluding remarks.

1. THE SCALED VARIOGRAM AND ITS SAMPLING PROPERTIES

The Scaled Variogram

Cochrane (1988) and Campbell and Mankiw (1987) use a similar nonparametric procedure for detecting and quantifying a unit root in a time series, derived from the following elementary property of random walks. For any stochastic process $\{X_t\}$, let $\sigma^2(k) = \sigma^2(X_t - X_{t-k})$ denote the variance of the *kth difference* of $\{X_t\}$. This is the population *variogram* of $\{X_t\}$.[8] If $\{X_t\}$ is a random walk, then $\sigma^2(k) = k\sigma^2(1)$ holds in population for all positive k. We call the sequence $V(k) = \sigma^2(k)/k, k=1,..., n$, the *variogram rate of* $\{X_t\}$.[9] A plot of the variogram rate of a random walk against its lags k is then a horizontal line. If no unit root is present, $V(k)$ is asymptotically zero. If $\{X_t\}$ has a unit root, $V(k)$ has a positive asymptote.

Let the time series $x_0,..., x_n$ be a realization from the stochastic process $\{X_t\}$. For any positive integer k, first let

$$\hat{\sigma}^2(k) \equiv \sum_{t=k}^{n} [x_t - x_{t-k} - \frac{k}{n}(x_n - x_0)]^2 \ / \ (n-k) \quad (1)$$

be an estimator of $\sigma^2(k)$. Following Cochrane (1988), we multiply $\hat{\sigma}^2(k)$ by $n/(n-k)$ to adjust for the bias due to the overlap in consecutive differences. Our estimator of the variogram rate is then

[7]In a paper that came to our attention after this one was completed, Cogley (1990) uses the century-long annual data to arrive at conclusions similar to ours.

[8]The variogram is a one-dimensional (time) special case of a technique, known for some years in the geostatistics and meteorological literatures, for analyzing spatial nonstationarity and autocorrelation in two or more dimensions. We have appropriated the term variogram from this literature. See Cressie (1989) and references therein, especially Matheron (1971). Variants of the variogram have recently appeared in the finance literature; cf. Lo and MacKinley (1987a, b), French and Roll (1987), Huizinga (1987), and Poterba and Summers (1988).

[9]Noel Cressie (personal communication) suggested this term.

$$\hat{V}(k) \equiv \frac{n}{k(n-k)} \hat{\sigma}^2(k) . \tag{2}$$

We then scale $\hat{V}(k)$ by the variance of first differences, $\hat{V}(1)$, to obtain the *scaled variogram*, with typical element $\hat{R}(k) \equiv \hat{V}(k) \div \hat{V}(1)$.

The scaled variogram is a dimensionless quantity independent of the units in which the underlying data x_t are measured. It is a function only of the length of the series and of the autocorrelations of its first differences; its sampling properties do not depend on any other nuisance parameters. The scaled variograms from series with similar lengths can be meaningfully compared and plotted together along the same set of coordinates. Hence the scaled variogram is particularly useful for comparing data across countries. The expected value of $R(k)$ computed from a random walk is 1, for all k. As is the case for $V(k)$, if a series contains a unit root, then $R(k)$ has a positive asymptote. If this asymptote lies in the [0,1] interval, it can be interpreted as the fraction of the variance of a series due to permanent shocks. If no unit root is present, $R(k)$ asymptotes to zero.

The scaled variogram summarizes the covariance properties of a time series and hence is related to the correlogram. As Cochrane (1988) and Campbell and Mankiw (1987) show,

$$R(k) = 1 + 2 \cdot \sum_{j=1}^{k-1} \frac{(k-j)}{k} \rho(j) \tag{3}$$

holds in population, so that $R(k)$ is a linear combination of the first $k-1$ autocorrelations ($\rho(j)$) of the differenced series.

The Sampling Distribution of R(k) Computed from a Pure Random Walk

Since $R(k)$ is proportional to a ratio of variances divided by their degrees of freedom, it resembles an F-statistic. The similarity is not exact because the kth differences underlying $V(k)$ are not statistically independent. Nonetheless, the sampling distribution can be easily simulated, as it has only two parameters, n and k. Table 1A shows the sampling distribution of $R(k)$, $k = 3, 10, 20$, and 50, computed from 1,000 simulated random walks of length 117, corresponding to the period 1869–1985.[10]

The major fact we wish to point out about the sampling distribution of $R(k)$ is its pronounced skewness, which increases with k. In particular, whereas the sample mean of $R(k)$ is essentially 1 for all k, so that $R(k)$ is unbiased, *the sample medians are biased below one, and this median bias increases with k*. This skewness (expected by analogy with the F distribution) renders inappropriate sym-

[10]The simulations and estimates reported in this paper were done with version 2.12 of RATS on a microcomputer. The programs are available upon request in machine readable form from the authors. A more comprehensive version of this paper, Kormendi and Meguire (1987), is also available upon request.

TABLE 1

SIMULATED SAMPLING DISTRUBTION OF SCALED VARIOGRAM FOR RANDOM WALK. 1,000 REPLICATIONS

1A
Homoskedastic Disturbances (length 117)

Lag K	Min	5	10	25	50	Mean	75	90	95	Max
				Fractiles						
3	.57	.79	.84	.90	.99	1.00	1.09	1.17	1.23	1.49
10	.35	.55	.62	.76	.95	.99	1.15	1.40	1.58	2.65
20	.16	.37	.46	.64	.87	.97	1.21	1.62	1.89	3.85
50	.10	.21	.28	.45	.76	.99	1.28	1.96	2.52	6.01

1B
Heteroskedastic Disturbances (length 117)

Lag K	Min	5	10	25	50	Mean	75	90	95	Max
				Fractiles						
3	.44	.71	.76	.86	1.00	1.01	1.15	1.26	1.36	1.75
10	.29	.48	.58	.72	.94	1.05	1.28	1.67	2.03	3.24
20	.19	.36	.43	.61	.90	1.09	1.37	1.97	2.54	4.77
50	.07	.20	.26	.42	.81	1.11	1.43	2.36	3.19	6.16

1C
Homoskedastic Disturbances (length 36)

Lag K	Min	5	10	25	50	Mean	75	90	95	Max
				Fractiles						
3	.33	.62	.68	.82	.98	1.00	1.16	1.35	1.43	2.13
10	.12	.31	.38	.55	.86	1.00	1.30	1.83	2.15	3.75
20	.08	.23	.31	.47	.80	1.01	1.34	2.00	2.59	5.06

NOTE: The model simulated is $X_t = \delta + X_{t-1} + k_t\epsilon_t$, where ϵ_t is a simulated drawing from a $N(0,1)$ distribution. In 1A, $k_t = .054$ for all t. In 1B, k_t is set to the standard deviation, given in footnote 12, of U.S. GNP for the period that includes t. In 1C, $k_t = .028$. For each simulated random walk, δ and X_0 were set equal to their estimated (actual) values using the log of U.S. annual per capita real GNP.

metric standard error bands about simulated or actual (scaled) variograms.[11] For this reason, we will report selected fractiles from our empirical pdfs rather than standard errors, and base inferences on these fractiles rather than on simulated means and standard errors.

The dispersion of the estimates also increases with k. Taking the 5 percent and 95 percent fractiles as the lower and upper bounds of a 90 percent "confidence interval" under the random walk null, this interval is quite wide, especially for the larger k. For example, the interval is about [.4, 1.9] for $k = 20$, and about [.2, 2.5] for $k = 50$. This large sampling variability reveals the limits of the power of the scaled variogram to detect a unit root in a single time series, even one 117 years long, and motivates our desire to increase the number of countries under evaluation.

[11]In virtually all work to date using the variogram and analogues thereof, for example, Cochrane (1988) and Campbell and Mankiw (1987), symmetric standard error bands are assumed (at least implicitly). Lo and MacKinley (1987a) simulate and derive analytically the asymptotic properties of a statistic, called M_rq in their paper, very similar to $R(k)$. $R(k) = M_r(q) + 1$ when k is substituted for q and n for nq, q=1,...,nq−1 in their equations (9) and (14c). However, they fail to recognize the strong right skewness of the (scaled) variogram computed from finite samples.

2. THE SCALED VARIOGRAM OF REAL OUTPUT ACROSS TIME AND COUNTRIES

The Long Series for the United States and United Kingdom

Our long series for the United States is real GNP from the National Income and Products Accounts for the period 1929–86, spliced to C. Romer's (1989) new estimates of real GNP for the period 1869–1928. The analogous series for the United Kingdom is annual real GDP for 1870–1947 from Feinstein (1972), spliced to the IFS data for the period 1948–86.[12] Both series are divided by population and then logged. The scaled variograms through lag fifty of U.S. GNP and U.K. GDP are shown in Figure 1, along with the 5 percent, 50 percent, and 95 percent fractiles of the simulated sampling distribution under a Gaussian random walk null. Numerical values corresponding to the lags shown in Table 1 are given in Table 2.

The U.S. variogram through lag 30 is quite similar to Figure 1 in Cochrane (1988). Substantially above 1 at low lags, the variogram then declines gradually from a peak at about lag 4. Although this pattern is generally not what we would expect from a Gaussian random walk, note that the 5 percent lower bound in Figure 1 is never crossed at any lag. In fact, the variogram for the United States generally lies above the first decile of the sampling distribution under a random walk, and $R(50)$ lies close to the 25 percent fractile.

Figure 1 likewise shows the scaled variogram for the long series for U.K. GDP. While also an improbable realization from a random walk, the reason is diametrically opposite that for the United States: the U.K. ordinates are too large relative to Table 1A. In fact, $R(k)$ is everywhere greater than 1, with many ordinates equaling or exceeding the 90 percent fractile.

In order to reconcile Cochrane's and our results for the long U.S. data with those of Nelson and Plosser (1982) and Campbell and Mankiw (1987), we have also computed the scaled variogram for the sample periods used in those studies. These studies have typically examined total rather than per capita GNP. For this reason, Table 2 presents variogram ordinates for both total and per capita output. Table 2 reveals that variogram estimates can be quite sensitive to the choice of sample period and that this may be an important factor in explaining previous findings.[13]

[12]The data and their sources are described in a Data Appendix, available from the authors on request. The United Kingdom data from before WWI may be of higher quality than the U.S. data from the same period because (a) the United Kingdom had income taxation throughout the period, and (b) estimating U.S. GNP prior to 1909 requires nontrivial assumptions (Romer 1989).

[13]The following summary statistics by subperiod reveal significant heteroskedasticity. As Lo and MacKinley (1987a) have recognized, the sampling distribution of the variogram for a random walk may be sensitive to departures from homoskedasticity in the random walk innovations.

U.S. GNP

Period	SD
1869–1929	.039
1930–1954	.096
1955–1985	.024

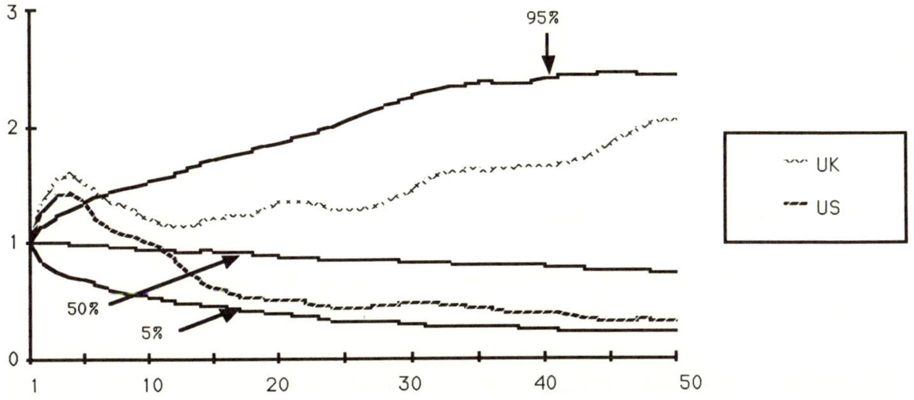

FIG. 1. Scaled Variograms of U.S. and U.K. Long Data

TABLE 2

LONG DATA FOR THE UNITED KINGDOM AND THE UNITED STATES
SELECTED SCALED VARIOGRAM ORDINATES OF LOG AGGREGATE REAL OUTPUT BY SUBPERIODS

	First Row: Per Capita			K	Second Row: Total	
Period	3	5	10	20	30	50
United States						
1869–1986	1.55	1.51	1.15	.54	.49	.43
	1.57	1.54	1.20	.63	.64	.48
1909–1970	1.81	1.87	1.53	.97	.61	—
	1.82	1.86	1.53	.94	.66	—
1948–1986	1.17	.90	.67	.32	—	—
	1.21	.96	.78	.67	—	—
1953–1986	1.15	1.00	.90	.79	—	—
	1.14	1.03	1.16	.82	—	—
United Kingdom						
1870–1986	1.44	1.58	1.41	1.69	1.88	2.77
	1.41	1.52	1.27	1.35	1.29	1.61

NOTE: Data are the long series for the United States and United Kingdom described in the Data Appendix.

Turning first to Nelson and Plosser, we find that their sample period, 1909–70, yields the largest variogram ordinates of any subperiod shown. This explains their unambiguous finding of a unit root in total GNP using Dickey-Fuller tests. Table 2 suggests three reasons why Campbell and Mankiw (1987) find a larger role for a unit root than Cochrane (1988) does. First, their maximum differencing interval of 60 in quarterly data corresponds to $k=15$ in annual data.

Table 1B shows the sampling distribution of selected variogram ordinates computed from a random walk, again 117 observations long, but now with heteroskedasticity patterned after the United States. Relative to the homoskedastic case shown in 1A, the lower fractiles decrease, and the dispersion increases, but both only slightly. Overall, allowing for the observed heteroskedasticity does not alter our interpretation of Figure 1.

For k in the range of 3 to 15, the scaled variogram for the United States is generally consistent with a significant unit root, regardless of sample period. As Cochrane emphasizes, it is only at horizons of twenty to thirty years that the importance of a unit root in the U.S. data becomes questionable. Second, their sample period is close to the period 1953–86, for which our results are fully consistent with a unit root. Note, however, that the estimates for the period 1948–86 are much lower, which suggests why Cochrane's findings for the long data also hold for the postwar subperiod he chooses to examine, 1947–86. Finally, total output generally yields somewhat larger variogram ordinates than per capita output.

The Evidence from Long and Short International Data

The radically different results for the United States and United Kingdom suggest two competing explanations. One is that the long term properties of aggregate output in the two countries are fundamentally different. The other is that the United States and United Kingdom are merely different realizations from the same stationarity class of stochastic processes, and that the seeming differences in their variograms are due to sampling variation. These possibilities motivate an investigation of the data from additional countries.

The source of international data for the postwar era is the International Financial Statistics (IFS) of the International Monetary Fund, which reports continuous series for both real GDP (GNP) and population in thirty-two countries over the period 1950–83. We refer to these data, as the "IFS" or "short" data. Of particular interest, given Cochrane's results, is the longer data for countries other than the United States and the United Kingdom, which consist of Maddison's (1982) series on population and index numbers of real GDP in ten countries. We spliced these data to the postwar IFS data to compute a series for real per capita GDP covering the period 1870–1986 (in two countries the data begin in 1900). We refer to these data, plus the analogous ones for the United States and United Kingdom, as the "Maddison" or the "long" data.[14]

The added power from examining such international data is inversely related to the intercorrelation among the growth rates for each country. If these growth rates are perfectly correlated, there is no added power. More generally, the greater the interdependence among countries' growth rates, the fewer the effective degrees of freedom added, and the smaller the incremental power. Table 3 gives the mean cross-country pairwise correlation for k-year growth rates of real output. The mean correlation of annual growth rates is less than .25 for both data sets. For both the IFS and Maddison data, the mean correlation initially increases as the horizon k lengthens and then levels off at about .4. While there appears to be more common movement in the series as the horizon lengthens, the mean correlations appear small enough to admit significant additional power.

[14]Maddison made a serious effort to assure that his series were as comparable as possible across countries and through time. His U.S. and U.K. data for the period 1870–1947 are not identical to those already analyzed but yield quite similar variogram estimates.

TABLE 3

MEAN CROSS-COUNTRY CORRELATION OF THE GROWTH RATE OF REAL OUTPUT FOR VARIOUS HORIZONS

Number of Countries	Number of Correlations	Horizon K in Years 1	5	10	20	30
Maddison data: 1870–1986						
10	45	.12	.18	.24	.44	.42
IFS Data: 1950–86						
31	465	.21	.34	.35	.36	—

The scaled variograms for the Maddison data are graphed in Figure 2, along with the simulated median and 90 percent confidence interval for a Gaussian random walk 117 observations long, corresponding to panel A of Table 1. The corresponding values of $R(k)$ by country for $k = 20$ and 50 are shown in Table 4. Most $R(k)$ are greater than 1, with only three out of twelve values of $R(50)$ being less than the median value predicted by a random walk. Viewed as a whole, it is very likely that the twelve series contain significant unit root components. That most variogram ordinates graph above the simulated median line suggests that real GDP is on the whole somewhat more persistent than a random walk. After lag 10 or so, the scaled variogram for the United States serves as a lower envelope. Hence the time series behavior of U.S. real output is not at all typical among the countries examined.

Before turning to the results computed from the IFS data, we need to address the shortness of these series. With only thirty-six years of data per country, one might well question whether series so short have anything to say about a long-run property such as the presence of a unit root. Clearly, we can say absolutely nothing about any properties of real output that emerge over horizons longer than thirty-six years. However, if the economic structure governing the nonstationarity of real output is similar across a set of countries, one can examine whether real output *for the set as a whole* contains a unit root by studying the pattern of the $R(k)$ across countries. This approach was implicit in our study of the Maddison data, where data length was not at issue. Moreover, the short sample period is to some extent offset by the relatively low mean cross-country correlations for the IFS data shown in Table 3.[15]

Panel C of Table 1, which should be compared with A, shows the simulated sampling distribution of $R(k)$ computed from a Gaussian random walk of length 36. This length was chosen to correspond to the period 1950–1985, the typical period for which *IFS* reported real output as of this writing. The peculiarities of the sampling distribution of $R(k)$, namely its dispersion, left skewness and downward median bias, are all more pronounced for $n = 36$ than for $n = 117$.

[15]Cochrane (1988) argues that a "rough guide" to the number of degrees of freedom associated with inferences for a lag k horizon is the number of nonoverlapping period of length k contained in a sample of size n, that is, n/k. By this notion, the "long" U.S. time series for GNP has roughly 6 degrees of freedom for inferences about twenty-year horizons, and the postwar data has only 2 or so. Correspondingly, for twelve countries worth of independent "long" data, one would obtain approximately 72 degrees of freedom for inferences; for thirty-two countries of postwar data, approximately 64 degrees of freedom.

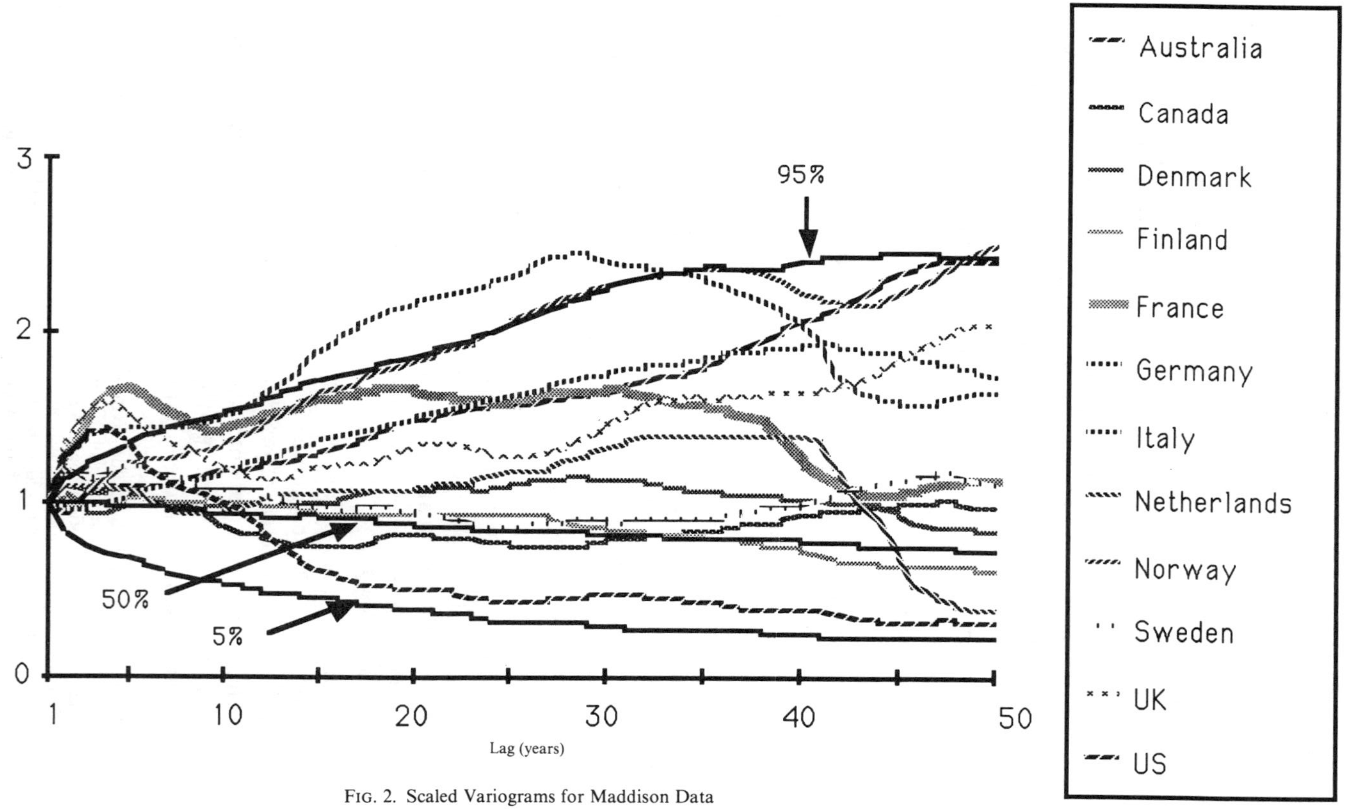

FIG. 2. Scaled Variograms for Maddison Data

TABLE 4

MADDISON DATA: ESTIMATED $R(20)$ AND $R(50)$, SIMULATED MSLS; AND PROBABILITIES, CONDITIONAL ON THE ESTIMATED TS AND DS MODELS

Country	K	$R(K)$	MSL_{TS}	MSL_{DS}	$MSL_{DS}>MSL_{TS}$
Australia	20	1.49	.21	.76	yes
	50	2.39	.07	.88	yes
Canada	20	.82	.32	.36	yes
	50	.98	.13	.52	yes
Denmark	20	1.08	.07	.77	yes
	50	1.83	.07	.77	yes
Finland	20	.94	.10	.64	yes
	50	.61	.06	.31	yes
France	20	1.67	.20	.53	yes
	50	1.17	.25	.44	yes
Germany	20	1.50	.01	.91	yes
	50	1.74	.01	.88	yes
Italy	20	2.17	.06	.89	yes
	50	1.67	.17	.67	yes
Netherlands	20	1.10	.08	.72	yes
	50	.38	.63	.14	no
Norway	20	1.84	.01	.79	yes
	50	2.51	.01	.85	yes
Sweden	20	.94	.12	.46	yes
	50	1.12	.03	.61	yes
United Kingdom	20	1.34	.27	.52	yes
	50	2.07	.07	.76	yes
United States	20	.50	.23	.04	no
	50	.31	.12	.11	no

This is to be expected by analogy with the F distribution with few degrees of freedom.

The lag 20 values of the scaled variograms for the IFS data are shown in Table 5. The findings here are quite similar to those that emerged from the Maddison data. The vast majority of ordinates are again greater than 1. In fact, for several countries $R(20)$ lies above 2, the 90 percent fractile under a random walk null shown in panel C of Table 1. The United States still has the lowest variogram, even when compared with nearly all of its industrial peers. Recall from Table 2, however, that when the sample period is 1953–86, $R(20)$ for the United States is .79, a value much more consistent with those shown in Table 5 for the other countries.

3. DISCRIMINATING BETWEEN THE TREND STATIONARY AND DIFFERENCE STATIONARY CLASSES

So far we have compared scaled variograms only with a simple random walk null. We now expand the set of hypotheses considered and set out a simulation method for evaluating unit roots when a richer set of hypotheses obtains. To this end, we define two classes of univariate models: a trend stationary (TS) class consisting of ARMA deviations from linear trends, and a difference stationary (DS) class consisting of ARIMA (p,1,q) models. We simulate parsimonious models from both classes, using parameter values estimated from the actual data,

TABLE 5

IFS Postwar Data: Estimated $R(20)$ and Simulated MSLs; Conditional on the Estimated TS and DS Models

Country	$R(20)$	MSL_{TS}	MSL_{DS}	$MSL_{TS}>MSL_{DS}$
Australia	.82	.12	.78	yes
Austria	3.29	.02	.85	yes
Canada	.76	.27	.40	yes
Colombia	2.05	.23	.73	yes
Denmark	2.76	.01	.90	yes
Dominican Republic	.80	.27	.52	yes
Ecuador	1.56	.23	.43	yes
Finland	.87	.28	.48	yes
France	7.14	.95*	.85	no*
Germany	4.12	.00	.93	yes
Greece	4.21	.10	.80	yes
Guatemala	4.28	.01	.86	yes
Honduras	.81	.15	.45	yes
Iceland	1.15	.04	.73	yes
Ireland	2.30	.06	.85	yes
Israel	4.74	.01	.90	yes
Italy	4.44	.01	.83	yes
Mexico	1.40	.01	.75	yes
Netherlands	2.56	.03	.65	yes
Norway	1.13	.07	.58	yes
Panama	2.12	.13	.79	yes
Paraguay	2.62	.10	.61	yes
Philippines	.95	.95	.00*	no*
South Africa	1.71	.07	.86	yes
Sri Lanka	2.06	.00	.70	yes
Sweden	3.89	.00	.95	yes
Switzerland	1.96	.04	.76	yes
Thailand	2.27	.00	.78	yes
Turkey	.50	.49	.20	no
United Kingdom	.82	.13	.71	yes
United States	.35	.63	.18	no
Venezuela	3.74	.96*	.34	no*

*The AR coefficients in the estimated model sum to more than 1, indicating an explosive process, which renders the comparisons of MSLs problematic.

by adding iid Gaussian disturbances. We then compute the scaled variogram at selected lags for each simulated series. Our estimate of the sampling distribution of $R(k)$ is then the empirical distribution (pdf) of the simulated $R(k)$.

Let ϕ_{TS} be the pdf simulated under the parsimonious TS model and ϕ_{DS} the pdf under the parsimonious DS model. We wish to compare TS and DS models in a manner that treats the two null hypotheses *symmetrically*. To this end, we compare the relative probabilities of observing the actual values of $R(k)$ given the empirical pdfs. Under the TS null, that is, given ϕ_{TS}, the probability of finding variogram values *greater than* the observed $R'(k)$ is the standard marginal significance level for rejecting TS in favor of the DS alternative. Correspondingly, given ϕ_{DS} the probability of finding variogram values *less than* the observed $R'(k)$ is the standard marginal significance level for rejecting DS. That is,

$$MSL_{TS} = \text{Prob}[R(k) > R'(k)] = \int_{R'(k)}^{\infty} \phi_{TS}(s)ds \ .$$

$$MSL_{DS} = \text{Prob}[R(k) < R'(k)] = \int_0^{R'(k)} \phi_{DS}(s)ds\,. \qquad (4)$$

The smaller the MSL, the less probable the model. A simple comparison of the two MSLs across countries forms the basis for choosing among the two hypotheses.[16] For a hypothetical $R'(k)$, the two MSLs are illustrated in Figure 3. In this illustration, the observed $R'(k)$ produces a MSL_{DS} somewhat larger than MSL_{TS}.

For simplicity and parsimony, we restrict ourselves to one low-order model from each class: an AR(3) about a linear trend, and an ARIMA (3,1,0).[17] For the series used in this study, three AR terms generally suffice to yield residuals whose standard diagnostics are consistent with white noise.[18] Table 4 gives the corresponding simulated MSLs of DS and TS at lags 20 and 50 for the Maddison data. Table 4 shows that DS is more probable than TS in twenty-one out of twenty-four possible comparisons. At lag 20, the DS model dominates in all countries but the United States. At lag 50, DS is superior in all countries except the United States and the Netherlands. Table 5 shows analogous results for the postwar IFS data at lag 20. DS is more probably in twenty-seven out of thirty-two countries. Of the five that apparently favor TS, three have estimated AR parameters under either TS or DS that imply an explosive process, which contradicts the implicit assumption that all of the nonstationarity in the data can be accounted for either by a linear trend or by a unit root. Of the two remaining, one is again the United States, but recall the results in Table 2 in which the United States over 1953–86 appears to have a significant unit root.

For a given null, the marginal significance levels corresponding to that null should be uniformly distributed across countries between 0 and 1. Table 6 gives a frequency count of the MSLs for $R(50)$ for the Maddison data and for $R(20)$ for the IFS data.

The MSLs under TS are clustered toward 0, indicating that TS cannot account for values of $R(20)$ and $R(50)$ as high as those actually observed. On the other hand, DS yields too many MSLs in the upper half of [0,1], especially for the IFS data, so that DS also cannot fully account for the large observed values of $R(20)$ and $R(50)$.

Thus, restricting the DS class to a parsimonious subset such as ARI(3,1) does not do full justice to the long-run properties of these series. However, instead of being "too nonstationary," as Cochrane concluded for the United States, parsi-

[16]An alternative statistic to MSL for comparing the likelihood of DS to TS would be the posterior odds ratio of ϕ_{DS} to ϕ_{TS} at $R'(k)$. In the context of Figure 3, the posterior odds would be the ratio of the empirical densities in the neighborhood of $R'(k)$.

[17]As Cochrane (1987) argues, without a priori restrictions, there is no power to discriminate between TS and DS classes. Our restriction in this regard is parsimony, that is, restricting ourselves to models of low order.

[18]With respect to the DS class, estimates of low-order ARIMA models with MA components generally yielded results similar to the ARIMA(3,1,0) case. Finally, models with two unit roots typically showed evidence of overdifferencing. Hence using standard diagnostic methods, no *low-order* ARIMA model seemed superior overall to the (3,1,0).

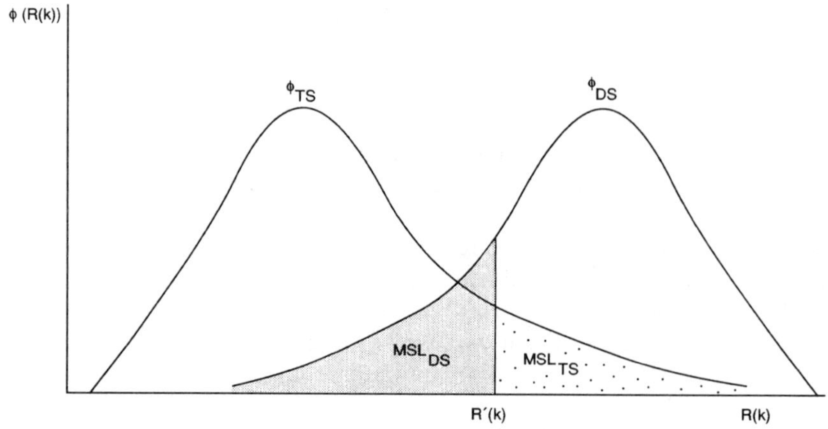

FIG. 3. Illustration of Marginal Significance Levels (MSLs) for an Observed $R'(k)$ under TS and DS Nulls

TABLE 6

FREQUENCY COUNT OF MSLS: IFS POSTWAR DATA, R (20)

Interval		*TS*	*DS*
0	.2	22	2
.2	.4	5	2
.4	.6	1	6
.6	.8	1	11
.8	1.0	3	11

MADDISON DATA, $R(50)$

Interval		*TS*	*DS*
0	.2	10	2
.2	.4	1	1
.4	.6	0	2
.6	.8	1	4
.8	1.0	0	3

monious ARIMA models are generally *insufficiently* nonstationary to simulate with reasonable frequency the large $R(k)$ we actually observe. In other words, the data show some "excess nonstationarity" relative to an ARI(3,1).

4. CONCLUSION

We define the scaled variogram and use it to determine whether the log of annual real per capita output in a number of countries contains a unit root. We confirm recent findings that the long data for the United States, when viewed in isolation, provide questionable evidence in support of a unit root. Viewed as a whole, however, the variograms computed from a variety of countries are overwhelmingly consistent with the presence of a unit root. Our simulations show that a (DS) ARIMA (3,1,0) is almost always a more "probable" model for the data than stationary (TS) AR(3) deviations from a linear trend.

As Cochrane has observed, parsimonious ARIMA models tend to sacrifice goodness of fit at the lowest frequencies in exchange for a better average fit over the entire spectrum. Therefore, such models, while doing justice to the short-run dynamics of a series, may well misrepresent its long-run behavior.[19] In this regard, Cochrane found that the variogram for the U.S. long data is too small to be captured by parsimonious unit root models. While confirming Cochrane's results for the United States, we find that for most other countries, the estimated variogram at long lags is *too large* to be modeled fully by parsimonious ARIMA models, that is, there appears to be "excess" nonstationarity. It should be noted, however, that parsimonious ARIMA models may not necessarily do violence to the *economically relevant* dynamics of a series, if agents appropriately discount the effects of current innovations on future income.

Data for this paper are available from the JMCB *editorial office.*

LITERATURE CITED

Brunner, Karl, "Fiscal Policy in Macro Theory: A Survey and Evaluation." In *The Monetary Versus Fiscal Policy Debate*, edited by R. W. Hafer. London: Rowman and Allanheld, 1986.

Campbell, John Y., and Angus Deaton. "Is Consumption Too Smooth?" National Bureau of Economic Research, Working Paper No. 2134, Spring 1987.

Campbell, J. Y., and N. G. Mankiw. "Permanent and Transitory Components in Macroeconomic Fluctuations." *American Economic Review* 77 (1987), 111–17.

______. "International Evidence on the Persistence of Economic Fluctuations." *Journal of Monetary Economics* 23 (1989), 319–34.

Clark, Peter K. "The Cyclical Component of U.S. Economic Activity." *Quarterly Journal of Economics* 102 (November 1987), 797–814.

Cochrane, John H. "A Critique of Tests for Unit Roots." University of Chicago Working Paper, 1987.

______. "How Big Is the Random Walk in GNP?" *Journal of Political Economy* 96 (1988), 893–920.

Cochrane, John H., and A. M. Sbordone. "Multivariate Estimates of the Permanent Components of GNP and Stock Prices." *Journal of Economic Dynamics and Control* 12 (1988), 255–96.

Cogley, Timothy. "International Evidence on the Size of the Random Walk in Output." *Journal of Political Economy* 98 (1990), forthcoming.

Cressie, Noel. "A Graphical Procedure for Determining Nonstationarity in Time Series." Preprint #87-28, Department of Statistics, Iowa State University, 1987.

______. "The Variogram." In Vol. 9 of the *Encyclopedia of Statistical Science*, edited by N. L. Johnson and S. Kotz. New York: Wiley, 1989.

[19]Yet our full simulations (see Kormendi and Meguire (1987) show that DS outperforms TS not only at the short lags, but even more so at the longer ones.

Deaton, Angus. "Life-cycle Models of Consumption: Is the Evidence Consistent with the Theory?" National Bureau of Economic Research, Working Paper No. 1910, Summer 1986.

Dickey, David A., William R. Bell, and Robert B. Miller. "Unit Roots in Time Series Models: Tests and Implications." *American Statistician* 40 (1986), 12–26.

Engle, Robert F., and Clive W. J. Granger. "Cointegration and Error Correction: Representation, Estimation and Testing." *Econometrica* 55 (1987), 251–76.

Fama, Eugene F. "Inflation, Output and Money," *Journal of Business* 55 (1982), 201–32.

Fama, Eugene F., and Kenneth French. "Permanent and Temporary Components of Stock Prices." *Journal of Political Economy* (1988), 246–73.

Feinstein, C. H. *National Income, Expenditure and Output of the United Kingdom*. Vol. 6 in *Studies in the National Income and Expenditure of the United Kingdom*, series editor Richard Stone. London: Cambridge University Press, 1972.

French, Kenneth R., and R. Roll. "Stock Return Variances: The Arrival of Information and the Reaction of Traders." *Journal of Financial Economics* 19, 3–30.

Granger, Clive W. J., and P. Newbold. "Spurious Regressions in Econometrics." *Journal of Econometrics* 2 (1974), 111–20.

Harvey, A. C. "Trends and Cycles in Macroeconomic Time Series." *Journal of Business and Economic Statistics* 3 (July 1985), 216–27.

Huizinga, John. "An Empirical Investigation of the Long-Run Behavior of the Real Exchange Rate." *Carnegie-Rochester Conference Series on Public Policy* 27 (1987), 149–214.

International Monetary Fund, *International Financial Statistics (IFS)*. Washington: International Monetary Fund, various years.

King, Robert G., and Sergio Rebelo. "Business Cycles with Endogenous Growth." Unpublished manuscript, University of Rochester, 1986.

Kormendi, Roger C. "Government Debt, Government Spending, and Private Sector Behavior." *American Economic Review* 73 (December 1983), 994–1010.

Kormendi, Roger C., and Laura LaHaye. "Cross-Regime Tests of the Permanent Income Hypothesis." Working Paper, University of Michigan, May 1987.

Kormendi, R. C., and P. G. Meguire. "Cross-Regime Tests of Macroeconomic Rationality." *Journal of Political Economy* 92 (1984), 875–908.

______. "Government Debt, Government Spending and Private Sector Behavior: Reply." *American Economic Review* 76 (1986), 1180–87.

______. "The Non-Stationarity of Aggregate Output: A Multicountry Perspective." Working Paper, University of Michigan, 1987.

______. "Fiscal Policy and Private Sector Behavior Revisited." *American Economic Review* (1990), forthcoming.

Lo, A., and A. C. MacKinley. "Stock Market Prices Do Not Follow Random Walks: Evidence from a Simple Specification Test." Working Paper, Rodney L. White Center for Financial Research, University of Pennsylvania, 1987. (a)

______. "A Simple Specification Test of the Random Walk Hypothesis." Working Paper, Rodney L. White Center for Financial Research, University of Pennsylvania, 1987. (b)

Lucas, Robert E. "On the Mechanics of International Development." *Journal of Monetary Economics* 22 (1988), 3–42.

Maddison, Angus. *Phases of Capitalist Development*. London: Oxford University Press, 1982.

Mankiw, N. Gregory, and Matthew Shapiro. "Trends, Random Walks and Tests of the Permanent Income Hypothesis." *Journal of Monetary Economics* 16 (September 1985), 163–74.

Mankiw, N. Gregory and Lawrence Summers. "Money Demand and the Effects of Fiscal Policies." *Journal of Money, Credit, and Banking* 18 (November 1986), 415–29.

Matheron, G. *The Theory of Regionalized Variables and Its Applications.* Cahiers du Centre de Morphologie Mathematique, No. 5, Fontainebleau, 1971.

Nelson, Charles R., and Heejon Kang. "Spurious Periodicity in Inappropriately Detrended Time Series." *Econometrica* 49 (May 1981), 741–51.

Nelson, Charles R., and Charles I. Plosser. "Trends and Random Walks in Macroeconomic Time Series: Some Evidence and Implications." *Journal of Monetary Economics* 10 (September 1982), 139–62.

Phillips, P. C. B. "Understanding Spurious Regressions in Econometrics." *Journal of Econometrics* 33 (December 1986), 311–40.

Plosser, Charles I., and G. William Schwert. "Money, Income and Sunspots: Measuring Economic Relationships and the Effects of Differencing." *Journal of Monetrary Economics* 4 (November 1978), 637–60.

Poterba, James M., and Lawrence H. Summers. "Mean Reversion in Stock Prices: Evidence and Implications." *Journal of Financial Economics* 22 (1988), 27–60.

Romer, Christina. "The Prewar Business Cycle Reconsidered: New Estimates of Gross National Product, 1869–1928." *Journal of Political Economy* 97 (1989), 1–37.

Romer, Paul. "Increasing Returns and Long Run Growth." *Journal of Political Economy* 94 (1986), 1002–37.

Rose, Andrew K. "Four Paradoxes in GNP." *Economics Letters* 22 (1986), 137–41.

Rush, Mark. "Unexpected Money and Unemployment: 1920–1983." *Journal of Money, Credit and Banking* 18 (August 1986), 259–74.

Schwert, G. William. "Effects of Model Specification on Tests for Unit Roots in Macroeconomic Data." *Journal of Monetary Economics* 20 (July 1987), 73–104.

Stock, James H. "Asymptotic Properties of Least Squares Estimators of Cointegrating Vectors." *Econometrica* 55 (1987), 1035–56.

Stock, James H., and Mark W. Watson. "Does GNP Have a Unit Root?" *Economics Letters* 22 (1986), 147–51.

Stock, James H., and K. D. West. "Integrated Regressors and Tests of the Permanent Income Hypothesis." *Journal of Monetary Economics* 21 (1988), 85–96.

Watson, Mark W. "Univariate Detrending Methods with Stochastic Trends." *Journal of Monetary Economics* 18 (July 1986), 49–75.

West, Kenneth D. "The Insensitivity of Consumption to News about Income." *Journal of Monetary Economics* 21 (1988), 17–34. (a)

ATHANASIOS G. NOULAS
SUBHASH C. RAY
STEPHEN M. MILLER

Returns to Scale and Input Substitution for Large U.S. Banks

THE UNITED STATES COMMERCIAL BANKING INDUSTRY has experienced significant changes in recent years. The recent wave of mergers and the near-term prospects of interstate banking suggests that the industry is moving toward much larger average banking organizations (Rhoades 1985). Will a more concentrated banking industry result in lower costs due to scale economies? We address this question by examining the cost function for large banks.

Numerous studies of economies of scale in banking exist, generally tracing their roots to the classic papers by Benston (1965) and Bell and Murphy (1968). A good review of the most recent studies can be found in Clark (1988). The majority of the papers uses samples of smaller banks (that is, under $1 billion in deposits), finding generally that economies of scale are quickly exhausted and that further increases in bank size occur at constant, or possibly increasing, cost.

The extrapolation of previous findings for samples of smaller banks to large banks may be problematic, especially in the current environment. First, large banks service a different mix of markets and customers than small banks, suggesting that large and small banks probably face different cost structures. Second, the process of deregulation may have rendered the results of prior studies moot, since the data pertain to periods before significant deregulation. Since we

The authors acknowledge the help of N. B. Murphy, who provided valuable counsel and made the data available through the Center for Research Development in Financial Services at the University of Connecticut. They also acknowledge the support of the University of Connecticut Computer Center.

ATHANASIOS G. NOULAS *is visiting assistant professor,* SUBHASH C. RAY *is associate professor, and* STEPHEN M. MILLER *is professor of economics at the University of Connecticut, Storrs.*

Journal of Money, Credit, and Banking, Vol. 22, No. 1 (February 1990)

employ 1986 data, the banks have had some time to adjust to the regulatory activity of the early 1980s. Thus, our analysis provides additional, and up-to-date, evidence on the cost structure of large banks.

A number of studies consider banks with deposits above $1 billion (Humphrey 1987, Hunter and Timme 1986, Nelson 1985, and Shaffer and David 1986). But these studies, except for Nelson, do not disaggregate output, treating it as a single composite commodity. Aggregation assumes that the cost function is separable in output. That is, the relative marginal cost of any two outputs is independent of input prices. If the separability assumption does not hold, then the scale results may be biased.[1] We disaggregate output and discover that the separability assumption is invalid.

In sum, we examine banks with assets in excess of $1 billion, treating banks as multiproduct firms. A translog variable cost function with four outputs, four variable inputs, and a quasi-fixed input is specified and estimated. Section 1 specifies the model. Section 2 describes the data. Section 3 provides test results of various hypotheses; calculates elasticities of substitution, elasticities of input demands, and economies of scale; and compares our findings to previous studies. Section 4 is the conclusion.

1. THE MODEL

A bank's short-run cost-minimization problem can be formulated as

$$\text{Minimize } \mathbf{p}'\,\mathbf{x} \qquad \text{Subject to } T(\mathbf{q},\mathbf{x},\mathbf{z}) = 0 \,. \tag{1}$$

where $\mathbf{q}$ is a prespecified output bundle; $\mathbf{x}$ and $\mathbf{p}$ are the vectors of variable input quantities and prices, respectively; and $\mathbf{z}$ is the vector of quasi-fixed inputs. The production technology is specified by the transformation function $T(\mathbf{q},\mathbf{x},\mathbf{z})$. The optimal solution of (1) yields the dual variable cost function

$$VC = \Sigma p_j x_j = VC(\mathbf{p},\mathbf{q},\mathbf{z}) \,. \tag{2}$$

We use the translog form as a quadratic approximation to the cost function of the bank. We estimate two models. Model P estimates the cost function at the plant level by keeping the number of branches constant. Model F estimates at the firm level by allowing the number of branches to change, where branches are a function of output. The translog variable cost function for Model P is as follows:

[1] Kim (1986) shows that increasing returns to scale exist at the plant level and constant returns at the firm level when no aggregation is imposed. But, with aggregation, the firm experiences increasing returns to scale. Thus, aggregation bias may lead to erroneous conclusions.

$$\ln VC = \alpha_0 + \sum_{i=1}^{m}\alpha_i \ln q_i + \sum_{j=1}^{n}\beta_j \ln p_j + \frac{1}{2}\sum_{i=1}^{m}\sum_{r=1}^{m}\gamma_{ir} \ln q_i \ln q_r$$

$$+ \frac{1}{2}\sum_{j=1}^{n}\sum_{k=1}^{n}\delta_{jk} \ln p_j \ln p_k + \sum_{i=1}^{m}\sum_{j=1}^{n}\theta_{ij} \ln q_i \ln p_j + \phi_0 \ln z$$

$$+ \sum_{i=1}^{m}\phi_i \ln q_i \ln z + \sum_{j=1}^{n}\psi_j \ln p_j \ln z + \frac{1}{2}\mu(\ln z)^2 + \lambda_0 \ln b$$

$$+ \sum_{i=1}^{m}\lambda_i \ln q_i \ln b + \sum_{j=1}^{n}\zeta_j \ln p_j \ln b + \frac{1}{2}\pi(\ln b)^2$$

$$+ \nu \ln b \ln z + u_i \; ; \qquad (3)$$

where $\ln VC$ is the natural logarithm of the variable cost; $\ln q_i$ is the natural logarithm of the ith output ($i = 1,...,4$); $\ln p_j$ is the natural logarithm of the jth input price ($j = 1,...,4$); $\ln z$ is the natural logarithm of the quantity of the fixed input; and $\ln b$ is the natural logarithm of the number of branches.

Symmetry requires that $\gamma_{ir} = \gamma_{ri}$ for all i and r, and $\delta_{jk} = \delta_{kj}$ for all j and k. Linear homogeneity of the variable cost function in the input prices implies that

$$\sum_{j=1}^{n}\beta_j = 1; \sum_{j=1}^{n}\delta_{jk} = 0, \forall\ k; \sum_{j=1}^{n}\theta_{ij} = 0, \forall\ i; \sum_{j=1}^{n}\zeta_j = 0, \text{ and } \sum_{j=1}^{n}\psi_j = 0\,. \qquad (4)$$

These symmetry and linear homogeneity restrictions are imposed, a priori, in all versions of the model estimated.

By Shephard's lemma, we have that

$$\frac{\partial \ln VC}{\partial \ln p_j} = \frac{\partial VC}{\partial p_j}\,\frac{p_j}{VC} = \frac{p_j x_j}{VC} = S_j\,, \qquad (5)$$

where S_j is the share of the jth input in the total variable cost. Hence, the share equations are as follows:

$$s_j = \beta_j + \sum_{j=1}^{n}\delta_{jk} \ln p_k + \sum_{i=1}^{m}\theta_{ij} \ln q_i + \sum_{j=1}^{n}\psi_j \ln z + \sum_{j=1}^{n}\zeta_j \ln b$$

$$+ u_j; j = 1, \dots, 4\,. \qquad (6)$$

The translog cost function usually contains too many coefficients to be efficiently estimated. But, one can append the system of share equations to the cost function and estimate the full dual system subject to the restrictions that parameters appearing in more than one equation should have unique estimated values. Typically, estimates obtained from the full dual system are more precise and are more likely to be consistent with concavity and other restrictions. Given that the subsystem of the share equations is singular by virtue of the adding-up constraint, one of the share equations is excluded at the estimation stage. Thus, our model consists of equations (3) and (6) and is subject to across-equation restrictions on coefficients. Model F is the same as Model P, but with the additional restrictions that $\lambda_0 = 0$, $\pi = 0$, $\nu = 0$, $\lambda_i = 0$, and $\zeta_i = 0$, for all i.

The translog function is an approximation to the true cost function; we take the mean value of all variables as the point of approximation. Each variable has been divided by its mean before taking logarithms. In doing so, the linear coefficients are interpreted as elasticities at the point of approximation. The cost function and three cost shares are jointly estimated using Zellner's iterative procedure, where one cost share is dropped to avoid singularity.[2] Various tests are calculated at the overall mean and at the mean of four groups of banks. Table 1 identifies group sizes and number of banks.

2. DATA

The definition and measurement of output and cost, the treatment of branching, and the data sources vary across studies of the banking industry. Two approaches dominate, the *production* and *intermediation approaches*. The production approach measures output by the number of accounts and considers only operating cost. The intermediation approach measures output by the dollar value of accounts and considers both operating and interest costs.

The studies that use operating cost argue that they are interested in the production, and not the intermediation, process. But using only operating cost may bias results. For example, larger banks fund a larger proportion of assets with nondeposit accounts, which have low operating, but high interest, costs. Thus, we may find, using only operating cost, higher economies of scale than, in fact, exist. We adopt the intermediation approach, and define cost to include both operating and interest costs.

TABLE 1

BANK GROUPS AND THEIR TOTAL ASSETS (IN BILLIONS)

Bank Size	Total Assets	Number of Banks
G(1–3)	\$1–3	186
G(3–6)	\$3–6	62
G(6–10)	\$6–10	28
G(10+)	\$10+	32

[2]The estimates so obtained are invariant to which cost share equation is dropped.

We measure output by the dollar value of items on the asset side of the bank's balance sheet and consider deposits as inputs. We follow recent studies and allow the branch variable to interact with all other variables (Berger, Hanweck, and Humphrey 1987, and Mester 1987). By holding the number of branches constant during the estimation, economies of scale are estimated at the plant and not at the firm level. To find economies of scale at the firm level, the number of branches is also allowed to vary. In so doing, it is possible to find economies of scale at the plant, but diseconomies at the firm, level. This can occur when banks open new branches before the existing ones reach the minimum average cost.

Our model includes four outputs and four variable inputs. The outputs are as follows: loans to individuals for household, family, and other personal expenses (q_1); loans secured by real estate (q_2); commercial and industrial loans (q_3); and federal funds sold, securities, total investment securities and assets held in trading accounts (q_4). The variable inputs are interest bearing deposits except certificate of deposits above \$100,000 (deposits) (x_1); the sum of certificate of deposits above \$100,000, federal funds, demand notes, and other borrowed money (funds) (x_2); number of employees (labor) (x_3); and premises and fixed assets (capital) (x_4).

Input prices are calculated as follows: average interest cost per dollar of interest bearing deposits except certificate of deposits above \$100,000 (average price of deposits) (p_1); average interest cost per dollar of certificate of deposits above \$100,000 federal funds purchased, demand notes, and other borrowed money (average price of funds) (p_2); the average annual wage per employee (average price of labor) (p_3); and the average cost of premises and fixed assets (average price of capital) (p_4).

The dependent variables include variable cost (VC) and cost shares (S_j). Variable cost includes (1) interest cost on all deposits, (2) cost of federal funds purchased and securities sold under agreements to repurchase, (3) interest on demand notes issued to the U.S. Treasury, (4) interest on other borrowed money, (5) salaries and employee benefits, and (6) expenses on premises and fixed assets. The cost shares are defined as follows: interest cost on all deposits minus large certificate of deposits per dollar of variable cost (deposit cost share) (S_1); cost of large certificate of deposits plus cost of federal funds and securities plus interest on demand notes issued to the Treasury plus interest on other borrowing money per dollar of variable cost (funds cost share) (S_2); salaries and employee benefits per dollar of variable cost (labor cost share) (S_3); and expenses on premises and fixed assets per dollar of variable cost (capital cost share) (S_4).

We treat non-interest-bearing deposits as a quasi-fixed input. Since banks can not attract more of these deposits by offering interest, such deposits can be regarded as exogenously determined. In other words, banks are considered to be quantity-takers with respect to this input. Of course, banks can offer certain services and other incentives to attract non-interest-bearing deposits. But, since no explicit price exists for this input, its quantity rather than its price is included in the cost function.

Most studies of the banking industry use functional cost analysis (FCA) program data of the Federal Reserve System. Two problems arise with this data. First, it excludes large banks, and does not appropriately sample the banking industry. Heggestad and Mingo (1978) examine the FCA program, finding that banks in the FCA program have lower expense ratios, and that the influence of bank size on cost is different for FCA banks. Second, the sample is not random since the program is voluntary.

Our data are taken from the 1986 Income and Condition Reports for banks with total assets above \$1 billion, a total of 330 banks. Out of these, 309 have branches while the rest are unit banks. The analysis is based on 308 banks with branches.[3] A problem with our data, however, is that detailed cost information for each account is not given.

3. EMPIRICAL RESULTS AND TESTS OF HYPOTHESES

The estimated parameters along with the asymptotic t ratios are reported in Table 2. All output and price coefficients are positive and statistically significant, implying positive cost elasticities and input shares. The branch coefficient is positive and statistically significant. The fixed input coefficient is negative, but not statistically significant.

Different variants of the model are estimated in order to test various hypotheses about the production technology in the banking industry. Our estimates are asymptotically equivalent to maximum likelihood estimates. Hence, the variance covariance matrices obtained in the final iteration can be reasonably used to perform likelihood ratio tests.[4]

We first test for constant returns to scale, both in the short and long run, and for homotheticity. Returns to scale are difficult to conceptualize in a multiproduct context. Moreover, when one or more inputs remain fixed, the meaning of a change in the scale of production becomes fuzzy. Drawing on the analogy with the single-product case, however, we can characterize short-run constant returns to scale as the situation in which the total variable cost increases proportionately when all outputs are expanded by the same proportion, implying that the variable cost function is homogeneous of degree one in q. For the translog case, short-run constant returns to scale implies the following restrictions:

[3]One bank was eliminated due to data problems.

[4]The basic test procedure is as follows. Let $\Sigma = (\sigma_{ij})$ be the matrix of variance-covariances of the disturbances across equations. Let $\hat{\Sigma}_R$ and $\hat{\Sigma}_{UR}$ be the maximum likelihood estimates of Σ with and without restrictions. Then, under the multivariate normality assumption about the disturbances, the likelihood ratio (LR) is given by $LR = \{(\det(\hat{\Sigma}_R)/\det(\hat{\Sigma}_{UR})\}^{-n/2}$ where det is the determinant and n equals the number of observations. Therefore, $-2 \ln LR$ has a X^2 distribution with degrees of freedom equal to the number of restrictions being tested.

TABLE 2

NONLINEAR ITERATED ZELLNER PARMETER ESTIMATES

Para-meter	Model P	Model F	Para-meter	Model P	Model F
α_0	−0.0856 (−5.28)	−0.0931 (−6.08)	θ_{23}	−0.0148 (−3.73)	−0.0060 (−1.49)
α_1	0.1464 (5.46)	0.2010 (9.91)	θ_{24}	−0.0000 (−0.11)	0.0023 (1.11)
α_2	0.1874 (7.05)	0.1804 (7.36)	θ_{32}	0.0552 (5.45)	0.0598 (5.28)
α_3	0.4170 (14.36)	0.4018 (13.99)	θ_{33}	−0.0437 (−10.10)	−0.0453 (−9.80)
α_4	0.2593 (11.87)	0.2497 (11.64)	θ_{34}	−0.0171 (−7.31)	−0.0178 (−7.47)
β_2	0.2534 (36.35)	0.2635 (34.11)	θ_{42}	0.0345 (3.50)	0.0387 (3.49)
β_3	0.2211 (75.39)	0.2182 (70.24)	θ_{43}	−0.0398 (−9.62)	−0.0412 (−9.34)
β_4	0.0755 (47.44)	0.0745 (46.36)	θ_{44}	−0.0129 (−5.79)	−0.0137 (−6.01)
γ_{11}	0.1037 (2.90)	0.0667 (2.46)	λ_0	0.0458 (2.09)	— —
γ_{12}	−0.0091 (−0.29)	0.0154 (0.60)	λ_1	−0.0135 (−0.06)	— —
γ_{13}	−0.1733 (−6.05)	−0.1200 (−5.29)	λ_2	0.0119 (0.63)	— —
γ_{14}	−0.0633 (−2.04)	−0.3418 (−1.36)	λ_3	0.0615 (2.57)	— —
γ_{22}	0.0830 (2.66)	0.0864 (2.97)	λ_4	0.0162 (0.79)	— —
γ_{23}	0.0086 (0.27)	0.0296 (1.03)	ζ_2	−0.0616 (−9.15)	— —
γ_{24}	−0.0619 (−2.45)	−0.0745 (−3.08)	ζ_3	0.0192 (6.72)	— —
γ_{33}	0.1110 (2.95)	0.1501 (4.19)	ζ_4	0.0051 (3.28)	— —
γ_{34}	−0.0497 (−1.54)	−0.0548 (−1.72)	π	0.0053 (0.021)	— —
γ_{44}	0.1849 (4.79)	0.1805 (4.67)	ϕ_0	−0.0268 (−0.71)	−0.0159 (−0.42)
δ_{22}	0.0564 (2.54)	0.0419 (1.68)	ϕ_1	0.1855 (4.95)	0.1079 (3.50)
δ_{33}	0.1049 (10.32)	0.1018 (9.83)	ϕ_2	−0.0677 (−1.83)	−0.1095 (−3.56)
δ_{44}	0.0230 (11.10)	0.0232 (11.31)	ϕ_3	0.1108 (2.25)	0.0369 (0.85)
δ_{23}	−0.0334 (−3.79)	−0.0304 (−3.23)	ϕ_4	−0.0234 (−0.55)	−0.0093 (−0.22)
δ_{24}	−0.0120 (−2.72)	−0.0144 (−3.15)	ψ_2	−0.0210 (−1.42)	−0.0052 (0.33)
δ_{34}	0.0083 (2.47)	0.0106 (3.14)	ψ_3	0.0690 (11.15)	0.0615 (9.50)
θ_{12}	−0.0134 (−1.32)	−0.0706 (−7.86)	ψ_4	0.0256 (7.69)	0.0237 (7.13)
θ_{13}	0.0086 (1.99)	0.0260 (6.88)	μ	−0.1674 (−2.10)	−0.0578 (−0.82)
θ_{14}	0.0009 (0.37)	0.0057 (3.00)	ν	−0.1124 (−3.35)	— —
θ_{22}	0.0063 (0.68)	−0.0209 (−2.14)			

NOTE: Numbers in parentheses following parameter estimates are asymptotic t ratios.

$$\sum_{i=1}^{m} \alpha_i = 1; \sum_{i=1}^{m} \gamma_{ir} = 0, r = 1, 2, \ldots, m;$$

$$\sum_{i=1}^{m} \theta_{ij} = 0, j = 1, 2, \ldots, n; \sum_{i=1}^{m} \phi_i = 0; \text{and} \sum_{i=1}^{m} \lambda_i = 0 . \tag{7}$$

If we assume competitive product markets and marginal-cost pricing for each output, constant returns to scale means that economic profit is zero in the long run. Moreover, in the long run, the levels of the quasi-fixed inputs are such that their respective shadow prices equal their market prices (Berndt and Hesse 1986). Let p_t represent the shadow price, where $p_t = -\frac{\partial VC}{\partial z_t}$, and let u_t represent the market price of the quasi-fixed input z_t. Then, long-run equilibrium implies that $u_t = p_t = -\frac{\partial VC}{\partial z_t}$ for $t = 1, 2, \ldots, l$. Then, the shadow value of the fixed inputs is

$$\sum_{t=1}^{l} u_t z_t = - \sum_{t=1}^{l} \frac{\partial VC}{\partial z_t} z_t \, . \tag{8}$$

Economic profits are

$$\sum_{i=1}^{m} w_i q_i - VC - \sum_{t=1}^{l} u_t z_t \, , \tag{9}$$

where w_i is the price of output. Zero economic profit implies that

$$VC = \sum_{i=1}^{m} w_i q_i - \sum_{t=1}^{l} u_t z_t = \sum_{i=1}^{m} \frac{\partial VC}{\partial q_i} q_i + \sum_{t=1}^{l} \frac{\partial VC}{\partial z_t} z_t \, . \tag{10}$$

Thus, long-run constant returns to scale implies that the variable cost function is homogeneous of degree one in outputs and quasi-fixed inputs. For the translog case, long-run constant returns to scale implies the following restrictions:

$$\sum_{i=1}^{m} \alpha_i + \phi_0 + \lambda_0 = 1;$$

$$\sum_{r=1}^{m} \gamma_{ir} + \sum_{i=1}^{m} \phi_i + \sum_{i=1}^{m} \lambda_i = 0, i = 1, 2, \ldots, m \, ;$$

$$\sum_{i=1}^{m} \theta_{ij} + \sum_{j=1}^{n} \psi_j + \sum_{j=1}^{n} \zeta_j = 0, j = 1, 2, \ldots, n \, ;$$

$$\sum_{i=1}^{m} \lambda_i + \pi + \nu = 0; \text{and} \sum_{i=1}^{m} \phi_i + \mu + \nu = 0 \, . \tag{11}$$

The test statistics for short-run and long-run constant returns to scale are 131.6 and 65.5, far exceeding the 5 percent critical X^2 value of 18.3 with 10 degrees of freedom. Hence, short-run and long-run constant returns to scale are rejected.

Next, we test for homotheticity in the form of separability of the variable cost function in the outputs and all other variables. For the translog case, the testable restrictions for homotheticity are $\theta_{ij} = 0, \phi_i = 0$, and $\lambda_i = 0$ for all i and j. The test statistic of 249.0 with 20 degrees of freedom, which exceeds the 5 percent critical X^2 value of 31.4. The failure of the homotheticity restrictions implies that the unspecified transformation function underlying the cost function is not separable in outputs and all other variables. Therefore, a valid aggregation of outputs into a single index does not exist. The analysis must take explicit account of the multiproduct nature of large banks.

Overall Economies of Scale

Overall scale economies (SCE) measures the elasticity of cost with respect to proportional changes in the scale of outputs holding the product mix unchanged. Thus, by differentiating the translog function with respect to outputs, we have

$$SCE = \sum_{i=1}^{m} \frac{\partial \ln VC}{\partial \ln q_i} = \sum_{i=1}^{4} \alpha_i + \sum_{i=1}^{4} \sum_{r=1}^{4} \gamma_{ir} \ln q_r + \sum_{i=1}^{4} \sum_{j=1}^{4} \theta_{ij} \ln p_j$$

$$+ \sum_{i=1}^{4} \lambda_i \ln b + \sum_{i=1}^{4} \phi_i \ln z \, . \tag{12}$$

If $SCE > 1$, cost increases more than proportionately with scale, implying diseconomies of scale. If $SCE < 1$, increasing returns exist, and if $SCE = 1$, constant returns.

We measure scale economies at different data points to examine how changes in scale affect total cost. To neutralize input prices changes, we evaluate overall scale economies using constant input prices. We also have the number of branches and level of non-interest-bearing deposits as two additional variables. Ideally, these variables should also be held constant across observations. Using the same input prices for all banks has a natural perfect competition interpretation. The use of the overall mean number of branches and the overall mean level of the quasi-fixed input for every bank is not so easily justified, since the level of the quasi-fixed input or the number of branches are themselves indices of scale. We can, therefore, measure overall scale economies using the mean values of the quasi-fixed input and the mean number of branches for different groups while using the overall mean levels of variable input prices. Needless to say, our overall scale economy measure is interpreted broadly.

Table 3 reports the overall scale economies for the whole sample and for each group. We present two methods of estimation, labeled "at mean" and "average." The "at mean" estimates use the mean of the variables for each group, holding the prices of inputs constant at the overall mean. In a sense, these estimates correspond to the *representative* bank of each group. The estimates labeled "average" represent measures for the average of each group. The estimation holds prices constant, but the quasi-fixed input and the branches are allowed to have the actual values for each bank. Table 3 shows that some economies of scale exist in the first group (that is, banks between \$1 and \$3 billion). Economies of scale are exhausted somewhere in the second group, and diseconomies emerge in the third group, becoming more pronounced in the fourth group. This general conclusion holds at the plant and firm levels. Thus, banks between \$1 and \$3 billion can

TABLE 3

OVERALL ECONOMIES OF SCALE

Bank Size	Method	Model P	Model F
G(1–3)	at mean	0.97	0.99
	average	0.96	0.98
G(3–6)	at mean	1.02	1.01
	average	1.01	1.02
G(6–10)	at mean	1.07	1.03
	average	1.04	1.04
G(10+)	at mean	1.09	1.08
	average	1.05	1.08
All	at mean	1.01	1.03

increase their size and banks above $6 billion can decrease their size to become more cost efficient.

How do our results compare with other large bank evidence?[5] Shaffer and David (1986) come the closest to our analysis, defining output as the total value of assets and costs to include operating costs and interest expenses. They estimate a hedonic translog cost function for the one hundred largest banks in 1983, which excludes the lowest class size in our sample. Economies of scale are found up to $37 billion in assets. We, however, find no evidence of scale economies beyond our lowest class size.[6]

Hunter and Timme (1986) estimate a translog cost function for a sample of ninety-one large banks from 1972 to 1982. They define output more broadly to include the dollar volume of loans, securities, and deposits and consider two cost measures: operating cost, and operating cost plus interest expenses. Significant scale economies emerge when cost is defined narrowly to include only operating costs. When cost is more broadly defined to include interest expenses, no significant scale economies exist. That is, their results come closer to ours than do those of Shaffer and David (1986).

Partial Scale Economies

Partial scale economies (PSCE) reflect the elasticity of total variable cost with respect to any individual output when other outputs and input prices are held constant. Moreover, they reflect each output's contribution to the overall scale economies. For the translog cost function, we have

[5]Nelson (1985) and Humphrey (1987), who examine large banks, employ markedly different methodologies. Nelson finds using 1979 data significant scale economies at the branch level, but no economies from expansion by further branching. He surmises that branching networks service customer convenience, thus rationalizing his results. Humphrey finds using 1980 and 1984 data generally scale diseconomies for large banks (banks between $5–10 billion were sometimes the exception).

[6]For comparison purposes, we also estimate the translog model using the one hundred largest banks in our sample. At the overall mean, we find significant diseconomies of scale (1.036).

$$PSCE_i = \frac{\partial \ln VC}{\partial \ln q_i} = \alpha_i + \sum_{r=1}^{4} \gamma_{ir} \ln q_r + \sum_{i=1}^{4} \theta_{ij} \ln p_j + \lambda_i \ln b$$
$$+ \phi_i \ln z \, . \tag{13}$$

Tables 4 reports partial scale economies. Partial scale economies for all outputs are generally significant. Loans to individuals (that is, q_1) and loans secured by real estate (that is, q_2) have the lowest cost elasticity for all groups, possibly because the volume of these loans is smaller than the other two outputs. One major difference is apparent. The partial scale economy of loans secured by real estate becomes smaller as the size of the bank increases, probably because banks in the first two groups invest more heavily in real estate loans than banks in the last two groups. But, for commercial and industrial loans (that is, q_3), the value of the partial scale economy increases with the bank size, likely because larger banks invest more heavily in commercial and industrial loans.

Elasticities of Substitution

For the translog cost function, the Allen-Uzawa elasticities of substitution (σ_{ij}) can be calculated as follows (Binswanger 1974):

$$\sigma_{jk} = 1 + \frac{\delta_{jk}}{S_j S_k}, \text{ for } j \neq k \text{ ; and } \sigma_{jj} = \frac{\delta_{jj} + S_j(S_j - 1)}{S_j^2} \, . \tag{14}$$

Using the σ_{jk}, we can directly compute the own and cross-partial elasticities (ϵ_{jk}) of the conditional input demand using the following formulas:

$$\epsilon_{jk} = \sigma_{jk} S_k, \text{ for } j \neq k, \text{ and } \epsilon_{jj} = \sigma_{jj} S_j \, . \tag{15}$$

Table 5 reports the Allen partial elasticities of substitution, which have been calculated at the plant and firm levels. The following conclusions emerge. First, all inputs are substitutes. Despite substitutability between all pairs of variable inputs, greater substitutability occurs between the physical inputs (that is, labor and capital) and between financial inputs (that is, purchased funds and interest bearing deposits) than between any financial input and any physical input. Moreover, pairwise elasticities generally change monotonically with the size group. Funds become increasingly substitutable for deposits, labor, and capital with firm size. But, substitutability between deposits and physical inputs declines with bank size. These results probably reflect the increasing importance of purchased funds as bank size rises.

Table 6 reports the own- and cross-price elasticities of conditional input demands.[7] All own-price elasticities are negative in accordance with theory. More-

[7]The elasticities relate to the conditional input demands functions where outputs are held constant. Therefore, these magnitudes do not reflect adjustments in output in response to input price changes.

TABLE 4

PARTIAL ECONOMIES OF SCALE

Bank Size	Method	q_1 P	q_1 F	q_2 P	q_2 F	q_3 P	q_3 F	q_4 P	q_4 F
		Output Varied							
G(1–3)	at mean	.18	.22	.23	.23	.27	.26	.28	.27
	average	.18	.22	.23	.24	.26	.25	.29	.27
G(3–6)	at mean	.18	.22	.20	.19	.37	.34	.26	.25
	average	.16	.21	.19	.18	.38	.36	.28	.27
G(6–10)	at mean	.21	.24	.16	.14	.44	.39	.26	.25
	average	.20	.23	.16	.14	.42	.40	.26	.26
G(10+)	at mean	.16	.22	.13	.10	.55	.52	.25	.25
	average	.14	.20	.12	.10	.52	.51	.26	.27
All	at mean	.14	.20	.18	.18	.42	.40	.26	.25

NOTE: q_1 = loans to individuals for household, family, and other personal expenses;
q_2 = loans secured by real estate;
q_3 = commercial and industrial loans;
q_4 = federal funds purchased, securities, total investment securities, and assets held in trading accounts.

TABLE 5

ELASTICITIES OF SUBSTITUTION BETWEEN PAIRS OF INPUTS

Inputs	G(1–3) P	G(1–3) F	G(3–6) P	G(3–6) F	G(6–10) P	G(6–10) F	G(10+) P	G(10+) F	All P	All F
	Bank Size									
deposits-funds	.698	.780	.710	.800	.713	.797	.761	.862	.716	.800
deposits-labor	.262	.257	.228	.189	.208	.186	.073	.047	.246	.224
deposits-capital	.487	.481	.464	.448	.426	.448	.328	.320	.476	.472
funds-labor	.339	.370	.393	.470	.465	.512	.503	.532	.395	.488
funds-capital	.316	.143	.373	.280	.421	.307	.463	.336	.373	.250
labor-capital	1.45	1.58	1.45	1.58	1.43	1.55	1.56	1.72	1.45	1.57

NOTE: Pairwise elasticities of substitution are measured using predicted values of input shares. Figures reported are sample averages of values for each observation in each group.

TABLE 6

OWN- AND CROSS-PARTIAL ELASTICITIES OF CONDITIONAL INPUT DEMANDS

Demand for	Bank Size	Deposits P	Deposits F	Funds P	Funds F	Labor P	Labor F	Capital P	Capital F
		Price of							
Deposits	G(1–3)	−.29	−.31	.15	.17	.06	.06	.04	.04
	G(3–6)	−.30	−.33	.17	.20	.05	.04	.03	.03
	G(6–10)	−.30	−.34	.18	.21	.04	.04	.03	.03
	G(10+)	−.31	−.35	.24	.26	.00	.01	.02	.02
	All	−.29	−.32	.16	.19	.05	.05	.03	.03
Funds	G(1–3)	.32	.36	−.50	−.57	.06	.08	.02	.00
	G(3–6)	.30	.35	−.49	−.57	.08	.10	.02	.01
	G(6–10)	.29	.33	−.51	−.57	.10	.12	.03	.02
	G(10+)	.29	.33	−.48	−.54	.09	.11	.03	.02
	All	.31	.35	−.50	−.57	.07	.09	.02	.01
Labor	G(1–3)	.12	.11	.07	.08	−.30	−.31	.11	.12
	G(3–6)	.09	.06	.09	.11	−.29	−.30	.11	.13
	G(6–10)	.07	.07	.11	.13	−.30	−.32	.12	.13
	G(10+)	−.00	−.01	.15	.14	−.25	−.28	.11	.11
	All	.09	.00	.08	.16	−.29	−.31	.11	.12
Capital	G(1–3)	.21	.22	.05	.02	.35	.37	−.61	−.62
	G(3–6)	.18	.17	.08	.05	.34	.38	−.61	−.60
	G(6–10)	.17	.17	.10	.07	.35	.37	−.62	−.62
	G(10+)	.03	.05	.08	.04	.37	.41	−.48	−.50
	All	.18	.19	.06	.04	.35	.38	−.60	−.60

over, since own-price elasticities are less than one in absolute value, all input demands are inelastic. This result suggests some restriction on a bank's ability to use liability management. But liability management, if used, is more likely to involve funds since they are more price responsive than deposits. Further, funds respond more to a change in the price of deposits than deposits to the price of funds. That is, depositor behavior limits the ability of banks to implement liability management.

Humphrey (1981) reports own- and cross-price elasticities of substitution. He finds, using five inputs, that substitution exists only between federal funds and certificates of deposits, and between demand deposits and time deposits. The own-price elasticities of federal funds, demand deposits, time deposits, certificate of deposits, and capital are −0.30, −0.12, −0.51, −0.09, and −0.35, respectively. While a comparison of our results is somewhat speculative since our definition of inputs differs, one observation seems warranted. The level of substitutability appears to have risen somewhat since deregulation.

4. CONCLUSION

Empirical tests for scale economies or diseconomies in banking have a long history. Recent deregulation and subsequent bank response may have significantly altered the cost relationships in the banking industry. Our analysis provides information about the more recent state of scale economies or diseconomies and input substitution for large banks.

Humphrey (1987) provided two cautions against almost all previous studies of bank scale economies. First, estimates are more reliable when they are based on data disaggregated by class size. Our work is a step in that direction, since we examine only banks with assets in excess of $1 billion. Second, scale economy estimates based on one year's cross-section data may not generalize to other years. Humphrey's results span 1980 to 1984 when significant deregulation occurred. Our sample of 1986 provides another observation on the scale economy question further removed from the regulatory changes of the early 1980s.

We reject the hypotheses of short-run and long-run constant returns to scale. Banks with assets between $1–3 billion exhibit scale economies; diseconomies set in between $3–6 billion and continue through larger bank class sizes. But the economies and diseconomies are not large in magnitude. Thus, our evidence does not support the view that a few large megabanks will emerge as the economy moves toward an interstate banking environment based on cost economies. This, of course, does not exclude the emergence of megabanks as a result of noncost factors (that is, diversification of bank activities).

We also reject the hypothesis that the bank cost function is homothetic in output. Thus, single-product analysis (Shaffer and David 1986, and Hunter and Timme 1986) using total assets (or even any sophisticated index of aggregate output) is inappropriate; the results from such studies are suspect.

All variable inputs emerge as pairwise substitutes. All input demands are inelastic, suggesting that banks face some restrictions in the use of liability management. Labor and capital have the highest degree of substitutability among all inputs. But, more interestingly, our evidence suggests that substitutability may have risen since deregulation. If so, then banks have been given more flexibility in their operations because of deregulation.

We end with a note of caution. Our study is based on data from a single year. The industry is still adjusting due to deregulation. Therefore, our findings are tentative. Future study should throw more light on the issues.

LITERATURE CITED

Bell, Frederick W., and Neil B. Murphy. "Costs in Commercial Banking: A Quantitative Analysis of Bank Behavior and Its Relation to Bank Regulation." Research Report No. 41. *Federal Reserve Bank of Boston*, 1968.

Benston, George J. "Branch Banking and Economies of Scale." *Journal of Finance* 20 (May 1965), 312–31.

Berger, Allen N., Gerald A. Hanweck, and David B. Humphrey. "Competitive Viability in Banking: Scale, Scope, and Product Mix Economies." *Journal of Monetary Economics* 20 (1987), 501–20.

Berndt, Ernst R., and Dieter M. Hesse. "Measuring and Assessing Capacity Utilization in the Manufacturing Sector of the Nine OECD Countries." *European Economic Review* 30 (October 1986), 961–89.

Binswanger, Hans P. "A Cost Function Approach to the Measurement of Elasticities of Factor Demand and Elasticities of Substitution." *American Journal of Agriculture Economics* 52 (May 1974), 377–86.

Clark, Jeffrey A. "Economies of Scale and Scope at Depository Financial Institutions: A Review of the Literature." Federal Reserve Bank of Kansas City *Economic Review* 73 (September/October 1988), 16–33.

Heggestad, Arnold A., and John J. Mingo. "On the Usefulness of Functional Cost Accounting Data." *Journal of Bank Research* 9 (Winter 1978), 251–56.

Horvitz, Paul M. "Economies of Scale in Banking." In *Private Financial Institution*, edited by P. M. Horvitz et al., pp. 1–54, Englewood Cliffs, N.J., Prentice-Hall, 1963.

Humphrey, David B. "Intermediation and Cost Determinants of Large Bank Liability Composition." *Journal of Banking and Finance* 5 (June 1981), 167–85.

———. "Cost Dispersion and the Measurement of Economies in Banking." Federal Reserve Bank Of Richmond *Economic Review* 73 (May/June 1987), 24–38.

Hunter, William C., and Stephen G. Timme. "Technical Change, Organizational Form, and the Structure of the Bank Production." *Journal of Money, Credit, and Banking* 18 (May 1986), 152–66.

Kim, Moshe. "Banking Technology and the Existence of a Consistent Output Aggregate." *Journal of Monetary Economics* 18 (September 1986), 181–95.

Mester, Loretta J. "A Multiproduct Cost Study of Savings and Loans." *The Journal of Finance* 42 (June 1987), 423–45.

Nelson, Richard W. "Branching, Scale Economies, and Banking Cost." *Journal of Banking and Finance* 9 (June 1985), 177–91.

Rhoades, Stephen A. "Mergers of the Twenty Largest Banks and Industrials, All Bank Mergers (1960–1983), and Some Related Issues." *The Antitrust Bulletin* 30 (Fall 1985), 617–49.

Shaffer, Sherrill, and Edmond David. "Economies of Superscale and Interstate Expansion." Research Paper, Federal Reserve Bank of New York, November 1986.

NOTES, COMMENTS, REPLIES

The Forerunners of "New Monetary Economics" Proposals to Stabilize the Unit of Account

A Note by Scott Sumner

A recent paper by Cowen and Kroszner (1987) traced the historical roots of the "new monetary economics." This approach has two basic tenets. First, our current monetary system is a creation of government regulation. Second, an ideal monetary system would separate the function of unit of account from the medium of exchange. Greenfield and Yeager (1983) proposed a monetary system in which the government's only role would be to define the unit of account in terms of a comprehensive basket of commodities. They named this regime a "BFH system" after three important theorists: Black (1970), Fama (1980), and Hall (1983). A related approach, described by Wallace (1983) as the "legal restrictions theory of money," emphasizes the importance of legal barriers against the private issue of interest-bearing currency in creating the demand for non-interest-bearing fiat money.

Because the term "new monetary economics" covers several distinct schools of thought, this paper will focus solely on the forerunners of BFH system. In the early works of Arthur Kitson and Henry Meulen, Cowen and Kroszner (henceforth C–K) claim to have found antecedents of the modern BFH proposals for creating an abstract unit of account separated from the media of exchange.

This paper will demonstrate that although Kitson and Meulen did show some affinities to the new monetary economics approach (particularly the legal restrictions theory), the macroeconomic implications of their policy proposals fell far short of the modern BFH system. In fact, it is not clear they had any coherent policy at all. Contrary to the assertions of C–K, there is no convincing evidence that Kitson and Meulen proposed a system where the unit of account would be separate from the media of exchange.

C–K also noted that "the forerunners, more akin to the BFH theorists, stressed the gains to be secured by providing a stable unit of account and the diminished macroeconomic influence of changes in the supply and demand for exchange media" (p. 574). It does appear that the avoidance of deflation was the

SCOTT SUMNER *is associate professor of economics, Bentley College.*

Journal of Money, Credit, and Banking, Vol. 22, No. 1 (February 1990)

primary motivation of the BFH forerunners. It is not at all clear, however, that the system proposed by Kitson and Meulen would have provided a stable unit of account.

This paper will also demonstrate that the "compensated dollar" plans of Williams (1892) and Fisher (1920) featured a unit of account which corresponds much more closely to the ideas of modern BFH theorists than does the Kitson-Meulen system. In fact, proposals by Black (1981), Hall (1982), and Greenfield and Yeager (1983) share many of the strengths and weaknesses of the Williams-Fisher approach.

1. Henry Meulen

C–K call Henry Meulen the "the most interesting and most sophisticated contributor to the theory of legal restrictions," and term his treatise *Free Banking* (1934) "the only comprehensive book-length statement of NME." (1987, p. 582). Meulen's work does contain a proposal for the denationalization of money. But the unit of account discussed in Meulen's book is fundamentally different from the sort of unit envisioned by modern BFH theorists. And it is not clear that Meulen's proposal would actually separate the unit of account from the media of exchange.

Meulen is critical of the gold standard because of the instability created by fluctuations in the value of gold. C–K note that "Meulen claimed that an abstract unit of account is nonetheless superior to a laissez-faire gold standard because only the former can perfectly register changes in the value of gold" (1987, pp. 581–82). This suggests that Meulen expected his system to produce some sort of price stability since nominal prices only register real values when the price level is constant.

In discussing Meulen's system C–K also observed that

> Instead of being a claim to a certain weight of gold, bank notes would be a claim for their "face worth" of gold according to the market conditions of the metal. Under the gold standard, notes are claims to a varying worth of gold and, hence, *a varying worth of commodities.* (p. 583, italics added)

This also creates the impression that under the Meulen proposal bank notes would have a stable purchasing power. However, this is clearly not what Meulen means by "face worth."

In *Free Banking* Meulen defines the unit of account: "Hence, since no known commodity continuously evokes the same intensity of feeling, the monetary unit must not be a commodity . . . but a claim upon a certain satisfaction . . . Accordingly we select the *feeling* for a certain standard commodity, and call it one unit" (1934, p. 250). Later Meulen states: "Whether we build up our scale of prices by calling the price of our standard commodity 1 bank-note pound, unit, macute, feeling, or spasm, the result is the same: the unit of price, being a simple unit of feeling, remains absolutely invariable" (p. 273). Meulen's unit of account (which now seems similar to utility) is not defined clearly enough to make any judgments regarding its stability.

One might argue that Meulen intended the unit to have a fixed purchasing power and that the clumsy wording merely reflected the terminology of the day. In numerous other passages, however, Meulen makes it clear that price level stability was not his intention:

> Value is to-day conceived of in terms of only the *contemporary* feelings in respect of a standard commodity, and, since every known commodity fluctuates in human estimation, our "standard" is no standard at all. Under the invariable price unit system, the stability of the value unit would be unaffected by any excessive issue of paper exchange medium in terms of the unit. Commodity prices would rise on account of the excessive issue of purchasing power as compared with the production of commodities; but the unit would remain the expression of the normal desire and sacrifice feelings in respect of gold [sic] on a certain day in the past. The purchasing power of a given weight of gold at the time of the introduction of the unit system was, for example, 1; after the inflation of general prices, the purchasing power of the same weight of gold would be, perhaps, 3. This would indicate that the normal desire for gold, *expressed in purchasing power*, had increased threefold since the time of the establishment of the unit system. All other prices would similarly have risen, indicating simply that the supply of commodities had not kept pace with the demand. It may be objected that in this case human desire for commodities had not risen, that it was merely the volume of exchange medium which had been inflated. I reply that the volume of exchange medium would never had been introduced into the channels of exchange if the desire for commodities had not suddenly increased. Somewhere there must have been an individual, or individuals who were desirous of consuming inordinately—whose desire to consume exceeded considerably their contemporary power of production. (p. 258)

The proposition that the price level could triple with no diminution in the utility value of the unit of account, although theoretically defensible, would seem somewhat implausible. And the statement regarding the purchasing power of gold increasing threefold seems inconsistent with the statement that "all other prices would similarly have risen."

There is further evidence that Meulen did not intend a policy of price level stability in the footnote on page 262 where he provides a lengthy critique to Fisher's compensated dollar plan to stabilize the price level. Surprisingly, his critique is not based on the inability of Fisher's plan to stabilize the price level, but rather on the fact that, if successful, it would amount to a countercyclical monetary policy!

If Meulen had a coherent plan to stabilize the "worth" of the invariable unit of account, it would be interesting to see how the plan was to be implemented. His explanation was perhaps the most disappointing part of his proposal:

> All the present denominations of coins could be retained, the public could still reckon its purchases in pounds, shilling, and pence, the only difference being that gold coins would be gradually withdrawn from circulation, their place being taken by the pound and ten-shilling notes, and that the pound note would no longer indicate a certain weight, but a certain *worth* of gold at the market price of the metal, whatever that price might be. (p. 291)

In this statement Meulen appears to be suggesting that the ability of the pound note to buy a certain "worth" of gold distinguishes this regime from other monetary systems. But this criterion could be met by *any* monetary system; even throughout the hyperinflation of 1923 one (paper) German mark could be exchanged for gold "at the market price of the metal." Thus the "backing" Meulen seems to provide for the new pound notes would have no operational significance.

What then is to prevent overissue of banknotes and a depreciation in the unit of account? Meulen's discussion of the French paper "Assignats" is hardly reassuring:

> The notes themselves depreciated *in worth* and caused prices of commodities to be artificially enhanced only when the quantity issued began to exceed all reason . . . let it be noted that the Assignats were not issued as a true credit medium should be, namely, in advances to capable producers, but were issued to pay government debts, thus necessitating no balancing production of commodities. (p. 276)

The proposition that the French inflation could have been avoided had Assignats been issued only to "capable producers" seems very dubious. While an application of the "real bills doctrine" need not lead to price level indeterminacy when the unit of account is linked to a commodity, neither the French system, nor Meulen's proposal would have done so. In contrast, Fama (1980), Black (1981), Hall (1982), and Greenfield and Yeager (1983) all proposed systems whereby price level indeterminacy would be avoided either by linking the unit of account to one or more commodities, or through control of the stock of fiat currency.

C–K conclude their discussion of Meulen by asserting that his system would produce exchange media which fluctuated in value in terms of the "abstract" numeraire. However, as the previously cited quotation indicates (p. 291), Meulen intended prices to be quoted in pounds, and pound notes to continue to circulate (albeit privately issued). The evidence C–K cite from page 293 (p. 586, C–K) refers to the risk of the value of notes fluctuating in terms of a given *weight* of gold. But the numeraire was defined in terms of a given worth, not weight, of gold. Part of the confusion is due to the use of the word "abstract" when describing the unit of account. To an economist writing at the turn of the century, any unit of account which was not linked to a fixed weight of gold (or silver) would appear abstract.

C–K also claim that Meulen believed "confidence in the system will grow to the point at which bank notes would not be backed by any gold at all" (1987, p. 585). Meulen would probably agree with C–K's characterization of his views, although a close inspection of the text leaves one unclear as to exactly what is meant by "backed." Meulen states that eventually notes would not be "redeemable in gold at the bank of issue" and that the "holder of these notes must apply to the goldsmith when he desires gold" (1934, p. 309). This evolution does not imply any change in the backing but rather in the location at which notes could be redeemed. At *no time* would the notes be redeemable for anything but their "face worth" of gold (p. 291). Thus even before the system evolved to its purer form there would be no "backing" of notes in any meaningful sense.

2. *Arthur Kitson*

In contrast to Meulen, there is abundant evidence that Kitson intended his proposal to result in price level stability. In *The Money Problem* (1903) Kitson asserted that the adoption of an "invariable ideal unit of purchasing power" would eliminate interest and make general changes in the price level impossible (1903, pp. 153–54, 224). The unit would represent "a certain fraction of all the exchangeable wealth at a given time" (p. 217). Although a sympathetic reading might lead one to suppose Kitson intended to define the unit in terms of a fixed bundle of tangible assets, the text is vague on this point.

In *A Fraudulent Standard* (1917) Kitson spelled out the details of his proposal, if not with greater clarity, then at least with more specificity. To assure that the unit had stable purchasing power Kitson would define the pound as a given fraction of national wealth:

> For example suppose we start at noon, as stated, January 1, 1918. Our wealth is then X pounds. Suppose by noon, January 1, 1919, our wealth has increased 10 per cent., then our total wealth = (X + .1X) pounds and the pound which equalled 1/Xth of the national wealth, January 1, 1918—becomes 1/(X + .1X)th of the national wealth in January, 1919. (1917, p. 129)

Obviously, for this definition to be anything more than a tautology Kitson would have to mean *real* wealth. However, Kitson never seems to specify his unit in terms of a given basket of commodities. In fact it is unclear whether the term "wealth" is to include only physical assets, or financial assets as well. Later he states that "all additions and subtractions from such wealth would be additions or subtractions of so many pounds, that is, so many fractional parts of total wealth. It is not essential to transform the system into numbers" (1917, p. 142). But if price stability is the goal, then it is necessary to specify the unit of account in terms of numbers of commodities.

Kitson's explanation in *Liberty* (June 15, 1895, pp. 6–8) suggests that he meant the unit to represent a comprehensive bundle of commodities although he continued to deny the need to compute a price index to implement the system. In the same issue one reviewer argued that Kitson had admitted that his proposal was a commodity standard: "Then Mr. Kitson is, after all, advocating a concrete unit of purchasing power,—*viz.*, a composite unit agreeing in composition with that of the sum total of all wealth" (p. 2). Also in this issue, another reviewer noted that "as for Mr. Kitson's claim that the value of the unit need not be calculated, but will take care of itself, nothing could be more absurd" (p. 4).

At times Kitson himself seems confused about the issue. Regarding Fisher's proposal to back the dollar by gold of fixed purchasing power (rather than fixed weight), Kitson writes:

> The suggestion is ingenious, but more feasible in theory than in practice. It would be analogous to the legal establishment of a mercury-tube as our yard-stick, exposed to atmospheric influences which would involve an alteration in every yard measure and every foot-rule in the Kingdom whenever there was a change in temperature! (1917, p. 86)

Obviously Kitson does not understand what Fisher was proposing since elsewhere Kitson uses length as a metaphor for purchasing power. Fisher's proposal would eliminate changes in the "length" of the dollar. What is more puzzling is how Kitson could be so confused since he makes the same criticism of a gold standard based on a fixed *weight* of gold.

There are also numerous instances where Kitson belittles the fear that free issue of paper money might be inflationary. Were the unit of account clearly defined (as in the BFH system), then Kitson's view would be justifiable. Many of the examples he cites with approval, however, such as the greenbacks issued during the Civil War, do not support his assertion (1903, p. 228). Most of Kitson's (and Meulen's) references to price level instability refer to the problem of deflation. As with the silver proponents of the late nineteenth century, the actual method to be employed seems relatively unimportant in comparison to the objective of expanding the money supply.

C–K seem to accept Kitson's assertions regarding the invariable unit at face value. They state that Kitson's unit "can be defined by setting the value of any commodity on a given day equal to 'one' and pricing all commodities in terms thereof" (1987, p. 579). Yet this definition is either incorrect or redundant. The unit can be defined as the value of X ounces of gold on a given day, but to insure price stability it must also be defined in terms of a given basket of commodities (as in the Greenfield-Yeager system.) Otherwise, linking of the unit of account to the value of gold on a given day merely provides the unit with the *appearance* of having intrinsic value.

3. Precursors of the Modern BFH Theorists

The fact that both Kitson and Meulen repeatedly define the unit of account in terms of itself, indicates that these quotations represent something more than an accidental application of circular reasoning. Their proposal does bear a superficial resemblance to the system proposed by Greenfield and Yeager, and Yeager even discussed the possibility of indirect convertibility of currency into gold.[1] The crucial difference, however, is that under the Greenfield-Yeager system, each dollar's worth of currency would be redeemable for gold of fixed purchasing power (in terms of the standard bundle of commodities). In this respect the Greenfield-Yeager proposal is closer to the Williams-Fisher compensated dollar plan.

Williams (1892) proposed a plan whereby the gold weight of the pound would be adjusted daily in proportion to changes in the price of a specified bundle of

[1]See McCallum (1985), p. 37, footnote.

commodities. Fisher's (1920) plan differed slightly in that the adjustments would be made bimonthly, and on the basis of a more comprehensive price index (the Wholesale Price Index as measured by the Bureau of Labor Statistics).[2]

Black's (1981) proposal is almost identical to Fisher's compensated dollar plan. Under the Black proposal, "when the price level starts to rise, the price of gold is dropped; and when the price level starts to fall, the price of gold is raised. The only delays in this process should be due to the time it takes to measure the level of the price index" (p. 118).

Fisher had recognized that the existence of an information lag in measuring the price level could lead to destabilizing speculation in the gold market when there was an expectation of an imminent change in the price index. He therefore proposed what he termed a "brassage charge" (that is, spread or turnaround fee) of 1 percent on all gold transactions with the central bank. Fisher noted that the spread should be set at a high enough level to insure that it was larger than any probable change in the gold weight of the dollar (which is the inverse of the change in the price index).

Although this type of spread would eliminate the problem of speculation, it would simultaneously eliminate the ability of private individuals to arbitrage small gaps between the official price of gold and its free market price. In that case there would be no obvious mechanism by which changes in the price of gold could generate corresponding changes in the price level. Instead it appears that the policy would become operational only through changes in the currency stock.

Under Fisher's proposal gold coins would be withdrawn from circulation and replaced with gold notes. Under the "rules of the game" governments maintained a fixed currency/gold stock ratio. If the price index announcement showed a 1 percent decrease, then the government would increase in the official price of gold by 1 percent, which would increase the (nominal) monetary gold stock by 1 percent, and thus the government would increase the stock of currency by 1 percent. It is the change in the currency stock, not the official gold price, which *causes* the price level to rise.

Because the spread must be large enough to prevent speculation (and arbitrage) Fisher might just have well proposed a system with a 1,000 percent spread. This would have more clearly highlighted the similarity of Fisher's plan to modern money rules such as McCallum's (1984) proposal to adjust the monetary base inversely to announced shifts in velocity.

Under Fisher's plan the currency stock would show a discrete jump when the price index was announced, yet there would be no discontinuous changes in either the market price of gold or the exchange rate in response to the *anticipated* portion of the price level announcement. (Note: If foreign countries were on a

[2]Rooke (1824) proposed a plan similar to the Williams-Fisher compensated dollar plan. Rooke suggested that the official price of gold be adjusted inversely to changes in the average nominal wage rate. He argued that this would prevent major price level changes while still allowing some price level fluctuations due to "non-monetary" factors. Surprisingly, Rooke's plan is in some ways actually more "modern" than the Williams-Fisher plan in that it would be accommodative toward supply shocks.

gold standard, then the exchange rate would be linked through arbitrage to the *market* price of gold.) Thus, the system would not be vulnerable to speculative attacks.

In a letter to McCallum (1985, p. 37) Yeager indicated that under the Greenfield and Yeager proposal "competition would probably lead institutions to cash checks (if their holders so desired) and redeem currencies and deposits in whatever quantities of a convenient redemption medium (such as gold or actively traded securities) equalled in total value as many standard commodity bundles as the number of units of account denominating the obligations to be redeemed." McCallum noted that "the Greenfield and Yeager claim that their system 'is not a variant of the often-proposed composite-commodity or commodity-reserve money' system (1982, p. 303) would seem highly misleading" (1985, p. 37). It might also be noted that their plan is susceptible to the same speculation problem that Fisher was concerned about.

By linking the price of gold to a price index containing only the prices of actively traded commodities, Williams avoided the problem of discrete price index changes generated by an information lag. Hall's (1982) proposal to link the unit of account to a specified quantity of four commodities (aluminum, copper, plywood, and ammonium nitrate) shares this advantage.[3] Of course, both proposals are susceptible to price level instability if the relative price of the specified commodity bundle is not stable.

4. Concluding Remarks

The work of Kitson and Meulen was further from the ideas of the modern BFH proponents than one might infer from the C–K paper. It is true that they did anticipate some of the tenets of the new monetary economics, particularly in the area of free banking and deregulation. And it might be argued that the inability of Kitson and Meulen to construct a stable unit of account is a relatively minor defect, were it not for the fact that both the BFH forerunners and the modern BFH proponents place great importance on this issue. Yeager (1983) begins his discussion of the new monetary economics with the assertion that the instability of our unit of account is the central defect of our current system. Black (1981), Fama (1983), Hall (1983), and Greenfield and Yeager (1983) have all proposed systems which would result in approximate price stability.

Given the importance many NME theorists place on the stability of the unit of account, it is surprising that C–K did not give more attention to the Williams-Fisher system. C–K lumped the compensated dollar plans in with Jevons' tabular standard as mere "indexation schemes" (1987, p. 571) although, unlike the Jevons plan, they are clearly policies designed to prevent price level fluctuations, not to index contracts against such fluctuations. Although the unit of account in the compensated dollar plan is linked to a quantity of gold of fixed purchasing power, at a more fundamental level it is the underlying basket of commodities by

[3]Hall chose this commodity bundle because its price closely tracked the cost of living.

which the purchasing power is measured that constitutes the unit of account. Gold is merely the *medium* by which the purchasing power of notes is guaranteed.[4]

Greenfield and Yeager went far beyond Williams and Fisher in their proposal for a laissez-faire monetary system. It is not clear, however, that the macroeconomic implications of their proposal are much different from the compensated dollar plan.

LITERATURE CITED

Black, Fischer. "Banking and Interest Rates in a World without Money: The Effects of Uncontrolled Banking." *Journal of Banking Research* 1 (Autumn 1970), 8–20.

______. "A Gold Standard with Double Feedback and Near Zero Reserves." Unpublished, MIT, December 1981.

Cowen, Tyler, and Randall Kroszner. "The Development of the New Monetary Economics." *Journal of Political Economy* 95 (June 1987), 567–90.

Fama, Eugene. "Banking in the Theory of Finance." *Journal of Monetary Economics* 6 (January 1980), 39–57.

______. "Financial Intermediation and Price Level Control." *Journal of Monetary Economics* 12 (July 1983), 7–28.

Fisher, Irving. *Stabilizing the Dollar: A Plan to Stabilize the General Price Level without Fixing Individual Prices.* New York: Macmillan, 1920.

Greenfield, Robert L., and Leland B. Yeager. "A Laissez-Faire Approach to Monetary Stability." *Journal of Money, Credit, and Banking* 15 (August 1983), 302–15.

Hall, Robert. "Explorations in the Gold Standard and Related Policies for Stabilizing the Dollar." In *Inflation: Causes and Effects*, edited by R. Hall, pp. 111–22. Chicago: University of Chicago Press, 1982.

______. "Optimal Fiduciary Monetary Systems." *Journal of Monetary Economics* 12 (July 1983), 33–50.

Jevons, William Stanley. *Money and the Mechanism of Exchange.* New York: Appleton, 1876.

Kitson, Arthur. *The Money Problem.* London: Grant Richards, 1903. (Originally published as *A Scientific Solution to the Money Question.* Boston: Arena, 1895).

______. *A Fraudulent Standard: An Exposure of the Fraudulent Character of Our Monetary Standard.* London: King, 1917.

Liberty, edited by Benjamin Tucker. Westport, Conn.: Greenwood Reprint, 1970.

McCallum, Bennett T. "Monetarist Rules in the Light of Recent Experience." *American Economic Review* 74 (May 1984), 388–91.

______."Bank Deregulation, Accounting Systems of Exchange, and the Unit of Account: A Critical Review." In *The "New Monetary Economics," Fiscal Issues and Unemployment*, edited by K. Brunner and A. Meltzer, pp. 13–45. Amsterdam: North-Holland, 1985.

Meulen, Henry. *Free Banking: An Outline of a Policy of Individualism.* London: Macmillan, 1934.

[4]Black seems to have recognized this point since his system calls for "near zero reserves."

Rooke, John. *Inquiry into the Principles of National Wealth*. Edinburgh, 1824.

Wallace, Neil. "A Legal Restrictions Theory of the Demand for 'Money' and the Role of Monetary Policy." Federal Reserve Bank of Minneapolis *Quarterly Review* (Winter 1983), 1–7.

Williams, Aneurin. "A 'Fixed Value of Bullion' Standard—A Proposal for Preventing General Fluctuations of Trade." *Economic Journal* 2 (June 1892), 280–89.

Yeager, Leland B. "Stable Money and Free-Market Currencies." *Cato Journal* 3 (Spring 1983), 305–26.

Market Discipline and Bank Subordinated Debt

A Note by Gary Gorton and Anthony M. Santomero

A lengthy literature in banking has addressed the question of whether the market prices of liabilities respond to individual bank risk-taking activity, that is, whether any "market discipline" exists. However, despite the obvious importance of this question the current record has led to no consensus on the issue. Results have been contradictory. In this *Journal* alone Hannan and Hanweck (1988) conclude that the market does extract at least some price for risk-taking, while Avery, Belton, and Goldberg (1988) find no such evidence.

In this study we argue that this line of inquiry has a serious flaw in that it fails to use theoretical models of bank instrument valuation to determine the appropriate testing of market discipline. Therefore, the empirical models have lacked the necessary exactness to isolate the appropriate null hypotheses. To redress this shortcoming and advance the methodology of this area of the literature, we use a pricing model which comes to the banking area from the options pricing literature to look at the yield spread on bank liabilities. Using this model it is clear that the value of large, uninsured, bank liabilities cannot be described as a linear, monotonic, function of risk. Moreover, current bank regulation affects the assumed role risk measures play in the pricing of such debt instruments. Both of these complications mean that simple regressions are not likely to adequately address the relationship between the value of debt and underlying risk. In the final section we empirically investigate the presence of market discipline using contingent claims pricing. We find that accounting measures of bank risk still have little predictive value in explaining yield spreads, and therefore, offer little evidence of meaningful market discipline.

1. The State of the Literature

The literature on market discipline of the banking firm tests for the existence of market sensitivity to bank risk by regressing the relative cost of bank funds on balance sheet and/or income statement measures of risk, return, and market

The authors thank Robert Avery for sharing his data and for patiently answering all our questions, two anonymous referees, and Huston McCulloch whose comments considerably improved the paper.

GARY GORTON *is assistant professor and* ANTHONY M. SANTOMERO *is professor, The Wharton School, University of Pennsylvania.*

Journal of Money, Credit, and Banking, Vol. 22, No. 1 (February 1990)

position. The issue is whether the measures of risk are significantly related to movements in liability or equity prices. If they are, then some "market discipline" is said to exist.

In the debt area there have been constant contributions. Recent papers include Cramer and Rogowski (1985) and Goldberg and Lloyd-Davies (1985) who offer contradictory conclusions. These were followed by Baer and Brewer (1986) who find large liability rates positively related to risk measures over the period 1979:4 to 1982:3, and the previously cited Hannan and Hanweck (1988) who conclude that the market extracts a price for bank risk taking. However, in both studies the explanatory power of risk measures was quite small, rarely accounting for more than 10 percent of the overall variation in debt prices. This was followed by the aforementioned Avery, Belton, and Goldberg study of subordinated debt for both 1983 and 1984. Examining the spread over comparable Treasury yields these authors were unable to demonstrate any effect of balance sheet structure or income statement data on bank costs. Taken as a whole, the literature suggests that market self-regulation of risk taking is not clearly evident in the banking industry.

However, failure to observe such a relationship may derive from several factors, as the search for some market discipline involves several joint hypotheses. These may be listed as follows:

(i) Accounting measures of risk are accurate proxies for true risk;
(ii) The model, a linear regression, is correct;
(iii) The FDIC has well-defined and well-understood closure rules.

The first of these has its shortcomings, but is generally accepted. Accounting data are presumed to have noise, but are assumed to be unbiased measures of underlying risk both here and in other areas of financial research. Given the lack of an explicit pricing theory, condition (ii) is taken as a first approximation. Thus, explanations for differential findings involve recourse to the last assumption. If discipline is found, it is alleged that the market responds to risk. If not, it must be the result of market naïveté or a deference to the regulator's role as monitor.

In this study we choose to concentrate on the need for an explicit pricing model, as well as narrowly defined alternatives as to regulatory behavior. Consistent with previous work in the area we, too, assume the general usefulness of accounting data. However, we plan to show that with the aid of recent theory we can be more precise about bank liability pricing and the effect of different FDIC closure rules on subordinated debt pricing.

2. *Contingent Claims Valuation of Bank Subordinated Debt*

The contingent claims valuation model, derived by Black and Scholes (1973), has been applied by Merton (1974) to liability pricing in the case of a single issue of nonconvertible debt. Black and Cox (1976) subsequently expanded the model to consider multiple debt claimants. This is the relevant version for the current study's interest in subordinated debt.

Consider a firm that has a capital structure composed of equity and two types of debt, differentiated by their priorities as claimants on the firm. Assume that both have the same maturity date. If, at maturity, the value of the firm is greater than the promised repayment on the senior debt, denoted as X_1, then the senior debt is paid in full. Otherwise, the senior debt holders receive the value of the firm and the holders of junior debt and equity get nothing. If the value of the firm at maturity is greater than the sum of the promised repayments to both the junior and senior debt, $x_1 + X_2$, then all the debt is paid and the equity holders get the residual. If the value of the firm at maturity, V^*, is between X_1 and $X_1 + X_2$, that is, $X_1 < V^* < X_1 + X_2$, then the junior debt receives the difference between the value of the firm, V^*, and X_1. Therefore, at maturity the value of these claims on the assets of the firm may be written as

$$D_1^* = \min[V^*, X_1] \tag{1}$$

$$D_2^* = \max[\min(V^* - X_1, X_2), 0] \tag{2}$$

$$E^* = \max[V^* - (X_1 + X_2), 0] \tag{3}$$

where E^* is the value of equity at maturity; $D_1^* =$ is the value of senior debt at maturity; $D_2^* =$ is the value of the junior debt at maturity.

Using Black-Scholes methodology, it is well known that the current values of the claims on the firm can be obtained, under the assumption of log-normality, by solving a partial differential equation which is a function of firm value, V, and time. Following the work of Black and Cox (1976), the solution for the current value of the subordinated debt is

$$\begin{aligned} D_2 = {} & V[N(d_1) - N(\hat{d}_1)] - X_1\exp[-R_f\tau]N(d_2) \\ & + (X_1 + X_2)\exp[-R_f\tau]N(\hat{d}_2) \end{aligned} \tag{4}$$

where $d_1 = [\ln(V/X_1) + (R_f + \sigma^2/2)\tau]/\sigma\tau^{\frac{1}{2}}$, $d_2 = d_1 - \sigma\tau^{\frac{1}{2}}$,

$\hat{d}_1 = [\ln(V/(X_1 + X_2)) + (R_f + \sigma^2/2)\tau]/\sigma\tau^{\frac{1}{2}}$, and $\hat{d}_2 = \hat{d}_1 - \sigma\tau^{\frac{1}{2}}$. σ^2 is the volatility of the logarithm of the value of the firm and $N(z)$ is the univariate cumulative normal distribution. In what follows attention will focus on σ^2 because it measures the risk of the firm. In particular, the price of subordinated debt relative to the risk free rate is a function of σ^2. To see this, note that equation (4) can be rearranged so that the default risk premium can be expressed as the spread between the yield on subordinated debt, R_2, and the riskless rate, R_f, of the same maturity:

$$\begin{aligned} R_2 - R_f = {} & -\ln\{V/X_2\exp(R_f\tau)\,[N(d_1) - N(\hat{d}_1)] - (X_1/X_2)N(d_2) \\ & + ((X_1 + X_2)/X_2)N(\hat{d}_2)\}/\tau\,. \end{aligned} \tag{5}$$

This risk premium is a function of V/X_2 and $(X_1 + X_2)/X_2$ which are the two leverage terms, as well as σ^2 and maturity, τ.

This may be compared to the default risk premium in the case of a single class of debt issue:

$$R - R_f = -\ln[(V/X)\exp(R_f\tau)\, N(-d_1) + N(d_2)]/\tau \tag{6}$$

where d_1 and d_2 are defined as before with X replacing X_1. As others have noted, the value of the junior debt behaves differently than does senior debt with respect to time to maturity (τ), the volatility of the firm's assets (σ^2), and the riskless rate (R_f). Unlike the case of a single debt issue, the response of junior debt to these variables is ambiguous. If the promised payment of the senior debt is close to the value of the firm, then junior debt is effectively the residual claimant and will behave like an equity claim. If, however, the value of the firm is significantly higher than the promised payment on the senior debt, then the junior debt will behave like debt.

Black and Cox (1976) were the first to point this out. They show that junior debt is initially a convex function of the value of the firm and then becomes a concave function at a high enough value of the firm. Importantly, there is a single inflection point, $\hat{V}$, given by

$$\hat{V} = [X_1(X_1 + X_2)]^{\frac{1}{2}} \exp[-(R_f + \frac{\sigma^2}{2})\tau] . \tag{7}$$

Unlike senior debt, the default risk premium on junior debt is a *decreasing function* of σ^2 when V is less than $\hat{V}$ and an *increasing function of* σ^2 when V is greater than $\hat{V}$.[1]

This fact is potentially important when addressing the question of "market discipline." Consider the usual procedure employed to empirically verify its existence. Measures of bank risk, proxying for σ^2, are regressed on bank default risk premia, that is, spreads like $R_2 - R_f$. It should be clear from the above that no inferences can be drawn from the results about "market discipline" unless it can be stated ahead of time that linearity of the pricing equation is a good approximation of the underlying nonlinear relationship contained in either (5) or (6), and that the entire sample of banks is on one side of the inflection point given by equation (7) for subordinated debt.

An empirical investigation of the pricing of bank liabilities is also complicated by regulatory authorities that have broad discretionary powers. The FDIC may keep a troubled bank open; it may liquidate the bank; it may undertake some modified payoff approach or use the purchase and assumption method of dealing with the bank. In order to use contingent claims pricing some assumption must

[1]It is important to keep in mind that this is a statement about cross-sections of firms. A maintained assumption of the Black-Scholes option-pricing model is that σ^2 is constant.

be made about the regulatory authority's closure rules. Typically researchers have faced this difficulty by assuming an exogenously given closure rule. Merton (1978), when calculating the value of FDIC insurance, assumes that banks are audited once a year and that a bank will be closed if, at that time, its assets-to-deposits ratio is below one. Ronn and Verma (1986) also assume an annual audit with an exogenously given assets-to-deposits ratio below which the bank is closed.

Recent theoretical work by Acharya and Dreyfus (1988) indicates that realistic closure rules are much more complicated than the exogenous rules which have been considered in the literature. They solve for the optimal closure rule and insurance premium simultaneously. In this case, the optimal closure rule is endogenous and bank-specific.

The strategy we will follow is to proceed by specifying two possible closure rules. The first approach assumes the traditional annual horizon based on the fact that banks are examined each year. With the arrival of the regulators the stockholders have a choice of satisfying the regulator's criteria or forfeiting the bank to the regulators. That is, we adopt, as one case, the assumption that the effective maturity of the debt is one year.

The other extreme is to assume that the regulators do not impose any additional closure rules over the life of the subordinated debt. In this case visits by examiners are of no consequence to the holders of longer term subordinated debt. The appropriate boundary maturity under this set of assumptions depends on the maturity of the junior debt.[2] In the section below we will explore the empirical methodology associated with these two polar cases and attempt to determine whether the results obtained concerning the issue of market discipline vary under these two scenarios.

3. *Empirical Methodology Implied by the Pricing Model*

Contingent claims pricing demonstrates that the price of a corporate liability is a function of a small number of variables, including, τ, σ^2, and R_f. For our current interest, the variance of the firm's assets is the underlying driving variable. The riskiness of a firm is completely captured by this variance or volatility. Thus, the basic empirical strategy that must be subsequently implemented to investigate the presence of market discipline begins by calculating the variance which is implied by the current price of the debt instrument. Using the yield spreads on the bank liability over Treasuries of the same maturity, one can calculate implied volatilities using either formula (5) or (6). The formula is simply inverted to find the volatility implied by that market spread. This procedure is similar to the one employed by Ronn and Verma (1987) in a different context.

Implied volatilities of bank assets calculated for a cross-section of banks, the σ^2s, may then be regressed on the measures of bank risk as in previous studies.

[2]By assumption banks do not default on their coupon payments, which presumably can be financed by borrowing if necessary.

Once the risk measures have been calculated the approach is similar to previous studies. However, the procedure has the advantage of being able to directly assess whether accounting measures of risk are correlated with market risk while avoiding direct use of the yield spreads which are neither linearly nor monotonically related to bank asset risk.

In order to calculate the risk measures from contingent claims pricing, the usual assumptions needed to use the Black-Scholes formula must be employed.[3] In addition, some calculations of the implied risk measure require that the following be assumed:

1. Deposit insurance is fairly priced.
2. Aggregation of a bank's multiple issues of debt by weighted averages of yields and maturities is a good approximation.
3. The book values of balance sheet items are unbiased estimates of their market value, in cross-section.

Some of these assumptions are more restrictive than others. For example, the assumption that deposit insurance is fairly priced has received empirical support from Pennacchi (1987). However, McCulloch (1985) presents evidence to suggest that it is underpriced. Assumption (2) is necessitated by the fact that some banks have multiple issues of a particular debt form with differing maturities, requiring some form of aggregation. The last assumption is adopted because market valuation does not exist in reported data, and in some cases, may be impossible to obtain.

4. An Empirical Application of the Implied Technique

To see how such an approach may be employed we have investigated the use of this methodology on subordinated debt yield spreads. This area was examined by Avery, Belton, and Goldberg (1988) (hereafter referred to as ABG) and seems most applicable due to the explicit subordination of these debt issues. ABG collected (sale or bid) prices of all publicly traded bank subordinated notes and debentures for the one hundred largest U.S. bank holding companies (BHC) as of December 31, 1983, and December 31, 1984. As explained by ABG, some issues were dropped for various reasons, leaving a final sample of 137 issues from seventy-one BHC. Next ABG compute the spread, $R_2 - R_f$, by "first computing the price of a Treasury bond identical in maturity and callability to each issue and solving for the difference in yield to maturity from that actually quoted for each bank holding company issue" (p. 599). ABG provide some stylized facts about the computed spreads. See ABG for more detail.

ABG used the average premium of all outstanding issues for each bank holding company for each year as the dependent variable in their study. We use the aver-

[3]The implied volatility measures assume a normal distribution. As McCulloch (1985) points out, for non-Gaussian distributions these estimates will be systematically biased. In addition, the interest rate is assumed nonstochastic. Ronn and Verma (1986) show that the relative contribution of interest rate variance to overall variance appears small.

age premium outstanding for each BHC for each year as the input into calculating each BHC's volatilities, using the above procedure. These σ^2s are then used as the dependent variable in regressions on measures of bank risk. The implied values from this procedure are contained in Table 1. Panel (A) of the table lists computed σ^2s for the fourth quarter of 1983; Panel (B) lists those for the fourth quarter of 1984. For each institution the reported volatility represents the value implied by the aggregation of all its junior debt.[4]

The volatilities in Table 1 differ by maturity and subordination assumption. The first two columns assume that debt maturity is one year. In the first case, column 1 reports computed volatilities with full recognition of the different claimant classes, junior and senior debt. In the second case, the subordinated debt is combined with all other liabilities as equal claimants. In other words, regulators are treated as if they were insuring the entirety of bank debt over the one-year horizon. Column 3 assumes the averge maturity of the subordinated debt with full recognition of its claimant position.

The next step is to examine whether these measures of bank risk implied by spreads on subordinated debt are statistically related to accounting measures of risk contained in the balance sheet. To investigate this question we regress the cross-section values of σ^2 on accounting risk measures. In each case proxies for both credit and interest rate risk are used.[5] Data used to form measures of bank risk are from the Call and Income *Reports* and were found by aggregating all banks within a holding company. Credit risk was measured by the ratios of nonaccruals, charge-offs, or nonperforming loans to assets alternatively, while interest rate risk uses the one-year gap measure, that is, the book value of assets minus the book value of liabilities that will be repriced within one year. A representative sample of results is present in Table 2 for various assumptions about seniority and maturity.

Columns 1 and 2 of Table 2 report the results for the case of debt of one-year maturity. In all cases the volatility measures used correspond to those in the respective columns of Table 1. Column 1 reports the results for the case of one-year debt when junior and senior debt are distinguished. While several different measures of credit and interest rate risk were examined, only one of each is reported. The results are, at best, only marginally supportive of the market discipline hypothesis. The interest rate measure is significant, while the credit risk measure is not. The R^2s are uniformly low, and consistent with the levels contained in previously cited studies.

In column 2 of Table 2, which treats all debt as equal claimants, there is no statistical evidence of market discipline. A similar finding is contained in column 3 for the case where the maturity of the bank subordinated debt is assumed to be the average maturity of these instruments.

[4]Results are very similar to those reported if instead of averaging the yields on subordinated debt σ^2s are calculated using the yield on the largest issue of subordinated debt for each bank.

[5]The significance of different risk proxies varied somewhat across the sample of σ^2s in the study. In general, we report the best explanatory variable in the accompanying tables.

TABLE 1

IMPLIED VOLATILITIES

Bank Name	(A) Computed σ^2's for Fourth Quarter of 1983 SIGMA1	SIGMA2	SIGMA3	(B) Computed σ^2's for Fourth Quarter of 1984 SIGMA1	SIGMA2	SIGMA3
First Interstate Bancorp	0.24	0.15	0.54	0.20	0.09	0.45
Barnett Banks Inc.	1.84	0.08	0.45	0.38	0.09	0.51
Shawmut Corp.	0.23	0.10	0.57	0.23	0.10	0.56
First Bank System Inc.	0.25	0.09	0.46	0.26	0.09	0.48
Norwest Corp.	0.18	0.07	0.44	0.17	0.08	0.43
First City Bancorp (Texas)	0.21	0.10	0.53	0.21	0.08	0.49
Irving Bank Corp.	0.27	0.08	0.50	0.26	0.08	0.52
Southeast Bank Corp.	0.10	0.10	0.40	0.21	0.05	0.47
Commerce Bancshares Inc.	0.21	0.05	0.48	0.16	0.07	0.41
Banc One Corp.	0.19	0.05	0.43	0.19	0.08	0.40
United Jersey Banks	0.19	0.10	0.55	0.20	0.00	0.51
Boatmen's Bancshares Inc.	0.33	0.21	0.86	0.23	0.18	0.69
Mercantile Bancorporation	0.20	0.09	0.49	0.22	0.10	0.48
Texas Commerce Bancshares	0.23	0.05	0.43	0.23	0.11	0.43
Northern Trust Corp.	0.26	0.08	0.49	0.26	0.08	0.50
Keycorp	0.18	0.14	0.70	4.08	0.15	2.41
Security Pacific Corp.	0.21	0.05	0.44	0.24	0.09	0.52
Sovran Financial Corp.	0.23	0.10	0.46	0.21	0.07	0.43
Allied Bancshares Inc. - TX	0.15	0.08	0.47	0.16	0.10	0.44
Hartford National Corp.	0.15	0.08	0.50	0.16	0.08	0.51
Bank of Boston Corp.	0.23	0.10	0.50	0.23	0.13	0.50
Fleet Financial Group Inc.	0.25	0.10	0.53	0.31	0.10	0.60
Manufacturers Hanover Corp.	0.23	0.07	0.45	0.26	0.10	0.60
Morgan (J.P.) & Co.	0.26	0.08	0.45	0.30	0.12	0.43
Chase Manhattan Corp.	0.25	0.08	0.50	0.28	0.09	0.50
Citicorp	0.30	0.11	0.53	0.26	0.09	0.48
Mellon Bank Corp.	0.30	0.05	0.47	0.29	0.11	0.49
Fidelcor	0.23	0.15	0.60	0.24	0.08	0.60
First Union Corp. (N.C.)	0.28	0.10	0.53	0.33	0.15	0.55
NCNB Corp.	0.25	0.10	0.51	0.25	0.15	0.54
First Chicago Corp.	0.20	0.06	0.41	0.25	0.10	0.48
Texas American Bancshares	0.22	0.13	0.60	0.21	0.14	0.62
US Bank Corp.	0.30	0.14	0.70	0.25	0.15	0.60
Bankamerica Corp.	0.19	0.05	0.44	0.18	0.08	0.42
Rainier Bancorporation	0.22	0.15	0.49	0.23	0.10	0.42
Wells Fargo & Co.	0.18	0.07	0.48	0.19	0.08	0.48

NOTES: SIGMA1 distinguishes between junior and senior debt and imposes a one year maturity.
SIGMA2 treats all debt as homogeneous and imposes a one year maturity.
SIGMA3 distinguishes between junior and senior debt and sets the maturity equal to the average of the subordinate debt.

TABLE 2

REGRESSIONS OF IMPLIED VOLATILITY ON RISK MEASURES

Independent Variables	Dependent Variables (1) SIGMA1	(2) SIGMA2	(3) SIGMA3
Intercept	0.228*	0.107*	0.539*
	(17.06)	(11.726)	(25.09)
NONACC	0.0776	−0.772	−2.46
	(0.088)	(1.29)	(1.74)
1YRGAP	0.005*	0.007	0.001
	(2.22)	(0.509)	(0.209)
R^2	.070	.024	.043

T-statistics are in parentheses.
NONACCC ≡ nonaccruals divided by total bank assets.
1YRGAP ≡ the one-year gap, that is, the difference between assets and liabilities subject to repricing within the next year. All data are from the Call and Income Reports.

We next investigated the inflection point issue raised in equation (7) for the ABG data. We calculated the inflection for each bank in the sample to see if the data support the notion that bank subordinated debt pricing corresponds to standard debt pricing behavior, or equity-like behavior. For the ABG data set of large commercial bank subordinated debt issuers, the calculated inflection point using our estimated σ^2s always implies that all the banks have $V > \hat{V}$. This should be expected given the nature of banks in the sample, but should not imply that the issue is unimportant for the industry in general.

Taken as a whole these results offer little support for the presence of market discipline in the subordinated debt market. However, the results do suggest that assumptions concerning the behavior of the regulatory authorities may be important. The case where the results are strongest correspond to those measures of implied volatility which imposed subordination of junior debt, relatively short maturity for the implied option, and close regulatory supervision.

5. *Summary and Conclusion*

If market prices of uninsured bank liabilities reflect the risk of default, then the market is at least partially "disciplining" banks. The usual approach to question whether market prices of uninsured bank debt contain individual bank risk premia is to regress the yield spread against accounting measures of bank risk. To date, these results have been mixed. However, we know theoretically that uninsured liabilities are subordinated claimants which are not linearly or monotonically functions of bank risk. In addition, the underlying risk is dependent upon regulatory behavior. Without recognizing these complications linear regressions may have difficulty addressing the question.

In this paper we used contingent claims valuation to derive an explicit pricing model for subordinated debt. Without exact knowledge of the regulatory closure rules we adopted the approach of modeling two polar cases in our application. In addition, we explicitly examined variation in the treatment of the subordination of noninsured debt. For each of these cases the implied volatilities were extracted and correlated with accounting measures of risk in an application to subordinated debt. The results generally confirm earlier work in the area. Accounting measures of risk turn out to only marginally predict the volatility of bank assets. Interest rate risk has some statistical effect, but credit risk proxies offer little evidence.

We believe that the methodological issues raised here are, at least, as important as any of our results.

LITERATURE CITED

Acharya, Sankarshan, and Jean-Francois Dreyfus. "Optimal Bank Reorganization Policies and the Pricing of Federal Deposit Insurance." Mimeo, Graduate School Of Business, New York University, 1988.

Avery, Robert B., Terrence M. Belton, and Michael A. Goldberg. "Market Discipline in

Regulating Bank Risk: New Evidence From Capital Markets." *Journal of Money, Credit, and Banking* 20 (November 1988), 597–610.

Baer, Herbert, and Elijah Brewer. "Uninsured Deposits as a Source of Market Discipline: Some New Evidence." Federal Reserve Bank of Chicago, *Economic Perspectives* (September/October 1986), 23–31.

Black, Fischer, and John C. Cox. "Valuing Corporate Securities: Some Effects of Bond Indentures." *Journal of Finance* 31 (May 1976), 351–67.

Black, Fischer, and Myron Scholes. "The Pricing of Options and Corporate Liabilities." *Journal of Political Economy* 81 (May/June 1973).

Cramer, Robert H., and Robert J. Rogowski. "Risk Premia on Negotiable Certificates of Deposit and the Continental Illinois Bank Crisis." mimeo.

Goldberg, Michael A., and Peter R. Lloyd-Davies. "Standby Letters of Credit: Are Banks Overextending Themselves?" *Journal of Bank Research* 16 (Spring 1985), 29–39.

Hannan, Timothy, and Gerald Hanweck. "Bank Insolvency Risk and the Market for Large Certificates of Deposits." *Journal of Money, Credit, and Banking* 20 (May 1988), 203–11.

McCulloch, J. Huston. "Interest-Risk Sensitive Deposit Insurance Premia." *Journal of Banking and Finance* 9 (March 1985), 137–56.

Merton, Robert C. "On the Pricing of Corporate Debt: The Risk Structure of Interest Rates." *Journal of Finance* 29 (May 1974), 449–70.

______. "On the Cost of Deposit Insurance When There Are Surveillance Costs." *Journal of Business* 51 (July 1978), 439–76.

Pennacchi, George C. "A Reexamination of the Over-(or Under) Pricing of Deposit Insurance," *Journal of Money, Credit, and Banking* (August 1987), 340–60.

Ronn, Ehud, and Avinash Verma. "Pricing Risk-Adjusted Deposit Insurance: An Option-Based Model." *Journal of Finance* 41 (September 1986), 871–95.

______. "A Multi-Attribute Comparative Evaluation of Relative Risk for a Sample of Banks." *Journal of Banking and Finance* 11 (September 1987), 499–523.

BOOK REVIEWS

Toward a World of Economic Stability: Optimal Monetary Framework and Policy, edited by Yoshio Suzuki and Mitsuaki Okabe. Tokyo: University of Tokyo Press, 1988. 370 pp. $45.00.

This volume represents the proceedings of the third biennial International Conference sponsored by the Institute for Monetary and Economic Studies of the Bank of Japan, which was held in Tokyo, June 3–5, 1987. This conference has gained an international reputation in a short period of time because of the large number of innovative and interesting papers that have been presented over the years by some of the most respected scholars in the fields of macroeconomics and international finance. Moreover, all of the conferences have been based on a particular theme with important implications for economic policy. The third biennial conference was no exception, and the resulting conference volume is an excellent collection of papers all touching upon the common theme of economic stability and its relation to policy regimes and the conduct of monetary policy.

A conference volume of this nature is usually difficult to summarize and review because of the breadth of material covered—the wide variety of data, countries examined, models considered, and views expressed. But in this case, my task has been simplified considerably in two ways. First, the conference papers and discussion are loosely focused around a common theme. Second, two excellent summary papers written after the conference by Andrew D. Crockett and John B. Taylor are included in the volume.

The volume consists of an introduction by the editors, two overview and summary pieces, two keynote addresses, one statistical summary of economic performances in the major industrial countries, and six research papers complete with formal discussions covering three main topics—the causes of domestic instability since 1973, the causes of international imbalances in the 1980s, and issues of optimal monetary policy.

In the two summary papers, Crockett nicely summarizes each of the papers and the major points brought out in the conference. Taylor complements this by carefully analyzing the papers and discussions and organizing the material around a coherent and manageable set of results, on which there was considerable agreement emerging at the conference. These results are presented in three areas: empirical facts of macroeconomic performance, analytical results, and international monetary policy implications. Taylor manages to place the various strands of material into a coherent framework, and also critically evaluates each piece of research.

The two keynote speeches were provided by James Tobin, "Are There Reliable Adjustment Mechanisms?", and Allan H. Meltzer, "Monetary Stability and Monetary Reform." Tobin argues for the importance of international price adjustments in helping to restore full employment, and shows how many governments often adopt inappropriate policies in an attempt to hinder this adjustment process. He then focuses on shifts in effective demand and absorption as an alternative approach to achieve external and internal balance, and in this context reviews the monetary and fiscal policy mix in the United States in the 1980s. Tobin concludes that a gradual fiscal contraction is an essential part of restoring balance to the world economy, just as a fiscal expansion was the major initial source of the problem. Meltzer, in contrast, focuses on the issue of discretion versus rules in the conduct of monetary policy. He argues that our ability to forecast is so limited that discretionary policy, which may appear superior in principle, is far worse in practice than a simple monetary rule.

The statistical summary of economic performances of the major industrial countries, written by Yoshio Suzuki, provides a useful set of stylized facts that the discussion in the conference revolved around.

The first two full-length research papers included in the volume (Chapters 6 and 7) investigate the causes of domestic instability since 1973. Michael Parkin writes on "Monetary Policy and Aggregate Fluctuations," and empirically investigates the links between money, supply shocks, output, and prices for both an aggregative model of a single "world economy" and the seven major industrial countries individually. Parkin, on the basis of his empirical analysis, concludes that (i) the major sources of output fluctuations in recent years have been real shocks to technology, (ii) countries which have pursued highly stable targeting of a broad monetary aggregate have experienced lower output variability, and (iii) inflation has been generated mainly through monetary policy.

The second paper investigating empirical issues is by Stanley Fischer: "Monetary Policy and Economic Performance, 1973–1986." This is an nontechnical paper which uses descriptive data to make a general evaluation of the relationship between the conduct of monetary policy and economic stability in the United States, Germany, Japan, and the United Kingdom. He addresses issues of the role of monetary targets, gradualism in policy implementation and central bank credibility, and their contribution to differences in economic performance. Although he doesn't reach definite conclusions on these issues, Fischer convincingly dismisses the notion that simple lessons can be gleaned from cross-country comparisons. The nature of the policies conducted in each country have either been too complicated to allow simple comparisons, or the outcomes of similar policies so divergent that generalizations are difficult.

Chapters 8 and 9 investigate the causes of international imbalances in the 1980s. Chapter 8, written by Jürg Niehans, is entitled "Generating International Disturbances." This is an interesting and innovative theoretical paper in which Niehans is able to analyze the dynamic effects of fiscal and monetary policy fluctuations within the context of a two-country, perfect foresight model. The emphasis is on the influence of differences in the degree of capital mobility, represented by Niehans as the presence of differential investment lags ("gestation lags"), in the dynamic adjustment process. One major conclusion that Niehans reaches is that floating rates do not insulate an economy from foreign fiscal shifts, and there is no domestic policy response that would provide such insulation. Moreover, he suggests that while more stable U.S. fiscal and monetary policies would help reduce international imbalances, the task of international policy coordination under the present political circumstances is virtually hopeless.

Chapter 9 is entitled "Sources of Macroeconomic Imbalances in the World Economy: A Simulation Approach" and is written by Jeffrey Sachs and Nouriel Roubini. This paper uses a well-specified and consistent global macroeconomic simulation model to identify the factors that have contributed to global trade and financial imbalances in the 1980s. A complete set of monetary and fiscal policy simulations in the United States, Japan, and the remainder of the OECD nations form the bulk of the paper. One of the central questions posed is whether the budgetary shifts in the OECD economies in the 1980s can account for the bulk of trade and exchange rate movements, as conventional wisdom suggests. They find that the combination of sharply higher budget deficits in the United States and sharply reduced deficits in Japan goes far to explain the movements of the trade balances and the appreciation of the dollar, but has difficulty explaining the depreciation of the dollar since 1985.

The final two papers of the volume, Chapters 10 and 11, consider issues of optimal monetary regime and policy management for economic stability. Chapter 10, "Monetary Policy under Interest-Rate Targeting and Other Arrangements," is written by Robert Barro. In this paper the focus is on the closed economy and the familiar Poole result is derived that when shocks to the LM curve are large it is better to smooth out interest rate fluctuations, but when IS shocks are large it is better to let interest rates fluctuate and thereby smooth out the fluctuations in aggregate demand. Somewhat surprisingly, Barro argues that interest-rate rules on the part of the central bank have a number of desirable characteristics in stabilizing the economy.

Chapter 11, written by Shin-ichi Fukuda and Koichi Hamada, is entitled "Toward the Implementation of Desirable Rules of Monetary Coordination and Intervention" and is also concerned with the optimal monetary regime. Their analysis is carried out in the context of a stochastic two-country version of the sluggish price Dornbusch overshooting model, and also in the context of a neoclassical flex-prices model where the focus is on price "surprises." The focus of the paper is to characterize the nature of simple, appropriate rules for monetary management in the world economy under uncertainty. One particularly interesting innovation of the Fukuda-Hamada paper is that they show the familiar Poole result holds when there are country-specific shocks to the IS and LM curves. When there are country-specific shocks to the LM curve, they show that interest rate and exchange rate smoothing is desirable. When country-specific shocks to the IS curve are predominant, then interest rate and exchange rate variability is desirable.

In summary, I found this an interesting, informative, and well-focused conference volume of excellent papers by leading scholars in the fields of international and macroeconomics. Standing alone, the research papers make valuable reading. They are well complemented, however, by the many insightful commentaries by conference participants which are also included in the volume. The combination of academics together with economists from central banks and international organizations created an atmosphere that allowed a highly productive integration of academic research with discussion of important policy issues.

MICHAEL M. HUTCHISON

University of California at Santa Cruz

Money, Interest, and Banking in Economic Development, by Maxwell Fry. Baltimore: The Johns Hopkins University Press, 1988. xx + 522 pp.

The book provides an excellent survey of issues related to money, interest, and banking in economic development. Unlike the works of McKinnon (1973) and Shaw (1973), the book is, for the most part, based on previously published material. Hence, its main contribution is in integrating, comparing, and contrasting existing studies to highlight various methodologies and critically evaluate the theoretical and empirical results. It is important to mention, though, that the book includes many recent extensions to studies previously conducted by the author, especially in the section on econometric testing of financial development models.

The book is a must for academicians and policymakers involved in studying the financial environment, institutions, markets, monetary theory, and policy in economic development. Since the path-breaking work of McKinnon and Shaw in 1973, a myriad of literature has emerged on money in development finance and monetary policy in regulated financial settings. Coats and Khatkhate (1980) provided us with a survey of issues and evidence in an edited book comprising a set of previously published journal articles. The advantage of Maxwell Fry's book is in its updating of the findings and its highlighting of the important issues in an integrated framework. Some parts of the book are also likely to be of interest to economists involved in the working of monetary policy under various regulatory measures such as issues of fixed versus flexible deposit and loan rates.

The book is divided into four major parts including seventeen chapters. Part I comprises five chapters in which theoretical models of financial development are discussed. The author posits McKinnon-Shaw-type financial development models in their steady-state and dynamic forms, and their open-economy extensions. Then, he specifies some neostructuralist development models to analyze the controversy between the McKinnon-Shaw school and the neostructuralist school. The main conclusion is that the effects of financial liberalization depend on the assumptions regarding the efficiency of the official banking system and the curb market. If the former is more efficient at allocating investible funds (McKinnon-Shaw school), when the real deposit rate increases, financial liberalization raises the rate of economic growth. If the curb market is more efficient (neostructuralist school), the opposite results hold.

Since theory does not provide us with definite answers, the author embarks in part II on analyzing in four chapters the econometric testing of financial development models. He reports the results of studies that have examined the effects of financial conditions on saving, investment, growth, and inflation. He also addresses the empirical literature on transmission mechanisms, income distribution, and some causes and effects of monetary policies in some developing countries. The conclusions of this part largely support the McKinnon-Shaw view that financial liberalization increases savings and the rate of economic growth. There is also some contradictory evidence to this view showing that raising the time deposit rate reduces economic growth because it reduces the aggregate supply of credit. Evidence on the transmission mechanism suggests that institutional interest rates affect portfolio allocation. This portfolio effect may be the channel through which a change in the real deposit rate is transmitted to the output-capital ratio.

Part III includes three chapters highlighting the microeconomic institutional aspects of financial development. The author addresses issues related to financial intermediaries, institutions, and markets. He concludes that in most cases, removing the impediments to competitive financial intermediation accelerates the pace of economic development. He also supports the view that curb markets can play a productive role in the development process. Financial development programs, in his opinion, should address the issues of market structure to eliminate cartelized or oligopolistic banking for the purpose of assuring efficient intermediation between savers and investors. In a separate chapter, the author shows that government intervention in the financial system is rarely benign because of vested interests, the legal framework under which financial intermediaries operate, and the overtaxing of this system.

The last part provides in five chapters an overview of monetary and financial policies in economic development with special emphasis on interest rate policies and selective credit policies. The author shows that inflationary macroeconomic policies have negatively affected the efficiency of financial sectors and have been accompanied by increased financial instability and crises. He also argues against selective credit policies because evidence shows that subsidized credit makes the distribution of income and wealth more unequal without any benefits in terms of increased productivity. This part also highlights in one chapter monetary and financial policies in four high-growth developing countries, namely, Hong Kong, Singapore, Taiwan, and Korea.

I can think of three important money and banking issues that the book could have also addressed or analyzed differently. The first deals with the recent use of open-market operations to affect reserves in a few less-developed countries. For example, the author states on pp. 369–70:

> "As in most other developing countries, in Taiwan, open-market operations have been impossible because of the absence of a functioning bond market (Landberg 1979, p. 279)."

By relying on a 1979 source in support of his argument, the author misses the point that Taiwan started conducting open-market operations in 1979. Since that year, the Central Bank of China has conducted these operations on a regular basis, trading treasury bills and other money market instruments (Central Bank of China, *Annual Reports*, 1979–1987). It is true that the market for government securities in Taiwan remains inefficient. Therefore, in conducting open-market operations, the Central Bank of China did not rely solely on the thin stock of government securities but also on assets created in the mid-seventies such as banker's acceptances, negotiable certificates of deposits, and commercial paper.

Second, the author could have examined the issue of money supply implications of financing budget deficits through commercial banks when they are captive buyers of government securities. This phenomenon is common in many less-developed countries. The issue is of importance because it is believed that the stabilization consequences of budget deficits are closely related to their impact on money supply. This impact cannot always be predicted since it depends on the behavior of the money multiplier through changes in loans, excess reserves, or other assets (Coats and Khatkhate 1978) and the behavior of curb market participants (Shahin 1989).

The third issue concerns monetary targeting now that some less-developed countries are not totally fixing or pegging their exchange rates. The author discusses, in chapter 9, issues of capital flows, economic growth, and monetary policy regimes. It would be interesting to examine, at a theoretical level, the possibilities of having money or credit targets in the presence of the salient features characterizing less-developed financial markets. Specifically, is there a limit to the stabilizing role of money or credit in development finance in a system of authority-determined interest rates, captive buyers of government securities, and curb markets?

As it stands, the book is a commendable piece of work that deals with significant research issues in development finance.

WASSIM SHAHIN

DePauw University

LITERATURE CITED

Central Bank of China. *Annual Reports*, various issues.

Coats, Warren L., and Deena R. Khatkhate, eds. "Money Supply Implications of Commercial Banks' Financing of Government Debt in Developing Countries." *Oxford Bulletin of Economics and Statistics* 40 (May 1978), 179–93.

———. *Money and Monetary Policy in Less Developed Countries*. Great Britain: Pergamon Press, 1980.

McKinnon, Ronald. *Money and Capital in Economic Development*. Washington D.C.: Brookings, 1973.

Shahin, Wassim N. "Money Supply Implications of Financing Deficits through Captive Buyers in a Dual Loan System." *Quarterly Review of Economics and Business* 29 (Summer 1989), 87–95.

Shaw, Edward. *Financial Deepening in Economic Development*. New York: Oxford University Press, 1973.

STATEMENT OF OWNERSHIP, MANAGEMENT AND CIRCULATION
(Required by 39 U.S.C. 3685)

Publication: *Journal of Money, Credit, and Banking*
Publication Number: 0922-2879
Filing Date: 9-12-89
Frequency of Issue: Quarterly
No. of Issues Published Annually: 4
Annual Subscription Price: $45.00
Office of Publication: 1070 Carmack Rd., Columbus, OH 43210-1002
General Business Office: (same as above)
Publisher: Ohio State University Press, 1070 Carmack Rd., Columbus, OH 43210-1002
Editor: J. Huston McCulloch and Stephen A. McCafferty, Dept. of Economics, OSU, Columbus, OH 43210-1320
Managing Editor: Margaret Starbuck, OSU Press, 1070 Carmack Rd., Columbus, OH 43210-1002
Owner: OSU Press, 1070 Carmack Rd., Columbus, OH 43210-1002

Extent & Nature of Circulation	Average No. Copies Each Issue During Preceding 12 Months	Actual No. Copies of Single Issue Published Nearest to Filing Date
Total No. Copies (Net Press Run)	3,901	3,959
Sales Through Dealers, etc.	-0-	-0-
Mail Subscription	3,277	3,385
Total Paid Circulation	3,277	3,385
Free Distribution	53	55
Total Distribution	3,330	3,440
Copies Not Distributed	572	519
Return from News Agents	-0-	-0-
Total	3,901	3,959

I certify that the statements made by me above are correct and complete.
Margaret Starbuck

Instructions to Authors

Manuscripts should be submitted in triplicate to the editors, *Journal of Money, Credit, and Banking*, Department of Economics, Ohio State University, 1945 North High Street, Columbus, Ohio 43210. Papers must be in English, must contain original unpublished work, must not be under consideration for publication elsewhere, and should not exceed 30 pages in overall length. Submission fee: individual subscribers U.S. $30; nonsubscribers U.S. $40. Checks are to be made payable to the Ohio State University–JMCB and enclosed with submitted manuscripts.

Books for review should be sent to the editors at the address above.

Manuscripts should be typewritten, double-spaced, on one side only of white bond paper 8½ × 11 inches in size, with margins at least 1 inch wide. An abstract, double-spaced, must accompany the article. It should summarize the main points of the paper in *no more* than 100 words. Authors must supply their professional title, department, and the name of the institutions with which they are affiliated on both the title page and the abstract.

Literature Cited. All works cited should be listed separately by author in a double-spaced list at the end of the manuscript. Examples:

Barro, Robert J. "Unanticipated Money Growth and Economic Activity in the U.S." In *Money, Expectations, and Business Cycles*, edited by Robert J. Barro, pp. 137–69. New York: Academic Press, 1981.

Box, George E., and Gwylim M. Jenkins. *Time Series Analysis: Forecasts and Control*, 2nd ed. San Francisco: Holden Day, 1976.

Hopewell, Michael H., and George G. Kaufman. "The Cost of Inefficient Coupons on Municipal Bonds." *Journal of Financial and Quantitative Analysis* 9 (March 1974), 155–64 (a).

______. "Costs to Municipalities of Selling Bonds by NIC." *National Tax Journal* 27 (December 1974), 531–41 (b).

References to the literature in the text and footnotes should be made by means of the last name(s) of the author(s) followed by the year of publication enclosed in parentheses, without punctuation: Barro (1981). When a particular page, section, or equation is referred to, the references should also be placed within parentheses: (Box and Jenkins 1976, p. 361), (Hopewell and Kaufman 1974a, eq. 3).

Footnotes. Footnotes should not be used for the purpose of citation. In the final draft, footnotes must be double-spaced on a separate page at the end of the manuscript.

Mathematics. Equations must be typed and important displayed equations identified by consecutive arabic numbers in parentheses on the right. Expressions should be aligned and compound subscripts and superscripts clearly marked if there is any potential for confusion. Handwritten symbols should be identified in the margin the first time they appear. Equations should not be unnecessarily numerous or complex. A slash (/) should be used to separate the numerator and denominator of all in-text fractions and short displayed fractions. Multiple dots and bars over expressions should be avoided where primes can be used. Indicate boldface characters by drawing a wavy line (a) under them; a single underline (a) means italic to a printer.

Illustrations. Illustrations submitted with the final draft must be of professional quality, ready for reproduction, executed on white paper or vellum, in black ink, with clear, medium weight, black lines and figures. All lettering on figures should be executed by an artist in pen and ink, by means of dry transfer letters, or by applying typeset material to the prepared artwork. Typewritten lettering should not appear in illustrations. Figures should be capable of legible reduction to a size no larger than 4½ × 7 inches (full page) and preferably no larger than 4½ × 3½ inches (half page); they should be numbered consecutively, and the number and author's name should be penciled lightly on the back of each. All illustrations must have captions, which should not appear on the artwork but should be typed, double-spaced, on a sheet at the end of the manuscript. If there is any potential for doubt, the word "top" should be written on the back of the illustration.

Tables. Tables should be numbered consecutively throughout the article and typed on separate sheets at the end of the manuscript. Each table must include a descriptive title and headings to columns. Gather general footnotes to tables as "Note:" or "Notes:", and use *a, b, c*, etc., for specific footnotes. Asterisks * and/or ** indicate significance at the 5 percent and 1 percent levels, respectively, if used.

Copyrighted Material. Permission to reprint any previously published material (e.g., tables, illustrations, text extracts) must be obtained by the author from the copyright holder and copies of the grants of permission must be submitted to the editors with the final draft of the manuscript.

Institut für Weltwirtschaft an der Universität Kiel

Services in World Economic Growth

Symposium 1988

Edited by Herbert Giersch. Tübingen 1989. VII, 275 pages.
Paper DM 66.–, ISBN 3-16-345482-8. Cloth DM 86.–, ISBN 3-16-345483-6.

I. Services and the Changing Economic Structure

Modern Service Sector Growth: Causes and Effects, Herbert G. Grubel, Michael A. Walker
Discussant: Richard Blackhurst

Defining and Measuring Output and Productivity in the Service Sector, Domenico Siniscalco
Discussant: Frank D. Weiss

II. International Aspects

International Transactions Involving Interactions: A Conceptual Framework Combining Goods and Services, Seev Hirsch

Services and Comparative Advantage Theory, H. Peter Gray
Discussant: Henning Klodt

Trade and Foreign-Owned Production in Services: Some Conceptual and Theoretical Issues, John H. Dunning

Discussant: Pan Yotopoulos

III. Sectoral Analysis

Telecommunications and the Scope of the Market in Services, Gerald R. Faulhaber
Discussant: Axel Busch

Telecommunications Policy – Assessing Recent Experience in the US, Japan and Europe and Its Implications for the Completion of the Internal Common Market, Günter Knieps
Discussants: Tyll Necker, Herbert Ungerer

Protection and the Structure of the Banking Industry in an International Context, Robert Z. Aliber
Discussant: Norbert Walter

Integrated World Markets in Services: Problems and Prospects, Brian Hindley

Discussant: Jürgen Müller

IV. Services and International Division of Labour

North-South Trade in Services – Some Empirical Evidence, Rolf J. Langhammer
Discussant: J. Michael Finger

J. C. B. Mohr (Paul Siebeck) Tübingen
Postfach 20 40, D-7400 Tübingen

ACKNOWLEDGMENTS

Supporting Subscribers

PITTSBURGH NATIONAL BANK

SECURITY PACIFIC NATIONAL BANK

STATE SAVINGS CO.

Referees

Richard K. Abrams
F. Charles Adams
Richard G. Anderson
Michael Artis
David A. Aschauer
Robert D. Auberbach
Leonardo Auernheimer
James Barth
Michael T. Belongia
Arthur Benavie
Gerald O. Bierwag
Harold J. Black
Keith Blackburn
John F. Boschen
John H. Boyd
Philip L. Brock
John B. Burbidge
Tim S. Campbell
John A. Carlson
Binky Chadha
Jeffrey A. Clark
John H. Cochrane
Michael B. Connolly
J. S. Cramer
David Currie
Betty C. Daniel
Asli Demirguc-Kunt
Mark Denbaly
Michael Dotsey
John Driffill
Donald Dutknowky
Andrew J. Economopoulos
Robert A. Eisenbeis
Charles M. Engel
Paul D. Evans
Ray C. Fair
Roger E. A. Farmer
Alexander J. Field
Joel Fried
Richard Froyen
Maxwell J. Fry
William T. Gavin
Linda S. Goldberg
Marvin Goodfrind
Gikas A. Hardouvelis
Richard Hartman
Richard J. Herring
James D. Hess
Robert L. Hetzel
Arthur J. Hosios
Roger D. Huang
Steven Husted
James M. Johannes
Kent P. Kimbrough
Allan W. Kleidon
Kees Koedijk
Randall S. Kroszner
Finn E. Kydland
Paul A. Leonard
Deborah J. Lucas
W. Douglas McMillin
Michael T. Melvin
Loretta J. Mester
Stephen M. Miller
Gene Mumy
James M. O'Brien
Gerald P. O'Driscoll
Dale K. Osborne
Douglas Pearce
George C. Pennacchi
Edmund S. Phelps
Paul J. Pieper
Annette Poulsen
David H. Pyle
Leslie A. Robb
Richard Roll
Julio J. Rotemberg
Donald E. Schlagenhauf
Sherrill Sheffer
Thomas D. Simpson
Joseph F. Sinkey, Jr.
Michael Smirlock
Chester Spatt
Sanjay Srivastava
James H. Stock
Alan C. Stockman
John A. Tatom
Anjan V. Thakor
Charles Trzcinka
Christopher Waller
Carl E. Walsh
Kenneth D. West
John Williamson
Stephen D. Williamson
David F. Winter
Geoffrey Woglom

Ohio State
University Press

ISSN 0022-2879

BOOK REVIEWS

(continued from front cover)

Toward of World of Economic Stability: Optimal Monetary Framework and Policy, edited by Yoshio Suzuki and Mitsuaki Okabe — *Reviewed by Michael M. Hutchison*

Money, Interest, and Banking in Economic Development by Maxwell Fry — *Reviewed by Wassim Shahin*

JOURNAL OF MONEY, CREDIT AND BANKING

May 1990

ARTICLES

Money Supply Announcements and the Market's Perception of Federal Reserve Policy *Steven Strongin and Vefa Tarhan*

Money Supply Announcements and Market Reactions in an Open Economy *Richard Deaves*

Inflation and Reputation with Generic Policy Preferences *Herschel I. Grossman*

Loan Commitments and Optimal Monetary Policy *John V. Duca and David VanHoose*

Foreign Inflation Transmission under Flexible Exchange Rates and Currency Substitution *John H. Rogers*

The International Debt Crisis, Investor Contagion, and Bank Security Returns in 1987 *James J. Musumeci and Joseph F. Sinkey, Jr.*

The Effect of State Foreclosure Laws on Loan Losses *Terrence M. Clauretie and Thomas Herzog*

Savings, Commodity Market Rationing, and the Real Rate of Interest in China *Andrew Feltenstein, David Lebow, and S. van Wijnbergen*

NOTES, COMMENTS, REPLIES

Do Liquidity Constraints Vary over Time? *A Note by Gary S. Fissel and Tullio Jappelli*

The Effect of Import Price Changes on Domestic Inflation *A Note by Farhad Rassekh and Barry Wilbratte*

(continued on back cover)

JOURNAL OF MONEY, CREDIT AND BANKING

Manuscripts should be submitted in triplicate to the Editors, *Journal of Money, Credit, and Banking*, Department of Economics, Ohio State University, 1945 North High Street, Columbus, Ohio 43210–1172. Carolyn South, Secretary to the Editors. Submission fee: individual subscribers U.S. $30; nonsubscribers U.S. $40. Checks are to be made payable to THE OHIO STATE UNIVERSITY –JMCB and enclosed with submitted manuscripts. Instructions for preparing text and illustrations appear in the February issue.

JOURNAL OF MONEY, CREDIT AND BANKING

VOLUME 22 NUMBER 2 MAY 1990

ARTICLES

Money Supply Announcements and the Market's Perception of Federal Reserve Policy *Steven Strongin and Vefa Tarhan* 135

Money Supply Announcements and Market Reactions in an Open Economy *Richard Deaves* 154

Inflation and Reputation with Generic Policy Preferences *Herschel I. Grossman* 165

Loan Commitments and Optimal Monetary Policy *John V. Duca and David VanHoose* 178

Foreign Inflation Transmission under Flexible Exchange Rates and Currency Substitution *John H. Rogers* 195

The International Debt Crisis, Investor Contagion, and Bank Security Returns in 1987: The Brazilian Experience *James J. Musumeci and Joseph F. Sinkey, Jr.* 209

The Effect of State Foreclosure Laws on Loan Losses: Evidence from the Mortgage Insurance Industry *Terrence M. Clauretie and Thomas Herzog* 221

Savings, Commodity Market Rationing, and the Real Rate of Interest in China *Andrew Feltenstein, David Lebow, and S. van Wijnbergen* 234

NOTES, COMMENTS, REPLIES

Do Liquidity Constraints Vary over Time? Evidence from Survey and Panel Data *A Note by Gary S. Fissel and Tullio Jappelli* 253

The Effect of Import Price Changes on Domestic Inflation: An Empirical Test of the Ratchet Effect *A Note by Farhad Rassekh and Barry Wilbratte* 263

BOOK REVIEWS

Day of Reckoning, by Benjamin M. Friedman
Reviewed by John A. Tatom 268

JOURNAL OF MONEY, CREDIT, AND BANKING (ISSN 0022-2879). Published quarterly in February, May, August, and November by the Ohio State University Press, 1070 Carmack Road, Columbus, Ohio 43210. Margaret Starbuck, Managing Editor; Peg Carr, Production Editor; Tom Kangas, Subscriptions Manager. Second-class postage paid at Columbus, Ohio, and at additional mailing offices. *Postmaster:* Send address to: *Journal of Money, Credit, and Banking*, Ohio State University Press, 1070 Carmack Road, Columbus, Ohio 43210.

SUBSCRIPTIONS. Individual: U.S. $27.50 per year; library: U.S. $45; student: U.S. $20.00; additional subscriptions to the same address: U.S. $20.00 per subscription. Postage outside the United States: add $5.00 per year. Sponsoring Subscriptions: U.S. $1000 per year. Sustaining Subscriptions: U.S. $500 per year. Supporting Subscriptions: U.S. $100 per year. Claims for missing issues must be made within four months of the date of publication. Allow six weeks for address change. Checks should be made payable to the Ohio State University Press, 1070 Carmack Road, Columbus, Ohio 43210.

BACK ISSUES, REPRINTS, AND MICROFILM. Most back issues from 1983 to the present are available from the Ohio State University press. Microfilms of back volumes and reprints of articles may be obtained from University Microfilms International, 300 North Zeeb Road, Ann Arbor, Michigan 48106. Back volumes from 1969 through 1982 in reprint edition may be obtained from Schmidt Periodicals GmbH, Dettendorf, D-8201 Bad Feilnbach 2, West Germany.

STEVEN STRONGIN
VEFA TARHAN

Money Supply Announcements and the Market's Perception of Federal Reserve Policy

IN THIS PAPER WE EXAMINE the unsettled question of why interest rates rose in response to positive innovations in the money supply during the early and mid-1980s.[1] Two major hypotheses have been advanced in the literature.[2] The liquidity premium hypothesis holds that the market expects that the

[1]In recent years, the effect of money supply announcements on interest rates has been studied extensively (Cornell 1979, 1983, Urich and Wachtel 1981, 1984, Roley 1983, Grossman 1981). The impact of unanticipated movements in money on stock returns (Pearce and Roley 1983, 1985 and Lynge 1981) and on foreign exchange rates has also been investigated (Hardouvelis 1984, Cornell 1982, Engel and Frankel 1984). Generally, these studies find that the anticipated component of money supply announcements has no effect on capital market prices. On the other hand, unanticipated changes in money generate an interest-rate response in the same direction that is both significant and prompt. Both short- and long-term interest rates are affected. These studies also find that the impact of announcement shocks on market rates became more pronounced following the Federal Reserve's decision in October 1979 to switch to an operating procedure that targeted nonborrowed reserves, and then declined again following the policy to deemphasize M1 in October 1982.

[2]Additionally, signaling models have been advanced in the literature to explain the reaction of interest rates to money announcement surprises. For example, see Cornell (1983), Siegel (1985) and Nicholas, Small, and Webster (1983). In Cornell's case, money surprises are a signal about future real activity. In Siegel's model, the announced money supply reveals information about both the current and future states of real economic activity. The response of interest rates depends upon the variance-covariance matrix of real output, interest rates, and money. Nicholas, Small, and Webster argue that when announced money exceeds expectations, this is a signal that future money demand will be

Vefa Tarhan received partial financial support for this paper from the James S. Kemper Foundation. The authors thank David Aschauer, Paul Spindt, three anonymous referees of this journal, and the participants of the quantitative methods workshop at the Board of Governors of the Federal Reserve System and the University of Michigan economics department seminar series. Eric Klusman and Don Wilson provided excellent research assistance.

STEVEN STRONGIN *is senior economist and assistant vice president, Federal Reserve Bank of Chicago.* VEFA TARHAN *is associate professor of finance, J. L. Kellogg Graduate School of Management, Northwestern University, on leave from Loyola University of Chicago.*

Journal of Money, Credit, and Banking, Vol. 22, No. 2 (May 1990)

Federal Reserve will respond to a positive innovation in the money supply by raising reserve pressures and thereby raising interest rates. The alternative hypothesis, the expected inflation hypothesis, holds that the market expects that the Federal Reserve will accommodate the excess money growth and this in turn will raise the market's expectations of future inflation, again raising interest rates. The two hypotheses have opposite assumptions about Federal Reserve behavior, yet have identical implications for nominal interest rates.

Previous studies attempted to distinguish between the two hypotheses by examining the market's perceptions of how the Fed intends to respond to money surprises in indirect ways (for example, by examining the reaction of exchange rates).[3] These techniques suffered from two major drawbacks. First, since the tests were indirect they could at best provide inferential evidence. Second and more important, they implicitly held both Federal Reserve policy and the market's perceptions of that policy constant, subjecting the models to potential parameter biases and instabilities of the sort outlined in Lucas's econometric critique (1976). Empirically, such parameter instability has been found to be large by Loeys (1985). We intend to show that we can both directly distinguish between the expected liquidity and expected inflation hypotheses and explain previously observed parameter instability, by developing a model which directly accounts for the market's current perceptions of Federal Reserve policy stances.

Using Irving Fisher's separation of nominal interest rates into two components, the real part and the inflation premium, we can gain some further understanding of the liquidity premium and expected inflation hypotheses. Liquidity premium hypothesis assumes that the Fed will attempt to offset unexpected

---

higher. This being the case, they argue that interest rates will rise in response, if investors believe that the shock to money demand will dissipate more slowly than the equally large shock to money supply.

Cornell (1983) proposes another channel through which money surprises may cause interest rates to change. He argues that innovations in money announcements may influence nominal interest rates by affecting the aggregate level of risk aversion.

The goal of this paper is to discriminate empirically between the liquidity premium and expected inflation hypotheses. Our model in its present form does not enable us to assess the empirical content of the signaling and risk premium hypotheses.

[3]Attempts have been made in the literature to discriminate between these two hypotheses on empirical and theoretical grounds. Engel and Frankel (1984), for example, study the response of exchange rates to money announcements. They suggest that the spot value of the dollar (vis-á-vis the German mark in their study) would increase when money exceeds expectations if the expected liquidity hypothesis is correct, and decline if the inflation premium hypothesis holds. The empirical results presented in their study support the expected liquidity hypothesis. Cornell (1982) also comes to the same conclusion on the basis of examination of the exchange rates between the dollar and five other currencies. However, Cornell in another paper (1983) argues that the strong reaction of long term bond rates to money announcements is compatible with the inflation premium hypothesis.

Cornell (1983) carefully lays out and tests the implications of the expected liquidity and the inflation premium hypothesis, as well as the risk premium and signaling models. While he does find that money supply announcements have an impact on the real rate, he concludes that no single hypothesis fully explains the data.

Hardouvelis (1984) extends the previous empirical work by using forward exchange rates and also by examining the response of expected future exchange rates and foreign interest rates. Like Cornell, he concludes that, taken in isolation, neither of the two hypothesis is consistent with the data. He instead offers an alternative hypothesis which combines the two hypotheses in question. He argues that his results are compatible with a scenario where both the expected liquidity and inflation premium effects are present.

money growth by restraining the availability of credit. Thus, if the Federal Reserve is attempting to constrain money growth to a predetermined path, then a positive innovation in the money supply will force the Federal Reserve to increase reserve pressures. The increase in reserve pressures reduces the current supply of credit and thus raises its real price.

The expected inflation hypothesis, on the other hand, works through the inflation part of the interest rate. If the Federal Reserve is unwilling to increase reserve pressures enough to return monetary growth to its original path, then an increase at some point in the future in the rate of inflation is the inevitable result. This increase in the rate of inflation, while having no immediate effect on the supply of credit, raises the inflation premium that investors require. However, since the market does not distinguish which part of the interest rate becomes higher, in both cases all we observe is a higher nominal interest rate.

Most of the early attempts to distinguish directly between the two hypotheses did not yield clear-cut results because the hypotheses are not mutually exclusive. For example, it was argued that since the liquidity effect is immediate and temporary and the expected inflation effect should affect only the future, all that was necessary to determine which hypothesis was correct was to examine which parts of the term structure were affected. But, while the early part of the yield curve was affected the most, buttressing the case for the liquidity hypothesis, the effects lasted far too long into the yield curve to be explained solely by short-term liquidity considerations. This paradox can be easily explained if the Federal Reserve is allowed to *partially* offset innovations in the money supply, allowing both effects some play.

The key to quantifying the dual operation of these hypotheses is the observation that the liquidity effect should be greater the more the market is convinced that the Federal Reserve is attempting to constrain the growth of the money supply, while the inflation effect is reduced by such beliefs. Thus, by correlating the market's perception of the tightness of the Federal Reserve's policy stance with the size of the interest rate response to money supply innovations, we can determine which of the two hypotheses dominates and also examine if that dominance changes with the term of the asset.[4]

Intrinsic to this way of looking at the problem is the idea that money supply innovations affect interest rates by varying amounts over time. As mentioned earlier, parameter instability has been found empirically. If this instability is a natural part of the economic relationship, much of the previous empirical work on this topic must be reconsidered. This need to formally consider changes in the posture of monetary policy is not surprising as both of the major hypotheses rely primarily on the effects of anticipated Federal Reserve policy. Unless the Federal

[4]It is conceivable that both effects are present simultaneously. Some plausable scenarios where both factors may be present simultaneously are discussed below. Since the two hypotheses imply opposite signs for the d coefficient, in our model the term "dominance" is used simply to refer to the fact that, if both effects are present, the sign of the estimated d coefficient can be interpreted to mean that one effect outweighs the other.

Reserve's policy and consequently the market's perception of the Federal Reserve's short-run policy stance were nearly constant throughout the sample period, a model that ignores changes in policy may not be able to cope with the phenomenon. In light of Lucas (1976), models that are designed to explain market responses in the context of changing monetary policy actions, need to formally take into account shifts in expected monetary policy of those changes.

Section 1 describes a model that allows the magnitude of the interest rate response to innovations in the money supply to vary according to the market's perception of the contemporaneous Federal Reserve policy stance. Section 2 discusses the data used in the estimation of the models. Section 3 presents the empirical results. Finally, section 4 summarizes our conclusions.

1. THE MODEL

The usual model in the literature is

$$di_t = a + bM_t^u + e_t \tag{1}$$

where di_t is the change in the interest rate and M_t^u is the innovation in the money supply. The estimates of (1) reported in the literature indicate that b is positive. It can be argued that, by viewing b as constant even though there were significant changes in the manner monetary policy was conducted, previous studies have suffered from a misspecification problem. In this study we argue that b must be viewed as a function of the market's perception of how tight the contemporaneous Federal Reserve short-run policy stance is. We write this:

$$b_t = c + dT_t \tag{2}$$

where T_t is a measure of the market's perception of Federal Reserve policy tightness.[5] We claim that on the basis of the sign of the d coefficient in (2), it is possible to differentiate empirically between the two hypotheses. To see this, assume announced money exceeds expectations. It has been established that this triggers an increase in interest rates. If the liquidity premium hypothesis is correct (that is, if it is true that interest rates rise because the Fed is expected to offset the innovation), it should be the case that the tighter is the perception of monetary policy (high values for T_t), the stronger should be the reaction of investors (the larger the magnitude of the interest rate increase). This means that a positive sign for d supports the liquidity premium hypothesis. A negative sign for d, on the other hand, will be consistent with the expected inflation hypothesis. Assume again that announced money exceeds expected money. If interest rate increases that

[5]The market's perception of "tightness" refers to how the market participants view the current short-run Federal Reserve monetary stance conditional on their current information set—in other words, given the prevailing conditions in the economy (GNP growth, the unemployment level, the inflation rate, etc.), the degree of monetary restraint they think the Fed intends to follow.

accompany this event are driven by inflationary considerations, it should be the case that when the Fed policy is perceived to be accommodative (low values for T_t), the market's reaction should be stronger than when the monetary policy is considered to be tight. Such an inverse relationship between the degree of the market's reaction (size of b_t) and perceived tightness (size of T_t) implies that a negative estimate for the d coefficient will support the expected inflation hypothesis.

Substitution of equation (2) into (1) yields

$$di_t = a + cM_t^u + dT_tM_t^u + e_t \; . \tag{3}$$

The primary problem in estimating equation (3) is finding a good proxy for T_t. Ideally the measure used should be available on a weekly basis and relfect the market's perception of how the Fed will respond to a given innovation in money. For our sample period, there is strong evidence indicating that the market participants used net borrowed reserves as the measure of monetary policy tightness. For example, one Fed watcher notes,

> [U]nder the operating procedures in effect, with modifications, since late 1979, the key link between the Fed and the federal funds rate is the amount of reserves that the banks must borrow from the Fed's discount window. Consequently, the best single indicator of the degree of pressure the Fed is putting on the reserves market is the amount of borrowed reserves. . . . [The net borrowed reserves] is simply borrowed reserves minus excess reserves. Since the level of excess reserves is typically relatively modest, looking at one is often just as good as looking at the other. . . . Nevertheless, (net) borrowed reserves is usually the best indicator of the degree of pressure that the Fed is putting on the reserves market.[6]

Investors' reliance on net borrowed reserves as an indicator of monetary policy appears to be justified. During the sample period lagged reserve accounting (LRA) was in effect. LRA has the interesting property that it cleanly separates supply and demand shocks in the reserve market. The demand for reserves is set two weeks before the reserves are actually held. Thus, changes in the borrowed-non-borrowed reserve mix (that is, reserve pressures) that occur can be attributed almost in their entirety to Federal Reserve actions.[7] The only exception to this is excess reserve demand. However, since this is both small and usually fully accommodated by the Federal Reserve, it can be subtracted from borrowings. Net borrowed reserves obtained in this manner performs well as a tightness measure since the level of net borrowed reserves is simply the arithmetic difference between the amount of reserves banks need to have to satisfy their reserve requirements and the amount which the Fed is willing to supply.

While it appears that the actual level of net borrowed reserves is a good proxy

[6]See Melton 1985, pp. 129–30. Spindt and Tarhan (1987) develop an algorithm for the manner in which operating procedures were conducted in the post-1979 period.

[7]Note that monetary policy that relied on free reserves was criticized in the 1960s for its indeterminancy. However, during this period contemporaneous reserves accounting was in effect. Under this reserve accounting regime, it is difficult to sort out the demand and supply shocks in the reserves market.

for the degree of tightness in monetary policy and was used as such by investors, what is needed for our model is the market's *perception* of tightness. For this we used a survey of expected net borrowed reserves that money market services conducted on a weekly basis. Thus, the model we estimate becomes[8]

$$di_t = a + cM_t^u + dB_t^e M_t^u + e_t \tag{4}$$

where B_t^e is expected net borrowed reserves, and e_t is the estimation error.

2. THE DATA

The sample period for this study is May 2, 1980, to January 6, 1984. The eleven interest rates used are the Federal funds rate, the rates on Treasury bills of three-, six-, and twelve-month maturities, and constant maturity security rates (1, 3, 5, 7, 10, 20, and 30 years). Summary statistics on the variables used in this study are provided in Table 1.

Surveys of money supply and net borrowed reserves expectations are obtained from the Money Market Services.[9] Both were conducted on Tuesdays and measured fifty to sixty market participants' responses. The "money supply survey" solicited participants' estimates of the change in M1 from one week to the following week to be announced on the coming Friday.[10]

Note that the actual M1 change took place during the statement week that ended nine days prior to an announcement (see Figure 1). Also, market participants already had information about the actual level of the reserves for the statement week in question. The major source of the uncertainty about the money figure to be announced was that the market did not know how the Fed's actions (supply of reserves) and the activities of the public (currency and the type of deposits the public chose to hold) interacted to create the equilibrium level of M1.

In the "net borrowed reserves survey" the survey participants were asked each Tuesday to estimate what the Fed's net borrowed reserves target for the current statement week, ending the next day (Wednesday), was going to be (see Figure 1). Net borrowed reserves is defined as adjusted borrowings minus excess reserves (where adjusted borrowing is defined as total borrowings minus extended credit).

[8]Tests were performed to determine if a nonlinear specification might have been more appropriate. However, polynomial and other standard transforms did not provide any additional explanatory power. Additionally, the expected Fed funds rates was used as a proxy variable for monetary policy tightness. Our results indicated that the funds rate was not a good indicator of degree of tightness in monetary policy. We estimate our model for a sample period that starts on May 2, 1980, because our data on net borrowed reserves survey start on this date.

[9]We would like to thank Raul Nicho and Kim Rupert of the Money Market services for making the data available to us.

[10]Money announcements were made on Thursdays prior to February 8, 1980. Since February 16, 1984, the announcement day has been switched back to Thursdays. During the sample period, the announcement days did not always fall on a Friday due to holidays. To measure the response of interest rates over a consistent length of time, all non-Friday announcement dates were deleted from the sample, a loss of seventeen observations.

TABLE 1

SUMMARY STATISTICS ON SELECTED VARIABLES

	Mean	Standard Deviation	Minimum Value	Maximum Value	Standard Error of Mean
B^A	466.14	578.04	−456	2,276	43.82
B^E	504.98	527.79	−300	2,000	40.012
M^A	0.71	2.88	−5.9	11.4	0.21
M^E	0.34	1.57	−4.2	6.8	0.11
FF	0.037	0.047	−1.86	1.48	0.036
*TB*3	0.049	0.31	−0.94	1.34	0.023
*TB*6	0.057	0.29	−0.78	1.17	0.022
*TB*12	0.029	0.23	−0.61	0.88	0.018
*CM*1	0.036	0.29	−0.77	1.1	0.022
*CM*3	0.026	0.22	−0.77	0.83	0.017
*CM*5	0.029	0.20	−0.68	0.72	0.015
*CM*7	0.030	0.18	−0.58	0.58	0.014
*CM*10	0.027	0.16	−0.55	0.50	0.013
*CM*20	0.023	0.16	−0.45	0.49	0.012
*CM*30	−0.024	0.15	−0.47	−0.47	0.012

B^A = Actual net borrowed reserves
B^E = Expected net borrowed reserves
M^A = Actual (announced) money
M^E = Expected money
*CM*1, *CM*3, *CM*5, *CM*7, *CM*10, *CM*20, *CM*30 = constant maturity bond rates of 1, 3, 5, 7, 10, 20, 30 years (all Friday to Monday closings).
*TB*3, *TB*6, *TB*12 = Returns on T-bill rates of 3 months, 6 months and 12 months. All Friday to Monday closings.
FF = Fed funds rate (all Friday to Monday closings).

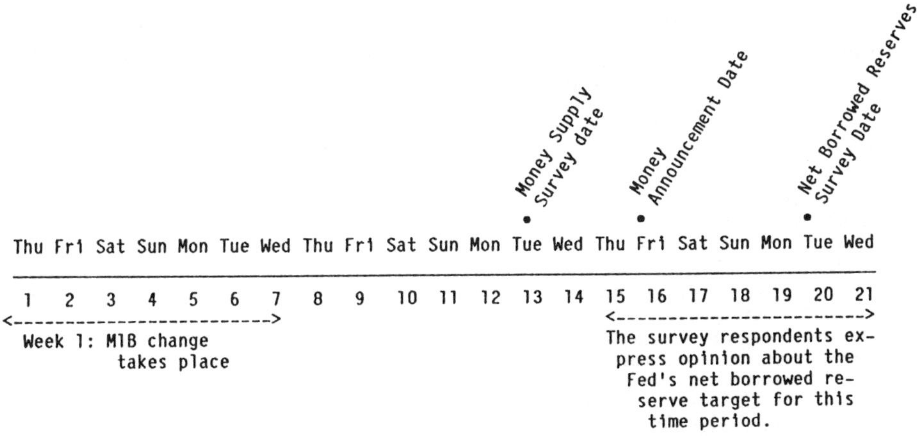

FIG. 1. Time Line for Money Supply and Net Borrowed Reserves Target Surveys

Thus, net borrowed reserves is the negative of free reserves. As discussed above, higher values for this variable indicate monetary tightness.

As shown in Figure 1, survey participants reveal their expectations on Tuesday, day 13, about the money supply for the statement week that ended six days before, that is, days 1–7.[11,12] On Friday, day 16, the actual money supply for the week that ended on the 7th is announced. The market's policy expectations regarding the Fed's net borrowed reserves target for the statement week covering days 15–21 are expressed on the Tuesday following the announcement (day 20). The announcement surprise is discovered on Friday (day 16). In this study the market's response is measured on the following Monday.[13] On Tuesday, day 20, the market participants are asked to express their views on the Fed's target net borrowed reserves figure for days 15–21. They already know the extent of money deviation, and have responded to it on Monday on the basis of what they think the Fed will do (they have watched the Fed on Thursday, Friday, and Monday). Thus, on that Tuesday they reveal their beliefs about how the Fed decided to respond to the money shock.[14]

The net borrowed reserves survey data were examined for unbiasedness, efficiency, and forecast performance.[15] The results of these tests are summarized in Table 2.[16]

To test for unbiasedness, the following equation is estimated.

$$B_t^A = a_0 + a_1 B_t^E + e_t \tag{5}$$

where B_t^A is the actual net borrowed reserves.

The survey data is considered to be unbiased if $a_0 = 0$ and $a_1 = 1$. The test results indicate that unbiasedness cannot be rejected at the 10 percent level of significance.

The efficiency test considered is based on the premise that if the actual data on net borrowed reserves are generated by an autoregressive process, the market's expectation should conform with the same process. This implies that the lagged values of the actual data should turn out to be insignificant as explanatory variables in an equation where the dependent variable measures the forecast errors.

[11]On the same day, they also express their opinions regarding the expected net borrowed reserves for the statement week covering days 8–14. This, however, is not marked on the diagram so as not to cause confusion. The relevant net borrowed reserves survey for our purposes is the one that takes place on Tuesday the 20th.

[12]Only the median value of the survey is made public. The subscribers get information on the distribution of responses.

[13]In some studies the market response is measured from 3:30 to 5:00 P.M. on the day of the announcement. Other studies measure the response over close of business on announcement day and the opening rates the following day. In this study we measure the responses over closing rates on announcement dates and the closing rates the following business day.

[14]A referee pointed out the possibility that Tuesday's survey responses may be affected by Monday's interest rates. This has the potential to generate an inconsistent estimator problem. We believe that relying on a survey that is conducted on the Tuesday following the money supply innovation enables us to use the most up-to-date market assessment of expected Fed behavior. However, reestimating the model with previous Tuesday's survey data produced essentially identical results. This indicates that information biases introduced by the timing of the survey are small.

[15]Grossman (1981) and Pearce and Roley (1983) conduct these tests for the survey data on expected money. Their results show that the money survey data passes the tests of unbiasedness and efficiency and has lower RMSE compared with an autoregressive model of actual money.

[16]Note that the survey data reveal the investors' perception of the expected Fed policy. Thus all tests conducted are joint tests of unbiasedness, efficiency, etc., and also the hypothesis that the Fed is able to achieve its net borrowed reserves objectives.

TABLE 2

TESTS ON NET BORROWED RESERVES TARGET SURVEY DATA

Unbiasedness: $B_t^A = a_0 + a_1 B_t^E + U_t$

a_0	a_1	R^2 (Summary Statistics)	D-W (Summary Statistics)	$H_0: a_0 = 0\ a_1 = 1$	
−12.35	0.94	0.75	2.14	$F(2,172)$	Prob > F
(−0.4)	(22.6)			2.33	0.09

Efficiency: $B_t^A - B_t^E = b_0 + b_1 B_{t-1}^A + b_2 B_{t-2}^A + b_3 B_{t-3}^A + b_4 B_{t-4}^A + U_t$

b_0	b_1	b_2	b_3	b_4	R^2 (Summary Statistics)	D-W (Summary Statistics)	$H_0: b_0 = b_1 = b_2 = b_3 = b_4 = 0$	
6.4	−0.1	−0.05	−0.06	−0.0	0.05	1.91	$F(4.165)$	Prob>F
(0.2)	(−1.7)	(−0.97)	(1.09)	(0.1)			2.10	0.08

Survey Forecast Performance: $B_t^A = c_0 + c_1 B_{t-1}^A + c_2 B_{t-2}^A + c_3 B_{t-3}^A + c_4 B_{t-4}^A$

c_0	c_1	c_2	c_3	c_4	R^2 (Summary Statistics)	D-W (Summary Statistics)	Forecast RMSE	
63.2	0.33	0.21	0.19	0.09	0.53	1.97	Auto	Survey
(1.5)	(4.4)	(2.71)	(2.49)	(1.17)			391.46	291.19

NOTES: t-statistics are reported in parentheses.

B_t^A = actual net borrowed reserves.

B_t^E = market's perception of the Fed's net borrowed reserves target as indicated by the survey data.

R^2 = multiple correlation coefficient.

D-W = Durban Watson statistic.

Auto = the autoregressive model.

The results in Table 2 show that efficiency cannot be rejected at the 10 percent significance level.

The third test is concerned with the forecast performance of the survey data. In this test the forecast performance of the survey data is compared with that of a simple autoregressive model. As can be seen from Table 2, the root mean square error associated with the survey is lower than that of the simple autoregressive model.

3. EMPIRICAL RESULTS

Equation (4) was estimated for the eleven interest rates by the ordinary least squares procedure. The OLS estimates are reported in Table 3.[17] Additionally the

[17]The survey on money is conducted on Tuesdays but the money is announced on Fridays. Since expectations can change between Tuesday and Friday, the difference between the announced and expected money may not truly represent the "surprise." To overcome this potential problem, Roley (1983) suggests that changes in the Fed funds rate from Tuesday to Friday can be used as a proxy for the change in expectations. We estimated our model with this correction. The variable in question turned out to be insignificant. Additionally, it did not affect the relative sizes and significance of the estimates for the other variables.

TABLE 3

MARKET RESPONSE TO MONEY SUPPLY ANNOUNCEMENTS

$di_t = a + cM_t^U + d_1 \; M_t^U \times B_t^E, + e_t, \bar{b}_t = c + d_1 \; \bar{B}_t^E$

Dependent Variable	a $\times 10^2$	c $\times 10^2$	d $\times 10^5$	$\bar{b}_t$ $\times 10^2$	D-W	R^2	F-Test†
FF	2.38	4.37	−.25	4.1	2.7	0.041	1.48
	(0.7)*	(1.9)*	(−.08)*				(0.32)**
*TB*3	4.15	2.37	5.90	22.0	1.7	0.221	0.57
	(1.9)	(1.7)	(3.3)				(.64)
*TB*6	4.7	3.17	4.43	22.2	2.0	0.222	0.92
	(2.3)	(2.4)	(2.6)				(.43)
*TB*12	2.03	2.87	3.27	23.1	2.0	0.221	0.80
	(1.2)	(2.8)	(2.4)				(.49)
*CM*1	2.49	3.49	4.19	23.8	2.0	0.238	0.69
	(1.3)	(2.7)	(2.5)				(.56)
*CM*3	1.73	2.91	2.74	23.5	2.0	0.235	0.63
	(1.2)	(3.0)	(2.2)				(.60)
*CM*5	2.14	2.57	2.03	20.0	2.1	0.201	0.85
	(1.6)	(2.9)	(1.7)				(.46)
*CM*7	2.30	2.4	1.55	18.3	2.1	0.183	0.75
	(1.8)	(3.0)	(1.5)				(.53)
*CM*10	2.15	1.75	1.43	13.6	2.0	0.136	0.37
	(1.8)	(2.3)	(1.4)				(.46)
*CM*20	1.88	1.39	1.24	9.5	2.0	0.096	0.98
	(1.6)	(1.8)	(1.24)				(.40)
*CM*30	2.01	1.34	1.36	10.2	2.0	0.102	1.19
	(1.7)	(1.7)	(1.39)				(0.3)

NOTES: B_t^E = expected net borrowed reserves. M_t^u = unanticipated money.

FF = Fed funds rate. *TB*3 = 3-month T-bill rate, *TB*6 = 6-month T-bill rate, *TB*12 = one-year T-bill rate, *CM*1 to *CM*30 are one-year constant maturity rate to thirty-year constant maturity Treasury bond rates.

† = F-test is a chow test for stability of parameters with October 1982 as the sample split date.

* = t-statistics.

** = p values.

equations were estimated using an autoregressive procedure and checked for heteroskedasticity. The results indicated that no corrections were necessary and therefore we do not report those regressions.

It appears that interest rates of all maturities respond significantly to money announcement surprises. In all cases the c coefficient has the expected positive sign. In general, the size of the response declines as maturity increases. This result is along the same lines as those reported in the literature.[18]

As can be seen from Table 3, the sign of the d coefficient is positive across the maturity spectrum, supporting the liquidity premium hypothesis. What is more, ignoring the Fed funds equation for the moment, the coefficient in question declines both in magnitude and in statistical significance as maturity increases.[19] This implies that the expected liquidity effect is the dominant factor in the response of the short-term rates (up to three years). Its influence declines beyond

[18]For example, Cornell (1983) finds that the magnitude of the Fed funds rate response is the largest and is about three times the response shown by the thirty-year bond rate.

[19]The decline in the size of the coefficients is not monotonic. In fact, the estimated coefficient for the one-year bond exceeds that of the twelve-month bills. This, however, is not unexpected since bonds pay coupons and have lower effective maturities relative to bills, and bills are quoted on a discount basis.

three years. The fact that the estimates of this coefficient are statistically significant only in the equations for short-term interest rates is additional evidence in favor of the liquidity premium hypothesis. If interest rates are responding to money surprises because of expected liquidity considerations (and not due to changes in inflationary expectations), the response should by and large be confined to the shorter end of the maturity spectrum.

While the empirical evidence presented in Table 3 shows the existence of strong expected liquidity effects for maturities up to three years, it also appears that changes in inflationary expectations play at least a minor role in the response of longer-term interest rates. Since the expected sign for d is negative for the expected inflation, but positive for the liquidity premium hypothesis, the positive sign of the estimated d coefficient is consistent with a scenario where both effects are present, but the liquidity effect dominates inflation considerations. It is conceivable that, as the term to maturity increases, the importance of liquidity effects declines relative to expected inflation effects, with neither dominating.

There are a number of possible explanations of this. If a classical view of monetary policy is assumed, then the liquidity effects would decline through time and the inflationary effects grow. This is because, while the Federal Reserve may be able to raise real rates temporarily by reducing the rate of monetary growth, such effects dissipate as time passes. If the reduction in the rate of monetary growth is not all the way back to previous money growth expectations, inflation will rise. In this case, liquidity effects predominate in the early part of the term structure, but, depending on the extent to which money growth is allowed to stay above previous expectations, inflation effects will be relatively stronger on the longer end of the term structure.

An equivalent explanation of the behavior of the coefficient across the maturity spectrum follows from a belief that the Federal Reserve will tighten for some period of time, but will ease policy at some point in the future. This is also a mixed hypothesis, but the mix occurs across time, rather than at a point in time.

One puzzle that needs to be addressed is that the estimate for the d coefficient in the Federal funds rate equation is insignificant. It might be argued that the expected liquidity effect should be largest in this equation because the underlying instrument has the shortest maturity. Urich and Wachtel (1984), for instance, claim that the strong reaction of the funds rate to the money innovations is evidence supporting the expected liquidity hypothesis.[20] However, this is not necessarily the case. The increase in the funds rate, triggered by a positive innovation in money, does not necessarily mean the Fed intends to offset the innovation. The reason for this is related to the lagged reserve accounting. Under this regime, which was in effect during the sample period, the reserve requirements of banks are set two weeks before reserves are actually held. The money figure is announced with a nine-day lag, which means banks are already two days into the

[20]Hardouvelis (1984) makes a point in a footnote which is similar to Urich and Wachtel's argument. He claims that the strong reaction of the Fed funds rate under lagged reserve accounting regime supports the expected liquidity hypothesis.

reserve settlement period when the announcement is made. Prior to the money announcement, the banks' assessment of the banking system's reserve demand is determined on the basis of expected money. When actual money exceeds expectations, the banks' estimate of the system's demand for reserves must be revised upwards, since the demand for reserves will be higher than expected. This could cause the Fed funds rate to go up regardless of expected Federal Reserve policy. Further, since the Federal Reserve does not allow intertemporal arbitrages in the reserve market, future actions on the part of the Federal Reserve should not have any effect.[21]

To see that even under conditions of inflationary expectations, the Federal funds rate may go up, consider a positive innovation in money. Assume also that the Fed intends to accommodate this shock, and the market expects the Fed to behave in this manner. Even under these conditions, the funds rate will go up unless the injection of reserves by the Fed is both immediate and of such a magnitude that it completely offsets the excess demand for reserves. The funds rate may increase in spite of an accommodative policy environment since the banks operate under a constraint in which the reserve requirements need to be met in the current reserve week. Thus, the fact that the funds rate rises in reaction to positive innovations in money should not be considered evidence that the market expects the Fed to offset the innovations in money.

Based on our empirical results, in the Fed funds market the reserve demand implications of money shocks under lagged reserve accounting apparently dominate any expected liquidity or inflation premium considerations. This appears to be the primary reason for a positive and significant c and a small and insignificant d in the Fed funds rate equation.

Table 3 also includes the average response of interest rates to money announcements, calculated in the following manner:

$$\bar{b}_{it} = \hat{c}_i + \hat{d}_i \bar{B}^e \tag{6}$$

where $\hat{c}_i$ and $\hat{d}_i$ for each interest rate is obtained from the estimation of (3) and $\bar{B}^e$ is the average value of the expected net borrowed reserves for the sample period.

Figures 2 and 3 show the estimated response of each interest rate to money surprises over time. This response is calculated

$$\hat{b}_{it} = \hat{c}_j + \hat{d}_j B^e_t \tag{7}$$

where, as before, the slope and intercept coefficients are obtained from estimating (4) and B^e_t is the value of the market's weekly forecast of net borrowed reserves. The response of interest rates over time appears to be similar to those

[21] Under the lagged reserve accounting regime, a bank could carry forward a surplus or deficit up to 2 percent of its required reserves provided it does not carry forward deficits two weeks in a row. However, this in all likelihood did not change the intertemporally segmented nature of the market, since the size of the carryover provision is rather insignificant. See Spindt and Tarhan (1987) for the implications of the carryover provision in an intertemporal reserve arbitrage framework.

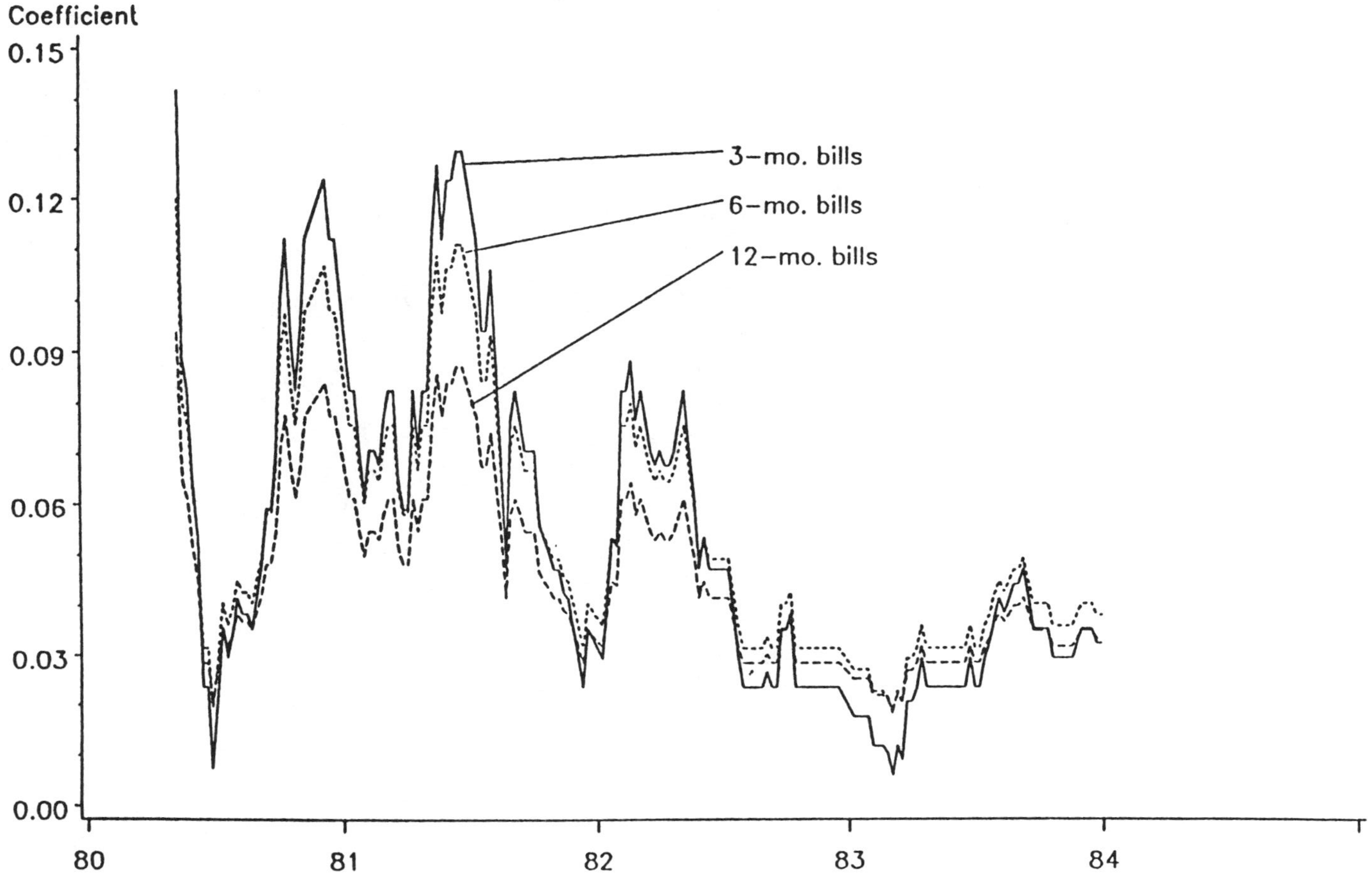

FIG. 2. The Value of b_t through Time: The Bills

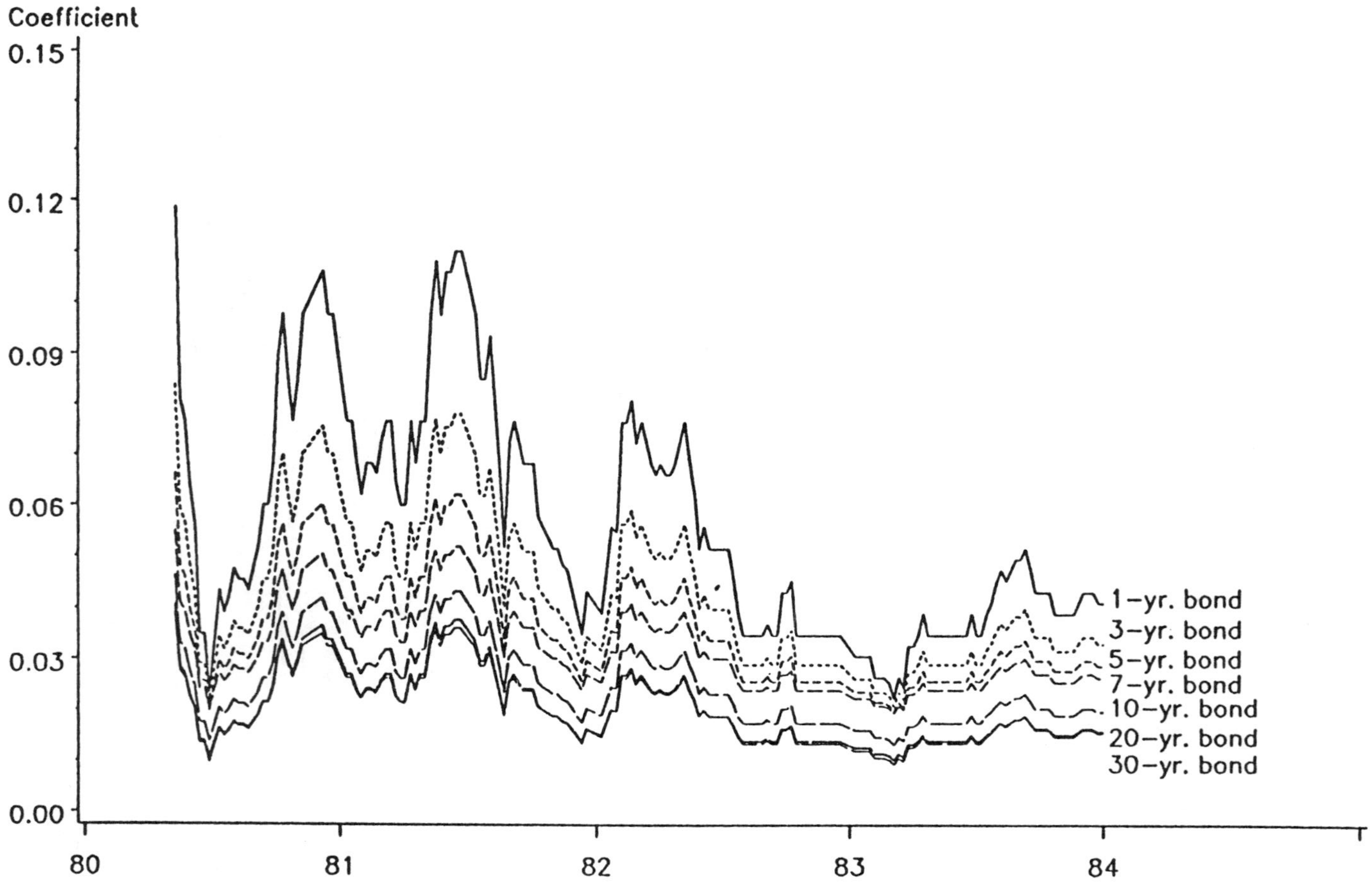

FIG. 3. The Value of b_t through Time: The Bonds

reported by Loeys (1986), who estimated the reaction of interest rates to money by "moving" regressions. The sample length in his regressions is fixed at one year, but each subsample moves over the six-year master sample at two-month intervals.

To better see the extent of the similarity, we duplicated his results for our sample period, using the rolling regression methodology he employed. We used forty-eight-week subsample periods in the rolling regression. Then, we constructed the time path of interest rate response coefficients from our model by

$$\hat{b}_{it} = \hat{c}_j + \hat{d}_j \bar{B}^e_t \quad (8)$$

where $\bar{B}^e_t$ is the expected net borrowed reserves averaged for each rolling regression subsample period. The time paths for the ninety-day Treasury bill rate response coefficients obtained from his model and our model are graphed together in Figure 4. The similarity between the two time paths, especially over the period when there is complete information on $\bar{B}^e_t$, is striking. Estimating (4) by use of a rolling regression methodology, and testing if the estimate for the parameter c (and d) is relatively constant throughout the sample period would show the extent to which our model explains the time variation found by Loeys.[22] To test

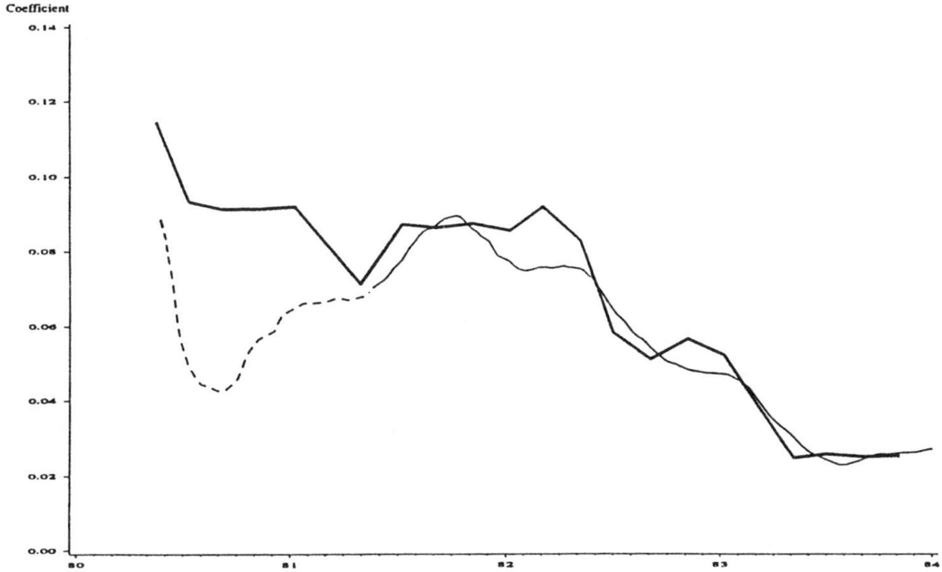

Thick line = Loeys' rolling regression coefficients.
Thin line = coefficients constructed from equation (8),
where dashes represent less than 48 lags of net borrowed reserves.

FIG. 4. Time Path of Interest Rate Response Coefficients (90-day treasury bill rate)

[22]We are indebted to an anonymous referee for his suggestion that we pursue just how much of the time variation documented by Loeys is captured by our model.

whether or not c varies over the sample period, we estimated the following equation:

$$d_{it} = a + cM_t^u + c'M_t^u I(s_j) + dM_t^u \bar{B}_t^e + d'M_t^u \bar{B}_t^e I(s_j) + e_t \qquad (9)$$

where $I(s_j)$ is an indicator function which takes on a value of 1 for each subsample period, and zero otherwise. The level of significance on $\hat{c}_j$ tests whether or not the coefficient in each subsample period differs compared with the rest of the sample period. Figure 5 plots the values associated with $\hat{c}_j$. In our sample period there are twenty-two subsample periods. As can be seen from Figure 5, we are unable to reject the null hypothesis of constancy in any of the cases.

The t values associated with d_j are plotted in Figure 6, and again constancy cannot be rejected in any of the cases. Thus $\hat{c}$ and $\hat{d}$ individually do not have time-varying character that Loeys found.

As an additional point of interest, while our sample period does not include the October 1979 period, it does cover fall 1982 when the Fed made a major policy change by deemphasizing M1. Both Figures 2 and 3 show that this was a critical period, in that the reaction of interest rates shows a marked difference after fall 1982. However, when the parameter stability tests are done by splitting the sample period at October 1982, we find no evidence of structural instability in our

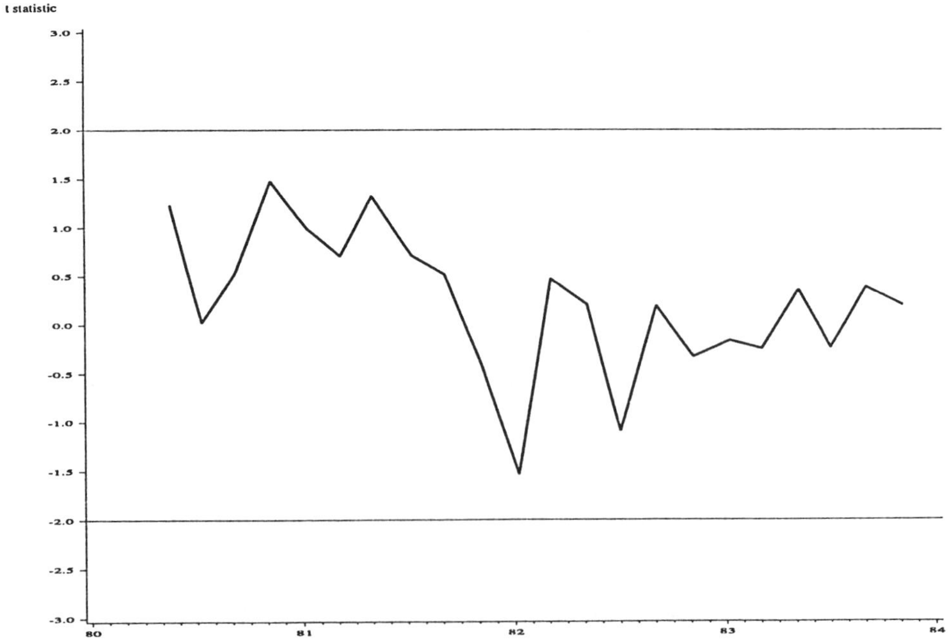

FIG. 5. t-Statistics for Estimates of c across Rolling Regression Subsample Periods (90-day treasury bill rate)

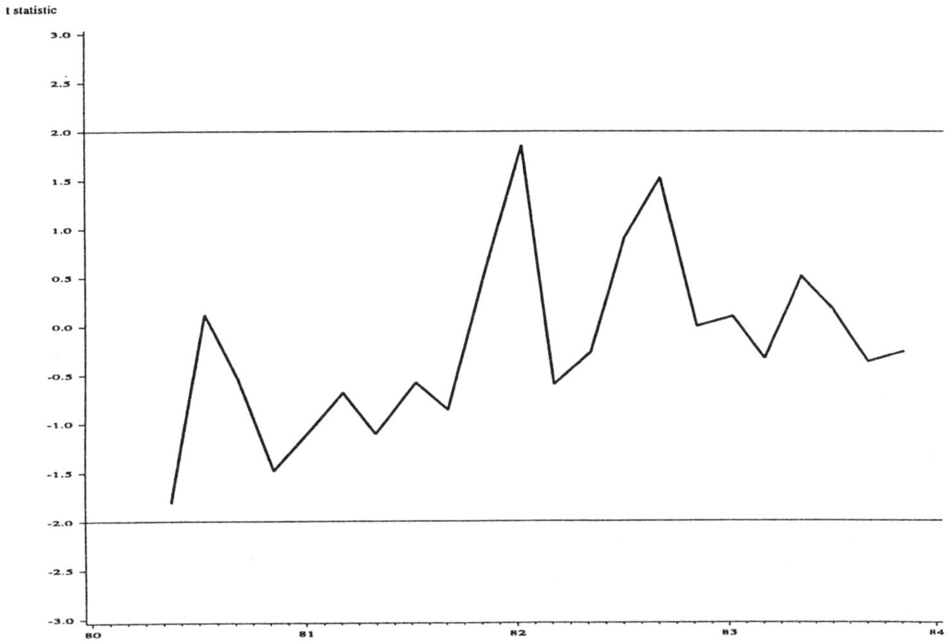

FIG. 6. t-Statistics for Estimates of d across Rolling Regression Subsample Periods (90-day treasury bill rate)

model, unlike the standard models such as Loeys' which show substantial instability. This can be seen in the F statistics reported in Table 3.

4. SUMMARY AND CONCLUSIONS

This paper attempts to distinguish between alternative hypotheses regarding the positive correlation between money announcement surprises and interest rates. The issue was examined directly by taking into account investor expectations about the Fed's net borrowed reserves target immediately following an announcement surprise. The ability of the estimates obtained from our model to mimic the results of a rolling regression methodology used by Loeys indicate that reduced-form models that allow for policy changes can be useful across different policy regimes.

Based on our empirical results the conclusions of this paper can be summarized: (1) Interest rates respond to unanticipated money. (2) The magnitude of this response declines with the maturity of the instrument. (3) The expected liquidity hypothesis explains the reactions at the shorter end of the maturity spectrum. (4) While the liquidity effects still outweigh the inflation premium effects, the reaction of the long rates appears to be caused by the combination of both factors. (5) The response of the Fed funds rate cannot be explained by either effect, but instead by the peculiar way money shocks are transmitted to the reserves market under lagged reserve accounting. (6) While the reaction of interest rates changes after October 1982, there is no evidence of structural instability. (7) The inclusion of a policy variable explains previously documented instabilities in parameter estimates.

LITERATURE CITED

Cornell, Bradford. "Do Money Supply Announcements Affect Short-Term Interest Rates?" *Journal of Money, Credit, and Banking* 11 (February 1979), 80–86.

______. "Money Supply Announcements, Interest Rates, and Foreign Exchange Rates." *Journal of International Money and Finance* (August 1982), 201–08.

______. "Money Supply Announcements and Interest Rates: Another View." *Journal of Business* 56 (January 1983), 1–23.

______. "The Money Supply Announcement Puzzle: Review and Interpretation." *American Economic Review* 83 (September 1983), 644–57.

Engel, Charles M., and Jeffery A. Frankel. "Why Interest Rates React to Money Announcements: An Explanation from the Foreign Exchange Markets." *Journal of Monetary Economics* 13 (January 1984), 31–39.

Grossman, Jacob. "The 'Rationality' of Money Supply Expectations and the Short-Run Response of Interest Rates to Monetary Surprises." *Journal of Money, Credit, and Banking* 13 (November 1981), 409–24.

Hardouvelis, Gikas. "Market Perceptions of Federal Reserve Policy and the Weekly Monetary Announcements." *Journal of Monetary Economics* 14 (September 1984), 255–40.

Loeys, Jan. "Changing Interest Rate Responses to Money Announcements: 1977–1983." *Journal of Monetary Economics* 15 (May 1985), 323–32.

Lucas, Robert E., Jr. "Econometric Policy Evaluation: A Critique." *Journal of Monetary Economics* 1, Suppl. (1976), 19–46.

Lynge, Morgan. "Money Supply Announcements and Stock Prices." *Journal of Portfolio Management* 8 (Fall 1981), 40–43.

Melton, William C. *Inside the Fed.* Homewood, Ill.: Dow-Jones Irwin, 1985.

Nicholas, Donald A., David H. Small, and Charles E. Webster, Jr. "Why Interest Rates Rise When an Unexpectedly Large Stock of Money Is Announced." *American Economic Review* 73 (June 1983), 383–88.

Pearce, Douglas D., and Vance Roley. "The Reaction of Stock Prices to Unanticipated Changes in Money: A Note." *Journal of Finance* 38 (September 1983), 1323–33.

______. "Stock Prices and Economic News." *Journal of Business* 58 (January 1985), 49–67.

Roley, Vance. "The Response of Short-Term Interest Rates to Weekly Money Announcements." *Journal of Money, Credit, and Banking* 15 (August 1983), 344–54.

Siegel, Jeremy J. "Money Supply Announcements and Interest Rates: Does Monetary Policy Matter?" *Journal of Monetary Economics* 15 (March 1985), 163–76.

Smith, Richard G., and Charles A. E. Goodhart. "The Relationship between Exchange Rate Movements and Monetary Surprises: Results for the United Kingdom and the United States Compared and Contrasted." *The Manchester School* 53 (March 1985), 2–22.

Spindt, Paul A., and Vefa Tarhan. "The Fed's New Operating Procedures: A Post-Mortem. *Journal of Monetary Economics* 19 (January 1987), 107–23.

______. "Bank Reserve Adjustment Process and Use of Reserve Carryover as a Reserve Management Tool." *Journal of Banking and Finance* 8 (March 1984), 5–20.

Urich, Thomas J. "The Information Content of Weekly Money Supply Announcements." *Journal of Monetary Economics* 10 (July 1982). 73–88.

Urich, Thomas, and Paul Wachtel. "Market Response to the Weekly Money Supply Announcements in the 1970s." *Journal of Finance* 36 (December 1981), 1063–72.

______. "The Effects of Inflation and Money Supply Announcements on Interest Rates." *Journal of Finance* 39 (September 1984), 1177–88.

RICHARD DEAVES

Money Supply Announcements and Market Reactions in an Open Economy

Reactions in money, bond, and foreign exchange markets induced by the Federal Reserve's weekly money supply announcement have been extensively documented and interpreted. The most consistent finding has been that short-term interest rates tend to increase (decrease) in response unexpectedly high (low) week-to-week monetary growth. Most researchers have sought to account for this and other empirical regularities by positing a certain view of market perceptions of central bank behavior. For example, the policy anticipations school argues that it is the real component of interest rates that increases after positive money surprises,[1] since market participants believe the Fed will seek to counteract these demand-based shocks in the coming weeks.[2] This view is strengthened by the tendency (observed in some sample periods) for the value of the dollar to also increase after positive surprises.[3]

[1]As a verbal abbreviation, I will often speak of typical reactions to positive surprises. There is no intention to imply any asymmetries (i.e., responses to negative surprises which are not equal in absolute value and of opposite sign to those of positive). In fact, in the clearest test for such asymmetries (for three-month U.S. T-bill reactions), Belongia and Kolb (1984) were unable to reject the null that responses to positive and negative surprises were symmetrical.

[2]These are shocks to the money multiplier since the corresponding level of the monetary base is announced the previous week. This is true in both Canada and the United States, where, in both cases, money supply announcements are weekly.

[3]A conflicting view, the expected inflation hypothesis, argues that interest rates increase because the inflation premium is increasing. Thus market participants expect the Fed to accommodate (at least partially) money surprises by raising monetary growth rates. Not all see the phenomenon as reflecting market perceptions of the central bank's reaction function. For example, Siegel (1985) has

The author acknowledges the helpful comments of James E. Pesando and two anonymous referees.

Richard Deaves *is assistant professor of finance and business economics on the faculty of business, McMaster University.*

Journal of Money, Credit, and Banking, Vol. 22, No. 2 (May 1990)

This line of research has been extended by examining market reactions induced by non-U.S. money supply announcements—in particular, for the United Kingdom (Smith and Goodhart 1985 and Goodhart and Smith 1985) and for Canada (Deaves 1989). Consistent with U.S. findings, there is evidence that, at least for some sample periods, the domestic currency tends to appreciate in response to positive surprises. There is, however, no indication that non-U.S. short-term interest rates are affected by domestic money surprises.[4]

This paper proposes an open-economy model of the money supply announcement–financial market reaction phenomenon which may account for the apparent divergence of this recent research from U.S. experience, and at the same time identifies an additional channel of influence of money surprises on interest rates for the United States. An implication of the model is that not only the magnitude but even the sign of short-term interest rate responses to money surprises is a function of the parameters of the model. In addition, the response is more likely to be small (if not zero or negative) in the case of countries such as Canada and the United Kingdom with high ratios of imports to GNP.[5]

A policy-anticipations view of central bank behavior is imposed, or, equivalently, long-term target levels for the money supply are assumed to be unaffected by unanticipated deviations from target. Previous modeling based on this view of central bank behavior in the context of the U.S. literature has been done by Urich (1982), Nichols, Small, and Webster (1983), and Roley and Walsh (1985) for closed economies, while Engel and Frankel's (1984) model is the principal open-economy predecessor. The latter, which predicts a positive correlation between interest rate changes and money surprises, is in some respects similar to a special case of the model presented here.[6]

The paper is structured as follows. Section 1 presents the basic model. The next section derives predictions of exchange rate and interest rate reactions induced by monetary innovations. Finally in section 3 brief consideration is given to the role that this model may play in explaining the stylized facts in the money supply announcements literature.

1. THE OPEN-ECONOMY MONEY MARKET MODEL UNDER POLICY ANTICIPATIONS

As a framework, a simplification of Mussa's (1982) generalization of Dornbusch's "overshooting" model (1976) is employed. The general price level at t

formulated a model that abstracts from central bank behavior and accords to monetary announcements a signaling role on the future prospects for the economy. The U.S. weekly money supply announcements empirical literature (and interpretations of it) are recently reviewed by Sheehan (1985) and Deaves (1987).

[4]Ito and Roley (1987) find that the yen/dollar exchange rate does not (for the most part) respond to Japanese money surprises. They did not test for any interest rate effects.

[5]For example, in 1987 the ratios were (according to the IMF's *International Financial Statistics*) 26.9 percent, 26.3 percent, and 10.7 percent for the United Kingdom, Canada and the United States, respectively.

[6]In Engel and Frankel interest rates and the exchange rate are linked through open interest parity

(P_t), measured as a logarithm, is a weighted average of domestic money prices of domestic goods and foreign goods:

$$P_t = \sigma p_t + (1 - \sigma)(e_t + p_t^*) , 0<\sigma<1 \tag{1}$$

where p_t = log of domestic money price of domestic goods;
p_t^* = log of foreign price level;
e_t = log of exchange rate, defined as the price of a unit of foreign money in terms of domestic;
σ = expenditure share on domestic goods.

Since the object is to investigate how asset prices deviate from their steady-state levels in response to domestic information of a transitory nature, it will be harmless to assume that all foreign magnitudes, including the price level, are constant, and that domestic steady-state variable values are constant.[7] If market participants hold a policy-anticipations view, then they believe that any demand-based money surprises will eventually be counteracted by the monetary authority (hereafter MA). If domestic goods prices are somewhat sticky in response to new information (even without counteractive monetary policy), then it may be a reasonable approximation to assume that the domestic price level can be treated as constant.[8] Normalizing the foreign price level at unity, equation (1) can be rewritten as

$$P_t = \sigma p + (1 - \sigma)e_t . \tag{1a}$$

Note that only one of P_t and e_t is independent. Forward differencing of (1a) yields

$$DP_t = (1-\sigma)De_t \tag{1b}$$

where $Dx_t = x_{t+1} - x_t$.

Money demand, open interest parity, and the Fisher equation have standard forms:

(as here). As will become clear, I go one crucial step further by incorporating the exchange rate (via import prices) in the general price level, which then feeds back into the monetary sector (through money demand).

[7]Foreign constant variables and domestic steady state variable values will be indicated by the relevant variable symbols without a time subscript. Steady-state growth in variables (such as monetary expansion and inflation) could readily be incorporated, and all asset price changes could then be viewed as deviations from trend.

[8]Many models of price adjustment allow for gradual movement of the price level toward its level in a world without any price inflexibility. In the model presented here the gap between these two gradually diminishes in any case (except perhaps, as will be shown, for an initial phase when it could potentially widen).

$$m_t^d = k_t + P_t - \eta i_t = m_t , \quad \eta > 0 \tag{2}$$

$$i_t = i^* + E_t(De_t) , \tag{3}$$

$$i_t = r_t + E_t(DP_t) , \tag{4}$$

where m_t^d, m_t = log of nominal money demand, supply;
i_t = domestic single-period nominal interest rate[9];
η = interest elasticity;
k_t = real money demand shift component;
i^* = foreign nominal interest rate (assumed constant);
r_t = real ex ante rate of interest.

Substituting (3) and (1b) into (2) allows derivation of the following first-order difference equation:

$$P_t - (1/c)E_t(DP_t) = w_t \tag{5}$$

where $c = (1 - \sigma)/\eta$;
$w_t = m_t - k_t + \eta i^*$.

Using recursive substitution, it is straightforward to show that its solution is a weighted average of the current and expected future values of w_t:

$$P_t = \sum_{j=0}^{\infty} c[1/(1+c)]^{j+1} E_t(w_{t+j}) . \tag{6}$$

Thus specification of the $E_t(w_{t+j})$ path, or, equivalently, the expected paths of money demand and supply are sufficient to derive current and expected future values for the general price level and [by (1a)] for the exchange rate. Current and expected future interest rates are then determined from (2), and ex ante real interest rates from (4).

Next the monetary process is specified.[10] There are two reasons why the MA is not able to exercise perfect monetary control, even if it desired to do so: shocks to money demand and a lag in information. Shocks to money demand occur through the real money demand shift component. It is assumed that

$$k_t = k + u_t \tag{7}$$

[9]Arguably the demand for money function would more normally have as its cost argument a longer-term interest rate (e.g., a thirteen-week Treasury bill rate) than the span from one money supply announcement to another. Deaves (1987) makes this adjustment and no substantive results change.

[10]The stochastic nature of money demand and the reaction function of the monetary authority share common features with those of Roley and Walsh (1985). For this reason, interest rate predictions for the zero import special case (with σ=1) are similar to those of Roley and Walsh.

where k = steady-state shift factor level;

$u_t = \rho u_{t-1} + \epsilon_t, 0 < \rho < 1,$

and ϵ_t is white noise. Thus shocks to money demand are both transitory and persistent.[11]

Because of an information lag, the MA becomes aware of demand shocks only after they take place. Until this time under most operating procedures some temporary central bank accommodation of unobservable money demand shocks occurs. In fact, this accommodation will be total under an interest rate instrument. This procedure will be assumed here.

Based on the information available to it, the MA plans to "set" single-period interest rates so as to achieve its target path for the money supply. To correspond with Canadian and U.S. institutional practice, it is assumed that the money supply is calculated with a two-period (that is, two-week) lag. Thus the MA learns of the level of the money supply at $t-2$ just before setting interest rates at t. It then revises its planned future single-period interest rate settings so as to counteract any surprises at a rate of λ percent per period:

$$T_t(m_{t+j}) - T_{t-1}(m_{t+j}) = (1-\lambda)^{j+1}[E_t(m_{t-1}) - T_{t-1}(m_{t-1})], j = 0,1,2,... \quad (8)$$

where $T_t(m_{t+j})$ = target money stock for $t+j$ based on information known to MA at t.

It is assumed that $0 \leq 1-\lambda < \rho$. In other words, the MA acts in such a way that the money supply reverts to target levels more quickly than it would otherwise "unwind."[12]

It should be stressed that the model is not based on any informational advantage. As soon as the monetary authority gathers the data (at the beginning of week t), it releases the money supply figure. The stochastic nature of money demand, the money supply target path and its adjustment to new information are common knowledge. Therefore, any changes in asset prices that take place will be consistent with the plans of the monetary authority and are simply market anticipations of these plans.

2. MARKET REACTIONS TO MONEY SURPRISES

To simplify the analysis, assume that the economy, beginning in the constant steady state at $t-3$, experiences a shock to money demand at $t-2$. Unknown to

[11]Since the shocks are weekly, it is probable that they would possess a high degree of serial correlation.

[12]If $\lambda=1$, the target levels of the money stock do not change, and the shock would be totally reversed in the next period. In all other cases temporary partial accommodation is implied. The reason that $\rho \leqslant 1-\lambda$ has been disallowed is as follows. In the case of the strict inequality (which always includes $\lambda=0$ since $\rho<1$), the implication is that the MA illogically compounds a surprise. As for the equality, by allowing the surprise to "unwind" at its own rate, the MA would have no role in the monetary process. In the strict context of the model this would actually be optimal, as there would be

the MA until t, it is at first accommodated. When at t the surprise is observed, the MA revises its planned interest rate settings so as to counteract it over time. The market becomes aware of this with the announcement at t of the money supply at $t-2$. Thus the general price level, the exchange rate, and interest rates are perturbed from their initial levels (P, e, and i, respectively). The forward-looking analysis will be simplified by assuming perfect foresight, with all error terms except for the original being set equal to zero.[13] Eventually the system converges to its original steady state. The object is to examine the impact of the shock on current levels of (and the path of) the endogenous variables before the reestablishment of long-term equilibrium.

Given the stochastic nature of money demand and the reaction function of the MA, and the fact that the system began in the steady state, (8) can be rewritten as

$$m_{t+j} - m = (1-\lambda)^{j+1}[\rho\epsilon_{t-2}], \qquad j=0,1,2,... \tag{8a}$$

where m = constant steady state level of money supply.

To calculate the immediate change in the general price level (as well as its future path) after the announcement, notice that [using (7) and (8a)] the following perceived shift in the path of w_t has taken place:

$$\begin{aligned} \Delta w_{t+j} &= \Delta m_{t+j} - \Delta k_{t+j} + \Delta\eta i^* ; \\ &= (1-\lambda)^{j+1}(\rho\epsilon_{t-2}) - \rho^{j+1}(\rho\epsilon_{t-2}) ; \\ &= \rho\epsilon_{t-2}[(1-\lambda)^{j+1} - \rho^{j+1}] ; \qquad j=0,1,2,... \end{aligned} \tag{9}$$

At t, just prior to the announcement, the general price level will still be at P (that is, $P_t^b = P$ where b denotes "before the announcement"), as the public will have no reason to expect that a monetary disturbance has taken place. After the announcement, the general price level will shift to P_t^a (where a denotes "after the announcement"). Its change (j=0) and the expected change in its path (j>0) is [from (6) and (9)]

$$\Delta P_{t+j} = P_{t+j}^a - P_{t+j}^b = P_{t+j}^a - P ;$$

no price level or interest rate consequences, but the model ignores the formation of inflation expectations, and the public's observation of an increase in monetary expansion might lead to revisions in future expected inflation, which is after all what a policy of targeting is designed to prevent.

[13]The following equations describe the money market up to t:

At $t-3$: $m = P + k - \eta i$ (steady state);
At $t-2$: $m + \epsilon_{t-2} = P + k + \epsilon_{t-2} - \eta i$ (shock accommodated);
At $t-1$: $m + \rho\epsilon_{t-2} = P + k + \rho\epsilon_{t-2} - \eta i$(shock again accommodated; $\epsilon_{t-1} = 0$).

It would be straightforward to repeat the analysis in terms of a fully stochastic world (with the appropriate substitution of expectations).

$$= \sum_{i=0}^{\infty} c[1/(1+c)]^{i+1} \Delta w_{t+j+i} \; ;$$

$$= c\rho\epsilon_{t-2} \left[\frac{(1-\lambda)^{j+1}}{(1+c)} \sum_{i=0}^{\infty} \left[\frac{(1-\lambda)}{(1+c)} \right]^i - \frac{\rho^{j+1}}{(1+c)} \sum_{i=0}^{\infty} \left[\frac{\rho}{(1+c)} \right]^i \right] ;$$

$$= c\rho\epsilon_{t-2} \left[\frac{(1-\lambda)^{j+1}}{(1+c-(1-\lambda))} - \frac{\rho^{j+1}}{(1+c-\rho)} \right] , \qquad j=0,1,2,... \tag{10}$$

Note that, if the surprise is positive, the current level of the general price level will decline.[14] Also it is clear that $P_{t+\infty} = P$. There may in fact be, depending on the magnitudes of λ and ρ, additional falls in the price level (after the initial decline). Eventually, if not immediately, the general price level must "turn around" and asymptotically reach P, its steady-state level.[15]

Implied movements in the spot and forward exchange rates are [from (10) and (1a)

$$\Delta e_{t+j} = e^a_{t+j} - e^b_{t+j} = e^a_{t+j} - e \; ;$$

$$= (1/(1-\sigma))c\rho\epsilon_{t-2} \left[\frac{(1-\lambda)^{j+1}}{[1+c-(1-\lambda)]} - \frac{\rho^{j+1}}{(1+c-\rho)} \right] ;$$

$$= (\rho/\eta)\epsilon_{t-2} \left[\frac{(1-\lambda)^{j+1}}{[1+c-(1-\lambda)]} - \frac{\rho^{j+1}}{(1+c-\rho)} \right] , \qquad j=0,1,2,... \tag{11}$$

A zero import special case is derived by setting $\sigma=1$ (implying $c=0$):[16]

$$\Delta e_{t+j} = (\rho/\eta)\epsilon_{t-2} \left[\frac{(1-\lambda)^{j+1}}{[1 - (1-\lambda)]} - \frac{\rho^{j+1}}{(1 - \rho)} \right] , \qquad j=0,1,2,... \tag{11Z}$$

In response to a positive surprise the value of the domestic currency unequivocally rises (that is, e_t falls). Over time it too asymptotically returns to its initial steady-state value. This is true for both the general model and the zero import special case.[17]

[14]This immediately follows from $\rho > 1 - \lambda$.

[15]For example, if η=.5, σ=.5, λ=.5, and ρ=.965, the general price level will continue to fall for several more periods, after which it begins to climb toward its steady-state level. After thirteen weeks it is approximately equal to its postannouncement level. See Deaves (1987) for a simulation using these parameter values.

[16]Note that the existence of an exchange rate is still valid in the zero import case because of international capital movements, and the possibility that the country may be exporting without importing at all. Also, in this case $\Delta P_{t+j} = 0$, since the general price level is equivalent to the price of domestic goods which is fixed by assumption. In fact equation (6) is not defined for this case.

[17]In the zero import case the linkage between the (now constant) general price level and the exchange rate is terminated. Exchange rate movements are determined *purely* from interest parity.

Next interest rate reactions are considered.[18] After the announcement, the current level of the weekly interest rate, which the MA intends to set, and expected future levels will be clear to the public. Thus both the current weekly rate and longer-term rates will immediately change in such a way as to clear the money market given P_t^a and the expected levels of the money supply and demand shift factor. In the appendix it is shown that current and future single-period and multiperiod interest rate changes are[19]

$$\begin{aligned}\Delta i_{t+j} &= i^a_{t+j} - i^b_{t+j} = i^a_{t+j} - i\,;\\ &= (\rho/\eta)\epsilon_{t-2}\left[c\left[\frac{(1-\lambda)^{j+1}}{[1+c-(1-\lambda)]} - \frac{\rho^{j+1}}{(1+c-\rho)}\right]\right.\\ &\quad \left.+ [\rho^{j+1}-(1-\lambda)^{j+1}]\right], \qquad j=0,1,2,... \end{aligned} \tag{12}$$

$$\begin{aligned}\Delta i_{k,t+j} &= i^a_{k,t+j} - i^b_{k,t+j} = i^a_{k,t+j} - i\,;\\ &= (\rho/k\eta)\epsilon_{t-2}\left[c\left[\frac{(1-\lambda)^{j+1}[1-(1-\lambda)^k]}{\lambda[1+c-(1-\lambda)]} - \frac{\rho^{j+1}(1-\rho^k)}{(1-\rho)(1+c-\rho)}\right]\right.\\ &\quad \left.+ \left[\frac{\rho^{j+1}(1-\rho^k)}{(1-\rho)} - \frac{(1-\lambda)^{j+1}[1-(1-\lambda)^k]}{\lambda}\right]\right],\\ &\quad j=0,1,2,...;k=1,2,3,... , \end{aligned} \tag{13}$$

where $i_{k,t}$ = k-period interest rate at t.

Setting c=0 for the zero import special case, we have

$$\Delta i_{t+j} = (\rho/\eta)\epsilon_{t-2}\,[\rho^{j+1} - (1-\lambda)^{j+1}], \qquad j=0,1,2,... \tag{12Z}$$

$$\begin{aligned}\Delta i_{k,t+j} &= (\rho/k\eta)\epsilon_{t-2}\left[\frac{\rho^{j+1}(1-\rho^k)}{(1-\rho)} - \frac{(1-\lambda)^{j+1}[1-(1-\lambda)^k]}{\lambda}\right],\\ &\quad j=0,1,2,...;k=1,2,3,... \end{aligned} \tag{13Z}$$

For the general case, the direction of these interest rate movements is indeterminate and depends on the relevant parameter values. To see this, consider the current single-period rate reaction. It is apparent that it is made up of two terms $c\{[(1-\lambda)/(1+c-(1-\lambda))] - \rho/(1+c-\rho)\}$ and $\rho-(1-\lambda)$ (whose sum is multiplied

[18]Note that, as is appropriate for an open economy, monetary forces drive the exchange rate and interest yields accommodate themselves appropriately. The monetary authority can only "set" nominal interest rates if the settings are consistent with the implied differences between money supply and demand and the value of the exchange rate.

[19]Note that, for simplicity, I am assuming the unbiased expectations theory of the term structure to be appropriate. Also, long-term interest rates are expressed as arithmetic rather than geometric averages of short-term rates.

by the product of ρ/η, which is positive, and the surprise). Since $\rho > 1-\lambda$, the first term is negative and the second positive. Only the second term, which constitutes an "anticipated counteraction" effect, is present for zero import economies (since $c=0$ implies that the first term is zero). This effect leads to increases (decreases) in interest rates in response to positive (negative) surprises, as the public anticipates future monetary tightening (loosening). The first term, a "price level" effect, works in the direction of interest rate decreases (increases) after positive (negative) surprises.[20] The more the general price level (driven by the exchange rate) falls (rises), the more real balances rise (fall). For this reason interest rates, through money demand, are pushed lower (higher).[21]

3. CONCLUDING REMARKS

A brief recapitulation of the predictions of the open-economy model under policy anticipations is in order. To concentrate on movements in spot variables (rather than expected paths), the formulation presented here suggests that, in response to positive money surprises, the value of the domestic currency tends to increase. This is true for both the general model and the zero import special case. Interest rates movements are another matter. For the zero import case, under policy anticipations, they will always increase in anticipation of future central bank tightening. In the general case, however, changes in interest rates may be positive, zero, or negative depending on parameter values and maturity.

Goodhart and Smith (1985) showed that, for the United Kingdom during a 1977–83 sample period, changes in the value of the pound were positively correlated with positive money surprises, while Deaves (1989) showed a similar result for Canada during a 1978–79 sample period. In both cases, however, three-month T-bill yields were not significantly affected. In light of the model presented here, and the fact that the United Kingdom and Canada have high imports to GNP ratios, these results need not be surprising. Empirical differences in short-term interest rate responses between the latter two nations versus the United States may thus be attributable to different parameter values. The "price level" effect, though present in the United States, is simply dominated by the "anticipated counteraction" effect.

[20]As pointed out by an anonymous referee, the magnitude of the "price level" effect is likely to be altered by the consideration of various factors abstracted from in my analysis. For example, this effect will be greater if domestic price flexibility (i.e., instantaneous inflexibility followed by gradual adjustment toward equilibrium levels) is allowed, since the rising value of the domestic currency will put downward pressure on the domestic price level causing the general price level to fall even further after positive surprises. Also, future real income increases induced by positive surprises will tend to further lower prices.

[21]As shown in Deaves (1987), investigating real interest rate movements provides an important clue on the direction of nominal rate movements. In fact it can be shown that changes in k-period real rates of interest move in the same direction as changes in expected movements in the general price level from t to $t+k$ $(\Delta P_{t+k} - \Delta P_t)$, which implies that nominal rates move in the same direction as both the real rate and the inflation premium.

APPENDIX: DERIVATION OF INTEREST RATE REACTIONS

First the immediate change in the single-period rate is derived. Consider how perceptions of the elements of the money demand and supply change after the announcement:

$$\Delta m_t = \Delta k_t + \Delta P_t - \eta \Delta i_t$$

$$\Rightarrow (1-\lambda)\rho\epsilon_{t-2} = \rho^2\epsilon_{t-2} + c\rho\epsilon_{t-2}\left[\frac{(1-\lambda)}{(1+c-(1-\lambda))} - \frac{\rho}{(1+c-\rho)}\right] - \eta\Delta i_t$$

$$\Rightarrow \Delta i_t = (\rho/\eta)\epsilon_{t-2}\left[c\left[\frac{(1-\lambda)}{[1+c-(1-\lambda)]} - \frac{\rho}{(1+c-\rho)}\right] + [\rho - (1-\lambda)]\right].$$

It is straightforward to generalize this to derive the path of single-period interest rates which gives us (12):

$$\Delta i_{t+j} = (\rho/\eta)\epsilon_{t-2}\left[c\left[\frac{(1-\lambda)^{j+1}}{[1+c-(1-\lambda)]} - \frac{\rho^{j+1}}{(1+c-\rho)}\right] + [\rho^{j+1}-(1-\lambda)^{j+1}]\right], \quad j=0,1,2,\ldots \qquad (12)$$

Equation (13) is derived from (12). We begin with current multiperiod rates:

$$\Delta i_{k,t} = (1/k)\sum_{j=0}^{k-1}\Delta i_{t+j};$$

$$= (\rho/k\eta)\epsilon_{t-2}\left[c\left[\sum_{i=0}^{k-1}\frac{(1-\lambda)^{i+1}}{[1+c-(1-\lambda)]} - \sum_{i=0}^{k-1}\frac{\rho^{i+1}}{(1+c-\rho)}\right] + \left[\sum_{i=0}^{k-1}\rho^{i+1} - \sum_{i=0}^{k-1}(1-\lambda)^{i+1}\right]\right];$$

$$= (\rho/k\eta)\epsilon_{t-2}\left[c\left[\frac{(1-\lambda)(1-(1-\lambda)^k)}{\lambda(1+c-(1-\lambda))} - \frac{\rho(1-\rho^k)}{(1-\rho)(1+c-\rho)}\right] + \left[\frac{\rho(1-\rho^k)}{1-\rho} - \frac{(1-\lambda)(1-(1-\lambda)^k)}{\lambda}\right]\right].$$

To derive the expected path of multiperiod rates, note tat all summations now are indexed from $i=j$ to $j+k-1$. Consider the third summation, for example:

$$\sum_{i=j}^{j+k-1} \rho^{i+1} = \rho^{j} \sum_{i=0}^{k-1} \rho^{i+1} \; .$$

Thus (13) clearly holds. The zero import equations (12Z) and (13Z) are derived by setting c=0.

LITERATURE CITED

Belongia, Michael T., and Frederic Kolb. "Risk Aversion and Weekly Money: Does the Market Expect the Fed to Offset Large Increases in M1?" *Economics Letters* 16 (1984), 327–30.

Deaves, Richard. "Money Supply Announcements and Canadian Financial Markets." Ph.D. dissertation, University of Toronto, 1987.

———. "Canadian Weekly Money Supply Announcements and Financial Market Reactions in the First Years of Targeting: A View of Market Perceptions of Bank of Canada Policy." Paper, McMaster University, October 1989.

Dornbusch, Rudiger. "Expectations and Exchange Rate Dynamics." *Journal of Political Economy* 84 (December 1976), 1161–76.

Engel, Charles M., and Jeffrey A. Frankel. "Why Interest Rates React to Money Announcements: An Explanation from the Foreign Exchange Market." *Journal of Monetary Economics* 13 (January 1984), 31–39.

Goodhart, Charles A. E., and Richard G. Smith. "The Impact of News on Financial Markets in the United Kingdom." *Journal of Money, Credit, and Banking* 17 (November I 1985), 507–11.

International Monetary Fund. *International Financial Statistics* 42 (July 1989). IMF: Washington.

Ito, Takatoshi, and V. Vance Roley. "News from the U.S. and Japan: Which Moves the Yen/Dollar Exchange Rate?" *Journal of Monetary Economics* 19 (March 1987), 255–77.

Mussa, Michael. "A Model of Exchange Rate Dynamics." *Journal of Political Economy* 90 (February 1982), 74–104.

Nichols, Donald A., David H. Small, and Charles E. Webster, Jr. "Why Interest Rates Rise When an Unexpectedly Large Money Stock Is Announced." *American Economic Review* 73 (June 1983), 383–88.

Roley, V. Vance, and Carl E. Walsh. "Monetary Policy Regimes, Expected Inflation, and the Response of Interest Rates to Money Announcements." *Quarterly Journal of Economics* 100 (December supplement 1985), 1011–39.

Sheehan, Richard G. "Weekly Money Announcements: New Information and Its Effects." *Federal Reserve Bank of St. Louis Review* 67 (August/September 1985), 25–34.

Siegel, Jeremy J. "Money Supply Announcements and Interest Rates: Does Monetary Policy Matter?" *Journal of Monetary Economics* 15 (March 1985), 163–76.

Smith, Richard G., and Charles A. E. Goodhart. "The Relationship between Exchange Rate Movements and Monetary Surprises: Results for the United Kingdom and the United States Compared and Contrasted." *The Manchester School* 53 (March 1985), 2–22.

Urich, Thomas J. "The Information Content of Weekly Money Supply Announcements." *Journal of Monetary Economics* 10 (July 1982), 72–88.

HERSCHEL I. GROSSMAN

Inflation and Reputation with Generic Policy Preferences

THIS PAPER DERIVES A REPUTATIONAL EQUILIBRIUM for inflation under the generic assumption that monetary policy reflects proximate preferences for low expected inflation and positive unexpected inflation. The analysis shows how policymaker concern about reputation affects qualitative properties of equilibrium behavior. Specifically, the desire to signal that their mode of behavior is rational, as opposed to opportunistic, causes policymakers to behave as if they are concerned about controlling inflation, even if they do not have a separate preference for low actual inflation.

This paper also analyzes how the equilibrium inflation rate depends on the length of the relevant decision interval that determines how fast private agents would react to opportunistic behavior by the policymaker. This decision interval is related to the underlying real objectives of monetary policy and to the structure of the economy. The analysis shows that the shorter is this decision interval, the smaller are the potential gains from unexpected inflation and the lower is the equilibrium inflation rate.

This paper reports in part research done in connection with the author's appointment as visiting professor at the Institute for Advanced Studies (Vienna). He thanks members of the Institute and participants in the Economic Theory Research Seminar of the Viennese Universities and in the NBER/FMME Summer Institute for useful comments on earlier versions of this paper. The author also has benefited from discussions with John Van Huyck and Guido Tabellini and from comments from anonymous referees and, especially, from J. Huston McCulloch.

HERSCHEL I. GROSSMAN *is Merton P. Stoltz Professor in the Social Sciences and professor of economics at Brown University.*

Journal of Money, Credit, and Banking, Vol. 22, No. 2 (May 1990)

1. POLICY OBJECTIVE

Assume that over month τ the realization of the policymaker's proximate preference function, denoted by u_τ, is

$$u_\tau = u(e_\tau, p_\tau - e_\tau) \tag{1}$$

with $u_1 \gtreqless 0$ as $e_\tau \gtreqless \tilde{e}$, $u_{11} < 0$,

$u_2 \gtreqless 0$ as $p_\tau - e_\tau \gtreqless \Pi > 0$, $u_{22} < 0$,

$u_{12} \approx 0$, and $p_\tau \leqslant \bar{p} \leqslant \infty$,

where e_τ is the expected inflation rate on which private agents base their behavior in month τ and p_τ is the actual inflation rate during month τ. The monthly evaluation of the policymaker's preference function presumes that in the case of a preference function involving inflation a cognitive interval corresponds to the monthly interval at which inflation data is usually gathered. As we shall see, the analysis distinguishes this cognitive interval from the relevant decision interval, which is the time between points at which private agents reconsider the expectation of inflation on which they base their behavior.

The policymaker's preference function has a maximum with respect to e_τ at e_τ equal to $\tilde{e}$, and a maximum with respect to $p_\tau - e_\tau$ at $p_\tau - e_\tau$ equal to Π. Whereas $\tilde{e}$ can be positive, negative, or zero, Π is strictly positive—that is, whatever the expected inflation rate, the policymaker prefers a positive, and not necessarily finite, amount of unexpected inflation. In the absence of a general presumption about the sign of u_{12}, the analysis takes this cross-partial derivative, wherever it is relevant, to be approximately zero. Accordingly, the analysis treats $\tilde{e}$ and Π as approximately constant. The maximum possible inflation rate per month is $\bar{p}$, which also could be infinite. Finally, it is convenient to scale the preference function such that $u(\bar{p}, 0)$ equals zero. The analysis assumes that $u(\cdot)$ is common knowledge.

The policymaker's proximate concern about expected inflation presumably reflects concern about the demand for real money balances and could derive from such underlying real objectives of monetary policy as allocative efficiency or enhancement of revenue prospects, especially potential seigniorage. The policymaker's preference for positive unexpected inflation can reflect such objectives as high aggregate economic activity, low real cost of servicing nominally denominated debts, or high revenue from seigniorage. As they are attributable to a variety of real objectives involving resource allocation, income distribution, aggregate economic activity, or the public finances, the discussion refers to these proximate preferences for low expected inflation and positive unexpected inflation as generic.

The preference function $u(\cdot)$ presumes that the policymaker, although concerned about expected inflation and unexpected inflation, is not separately concerned about actual inflation. Specifically, a property of the function $u(\cdot)$ is that, for a given value of e, $\partial u/\partial p$ equals $\partial u/\partial(p-e)$, rather than being less than $\partial u/\partial(p-e)$ as would be the case if the policymaker had a separate preference for low actual inflation. In this respect, the policy objective implied by equation (1) differs from the setup used by Kydland and Prescott (1977), by Barro (1983), and by Barro and Gordon (July 1983, August 1983), all of whom assume that the policymaker exhibits aversion to high inflation per se, in addition to a preference for positive unexpected inflation.

These earlier analyses incorporated separate concern about actual inflation apparently because this assumption seemed to be the only way to avoid the implication, derived by Calvo (1978) for the case of a preference for positive unexpected inflation alone, that a unique equilibrium exists at the maximum feasible inflation rate. The problem with assuming aversion to high inflation per se, however, is that if the underlying objectives of monetary policy involve only real economic outcomes, then, as earlier authors recognized, the policymaker has no apparent reason to be separately concerned about actual inflation. If private agents do not suffer from money illusion, then, for given expected inflation, actual inflation would seem to affect real outcomes only as a component of unexpected inflation.

The analysis that follows shows how the introduction of reputational considerations avoids this modeling problem. Even if, as in the preference function $u(\cdot)$, the policymaker does not have a separate preference for low actual inflation, we see that with a reputational linkage between current policy and expected future policy, preference for low expected inflation can produce an equilibrium in which actual inflation is realistically low.

2. DECISION INTERVALS

To complete the specification of the policy objective, assume that the policymaker is concerned about the discounted sum of present and future realizations of its preference function over an infinite horizon. In any month zero this discounted sum, denoted by U_0, is given by

$$U_0 = \sum_{\tau=0}^{\infty} \beta^{\tau} u_{\tau}, \; 0 < \beta \leqslant 1, \tag{2}$$

where β is the policymaker's discount factor. For simplicity, equation (2) also implicitly assumes that the policymaker controls the actual inflation rate exactly and can predict future expected inflation rates exactly.

As we shall see, the reputational model developed below, in which rational policymakers want to signal their rational mode of behavior, readily accommodates an infinite planning horizon. In contrast, in models in which policymakers attempt to conceal private information or attributes—see, for example, Barro

(1986)—nontrivial equilibria apparently require the implausible assumption that the policymaker's planning horizon has a finite deterministic terminal date that is common knowledge. Grossman and Van Huyck (1988) explicitly derive an infinite-horizon setup like equation (2) in a model in which the terminal date is a random variable corresponding to the prospective longevity of the sovereign's survival in power, and the discount factor depends on the stochastic process that governs the sovereign's survival. Grossman and Noh (1989, 1990) extend this model to allow the sovereign's survival to depend in part on the policy choice, thereby endogenizing the discount factor.

As mentioned above, the length of a cognitive interval, which is presumed to be a month and is dated by the index τ, does not necessarily equal the length of the interval between points in time at which private agents reconsider the expectation of inflation on which they base the behavior. The length of the relevant decision interval depends on the underlying real objectives of monetary policy—specifically, on the reason for the policymaker's preference for positive unexpected inflation—and on the structure of the economy. For example, if the policymaker wants to depress real wages in order to stimulate aggregate economic activity, then the relevant decision interval reflects the frequency with which nominal wages are adjusted. If the policymaker wants to reduce the real return on nominally denominated assets, then the relevant decision interval reflects the maturity of these assets. If the policymaker is mainly interested in seigniorage, then the relevant decision interval reflects the frequency with which private agents adjust their transactions patterns.

To highlight the importance of this decision interval,the analysis assumes that private agents make all relevant decisions involving inflationary expectations simultaneously at intervals that each consist of λ monthly cognitive intervals, $\lambda \geqslant 1$. The policymaker has a relevant decision to make about monetary policy at these same decision intervals. [Although the present analysis treats λ as an exogenous parameter, a useful extension would be to recognize that the relevant decision interval is also subject to choice and to analyze its joint determination with the equilibrium inflation rate.]

Using the index t to date the decision intervals, let e_t and p_t represent the fixed expected and actual monthly inflation rates that obtain during decision interval t, and let u_t represent the fixed value per month of the policymaker's proximate preference function that obtains during decision interval t. Thus, aggregating monthly cognitive intervals into decision intervals, we have

$$e_\tau = e_t, p_\tau = p_t, \text{and } u_\tau = u_t \quad \text{for } \tau = t\lambda, \ldots, (t+1)\lambda - 1,$$

where $u_t = u(e_t, p_t - e_t)$. Accordingly, the discounted sum given by equation (2) can also be expressed as

$$U_0 = \sum_{t=0}^{\infty} u_t \sum_{\tau=t\lambda}^{(t+1)\lambda-1} \beta^\tau , \tag{3}$$

or, equivalently, as

$$U_0 = \frac{1-\beta^{\lambda}}{1-\beta} \sum_{t=0}^{\infty} \beta^{\lambda t} u(e_t, p_t - e_t) . \tag{4}$$

In equation (4), in summing realizations of the policymaker's preference function over present and future decision intervals, the discount factor is adjusted for the number of months in a decision interval.

3. A COMMITTED MONETARY POLICY

Suppose that the policymaker could irrevocably commit monetary policy to be consistent with an announced path of future inflation rates. Such an irrevocable commitment would determine inflationary expectations. In this case, the policymaker's problem would be to choose the program $\{e_t, p_t\}_{t=0}^{\infty}$ to maximize U_0 as given by equation (4) subject to the constraint that p_t must equal e_t for all t. The first-order condition for this problem would be

$$u_1(e_t, 0) = 0 \quad \text{for all } t . \tag{5}$$

The unique value of e_t that would satisfy equation (5) is $\tilde{e}$. Thus, with a hypothetically committed monetary policy, the inflation rate would be

$$p_t = e_t = \tilde{e} \quad \text{for all } t . \tag{6}$$

Substituting equation (6) into equation (4) gives

$$U_0 = (1-\beta)^{-1} u(\tilde{e}, 0) > 0 . \tag{7}$$

Equation (7) says that, if the policymaker could make an irrevocable commitment, he would be able to achieve the positive expected value of realizations of its preference function associated with the best expected inflation rate and zero unexpected inflation. In equation (7), because $u(\cdot)$ is constant, it turns out that U_0 does not depend on λ.

4. AN OPPORTUNISTIC MONETARY POLICY

In reality, monetary policy is not subject to irrevocable commitments. Accordingly, although providing a useful benchmark, the preceding case does not provide an empirically relevant analysis of monetary policy.

To consider another useful benchmark case, suppose that the policymaker, in addition to being incapable of making irrevocable commitments, sets monetary policy opportunistically without regard either for his own announcements about policy intentions or for any effect that the actual inflation rate has on inflationary expectations. This strategy means that the policymaker chooses the program $\{p_t\}_{t=0}^{\infty}$ to maximize U_0, taking $\{e_t\}_{t=0}^{\infty}$ as given. The first-order condition for this problem would be for all t

$$\begin{aligned} &\text{either } u_2(e_t, p_t - e_t) = 0 \quad \text{with } p_t = e_t + \Pi \leqslant \bar{p} \\ &\text{or } u_2(e_t, p_t - e_t) > 0 \quad \text{with } p_t = \bar{p} < e_t + \Pi \,. \end{aligned} \tag{8}$$

Condition (8) implies that, with a hypothetically opportunistic monetary policy, the inflation rate would satisfy

$$p_t = \min(e_t + \Pi, \bar{p}) \quad \text{for all} \quad t \,. \tag{9}$$

In other words, the policymaker increases the actual inflation rate either until it exceeds expected inflation by the amount Π or until it reaches the maximum possible inflation rate.

Assuming that private agents correctly perceive the policymaker's opportunistic strategy, expected inflation would be consistent with equation (9)—that is, expected inflation would satisfy

$$e_t = \min(e_t + \Pi, \bar{p}) \quad \text{for all} \quad t \,, \tag{10}$$

which, given $\Pi > 0$, implies

$$e_t = \bar{p} \quad \text{for all} \quad t \,. \tag{11}$$

Equation (11) obtains because private agents know that, if expected inflation were less than the maximum inflation rate, the opportunistic policymaker would create actual inflation higher than expected inflation. The key to this result is the assumption that Π is strictly positive, which implies that $u_2(e_t,0)$ is strictly positive.

Combining equations (9) and (11) yields a unique equilibrium in which

$$e_t = p_t = \bar{p} \quad \text{for all} \quad t \,. \tag{12}$$

Equation (12) says that, as in Calvo's analysis, an opportunistic monetary policy would result in expected and actual inflation equal to the maximum inflation rate. In other words, an opportunistic monetary policy would imply hyperinflation.

As mentioned above, Kydland and Prescott, Barro, and Barro and Gordon avoided this conclusion by assuming that the policymaker is averse to high actual inflation rather than to high expected inflation. For example, if we changed the first argument of the $u(\cdot)$ function from e_t to p_t, without changing any other properties of this function, then the first-order condition for opportunistic maximization of U_0 could be $u_1 + u_2 = 0$ with $\tilde{e} < e_t = p_t < \bar{p}$.

Returning to the present model, substituting equation (12) into equation (4) gives

$$U_0 = (1-\beta)^{-1} u(\bar{p},0) = 0 . \tag{13}$$

Equation (13) confirms the general result that an opportunistic monetary policy would yield an expected value of realizations of the preference function unambiguously smaller than would a committed monetary policy.

5. A REPUTATIONAL MODEL

The analysis in the preceding sections considered two hypothetical cases. In one the policymaker irrevocably commits himself to a path of future inflation rates, and actual and expected inflation equal the best expected inflation rate. In the other the policymaker behaves opportunistically, and actual and expected inflation equal the maximum possible inflation rate. To develop a more realistic analysis, consider the following reputational model, which is a simplified version of a model of expectation formation developed in previous analysis of a reputational equilibrium for public debt—see Grossman and Van Huyck (1988).

This model focuses on the different modes of behavior of rational policymakers and compulsively opportunistic policymakers. A rational policymaker is able to resist the temptation to act opportunistically whenever the short-term gains from opportunistic behavior are not larger than its long-term costs. In contrast, a compulsively opportunistic policymaker behaves as a rational policymaker would behave if its discount factor were zero—that is, as if he is concerned only with the current realization of his preference function. Because the preference for positive unexpected inflation derives from the underlying objectives of monetary policy, it seems natural in modeling reputation to think of the policymaker as the institution that carries out the policies mandated by the political process, rather than as the set of individuals who are currently making policy.

The model assumes that policymakers always behave rationally, except that there is a positive, but infinitesimal, probability that at any date a policymaker's behavior becomes compulsively opportunistic. The model also assumes that private agents would view such a loss of rational restraint to be an irreversible change in the policymaker's mode of behavior.

These assumptions imply that a policymaker has a reputation for rationality and private agents expect rational behavior with probability of approximately unity as long as the policymaker has never exhibited opportunistic behavior. If, alternatively, the policymaker were ever to behave opportunistically, then the policymaker would lose permanently its reputation for rationality. [We can easily extend this analysis to allow producers to ignore an isolated instance of opportunistic behavior or to forget distant past behavior. In Grossman and Van Huyck (1988), memory is a stochastic process.]

This analysis is concerned only with the expectations of atomistic private agents and does not require or involve collusive strategic behavior by private agents. Although the assumed reaction of inflationary expectations to opportunistic behavior and the trigger punishment strategy assumed by Friedman (1971, 1977) in his analysis of supergames impose similar constraints on the policymaker's choice problem, we must be careful not to press this formal similarity too far. Specifically, we cannot appeal to strategic considerations to provide an a priori rationale for assumptions about the expectations of atomistic private agents. In some situations, of course, either the relevant private agents are large, like labor unions or consortia of creditors, or the relevant interactions involve a few large participants in the policy-making process, like different political parties, different branches of government, or even different governments. In these cases, a theory of punishment strategies rather than a theory of expectations and reputation would be relevant.

Given how private agents form their expectations, a rational policymaker, in choosing policy to maximize U_0, the expected value of present and future realizations of his preference function, has to signal that his mode of behavior is in fact rational, in order to avoid being mistakenly thought to have become compulsively opportunistic. To transmit the desired signal, a rational policymaker, given the fixed nonstochastic structure of the model, announces in decision interval zero a time-invariant path of inflation rates, $\{p_t\}_{t=0}^{\infty} = p^*$, such that p^* satisfies

$$(1-\beta)^{-1}u(p^*,0) \geqslant (1-\beta)^{-1}(1-\beta^{\lambda})\, u[p^*, \min(\Pi, \bar{p}-p^*)]\ . \tag{14}$$

The lhs of condition (14) gives the value of U_o that results from setting p_t equal to p^*, given e_t equal to p^*, for all $t \geqslant 0$. This value is calculated by substituting p^* for p_t and e_t in equation (4). Because $u(\cdot)$ is constant, this value does not depend on λ.

The rhs of condition (14) gives the value of U_o that would result from setting p_o equal to $\min(p^* + \Pi, \bar{p})$, given e_o equal to p^*. To calculate this value, observe that by setting p_0 equal to $\min(p^* + \Pi, \bar{p})$, the policymaker would obtain a realization of his preference function in decision interval zero equal to $u[p^*, \min(\Pi, \bar{p}-p^*)]$. At the same time, such opportunistic behavior would cause the expected inflation rate beginning in decision interval one to equal $\bar{p}$ as in the equilibrium with an opportunistic monetary policy. In such an equilibrium, as indicated by equation (13), the policymaker would obtain a realization of zero for his preference function. Thus, we substitute in equation (4) $u_t = u[p^*, \min(\Pi, \bar{p}-p^*)]$ for $t = 0$ and $u_t = 0$ for $t > 0$. Because the positive realization of the preference function lasts for only one decision interval, the rhs of condition (14) is positively related to λ, the length of a decision interval.

Condition (14) implies that, if private agents expect the inflation rate to be p^*, then, by planning to validate expectations by setting p_t for all $t \geqslant 0$ equal to p^*, the policymaker achieves a value of U_0 at least as high as he could achieve by setting p_0 opportunistically. Accordingly with expected inflation equal to p^*, a rational policymaker, exhibiting appropriate concern for his reputation, would resist the temptation to behave opportunistically and would validate his announcement of $\{p_t\}_{t=0}^{\infty} = p^*$. Thus, because private agents expect rational behavior from a heretofore rational policymaker with probability of approximately unity, this announcement is credible. Hence, we also have $\{e_t\}_{t=0}^{\infty} = p^*$. The literature denotes such a credible time path of expected and actual inflation rates as "time consistent."

6. REPUTATIONAL EQUILIBRIUM

Taking account of its reputation, the rational policymaker's problem in decision interval zero is to choose the program $\{p_t\}_{t=0}^{\infty} = p^*$ to maximize U_0, as given by equation (4), subject to the constraint given by condition (14). The actual announcement of p^*, of course, can be implicit, because the private agents can infer what the policymaker would explicitly announce. [In a stochastic model, the policymaker might want to announce a state-contingent inflation rate, which could present a difficult communication problem. Grossman and Van Huyck (1988) develop the theoretical form for this generalization in a model that treats sovereign debts as contingent claims.]

In analyzing the hypothetical case of a committed monetary policy, we found that the value of p_t that maximizes U_0, given p_t equal to e_t for all $t \geqslant 0$, is $\tilde{e}$. Accordingly, if condition (14) is not a binding constraint on the choice of p^*, then p^* also equals $\tilde{e}$—that is, the reputational equilibrium would be the same as the outcome of a hypothetically committed monetary policy.

To determine whether condition (14) is a binding constraint, it is necessary to evaluate condition (14) under the hypothesis that p^* equals $\tilde{e}$. Making the appropriate substitutions in condition (14), the necessary and sufficient condition for p^* to equal $\tilde{e}$ is

$$u(\tilde{e},0) \geqslant (1-\beta^{\lambda})\, u[\tilde{e}, \min(\Pi, \bar{p}-\tilde{e})] \,. \tag{15}$$

Condition (15) holds if $1-\beta^{\lambda}$, which is the ratio of the capitalization factor for the realization associated with opportunistic behavior to the capitalization factor for the realization associated with the hypothetically committed monetary policy, is sufficiently small. The ratio $1-\beta^{\lambda}$ is smaller the larger is β, which is the weight given to future months in calculating U_0, and the smaller is λ, which is the length of the relevant decision interval that determines how fast private agents would react to opportunistic behavior by the policymaker. The value of λ is critical because, as the lag in the adjustment of inflationary expectations becomes small, the potential gain from opportunistic behavior also becomes small.

Condition (15) also can be satisfied if the ratio of the monthly realization of the preference function associated with opportunistic behavior, given expected inflation equal to $\tilde{e}$, to the monthly realization of the preference function associated with the hypothetically committed monetary policy, is sufficiently small. Given the form of the $u(\cdot)$ function, if $\Pi < \bar{p} - \tilde{e}$, then this ratio is smaller the smaller is Π.

If condition (15) is not satisfied, then condition (14) is a binding constraint and p^* cannot equal $\tilde{e}$, Moreover, the value of $(1-\beta)^{-1}u(p^*,0)$ decreases monotonically as p^* diverges from $\tilde{e}$. Accordingly, if p^* does not equal $\tilde{e}$, then p^* is the member of the set of values of p that could satisfy condition (14) that is closest to $\tilde{e}$.

A value of p^* equal to $\bar{p}$ would satisfy condition (14) for any value of β^λ. Also, $u[p^*, \min(\Pi, \bar{p}-p^*)]$ is larger than $u(p^*,0)$ for any value of p^* less than $\bar{p}$. Thus, if β were zero—that is, if the policymaker disregarded future realizations of its preference function—or if λ were infinite—that is, if the private agents would wait forever to react to opportunistic behavior—then $\bar{p}$ would be the only value of p^* that would satisfy condition (14). In this case, p^* would equal $\bar{p}$.

The interesting question is whether, with condition (14) as a binding constraint, but with β positive and λ finite, p^* can be less than $\bar{p}$. The answer to this question is positive if there exists a nonempty set of values of p that satisfy

$$u(p,0) \geqslant (1-\beta^\lambda)\, u[p, \min(\Pi, \bar{p}-p)]\,, \tag{16}$$

where $\bar{p} > p \neq \tilde{e}$ and

$$u(\tilde{e},0) < (1-\beta^\lambda)\, u[\tilde{e}, \min(\Pi, \bar{p}-\tilde{e})]\,.$$

Condition (16) requires the existence of a nonempty set of values of p that satisfy

$$u[\tilde{e}, \min(\Pi, \bar{p}-\tilde{e})] - u[p, \min(\Pi, \bar{p}-p)] > (1-\beta^\lambda)^{-1}\,[u(\tilde{e},0) - u(p,0)] \tag{17}$$

where $\bar{p} > p \neq \tilde{e}$.

With $u_{12} \approx 0$, condition (17) can be satisfied only for values of p such that

$$\min(\Pi, \bar{p}-\tilde{e}) > \min(\Pi, \bar{p}-p)\,. \tag{18}$$

Regardless of whether Π is larger or smaller than $\bar{p}-\tilde{e}$, condition (18) requires

$$p > \tilde{e} \quad \text{and} \quad p > \bar{p} - \Pi\,. \tag{19}$$

Condition (19) says that p^* has to be both higher than $\tilde{e}$ and sufficiently high that $\bar{p} - p^*$ is less than Π. In other words, p^* has to be sufficiently high that the policymaker could not create unexpected inflation as high as Π even by choosing the maximum possible inflation rate. [We could relax this latter condition by assuming $u_{12} < 0$ or, more radically, by assuming, as in the reputational model of Barro and Gordon (July 1983), that policymaker preferences are a convex function of actual inflation rather than expected inflation.]

Condition (17) also implies that the larger is $1-\beta^{\lambda}$ the smaller can be the difference between $\min(\Pi, \bar{p}-\tilde{e})$ and $\min(\Pi, \bar{p}-p)$ and, hence, the larger is the set of values of p that satisfy condition (18). This result obtains because the larger is $1-\beta^{\lambda}$ the more rapidly the value of opportunistic behavior declines as e becomes higher. Thus, the larger is $1-\beta^{\lambda}$ the lower can p^* be relative to $\tilde{e}$ and $\bar{p}-\Pi$. In sum, taken together conditions (15) and (17) imply that, if Π and $1-\beta^{\lambda}$ are small, then p^* is likely to equal $\tilde{e}$, whereas, if Π and $1-\beta^{\lambda}$ are large, then p^* is likely to be larger than $\tilde{e}$, but it is possible for p^* to be small relative to $\bar{p}$.

7. SUMMARY

In this paper monetary policy attempts to maximize the expected value of present and relevant future realizations of a generic function that involves proximate preferences for low expected inflation and positive unexpected inflation. Importantly, this proximate preference function does not involve actual inflation other than as a component of unexpected inflation.

To analyze policymaker strategy, the paper focussed on the linkage between current policy actions and expected future policy actions associated with a reputation for rationality. The main qualitative effect of this linkage is to cause rational policymakers, in order to signal that their mode of behavior is rational, to behave as if they are concerned about controlling inflation even though they do not have a direct preference for a low actual inflation rate. As a result, the set of time-consistent inflation rates, which without either irrevocable commitments or reputational effects would include only the pathological outcome of hyperinflation, can expand to include patterns of monetary policy that are both realistic and relatively benign. This effect creates a presumption that reputation plays an essential role in the actual formulation of monetary policy. [An analogous result, derived in the reputational model of sovereign debt analyzed in Grossman and Van Huyck (1988), is that the sovereign faithfully meets its debt-servicing obligations even though it has no moral compulsion not to repudiate its debts.]

In the reputational equilibrium the actual and expected inflation rates are equal to the best credible expected inflation rate. A credible expected inflation rate has the property that, if private agents expect this inflation rate, then the value to the policymaker of maintaining a reputation for rationality by resisting the temptation to act opportunistically is at least as large as the value of creating unexpected inflation. If the set of credible expected inflation rates contains the inflation rate that would be optimal with a hypothetically committed monetary policy, then that inflation rate is also the reputational equilibrium. In this case, reputation serves as a perfect substitute for infeasible commitments. Otherwise, the inflation rate in the reputational equilibrium is higher than the inflation rate under a hypothetically committed monetary policy, but it is the lowest inflation rate in the set of credible expected inflation rates. The analysis shows that reputation is more likely to be a perfect substitute for infeasible commitments, the smaller is the increment in the realization of the policymaker's preference function that would result from opportunistic behavior, the larger is the policymaker's discount factor, and perhaps most importantly, the shorter is the decision interval that determines how fast private agents would react to opportunistic behavior by the policymaker.

This decision interval depends on the nature of the underlying real objectives of monetary policy and on the structure of the economy. Specifically, the analysis implies that if, for example, the policymaker's preference for positive unexpected inflation results from its effect on real wages and aggregate economic activity, then inflation is lower the more frequently are nominal wages adjusted. Alternatively, if the policymaker is interested in reducing the real return on nominally denominated assets, then inflation is lower the shorter is the average maturity of these assets. If, instead, the policymaker is mainly interested in seigniorage, then inflation is lower the more frequently that private agents would adjust their transactions patterns.

In this analysis private agents know that the policymaker prefers positive unexpected inflation and is not separately concerned about actual inflation. Thus, the analysis shows that a low equilibrium inflation rate does not require the existence, or potential existence, of a policymaker who prefers low inflation or who does not prefer positive unexpected inflation. A good outcome, if it occurs, can be unrelated to good intentions.

LITERATURE CITED

Barro, Robert J. "Inflationary Finance under Discretion and Rules." *Canadian Journal of Economics* 16 (February 1983), 3–16.

______. "Reputation in a Model of Monetary Policy with Incomplete Information." *Journal of Monetary Economics* 17 (January 1986), 3–2.

Barro, Robert J., and Donald B. Gordon. "Rules, Discretion, and Reputation in a Model of Monetary Policy." *Journal of Monetary Economics* 12 (July 1983), 101–21.

______. "A Positive Theory of Monetary Policy in a Natural Rate Model." *Journal of Political Economy* 91 (August 1983), 589–610.

Calvo, Guillermo. "Optimal Seigniorage from Money Creation." *Journal of Monetary Economics* 4 (August 1978), 503–17.

Friedman, James W. "A Noncooperative Equilibrium for Supergames." *Review of Economic Studies* 38 (January 1971), 1–12.

______. *Oligopoly and the Theory of Games*. Amsterdam: North-Holland, 1977.

Grossman, Herschel I., and Suk Jae Noh. "A Theory of Kleptocracy with Probabilistic Survival and Reputation." Unpublished manuscript, December 1989.

______. "Proprietary Public Finance and Economic Welfare." Unpublished manuscript, January 1990.

Grossman, Herschel I., and John B. Van Huyck. "Sovereign Debt as a Contingent Claim: Excusable Default, Repudiation, and Reputation." *American Economic Review* 78 (December 1988), 1088–97.

Kydland, Finn E., and Edward C. Prescott. "Rules Rather than Discretion: The Inconsistency of Optimal Plans." *Journal of Political Economy* 85 (June 1977), 473–92.

JOHN V. DUCA
DAVID D. VANHOOSE

Loan Commitments and Optimal Monetary Policy

THERE IS A GROWING RECOGNITION that standard models of the monetary policy process are "sterile" in that they oversimplify the role of bank credit. Recent work (notably Bernanke 1983, Bernanke and Blinder 1988, and Gertler 1988) has attempted to enrich the traditional paradigm by incorporating bank lending as a fundamental part of the monetary policy transmission mechanism. Coinciding with this renewal of interest in credit has been the increased use by individuals and firms of bank loan commitment contracts. Figure 1 illustrates how the sizable portion of all short-term bank business loans (of one year or less in maturity) taken down under commitment has increased since the early 1980s. This trend has led to a significant amount of work to understand the microeconomics of loan commitment contracts (for example, James 1981, Thakor 1982, Melnik and Plaut 1986, and Kanatas 1987).

Although some earlier work briefly discusses the implications of changing loan contract structures for monetary policy [for example, Deshmukh, Greenbaum, and Kanatas (1982, pp. 935–37) and Campbell (1978, pp. 242–43)], only recently has any serious work focused specifically on this issue. Recent preliminary work by Sofianos, Wachtel, and Melnik (1987) and by Glick and Plaut (1987) has

Work on this paper was initiated while VanHoose was a visiting economist at the Board of Governors of the Federal Reserve System and was completed while he was a visiting scholar at the Federal Reserve Bank of Kansas City. The authors are grateful for very helpful comments from Allen Berger, Joshua Feinman, Vincent Reinhart, Gregory Udell, William Whitesell, Bill Witte, and two anonymous referees. All views expressed are solely those of the authors and do not necessarily correspond to those held by the Board of Governors, or the Federal Reserve Bank of Kansas City.

JOHN V. DUCA *is an economist in the Division of Monetary Affairs, Board of Governors of the Federal Reserve System.* DAVID D. VANHOOSE *is assistant professor of economics, Indiana University.*

Journal of Money, Credit, and Banking, Vol. 22, No. 2 (May 1990)

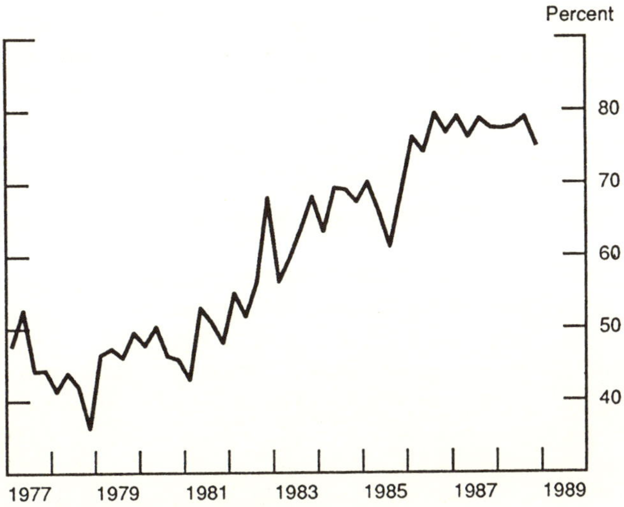

FIG. 1. Commitment Share of C & I Loan Extensions with Maturities under One Year

explored how loan commitments insulate borrowers from credit rationing. According to Sofianos et al., monetary policy works through the two channels of quantity restrictions and interest rate effects; greater use of loan commitments reduces the importance of the former channel and thereby places a greater burden upon the latter. Glick and Plaut go further, arguing that "monetary policy becomes potent *only* when agents are rationed by credit ceilings, and otherwise loses its effectiveness" (p. 3), and that "as a result of credit advanced through off-balance-sheet facilities, the monetary authorities can lose control over liquidity, interest rates, and real activity, at least when 'control' is being exercized in the form of fine tuning through open-market operations" (p. 28). Hence, both of these papers stress how commitments enable firms to avoid credit rationing, thereby reducing the potency of monetary policy.

In contrast, this paper focuses upon how increased commitment lending affects the optimal conduct of monetary policy when the central bank uses an interest-rate-based transmission mechanism. Survey evidence in Avery and Berger (1988) and Duca (1988) suggests that loan commitments may not significantly reduce the incidence of quantity rationing of businesses in the aggregate. Recent theoretical models of rationing suggest that lenders most likely will ration the least creditworthy loan applicants or those whose creditworthiness has declined. Avery and Berger (1988) find that loans taken down under commitment have lower default rates than other business loans, suggesting that firms posing relatively less credit risk are more likely to borrow under commitments. Duca (1988) finds that the firms most likely to be rationed tend to face more binding limits on the funds available from commitments. In addition, the vast majority of commitments have loan covenants (material adverse change clauses) that allow banks to void contracts if a borrower's creditworthiness declines. This reduces the ability of firms to insulate themselves from quantity rationing with loan commitments. Moreover, data from the Federal Reserve's Survey of Terms of Bank Lending show that the share of business loans borrowed under commitment tends to rise with loan size. This suggests that large firms, which probably pose less credit risk and are thus less likely to be rationed, tend to borrow under commitments to a greater extent than smaller, and probably less secure, firms.[1] Together, this empirical evidence suggests that commitments do not appreciably limit the incidence of credit rationing.[2]

Whereas other work has emphasized the role of loan commitments as a means of avoiding quantity rationing, the model constructed here highlights the increased flexibility commitments give agents to respond to contemporaneous changes in income that were unanticipated when loan contracts were negotiated, at the cost of an increased susceptibility to capital losses resulting from unanticipated interest rate variations. Because this trade-off determines agents' choices between flexible-rate commitments and more traditional fixed-rate loans, the extent to which monetary policy constrains interest rate and income volatility is crucial. In turn, changes in the share of firms using flexible-rate commitments can significantly influence how exogenous structural disturbances affect nominal income and interest rates and thereby can alter the optimal monetary policy. This study attempts to capture, in a stylized model, the implications of this feedback between loan contract choice and the determination of an optimal interest-rate-conditioned monetary policy. Essentially, this approach represents a way of dealing with the "Lucas critique" and of demonstrating a situation where it likely has empirically important implications for policy.

A very interesting implication of the analysis is that, as discussed by Bernanke and Blinder (1988) and Brunner and Meltzer (1988), inclusion of an important role for bank credit in the monetary policy transmission mechanism eliminates the separation between the financial and goods sectors presumed by standard models couched in an IS–LM framework. Although this result does not rule out a potential usefulness for the IS–LM paradigm when bank credit is explicitly incorporated, it does imply that some of the policy implications from this framework must be modified. One specific example highlighted is a result from Poole's (1970) seminal analysis, which is that greater money demand variability should be offset by increased interest rate smoothing by the monetary authority. Our model indicates that this result does not necessarily follow when loan contracting is endogenous.

The analysis begins by constructing a stylized Poole (1970)-type IS–LM structure in section 1. The model parallels that of Bernanke and Blinder (1988) by integrating explicitly the interaction between credit and goods market clearing. Section 2 investigates the response of an optimal combination policy to varia-

[1]For evidence on large versus small business credit risk see Churchill and Lewis (1985).

[2]This is not to say that small-sized agents are not credit rationed in the consumer loan, home mortgage, and small business loan markets. In addition, households with home equity loans, which are a type of household loan commitment, are, according to Federal Reserve survey data, higher wealth and income households that are least likely to be rationed.

tions in the proportion of bank lending under commitments. In section 3, the choice between traditional fixed-rate loans and floating-rate commitment loans is modeled and is used to determine the share of bank loans that are negotiated as commitments. Based on the results of the previous two sections, section 4 derives implications for the interaction between the use of commitments and optimal monetary policy. Section 5 summarizes conclusions and discusses some future directions for research.

1. THE MODEL

It is assumed that all firms make decisions concerning investment financing at time $t-1$, prior to the realizations of exogenous disturbances in the economy. There are two types of firms in the economy. A fraction $(1-\theta)$ negotiates traditional (that is, noncommitment) fixed-rate bank loan contracts at time $t-1$ that set the loan rate that will prevail for time t, along with the amount of the loan during period t. The remainder (θ) negotiates floating-rate commitment loan contracts in which the firms pay a markup over the spot rate at time t, but have the discretion to borrow as needed or pay down any principal.[3]

Throughout, we assume that banks are risk neutral and offer floating-rate commitments and fixed-rate, noncommitment loans at the same expected markup over market interest rates expected to prevail during loan contracts. The latter follows from the risk neutrality assumption and from the additional assumptions that banks can issue liabilities or reduce holding of securities to fund fixed-rate traditional loans without exposing themselves to rate risk and that banks hold enough securities to meet unexpected commitment loan demand at virtually no extra cost to themselves.

The floating rate paid under commitments is given by

$$r_t^c = r_t^s + \gamma , \tag{1}$$

where $r_t^c \equiv$ actual commitment loan rate, $r_t^s \equiv$ spot market interest rate, and $\gamma \equiv$ constant intermediation costs (for example, default risk). Thus, a bank that

[3]Such commitment loans are called "demand loans." Other commitment loans allow a firm to borrow up to a limit, but penalize the firm if it pays down any principal before the loan's fixed maturity ends. These other commitment loans are more likely to have fixed rates, but the pay-down penalties limit the flexibility of a firm by reducing its ability to exploit an option against the bank.

In practice, some firms rely upon both commercial paper and bank loan financing. Allowing for this possibility would not qualitatively affect the results, but would unnecessarily clutter them. Furthermore, some firms obtain bank loan commitments to back up commercial paper [see Duca (1988)]. Kanatas (1987) argues that this is done to signal open market lenders that the commercial paper issuer is creditworthy in an incentive-compatible way. Since such commitments are primarily used for information signaling reasons and to guarantee ("back up") commercial paper issuance, they are irrelevant to the focus of this paper and probably amount to a small share of actual loans taken down under commitment. For these reasons,they are ignored.

Of course, many established firms have access to the commercial paper market. However, if one assumes that the share of firms that issue paper is constant over the horizon relevant for policy analysis, the qualitative results of this model are not changed [see an earlier version of this study—Duca and VanHoose (1988)].

negotiates a commitment loan precommits itself to making credit available to a firm during period t using a spot rate as an index,[4] and such a firm precommits itself to paying a variable rather than a fixed-loan rate. The interest rate negotiated with banks by the fraction $(1-\theta)$ of firms that choose fixed-rate bank loan contracts is

$$r_t^f = E_{t-1}r_t^s + \gamma , \tag{2}$$

which is the $t-1$ expectation of the bank commitment rate (that is, the sum of intermediation costs and the expected spot rate), where $E_{t-1} \equiv$ the expectation based on time $t-1$ information.

The quantity of traditional fixed-rate loans demanded equals

$$L_t^f = \alpha_0 + \alpha_1 E_{t-1} Y_t - \alpha_2 r_t^f , \tag{3}$$

where $Y_t \equiv$ nominal income. Equation (3) implies that the amount of fixed-rate credit demanded depends positively upon expected time t income (sales) at the time contracts are written and negatively upon the negotiated loan rate.

The volume of commitment loans demanded is given by

$$L_t^c = \alpha_o + \alpha_1 E_{t-1} Y_t - \alpha_2 r_t^c + \alpha_3(Y_t - E_{t-1} Y_t) . \tag{4}$$

Loan demand of firms with commitments depends positively upon the expectation of time t income when the contract was written in period $t-1$ and depends negatively upon the prevailing commitment rate at time t following the realization of time t disturbances and the resulting implied capital losses or gains for these firms. Although firms with commitments are exposed to such unanticipated losses or gains, they gain flexibility to adjust their desired credit takedowns to changes in income that were unanticipated when bank loan contracts were negotiated, in contrast to precommitting themselves to borrow a prenegotiated amount with a traditional loan. Hence, time t loan demand of these com-

[4]Throughout the analysis, all commitments are assumed to have floating rates. Recent issues of the *Federal Reserve Bulletin* indicate that there are sizable bank *extensions* of short-term fixed-rate commitments [about $26 billion, according to a terms of lending survey summarized in the September 1988 *Bulletin* (p. A70)] as well as floating-rate commitments (about $17 billion for the same time period). However, roughly half of these fixed-rate commitment loans are overnight reverse repurchase arrangements with Treasury securities which are typically used for liquidity management purposes. Of the remaining $13 billion in fixed-rate commitments, only $3 billion are demand loans, whereas the remainder are commitment loans which usually penalize borrowers if they pay down any principal before the fixed, stated maturity. According to this survey, demand loans comprised roughly half of all nonovernight, short-term loans. Fixed-rate commitments constitute only 1/6 of demand loans, the type of commitment modeled (see footnote 3). Therefore, the stylized simplification that all demand-loan-type commitments are made on a floating-rate basis is not unreasonable on empirical grounds. From a theoretical perspective, floating-rate contracts are optimal under our model's simplifications and the assumption that noncommitment and commitment loans are offered at the same expected markup over market interest rates. The reason is that banks would need to charge a larger markup on fixed-rate commitments to offset the option value to borrowers of taking advantage of the bank's exposure to interest rate risk.

mitment borrowers depends positively upon contemporaneous innovations in income.

Equations (1) through (4) imply that total loan demand is

$$\begin{aligned} L_t &= \theta L_t^c + (1-\theta)L_t^f . \\ &= \alpha_0 + \alpha_1 E_{t-1} Y_t - \alpha_2(1-\theta)E_{t-1}r_t^s - \alpha_2\gamma - \alpha_2\theta r_t^s \\ &\quad + \alpha_3\theta(Y_t - E_{t-1} Y_t) . \end{aligned} \tag{5}$$

Nominal income is assumed to depend positively upon the quantity of credit extended, according to

$$Y_t = \omega_0 + \omega_1 L_t + \delta_t, \text{ with } \delta_t \sim N(0,\sigma_\delta^2) . \tag{6}$$

Equations (5) and (6) imply the following semi-reduced-form IS schedule:

$$\begin{aligned} (1 - \beta_3\theta)Y_t = \beta_0 + (\beta_1 - \beta_3\theta)E_{t-1} Y_t - \beta_2(1-\theta)E_{t-1}r_t^s - \beta_2\gamma \\ - \beta_2\theta r_t^s + \delta_t , \end{aligned} \tag{7}$$

where $\beta_0 \equiv \omega_0 + \omega_1\alpha_0, \beta_1 \equiv \omega_1\alpha_1, \beta_2 \equiv \omega_1\alpha_2, \beta_3 \equiv \omega_1\alpha_3$, and β_3 can be interpreted as the marginal propensity to spend out of unanticipated income for commitment borrowers, which is assumed to be less than 1.

The quantity of deposits held at banks is determined by a deposit (D_t) demand function of the form

$$D_t = \mu_0 + \mu_1 Y_t - \mu_2 r_t^s + \nu_t, \nu_t \sim N(0,\sigma_\nu^2) . \tag{8}$$

Banks must meet reserve requirements and hold excess reserves that bear an opportunity cost governed by the spot interest rate, implying the following rearranged reserve (R_t) demand function:

$$D_t = \zeta_0 + \zeta_1 R_t + \zeta_2 r_t^s . \tag{9}$$

The central bank supplies reserves to the banking system according to

$$R_t = \bar{R} + \lambda r_t^s , \tag{10}$$

where λ is a Poole (1970)-type combination policy parameter; for $\lambda = 0$, the level of reserves is fixed by the central bank, while $\lambda \rightarrow \infty$ implies that reserves are varied to stabilize the spot interest rate r_t^s. Finite, nonzero values of λ correspond to use of a combination policy.

The LM schedule follows directly from (8), (9), and (10):

$$r_t^s = (\mu_0 - \zeta_0 + \mu_1 Y_t - \zeta_1 \bar{R} + \nu_t) \,/\, (\zeta_2 + \mu_2 + \zeta_1 \lambda) \,. \tag{11}$$

Substituting (11) into (5) gives a semi-reduced-form for nominal income:

$$\begin{aligned}[\Omega(1 - \beta_3\theta) + \beta_2\mu_1\theta]Y_t = \; & \Omega\beta_0 + \Omega(\beta_1 - \beta_3\theta)E_{t-1}Y_t \\ & - \Omega\beta_2(1-\theta)E_{t-1}r_t^s - \Omega\beta_2\gamma \\ & - \beta_2\theta(\mu_0 - \zeta_0 - \zeta_1\bar{R}) \\ & - \beta_2\theta\nu_t + \Omega\delta_t \,,\end{aligned} \tag{12}$$

where $\Omega \equiv \zeta_2 + \mu_2 + \zeta_1\lambda$.

To solve for Y_t, propose the solution form

$$Y_t = \pi_0 + \pi_1\nu_t + \pi_2\delta_t \,, \tag{13}$$

so that

$$E_t Y_{t+1} = \pi_0 \,. \tag{14}$$

Using equations (12) through (14) yields the solutions:

$$\pi_0 = \frac{\Omega\beta_0 - \beta_2(\mu_0 - \zeta_0 - \zeta_1\bar{R}) - \Omega\beta_2\gamma}{\Omega(1-\beta_1) + \mu_1\beta_2} \,,$$

$$\pi_1 = \frac{-\beta_2\theta}{\Omega[1 - \beta_3\theta] + \beta_2\mu_1\theta} \,,$$

and

$$\pi_2 = \frac{\Omega}{\Omega[1 - \beta_3\theta] + \beta_2\mu_1\theta} \,, \tag{15}$$

The reduced-form expression for nominal income is thus

$$\begin{aligned} Y_t = \; & [\Omega\beta_0 - \beta_2(\mu_0 - \zeta_0 - \zeta_1\bar{R}) - \Omega\beta_2\gamma] \,/\, [\Omega(1-\beta_1) + \mu_1\beta_2] \\ & + \frac{\Omega\delta_t - \beta_2\theta\nu_t}{\Omega(1 - \beta_3\theta) + \beta_2\mu_1\theta} \,. \end{aligned} \tag{16}$$

This expression indicates that both the proportion of lending under commitments (θ) and the choice of the combination policy parameter (λ) affect how exogenous disturbances influence the actual level of income.

2. OPTIMAL MONETARY POLICY AND THE COMMITMENT SHARE OF LENDING

For the sake of simplicity, the central bank is assumed to minimize the quadratic objective $E_{t-1}(Y_t - Y^*)^2$, where Y^* is a target level of nominal income. Using (16), the value of this objective is

$$E_{t-1}(Y_t - Y^*)^2 = (E_{t-1}Y_t - Y^*)^2 + E_{t-1}(Y_t - E_{t-1}Y_t)^2 =$$
$$(\{[\Omega\beta_0 - \beta_2(\mu_0 - \zeta_0 - \zeta_1\bar{R}) - \Omega\beta_2\gamma] /$$
$$[\Omega(1-\beta_1) + \mu_1\beta_2]\} - Y^*)^2$$
$$+ \frac{\Omega^2\sigma_\delta^2 + \beta_2^2\theta^2\sigma_\nu^2}{\{\Omega[1 - \beta_3\theta] + \beta_2\mu_1\theta\}^2} . \quad (17)$$

The bias term in (17) can be eliminated via an appropriate setting for $\bar{R}$, leaving the setting for λ to minimize the variance term. The optimal value for λ can be computed to be

$$\lambda^* = \frac{\beta_2[1 - \beta_3\theta]\theta\sigma_\nu^2}{\zeta_1\mu_1\sigma_\delta^2} - [(\zeta_2 + \mu_2)/\zeta_1] . \quad (18)$$

Equation (18) implies that, when θ is exogenous, if the monetary authority aims to remove the contemporaneous effects of loan demand/spending disturbances (δ_t), then the optimal policy sets λ to yield $\Omega = 0$. This policy produces a vertical LM schedule, thereby offsetting the effects of these disturbances. In contrast, neutralizing the contemporaneous effects of LM shocks (ν_t) requires $\Omega \rightarrow \infty$ ($\lambda \rightarrow \infty$). Both results are consistent with the Poole analysis, provided that θ is exogenous.

It also follows from (18) that the effect on the optimal combination policy of an increase in the proportion of firms that use floating-rate bank commitment contracts is given by

$$\partial\lambda^*/\partial\theta = \beta_2\sigma_\nu^2[1-2\beta_3\theta] / \zeta_1\mu_1\sigma_\delta^2 \gtrless 0 . \quad (19)$$

Hence, an increase in the share of firms with commitments has a indeterminate effect on the optimal combination monetary policy. This ambiguity arises because a rise in θ has three effects, one which increases λ^* and two which decrease λ^*. Equation (7) implies that the slope of the IS schedule, $\partial r_t^s/\partial Y_t = -\{1-\beta_3\theta\} / \beta_2\theta$, becomes less steep, so that the interest-sensitivity of income increases as θ rises. Hence, a given IS shift has a smaller effect on equilibrium income, ceteris paribus. This implies that there is less loss incurred by flattening the LM schedule in order to offset IS shocks by enlarging λ^*. In addition, LM disturbances have a greater effect on income when the IS schedule is less steep, which increases the policy gain from flattening the LM schedule. Therefore, this effect tends to produce an unambiguously positive relationship between λ^* and θ.

This point is illustrated in Figure 2, which depicts an initial equilibrium where the certainty equivalent level of income is at the target Y^* where the LM schedule LM ($\nu_t = 0$) intersects two alternative IS schedules. A positive money demand disturbance shifts the LM schedule to the left, resulting in an equilibrium income level of $Y'_t | \theta_0$ at point B for some fixed initial θ_0. For a larger θ, $\theta_1 > \theta_0$, the reduced steepness of the IS schedule would imply a greater fall in income to $Y'_t | \theta_1$ at point C. In the limiting case, elimination of the enlarged effects of these shocks requires $\lambda^* \rightarrow \infty$. Given no change in the variability of IS disturbances, increasing λ^* would be optimal.

However, (7) indicates that the multiplier linking spending shocks (δ_t) to nominal income, $1/(1 - \beta_3\theta)$, where $\beta_3\theta$ is the average firm marginal propensity to spend contemporaneously, is increasing in θ. This effect is enlarged by a greater value of $\beta_3 \equiv \omega_1\alpha_3$. Hence, the more flexibility derived by firms through use of commitments (that is, as α_3 rises), the larger is the aggregate propensity by firms to respond to income innovations. In turn, a larger θ implies an increased share of firms that contemporaneously respond to income innovations, and therefore, an IS schedule which is more sensitive to spending disturbances (δ_t).

Ceteris paribus, these combined effects require a steeper LM schedule, as shown in Figure 3. Point A in the figure is an initial certainty equivalent equili-

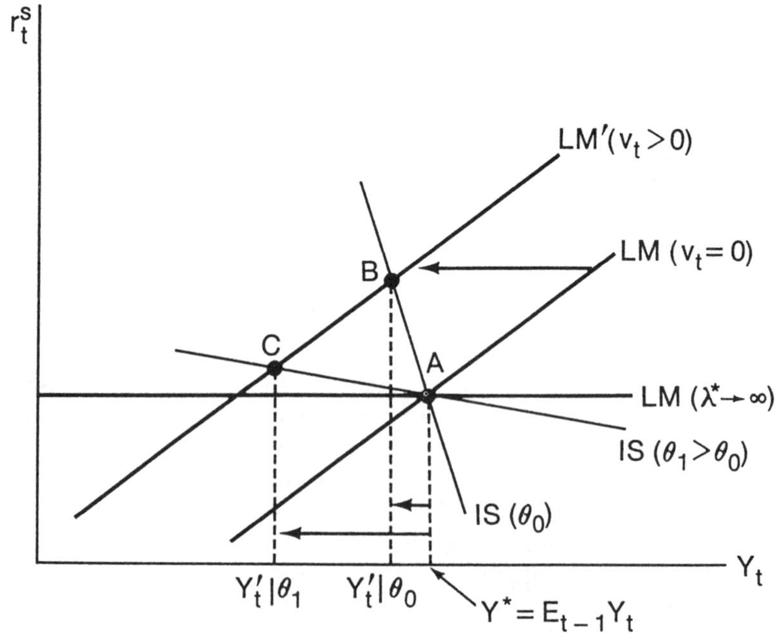

FIG. 2. The Effects of LM Shocks as Commitment Share (θ) Increases

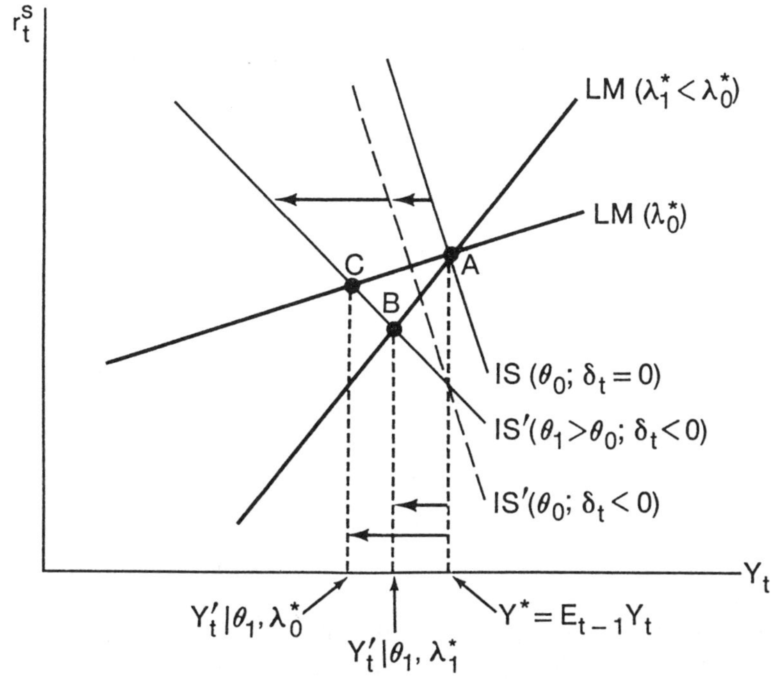

FIG. 3. The Enlarged Effects of IS Shocks as Commitment Share (θ) Increases

brium point for an initial value of θ of θ_0 and for two alternative choices for λ^*. An IS disturbance ($\delta_t < 0$) shifts the IS schedule downward and to the left and, for a greater value of θ, say $\theta_1 > \theta_0$, has a larger effect than otherwise would have been the case. Income under a smaller value of λ^*, say $\lambda_1^* < \lambda_0^*$, falls by less (to $Y_t' | \theta_1, \lambda_1^*$) as compared to the case of a larger λ^* (where income falls to $Y_t' | \theta_1, \lambda_0^*$). Hence, these effects imply a smaller optimal value for λ^*.

Equation (19) implies that $\partial \lambda^* / \partial \theta \gtrless 0$ as $\beta_3 \lesseqgtr 1/2\theta$. Hence, the effect of increased firm use of bank loan commitment contracts upon optimal monetary policy depends crucially upon the flexibility available to firms to respond to contemporaneous income innovations by adjusting their credit take-downs appropriately. As the marginal propensity to spend contemporaneously increases, the effect of a higher θ on the optimal λ is reduced. Therefore, the relative magnitude of the parameter β_3, which influences the size of the nominal spending multiplier, determines the direction of the optimal monetary policy response to an increase in the use of commitments.

3. FIRM CHOICE BETWEEN COMMITMENT AND TRADITIONAL LOAN CONTRACTS

Taken alone, the analysis of the previous sections suffers from the "Lucas critique" problem in that the proportion of firms that use commitments is exogenous. In fact, firms generally will find it optimal to adjust the type of loan contract chosen in light of anticipated economic conditions, which depend upon the conduct of monetary policy. Therefore, the analysis would be incomplete if it did not account for an endogenous response of firms' loan contract choices to central bank policy decisions. This section provides an intuitive model of loan contract choice which characterizes the trade-offs inherent in deciding between the two contract types and which permits tractable solutions.

Each firm borrows to finance irreversible one-period investments and variable working capital needs. The latter are assumed to be proportional to average output per firm Y/n, with the distribution:

$$\omega_t^i \sim N(\eta^i \mu Y/n, (\eta^i/n)^2 \sigma_Y^2) , \tag{20}$$

where $\sigma_Y^2 \equiv E_{t-1}(Y_t - E_{t-1} Y_t)^2$, μ is a constant, and η^i represents the sensitivity of firm i's working capital needs with respect to income, with η^i distributed uniformly over the interval [0,1]. A firm that negotiates traditional fixed-rate contracts can borrow an amount equal to its investment plus its expected working capital needs. In contrast, a firm with a flexible-rate loan commitment can borrow an amount equal to its investment plus its expected working capital needs plus or minus an amount that can offset any actual disturbance to working capital that occurs during the contract. The flexibility of commitments thereby insulates a firm from over- or underborrowing when there are working capital shocks that were not anticipated when the loan contract was negotiated.

Working capital shocks may asymmetrically affect a firm with fixed-rate loans. If such a firm has overborrowed, it can invest in a security yielding an expected rate of $E_{t-1} r_t^s$, which is γ less than the loan rate. Therefore, its actual loss depends upon the amount of the markup γ and the amount of overborrowing, $\eta^i(E_{t-1} Y_t - Y_t) < 0$. It is assumed that a firm adjusts the scale of its operations (that is, its capital stock) in a linear relation to the present value of its net worth and that the transactions costs of doing so are proportional to the squared amount of upsizing or downsizing. This last assumption is made to make the model ultimately solvable for θ in terms of σ_r^2 and σ_Y^2, which permits tractable solutions for λ. It follows that the expected cost arising from adjusting to unanticipated capital losses from overborrowing with a fixed-rate loan can be approximated by

$$E_{t-1} \int_0^\infty [g\{(\gamma\eta^i)(E_{t-1} Y_t - Y_t)\}^2] \, d(E_{t-1} Y_t - Y_t) = g\gamma^2 (\eta^i)^2 \sigma_Y^2 / 2 , \tag{21a}$$

where $\sigma_Y^2 \equiv E_{t-1}(Y_t - E_{t-1} Y_t)^2$.

In addition to overborrowing, if the firm has borrowed too little, it produces less efficiently and suffers a loss that is increasing in the shortfall.[5] In order to

[5]The model explicitly assumes that these firms are rationed, ex post. Realistically, it is possible that such firms could take down loans on a spot loan market to make up the unanticipated shortfall. However, costs of the type modeled here would prohibit firms from making up the entire amount of the shortfall. Rather than complicate the model considerably by allowing for this possibility, which

keep the model tractable, it is assumed that profits fully absorb such inefficiencies, leaving output unaffected. For simplicity, assume that the loss from underborrowing [that is, when $Y_t > E_{t-1}Y_t$] equals $p[\eta^i(Y_t - E_{t-1}Y_t)]^2$, where $p \equiv j/n^2$ and $j > 0$ is a constant.[6] Since the innovation $Y_t - E_{t-1}Y_t$ is distributed normally, the expected loss from underborrowing equals

$$E_{t-1}\int_0^\infty \{p[\eta^i(Y_t - E_{t-1}Y_t)]^2 d(Y_t - E_{t-1}Y_t)\} = p(\eta^i)^2\sigma_Y^2/2 , \quad (21b)$$

which is increasing in the sensitivity of firm i's product demand (working capital needs) to output. Using (21a) and (21b), the expected loss from under- and overborrowing with a traditional loan is given by

$$l^f = c(\eta^i)^2\sigma_Y^2/2 , \quad (21c)$$

where $c \equiv p+g\gamma^2$. This result has the plausible implication that the disadvantage of foregoing the flexibility of a commitment is greater when unanticipated loan demand is more variable.

Although commitments have the advantage over traditional fixed-rate loans of insulating a firm from short-term working capital shocks, they make a firm vulnerable to unexpected capital losses. Since $r_t^s - E_{t-1}r_t^s$ is distributed normally with a mean of zero, the present value of a firm with a commitment is a random walk. The reason is that a loss suffered last period is not expected to be offset by a future capital gain or loss which has a mean of zero. Hence, an unanticipated capital loss last period results in costly downsizings this period. It follows that the expected cost of losses arising from adjusting to unanticipated capital losses or gains from commitments loans is

$$l^c = E_{t-1}\int_{-\infty}^\infty [m(r_t^s - E_{t-1}r_t^s)^2]\, d(r_t^s - E_{t-1}r_t^s) = m\sigma_r^2 , \quad (22a)$$

where $\sigma_r^2 \equiv E_{t-1}(r_t^s - E_{t-1}r_t^s)^2$. The loss function in (22a) overlooks the hedging opportunities available to firms. Since the loss is proportional to σ_r^2, so is the incentive to hedge. However, since hedging usually entails a mean-variance trade-off, its cost is roughly linear in the amount of risk insured against. Thus, this expected loss, when there are hedging opportunities, can be approximated by

$$l^c = k\sigma_r^2, \quad (22b)$$

where $k \equiv hm$ and h is the "hedging cost" per unit of variance.

Each firm i chooses the loan type which minimizes its expected losses from

would have no qualitative implications on our results, we have chosen to simplify by assuming the costs to these firms is so great that they do not participate in a spot market.

[6]This assumption is consistent with a production function in which other inputs exhibit declining marginal products that increase as working capital rises.

underborrowing via a traditional fixed-rate loan and the expected losses from unanticipated capital losses with a flexible-rate commitment. It is assumed that the parameter values are such that, for the proportion θ of firms, $c(\eta^i)^2\sigma_Y^2/2 > k\sigma_r^2$. The degree of sensitivity (η^c) to working capital disturbances at which firms are indifferent between fixed-rate loans and flexible-rate commitment loans is

$$\eta^c = (2k/c)^{1/2}(\sigma_r/\sigma_Y) . \tag{23}$$

Since $\eta^i \sim U[0,1]$ and since k and c are constants, θ can be written as

$$\theta = \max(\eta^i) - \eta^c = 1 - \eta^c . \tag{24}$$

Because σ_r and σ_Y depend upon the conduct of monetary policy, the proportion of bank loan contracts negotiated as floating rate commitments endogenously adjusts to central bank behavior.

Indeed, (23) suggests that the adoption of monetarist operating procedures, which tend to increase the variance of unanticipated interest rate movements, would tend to lower the use of commitments and that the adoption of an interest rate conditioned policy would boost the reliance on commitment borrowing. This is not inconsistent with the slight decline in the commitment share of short-term business loans, shortly after the Fed began targeting nonborrowed reserves in late 1979, and with the sharp increase in this share shortly after the Fed switched to an interest rate-conditioned policy in late 1982 (see Figure 1).[7]

4. THE INTERACTION OF LOAN COMMITMENTS AND OPTIMAL MONETARY POLICY

Substituting income [(16)] into the LM schedule [(11)], the conditional variance of the spot interest rate can be computed as

$$\sigma_r^2 \equiv E_{t-1}(r_t^s - E_{t-1}r_t^s)^2 = \frac{\mu_1^2\sigma_\delta^2 + \beta_3^2\theta^2\sigma_\nu^2}{\{\Omega[1 - \beta_3\theta] + \beta_2\mu_1\theta\}^2} . \tag{25}$$

Substituting (25), the solution for σ_Y^2 from (17), and the solution for λ from (18) into (23) and (24) ultimately yields

$$\theta^* = \frac{\sigma_\nu + [\sigma_\nu(\sigma_\nu - 4\phi\sigma_\delta)]^{1/2}}{2\sigma_\nu} , \tag{26}$$

where $\phi \equiv (\mu_1/\beta_2)(2k/c)^{1/2}$, is a meaningful solution (that is, this rules out economically meaningless corner solutions). This expression for θ^* implies that,

[7]The upward trend since 1983 may reflect that agents gained ability in predicting interest rates or better opportunities to hedge rate risk.

as LM disturbances become predominant relative to spending disturbances (that is, as $\sigma_\nu / \sigma_\delta \rightarrow \infty$), $\theta^* \rightarrow 1$. The economic intuition behind this result is as follows. When monetary (LM) variability overwhelms goods market (IS) variability, optimal monetary policy [see (18)] requires that the monetary authority produce a horizontal LM schedule via the policy setting $\lambda^* \rightarrow \infty$. This setting automatically neutralizes the effects of LM disturbances on interest rate variability, eliminating the role of unanticipated capital losses as a factor influencing the choice of loan contract type. In the absence of the potential for incurring such costs via use of loan commitments, all firms use floating-rate commitments. For nonzero, finite values of σ_ν and σ_δ, this special case implies that θ^* is an increasing function of the variation of velocity.

If (26) is substituted into (18), the reduced-form expression for the optimal monetary policy setting is

$$\lambda^* = \frac{-(\xi_2 + \mu_2)}{\xi_1} + \frac{\beta_2\{(1-\beta_3)2\sigma_\nu\{\sigma_\nu + [\sigma_\nu(\sigma_\nu - 4\phi\sigma_\delta)]^{1/2}\} - \beta_3\sigma_\nu(\sigma_\nu - 4\phi\sigma_\delta)\}}{4\xi_1\mu_1\sigma_\delta^2\sigma_\nu^2} . \quad (27)$$

The partial derivatives $\partial\lambda^*/\partial\sigma_\nu$ and $\partial\lambda^*/\partial\sigma_\delta$ are ambiguous in sign. The intuition behind this result can be seen from the fact that

$$\frac{\partial\lambda^*}{\partial\sigma_j} = \left.\frac{\partial\lambda^*}{\partial\sigma_j}\right|_{\theta^*} + \left(\frac{\partial\lambda^*}{\partial\theta^*}\right)\left(\frac{\partial\theta^*}{\partial\sigma_j}\right); \; j = \nu,\delta . \quad (28)$$

The first term on the right-hand side of (28) is the direct effect of a change in the standard deviation of a disturbance on optimal policy, holding the proportion of firms using commitments constant. For each disturbance, this direct effect can be computed from (18). As in the standard Poole analysis, $\partial\lambda^*/\partial\sigma_\nu|_{\theta^*} > 0$ and $\partial\lambda^*/\partial\sigma_\delta|_{\theta^*} < 0$.

However, when θ is endogenous, as in this model, alterations in θ feed back to influence how these disturbances affect the variability of income and, therefore, the optimal monetary policy response. This feedback effect is captured in the second (multiplicative) term in (28), which measures the change in optimal policy resulting from a change in the proportion of firms using commitments following an increase in a structural variance. Equation (26) implies that $\partial\theta^*/\partial\sigma_\nu > 0$ and $\partial\theta^*/\partial\sigma_\delta < 0$ hold unambiguously. Nevertheless, as discussed in section 2, the value of β_3 determines the size of the nominal spending multiplier and, hence, the qualitative effect of a change in θ^* on λ^*. Consequently, $\partial\lambda^*/\partial\theta^* \gtrless 0$ in (28). Whether or not this ambiguous effect outweighs the first, direct effect is an empirical issue. However, theoretically this result could follow for a range of combinations of underlying parameters and initial values of standard deviations of disturbances.

It should be noted that the magnitude of β_3 depends upon features of the commitment negotiation process not modeled explicitly here. For instance, the flexibility of firms to respond to unanticipated changes in income depends largely upon the commitment limits available. In light of material adverse change clauses that are relatively standard in commitment contracts, this flexibility also potentially depends upon the extent to which firms' creditworthiness changes in response to variations in income and interest rates that arise given choices of λ^* and θ^*. Hence, although this model provides a good characterization of some of the key forces that influence monetary policy and choices of loan contract type, it does not tell a complete story of that process.

5. CONCLUSION

The key implication of this paper is that, if the endogenous response of loan contract choices is taken into account, the optimal formulation of monetary policy is less clearcut than it otherwise would seem. Hence, the results of this paper support the view that the separation between the goods and financial sectors implicit in the standard IS–LM paradigm breaks down when credit market considerations are incporated. Furthermore, the results highlight an example of a situation in which this failure of the traditional paradigm, in conjunction with the Lucas critique, has important policy implications.

Specifically, an optimal combination monetary policy could potentially steepen the LM schedule in the presence of greater monetary variability, in contrast to the results of the more traditional model that ignores the feedback between policy and credit contracting decisions. This result arises because the conduct of monetary policy alters the variability of income and interest rate forecast errors, thereby altering the trade-off faced by borrowers. Changes in loan contract type in turn influence how structural disturbances (that is, monetary disturbances) impinge upon income and interest rates, altering the optimal conduct of policy. Whether or not such a potentially "perverse" result arises depends crucially upon the flexibility available to those firms with commitments. In any case, the endogeneity of loan contract choice encourages the central bank to stabilize interest rates to a smaller degree in the presence of velocity shocks.

This study suggests several lines of research. Clearly, it would be preferable to model the flexibility in commitment contracts in a more concrete manner and to endogenize this flexibility. This is crucial for proper specification of the IS side of the economy. In particular, the loan choice functions of borrowers need to be specified and their parameters identified. The fact that the optimal combination policy response to a change in the commitment share of lending is theoretically ambiguous indicates a need for empirical examination of this issue. One possible approach would be to use a central bank reaction function model that explicitly incorporates a combination policy rule, as in Bradley (1984), which might enable one to empirically determine how monetary policy has responded to and influenced the greater use of commitments. Given that there have been three different monetary policy regimes over the last eleven years, it is an open question whether there are enough data to adequately estimate such functions at this time. If these parameters are hard to observe, then it will be difficult to use a combination policy without running into practical Lucas critique problems which may appear in the form of evolving or unstable interest rate elasticities.

On a more general level, our intentionally stylized analysis indicates that research on optimal monetary policy that ignores credit markets and their associated institutional features could have misleading policy implications. Efforts to extend the traditional paradigm of the monetary policy transmission mechanism by including such considerations should continue.

LITERATURE CITED

Avery, Robert B., and Allen N. Berger. "Loan Commitments and Bank Risk Exposure." Working Paper No. 36, Board of Governors of the Federal Reserve System (August 1988).

Bernanke, Ben S. "Non-Monetary Effects of the Financial Crisis in the Propagation of the Great Depression." *American Economic Review* 73 (June 1983), 257–76.

Bernanke, Ben S., and Alan S. Blinder. "Credit, Money, and Aggregate Demand." *American Economic Review* 78 (May 1988), 435–39.

Bradley, Michael D. "Federal Deficits and the Conduct of Monetary Policy." *Journal of Macroeconomics* 6 (Fall 1984), 411–31.

Brunner, Karl, and Allan Meltzer. "Money and Credit in the Monetary Transmission Process." *American Economic Review* 78 (May 1988), 446–51.

Campbell, Tim S. "A Model of the Market for Lines of Credit." *Journal of Finance* 33 (March 1978), 231–44.

Churchill, Neil C., and Virginia L. Lewis. "Profitability of Small-Business Lending." *Journal of Bank Research* 16 (Summer 1985), 63–71.

Deshmukh, Sudhakar D., Stuart I. Greenbaum, and George Kanatas. "Bank Forward Lending in Alternative Funding Environnments." *Journal of Finance* 37 (September 1982), 925–40.

Duca, John V. "The Relevance of Loan Commitment Theories: Evidence from Survey Data." Unpublished Working Paper, Board of Governors of the Federal Reserve System, September 1988.

Duca, John V., and David D. VanHoose. "Loan Commitments and Optimal Monetary Policy." Working Paper No. 44, Board of Governors of the Federal Reserve System (August 1988).

Federal Reserve Bulletin. "Terms of Lending at Commercial Banks: Survey of Loans Made, May 2–6, 1988." Volume 74 (September 1988), Table 4.23, A70.

Gertler, Mark. "Financial Structure and Aggregate Economic Activity: An Overview." *Journal of Money, Credit, and Banking* 20 (August 1988, Part 2), 559–88.

Glick, Reuven, and Steven E. Plaut. "Off-Balance-Sheet Liquidity and Monetary Control." Federal Reserve Bank of San Francisco Working Paper No. 87-12 (December 1987).

James, Christopher. "Self-Selection and the Pricing of Bank Services: An Analysis of the Market for Loan Commitments and the Role of Compensating Balance Requirements." *Journal of Financial and Quantitative Analysis* 16 (December 1981), 725–46.

Kanatas, George."Commercial Paper, Bank Reserve Requirements, and the Informational Role of Loan Commitments." *Journal of Banking and Finance* 11 (September 1987), 425–48.

Melnik, Arie, and Steve E. Plaut. "The Economics of Loan Commitment Contracts: Credit Pricing and Utilization." *Journal of Banking and Finance* 10 (June 1986), 267–80.

Poole, William. "Optimal Choice of Monetary Policy Instruments in a Simple Stochastic Macro Model." *Quarterly Journal of Economics* 84 (May 1970), 197–216.

Sofianos, George, Paul Wachtel, and Arie Melnik. "Loan Commitments and Monetary Policy." National Bureau of Economic Research Working Paper No. 2232 (May 1987).

Thakor, Anjan V. "Toward a Theory of Bank Loan Commitments." *Journal of Banking and Finance* 6 (March 1982), 55–83.

JOHN H. ROGERS

Foreign Inflation Transmission under Flexible Exchange Rates and Currency Substitution

A STRONG MOTIVATION FOR MOVING AWAY from a system of fixed exchange rates in the 1970s was the belief that a country would be provided with insulation from foreign price shocks by floating its currency. A system of floating exchange rates would allow individual nations—in which monetary policy otherwise may have been dominated by inflationary trends in a large country—the liberty of using monetary policy for domestic purposes. The case for floating exchange rates dates back at least as far as Friedman (1953).

In this paper, I explore the possibility that the (theoretically expected) functioning of the floating exchange rate system may be altered under currency substitution.[1] I examine the effect of higher foreign inflation on the demand for domestic real balances, the domestic velocity of money, and particularly, the domestic inflation rate, under currency substitution, in a small, open economy (foreign interest and inflation rates are taken as given) with flexible prices and exchange rate. I identify and analyze in detail two features of the domestic economy which affect the insulation properties of flexible exchange rates: the elasticity of demand for, and initial stock of, foreign real balances.

Several papers examine the phenomena of concern here—the transmission of international disturbances and currency substitution—either jointly or separ-

[1]Currency substitution exists when foreign money is held and used in transactions alongside domestic money by domestic residents, and (relative) demand changes in response to changes in their relative opportunity costs.

This paper is taken from the author's Ph.D. dissertation. He thanks the members of his committee: Jon Eaton, Ron Michener, and especially Charles Engel for their assistance.

JOHN H. ROGERS *is assistant professor of economics, The Pennsylvania State University.*

Journal of Money, Credit, and Banking, Vol. 22, No. 2 (May 1990)

ately, theoretically or empirically. Darby and Lothian (1983) present abundant empirical evidence on international inflation transmission, analyzing several possible channels including currency substitution. This study, concentrating on the major industrialized countries during the Bretton Woods era, concludes that monetary factors, primarily due to U.S. monetary policy, rather than "special factors" such as oil price increases, explain the bulk of the inflation for these countries in this period. McKinnon (1982) explores empirically and theoretically the phenomenon of international inflation transmission in a currency substitution framework, concentrating his empirical analysis of currency substitution on the industrialized countries, as does Cuddington (1983). Flood and Marion (1982) develop a stochastic macroeconomic model to analyze the international transmission of both real and monetary disturbances to a small economy, in the absence of currency substitution, under both fixed and flexible exchange rates, in order to compare the insular properties of each system. Insulation from foreign disturbances is not necessarily a desirable policy goal. Rogers (1988) analyzes dollarization in Mexico during 1976–88 and finds currency substitution to be significant in this small-country setting, from estimates of (1) a model of relative money demand (innovations) from a vector autoregression, and (2) an error correction model.

This paper is constructed as follows. The full model is described in section 1. In section 2, a permanent, unanticipated rise in foreign inflation is shown to cause a change in domestic inflation between steady states which is positively related to the elasticity of demand for foreign currency. Moreover, the higher the initial stock of foreign real balances held domestically, all else constant, the greater the magnitude of the transmission effects. A specific example illuminates the results. Section 3 concludes.

1. THE MODEL

Residing in the small open economy are infinitely lived, utility-maximizing households with perfect foresight. A household's utility at any moment is a function $U(c,m,f) = u(c) + v(m,f)$ of the traded consumption good, c, and domestic and foreign real balances, m and f, respectively.[2] The domestic (foreign) price of the good is denoted P (P^*). Nominal money balances are deflated to give $m = (M/P)$ and $f = (F/P^*)$. The appropriate Inada conditions on the utility functions hold, so that c, m, and f are positive and no domestic money is held abroad. Purchasing power parity holds, so that $P = EP^*$, where E is the domestic price of foreign currency.

The household maximizes the discounted sum of future utility,

$$V = \int_0^\infty U(c_t,m_t,f_t)\exp(-\Delta_t)dt \; , \tag{1}$$

[2]By entering each currency into the utility function individually instead of entering aggregate real balances, the currencies are assumed to be imperfect substitutes; implicitly, foreign money balances provide services not provided by the domestic currency.

where the discount factor $\Delta_t = \int_0^t \delta_s ds$ varies over time. This implies

$$d\Delta/dt = \delta_s \, . \tag{2}$$

The discount rate, δ_s, is assumed to be a function of current utility,

$$\delta_s = \delta[U(c_s,m_s,f_s)] \, , \tag{3}$$

where it is assumed for convenience that δ', δ'', and $[\delta(U) - U \cdot \delta'(U)] > 0$.[3]

Define the household's real assets at any time t as

$$a_t = m_t + f_t + b_t \tag{4}$$

where b_t denotes the real value of foreign bonds in terms of the good.[4] It is useful to define the real value of foreign asset holdings, $A_t \equiv f_t + b_t$. Over time (a dot overhead represents that variable's time derivative),

$$\dot{a}_t = ra_t - (\pi_t+r)m_t - (\pi^*+r)f_t + \tau_t + (y-c_t) \, , \tag{5}$$

where τ denotes expected real transfers from the government, y is output, constant at capacity level, r the exogenous real interest rate, and domestic and foreign inflation, respectively, are given by $\pi = \dot{P}/P$ and $\pi^* = \dot{P}^*/P^*$.

The household is constrained by

$$\int_0^\infty \exp(-rt)[c_t+(\pi_t+r)m_t+(\pi_t^*+r)f_t]dt \leq a_0 + y/r + \int_0^\infty \exp(-rt)\tau_t dt \, . \tag{6}$$

The initial value of the household's endowment—M_0, F_0, b_0, the infinite stream of payments y, and a stream of money transfers, τ—is given in (real) present value terms by the right-hand side of (6). Agents cannot acquire goods and liquidity services through borrowing indefinitely, since from (6) (in present value terms) consumption of these can be no greater than endowment.[5]

[3]All of these conditions are in papers by Uzawa (1968), eqs. 13 and 14, Obstfeld (1981), eq. 5, and Obstfeld (1982), eq. 3, which do not analyze currency substitution. Obstfeld (1982), p. 254, notes that δ' and $\delta''>0$ are not the only assumptions consistent with endogenous time preferences, but that $\delta'>0$ (a rise in the level of consumption increases the rate of discount for all future consumption) is necessary for the small economy to converge to the steady state under perfect capital mobility [Obstfeld (1982), fn. 10]. If δ' were negative, any disturbance which, say, raises consumption above (lowers saving below) the steady-state level, would lead to more consumption, less saving, and wealth would approach zero. To assume $\delta=r$ would do away with the dynamics out of steady state. As in Obstfeld (1982), fn. 16, this would remove a feature of the model which drives an important result here: domestic inflation would be unaffected by a change in foreign inflation, as becomes clear later. The third condition ensures that discounted lifetime utility, $\bar{U}/\delta(\bar{U})$, is rising in $\bar{U}$, implying that between two stationary wealth streams, the one with higher instantaneous utility is preferred.

[4]The assumption that agents hold both foreign currency and bonds is appropriate for certain economies, small and very open, which also have developed capital markets. It is likely that in many countries, foreign interest-bearing assets are in the portfolios of businesses and other major domestic investors, while foreign currency circulates widely. Engel (1989) and Rogers (1988) both discuss the implications of allowing for traded bonds in a model of currency substitution.

[5]This model, similar to Calvo and Rodriguez (1977), Liviatan (1981), Calvo (1985), and Engel

The intertemporal optimization is defined by the objective function (1), the laws of motion of the state variables (2) and (5), and the boundary conditions (6). Thus, households maximize (1) subject to (2), (5), and (6). The current-value Hamiltonian is given by

$$H_t = U(c_t,m_t,f_t) + \lambda[ra_t-(\pi_t+r)m_t-(\pi^*+r)f_t+\tau_t+(y-c_t)] + q_t\delta(U) . \quad (7)$$

The necessary conditions for maximization of utility are

$$u'(c) = \lambda/[1+q\delta']\} , \quad (8a)$$

$$x^m(c,m,f) \equiv v_m(m,f)/u'(c) = \pi_t+r , \quad (8b)$$

$$x^f(c,m,f) \equiv v_f(m,f)/u'(c) = \pi_t^*+r , \quad (8c)$$

$$\dot{\lambda}_t = \lambda[c,m,f]\{\delta[U(c,m,f)]-\text{r}\} , \quad (8d)$$

$$\dot{q}_t = q\delta[U(c,m,f)] + [u(c)+v(m,f)] , \quad (8e)$$

where partial derivatives on the utility function $v(m,f)$ are denoted by subscripts, while the derivative of the $u(c)$ function is represented by a prime. I discuss in appendix C (available upon request) a methodological issue, noted by Kompas and Abdel-Razeq (1987), pertaining to models with endogenous time preferences, and related to the derivation of equations (7) and (8).

The government creates money (makes transfers) to keep the rate of money growth, $\dot{M}_t/M_t$, constant at μ. Thus $\tau_t = \mu m_t$, with μ chosen always to exceed $-r$, the rate at which the household "gains" from holding money as opposed to interest-bearing bonds. Since $\pi_t = \mu - \dot{m}_t/m_t$,

$$\dot{m} = [\mu + r - x^m(c,m,f)]m . \quad (9)$$

The accumulation of real foreign assets is given by

$$\dot{A} \equiv \dot{f} + \dot{b} = y - c + rA - (\pi^*+r)f . \quad (10)$$

The rest of the economy is characterized as follows. First, the necessary condition $x^f(c,m,f) = (\pi^*+r)$ implies an expression (derived in appendix B) for foreign real balances, f, in terms of c, m and (π^*+r), $f = 1[c,m,(\pi^*+r)]$. It follows

(1989), has two distinguishing features which make it particularly suitable for the purpose at hand. These are a nonzero foreign inflation rate and an endogenous rate of time preference. Calvo and Rodriguez (1977), Liviatan (1981), and Calvo (1985) do not consider changes in foreign inflation, while there are no dynamic effects from such changes in Engel's (1989) model because the rate of time preference is assumed constant and equal to the (given) world interest rate. As noted in fn. 3 and seen below, the endogenous rate of time preference implies gradual adjustment of the state variables, and allows for analysis of the transmission of foreign to domestic inflation, which takes place between steady states.

from (8a) that $\lambda_t = \lambda(c,m,q)$. Differentiating this expression for λ_t with respect to time and rearranging,

$$\dot{c} = (\lambda_c^{-1})\,[\dot{\lambda} - \lambda_m \dot{m} - \lambda_q \dot{q}]\,.$$

Substitution of equations (8d), (8e), and (9) into the above yields

$$\dot{c} = (\lambda_c^{-1})[\lambda(\delta - r) - \lambda_m(\mu + r - x^m)m - \lambda_q(q\delta + u + v)]\,. \tag{11}$$

The system (8e), (9), (10), and (11), written as a function of four endogenous variables (c,m,A,q), completely characterizes the evolution of the economy over time. For convenience, the system is reproduced:[6]

$$\dot{m} = \{\mu + r - x^m[c,m,1(c,m,r+\pi^*)]\}m\,,$$

$$\dot{A} = y - c - [(r+\pi^*)1(c,m,r+\pi^*)] + rA\,,$$

$$\dot{c} = (\lambda_c^{-1})\{\lambda[\delta - r] - \lambda_m[\mu + r - x^m]m - \lambda_q[q\delta + u + v]\}\,,$$

$$\dot{q} = q\delta + (u+v)\,.$$

2. THE STEADY-STATE AND DYNAMIC EFFECTS OF HIGHER FOREIGN INFLATION

In this section, I analyze the transmission effects of higher foreign inflation under currency substitution and a flexible exchange rate. The model provides a rich setting in which the dynamics are tractable, allowing analysis of the effects of a rise in π^* on the demand for (velocity of) m, and on π.

The conditions necessary for a steady state are (here, as throughout, a bar over a variable indicates its steady-state value):

$$[v_m(\bar{m},\bar{f})/u'(\bar{c})] = \mu + r\,; \tag{12a}$$

$$r = \delta[U(\bar{c},\bar{m},\bar{f})]\,; \tag{12b}$$

$$y - \bar{c} = -r\bar{b} + \pi^*\bar{f}\,; \tag{12c}$$

$$[v_f(\bar{m},\bar{f})/u'(\bar{c})] = \pi^* + r\,; \tag{12d}$$

$$\bar{q} = -(\bar{u} + \bar{v})/\bar{\delta}\,. \tag{12e}$$

[6]I show in appendix B that, when linearized about $\bar{c}$, $\bar{m}$, $\bar{A}$ and $\bar{q}$, the differential equation system possesses three positive characteristic roots (so there are three "jump" variables, c, m, and q), and one negative root (thus one "nonjumping" state variable, A, predetermined by past foreign asset accumulation). Therefore the system is locally saddlepath stable.

For simplicity, $\bar{f}$ is often used to represent the function $1(\bar{c},\bar{m},r+\pi^*)$.[7]

The Long-term Effects of a Change in π^*

Starting in steady state, the economy is disturbed by an unanticipated, permanent increase in foreign inflation. Conventional comparative statics gives, as derived in appendix A,

$$\frac{d\bar{c}}{d\pi^*} > 0, \quad \frac{d\bar{f}}{d\pi^*} < 0, \text{ while } \frac{d\bar{m}}{d\pi^*}, \frac{d\bar{b}}{d\pi^*}, \frac{d\bar{A}}{d\pi^*} \gtreqless 0 \,. \tag{13}$$

A sufficient condition for $d\bar{m}/d\pi^* > 0$ is that m and f are Edgeworth substitutes, that is, that $v_{mf} < 0$. Money demand functions which imply substitution into the foreign (domestic) currency when domestic (foreign) inflation rises are derived if and only if $v_{mf} < 0$.[8] This is assumed below, but I first show that the sign of the inflation transmission is independent of the sign of v_{mf}.

An *increase* in foreign inflation changes the relative attractiveness of the two currencies, leading to a shift away from foreign real balances. Consumption rises (fn. 7) and the trade balance worsens in steady state. The ambiguous effect of changes in π^* on $\bar{b}$ is indicated by (12c). If it is assumed that $\pi^*\bar{f}$ rises when π^* rises, then from (12c), $\bar{b}$ must be higher. However, if $\pi^*\bar{f}$ falls by a sufficient amount, $\bar{b}$ may fall. Thus, $\bar{A}$ $(\equiv\bar{f}+\bar{b})$ may rise, fall, or remain unchanged. The sign of $d\bar{A}/d\pi^*$, crucial for the dynamic analysis of the transmission effects, is *negatively* related to the elasticity of demand for foreign currency, as demonstrated in appendix A.

The Impact Effects and Transition Paths

The dynamic effects of a permanent, unanticipated rise in π^* are found by linearizing (8e), (9), (10), and (11) around $\bar{c}$, $\bar{m}$, $\bar{A}$, and $\bar{q}$. The linearized system possesses exactly one negative characteristic root, is therefore locally saddlepath-stable (see appendix B), and may be written

[7]Due to the small-country assumption, (12b) implies a constant level of felicity (instantaneous utility) in steady state, and provides intuition about the long-run effects of a rise in π^*: this leads to a lower level of felicity from real balances in steady state because the two currencies are assumed to be normal goods. This drop in felicity is accompanied in steady state by higher felicity from consumption, in order to keep utility equal to $\bar{U}$, and hence $\delta(\bar{U})$ equal to (the constant) r. In this way, changes in π^* affect domestic real variables in the long run.

[8]It is evident from the results in Liviatan (1981) and discussions in Calvo (1985) and Engel (1989) that signing v_{mf} is generally nontrivial. One way to approach the issue here is to totally differentiate 8b and 8c:

$$dm = Q[u''(v_m v_{ff} - v_f v_{fm})dc + (u')^2 v_{ff} d\pi - (u')^2 v_{mf} d\pi^*]$$
$$df = Q[u''(v_f v_{mm} - v_m v_{mf})dc + (u')^2 v_{mm} d\pi^* - (u')^2 v_{mf} d\pi] \,,$$

where $Q \equiv [1/u'(v_{mm}v_{ff} - v_{mf}^2)] > 0$, by the concavity condition. The substitution aspect of currency substitution is best reflected in these money demand functions when $v_{mf} < 0$, an argument also made by Engel (1989).

$$\begin{bmatrix} \dot{c} \\ \dot{m} \\ \dot{A} \\ \dot{q} \end{bmatrix} \approx \begin{bmatrix} z_{11} & z_{12} & z_{13} & z_{14} \\ z_{21} & z_{22} & z_{23} & z_{24} \\ z_{31} & z_{32} & z_{33} & z_{34} \\ z_{41} & z_{42} & z_{43} & z_{44} \end{bmatrix} \begin{bmatrix} (c-\bar{c}) \\ (m-\bar{m}) \\ (A-\bar{A}) \\ (q-\bar{q}) \end{bmatrix} = \theta \begin{bmatrix} (c-\bar{c}) \\ (m-\bar{m}) \\ (A-\bar{A}) \\ (q-\bar{q}) \end{bmatrix} \tag{14}$$

In (14), θ denotes the sole negative root; initial conditions are chosen in such a way that the three explosive roots have no influence on the dynamics of c, m, A, and q. This is done to ensure that (6) holds, and to satisfy the transversality conditions. The system therefore must contain exactly one state variable whose value is predetermined, in the sense that discrete jumps in this variable are precluded. Here, this variable is real foreign assets, A. Thus, A is constant immediately after an unanticipated change in π^*, while the other state variables take discrete jumps to place the economy on the transition path to steady state.

The convergent solution to the linearized system can be written (see appendix B for the derivations),

$$(m-\bar{m}) = \phi(A-\bar{A})\,,\ \phi > 0,\ (c-\bar{c}) = \beta(A-\bar{A})\,,\ \beta > 0,$$
$$(q-\bar{q}) = \alpha(A-\bar{A})\,,\ \alpha < 0\,. \tag{15}$$

The dynamic path of the economy is characterized by (13) and (15).

The Change in π along the Transition Path

The transmission of foreign to domestic inflation between steady states is derived using (14), (15), and our definition, $\pi = \mu - \dot{m}/m$. It is convenient to take from appendix A

$$(d\bar{A}/d\pi^*) = \bar{\Omega} + (\bar{f}/r)(1-\eta) \gtreqless 0\,, \tag{16}$$

where $\Omega > 0$, r and f are as above, η (> 0 by convention) is the elasticity of demand for foreign currency, and a bar indicates evaluation at the initial steady state. When demand for foreign currency is sufficiently elastic that $d\bar{A}/d\pi^* < 0$, then $(A-\bar{A}) > 0$ between steady states following a rise in π^*, since A is unchanged on impact. From (15), $(m-\bar{m}) > 0$, so that $\dot{m} \cong \theta(m-\bar{m}) < 0$, using (14). Since $\dot{m} < 0$, π *rises* above its long-term value μ during the transition to the new steady state. On the other hand, when $d\bar{A}/d\pi^* > 0$, then π *falls* below its long-run value between steady states, as $(A-\bar{A})$ and $(m-\bar{m}) < 0$, so that $\dot{m} > 0$, and $\pi < \mu$. The magnitude of the transmission effects (positive or negative), all else constant and ignoring the case in which $d\bar{A}/d\pi^* = 0$, is greater the larger is the economy's initial stock of foreign real balances, according to (16).

This result, independent of the sign of v_{mf} because (15) and (16) are (appendix B), is illuminated with the two cases in the following example, in which I make the simplifying assumption that $v_{mf} < 0$ to ease the exposition of the economic intuition. In footnotes 9 and 10 I provide an alternative interpretation of the transmission effects, using a different measure of π.

Case 1: Drop in $\bar{A}$ (Sufficiently Elastic Demand for Foreign Currency)

Since $\bar{A}$ falls in this case so that $(A-\bar{A}) > 0$, $(m-\bar{m})$ must be positive from (15). Thus, since $\bar{m}$ is higher (eq. 13), real holdings of domestic money balances must rise on impact above the steady-state level, and fall along the transition path. This pattern of adjustment has two implications. First, the domestic price level falls on impact, because m is higher while the nominal money supply, M, is unchanged. The drop in P equates the given quantity of nominal domestic money with the desired impact level of real balances. Second, π ($\equiv \dot{P}_t/P_t$) must rise above its steady-state level of μ along the transition path: since $\dot{m} < 0$ and $\pi = \mu - \dot{m}/m$, it follows that $\pi > \mu$ between steady states.

Intuitively, the drop in demand for domestic real balances during the transition (a negative rate of change in real money demand), increases the velocity of money in percentage terms (velocity is unity in steady state). With output and nominal money growth constant, domestic inflation rises.[9]

I make two final points about this case. First, from (16) and appendix B, the larger the initial stock of foreign real balances, $\bar{f}$, the higher is the inflation rate π along the transition path; $(A-\bar{A})$ is larger, and so $(m-\bar{m})$ and $\dot{m}$ rise in absolute terms with a rise in $\bar{f}$. Second, I avoid the issues raised by Kareken and Wallace (1981) concerning perfectly substitutable currencies, by the construction of $v(\cdot)$ (see fn. 2), since, in this framework, the assumption would require that m and f enter $v(\cdot)$ as some linear combination. This case is not analyzed here.

Case 2: Increase in $\bar{A}$ (Inelastic Demand for Foreign Currency)

Assume that $d\bar{A}/d\pi^* > 0$ alters the dynamic analysis, inasmuch as $(A-\bar{A})$, $(c-\bar{c})$, and $(m-\bar{m})$ are now negative in sign. Since $(d\bar{c}/d\pi^*)$ and $(d\bar{m}/d\pi^*)$ are positive while $(c-\bar{c})$ and $(m-\bar{m})$ are negative, the impact effects on c and m may be reversed (they were positive). No matter what the impact effects, c, m, and A each *rise* along the transition path.

Higher foreign inflation is again transmitted to the domestic economy between steady states, but *negatively* under the assumption of inelastic demand for dollars.[10] In this instance, $\dot{m} \approx \theta(m-\bar{m}) > 0$—the accumulation of domestic real

[9]It is seen that on impact P falls and P rises, while in the new long run $\bar{m}$ is higher than initially, and M is higher by μ percent. Thus, although the rate of change of P is higher between steady states than in steady state, when the new steady state is reached, P may be above, below, or the same as the initial price level. This depends on the difference between μ and the percentage change in $\bar{m}$, and brings up the issue of the appropriate measure of the domestic inflation rate. In the example above $\pi = \dot{P}/P$, and is measured along the transition path. This measure does not take into account the impact drop in P, which in theory may be quite large. A rise in π may not be transmitted positively in case 1, if we consider $\pi = \Delta P/P$, from steady state to steady state. As an example, an increase in π^* leads to domestic *deflation* when $\mu = 0$ and π is measured according to our second definition.

[10]Again, if π is measured as $\Delta P/P$ across steady states, the result that higher foreign inflation is transmitted negatively when demand for f is inelastic may no longer hold. As in case 1, this depends on (i) the direction and extent of the impact change in P, and (ii) the difference between the percentage change in m across steady states and μ.

balances lowers (in percentage terms) the velocity of money, and, with output and nominal money growth unchanged, leads to a lower rate of domestic inflation along the transition path. In addition, the higher is $\bar{f}$ initially, the lower is π between steady states.

The main result of the paper is established: the more elastic is the demand for foreign currency, the larger is the transmission effect of higher foreign inflation to domestic inflation during the transition to the new steady state. Intuitively, when demand for foreign currency is elastic, as in case 1 in which $\bar{A}$ falls, the substitution out of f and into m on impact is sufficiently great that the demand for domestic real balances falls along the transition path. This increase in velocity (growth), with y and μ unchanged, implies a rise in domestic inflation until the new steady state is reached. In the case of inelastic demand for f, the initial substitution into domestic real balances is not as large (m may even fall) and the household accumulates m along the transition path, in association with the temporarily lower domestic inflation rate.

Notice the importance of the currency substitution phenomenon in the model. In a "standard" model in which foreign money balances are not held, an increase in foreign inflation would give rise to an equivalent depreciation of the nominal exchange rate, without affecting the real return on any state variable. In the currency substitution model, the real return on foreign money balances is reduced when π^* rises producing real effects—shown to depend on the degree of currency substitution—on holdings of foreign money balances, on the demand for domestic real balances and velocity growth, and on the domestic inflation rate between steady states. Furthermore, all else constant, a higher initial level of foreign real balances makes domestic inflation more sensitive to changes in π^* between steady states.

Notice also the importance of the assumed properties of $\delta(U)$. Assuming that $\delta' > 0$ allows the small economy to attain a steady state under perfect capital mobility. A stationary state may also be reached had we assumed $\delta = r$, but the resulting model would imply that an unanticipated, permanent rise in π^*, when initially in steady state, has no effect on the domestic inflation rate. In this case, steady-state domestic real balances would be attained instantaneously through a jump in P, while π would always equal the (unchanged) money growth rate μ. In contrast, the assumption of endogenous time preference gives rise to a model in which there are transmission effects of foreign to domestic inflation.

3. CONCLUSION

This paper has analyzed the transmission effects of an unanticipated, permanent rise in foreign inflation under flexible exchange rates and currency substitution. I focus on the way in which the elasticity of demand for and initial stock of foreign real balances influences the change in domestic inflation, following the disturbance. Interesting and related issues such as the effects on the trade balance and current account, and incorporation of nontraded goods are passed over here for the sake of brevity, but investigated in Rogers (1988).

The paper supports the notion that, for a small, open economy which floats its currency, a degree of insulation from foreign price shocks may be lost in the presence of currency substitution. Therefore, when a foreign currency is a substitute for domestic money, the domestic monetary authority will experience a loss of independence in policy-making.

This is not to say that currency substitution makes a flexible exchange-rate regime exactly like one of fixed rates for a small country; under the latter, higher inflation abroad necessitates inflationary monetary policy domestically. This paper demonstrates that foreign inflation may be transmitted negatively under flexible exchange rates and currency substitution. Of course, as the foreign currency becomes a closer substitute for domestic money (and so, we would expect, the larger is η), the more the flexible exchange-rate system becomes like one of fixed rates, in the sense that higher foreign inflation is positively transmitted. It is established that the transmission of foreign inflation to domestic inflation during the transition to the new steady state is positively related to the elasticity of demand for foreign currency, and that the absolute magnitude of this transmission effect is positively related to the economy's initial stock of foreign real balances.

APPENDIX A. THE STEADY-STATE RESULTS

The long-run effects of changes in foreign inflation are derived by totally differentiating (12), holding the world interest rate constant:

$$\begin{bmatrix} -[\bar{u}''\bar{v}_m/(\bar{u}')^2] & \bar{v}_{mm}/\bar{u}' & \bar{v}_{mf}/\bar{u}' & 0 \\ \bar{\delta}'\bar{u}' & \bar{\delta}'\bar{v}_m & \bar{\delta}'\bar{v}_f & 0 \\ -[\bar{u}''\bar{v}_f/(\bar{u}')^2] & \bar{v}_{fm}/\bar{u}' & \bar{v}_{ff}/\bar{u}' & 0 \\ -1 & 0 & -\pi^* & r \end{bmatrix} \begin{bmatrix} dc \\ dm \\ df \\ db \end{bmatrix} = \begin{bmatrix} d\mu \\ 0 \\ d\pi^* \\ d\pi^* f \end{bmatrix}$$

The determinant of the 4×4 matrix, Δ, is equal to

$$\Delta = (\bar{\delta}\bar{\delta}'/\bar{u}')\{[\bar{u}''\bar{v}_m/(\bar{u}')^2](\bar{v}_m\bar{v}_{ff}-\bar{v}_f\bar{v}_{fm}) + (\bar{v}_{mm}\bar{v}_{ff}-\bar{v}_{mf}^2) + [\bar{u}''\bar{v}_f/(\bar{u}')^2](\bar{v}_f\bar{v}_{mm}-\bar{v}_m\bar{v}_{mf})\} .$$

From our concavity and normal goods assumptions, $(v_{mm}v_{ff} - \bar{v}_{mf}^2) > 0$, $(v_m v_{ff} - v_f v_{fm}) < 0$, and $(v_f v_{mm} - v_m v_{mf}) < 0$. As noted above, r, δ', u', v_m, and v_f are positive, while u'', v_{fm}, v_{ff}, and v_{mm} are negative. Thus $\Delta > 0$.

Setting $d\mu = 0$, and applying Cramer's Rule,

$$d\bar{c}/d\pi^* = (\bar{\delta}'\bar{\delta}/\Delta\bar{u}')[\bar{v}_m\bar{v}_{mf} - \bar{v}_f\bar{v}_{mm}] > 0 ,$$

$$d\bar{m}/d\pi^* = -(\bar{\delta}'\bar{\delta}/\Delta)[\bar{v}_{mf} + \bar{u}''\bar{v}_f\bar{v}_m/(\bar{u}')^2] \gtreqless 0 \text{ , but } > 0 \text{ for } v_{mf} < 0 \text{ ,}$$

$$d\bar{f}/d\pi^* = (\bar{\delta}'\bar{\delta}/\Delta)[\bar{v}_{mm} + \bar{u}''(\bar{v}_m)^2/(\bar{u}')^2] < 0 \text{ ,}$$

$$d\bar{b}/d\pi^* = (\bar{\delta}'/\Delta)[\pi^*\bar{v}_{mm}+\pi^*\bar{u}''(\bar{v}_m)^2/(\bar{u}')^2 - (\bar{v}_f\bar{v}_{mm}-\bar{v}_m\bar{v}_{mf})/(\bar{u}')] + (\bar{f}/\bar{\delta}) \gtreqless 0 \text{ ,}$$

$$d\bar{A}/d\pi^* = (\bar{f}/\bar{\delta}) + (\bar{\delta}'/\Delta\bar{u}')[\bar{v}_m\bar{v}_{mf} + \bar{u}''\bar{v}_m(r+\pi)(r+\pi^*)] \gtreqless 0 \text{ .}$$

The sign of $d\bar{A}/d\pi^*$ depends on the elasticity of demand for foreign currency, η. This is given by $\eta = -[df/d(r+\pi^*)][(r+\pi^*)/f]$. Examining the expressions for $d\bar{f}/d\pi^*$ and $d\bar{A}/d\pi^*$ above, note that

$$d\bar{A}/d\pi^* = [(\bar{\delta}'/\bar{u}'\Delta)(\bar{v}_m\bar{v}_{mf}-\bar{v}_f\bar{v}_{mm}) + (\bar{f}/r)(1-\eta)] \text{ .}$$

Since the first term is positive, as is η by convention, a sufficient condition for $d\bar{A}/d\pi^* > 0$ is that $\eta < 1$.

APPENDIX B. THE IMPACT EFFECTS AND TRANSITION PATHS

We must find (1) whether the system is saddlepath stable, and (2) the trajectory of the state variables along the saddlepath. Denote the transpose of the vector $\mathbf{x}$ by $[m\ c\ A\ q]$, so that $\dot{\mathbf{x}}^T = [\dot{m}\ \dot{c}\ \dot{A}\ \dot{q}]$, where $\dot{m}$, $\dot{c}$, $\dot{A}$, and $\dot{q}$ are given by (8e)–(11). Totally differentiating (8c) and (8a),

$$df[v_{ff}(1+q\delta')+q\delta''(v_f)^2] + dm[v_{fm}(1+q\delta')+q\delta''v_fv_m] + dc[q\delta''u'v_f]$$

$$= d\lambda[r+\pi^*] + d(r+\pi^*)[\lambda] - dq[v_f\delta'] \text{, and}$$

$$d\lambda = df[q\delta''v_fu'] + dm[q\delta''v_mu'] + dc[u''(1+q\delta')+q\delta''(u')^2] + dq[u'\delta'] \text{ .}$$

Substituting the latter into the former we obtain an expression defining $f = l[m,c,(r+\pi^*)]$, where $l_m = -v_{fm}/v_{ff} \gtreqless 0$ (< 0 for $v_{mf} < 0$), $l_c = (u''v_f/u'v_{ff}) > 0$, and $l_{r+\pi}{}^* = \lambda/v_{ff} < 0$. Therefore, equations (8e)–(11) may be written as a function of the endogenous variables c, m, A, and q.

Using a first-order Taylor series expansion of x around $\bar{x}$, we can write $\dot{x} \equiv f(x) = f(\bar{x}) + f'(x)(x - \bar{x})$. In steady-state $x = \bar{x}$, and so $f(x) = f(\bar{x})$. In terms of the variables in this paper, it follows that

$$\begin{bmatrix} \dot{c} \\ \dot{m} \\ \dot{A} \\ \dot{q} \end{bmatrix} \approx \begin{bmatrix} z_{11} & z_{12} & z_{13} & z_{14} \\ z_{21} & z_{22} & z_{23} & z_{24} \\ z_{31} & z_{32} & z_{33} & z_{34} \\ z_{41} & z_{42} & z_{43} & z_{44} \end{bmatrix} \begin{bmatrix} (c-\bar{c}) \\ (m-\bar{m}) \\ (A-\bar{A}) \\ (q-\bar{q}) \end{bmatrix} = \theta \begin{bmatrix} (c-\bar{c}) \\ (m-\bar{m}) \\ (A-\bar{A}) \\ (q-\bar{q}) \end{bmatrix} \qquad \text{(A1)}$$

where

$$
\begin{aligned}
z_{11} &= -\bar{m}\bar{\lambda}_m\bar{u}''(\bar{v}_m\bar{v}_{ff}-\bar{v}_f\bar{v}_{fm})/\bar{v}_{ff}(\bar{u}')^2\bar{\lambda}_{\dagger} > 0 & z_{13} &= 0 \\
z_{12} &= \bar{m}\bar{\lambda}_m(\bar{v}_{mm}\bar{v}_{ff}-\bar{v}_{mf}^2)/\bar{v}_{ff}\bar{u}'\bar{\lambda}_c < 0 & z_{14} &= -\bar{\lambda}_q\bar{\delta}/\bar{\lambda}_c > 0 \\
z_{21} &= \bar{m}\bar{u}''(\bar{v}_m\bar{v}_{ff}-\bar{v}_f\bar{v}_{fm})/\bar{v}_{ff}(\bar{u}')^2 < 0 & z_{23} &= 0 \\
z_{22} &= -\bar{m}(\bar{v}_{mm}\bar{v}_{ff}-\bar{v}_{mf}^2)/\bar{v}_{ff}\bar{u}' > 0 & z_{24} &= 0 \\
z_{31} &= -[\bar{v}_{ff}u'+u''(v_f)^2]/v_{ff}u' < 0 & z_{33} &= r > 0 \\
z_{32} &= [\bar{v}_f\bar{v}_{fm}/\bar{v}_{ff}) \ (> 0 \text{ for } v_{mf} < 0) & z_{34} &= 0 \\
z_{41} &= [\bar{v}_{ff}(\bar{u}')^2+\bar{u}''(\bar{v}_f)^2][\bar{\delta}-(\bar{u}+\bar{v})\bar{\delta}']/\bar{\delta}\bar{u}'\bar{v}_{ff} > 0 & z_{43} &= 0 \\
z_{42} &= (\bar{v}_m\bar{v}_{ff}-\bar{v}_f v_{fm})[\bar{\delta}-(\bar{u}+\bar{v})\bar{\delta}']/\bar{\delta}\bar{v}_{ff} > 0 & z_{44} &= r > 0\,.
\end{aligned}
$$

The signs given above are correct, since, from the first-order condition (8a), $\lambda = u'[1+q\delta']$, it follows that

$$
\begin{aligned}
\bar{\lambda}_m &= -\bar{u}'(\bar{u}+\bar{v})\bar{\delta}''(\bar{v}_m\bar{v}_{ff}-\bar{v}_f v_{fm})]/\bar{\delta}\bar{v}_{ff} < 0\,, \\
\bar{\lambda}_c &= \{\bar{u}''[\bar{\delta}-(\bar{u}+\bar{v})\bar{\delta}']/\bar{\delta}\} - \{\bar{u}'\bar{\delta}''(\bar{u}+\bar{v})[(\bar{u}')^2\bar{v}_{ff}+(\bar{v}_f)^2\bar{u}'']/\bar{\delta}\bar{v}_{ff}\bar{u}'\} < 0\,, \\
\bar{\lambda}_q &= \bar{u}'\bar{\delta}' > 0\,,
\end{aligned}
$$

where $[\bar{\delta}-(\bar{u}+\bar{v})\bar{\delta}'] > 0$ as noted in the text, $\bar{q} = -(\bar{u}+\bar{v})/\bar{\delta}$, and $\bar{\delta}'' > 0$. Notice also that $\bar{\lambda}\bar{\delta}' = \bar{\lambda}_q(1+\bar{q}\bar{\delta}')$.

The system is saddlepath stable if the **Z** matrix possesses exactly one negative characteristic root. Since the determinant of the matrix is the product of, while the trace is the sum of, the roots, and since one of the roots is r [examine the third column of **Z** in (A1)], a *negative* determinant and a trace $> r$ gives us the desired result. That is, if the determinant is negative, the system has either one or three negative roots; a positive trace which exceeds r is sufficient to rule out the latter.

The trace of **Z** is equal to $(z_{11}+z_{22}+2r) > r$, while the determinant, Det $\mathbf{Z} = z_{33}z_{44}(z_{11}z_{22}-z_{12}z_{21}) + z_{14}z_{33}(z_{21}z_{42}-z_{22}z_{41})$. Note that $(z_{11}z_{22}-z_{12}z_{21}) = 0$ and $z_{14}z_{33}(z_{21}z_{42}-z_{22}z_{41}) < 0$, so that Det $\mathbf{Z} < 0$. Thus the model of section one is *saddlepath stable*.

Equations (13) and (15) reveal the *impact effects* of changes in π^* on the endogenous variables, as well as the paths taken by these variables to the new steady state. Equations (15) are derived as follows. Denote the linearized system as written above, $\dot{\mathbf{x}} = \mathbf{Zx}$, where **Z** is a four-by-four matrix, and $\dot{\mathbf{x}}$ and $\mathbf{x}$ are vectors. Denote the negative characteristic root θ, let $\boldsymbol{\omega}$ represent an eigenvector belonging to θ (θ is found by taking Det $[\mathbf{Z} - \theta\mathbf{I}] = 0$, where **I** is the identity matrix) and k be an arbitrary constant determined by the value of A at time t. The elements of $\boldsymbol{\omega}$ are given by $\omega_{11}, \omega_{21}, \omega_{31}, \omega_{41}$. Any *convergent* solution is of the form

$$(m - \bar{m}) = \omega_{11} k \cdot \exp(\theta t) , \qquad (A - \bar{A}) = \omega_{31} k \cdot \exp(\theta t) ,$$

$$(c - \bar{c}) = \omega_{21} k \cdot \exp(\theta t) , \qquad (q - \bar{q}) = \omega_{41} k \cdot \exp(\theta t) ,$$

Clearly, $(m-\bar{m}) = [\omega_{11} / \omega_{31}](A-\bar{A})$, $(c-\bar{c}) = [\omega_{21} / \omega_{31}](A-\bar{A})$, and $(q-\bar{q}) = [\omega_{41} / \omega_{31}](A-\bar{A})$. From (15), ω_{11}, ω_{21}, and ω_{31} are of the same sign, while ω_{41} is of the opposite sign. Using equations A1, I show this as follows.

First, I prove (available from the author on request) by contradiction that no element of $\boldsymbol{\omega}$ may be zero without each of the others being zero, that is, each element must be strictly positive or strictly negative, otherwise each element must be zero. Second, I use this fact in setting $\omega_{41} = -1$, without loss of generality, and using $(\mathbf{Z} - \theta \mathbf{I})\boldsymbol{\omega} = 0$, directly calculate,

$$\omega_{11} = (z_{22}-\theta)(r-\theta)/[(z_{41}z_{22}-z_{21}z_{42})-z_{41}\theta] > 0 ,$$

$$\omega_{21} = -z_{21}(r-\theta)/[(z_{41}z_{22}-z_{21}z_{42})-z_{41}\theta] > 0 ,$$

$$\omega_{31} = [(z_{32}z_{21}-z_{31}z_{22})+z_{31}\theta]/[(z_{41}z_{22}-z_{21}z_{41})-z_{41}\theta] > 0 ,$$

Note that ω_{31} is independent of the sign of v_{mf} even though z_{32} is not:

$$\omega_{31} = \{[\bar{m}/v_{ff}(u')^3][(u')^2(v_{ff}v_{mm}-v_{mf}^2)+u''v_f(v_f v_{mm}-v_m v_{mf})]+\theta z_{31}\}/[\theta z_{41} - (z_{41}z_{22}-z_{21}z_{41})] .$$

LITERATURE CITED

Calvo, Guillermo A. "Currency Substitution and the Real Exchange Rate: The Utility Maximizing Approach." *Journal of International Money and Finance* 4 (June 1985), 175–88.

Calvo, Guillermo A., and Carlos A. Rodriguez. "A Model of Exchange Rate Determination under Currency Substitution and Rational Expectations." *Journal of Political Economy* 85 (June 1977), 617–25.

Cuddington, John. "Currency Substitution, Capital Mobility and Money Demand." *Journal of International Money and Finance* 2 (1983), 111–33.

Darby, Michael R., and James R. Lothian. *The International Transmission of Inflation.* Chicago and London: The University of Chicago Press, 1983.

Engel, Charles M. "The Trade Balance and Real Exchange Rate under Currency Substitution." *Journal of International Money and Finance* 8 (March 1989), 47–58.

Flood, Robert P., and Nancy P. Marion. "The Transmission of Disturbances under Alternative Exchange-Rate Regimes with Optimal Indexing." *Quarterly Journal of Economics* 97 (February 1982), 43–66.

Friedman, Milton. "The Case for Flexible Exchange Rates." In *Essays in Positive Economics*, 157–203. Chicago: University of Chicago Press, 1953.

Kareken, John, and Neil Wallace. "On the Indeterminacy of Equilibrium Exchange Rates." *Quarterly Journal of Economics* 96 (May 1981), 207–22.

Kompas, Tom, and Omar Abdel-Razeq. "A Note on Uzawa's Transformation of Two-state Variable Optimal Control Problems with an Endogenous Rate of Time Preference." Manuscript, 1987.

Liviatan, Nissan. "Monetary Expansion and Real Exchange Rate Dynamics." *Journal of Political Economy* 89 (December 1981), 1245–57.

McKinnon, Ronald. "Currency Substitution and Instability in the World Dollar Standard." *American Economic Review* 72 (June 1982), 320–33.

Obstfeld, Maurice. "Macroeconomic Policy, Exchange-Rate Dynamics, and Optimal Asset Accumulation." *Journal of Political Economy* 89 (December 1981), 1142–61.

______. "Aggregate Spending and the Terms of Trade: Is There a Laursen-Metzler Effect?" *Quarterly Journal of Economics* 97 (May 1982), 251–70.

______. "Exchange Rate Dynamics and Optimal Asset Accumulation, Revisited." Manuscript, August 1987.

Rogers, John. "Currency Substitution in International Monetary Analysis." Ph.D. dissertation, University of Virginia, August 1988.

Uzawa, Hirofumi. "Time Preference, the Consumption Function, and Optimum Asset Holdings." In *Value, Capital, and Growth: Papers in Honour of Sir John Hicks*, edited by J. N. Wolfe. Chicago: Aldine Press, 1968.

JAMES J. MUSUMECI
JOSEPH F. SINKEY, JR.

The International Debt Crisis, Investor Contagion, and Bank Security Returns in 1987: The Brazilian Experience

WHEN MEXICO ANNOUNCED ITS DEBT MORATORIUM in August 1982, disclosure requirements for bank loans to less-developed countries (LDCs) were absent and secondary markets for LDC debts did not exist. Because some private information existed, the numerous event studies of the Mexican debt crisis were ones of strong-form market efficiency.[1] Somewhat surprisingly these studies had conflicting findings.[2] When Brazil announced its debt moratorium on February 20, 1987, the environment was different in that disclosure

[1]Mexico's debt moratorium in August 1982 generated four independent event studies: Smirlock and Kaufold (1985, 1987), Schoder and Vankudre (1986), Cornell and Shapiro (1986), and Bruner and Simms (1987). Kane and Unal (1988) criticize these studies because the authors did not control for the possibility of parameter nonstationarity elsewhere in 1982. As a result, they may have falsely accepted or rejected their hypotheses.

[2]Although none of the authors (mentioned in footnote 1) reached the same conclusions regarding market efficiency, Bruner and Simms (B&S) and Smirlock and Kaufold (S&K) came close. B&S found evidence of *temporary* investor contagion, while S&K (1987), an extension of S&K (1985), found no such evidence. B&S used ordinary least squares, as we do, whereas S&K used seemingly unrelated regression. Since the choice between SUR with a dummy variable and OLS with its residuals does not explain the different contagion results estimated by B&S and S&K, we attribute the difference to either sample selection or choice of estimation period, or both.

The authors thank David Blackwell, Mitchell Collins,Mary Dehner, Jangsoon Han, Edward Kane, Van Son Lai, William Megginson, Annette Poulsen, Stephen D. Smith, James Thomson, Haluk Unal, Paul Wilson, and two JMCB referees for their helpful comments and suggestions. A preliminary version of this paper was presented at the 1988 Conference on Bank Structure and Competition sponsored by the Federal Reserve Bank of Chicago. A later version of the paper was presented at the 1988/1989 Federal Reserve Bank of Atlanta–Emory Business School Workshop in Money, Banking, and Finance.

JAMES J. MUSUMECI *is assistant professor of banking and finance, The University of Georgia.* JOSEPH F. SINKEY, JR., *is professor of finance and holds the Georgia Bankers Association Chair of Banking, The University of Georgia.*

Journal of Money, Credit, and Banking, Vol. 22, No. 2 (May 1990)

requirements and secondary markets existed and financial markets had experienced Mexico's default and numerous reschedulings of LDC debt. Because of these differences, Brazil's announcement merits analysis in its own right.

Using event-study methods, we examine bank security returns surrounding the announcement of Brazil's debt moratorium in 1987. Our tests, which are ones of semistrong-form market efficiency, present an opportunity to provide additional evidence regarding the pricing of bank security returns. In particular, we have two new angles: (1) the availability of bid and asked market prices for developing country debt allows us to compare changes in bank equity values with changes in the market prices of LDC debt and (2) the disclosure of debt levels by country allows us to test for "country contagion." For our sample of twenty-five large U.S. bank holding companies (BHCs), we reject the null hypotheses of no new information, irrational pricing, and country contagion.

Our paper proceeds in six sections. We briefly review the event studies related to the Mexican debt crisis in section 1. In section 2, we compare bank disclosure requirements and the development of secondary markets for LDC debt in 1982 with those in 1987. In the next four sections, we state our hypotheses; describe our sample BHCs, data, and methodology; present our empirical findings; and summarize and conclude our paper.

1. INVESTOR CONTAGION AND BANK SECURITY RETURNS IN 1982

Studies of the Mexican debt crisis analyzed (cross-sectionally) the risk-adjusted returns surrounding the announcement of Mexico's default on August 19, 1982. Schoder and Vankudre found a negative but insignificant market reaction on the announcement day. Using annual, biannual, monthly and selected daily returns, Cornell and Shapiro tested for a Latin American exposure effect. They postulated a "dribs-and-drabs" hypothesis whereby negative information was slowly released throughout 1982 and 1983. They found exposure to Latin American debt affected the annual returns in 1982 and over the two-year period 1982 to 1983, but did not affect monthly and selected daily returns (including the announcement day). They concluded that Mexico's announcement was not a material event compared to other events in 1982. Moreover, they argued that because of the dribs-and-drabs nature of information flows in 1982 and 1983, standard event-study methods would understate the effects of Latin American exposure on the relative pricing of bank equities.

Using daily data, Bruner and Simms (B&S, 1987) found a significant negative market reaction to the arrival of rumor and news about Mexico's default. In addition, they found that the degree of bank exposure to Mexico was *initially* positively related to risk-adjusted bank returns. This temporary investor contagion disappeared, however, after the fifth day of the published announcement. Like B&S, Smirlock and Kaufold (S&K, 1987) find a significant negative market reaction to the Mexican announcement. Unlike B&S, however, they find no evidence of contagion. Since B&S and S&K analyze the same event,their different findings regarding contagion are puzzling. We attribute the difference to either sample selection or choice of estimation period, or both.[3]

2. DISCLOSURE REQUIREMENTS AND THE DEVELOPMENT OF SECONDARY MARKETS FOR DEVELOPING COUNTRY DEBT: 1982 VERSUS 1987

In 1982, the year of the Mexican debt suspension, Bruner and Simms (1987) report "there were no reliable estimates of individual banks' lending exposure to Latin America" (p. 48).[4] In contrast, by 1987, the year of the Brazilian debt suspension, individual bank exposures to Brazilian and other LDCs were readily and widely available (see Table 1). Bid and asked market prices for LDC debt in secondary markets also became available in the mid-1980s. Although this traded debt was contractually similar to the LDC debt held by banks (that is, general obligation, floating-rate debt), traders acknowledged the secondary markets to be "thin." In addition, from August 1982 to February 1987 numerous debt reschedulings took place.

The existence of disclosure, secondary markets, debt reschedulings, and general improvement in information flows should permit markets to operate more efficiently (that is, to adjust prices more quickly and reliably). We think the market was likely to be more efficient in 1987 than 1982. Fundamentally, however, we test different hypotheses of market efficiency. In 1982, investors knew that large banks were making loans to developing countries as such deals (loan syndications) were announced regularly in the financial press (see Megginson, Poulsen, and Sinkey [1989]). What they did not know, however, were the individual banks' exact dollar exposures by country. Since some private information existed, the 1982 tests were ones of strong-form efficiency. With greater LDC disclosure, we test for semistrong-form market efficiency in 1987. Specifically, we test for two different types of contagion: investor contagion (that is, penalizing banks independent of their Brazilian exposure) and country contagion (that is, penalizing banks depending on their non-Brazilian exposure).[5]

3. HYPOTHESES

We pose hypotheses similar to those of Bruner and Simms (1987). Our first null hypothesis is that no new information was conveyed to the market by Braz-

[3]Although other differences exist between the methodologies used by B&S and S&K, they would not account for the differential findings. For example, SUR generally will provide more efficient estimates than OLS, but when the independent variables are the same (as they are in this case), both methods yield the same estimates. The dummy-variable technique used by S&K simply takes the OLS event-day residuals and converts them to coefficients. Thus, except for the inclusion of day 0 in the dummy-variable method, the two approaches produce identical results. Discussions with Stephen D. Smith, James Thomson, and Paul Wilson were helpful in clarifying these econometric issues.

[4]The one exception, reported by Bruner and Simms (1987, p. 48, fn. 3), was Manufacturers Hanover, which had voluntarily disclosed its exposure to Mexico during the spring of 1982.

[5]Although contagion typically is associated with irrationality, country contagion might be rational if expectations of non-Brazilian debt repayment changed.

TABLE 1

MAJOR BANKING COMPANIES CROSS-BORDER EXPOSURE TO BRAZIL, DECEMBER 31, 1986

Money-Center Group	$ millions	Percent of Primary Capital and Rank	
Bank America (24)	2,741	37.0%	23
Bankers Trust (20)	849	18.5	15
Chase Manhattan (23)	2,740	41.1	24
Chemical (22)	1,446	32.9	20
Citicorp (18)	4,600	36.0	22
Continental Illinois (15)	474	19.0	16
First Chicago (17)	733	22.1	17
J. P. Morgan (16)	1,926	30.1	19
Manufacturers Hanover (25)	2,317	42.9	25
Security Pacific (11)	605	14.6	11
Subtotal or average	18,431	26.7%	-
Regional Group			
Bank of Boston (12)	300	13.0%	9
Bank of New England (7)	82	5.9	7
First Bank System (8)	189	9.4	8
First Interstate (10)	504	14.8	12
First Union (1)	*	0.0	1
Irving (21)	398	24.9	18
Marine Midland (19)	621	36.3	21
M Corp (4)	34	2.0	4
Mellon (13)	347	13.9	10
NBD Bancorp (6)	46	3.3	5
NCNB (5)	85	5.0	6
Norwest (9)	147	16.4	13
PNC Financial (2)	*	6.6	2
SunTrust (3)	22	1.2	3
Wells Fargo (14)	594	16.5	14
Subtotal or average	3,510	11.2%	-
Grand total or average	21,941	17.4%	-

NOTES: The rank in the last column is based on "1" as the least exposed (safest). The number in parentheses beside the BHC name is its rank (1 = least exposed or safest) for the ratio of total LDC loans to *book* equity capital. The asterisk indicates an exposure of less than 0.75 percent of total assets. The money-center group of ten BHCs held 82 percent of Brazil's $22.4 billion in loans from U.S. banks.

Source: "Review of Major Banks' Loan Exposure to Less-Developed Countries." Fixed Income Research, First Boston, June 22, 1987, pp. 10–18.

il's announcement. Under this scenario, Brazilian debt would have already been discounted by the time its announcement was made on February 20, 1987, and reflected in the share prices of lending banks. If the Mexican debt crisis (and other events such as debt reschedulings) had led investors to fully anticipate this deterioration, then no significant market response to Brazil's announcement would occur. Our alternative hypothesis is that Brazil's announcement contained new information about the riskiness of bank LDC loans. Next, focusing on bank security returns cross-sectionally, we specify four hypotheses to determine causes of differential bank responses to Brazil's announcement:[6]

[6]If we accept our main null hypothesis, the remaining tests might appear to be irrelevant. Nevertheless, such tests still may provide information because even if the average residual is insignificantly different from zero, the individual residuals still could be significantly different from each other.

1. whether each BHC's abnormal return depends on its exposure to Brazilian debt (section 5.1),
2. whether the market penalized BHCs for their exposure to non-Brazilian debt (section 5.2),
3. whether Brazil's announcement inflicted more damage on the weaker banks than on the stronger ones (section 5.3), and
4. whether the change in the market price of Brazilian debt is the primary factor in any change in BHC share values (section 5.4).

Our hypotheses, along with empirical capsules for each test, are summarized in Table 2.

TABLE 2

A SUMMARY OF THE HYPOTHESES AND EMPIRICAL FINDINGS RELATED TO THE ANNOUNCEMENT OF BRAZIL'S DEBT MORATORIUM OF FEBRUARY 20, 1987

Hypothesis/Test	Finding and location in paper
1. No new information	1. Hypothesis rejected. BHC equities were negatively affected. See section 5 and Table 3.
2. Investor contagion or irrational pricing	2. Hypothesis rejected. The market reacted rationally and penalized banks in direct proportion to their exposure to Brazilian debt. See section 5.1.
3. Country contagion	3. Hypothesis rejected. Negative abnormal returns appear mainly related to Brazilian exposure. See section 5.2.
4. Capital adequacy or financial strength	4. Hypothesis rejected. Brazil's announcement inflicted more damage on BHCs with inadequate capital. See section 5.3
5. Market prices of Brazil's debt	5. Changes in BHC equity values are positively related to the change in the value of Brazil's traded debt. See section 5.4.

4. SAMPLE BANKING FIRMS, DATA, AND METHODOLOGY

Our sample banking firms and their outstanding loans to Brazil (as of December 31, 1986) are shown in Table 1. We analyze ten money-center or multinational banking companies and fifteen regional banking companies. At the time of Brazil's announcement, these banking companies were the twenty-five largest U.S. banks/BHCs as listed by the *American Banker* in its report of financial-services stocks. Although our sample is relatively small, it consists of the major U.S. lenders to LDCs. All of our sample BHCs had some LDC exposure. We group our stocks into three portfolios: money centers, regionals, and all twenty-five. Stock price and dividend data for these firms were collected from the *Daily Stock Price Record* and used to generate daily returns for our sample BHCs.

We employ standard event-study methods to generate our empirical findings.

Using a 140-day estimation period from day −143 through day −4, we center our event date on February 23, 1987, and designate day −3 to day +3 the event period. Within this event period, we examine one-, three-, five-, and seven-day windows. Since we do not test for significant market adjustments prior to day −4, we cannot rule out that such adjustments may have occurred earlier. Given the trade-off between the power of the test and the size of the window, we opted for a more powerful test by using a smaller window.

Each bank's daily return is regressed against the Value Line Index.[7] Since event-study results may be affected by the method used, we employ alternative return-generating processes to calculate abnormal returns (ARs) for each stock, which are then summed to obtain cumulative average returns (CARs).[8] Our portfolio standard deviations were estimated not by aggregating individual standard deviations, but by looking directly at the distribution of portfolio residuals.[9] As Jaffe (1974, 1974a) and Bruner and Simms (1987) point out, this latter method takes into account the cross-sectional correlation between residuals and reduces any problems arising from the presence of both calendar time and industry clustering.[10]

Kane and Unal (1988) criticize event-study researchers for ignoring confounding events and nonstationarity of return-generating processes. We find our event windows relatively clean of potential confounding events and our estimated betas stationary. We tested for stationarity by dividing our estimation period in half and applying Chow (1960) procedures. Moreover, alternative methods should work even in the presence of nonstationarity. Two such techniques are a market-adjusted approach (free of parameter estimation) and alternative estimation periods around our event windows. These methods gave us the same results.

5. EMPIRICAL FINDINGS

We summarize our hypotheses and empirical findings in Table 2. Our estimates of abnormal returns surrounding the announcement of Brazil's debt mor-

[7]Like the CRSP unweighted index, the Value Line index is unweighted, but it does have two relative disadvantages: (1) it does not include dividends and (2) it is calculated by Value Line as a cross-sectional geometric mean return. If dividends are paid out relatively continuously, then aggregate dividend payout would be a constant, and the first shortcoming would not be a serious problem. The extent to which the second point causes a problem is not known.

[8]To determine the significance of the CARs, we estimated the standard deviation of the CARs using the methods described by Brown and Warner (1980), Ruback (1982), and Jensen and Ruback (1983). We found no meaningful differences between the three results. We report standard deviations based on the Jensen and Ruback method, which multiplies the standard deviation of the daily residual by the square root of the number of days in the window. The alternative return-generating processes we employed included one- and two-factor market models (Stone 1974), a market-adjusted model, and the CAPM.

[9]Technically, the unbiased estimator of the variance of the sample residuals is a downward-biased estimator of the variance of the forecast errors (for example, see Kmenta 1971, p. 241). Although we did not make this adjustment, the maximum upward bias in our reported t-values is approximately 2 percent.

[10]Brown and Warner (1985) observe that direct estimation of the standard deviation of the portfolio residuals leads to less powerful tests than aggregating standard deviations of the individual residuals. Since our test is a less powerful one, we can be more certain of our results when the null is rejected.

atorium are shown in Table 3. The findings for the other hypotheses we test are presented in sections 5.1 through 5.4

After markets closed on February 20, 1987, Brazil announced an "open-ended" debt moratorium. *The Wall Street Journal* reported this on Monday, February 23. "Rumors" of a ninety-day moratorium, however, were reported in *The Wall Street Journal* February 19 and 20. Our findings clearly show significant negative market reaction to the stocks of money-center BHCs on February 23. Defining February 23 as day 0, we report two windows in Table 3: Day 0 and the three-day window [−1, +1]. The portfolio of money-center BHCs shows a significant negative reaction over both windows. Within the money-center portfolio, each BHC's abnormal return is negative. Although Fama (1976) has shown

TABLE 3

ABNORMAL RETURNS SURROUNDING THE ANNOUNCEMENT OF BRAZIL'S DEBT MORATORIUM ON FEBRUARY 23, 1987, ESTIMATED USING A SINGLE-FACTOR MARKET MODEL

Money-Center Group	Day 0 Residual	Day 0 *t*-value	3-day window [−1,+1] CARs	3-day window [−1,+1] *t*-value
Bank America	−4.75%	−1.41	−3.63%	−0.62
Bankers Trust	−2.61	−1.96	−5.04	−2.18
Chase Manhattan	−3.49	−2.23	−5.96	−2.20
Chemical	−4.58	−4.05	−4.77	−2.44
Citicorp	−5.66	−4.50	−8.01	−3.67
Continental Illinois	−6.32	−2.42	−6.31	−1.39
First Chicago	−0.81	−0.48	−0.75	−0.26
J. P. Morgan	−2.25	−1.85	−6.47	−3.07
Manufacturers Hanover	−1.96	−2.07	−5.05	−3.08
Security Pacific	−2.52	−2.35	−9.67	−5.21
Money-center portfolio (10)	−3.50%	−4.71*	−5.57%	−4.33*
Regional Group				
Bank of Boston	−5.34%	−3.29	−7.70%	−2.73
Bank of New England	1.20	0.75	3.24	1.18
First Bank System	−2.20	−1.66	−3.60	−1.57
First Interstate	−1.04	−0.83	−1.47	−0.68
First Union	−0.35	−0.26	4.40	1.85
Irving	−0.79	−0.64	−1.47	−0.69
Marine Midland	−1.58	−1.55	−0.16	−0.93
M Corp	−1.34	−0.44	0.46	0.09
Mellon	−0.07	−0.05	1.54	0.70
NBD Bancorp	−0.13	−0.09	0.09	0.04
NCNB	1.83	1.19	2.59	0.97
Norwest	1.47	1.03	2.68	1.09
PNC Financial	0.80	0.72	5.01	2.60
SunTrust	3.05	2.08	4.05	1.59
Wells Fargo	−0.76	−0.65	1.32	0.65
Regional bank portfolio (15)	−0.35%	−0.63	0.63%	0.66
Total portfolio (25 BHCs)	−1.61%	−3.27*	−1.85%	−2.17*

NOTES: The market portfolio is proxied by the Value Line Index. For the portfolio returns, an asterisk indicates significance at the 5 percent level. The estimated portfolio betas are .83, .99, and .93 moving down the table with corresponding *t*-values of 10.3, 16.3, and 17.3. Except for BankAmerica with an estimated beta of .47 (t=1.28) and Continental Illinois with an estimated beta of .05 (t=.19), all of the individual stock betas are statistically significant and ranged from .63 (t=4.58) for Mellon to 1.65 (t=10.6) for Norwest. Brown and Warner (1980), Ruback (1982), and Jensen and Ruback (1983) *t*-statistics were computed for the CARs. All three measures produced similar results. Jensen and Ruback *t*-values are reported here.

formal statistical significance cannot be attached to the t-values of individual securities' residuals,[11] it is interesting to note that seven of the ten abnormal returns for our event day are more than two standard deviations from zero. Combining our firms into an equally weighted portfolio, we find the money-center BHCs dominating the results with a portfolio AR of −1.61 percent ($t = -3.27$) on the event day and a CAR of −1.85 percent ($t = -2.17$) over the three-day window.

5.1 *Loan-Exposure Tests*

To test for the market's ability to distinguish among BHCs by degree of loan exposure to Brazil, we regressed the residuals shown in Table 3 against the exposure data shown in Table 1. The estimated relationship for the day 0 abnormal returns or residuals is

$$AR_j = -.0036 - \underset{(-3.42)}{.0311}\,(EX_j),\ R^2 = .3370 \text{ and } N = 25,$$

where AR_j is the abnormal return for the jth BHC on day 0 and EX_j is the Brazilian exposure (relative to "primary capital") for the jth BHC at year-end 1986. Our findings indicate a significant direct relationship between exposure and the market penalty.[12] When we deflated exposure by the market value of BHC equity, we found the following similar but slightly stronger relationship:

$$AR_j = -.0011 - \underset{(-3.72)}{.0398}\,(EXMV_j),\ R^2 = .3758 \text{ and } N = 25,$$

where $EXMV_j$ indicates the jth BHC's Brazilian exposure relative to the market value of its equity as of year-end 1986. For our three-, five-, and seven-day windows, we find similar results. In comparable tests for the Mexican debt crisis, Bruner and Simms (1987) found significant relationships only for their six-day and larger windows. Thus, the investor contagion found by Bruner and Simms from day 0 to day +5 is absent from our findings. We infer from these results that the better LDC information flows available in 1987 relative to 1982 enabled investors to adjust prices more quickly and efficiently for our total sample of twenty-five securities. In contrast, however, since Smirlock and Kaufold (1987) found no evidence of contagion associated with the Mexican announcement, our

[11]Fama (1976, chapter 1) analyzed individual security daily raw returns and found they are not normally distributed, but instead have "fatter tails." Brown and Warner (1985) found this also true of individual security daily residuals. For these reasons, formal statistical significance cannot be attached to the t-values for individual securities' residuals. When we grouped our 247 estimation and event days to estimate market-model parameters, we found almost exactly 5 percent of the individual daily residuals had t-values greater than 2.0. This finding suggests, on any given day, a null hypothesis of a zero daily residual for an individual BHC is rejected at about the same rate as a null hypothesis of a normal distribution.

[12]We also regressed our residuals against the ratio of total LDC debt relative to bank equity capital and found similar but slightly less significant relationships.

inference is not conclusive. As discussed in footnote 3, we attribute the difference in contagion findings estimated by B&S and S&K to differences in sample selection or choice of estimation period, or both.

5.2. *A Test for Country Contagion*

For our sample BHCs, the average exposure to Brazil was $878 million compared to an average total LDC exposure of $2.3 billion. If the announcement of Brazil's debt moratorium caused investors to devalue other LDC debt, this "country contagion" could help explain our estimated abnormal negative returns. However, because of the high correlation between banks' Brazilian and non-Brazilian LDC exposure ($r = .95$), neither a two-factor regression using both exposures nor a single-factor regression using both exposures nor a single-factor regression using only non-Brazilian LDC exposure was meaningful. Accordingly, we used a two-step procedure to test for country contagion. First, we orthogonalized the total dollar LDC exposure for each BHC (LDC_j) by regressing against each bank's dollar exposure to Brazil ($Brazil_j$) and found the following:

$$LDC_j = 239.1 + \underset{(26.5)}{2.415}\,(Brazil_j),\ R^2 = .9683 \text{ and } N = 25\ .$$

Next, we regressed the total dollar change in market equity for each BHC against the difference between the actual LDC exposure and the estimated LDC exposure. In effect, we regressed the dollar change in equity against the orthogonalized non-Brazilian exposure of each BHC. Since we did not find a statistically significant relationship for any of our windows, we find no evidence of country contagion (that is, the negative abnormal returns appear mainly related to Brazilian exposure).

5.3. *Capital-Adequacy Tests*

In banking, "capital adequacy" is a common measure of "safety and soundness" (that is, financial strength) by both the marketplace and bank regulators. It seems reasonable to hypothesize that the stronger a BHC's capital position, the more resistant it should be to bad news such as the announcement of a debt moratorium. To test this proposition, we regressed our abnormal returns against each BHC's ratio of market value of common equity to total assets as of year-end 1986. Using day 0 abnormal returns, we found the following positive and significant relationship:

$$AR_j = -.0433 + \underset{(2.74)}{.5664}\,(EAMV_j),\ R^2 = .2463 \text{ and } N = 25\ ,$$

where $EAMV_j$ is the market value of equity-to-asset ratio for the jth BHC. Using a *book* measure of total equity (defined to include preferred stock), the capital ratio had a t-value of only 1.34. Based on the more meaningful market-value capital ratio, we find that the market inflicted more damage on BHCs with "inadequate" capital than on those with "adequate" capital.[13]

5.4. *Tests Relating Changes in BHC Equity Values to Changes in Values of Brazil's Debt*

Based on bid and asked market prices for Brazil's debt (supplied by Shearson Lehman Brothers), the following prices (daily averages as a percentage of face value) were observed for the first three months of 1987:

Price	January	February	March	Dollar Change January to March
Bid	74	73.5	68	−6.00
Asked	76.5	75.5	70	−6.50
Average	75.25	74.5	69	−6.25

Since February prices are contaminated by Brazil's debt moratorium, we measured the price change from January to March. Since the market prices for the debt of other developing countries (not shown here) did not decline over this period, prima facie evidence of an absence of country contagion exists.

We first tested the relationship between changes in Brazilian debt values and changes in equity values and found:

$$\Delta E_j = 141.8 + \underset{(5.34)}{2.398}\,(\Delta D_j),\ R^2 = .5534 \text{ and } N = 25\ ,$$

where ΔE_j is the change in the jth BHC's total average equity January to March and ΔD_j is the change in the value of the jth BHC's Brazilian debt. This finding suggests that a decline in the market value of Brazil's debt of \$1.00 led to a \$2.40 drop in equity value for the average BHC in our sample. When we adjusted the change in each BHC's equity for the change in the value of our market index to obtain ΔEMA_j, we estimated the relationship to be[14]

$$\Delta EMA_j = -13.6 + \underset{(5.40)}{4.703}\,(\Delta D_j),\ R_2 = .5591 \text{ and } N = 25\ .$$

If the change in equity values were driven solely by the change in the value of Brazil's debt, we would expect a zero intercept and a slope coefficient of one.

[13]In joint tests for the significance of exposure and financial strength, we used various measures of the independent variables. None of these specifications resulted in statistical significance for any of our windows. We expect the strong negative correlation between exposure and strength accounts for this finding. For example, using market values of equity in both variables, the correlation between exposure and the capital-to-asset ratio was −.63. Even when exposure was defined as Brazilian debt over total assets, the correlation was −.43.

[14]The variable ΔEMA_j equals the actual value of the jth BHC's equity in March minus its January equity value adjusted for January through March market returns.

Since the coefficient is significantly greater than one, some other factor is influencing equity values or some bias/measurement error in the variables exists. We already have ruled out the possibility that an imputed reduction in the value of non-Brazilian debt influenced stock returns (see section 5.2 and our discussion above of the market prices for LDC debt). Another possibility is that the traded Brazilian debt and the Brazilian debt still held by banks have different values.[15] For example, if banks sold their higher quality LDC debt, we would expect their remaining (lower quality) debt to be more sensitive to default risk. Finally, since traders have described the secondary market for LDC debt as a thin one, another explanation is that the data are faulty.[16]

6. SUMMARY AND CONCLUSIONS

Greater disclosure requirements, the development of secondary markets for LDC debt, and investor experiences with the Mexican default announcement and numerous subsequent debt reschedulings distinguish the financial environment of the Mexican debt crisis of 1982 from the Brazilian one in 1987. Because of these differences, the Brazilian announcement merits analysis in its own right. Our contribution is testing for semistrong-form market efficiency for BHC equities in 1987. Our new angles on the problem revolve around the use of country exposure data and market data on LDC debt prices.

Although we find that the market reacted negatively to the announcement of Brazil's debt moratorium of February 20, 1987, we find no evidence of mispricing or investor contagion in its reaction. Specifically, investors reacted rationally to the debt suspension and penalized banks/BHCs based on their exposure to Brazilian debt. Moreover, the market did not penalize BHCs for their exposure to non-Brazilian debt and the change in the market price of Brazilian debt was the primary factor affecting any change in BHC share values. Finally, Brazil's announcement inflicted more damage on banks with weaker capital positions than on the stronger ones. On balance, we think that LDC disclosure requirements and the development of secondary markets for LDC debt have contributed to the efficiency of pricing BHC equities.

[15]We thank an anonymous referee for making this point.

[16]An anonymous referee suggested that thin markets have some implications for our regressions in this section. Specifically, an unbiased but noisy observation of any independent variable results in a downward-biased estimate of b, if the noise is uncorrelated with the dependent or independent variable. In our case, however, the observed independent variable has perfect correlation with the true independent variable. To illustrate, suppose our observed thin market price equals some random variable, k, times the price that would prevail in a liquid market. Unbiasedness implies $E(k) = 1$. We want to estimate $b = s_{xy}/s_x^2$, but we are able to estimate only $b = s_{xy}/ks_x^2$, where s_x^2 and s_{xy} are variance/covariance terms. If the noise factor k is uncorrelated with x or y, $E(b) = E[1/k]E[s_{xy}/s_x^2] = E[1/k]b$. Since k is always positive, $E[1/k] > 1/E[k] = 1$, and our estimated coefficients are biased upward. Although the extent of the bias is unknown, most likely it is small.

LITERATURE CITED

Brown, Stephen, and Jerold Warner. "Measuring Security Price Performance." *Journal of Financial Economics* 8 (September 1980), 205–58.

______. "Using Daily Stock Returns: The Case of Event Studies." *Journal of Financial Economics* 14 (March 1985), 3–32.

Bruner, Robert F., and John M. Simms, Jr. "The International Debt Crisis and Bank Security Returns in 1982." *Journal of Money, Credit, and Banking* 19 (February 1987), 46–55.

Chow, Gregory C. "Tests of Equality between Sets of Coefficients in Linear Regressions." *Econometrica* 28 (July 1960), 591–605.

Cornell, Bradford, and Alan C. Shapiro. "The Reaction of Bank Stock Prices to the International Debt Crisis." *Journal of Banking and Finance* 10 (March 1986), 55–73.

Daily Stock Price Record. NYSE and OTC, New York: Standard and Poor's, 1986 and 1987.

Fama, Eugene F. *Foundations of Finance.* New York: Basic Books, Inc., 1976.

Jaffe, Jeffrey F. "The Effect of Regulatory Changes on Insider Trading." *Bell Journal of Economics and Management Science* (Spring 1974), 93–121.

______. "Special Information and Insider Trading." *Journal of Business* 47 (July 1974a) 410–28.

Jensen, Michael, and Richard Ruback. "The Market for Corporate Control: The Scientific Evidence." *Journal of Financial Economics* 11 (April 1983), 5–50.

Kane, Edward J., and Haluk Unal. "Change in Market Assessments of Deposit-Institution Riskiness." *Journal of Financial Services Research* (June 1988), 207–29.

Kmenta, Jan. *Elements of Econometrics.* New York: Macmillan, 1971.

Megginson, William L, Annette B. Poulsen, and Joseph F. Sinkey, Jr. "Lending to Developing Countries: How the Stock Market Evaluated the Loans." *Issues in Bank Regulation* (Spring 1989), 27–31.

"Review of Major Banks' Loan Exposures to Less-Developed Countries." Fixed Income Research, First Boston, June 22, 1987.

Ruback, Richard. "The Effect of Discretionary Price Control Decisions on Equity Values." *Journal of Financial Economics* 10 (March 1982), 83–106.

Saunders, Anthony. "The Interbank Market, Contagion Effects, and International Financial Crises." In *Threats to International Financial Stability*, edited by Richard Portes and Alexander K. Swoboda, pp. 196–238. Cambridge: Cambridge University Press, 1987.

Schoder, Stewart, and Prashant Vankudre. "The Market for Bank Stocks and Banks' Disclosure of Cross-Border Exposure: The 1982 Mexican Debt Crisis." *Studies in Banking and Finance* 3 (1986), 179–202.

Smirlock, Michael, and Howard Kaufold. "Foreign Lending, Disclosure, and the Mexican Debt Crisis." In *Proceedings: A Conference on Bank Structure and Competition*, pp. 576–84. Federal Reserve Bank of Chicago, 1985.

______. "Bank Foreign Lending, Mandatory Disclosure Rules, and Reaction of Bank Stock Prices to the Mexican Debt Crisis." *Journal of Business* 60 (July 1987), 347–64.

Stone, Bernell K. "Systematic Interest-Rate Risk in a Two-Index Model of Returns." *Journal of Financial and Quantatitive Analysis* 9 (November 1974), 709–21.

TERRENCE M. CLAURETIE
THOMAS HERZOG

The Effect of State Foreclosure Laws on Loan Losses: Evidence from the Mortgage Insurance Industry

SEVERAL RESEARCH EFFORTS have focused on the effect of state laws on various aspects of credit markets. James (1984) found that the managerial efficiency of banks was adversely affected by state laws which restrict corporate acquisition of bank stock. Barth, Cordes, and Yezer (1986) found that state laws which restrict the exercise of credit remedies for personal loans in delinquency or default result in the imposition of net costs on all borrowers. Meador (1982) and Jaffee (1985) analyzed the effect of state foreclosure laws on mortgage rates. They found that contract rates were generally higher in states where the law extended the length and expense of the foreclosure process. Alston (1984) revealed that the farm foreclosure moratorium legislation during the 1930s led to fewer farm loans and higher rates in states which enacted such legislation. Clauretie (1987) has indicated that lenders' choice of either seeking a foreclosure or employing a nonforeclosure alternative is affected by state laws. He demonstrated that foreclosure rates on conventional loans are higher (lower) in states that facilitate (hinder) the foreclosure process.

An important implication of his findings is that foreclosure rates cannot be taken as a measure of risk per se. High rates may simply reflect the low cost of foreclosing in those states with facilitating laws. If this is so, dollar losses could actually be less in those states. To date, no research has focused on the losses incurred by lenders (or mortgage insurers) due to differences in laws that regulate the foreclosure process. That will be one purpose of this research.

TERRENCE M. CLAURETIE *is professor of finance and chairman of the Department of Finance at the University of Nevada, Las Vegas.* THOMAS HERZOG *is chief actuary of the Federal Housing Administration.*

Journal of Money, Credit, and Banking, Vol. 22, No. 2 (May 1990)

A related topic of inquiry concerns the relationship between foreclosure laws and incentive conflicts in the mortgage insurance market. There are major differences between private (PMI) and government (principally, FHA) mortgage insurance practices. These differences and the legal climate within the various jurisdictions combine to produce an incentive conflict between lenders and insurers. It will be shown that state foreclosure laws result in a differential risk according to the type of mortgage insurance for which the lenders contract. The evidence on the effect of state foreclosure laws on loan losses and on the incentive conflict will be taken from the claim experience of all private mortgage insurance companies and a large sample of claims made to the Federal Housing Administration.

In the following section we describe the basic differences in jurisdictional foreclosure laws and how they affect risk in mortgage lending. We also outline the nature of private and government mortgage insurance and indicate how differences here create an incentive conflict which results in a differential shift in risk. In the second section we propose a model to test the effect of foreclosure laws and the incentive conflict on risk. The empirical results follow in the third section. A final section offers a conclusion.

1. FORECLOSURE LAWS AND INCENTIVE CONFLICTS

Cost of the Foreclosure Process

To appreciate the effect of foreclosure laws on the cost of foreclosing and liquidating properties one need only review the various cost elements involved. They can be divided into three categories: transaction costs, property costs, and opportunity costs. Transaction costs include those that result from the foreclosure process or the liquidation of the property and include attorneys' fees, trustees' fees, sheriff's cost of sale, brokers' commissions, revenue stamps, and title charges. Property costs include property taxes, hazard insurance, utilities, and repairs and maintenance. Opportunity costs include the interest foregone on the investment value of the property. These three costs will be larger when the size of the loan and the length of the foreclosure and liquidation process are greater.[1] A foreclosure process which requires the greater use of the court system and extends the time period for liquidation of the property will impose larger property and opportunity costs on the lender or the lender's insurer. Such laws are described as follows.

[1]An early Federal Home Loan Bank Board study (1975) analyzed the losses of six savings and loans, two each in three states considered to have stringent, moderate, and lenient foreclosure laws (Illinois, California, and Texas, respectively). Considering all expenses and revenue from foreclosed properties the study revealed that the net losses averaged 53 percent of the mean loan balance in Illinois and only 6.4 percent in Texas.

State Foreclosure Laws

State foreclosure laws differ in three major and many minor respects. In this paper we concentrate on the major differences. We believe that modeling the many minor differences would not produce sufficiently different results to warrant the complications involved.[2] The first major difference is between a judicial (court action) and nonjudicial (power-of-sale) procedure. With the judicial procedure the lender must proceed through the court which acts on a complaint, issues a decree, and stipulates what notices should be provided. Where foreclosure laws can proceed by power-of-sale, the liquidation of the property often occurs quickly through a trustee with little legal expense.[3] In these states a deed-of-trust rather than a mortgage is the instrument which frequently secures the property.

A second major difference lies in the provision for a statutory right of redemption. This is a period (generally seventy-five days to eighteen months) subsequent to the foreclosure sale that the mortgagor is allowed to redeem the property for the amount of the delinquent payments and foreclosure expenses. In some states the mortgagor is allowed to remain in possession of the property during this period. In all states this provision extends the liquidation period, adds to carrying costs, and depresses bids at the foreclosure sale.

The third major difference reflects the state's legislative attitude towards a deficiency judgment. This judgment provides for a recovery for the difference between the unpaid loan balance and the property's liquidation value through the attachment of the mortgagor's personal assets. In states where the deficiency judgment is prohibited the lender's recourse is restricted to the value of the mortgaged property.[4] Although one might expect such a provision to materially affect the amount of the loss on defaulted loans, there are some factors which may mitigate the importance of this aspect of the law. Many states that allow a deficiency judgment restrict its use if the lender bids at the sale of the property, which is usually the case. Additionally, the ability of a mortgagor with few assets to declare personal bankruptcy may discourage lenders from undertaking the necessary legal expense to pursue the judgment. Nonetheless, the threat of its use may, in many cases, suggest a negotiated settlement such that the lender avoids the expense of pursuing the judgment and the mortgagor avoids the costs of bankruptcy and future credit restrictions. Ceteris paribus, the threat of judgment, where allowed, should mitigate lender losses. That is, the judgment itself need not be pursued in order for losses to be reduced through negotiated settlement.[5]

[2]For an in-depth discussion of the difference in the details of foreclosure laws see Durham (1986).

[3]In Texas a foreclosure sale can take place twenty-one days after notice has been posted in three places within the county.

[4]Six states, California being the largest, prohibit deficiency judgments.

[5]The importance of the judgment is evidenced by the provision in most private mortgage insurance contracts which reimburses lenders for the legal expense of pursuing it.

Incentive Conflicts in Mortgage Insurance

In the following we describe the nature of private and government (FHA) mortgage insurance and show how a difference in structure induces an incentive conflict in the latter that is not present in the former.

PMI Insurance

There are currently a dozen or so private mortgage insurance companies that insure conventional mortgages of greater than 80 percent loan-to-value ratio. The typical insurance contract is one of coinsurance. In the event of default the insurer is obligated to pay all of the losses up to a certain percentage of the exposure, typically around 20 percent. The exposure includes, among other costs, the direct costs discussed above: transaction, property, and interest foregone. If losses exceed this percentage a coinsurance relationship exists. Where the foreclosure process is costly and lengthy the claim will more likely exceed the exposure and the coinsurance feature will be triggered. To view the coinsurance feature consider a typical claim settlement.[6] Let

α = coverage ratio,
U = unpaid loan balance,
F = forgone interest from last payment to claim date,
Z, T, P = hazard insurance, property taxes, and property preservation expenses during the foreclosure process
C = court costs (exluding attorneys' fees),
A = attorneys' fees,
R = rental revenue,
H = value of the house,

The exposure, E, of the insurer is given by

$$E = U+F+Z+T+P+C+ \text{Min}\,[A, .03\,(U+F)\,] - R\,. \tag{1}$$

Attorney's fees are typically included in the exposure only up to 3 percent of the unpaid balance and foregone interest. The insurance payoff, I, is given by

$$I = \text{Min}\,[E-\text{H}, \alpha E]\,. \tag{2}$$

The lender's position on the defaulted property is $H+I$. This is equal to

$$E, \text{ if } E-H<\alpha E\,, \tag{3}$$

and

$$H+\alpha E, \text{ if } E-H>\alpha E\,. \tag{3'}$$

[6]For an example see Mortgage Insurance Companies of America (1988).

Since the lender's position prior to default is the unpaid balance, U, the lender's loss is

$$O, \text{ if } E-H<\alpha E \tag{4}$$

and

$$E-H-\alpha E, \text{ if } E-H>\alpha E\,. \tag{4'}$$

The lender suffers a potential loss whenever $E(1-\alpha)>H$.

Since the lender cannot affect the value of the house, he attempts to minimize E because he bears a loss equal to the complement of the coverage ratio on all items of exposure. From this model the effects of the legal structure can be seen clearly. A judicial procedure and statutory right of redemption (especially with possession by the mortgagor) will increase the exposure, E, and claims to PMI companies. The coinsurance feature will encourage lenders to mitigate the exposure by pursuing deficiency judgments or using the threat of a judgment to extract a settlement where they are allowed.

FHA Insurance

FHA insurance is similar to private mortgage insurance in regard to the types of foreclosure-related costs which are paid to the lender but different in terms of the coinsurance feature. The government program has no such arrangement; it pays all the expenses associated with the foreclosure of the mortgage and the liquidation of the property.[7] Since the lender is reimbursed for all elements of exposure with no coinsurance there is no incentive to expend managerial resources to mitigate losses. There are two principal ways in which lenders can reduce claims. One way is to assign the loan to the FHA, or, at the latter's request, process the foreclosure as quickly as legally possible. The other is to pursue or threaten to pursue a deficiency judgment to recover all or a portion of the exposure. Both these actions require the expenditure of resources, including managerial effort. Since the lender assumes none of the loss, he is not motivated to either foreclose quickly or pursue a deficiency judgment.[8]

In summary, legal restrictions on an expeditious foreclosure process (required judicial procedure and statutory right of redemption) are expected to increase the losses on residential properties and the claims made to both types of mortgage insurers. The provision for a deficiency judgment, whether frequently implemented or not, is expected to mitigate those losses. Furthermore, the difference

[7]The FHA program will also reimburse the lender for some foreclosure costs that are not covered under private contracts such as those related to the eviction of the mortgagor and the removal of personal property.

[8]Mulherin and Muller (1988) present a model where this incentive conflict exists in the private mortgage insurance arena. Where full coverage of all losses exist (that is, $E-H<\alpha E$), lenders have no incentive to expend resources to reduce the loss. Since this is always the case for the FHA program one can expect a greater occurrence of this conflict there.

in the coinsurance feature of private and government insurance will encourage lenders to mitigate losses through a more expeditious foreclosure and pursuit of a deficiency judgment on loans insured by the private sector but not on loans insured by the FHA.

2. MODEL AND DATA

The model employed here has two versions which differ from each other only slightly and are tested with data from private mortgage insurers and the FHA. An OLS technique is employed with the loss rate as the dependent variable and the predictor variables consisting of the state legal structure and control variables. The basic model is

$$L = f[F, E, M] \tag{5}$$

where L is the loss rate, F is a set of state foreclosure variables, E is a set of socioeconomic variables expected to affect defaults on residential properties, and M is a set of identifiable mortgage characteristics on defaulted loans.[9]

Variable Selection

The PMI and FHA loss data are somewhat different in form and therefore require slightly different versions of the basic model. The available PMI data consist of the direct loss paid as a percent of the previous end of year risk-in-force, by state, for all PMIs. No individual loans are identified. Losses are measured as a rate and not in dollars. Risk-in-force is defined as the exposure of the insurer in terms of policyholder limits. It is not adjusted, state-by-state, for factors such as the legal environment, and, because of the uniform nature of the contracts, is nearly a constant percentage of the balance of the insured loans. That is, risk-in-force is not systematically related to the states' legal structures. These data are available on an annual basis from 1980 through 1987 from Moody's Investor Service.[10] Over the period the loss rate has averaged 1.2 percent and has ranged from a low of zero in Hawaii in 1980 to 9.75 percent in Wyoming in 1987. The loss rate is a function of both the number of foreclosures and the per foreclosure expense, the latter affected to a great degree by state law.

The FHA data consist of approximately 163,000 loans for which the FHA has paid a claim (and calculated its loss) over the period 1972 through 1988.[11] The loss for each loan consists of the total claim paid to the lender less the value of the property (equivalent to $E-H$ from above). The loss rate is defined as the loss

[9]The loss rate is bounded by zero from below and unbounded from above. Inspection of the data suggests a distribution that is positively skewed and log-normal. The log of the loss rate is selected as the dependent variable in each version of the model.

[10]Moody's collects these and other data from PMIs because of their need to rate their claims-paying ability which is important to lenders.

[11]A description of the FHA data base is included in the data appendix.

divided by the original amount of the loan.[12] In each case the loss rate is expected to be larger for loans originated in states with a judicial foreclosure procedure and a statutory right of redemption. If lenders do not pursue deficiency judgments on FHA loans, then this variable should not have an impact (that is, not reduce losses).

Other variables expected to affect losses in each version of the model are as follows.

PMI Model

This version of the model is similar to Clauretie's (1987) except that insurers' loss rates replace foreclosure rates as the dependent variable as follows:

$$LR_{j,t} = f[R_t, P_{j,t}, X_{j,t}, L_{j,t}, \epsilon_t] \tag{6}$$

where

R_t = national mortgage interest rate in period t relative to an earlier rate.
$P_{j,t}$ = percent change in residential property prices in state j in period t over previous periods,
$X_{j,t}$ = socioeconomic variables in state j in period t,
$L_{j,t}$ = set of foreclosure laws in state j in period t,
ϵ_t = an error term.

A justification of the variable selection is as follows. Previous research has established that the greatest proportion of defaults and foreclosures on residential properties occurs within two to six years subsequent to origination.[13] Since, for the PMI data, information on the year of origination of each loan is unknown, alternative lags within this range are considered for two variables expected to affect default and foreclosure: loan value and property value (equity). In regard to the loan value, Mulherin and Muller (1987) demonstrate that lenders have a greater incentive to foreclose rather than seek an alternative (such as forebearance) when current rates are above the contract rate. This occurs because, while the loan's value is below its balance, it is the latter that is insured. On the other hand, a mortgagor is less likely to default on a loan with a value below its balance. The expected sign on this variable is, therefore, not unambiguous. Following Clauretie (1987) and Campbell and Dietrich (1983) this variable is entered as R_t

[12]The loss rate should be computed by dividing the loss by the amount of the balance at the time of default. This value is absent from the FHA data base, however. Because most defaults occur within a few years of origination there should be only a small difference between the original loan amount and the balance at the time of default.

[13]Studies that reveal lags of this duration include Campbell and Dietrich (1983), von Furstenberg (1970, 1974), and several U.S. government studies by the Federal Housing Administration (1963), the Housing and Home Finance Agency (1963), and the Veterans Administration (1962).

$=(r_r - r_o)/r_o$, where r_t is the current market rate and r_o is the rate at origination. Again, since for these data r_o is unknown, alternative lags are employed.

Loan losses are also expected to be inversely related to property price appreciation. The variable $P_{j,t}$ measures the percentage change in property prices in state j in period t relative to earlier years.

The socioeconomic variables include recent changes in unemployment and the divorce rate in each state. One could argue that default would not occur in the case of a property with positive equity regardless of the employment or other status of the owner. This is the basis of the equity versus the ability-to-pay theory of default. The former theory has been empirically supported by Jackson and Kaserman (1980) and Waller (1988) while Campbell and Dietrich (1983) have offered evidence that regional unemployment rates affect defaults.

Although there has been some discussion of these two "competing" theories in the literature, it should be recognized that there is no inherent conflict between them. If the mortgagor has a default option that is "in-the-money," in the sense that there is negative equity in the property, he may choose not to exercise the option if his combined consumer surplus in the present residence and the cost of default (such as a bad credit rating) exceed the value of the option. If an event such as divorce or unemployment occurs, an early exercise of the option becomes optimal. The loss of the residence and the bad credit rating become inevitable.[14] For completeness we include state divorce and unemployment variables in the PMI version of the model. A change in the unemployment rate is included rather than the level because variability of unemployment is expected to have the greater impact on defaults. Because it takes some time for the effect of the socioeconomic events to work through the default, foreclosure, and claim process, an approach that lags these variables is employed. In the case of all lagged variables in the model the selected lag is based on the best statistical relationship (coefficient t-value).[15]

Finally, state legal variables are included. Dummy variables indicate the lack or presence of the power-of-sale method of foreclosure, a statutory right of redemption (alternatively by itself and with possession by the mortgagor), and laws which allow a deficiency judgment.

FHA Model

The version of the model tested with the FHA data is somewhat different. With these data each defaulted loan for which a claim was paid is identified. Here, we can add an identifiable loan characteristic, its original loan-to-value ratio. We also drop the socioeconomic variables. They are dropped from this version of the model because, while the PMI data represent the ratio of claim losses to risk-in-force, the FHA loss ratio is computed only for defaulted loans. Given that a loan

[14]It is not our purpose here to test a model of the residential default option. The interested reader is referred to Foster and Van Order (1984), Epperson et al. (1985), or Cunningham and Hendershott (1984) for examples for such models.

[15]The results are not sensitive to the alternative lags used.

has defaulted, the magnitude of the loss is not affected by variables which may have caused the exercise of the default option. The size of the loss will, however, be affected by the remaining variables included in the PMI model. Property price appreciation in the state will affect the size of claims. Additionally, the interest rate variable remains in the model because it is expected to affect the size of the claim through lender behavior. If market rates have risen subsequent to the origination of the defaulted loan, the lender has an incentive to assign the loan to the FHA and foreclose on the property as quickly as legally possible (thereby reducing the carrying costs and the size of the claim). A low-rate loan is taken off the books and the proceeds loaned out at a higher rate. The reverse is true if market rates have declined. Here the lender has an incentive to delay the foreclosure process since foregone interest is a portion of the claim. The contract rate is identified for each loan in the data base. The market rate in the year of termination is employed to compute the interest relative, $(r_t - r_o)/r_o$.

3. EMPIRICAL RESULTS

The results of testing the model are displayed in Table 1. They support the dual hypothesis that state foreclosure laws affect lender losses (as evidenced by insurance claims) and that the form of the insurance contract creates an incentive conflict.

In both versions of the model the loss rate is increased by the existence of a

TABLE 1

OLS Estimates of PMI and FHA Loss Rate Equations

	PMI Model		FHA Model	
Constant	5.308 (30.45)***	5.257 (30.69)***	−1.3165 (29.914)***	−1.564 (17.31)***
$(r_t - r_o)/r_o$	−.857 (6.14)***	−.878 (6.38)***	−.0957 (11.249)***	−.2513 (9.81)***
$P_{t\text{-}3}$	−.129 (14.4)***	−.128 (14.34)***	−.0107 (15.79)***	−.0169 (5.70)***
$\Delta U_{t\text{-}2}$	.135 (4.31)***	.136 (4.40)***		
$D_{t\text{-}1}$	−.01 (.49)	−.001 (.04)		
L/V			.00061 (12.64)***	.0008 (7.97)***
PS	−.156 (1.89)*	−.181 (2.27)**	−.2906 (38.98)***	−.1411 (7.59)***
SRR	.298 (3.41)***		.1377 (28.74)***	.2436 (19.04)***
$POSS$		.398 (4.57)***		
DJ	−.308 (2.49)***	−.331 (2.80)***	.0107 (.962)	−.009 (.33)
$\bar{R}^2$	.56	.572	.04	.05
F-value	75.05***	78.68***	520.26***	92.38***
n	408	408	75,816	9,997

Note: One, two, and three asterisks represent significance at the .1, .05, and .01 levels, respectively.

statutory right of redemption and reduced by a power-of-sale provision. The PMI version was tested alternatively with a dummy variable for a statutory right of redemption and for possession during this period. The latter result was somewhat more powerful as indicated by the second column in Table 1.

The loss rate measured by PMI claims is negatively related to the existence of a deficiency judgment. This variable is insignificant in the equation tested with FHA data, however.[16] This result confirms the hypothesis of an incentive conflict.

For the most part the socioeconomic variables affect losses in the manner hypothesized. Rising property prices reduce losses as do rising interest rates. An increase in interest rates reduces the incentive for mortgagors to default (PMI data) and where a default occurs creates an incentive for lenders to expedite the foreclosure and liquidation process. Changes in unemployment rates affected PMI claims but the divorce rate proved to be insignificant.

One must be cautious in comparing the coefficients of the legal variables in each version of the model as the form of the dependent variable is not directly comparable. The loss rate for the PMI model is of the form, $(n \cdot l)/(\alpha \cdot m \cdot N)$, where, for a given state,

l is the average loss (claim),
n is the number of claims,
N is the total loans insured,
m is the average mortgage balance, and
α is the coverage ratio.

The numerator is the total amount of claims from a given state while the denominator is the risk-in-force. The measure is more nearly a measure of risk than is the dependent variable in the FHA model. That variable is of the form, l/m, for each of the loans in the data base. For each state the risk measure for the FHA is better approximated by the product of the loss per foreclosed loan and the relative number of such loans to the total insured.

An example of the modification necessary to measure the risk associated with the legal variables can be illustrated with the use of the last equation in Table 1. That equation results from testing the model with loans terminated by the FHA in 1984 only.[17] For loans terminated in this year the average loss was 45 percent of the average mortgage balance. The coefficient on the power-of-sale variable indicates that a judicial procedure adds, at the mean, .1475 to the log of the loss rate or 7 percentage points to the loss rate (a 16 percent increase). The risk of insuring

[16]When this equation was first tested the coefficient on the deficiency judgment variable was positive and significant. This result was puzzling. We hypothesized that because only six states prohibit a deficiency judgment (DJ=0) and by far the largest is California, the substantial increase in property values in that state over the period of the test caused a spurious result. The FHA equations in Table 1 result from a test which omits observations from California.

[17]This year was selected because data on the total number and amount of FHA insured loans by state are available for this year.

loans in such states is not 16 percent greater, however. It is significantly greater. Of the loans terminated in 1984, 59 percent were originated in states with a judicial procedure. Nationwide, only 50.6 percent of FHA insured loans were located in such states. Thus, a greater proportion of foreclosed loans were originated in states with a judicial foreclosure procedure than were insured in those states. The risk to the FHA is 60 percent greater.

Table 2 summarizes the interpretation of the coefficients of the legal variables in each version of the model taking into account the disproportionate number of claims which occur in states with a judicial foreclosure and statutory right of redemption. For the FHA model, estimates of risk are found by including the term n/N where, for each state, n is the number of claims and N is the number of loans insured.

TABLE 2

INCREASE IN RISK DUE TO STATE FORECLOSURE LAWS

	Effect on Log of Loss Rate		Percent Increase in Risk at Mean	
	PMI Model	FHA Model	PMI Model	FHA Model
Judicial Procedure	.1126	.1411	12.0	60.3
Statutory Right of Redemption	.2272	.2436	25.5	64.6
Deficiency Judgment	−.331	0	−29.2	0

4. CONCLUSION AND IMPLICATIONS

This study has demonstrated that state foreclosure laws affect the risk of residential mortgage lending. A judicial procedure and statutory right of redemption extend the foreclosure and liquidation process and add to loan losses. Furthermore, the nature of the insurance contract and state laws interact to affect losses. Where a coinsurance contract and a deficiency judgment exist, losses are reduced. Since PMIs and the FHA have historically charged uniform premiums they have absorbed much of this risk. One would not expect to see dramatic differences in contract rates under this arrangement. As the insurers become aware of the risks they may begin to price their policies accordingly. In such a development borrowers in states with onerous foreclosure laws could expect to bear the cost of the risk.

Additionally, if self-insured lenders in risky states incur large losses as a result of defaults and foreclosures, the federal supervisory agencies may consider submitting legislation that would, as in the case of usury laws in 1980, override state foreclosure laws as far as their members are concerned.

DATA APPENDIX

1. Legal Variables: Foreclosure Redemption Summary, in C. F. Sirmans, *Real Estate Finance*, pp. 83–85. Entered as dummy variable.

2. Mortgage Rate: Average Effective Interest Rate on Loans Closed, FHLBB Series, Federal Reserve Bulletin for the PMI model and the FHA rate, Federal Reserve Bulletin, for the FHA model. Entered as $(r_t - r_o)/r_o$.

3. Residential Property Prices: Monthly Report, Existing Home Sales, National Association of Realtors, data on a regional basis. Entered as percent change in year *t* over three years previous.

4. Unemployment: U.S. Bureau of Labor Statistics, Geographical Profile of Employment and Unemployment, 1986. Entered as change in the rate two years previous.

5. Divorce Rate: Vital Statistics of the United States. U.S. National Center for Health Statistics.

6. Loss Rate: for PMI model, Direct Loss Paid as a Percent of Previous Year End Risk, 1980–1987, Table 15, p. 31, Special Report: Moody's Annual Report of the Private Mortgage Insurance Industry. For the FHA model, loss on loan divided by original loan balance. Here the FHA computes its loss as the total claim less the liquidation value of the property. The data base includes 163, 165 loans for which are given the loss, endorsement year, contract rate, loan-to-value ratio, termination date, state of origin, type of property (new or existing), and program. Ninety percent of the loans were Section 203. Many loans did not have enough data to compute the loss rate or had missing data reducing the usable sample to approximately 85,000 loans.

LITERATURE CITED

Alston, Lee. "Farm Foreclosure Moratorium Legislation: A Lesson from the Past." *American Economic Review* 74 (June 1984), 445–57.

Barth, James R., Joseph Cordes, and Anthony Yezer. "Benefits and Costs of Legal Restrictions on Personal Loan Markets." *Journal of Law and Economics* 29 (October 1986), 357–80.

Campbell, Tim, and J. Kimball Dietrich. "The Determinants of Default on Insured Conventional Residential Loans." *Journal of Finance* 38 (December 1983), 1569–81.

Clauretie, Terrence M. "The Impact of Interstate Foreclosure Cost Differences and the Value of Mortgages on Default Rates." *Journal of the American Real Estate and Urban Economics Association* 15 (Fall 1987), 152–67.

Cunningham, Donald F., and Patric Hendershott. "Pricing FHA Mortgage Default Insurance." *Housing Finance Review* 3 (October 1984), 373–92.

Durham, James. "In Defense of Strict Foreclosure: A Legal and Economic Analysis of Mortgage Foreclosure." *South Carolina Law Review* (Spring 1986), 461–510.

Epperson, James F., James Kau, Donald Keenan, and Walter Muller. "Pricing Default Risk in Mortgages." *Journal of the American Real Estate and Urban Economics Association* 13 (Fall 1985), 261–72.

Foster, Chester, and Robert Van Order. "An Option Based Model of Mortgage Default." *Housing Finance Review* 3 (October 1984), 351–72.

Jackson, Jerry, and David Kaserman. "Default Risk on Home Mortgage Loans: A Test of Competing Hypotheses." *Journal of Risk and Insurance* 47 (December 1980), 678–90.

Jaffee, Austin. "Mortgage Foreclosure Law and Regional Disparities in Mortgage Financing Costs." Working Paper no. 85–80, Pennsylvania State University, 1985.

James, Christopher. "An Analysis of the Effect of State Acquisition Laws on Managerial Efficiency: A Case of Bank Holding Company Acquisitions." *Journal of Law and Economics* 27 (April 1984), 211–26.

Meador, Mark. "The Effect of Mortgage Laws on Home Mortgage Rates." *Journal of Economics and Business* 34 (1982), 143–48.

Mortgage Insurance Companies of America. *Fact Book and Directory: 1987–1988.* Washington, D.C., 1988.

Mulherin, J. Harold, and Walter J. Muller. "Volatile Interest Rates and the Divergence of Incentives in Mortgage Contracts." *Journal of Law, Economics, and Organization* (Spring 1987), 99–115.

———. "Resolution of Incentive Conflicts in the Mortgage Industry." *Journal of Real Estate Finance and Economics* 1 (April 1988), 35–46.

Touche, Ross & Co. *The Cost of Mortgage Loan Foreclosures: Case Studies of Six Savings and Loan Associations.* April 1975.

Waller, Neil. "Residential Mortgage Default: A Clarifying Analysis." *Housing Finance Review* 7 (Fall/Winter 1988), 321–33.

U.S. Government, Federal Housing Administration. FHA Experience with Mortgage Foreclosure and Property Acquisitions, 1963, Washington, D.C.

———, Housing and Home Finance Agency. Mortgage Foreclosures in Six Metropolitan Areas, 1963, Washington, D.C.

———, Veterans Administration. Report of Loan Service and Claims Studies, 1962, Washington, D.C.

von Furstenberg, George. "The Investment Quality of Home Mortgages." *Journal of Risk and Insurance* 37 (September 1970), 437–45.

———, and Jeffrey Green. "Home Mortgage Delinquencies: A Cohort Analysis." *Journal of Finance.* 29 (December 1974), 1445–48.

ANDREW FELTENSTEIN
DAVID LEBOW
SWEDER VAN WIJNBERGEN

Savings, Commodity Market Rationing, and the Real Rate of Interest in China

1. INTRODUCTION

DEVELOPING ADEQUATE THEORIES to describe household savings behavior has been a major element in modern economics. In this paper we attempt to develop such a theory for a highly nonmarket economy, and apply the resulting model to China, a country where private saving has undergone dramatic changes over the past thirty-five years. China is of particular interest for a variety of reasons. First, prior to the reforms carried out in 1979, it represented an extreme example of a repressed economy. Second, it is now undergoing a series of economic reforms that are quite possibly the most far-reaching ever undertaken by a socialist country; one of the first indicators of the impact of these reforms has come in the dramatic increase in the volume of savings. Finally, because the analysis of private savings allows one to derive an empirical measure of the degree to which markets are repressed in China, our results also refute the commonly stated notion that in planned economies such as China, consumers are subject to too many regime shifts to exhibit stable behavior characteristics.

A recent article by Chow (1985) demonstrates that it is, indeed, possible to estimate stable behavioral relationships in the Chinese economy, in this case a version of the permanent income hypothesis. Chow's article, however, makes an

The authors thank Morris Goldstein, Mohsin Khan, Francis Ng, Richard Portes, and two anonymous referees for helpful comments. The views expressed in this article are those of the authors and do not necessarily represent the opinions of the World Bank.

ANDREW FELTENSTEIN *is professor of economics at the University of Kansas.* DAVID LEBOW *is an economist at the Federal Reserve Board.* SWEDER VAN WIJNBERGEN *is lead economist in the Mexico department of the World Bank.*

Journal of Money, Credit, and Banking, Vol. 22, No. 2 (May 1990)

assumption that we wish to avoid, namely, that official price data indeed reflect the costs that people perceive themselves as facing. This is an especially important assumption in a model that attempts to explain savings since, in an economy with significant price controls, the official rate of inflation may distort the relative cost of present and future consumption. Our general assertion is that the Chinese consumer finds himself in a world in which goods markets do not, at least temporarily, clear because of government price controls. He has two possible views of the future; in one of these he expects markets to clear when prices eventually adjust, while in the other he expects markets to remain repressed indefinitely. In either of these circumstances the consumer's perception of the future purchasing power of his savings will be different than if he believed that he could satisfy his goods demands at existing official prices.

We demonstrate that ignoring non–market clearing phenomena in China causes false qualitative conclusions to be drawn about savings behavior. We will show, for example, that use of the official rate of inflation series leads one to conclude that there has been a regime shift affecting household savings. Using the measure of repressed inflation that we shall develop, however, we find that there have been no regime shifts. We will also demonstrate that a numer of neoclassical theories of savings are supported by our disequilibrium estimates and, perhaps more surprisingly, that household savings are responsive to real interest rates, if these rates are defined in terms of "virtual," or repressed, inflation rates.

There have been numerous studies of savings behavior in centrally planned economies (CPEs) [see Portes (1986) for a survey of this literature] with approaches to the problem falling essentially in one of two categories. In the first (for example, Portes and Winter 1978; Pickersgill 1976, 1980), there is no allowance made for the potential disequilibrium. The analysis assumes equilibrium and proceeds as if the CPEs were market-oriented economies. This is clearly inappropriate in the presence of substantial repressed inflation, as observed quantities will not be on the consumption demand curve. The estimation is quite simple, however, and may yield reasonable results if the macroeconomic disequilibrium is not "too" pervasive.

The second approach (for example, Portes and Winter 1980; Podkaminer 1982) involves explicit disequilibrium econometric techniques, which attempt to disentangle supple-and-demand schedules using a min-condition and discrete switching. This methodology is described in Fair and Jaffee (1972) and in Quandt (1982). The methodology is valid, although difficult to implement, and it requires specification of a supply equation in addition to demand. A methodology which does not fit into either approach is that of Howard (1976). Portes and Winter (1980) discuss the limitations of his approach.

This paper represents a third approach, that of "virtual prices." The concept of virtual prices is introduced and analyzed extensively in Neary and Roberts (1980). Feltenstein and Farhadian (1987) use virtual prices to explain money demand in China, and van Wijnbergen (1985) uses virtual prices to analyze the intertemporal consequences of commodity market rationing. The virtual price level is defined as that which would induce the observed quantity of consumption (and savings) in the absence of price controls. By specifying the relationship between virtual and official prices, we may use the (unobserved) virtual prices to estimate a demand schedule as if we were in equilibrium. This methodology thus takes the potential disequilibrium into account while maintaining the simplicity and clarity of the first methodology above.

The next section will give a brief overview of certain relevant aspects of recent Chinese economic history, while section 3 develops a theoretical disequilibrium model suitable for our analysis. Section 4 presents estimation results for a number of standard specifications of savings behavior. Section 5 estimates a neoclassical specification of savings based on real interest rates, while section 6 is a summary and conclusion.

2. INSTITUTIONAL CHANGES AND THE BEHAVIOR OF HOUSEHOLD SAVINGS IN CHINA

As indicated by Figure 1, household savings in China, after being a fairly stable fraction of national income for twenty-five years, rose sharply following the economic reforms instituted in 1979. These reforms are described in de Wulf (1985a, b) and de Wulf and Goldsborough (1986), while their monetary implications are discussed in Feltenstein and Farhadian (1987), as well as in Chow (1986) and Portes and Santorum (1987). We will summarize here those aspects of the Chi-

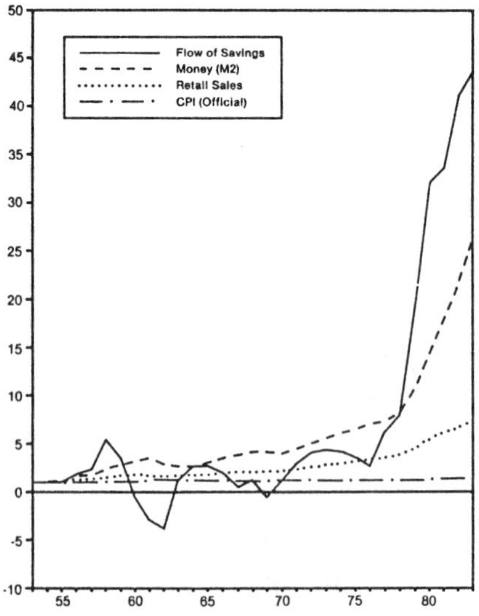

FIG. 1. China: Macroeconomic Indicators

nese economic system, both pre- and postreform, that are relevant for our analysis.

Prior to 1979, the Chinese system did not view private savings as being a source of investment funds. Rather, lending for investment came from the budget and was interest-free. Banks did offer low interest rates on deposits and used these deposits to make short-term loans to enterprises. Households, in turn, received wage payments in currency and although they were free to use their cash balances as they wished, the absence of financial assets forced them to distribute their income between current expenditure and savings deposits. The government, in turn, used a "cash plan" to attempt to determine the quantity of money held by households. It was felt that this quantity of money could have inflationary pressures if it grew too rapidly and was not channeled into savings.

"If social purchasing power much exceeds commodity supplies, then part of the purchasing power will not be realized and will become excess currency circulation on the market which will influence the stability of the market and currency. Of course, if it is the purchasing power of the urban and rural population that is not realized then currency will accumulate in their hands, or in the form of savings deposits.[1]

At various periods, the Chinese authorities have experienced major failures in controlling monetary expansion, with immediate implications for savings behavior. During the period of the Great Leap Forward (1958–59), credit policy became "Give as many loans as are needed whenever they are needed."[2] Currency in circulation thus rose by 140 percent between 1957 and 1961. The degree of repressed inflation rose steadily, and by 1961 could not longer be contained, with prices rising 16 percent, or about eight times the previous average rate of inflation. Consumers responded in a neoclassical fashion by reducing their bank deposits by 50 percent between 1959 and 1962. A similar situation occurred during the Cultural Revolution, particularly during 1966–69 and 1974–76.

Since 1979, considerable autonomy has been granted to enterprises in wage determination; in addition, they are being permitted to retain profits which they were previously required to remit to the government. The price system has not, however, been liberalized as rapidly as wages, and the result has been the rapid rise in savings. In addition, banks have been given greater autonomy with respect to interest rates among other things. "Banks may make use of methods such as extending or refusing loans, . . . , raising or lowering interest rates, rewarding the good and penalizing the bad."[3] As an attempt to control the rapid increase in liquidity, and fearing that the growing volume of saving deposits was "a tiger in a cage," the Chinese government in 1982 introduced the sale of Treasury bills to individuals, although the current volume of these sales is still quite low.

[1]Liu (1980), p. 169, quoted in Peebles (1983), p. 86.

[2]Li Chengrui (1981).

[3]"Strive to Implement the 1985 Credit Plan," Zhongguo Jinrong (1985).

3. A SIMPLE MODEL OF GOODS MARKET RATIONING AND SAVINGS BEHAVIOR

The purpose of this section is to derive a simple equation describing private savings behavior in the presence of commodity market rationing. The model is designed with empirical application in mind. We first present a market clearing version of the basic model, and then proceed to introduce commodity market rationing.

An Equilibrium Model of Price Determination and Savings Behavior

Consider a simple two-period, one-commodity-per-period world. Since we intend to focus on savings behavior rather than the intertemporal allocation of production through investment, we will assume output to be fixed in each period, at level X in period one and at level x in period two.[4] In addition, we will suppose that the economy is closed. Some of the output goes towards government expenditure. By assumption, the government is never rationed. G (g) is government expenditure in period one (two). We set g equal to zero for notational convenience.[5]

Consumer behavior is summarized through an expenditure function E which represents the minimum discounted value of current and future expenditure needed to achieve utility level U, given current and future prices:

$$E = E(P, \delta_N p; U) . \tag{1}$$

P (p) represents the current (future) price level. δ_N is the discount factor:

$$\delta_N = 1/(1 + i)$$

where i is the nominal rate of interest. The derivatives of E with respect to any price give the Hicksian demand function for the corresponding good (cf. Dixit and Norman (1980)). Therefore, the commodity market clearly requires

$$\begin{aligned} X &= G + E_1(P, \delta_N p; U) \\ &= G + E_1(1, \delta_N p/P; U) \end{aligned} \tag{2}$$

where E_1 stands for $\partial E/\partial P$, and we have used the fact that the Hicksian demand function is homogenous of degree zero in prices. A similar equation holds for second-period goods market clearing, but can be eliminated through Walras' law.

Under the simplifying assumptions that there are no first-period taxes and no

[4]We will use uppercase letters for first-period variables and lowercase letters for second-period variables.

[5]Government expenditure plays no important role in our theoretical analysis. It is introduced only as a counterpart to positive net private savings. Alternatively, we could have used an open economy model, allowing for a nonzero current account.

second-period government expenditure, the government budget constraint is

$$G = \delta t \tag{3}$$

where t is a second-period nondistortionary tax and δ the real discount factor, $\delta = p\delta_N / P$. Similarly, the private sector faces a budget constraint:

$$X + \delta x - \delta t = E(1, \delta, U) . \tag{4}$$

The mechanics of intertemporal trade are very simple since the asset choice is limited. Consumers can either hoard commodities, an opportunity which we will have to ignore for lack of relevant data, or deposit any income not spent in time deposit accounts in a bank. We ignore investment, so the only demand for bank loans comes from the government, since it raises no revenue through domestic credit to the banking sector. We assume, realistically, that consumers hold no interest-bearing government paper other than through the indirect channel we just sketched. We also assume, in accordance with the facts, that consumer loans are negligible. Banks face no reserve requirements and hold no reserves. Therefore, the only component of the monetary base is currency held by the public.

For simplicity, we assume in the theoretical analysis that the economy starts out with a stock of monetary base to which nothing is added over time. Consumers' demand for money is derived from a straightforward transaction technology: consumers need to accumulate money balances equal to the exact amount of any purchase before being able to make that purchase (a cash in advance constraint). Therefore money market equilibrium requires

$$PE_1 = Mv, pE_2 = mv . \tag{5}$$

M (m) is the first- (second-) period money stock, and $V(v)$ is first- (second-) period velocity. For convenience we assume $M = m$, although nothing hinges on that assumption.

The mechanics of the model can be described as follows. Through (5) the money stock determines the price level in each period. Commodity market clearing then requires a nominal interest rate that, in combination with the current and future prices from (5), implies a real rate that makes (2) hold. The commodity market clearing equation (2) in conjunction with the private and public sector budget constraints (3) and (4) imply that in equilibrium, private savings equal public dissaving. This of course reflects our assumptions of no capital accumulation and a closed economy.

Commodity Market Rationing, Virtual Prices, and the Real Rate of Interest

Consider now the possibility of rationing in goods markets. We will only introduce temporary (period-one) rationing, but will comment on the intertemporal aspects of permanent rationing later. In China, both prices and interest rates are still to a large extent administratively determined. We will therefore assume that prices and monetary policy are set up in such a way that excess demand results:

$$Mv/P = E_1(1,\delta; U) > X - G\,. \tag{6}$$

Hence observed ex post velocity $\tilde{v} = P(X - G)/M$ is not necessarily constant in the presence of commodity market rationing, even if ex ante velocity v is. Equation (6) then implies that when current price (or real interest rates) are "too" low, there is excess demand for current goods. Note that, although "ex ante" velocity $Mv/(PE_1)$ is constant, ex post velocity $Mv/(P(X-G))$ may vary. Ex post velocity has in fact been falling since 1979. In the empirical exercise below we also estimate a variant that allows for variable ex ante velocity.

We can now define a "virtual" real discount factor $\tilde{\delta}$ (or virtual price $\tilde{P}$, where $\tilde{\delta} = \delta_N p/\tilde{P}$), defined as the real discount factor at which consumers would be willing to consume the volume of goods available to them today, with the same level of utility that would hold if today's effective demand could be satisfied at official prices:

$$X - G = E_1(1, \tilde{\delta}; U)\,. \tag{7}$$

The notion that agents in a repressed economy act as if they face the virtual price level rather than the official price level may be understood in a definitional way and need not be taken literally.

Of course, virtual prices are not observable; we will therefore derive an approximation formula that expresses $\tilde{P}$ in terms of observable variables. Define, for convenience of notation, $R = X-G$ as the volume of goods available to the public.

Note that

$$Mv/P - R = E_1\,(1, \delta; U) - E_1\,(1,\tilde{\delta}; U) \tag{8}$$

or $$Mv/(PR) - 1 = (E_1\,(1, \delta; U) - E_1\,(1, \tilde{\delta}; U))/R\,. \tag{8a}$$

A first order Taylor expansion of (8a) yields

$$Mv/(PR) - 1 \approx (\delta E/R)(\delta - \delta)/\delta = \sigma\,(\tilde{\delta} - \delta)/\tilde{\delta}$$

where σ is the elasticity of real consumption with respect to the real discount factor. This can be written as an equation in virtual and actual prices, for given nominal interest rates and future prices:

$$(\tilde{P} - P)/P \approx 1/\sigma\,(Mv/(PR) - 1)\,. \tag{9}$$

$\tilde{\delta} - \delta P/\tilde{P}$ gives the link between $\tilde{P}$ and $\tilde{\delta}$. By definition, E_1 $(\tilde{P}, \delta_N p; U) = X - G$. In our empirical work we use a logarithmic approximation to (9):

$$\log\tilde{P} - \log P \approx 1/\sigma \log(Mv/(PR)) \tag{10}$$

which is the formula actually used in the next two sections.

If we therefore assume homothetic preferences, we can rewrite the demand function for current goods as

$$E_1 (\tilde{P}, \delta_N p; U) = E_1 (1, \tilde{\delta}; U) = c(\tilde{\delta}) E(1, \tilde{\delta}; U) \tag{11}$$

where $c(\tilde{\delta})$ is a share term independent of utility. Now $E(\tilde{P}, \delta_N p; U)$ equals the discounted value of wealth at virtual prices, something we cannot measure (even if we could measure wealth at actual prices). We know, however, that the intertemporal budget constraint holds at actual, not at virtual prices, since actual transactions take place at posted prices:

$$\begin{aligned} PR + \delta_N pr &= PE_1 (\tilde{P}, \delta_N p; U) + \delta_N p E_2 (\tilde{P}, \delta_N p; U) \\ &= E(\tilde{P}, \delta_N p; U) + (P - \tilde{P}) E_1 (1, \tilde{\delta}; U) \end{aligned}$$

or

$$\tilde{P}R + \delta_N pr = E(\tilde{P}, \delta_N p; U)$$

or

$$R + (\delta_N p/\tilde{P}) r = E(1, \tilde{\delta}; U) . \tag{12}$$

Combining this with (11) leads to the equation:

$$R = c(\tilde{\delta}) (R + \tilde{\delta} r) \tag{13a}$$

or, in terms of net discounted future expenditure (savings plus discounted future income),

$$(\delta_N/\tilde{P}) r = (1-c(\tilde{\delta})) (R + (\delta_N p/\tilde{P}) r) . \tag{13b}$$

Equations (13a) and (13b) underlie the empirical analysis presented in the next two sections. If intertemporal preferences are Cobb-Douglas, $(1 - c(\tilde{\delta}))$ is a constant; section 4 proceeds from that assumption. In section 5, we relax that assumption and estimate functional forms that allow for interest sensitive expenditure shares in wealth.

One further issue cannot be addressed in our two-period theoretical model, but needs to be resolved before (13a, b) can be tested against actual data: the issue of how long rationing is expected to last. Clearly nobody expects rationing to last ad infinitum, hence our assumption of period two goods market clearing. Permanent rationing would have no effect on the real interest rate since it would affect future prices as much as current prices; the relative price of future goods in terms of current goods would therefore not be affected and neither would savings behavior. But in practical terms, how long is period one? The issue matters for our empirical measure of permanent income $y_p = W/\gamma$ where wealth $W = R + \tilde{\delta} r$, and $\gamma = 1/(1-\delta)$.

Consider then a multiperiod world. Assume for simplicity that real income in periods with rationing equals $\tilde{y}$, and in nonrationing periods y. If rationing is expected to last until period T, wealth equals

$$W = \sum_{i=0}^{T-1} \delta^i \tilde{y} + \sum_{T}^{\infty} \delta^i y \,. \tag{14}$$

This can be written as

$$W = \sum_{i=0}^{\infty} \delta^i \tilde{y} + \sum_{T}^{\infty} \delta^i (y - \tilde{y}) \tag{15}$$

$$= \gamma \tilde{y} + \delta^T \sum_{0}^{\infty} \delta^i (y - \tilde{y})$$

$$= \gamma \tilde{y} + \delta^T \gamma (y - \tilde{y}) = \gamma\,((1-\delta^T)\tilde{y} + \delta^T y) \,.$$

So if there is no rationing, or rationing is expected to last for a negligible period, $W = \gamma y$; if rationing lasts forever, $W = \gamma \tilde{y}$. In section 4, these two extremes are tested against each other. Note that even if T is small and hence $W \approx y$, there may still be strong *substitution* effects that operate through $\tilde{\delta}$, not through W.

4. VIRTUAL PRICES AND COMMON SAVINGS FUNCTIONS

In this section, we estimate a number of common savings functions under the assumption that consumers respond to virtual prices, and show that this yields superior results to the same functions estimated using official prices. The savings equations in this section are based on the assumption of Cobb-Douglas intertemporal preferences, so that savings will depend on wealth only, not on intertemporal substitution effects.

Specification of the Empirical Model

The model consists of two equations: a virtual price level equation and a savings equation. The virtual price level is derived from equation (10):

$$\ln \tilde{P} = \ln P + \alpha \ln (M/PR) \quad (16)$$

where R is real retail sales, M is the stock of money and $\alpha = 1/\sigma$. The specification has a very natural "money chases goods" interpretation. If M and PR increase at the same rate, there is no additional divergence between the official and virtual price levels. When $\alpha = 0$ (the intertemporal substitution elasticity is infinite), the virtual price level collapses to the official price level. Feltenstein and Farhadian (1987) used a different specification for P. In our estimation, the variables P and M/PR were normalized to equal unity in the year 1953. This latter normalization corresponds to the inclusion of the velocity term v in equation (10).

We employ several common savings specifications, all involving real per capita disposal income as an explanatory variable for real per capita savings. The virtual price level is used to deflate nominal savings. The following specifications are tested:

$$S/\tilde{P} = b_0 + b_1 I^p + b_2 I^t \quad (17)$$

$$S/\tilde{P} = b_0 + b_1 (S/\tilde{P})_{-1} + b_2 (I - I_{-1}) \quad (18)$$

$$S/\tilde{P} = b_p + b_1 I + b_2 I_{-1} + b_3 I_{-2} \quad (19)$$

$$S/\tilde{P} = b_p + b_1 I \quad (20)$$

where S is per capital nominal savings and I is per capita real disposable income (divided into permanent and transitory components I^p and I^t). Equation (17) is a permanent income model, equation (18) an asset adjustment model, equation (19) a general distributed lag model, and equation (20) an absolute income model. We define permanent income (I^p) as a three-year moving average of I,[6] and transitory income (I^t) is defined by $I^t = I - I^p$. It is not our intention to propose any one savings specification appropriate for China; rather, we test a number of common specifications to demonstrate that deflating savings by the virtual price index is more reasonable than deflating by the official price index.

Substituting for $\tilde{P}$ from equation (16), equations (17) to (20) become

$$S/P = \left(\frac{M}{PR}\right)^{\alpha} \left(b_0 + b_1 I^p + b_2 I^t\right) ; \quad (21)$$

[6]Results will be presented for two definitions of I^P: backward-looking, where $I^P = 1/3\,(I + I_{-1} + i_{-2})$ and forward-looking, where $I^P = 1/3\,(I_{+1} + I + I_{-1})$.

$$S/P = \left(\frac{M}{PR}\right)^{\alpha} \left(b_0 + b_1 \left(\frac{S}{P}\right)_{-1} + b_2 \left(I - I_{-1}\right)\right) \quad ; \tag{22}$$

$$S/P = \left(\frac{M}{PR}\right)^{\alpha} \left(b_0 + b_1 I + b_2 I_{-1} + b_3 I_{-2}\right) \quad ; \tag{23}$$

$$S/P = \left(\frac{M}{PR}\right)^{\alpha} \left(b_0 + b_1 I\right) . \tag{24}$$

Again, note that when $\alpha = 0$, these equations reduce to the usual equations based on the official price level. Hence our hypotheses are nested, with no rationing ($\alpha = 0$) being a testable restriction.

The Data

Monetary data are taken from Byrd (1984) and from *International Financial Statistics*. Income, sales, and price data are taken from *Chinese Statistical Yearbook* (1984). Household savings is taken to be the change in urban and rural savings deposits over the year. As there is no disposable income series, we construct one using retail sales as a proxy for consumption, plus the savings variable. We employ two alternative definitions of real disposable income: one normalized by the official price index, the other by the virtual price index: $I_1 = R + S/P$, $I_2 = R + S/\tilde{P}$. Retail sales are measured in real units, so in both cases, reported nominal retail sales are normalized by the official price index to obtain R. Regarding the nominal savings component, however, it is less clear which is the more appropriate deflator, and we employ both. As argued in section 3, the choice of deflator should relate to the length of time the rationing is expected to last. Specifically, if rationing is expected to cease after one period, I_1 is the appropriate real income definition, and if rationing is expected to last forever, I_2 is the more appropriate definition.

We use a monetary aggregate corresponding to M2, equal to the sum of currency in circulation plus savings deposits.[7] We take the consumer price index, an average of retail and service price indices, as our official price index.[8]

Empirical Results

Equations (21) to (24) were estimated by the nonlinear maximum likelihood technique of Berndt, Hall, Hall and Hausman, on yearly data over the period 1955 to 1983. The model was similarly estimated under the constraint $\alpha = 0$, that is, the official price level is used to deflate nominal savings rather than the virtual price level. The results for the case of one-period expected rationing (income normalized by the official price level) are presented in Table 1.

[7]Results using currency in circulation as our definition of money are available upon request and are broadly similar to those obtained by using M2.

[8]Results using the retail price index are similar to these presented here.

TABLE 1

SAVINGS EQUATIONS

Equation	Period	α	$b_0(\times 10^{-3})$	b_1	b_2	b_3	LLF	$R^2_{(H)}$	DW	(α=0)
(17)[a]	1955–1983	1.427	−.510	.009	.082		166.7	.9494	1.86	
		(2.99)	(−.71)	(.96)	(2.97)					20.4
		0	−5.767	.081	.209		156.5	.8973	0.87	
			(−7.27)	(8.32)	(4.40)					
(17)[b]	1955–1982	1.346	−1.519	0.23	.064		153.9	.8931	1.05	
		(2.62)	(−1.44)	(1.64)	(1.63)					11.8
		0	−6.709	.096	.084		148.0	.8355	0.61	
			(−8.19)	(11.20)	(.82)					
(18)	1955–1983	1.796	.103	.560	.034		166.0	.9468	2.32	
		(3.79)	(1.44)	(4.04)	(2.27)				(−1.84)	10.4
		0	.017	.924	.120		160.8	.9237	2.07	
			(.07)	(12.20)	(3.62)				(−0.22)	
(19)	1955–1983	1.598	−.271	.044	−.002	−.036	168.0	.9536	1.86	
		(3.07)	(−.48)	(2.33)	(−.15)	(−2.69)				22.8
		0	−5.719	.159	−.024	−.055	156.6	.8977	0.85	
			(−6.96)	(4.23)	(−.39)	−1.28)				
(20)	1955–1983	.729	−2.933	.044			157.4	.9039	0.85	
		(2.18)	(−2.21)	(2.44)						7.4
		0	−6.831	.098			153.7	.8754	0.64	
			(−9.68)	(13.77)						

NOTES: [a] $I^P = \frac{1}{3}(I + I_{-2})$. [b] $I^P = \frac{1}{3}(I + I_{-1})$.

For all savings specifications, estimates for α are highly significant, as is clear from the t-statistics. Indeed, a likelihood ratio test decisively rejects the hypothesis $\alpha = 0$ in all specifications, as the χ^2 statistics range from 7.4 to 22.8. The .99 value of χ_1^2 is 6.63. This in itself is strong evidence in support of our virtual price level specification, since the models are nested and the estimates of α are quite stable across savings specifications. The hypothesis that the highest value of α (1.796) is equal to the lowest value (.729) cannot be rejected (the t-statistic on the difference is 1.184).

Further, in the official price model (that is, when α is constrained to equal zero), with the exception of the asset adjustment specification, which contains a lagged dependent variable, the Durbin-Watson statistic easily rejects the null hypothesis of zero first-order serial correlation at a 1 percent confidence level. In the virtual price model (when α is unconstrained), only the absolute income specification and the forward-looking permanent specification display serially correlated errors; for the other specifications, zero first-order serial correlation cannot be rejected at a 5 percent confidence level. The high degree of serial correlation in the official price residuals leads one to suspect the existence of a spurious correlation and is, in addition to the highly significant estimate of α, sufficient grounds for rejecting the model.

With regard to the parameter estimates, in all cases savings propensities out of income are much larger in the official price model than in the virtual price model. For example, in the backward-looking permanent income specification, the savings propensities out of transitory and permanent incomes are, respectively, .082 and .009 in the virtual price model, and .209 and .081 in the official price model. In both models, as we would expect, the propensity to save out of transitory income is much higher than that out of permanent income. However, only in the virtual price model do we fail to reject the theoretically attractive hypothesis that savings out of permanent income is zero.

Next, we show that in the official price level model, the parameter estimates are unstable. We employ a dummy variable which takes a value of unity from 1979–1983, the period of liberalization, and check for a change in slope during this period. In the permanent income model, we check the slope of transitory income. In the asset adjustment model, we check the slope of change in income. In the distributed lag and current income models, we check the slope of current income. Results are presented in Table 2.

In the virtual price model, only the absolute income specification yields a dummy parameter which is significantly different from zero at 5 percent. In the official price model, however, in four of the five specifications the dummy is significant, indicating a change in the slope during the liberalization period. Further, the inclusion of these slope dummies brings the parameters in the official price specifications closer to those estimated in the virtual price model. In the backward-looking permanent income specification, for example, the coefficient on savings out of transitory income declines from .209 to .148, whereas in the virtual price model the coefficient was estimated to be .082. By no means does

TABLE 2

TESTS FOR REGIME CHANGES

Equation	Period	α	$b_0(\times 10^{-3})$	b_1	b_2	b_3	Dummy[c]	LLF	R^2	D-W$_{(H)}$
(17)[a]	1955–1983	1.234	−.554	.010	.075		.039	168.5	.9552	1.79
		(2.65)	(−.75)	(1.03)	(3.10)		(1.29)			
		0	−4.183	.061	.148		.191	159.9	.9188	0.95
			(−4.41)	(5.23)	(3.01)		(2.57)			
(17)[b]	1955–1982	1.647	−1.076	.017	.034		.149	155.9	.9077	1.00
		(2.71)	(−1.20)	(1.38)	(.99)		(1.57)			
		0	−6.645	.095	.066		.364	148.3	.8391	0.56
			(−7.99)	(10.87)	(.63)		(0.74)			
(18)	1955–1983	.989	.144	.588	.040		.061	169.4	.9579	2.25
		(1.63)	(1.39)	(4.31)	(2.08)		(1.26)			(−1.28)
		0	.149	.753	.067		.181	168.0	.9536	2.15
			(.81)	(10.22)	(2.28)		(4.01)			(−.45)
(19)	1955–1983	.925	−.151	.056	−.008	−.042	.009	171.8	.9644	1.91
		(1.90)	(−.21)	(2.75)	(−.40)	(−2.77)	(1.45)			
		0	−1.655	0.95	−.013	−.053	.032	167.6	.9521	1.61
			(−1.71)	(3.27)	(−.31)	(−1.78)	(5.22)			
(20)	1955–1983	.249	−1.918	.033			.024	163.4	.9364	1.13
		(.80)	(−1.62)	(2.11)			(2.23)			
		0	−2.490	.042			.034	163.0	.9345	1.16
			(−2.40)	(3.30)			(4.84)			

NOTES: [a] ${}_IP = \frac{1}{3}(I + I_{-1} + I_{-2})$. [b] ${}_IP = \frac{1}{3}(I_{+1} + I + I_{-1})$. [c] Dummy tests for a change after 1979 in b_2 for (17) and (18), and b_1 for (19) and (20).

adjustment for the regime change eliminate the problems of the official price model; serial correlation is not eliminated and, in two of the specifications, the estimate of alpha is still significant. The result that the virtual price model is stable over the same period while the official price model indicates a regime shift is further evidence in favor of the virtual price model.

We now turn to the length of time that rationing is expected to continue. The above results were presented for the case in which rationing is expected to last for a negligible period of time. We similarly estimated the model under the assumption that rationing is expected to last forever: that is, nominal income is deflated by virtual prices. Qualitative results were similar, and we present only the values of the respective log likelihood functions in Table 3.

TABLE 3

LOG LIKELIHOOD VALUES UNDER TEMPORARY AND PERMANENT RATIONING

Equation	Temporary Rationing	Permanent Rationing
Permanent Income (Backward-looking)	166.7	164.0
Permanent Income (Forward-looking)	153.9	152.7
Asset Adjustment	166.0	163.0
Distributed Lag	168.0	165.3
Current Income	157.4	156.6

As the two income variables are highly collinear, it is not possible to imbed these in the same model and estimate the expected duration of rationing explicitly.[9] Nevertheless, in all cases the temporary rationing model leads to a higher likelihood value than does the permanent rationing model, which gives reason to believe that rationing was indeed expected to be temporary.

Finally, one may question the relevance of the estimated model in explaining events post-1983 in China. Real cash balances have increased by 130 percent between 1983.IV and 1987.IV,[10] leading to an initial indication that there continues to be monetary overhang and repressed savings.

5. SAVINGS AND THE REAL RATE OF INTEREST

In this section we move beyond the specifications of section 4 and allow savings to depend on real interest rates in addition to wealth. The real interest rate (ρ) is given by

[9]Ideally one would like to allow consumers to update their expectation on duration of rationing each period, incorporating the new information about rationing in that period. Data availability precludes estimation of such learning models.

[10]Here we are using M2 deflated by the CPI with data coming from International Financial Statistics.

$$1 + \rho = (1 + i)\, P/p = 1/\delta$$

in the market clearing model, or by

$$1 + \tilde{\rho} = (1 + i)\tilde{P}/p = 1/\tilde{\delta} \tag{25}$$

in the rationing model, where variables are defined as in section 3. Rationing this period which is expected to stop next period implies a lower "virtual" inflation rate (as current virtual prices are higher than current official prices) and hence a higher "virtual" real interest rate than would be the case if the current official price level were market clearing.

Our empirical specification is derived from equation (13a) in section 2.[11] Taking a log-linear approximation yields

$$\ln R = b_0 + b_1 \ln(1 + \tilde{\rho}) + b_2 \ln I$$

with I a proxy for permanent income or, equivalently, wealth. Substituting from equations (16) and (25) yields

$$\ln R = b_0 + b_1 \ln((1 + i)\, P/P_{+1}) + b_1\alpha \ln(M/PR) + b_2 \ln I\,.$$

Finally, allowing for differing responses to permanent and transitory incomes, and noting that $\ln(I^P + I^t) = \ln I^P + \ln(1 + I^t/I^p) \approx \ln I^p + I^t/I^p$, we obtain

$$\ln R = b_0 + b_1 \ln((1 + i)P/P_{+1}) + b_1\alpha \ln(M/PR) + b_2 \frac{I^t}{I^p} + b_3 \ln I^p\,. \tag{26}$$

We estimate equation (26) using the same two permanent income specifications as in section 4 above.[12] As current disposal income is correlated with current consumption, we instrument for this variable using two-stage least squares.[13] We similarly instrument for the unobserved future price. Instruments include all independent variables, a lagged dependent variable, and three additional variables thought to be correlated with income: government expenditure, fixed investment, and GNP in Japan (Japan being China's largest trading partner). Results are presented in Table 4.

[11]We use consumption rather than savings in this section as we wish to use the logarithmic specification and the flow of savings was negative for part of the sample.

[12]We present results only for the backward-looking permanent income specification. Results for the forward-looking specification are similar. It should be noted that these estimates are derived independently of the results of the previous section. In particular, new parameter values for α are estimated along with the b_is, rather than supply incorporating the values from Table 1.

[13]Similarly, we technically should have instrumented for disposal income in section 4 above. However, as our equations in that section are highly nonlinear, in parameters as well as variables, we were not able to carry this out. Further, in this section omitting the instruments leads to only a negligible change in the estimated parameters, indicating that the omission in section 4 would not be expected to affect the qualitative conclusions.

TABLE 4

RESTRICTIONS ON EQUATION (26), 1955–83

	α	b_0	b_1	b_2	$1\text{-}b_3$	LLF	R^2	χ_3^{2*}
(a)	.323 (5.72)	.0416 (6.01)	−.207 (−4.67)	.733 (23.42)	0	97.20	.9991	6.83
(b)	.172 (1.62)	−.0640 (−.98)	−.193 (−4.45)	.771 (20.22)	.033 (1.62)	99.05	.9992	4.41
(c)	0	−.0108 (−1.98)	−.005 (−.07)	.730 (12.33)	0	77.19	.9978	11.92
(d)	1.57 (.51)	.0174 (2.71)	−0.040 (−.49)	.759 (16.58)	0	87.55	.9983	13.20

NOTES: *This tests the hypothesis that the residuals are white noise to three autocorrelation lags. $\chi_3^2(.95) = 7.81$. $\chi_3^2(.99) = 11.34$).
(a) $b_3 = 1$.
(b) no restrictions.
(c) $b = 1$; $\alpha = 0$.
(d) $b_3 = 1$; $i = 0$.

In row a we make the theoretically plausible assumption that the elasticity of consumption with respect to permanent income is unity. As we see from row b, this assumption is justified—we cannot reject a unitary coefficient on permanent income. We see that the estimate for α in row a is highly significant, although smaller than in section 4. The most striking result, however, is that the estimate of b_1 is negative and significant. That is, consumption declines (savings increases) in response to an increase in real interest rates. Given the difficulty researchers have had in finding a significant savings response to real interest rates in developing countries (see, for example, Giovannini 1985), or, for that matter, in developed countries, we take this result to be of some interest.

As in section 4, when α is constrained to equal zero the errors display serial correlation and, in addition, the significance of the real interest rate disappears. Again, the virtual price model far outperforms the official price model.

We also estimate the model omitting the nominal interest rate—that is, b_1 now represents the consumption response to the inverse of the expected inflation rate. The results are presented in row d. In this equation b_1 is seen to be insignificant, indicating that the nominal interest rate is indeed important in explaining consumption behavior.

6. SUMMARY AND CONCLUSIONS

China has seen a rapid increase in personal savings since the economic liberalization began in 1979. We have attempted to explain this phenomenon in an intertemporal disequilibrium framework, using a virtual price technique. The virtual price level is defined as the price level that would induce the observed level of consumption in the absence of price controls. We first set out a simple theoretical model of savings behavior under rationing which, when combined with a cash-in-advance constraint, leads to a simple virtual price specification which links the virtual price to observable variables.

We then use the virtual price level to estimate a number of common savings functions. We find that normalizing savings by virtual prices explains savings behavior far better than does normalizing by the official price series. When official prices are used, that is, when equilibrium is imposed, the equations are found to be unstable and to indicate a regime shift during the liberalization. Allowing for disequilibrium by employing virtual prices eliminates this problem.

We next provide a test which lends support to the theory that rationing was perceived to be temporary, suggesting that intertemporal phenomena do play an important role in determining savings behavior. We therefore proceed to include real interest rates as a determinant of savings. Using virtual prices, we find a negative and significant real interest rate effect on consumption which, despite its intuitive appeal, has only rarely been empirically detected. As before, when we eliminate the virtual prices and assume equilibrium, the results deteriorate and we no longer detect a consumption response to real interest rates. This interest rate response indicates that savings does indeed respond to future market conditions, and is not simply an involuntary residual. Finally, we find that the nominal interest rate has considerable importance in influencing savings behavior, so that macroeconomic policy in China may be more effective than previously thought.

LITERATURE CITED

Byrd, William A. *China's Financial System: The Changing Role of the Banks.* Boulder, Col.: Westview Press, 1983.

Chinese Statistical Yearbook, Beijing, 1984.

Chow, Gregory. "A Model of Chinese National Income Determination." *Journal of Political Economy* 93 (August 1985), 782–92.

———. "Money and Price Level Determination in China." Econometric Research Program Research Monogram No. 327, Princeton University, 1986.

de Wulf, Luc. "Economic Reform in China." *Finance and Development* (December 1985), 19–22. (a)

———. "Financial Reform in China." *Finance and Development* (March 1985), 8–11. (b)

de Wulf, Luc, and David Goldsborough. "The Evolving Role of Monetary Policy in China." *International Monetary Fund Staff Papers* 33 (June 1986), 209–42.

Dixit, Avinash K. and V. Norman. *Theory of International Trade: A Duel General Equilibrium Approach.* Cambridge University Press, 1980.

Fair, Ray C. and Dwight M. Jaffee. "Methods of Estimation for Markets in Disequilibrium." *Econometrica* 40 (May 1972), 497–514.

Feltenstein, Andrew, and Ziba Farhadian. "Fiscal Policy, Monetary Targets, and the Price Level in a Centrally Planned Economy: An Application to the Case of China." *Journal of Money, Credit, and Banking* 19 (May 1987), 137–56.

Giovannini, A. "Savings and the Real Interest Rate in LDCs." *Journal of Development Economics* 18 (August 1985), 197–217.

Howard, David H. "The Disequilibrium Model in a Controlled Economy: An Empirical Test of the Barro-Grossman Model." *American Economic Review* 66 (December 1976), 871–79.

Li Chengrui. "The Balance of Finance and Credit." *Jingji Yanjiu* (Economic Research) 3 (March 1981), 3–12.

Liu, Hongru. *Problems of Socialist Money and Banking*. Peking: China Finance and Economics Publishing House, 1980.

Neary, J. P., and K. W. S. Roberts. "The Theory of Household Behavior under Rationing." *European Economic Review* 13 (January 1980), 25–42.

Peebles, Gavin. "Inflation, Money, and Banking in China: In Support of the Purchasing Power Approach." *Association for Comparative Economic Studies Bulletin* 25 (Summer 1983), 81–103.

Pickersgill, Joyce. "Soviet Household Saving Behavior." *Review of Economics and Statistics* 58 (May 1976), 139–47.

______. "Recent Evidence on Soviet Household Saving Behavior." *Review of Economics and Statistics* 62 (November 1980), 628–33.

Podkaminer, Leon. "Estimates of the Disequilibria in Poland's Consumer Markets 1965–1978." *Review of Economics and Statistics* 64 (August 1982), 423–31.

Portes, Richard. "The Theory and Measurement of Macroecon. Disequilibrium in Centrally Planned Economies." Center for Economic Policy Research Discussion Paper No. 91, 1986.

Portes, Richard, and A. Santorum. "Money and the Consumption Goods Market in China." *Journal of Comparative Economics* 11 (September 1987), 354–71.

Portes, Richard, and David Winter. "The Demand for Money and for Consumption Goods in Centrally Planned Economies." *Review of Economics and Statistics* 60 (February 1978), 8–18.

______. "Disequilibrium Estimates for Consumption Goods Markets in Centrally Planned Economies." *Review of Economics Studies* 47 (January 1980), 137–59.

Quandt, R. "Econometric Disequilibrium Models." *Econometric Review* 1 (March 1982), 1–63.

van Wijnbergen, Sweder. "Oil Price Shocks, Unemployment, Investment and the Current Account: An Intertemporal Disequilibrium Analysis." *Review of Economic Studies* 52 (October 1985), 627–45.

Zhongguo Jinrong (Chinese Finance). People's Bank of China (January 1985).

NOTES, COMMENTS, REPLIES

Do Liquidity Constraints Vary over Time? Evidence From Survey and Panel Data

A Note by Gary S. Fissel and Tullio Jappelli

1. *Introduction*

One of the most widely debated issues in the study of consumer behavior is the validity of the life cycle–permanent income hypothesis (LC–PIH). In its purest form, the LC–PIH posits the existence of rational, forward-looking agents, constrained only by expected lifetime income endowments, who smooth consumption over their entire life. Capital markets are assumed to be perfect so that agents may lend and borrow at will, and so are never constrained from their optimal consumption plans in any period. However, if capital markets are not perfect, consumers may be prohibited from satisfying their "desired" consumption plans, and are, as a result, "liquidity constrained."

Empirical tests of the LC–PIH have provided evidence that the model is not able to account for the behavior of all households. Much empirical work has been devoted to estimating the fraction of income held by consumers who do not obey the LC–PIH. Hall and Mishkin (1982) and Hayashi (1985b), among others, provide evidence on panel data that a significant fraction of consumers do not follow the LC–PIH without borrowing constraints. Hayashi (1982), Flavin (1985), and Campbell and Mankiw (1987) are only some of the recent studies performed on aggregate time series. There are two common features of these studies. First, since liquidity-constrained households are not observable, they rely on indirect evidence to assess the effect of borrowing constraints on consumption. Second, they assume that the consumers who do not follow the LC–PIH are *behaviorally* different from the others, in that they are assumed to consume their entire disposable income. If this very specific Keynesian consumption function describes correctly the behavior of consumers who are

The authors are indebted to Kit Baum and Bob Murphy for useful discussions and to two anonymous referees for helpful comments.

GARY S. FISSEL *is in the Division of Research and Statistics, Federal Deposit Insurance Corporation, Washington.* TULLIO JAPPELLI *is associate professor, Institute for Economic Studies, I.U.N., Naples, Italy.*

Journal of Money, Credit, and Banking, Vol. 22, No. 2 (May 1990)

liquidity constrained, then the assumption that the fraction of consumers who do not follow the LC–PIH is constant over time is internally consistent, although not very appealing from a theoretical point of view. If instead liquidity constraints affect consumers' behavior along the lines suggested by Zeldes (1989), then the fraction of people who are liquidity constrained is endogenous and cannot be taken as a constant over time. This paper attempts to provide independent and direct estimates of the degree of liquidity constraints and to determine whether the assumption of constancy of the fraction of liquidity-constrained housholds is empirically justified.

We estimate an approximate reduced form of the probability that a consumer is liquidity constrained—in the sense that his net resources fall below his desired consumption—as a function of his preferences, endowments, and the constraint imposed by lenders on his desired borrowing. Using both the Survey of Consumer Finances (SCF) and the Michigan Panel Study of Income Dynamics (PSID) we derive estimates of the proportion of consumers who are liquidity constrained from 1969 to 1982. We find that this proportion does vary significantly over time with apparent trend and cyclical components.

The fraction of income which accrues to liquidity-constrained consumers, rather than the proportion of constrained consumers, has the most important policy ramifications.[1] Thus, we provide estimates for the fraction of total income controlled by those consumers who are more likely to be liquidity constrained. Finally, we place our study in the context of the popular tests for liquidity constraints, the so-called "excess sensitivity tests." We conclude that these tests may suffer from endogeneity problems due to their treatment of the fraction of income controlled by liquidity-constrained consumers. They estimate as a parameter what is, instead, a variable which is endogenous to the consumer's maximization problem.

In section 2 we present the reduced form that leads to the estimation of the empirical model. In particular, we sketch the method used in determining the fraction of liquidity-constrained consumers and discuss the initial application of the model to the SCF data set. In section 3 we outline the procedures employed in combining the results of the SCF estimation with the data available in the PSID, and present estimates of the proportion of liquidity-constrained consumers, and of the fraction of income controlled by these consumers for the period 1969–1982. In section 4 we state our conclusions. The Appendix, which gives a

[1]The policy implications of liquidity constraints have recently come to the attention of researchers, especially with regard to tax policy analysis (Hubbard and Judd 1986). In particular, within the framework of the LC–PIH, knowledge of the proportion of liquidity-constrained consumers and of the fraction of total disposable income controlled by these liquidity-constrained consumers are important components in estimating the effectiveness of fiscal policy, progressive taxation, and temporary tax levies. Hayashi (1985a) and Yotsuzuka (1987) have presented models in which tax policies (specifically, a switch from debt to taxes) affects the consumer's borrowing constraint as well as his lifetime constraint. While in these models the so-called Ricardian proposition holds, Bernheim (1987) has pointed out that they require very specific assumptions. Furthermore, these models require that all agents participate in the loan market (nobody is denied loans), while our definition of liquidity constraints stresses the importance of quantity constraints on borrowing.

more detailed look at the model used in section 2 of this study, is available upon request.

2. *Evidence from Survey Data*

The type of liquidity constraints considered in this paper are quantity constraints on borrowing. In particular, we focus on consumers whose desired borrowing exceeds the amount that financial intermediaries are willing to lend them, and are therefore denied loans. Since the consumer's optimization problem in the presence of both resource constraints and borrowing constraints does not have a closed-form solution (Zeldes 1989), we follow a reduced-form approach also used by Jappelli (1990). We define a consumer to be liquidity constrained when his desired consumption (C^*) exceeds available resources, that is, net wealth (A), current disposable income ($Y + rA$), and the amount which intermediaries are willing to lend to that individual (B). If

$$C_{it}^* - Y_{it} - (1+r)A_{it} - B_{it} > 0 \, , \tag{1}$$

the consumer's excess demand for loans is positive, and so, he is liquidity constrained.[2] Since C^* and B are unobservable, it is assumed that they can be approximated by a set of variables observable in a cross-section. If the functional forms for desired consumption and for the borrowing constraint are linear, the probability that consumer i is liquidity constrained in period t is

$$P_{it} = Pr\{C^* - Y - (1+r)A - B > 0\} = F(\mathbf{X}_{it}\boldsymbol{\beta}_t) \tag{2}$$

where $\boldsymbol{\beta}_t$ is a vector of parameters, $\mathbf{X}_t$ a matrix of exogenous variables available in the SCF applicable to all individuals, and $F(.)$ a standard normal distribution function. If $\mathbf{X}_{it}\boldsymbol{\beta}_t > 0$, consumer i is said to be liquidity constrained in period t with probability P_{it}. We assume that the reduced form for P_{it} is a function of the variables affecting desired consumption (C^*), resources (Y and A) and of the borrowing constraint imposed by lenders. Even if all consumers face the borrowing constraint, at each point in time some are liquidity constrained and others are not. Thus, our approach stands in contrast to most of the existing literature where consumers are assumed to be either (a) always constrained, (b) never constrained, or (c) constrained until a certain age and not afterwards, depending essentially on the timing of their income stream.

Candidates for inclusion in the reduced-form vector equation (2) would be current resources (income and net wealth) and proxies for future resources (such

[2]Equation (1) is sufficient but not necessary for someone to be liquidity constrained. In models where liquidity constraints affect consumption behavior there is also the situation in which the consumer faces some probability of being constrained in the future (Zeldes 1989), which lowers current consumption below what it otherwise would be. Similarly, Mariger (1986) defines consumers to be liquidity constrained when they have short horizons (are constrained in the current period) as well as when they have multiperiod horizons (they expect to be constrained in the future). In these cases, desired consumption differs from observed consumption but equation (1) does not hold.

as age, schooling, sex, and race) that are likely to affect both C^* and B. In a life-cycle context, with plausible assumptions about the reduced form for desired consumption and the nature of the borrowing constraint, one would expect to find a negative relationship between P_{it} and current resources. On the other hand, an increase in expected future resources, holding current resources constant, increases desired consumption as well as borrowing, and has an ambiguous impact on P_{it} (Jappelli 1990). Having estimated values for P_{it} across individuals, we denote the mean of P_{it} in each yer as P_t, that is, $E(P_{it}) = P_t$. Thus, we refer to P_t as the fraction of liquidity-constrained consumers in year t.

As noted, in a cross-section C^* and B are not observable, but one can infer whether $\mathbf{X}_{it}\boldsymbol{\beta}_t > 0$ or $\mathbf{X}_{it}\boldsymbol{\beta}_t \leqslant 0$ from other data in the SCF. As an operational definition of liquidity-constrained consumers, we follow Jappelli (1990) by defining a consumer to be liquidity constrained ($\mathbf{X}_{it}\boldsymbol{\beta}_t > 0$) when he has been denied a loan by a lender or when the consumer thought of applying for credit but changed his mind because he thought that he would be refused a loan.[3] The SCF represents a cross-section data set taken in 1983 which pertains to 1982. In that year the estimated sample proportion of liquidity-constrained consumers, that is, the proportion of consumers for which we assume that desired consumption exceeds available resources, is 18.95 percent. This number is broadly consistent with the 20–25 percent range of consumers who do not seem to behave in accordance to the standard LC–PIH reported by King (1985). Having assumed that liquidity-constrained consumers can be observed, the model represented by (2) can be estimated using maximum likelihood.

The logit estimation performed on the SCF produces an estimate of $\boldsymbol{\beta}$, a vector of parameters that relate the observable variables (income, wealth, and individual characteristics) of the SCF to the probability that an individual is denied loans. These estimated parameters allow us to compute the proportion of liquidity-constrained households for years other than that covered by the SCF.

3. *Evidence from Panel Data*

In order to test our proposition of the variability in the proportion of liquidity-constrained consumers, we adopt the SCF parameter estimates for 1982 as our benchmark. Then we perform simulations on the PSID using the coefficients of the logit model derived from the SCF.[4] In what follows we assume that the average sample probability of being liquidity constrained in each period equals the proportion of all consumers who find themselves constrained in that period. By averaging the estimated P_{it} values in each year, we are also able to produce estimates of P_t (t=1969,..., 1982) for years other than 1982. These values of

[3]The Appendix provides a more exhaustive discussion of the validity of this proxy to identify constrained households. It also reports the exact wording of the relevant questions asked in the SCF and an exposition of the estimated logit equation and of the performance of the model.

[4]We present estimates starting with the PSID wave III (referring to the year 1969) through wave XVI (referring to the year 1982).

P_t vary from period to period, and from the benchmark year, because the underlying variables vary over time.

In order to carry out the above described simulation, we match variables in the PSID data set with those used in the SCF. A description of these variables can be found in the Appendix (available upon request), which also reports the values of the estimated coefficients used in the simulation. All dollar magnitudes are converted to 1982 dollars. The results of the simulation are presented in Table 1, where we display the average probability of being liquidity constrained derived for the fourteen PSID waves. The resulting $E(P_{it})$ values are denoted by "P" in column (1).

TABLE 1

THE PROPORTION OF THE POPULATION THAT IS LIQUIDITY CONSTRAINTED (P), THE AVERAGE FRACTION OF INCOME CONTROLLED BY LIQUIDITY-CONSTRAINED CONSUMERS (L), AND THE UNEMPLOYMENT RATE (U)

Year	PSID Wave	P (1)	L (2)	U (3)
1969	III	18.67	11.98	3.5
1970	IV	18.30	11.91	4.9
1971	V	17.86	11.41	5.9
1972	VI	17.45	11.14	5.6
1973	VII	17.47	11.05	4.9
1974	VIII	17.84	11.22	5.6
1975	IX	17.94	11.42	8.5
1976	X	17.87	11.10	7.7
1977	XI	17.79	11.10	7.1
1978	XII	17.67	11.28	6.1
1979	XIII	17.87	11.28	5.8
1980	XIV	18.32	11.31	7.1
1981	XV	18.66	11.86	7.6
1982	XVI	19.06	11.88	9.7

NOTE: The unemployment series is taken from the Economic Report of the President.

In 1982 the two surveys overlap, and it is encouraging that we obtain a value for P of 19.06 percent, a number which is very close to that found in the SCF data set (18.95 percent). Even if some of the variables—specifically, the wealth variable—are not fully comparable between the two data sets, the outcome of the simulation for the benchmark year is satisfactory.[5]

The pattern of the proportion of liquidity-constrained consumers is seen to follow a cyclical pattern and, possibly, a slightly increasing trend, visible especially in the second half of the sample period. If our procedure is correct, it is apparent that P_t must be treated as a variable determined endogenously by demographic characteristics and economic activity rather than, as in previous studies, as a parameter to be estimated from time series regressions and/or panel data studies.

If the fraction of liquidity-constrained individuals does vary over time with

[5]See the Appendix for a description of the difference between the definition of wealth in the two surveys, and for the approximation that we have used to match the two variables.

cyclical and trend components which depend on variables such as income, wealth, and age, then the years covered by the PSID provided a good sample for this proposition. Over this period there were significant peaks and troughs in the business and income cycles. We estimate that, from the minimum of 1972, there has been an increase of 1.61 percentage points in *P*. Even if the swings in *P* have not been dramatic over the fourteen years of our analysis, a *t*-test for the difference between the sample means in 1972 and 1982 is highly significant even at the 1 percent level.

A closer inspection of Table 1 reveals that *P* declined from 1969 to 1972, rose gradually from 1973 through 1975, decreased slightly in the 1976–78 period, and increased rapidly for the remainder of the sample period. There are a number of underlying factors which can explain this pattern. The cyclical movements in *P* are primarily driven by movements in average real family income and average real family wealth. In addition, social and demographic characteristics of the population (such as age, family size, and marital status) play important roles in the evolution of *P*. In the logit model estimated on the SCF, age, income, wealth, and being married are negatively correlated with the probability of being liquidity constrained, while family size is positively correlated with *P*.

The age structure of the population, despite the short period of our sample, increased until 1972 from an average of 42.7 years in 1969 to 43.2 years in 1972 (contributing to the corresponding decrease in *P*) and decreased for the remainder of the sample period to an average of 42 years in 1982. The proportion of the sample that were married or cohabitating and the average family size both steadily decreased from 1969 through 1982. While the marital status and family size variables have opposite effects upon *P*, these two phenomena are closely related, and, as noted below, both affect real family income. That is, smaller family size due to the absence of a spouse (and a potential wage-earner) will have a negative impact upon real family income.[6]

According to the PSID survey, average real family income peaked in 1973 and had distinct troughs which correspond to the recessionary periods of 1974–75 and 1981–82. The peaks and troughs of real family income closely match the troughs and peaks of *P*. These changes in family income reflect changes in the level of economic activity but, in part, may reflect differences in family composition.[7]

Real family wealth also contributes to the cyclical component of *P*. Real

[6]An increase in the number of families consisting of unmarried people (including single person families) contributed to a decrease in average family size between 1969 and 1982 and also put downward pressure on average family income. According to the PSID, average family size was 4.91 in 1969 as compared with 2.84 in 1982. Marital status and family size are taken into account in the logit estimation performed on the SCF: large families and singles are predicted to be more likely to be liquidity constrained.

[7]The average total family income, expressed in 1982 dollars, was $24,011 in 1969, climbed to a maximum of $25,307 in 1973 and reached a minimum of $22,745 in 1982. Thus, average family income at the beginning of the 1980s was lower by 5.3 percent than at the end of the 1960s, and by 11.3 percent relative to 1973. Similar results are obtained when one compares the 1970 Survey of Consumer Finances with the 1977 Consumer Credit Survey and the 1983 Survey of Consumer Finances (Avery et al. 1984).

wealth for the PSID sample generally increased over the 1969–1978 period, except for a slight decrease in the 1973–75 subperiod. However, real wealth decreased dramatically over the 1980–82 period from \$51,023 to \$43,850, which corresponds to the increase in P.[8]

As noted above, the cyclical movements in P are particularly visible in the recessions of 1974–75 and 1981–82. Real income, employment status, and real wealth capture this cyclical component most strongly since they are relatively sensitive to the level of economic activity. As a summary measure for aggregate economic activity, we report that the simple correlation between P and the official unemployment rate (reported in column 3 of Table 1) is 0.32. The fact that P tends to be higher during recessionary periods supports a finding by Flavin (1985) that individuals rationed in the labor market are more likely to be constrained in capital markets.

A caveat is in order at this point. As noted, the estimated coefficients reflect not only desired consumption (C^*), but also the nature of the constraint imposed by lenders on consumers (B). The supply of credit in the market is conditioned by the behavior of financial intermediaries in response to a variety of factors, including the current monetary and regulatory regimes as well as any institutional developments in the credit market. In using the estimated coefficients from the SCF in years other than 1982, we assume that the parameters of the reduced form for desired consumption, as well as those of the credit constraint, have remained constant. While it is very reasonable to assume that consumption changes slowly at best, the hypothesis of unchanging behavior by financial intermediaries can be questioned. While the 1980–82 period was typified by tight credit supplies by the monetary authority, this was not the case over the entire sample period. In addition, the early 1980s witnessed important institutional changes and financial innovations in the credit market, including the Depository Institutions Deregulation and Monetary Control Act of 1980 which, among other things, permitted savings and loan associations to become an increasing source of consumer credit.

Unfortunately, given the nature of the PSID survey and the operational definition of liquidity constraints that we have adopted in the SCF survey, we have found no satisfactory way of incorporating "supply side" effects in our analysis. For this reason, the estimate of P_t that we provide should be taken as merely indicative of its true value. More generally, our exercise is only meant to provide an example of how the changing behavior of P_t over time could be studied, and cannot account for all sources of variation that might have potentially affected P_t in recent years.

With these qualifications in mind, and having obtained an estimate of P_t, it is a simple task to compute the value of L_t, the fraction of total income that accrues to consumers who are predicted to be liquidity constrained. For this purpose we

[8]This phenomenon can be explained by two characterisitcs of the sample over the 1979–82 period. First, nominal home values appreciated only slightly in the 1980–81 period and depreciated in the 1981–82 period. Second, the proportion of the sample who were homeowners declined over the 1980–82 period, thus decreasing the equity portion of wealth.

compute the average income of the consumers with $P_{it} > E(P_{it})$ for t=1969,..., 1982, that is, the average income of those consumers that are on average more likely to be liquidity constrained. We denote this average as Y_{ct}. The variable L_t is then computed as $P_t(Y_{ct}/Y_{Nt})$, where Y_{Nt} is the average income of the sample population in year t. The results of the computation are also reported in Table 1 (column 2). The values of L_t oscillate from a minimum of 11.05 percent in 1973 to maximum values of 11.98 percent in 1969 and 11.88 percent in 1982.

As expected, L_t is lower than P_t since constrained consumers tend to control a lesser fraction of total income than do unconstrained consumers. However, it is apparent that L_t tracks P_t very closely. The swings in L_t are less pronounced than for P_t (about 0.83 percent from 1973 to 1982 for L_t and about 1.6 percent for P_t over the same period). Moreover, the ratio of L_t to P_t, which measures the average constrained family income to the average family income for the entire sample, has declined slightly, although not monotonically, over the sample period. The average ratio for the 1969–72 subperiod is 64.4 percent and 62.5 percent for the 1980–82 subperiod, indicating that the income distribution between constained and unconstrained consumers has moved against the former group. As a final note on the plausibility of our results, one can compare them with the above discussed existing empirical evidence, as well as with the theoretical simulation provided by Hubbard and Judd (1986, Table 3) who, in a nonstochastic environment predict P= 23.5 percent, and L= 14.9 percent. Our study provides empirical evidence broadly consistent with these simulations. In the next section we place our study in the context of the existing tests of liquidity constraints, and state our conclusions.

4. *Conclusions*

The most popular tests for liquidity constrained consumption behavior attempt to determine whether consumption behavior is "too" sensitive to anticipated current income, relative to the LC–PIH cum rational expectations model. These studies (see the references in section 1) rely on indirect evidence to estimate the effect of liquidity constraints on consumption and assume a constant value over time of the fraction of total disposable income held by constrained households (L). In light of our discussion in section 3, these tests are likely to suffer from endogeneity problems.

The value of L results from the combination of the proportion of liquidity constrained consumers (P), and from the distribution of income among constrained and unconstrained consumers. The variable P itself is the outcome of the maximizing behavior of consumers, the nature of the constraint imposed on consumers by financial intermediaries, and the individual shocks to income in each period. We have shown that the probability of an individual consumer being liquidity constrained in each period is an endogenous variable, and so, both the proportion of the population that is liquidity constrained (P) and the fraction of total income which is controlled by constrained consumers are endogenous.

As Hayashi (1985a) reports, estimates of the fraction of income that accrues to liquidity constrained consumers using panel data are usually more stable, precise, and uniform than are time-series estimates. Indeed, we have found that the point estimates of L are broadly consistent with those of Hall and Mishkin (1982) and the fluctuations in the fraction of constrained households have not been dramatic over the period 1968–82. These findings may be reconciled by noting that the sample period is relatively short, and that L probably does not vary widely in the short run. Nevertheless, our estimates of the movements in P and L are statistically significant. Hence, our study has identified what we believe to be an oversight in popular tests for liquidity-constrained consumers that should be considered in future work.

LITERATURE CITED

Avery, Robert B., Gregory E. Elliehausen, Glenn B. Canner, and Thomas A. Gustafson. "Survey of Consumer Finances." *Federal Reserve Bulletin* (September 1984), 679–92.

Bernheim, Douglas B. "Ricardian Equivalence: An Evaluation of Theory and Evidence." In *National Bureau of Economic Research Macroeconomic Annual 1987*, edited by Stanley Fischer, pp. 263–304. Cambridge: The Mit Press, 1987.

Campbell, John Y., and Gregory N. Mankiw. "Permanent Income, Current Income, and Consumption." National Bureau of Economic Research, Working Paper No. 2436, November 1987.

Flavin, Marjorie A. "Excess Sensitivity of Consumption to Current Income: Liquidity Constraints or Myopia?" *Canadian Journal of Economics* 18 (February 1985), 117–36.

Hall, Robert E. "Stochastic Implications of the Lifecycle-Permanent Income Hypothesis: Theory and Evidence." *Journal of Political Economy* 86 (December 1978), 971–87.

Hall, Robert E., and Frederich S. Mishkin. "The Sensitivity of Consumption to Transitory Income: Estimates from Panel Data on Households." *Econometrica* 50 (March 1982), 461–81.

Hayashi, Fumio. "The Permanent Income Hypothesis: Estimation and Testing by Instrumental Variables." *Journal of Political Economics* 90 (November 1982), 895–917.

______. "Tests for Liquidity Constraints: A Survey." National Bureau of Economic Research, Working Paper No. 1720, October 1985. (a)

______. "The Permanent Income Hypothesis and Consumption Durability: Analysis Based on Japanese Panel Data." *Quarterly Journal of Economics* 100 (November 1985), 1083–1113. (b)

Hubbard, Glenn R., and Kenneth J. Judd. "Liquidity Constraints, Fiscal Policy and Consumption." *Brookings Papers on Economic Activity* 1 (June 1986), 1–50.

Jappelli, Tullio. "Who Is Credit-Constrained in the U.S. Economy?" *Quarterly Journal of Economics* 105 (February 1990).

Mariger, Randall P. *Consumption Behavior and the Effects of Government Fiscal Policies.* Cambridge: Harvard University Press, 1986.

King, Mervyn A. "The Economics of Saving: A Survey of Recent Contributions." In *Frontiers of Economics*, edited by Kenneth J. Arrow and Seppo Honkapohja, pp. 227–94. Oxford: Basil Blackwell, 1985.

Yotsuzuka, Toshiki. "Ricardian Equivalence in the Presence of Capital Market Imperfections." *Journal of Monetary Economics* 20 (September 1987), 411–36.

Zeldes, Stephen P. "Consumption and Liquidity Constraints: an Empirical Investigation." *Journal of Political Economy* 97 (April 1989), 305–46.

The Effect of Import Price Changes on Domestic Inflation: An Empirical Test of the Ratchet Effect

A Note by Farhad Rassekh and Barry Wilbratte

The possibility of downward rigidity of wages and prices has been considered in the literature at least since Keynes' *General Theory*. Many argue that monopolistic forces such as oligopolies and unions respond to inflationary pressures by raising wages and prices but resist wage and price reductions.[1] To the extent that these entities resist downward wage and price movements, they contribute to the existence of a ratchet effect, in which wages and prices behave asymmetrically.

The issue of a possible ratchet effect is particularly important in the context of international price movements. Commonly known as the Mundell-Laffer hypothesis,[2] the ratchet effect implies an upward bias in the response of domestic prices to changes in import prices. Consider the effect of an exchange rate movement on prices. Depreciation raises import prices, thereby increasing the domestic price level. The question is whether appreciation causes an equal downward movement in prices. For example, a 10 percent exchange rate depreciation followed by 10 percent appreciation would leave the exchange rate intact, but may leave domestic prices higher than the original level. If prices adjust asymmetrically throughout the world, such an exchange rate movement would result in higher world prices.

Despite the attention this issue has received in the theoretical literature, little empirical work has been devoted to it. In a discussion of the literature, Ahmad (1984, p. 4) assumes the ratchet effect is significant and inflationary. In empirical research, Sachs (1985) and Feldman (1984), among others, make the opposite assumption. In the only paper devoted to empirical testing of the ratchet effect, Goldstein (1977) presents evidence that price movements are symmetric, but his

[1]See Mankiw (1985), Yellen (1984), and Katz (1986). In a recent paper, Katz (1988, p. 519) echoed the old argument regarding sticky wages: "Workers losing high-wage jobs tend to wait for reemployment in the high-wage sector and have quite long unemployment spells."

[2]See Ahmad (1984, chapter 8).

The authors are indebted to Jacques Melitz, Manouchehr Mokhtari, Hassan Shirvani, Gary Smith, and to several anonymous referees for helpful suggestions.

FARHAD RASSEKH *is assistant professor of economics, University of Hartford.* BARRY WILBRATTE *is professor of economics, University of St. Thomas, Houston.*

Journal of Money, Credit, and Banking, Vol. 22, No. 2 (May 1990)

conclusions are somewhat marred by the perverse statistical finding that prices decline more readily than they rise.

Because of the void in the literature with respect to empirical evidence concerning asymmetry, this paper investigates the possibility of a ratchet effect. This investigation focuses on five major OECD countries: the United States, the United Kingdom, Canada, Japan, and West Germany. The sample period covers the third quarter of 1972 through the second quarter of 1987. The empirical tests performed in preparation of this work were twofold: First, we investigate which model best explains inflation. We then test for asymmetry. We present evidence for each country individually and for the five countries in a pooled regression.

The Inflation Model

In investigating which model best explains inflation, we considered two general categories of models: monetarist and structuralist.

We estimated numerous variants of a monetarist model developed by Harberger (1963), but found in each case that the monetarist model simply fails to explain inflation in our sample countries.[3] We therefore discarded the monetarist model as a possible basis for investigating the ratchet effect.

We found that structuralist models performed more satisfactorily in explaining inflation. Considering the many structural inflation models in the literature, we postulate that the inflation rate is explained by import prices, unit labor costs, the unemployment rate, and the lagged inflation rate.[4] With all variables except the unemployment rate expressed as percentage changes, the appropriate reduced-form equation is

$$P^*_t = f(MP^*_t, ULC^*_t, U^{-1}_t, P^*_{t-1}) \qquad (1)$$

where P^* is the domestic inflation rate, MP^* is the rate of change in domestic import prices, ULC^* is the percentage change in unit labor costs, U is the unemployment rate, and P^*_{t-1} is the lagged inflation rate. We expect, a priori, the coefficient of each regressor to be positive.

The Ratchet Effect

This section tests the proposition that prices rise more readily than they fall in response to import price changes. Since exchange rates were flexible during our sample period, variation in domestic import prices originates with exchange rate fluctuations and/or with a movement of the foreign price of imported goods. The equation does not distinguish between the two sources of variation in the domestic price of imports.

[3]The monetarist model was successfully employed by Vogel (1974) in explaining inflation in several Latin American countries.

[4]For a survey of the structural models that formed the basis of our model, see Hooper and Lowrey (1979) and Goldstein (1977).

To conduct the asymmetry test, we generate a dummy variable and add it to the list of regressors of equation (1). With the dummy variable included, the equation is

$$P_t^* = a + b\,[MP_t^*] + c\,[UCLC_t^*] + d\,[U_t^{-1}] + e\,[P^*_{t-1}] + f\,[DMP_t^*] + E_t \qquad (2)$$

where E_t is the residual term and DMP^* is the dummy variable. The dummy variable is constructed as follows: $DMP^* = D \times MP^*$, where $D = 1$ if $MP^* < 0$ and $D = 0$ otherwise. Therefore, the sum $b + f$ indicates the effect of negative changes in MP^* on inflation while b indicates the effect of positive changes. Thus, if the coefficient of the dummy variable, f, is significantly negative, we interpret this as evidence of a ratchet effect: an increase in import prices has a stronger effect than a decrease. If the coefficient f is not significantly different from zero, we interpret this as evidence of symmetry.

The Empirical Results

Table 1 presents the results of our estimates of equation (2), with separate regressions performed for each country. The structural model performs well in terms of the overall explanatory power of the equation. The F-ratio for each of the five countries is statistically significant at the 1 percent level. In addition, the Durbin h-test indicates that the equation of each country except Canada is free of autocorrelation. In terms of the statistical significance of the regressors, the model performs best for Germany, Canada, and Japan, and less well for the United States and the United Kingdom.

TABLE 1

EMPIRICAL ESTIMATES OF EQUATION (2)

	Dependent Variable: P^*								
	C	MP^*	ULC^*	U^{-1}	P^*_{t-1}	DMP^*	$\bar{R}^2$	$F(5,54)$	SE
US	−0.0002	0.08	−0.05	0.02	0.70	−0.13	.69	25.41	.005
	(−0.04)	(2.83)	(−1.09)	(0.84)	(6.88)	(−1.36)			
UK	0.004	0.02	0.07	0.03	0.55	0.02	.49	11.57	.014
	(1.26)	(0.38)	(0.96)	(1.67)	(4.17)	(0.72)			
GR	0.004	0.09	0.084	0.002	0.32	0.0001	.60	19.06	.004
	(3.43)	(4.51)	(2.40)	(0.76)	(3.20)	(0.003)			
JP	−0.009	0.06	0.04	0.03	0.44	−0.03	.75	33.84	.010
	(1.76)	(3.25)	(0.77)	(2.47)	(3.03)	(−1.17)			
CN	0.002	0.07	0.008	0.04	0.56	0.02	.61	19.55	.005
	(0.77)	(2.16)	(1.41)	(1.83)	(5.67)	(0.74)			

Definitions of variables: P^* = domestic inflation rate, MP^* = percent change in import prices; ULC^* = percent change in unit labor costs; U^{-1} = inverse of the unemployment rate; P^*_{t-1} = lagged dependent variable; DMP^* = dummy variable described following equation (2). SE = standard error of the regression. Abbreviations of countries: US = United States; UK = United Kingdom; GR = West Germany; JP = Japan; CN = Canada.

The dummy variable is insignificant for each country, providing no evidence of a ratchet effect. Of course, the insignificance of this variable means little in the case of the United Kingdom because the underlying variable, MP^*, is statistically insignificant. Our tests thus indicate that prices respond symmetrically to variation in the rate of import price change.[5]

The unemployment rate is significant for Japan, Canada, and marginally significant for the United Kingdom, indicting a short-term Phillips-curve relationship for these countries. However, the growth of unit labor costs significantly explains inflation only for Germany.

Table 2 presents the regression results based on pooled data for the sample countries. These results are broadly consistent with the individual country estimates. For each country, different slopes of the import price (MP^*) and dummy (DMP^*) variables are estimated. Import prices (except for Germany) and the lagged inflation rate are significant while unit labor costs and the unemployment rate are not. Also, in the pooled regression in ratchet effect finds no support, as none of the dummy variables is significant.[6]

TABLE 2

POOLED REGRESSION ESTIMATES OF EQUATION (2)

Dependent Variable: P^*

U.S.		U.K.		Germany		Japan		Canada	
MP^*	DMP^*	MP^*	DMP^*	MP^*	DMP^*	MP^*	DMP^*	MP^*	DMP^*
0.07	0.13	0.11	0.002	0.05	0.08	0.08	−0.03	0.10	0.006
(2.31)	(1.00)	(4.35)	(0.14)	(1.25)	(1.06)	(4.20)	(−1.30)	(2.30)	(0.16)

Constant	ULC	U^{-1}	P^*_{t-1}
0.006	0.004	0.00007	0.56
(4.94)	(0.99)	(0.22)	(11.48)

$R^2 = .50$
SE = .009
$F(13,286) = 23.92$

Our finding that the domestic price level responds symmetrically provides support to other empirical works, which assume that the effects of exchange rate fluctuations on inflation is symmetric. Examples are the works of Sachs (1985) and Feldman (1984), cited earlier. Our results also provide indirect support to the work of Deardorff and Stern (1982), who used estimates performed by Hooper and Lowrey (1979) to analyze the sectoral employment impact of the dollar appreciation of the early 1980s. Hooper and Lowrey performed elasticity estimates for a period during which the dollar depreciated.

[5]We repeated the estimates of equation (2) with unit labor cost treated as endogenous. The results were similar to the coefficients reported in Table 1. Sepcifically, all the dummy variables were insignificant.

[6]We also performed a pooled regression with the rate of change of import prices of each country multiplied by the corresponding country's propensity to import (to adjust for the possibility that the sensitivity of domestic prices to import prices may vary with the propensity to import). This regression also failed to support the ratchet effect.

Conclusion

Our statistical estimates suggest several patterns. We find that a structural model explains inflation better than a monetarist model. The model's performance is strongest in the case of Germany and weakest in the case of the United Kingdom. Applying a structural model, we find no evidence of a ratchet effect with respect to import prices. All individual country estimates and the pooled estimate indicate that domestic prices respond symmetrically to variation in the rate of import price change.

LITERATURE CITED

Ahmad, Jaleel. *Floating Exchange Rates and World Inflation.* London: Macmillan, 1984.

Deardorf, Alan V., and Robert M. Stern. "The Sectoral Impact of the Recent Appreciation of the U.S. Dollar." Manuscript (April 1982), University of Michigan.

Feldman, Robert. "The Impact of the Recent Strength of the Dollar on the U.S. Merchandise Trade Balance: Some 'First-Round' Effects and Feedbacks from Exchange-Rate-Induced Changes in U.S. Relative Inflation." *Journal of Policy Modeling* (February 1984), 29–74.

Goldstein, Morris. "Downward Price Inflexibility, Ratchet Effects, and the Inflationary Impact of Import Price Changes: Some Empirical Evidence," *International Monetary Fund Staff Papers* 24 (November 1977), 569–612.

Harberger, Arnold. "The Dynamics of Inflation in Chile." In *Measurement in Economics: Studies in Mathematical Economics and Econometrics in Honor of Yehuda Grunfeld,* pp. 219–50. Stanford, 1963.

Hooper, Peter, and Barbara R. Lowrey. "Impact of the Dollar Depreciation on the U.S. Price Level: An Analytical Survey of Empirical Estimates." *Federal Reserve Bulletin* 65 (April 1979), 305–13.

Katz, Lawrence F. "Efficiency Wage Theories: A Partial Evaluation." In *Macroeconomics Annual,* vol. 1, edited by J. Fischer, pp. 235–75. National Bureau of Economic Research, 1986.

______. "Some Recent Developments in Labor Economics and Their Implications for Macroeconomics." *Journal of Money, Credit, and Banking* 20 (August 1988 Part 2), 507–22.

Mankiw, N. Gregory. "Small Menu Costs and Large Business Cycles: A Macroeconomic Model of Monopoly." *Quarterly Journal of Economics* 100 (May 1985), 529–39.

Sachs, Jeffrey D. "The Dollar and the Policy Mix: 1985." *Brookings Papers on Economic Activity* (1:1985), 117–85.

Vogel, Robert C. "The Dynamics of Inflation in Latin America, 1950–1969." *American Economic Review* 64 (March 1974), 102–13.

Yellen, Janet. "Efficiency Wage Models of Unemployment." *American Economic Review* 74 (May 1984), 200–205.

BOOK REVIEWS

Day of Reckoning, by Benjamin M. Friedman. New York: Random House, 1988. 298 pp. $19.95.

Benjamin Friedman has written the definitive book on the conventional analysis of what he calls Reagan's "new fiscal policy." He argues that the 1981 tax cut raised the budget deficit and set in motion a complex set of reactions that lowered the nation's output and raised foreign claims on that output. This policy entailed a permanent acceptance of a relatively large budget deficit and, hence, continuing and cumulating reductions in the future standard of living. Friedman offers an explanation of why such policies were put in place, what their effects were, why these effects occurred, and what should be done to end the continuing destructive influence of these policies. His solution is to raise the personal income marginal tax rates by 3 percentage points at each level of income. He argues that this would reduce the averge budget deficit by $50 to 75 billion from 1989 to 1996 and return total federal debt to 36 cents per dollar of GNP in 1996. Readers will find this solution strikingly ho-hum after the rhetoric that set the stage for it.

The principal linkages that Friedman lays out are these: 1981 tax cuts, in particular the phased reduction in personal marginal income tax rates, raised the federal budget deficit, which raised the real rate of interest. The higher real interest rate reduced domestic investment, which reduced productivity, output, and the future U.S. standard of living. In addition, the higher real rate of interest attracted a capital inflow from abroad, which raised the demand for dollars in international currency markets. The larger demand for the dollar raised the value of the dollar in terms of foreign currencies, which raised prices of U.S. goods abroad, so that U.S. exports fell, and lowered the dollar prices of foreign goods, so that U.S. imports rose. The larger trade deficit reflected a loss in U.S. competitiveness; that is, lower exports reduced employment and production of such goods, just as larger imports reduced U.S. employment and production of import-competing goods. Since the trade deficit entails domestic borrowing from abroad, the future servicing of this debt is a burden for future generations. It represents a larger claim on their already reduced output of goods and services, a double-whammy on future consumption possibilities. A concomitant result is that the future position of U.S. world leadership or influence has been reduced.

One of the most disturbing features of this book is that Friedman moves beyond positive analysis to the moral plane. His central thesis is that the new fiscal policy violated a basic moral principle to arrange our economic affairs so as to ensure a rising standard of living, a principle that had bound generations of Americans to their offspring. The cause of this broken faith, he argues, was either simply an erroneous set of policy conclusions endorsed in good faith by the Administration and voters and adhered to for several years or, more darkly, an intentional deceit by the Administration, "willful bankruptcy," "a carefully calculated plan for forcing the government to reduce its role in American life" (p. 23). In support of this claim, Friedman provides assertions but no evidence. One should have some misgivings about taking such a morally superior position when the great mass of voters, and many policy analysts, still do not agree that the initial Reagan program entailed cheating future generations or lying to the voters.

The book's central recurring theme and the linchpin of the analysis is that the Reagan economic policy planned for total federal spending to be at the levels that in fact occurred, and that it planned the personal income tax rate cuts; when the tax cuts led to a fall in tax receipts, there was a matching, and perhaps intentional, rise in the deficit. In this assessment there is no room for the effects on the budget of substantially poorer cyclical performance and of lower inflation than were anticipated by the Reagan administration. While Friedman emphasizes that 1986 total budget outlays were near the 1981 budget target anticipated five years earlier, he fails to indicate that the 1986 spending total was about 23.8 percent of GNP, up from 22 percent in 1980, and that this rise contrasts starkly with the targeted reduction of spending by 3 percent of GNP. The resulting 4.8 percentage-point rise in the share of spending in GNP, relative to the targeted proportion of GNP, provides an alternative accounting for the unintended budget deficit.

A $170 billion shortfall of 1986 primary receipts from the Reagan target of $921.3 billion was not due to the tax cut as Friedman argues, but to the slower growth of nominal income. Carlson (1989) shows that primary receipts in 1986 were reduced by $195.8 billion due to the shortfall of output and prices from the 1981 Reagan plan. The Reagan tax cut could not have been the impetus for this shortfall because it was largely offset by the other personal tax increases in the 1980s that Friedman conveniently ignores, such as bracket creep and social security tax hikes.

One of Friedman's strongest substantive statements for his claim that business investment fell in the 1980s, rather than being boosted as intended by the new fiscal policy, is "After allowing for inflation, the dollar value of net business investment declined by more than half between 1979 and the post-recession low in 1983. By 1986, after four years of expansion, we had not yet regained the 1979 level" (pp. 198–99). The statement is correct; real net nonresidential fixed investment (1982 prices) was $124.3, $50.4, and $80.5 billion in 1979, 1983, and 1986, respectively. The use of 1986 data is surprising since, elsewhere in the book, Friedman goes to some length to excoriate the Tax Reform Act of 1986, especially for its depressing effect on business investment. Such investment had been $103.3 and $116.1 billion in 1984 and 1985, respectively, still less than in 1979, but much higher than in 1986. Why was investment lower in 1984–85 than in 1979? The answer is more involved than Friedman indicates.

The data can be used to question Friedman's simple conclusion. In 1979, the civilian labor force rose by 2.7 million people, so that net real business fixed investment climbed by about $46 thousand per additional labor force participant, well above the $27.7 thousand per person ratio of the real net stock of capital at the beginning of 1979 to the 1979 labor force. In 1985, the civilian labor force rose 1.9 million, so real business capital rose $61.1 thousand per additional labor force participant, or nearly one-third more than in 1979. Even this rise understates the greater strength of capital formation in 1985 for two cycle-related reasons. First, capacity utilization was lower in 1985 than in 1979 so that, in 1985, employment of additional capital per worker was more readily available with existing facilities and without new investment than it was in 1979. Second, capacity utilization did not rise in 1985 as it had in 1979, so that demand for existing and new capital facilities was not expanding as fast.

From a longer perspective, the annual average pace of net real business investment in 1981–85 was little changed from 1975–80 or in 1980–85 compared with 1975–79; for these periods the annual average ranged from about $88 to $91 billion. On the basis of per additional member of the labor force, however, real net investment was 40 to 50 percent larger in the 1980s, depending on which pair of periods is used for comparison. The significance of this sharp rise in capital formation is enhanced by the fact that the civilian unemployment rate was over a full percentage point higher in the first half of the 1980s than in the last half of the seventies. Adjusted for cyclical and demographic considerations, Friedman's gloomy characterization of U.S. investment performance in the 1980s is reversed.

Friedman's analysis of the rise in the dollar and purported loss of U.S. competitiveness suffers from an excessive preoccupation with demand. His failure to note the decline in U.S. investment abroad (to expand investment at home) means missing the fact that it was the shift in the supply of dollars that caused the rise in the value of the dollar, not the shift in foreign demand that Friedman emphasizes. The overall supply of dollars for U.S. investment abroad and for U.S. imports fell relative to GNP from 1980 to 1985, principally due to the decline in the former item. For foreigners to invest more dollars in U.S. assets required that any increased foreign currency flow toward U.S. investment would have to exceed, in percentage terms, the relatively large rise in the price of the dollar. Because of the strength of the latter, the demand for dollars for foreign capital transactions measured relative to U.S. GNP fell from 1980 to 1985, the period of the rising dollar.

Friedman argues that the effect of a higher-priced dollar on demands for U.S. imports and exports can be used to explain the rise of the trade deficit and to assess the loss of domestic output. But the competitive performance of U.S. producers is not determined solely by the size of foreign markets or the appetite of U.S. consumers for foreign goods. Exports can decline without lowering domestic production, if U.S. purchases of such goods rise. Imports can rise with domestic production of import-competing goods, if domestic demand is increased. I have shown elsewhere (1988) that when the dollar rose, U.S. production boomed, especially in the very industries where the trade deficit rose the most. Production data in the United States and abroad fail to support Friedman's view of lost U.S. competitiveness. The strong dollar reflected an investment- and productivity-based improvement in U.S. competitiveness.

It is as easy to argue that investment and productivity boomed in the 1980s by comparing performance to the 1973–80 period, as it is for Friedman to argue that performance was poor compared to the 1948–73, or 1948–80 periods. Which comparison is more appropriate depends on the issue, but generally one should use the prior period over which conditions existed that the policies in question were intended to address. In this case, the first comparison is the relevant one. Friedman's chapter-long survey of the landscape on the investment and productivity issue is also superficial. A good example is his tongue-in-cheek assertion that a burst of public capital formation did not explain the budget deficit (p. 205). In point of fact, the cumulative NIPA total government budget deficit from the end of 1980 to the end of 1987 was $658.1 billion (excluding $97.1 billion added to the Fed's balance sheet), while the U.S. Department of Commerce shows the current dollar net government capital stock rose by $615 billion over the same period, 93.5 percent of the net debt increase. While a burst in capital spending did not cause the deficit, it did match most of it.

The readability of the book is impaired by tedious numerical comparisons; perhaps an editor decided that charts of the data would be intimidating. The comparisons would have been more persuasive, although perhaps not the same, had charts beeen used instead. For example, charts on the real rate and the deficit would have made it more difficult to assert, as Friedman does, that budget deficit movements were more clearly positively correlated with the real rate in the 1980s, while charts on the budget deficit and its components relative to GNP would have complicated the principal budget argument.

This book will be useful to students of the fiscal debate in the 1980s because it presents, in a readable fashion, one side of that debate. For this purpose, it should be popular with laymen and undergraduates. Such an accessible exposure to so well-integrated a set of theoretical linkages, which are also critical to the fiscal debate and its broader implications, is rare. Unfortunately, this is all the more reason to regret the partial nature of the argument and its complex web of inconsistent assumptions and insupportable conclusions. Arguments as intricantly woven and of such current relevance as Friedman's require attention and careful examination, most especially when they are, in principle and in fact, so questionable.

JOHN A. TATOM

Federal Reserve Bank of St. Louis

LITERATURE CITED

Carlson, Keith M. "Federal Budget Trends and the 1981 Reagan Economic Plan." Federal Reserve Bank of St. Louis *Review* (January/February 1989), 18–31.

Tatom, John A. "The Link between the Value of the Dollar, U.S. Trade and Manufacturing Output: Some Recent Evidence." Federal Reserve Bank of St. Louis *Review* (November/December 1988), 24–37.

The Ohio State University Department of Economics Offers Programs of Graduate Study in Economics

The Ohio State University is located in Columbus, capital city of Ohio and a metropolitan area of more than one million people. There are six other institutions of higher education in Columbus as well as the headquarters facility of Battelle Memorial Institute, the largest independent research organization in the world. University students number over fifty thousand, including about eight thousand graduate students. Ohio State is a major center for graduate education, ranking eighth in the nation in degrees conferred. The Ohio State University library system is one of the ten largest library systems in the United States.

Graduate Studies in Economics

The Department of Economics has a faculty of forty members with approximately ninety graduate students in residence at any point in time. The large faculty and relatively small graduate student body make possible in-depth graduate education through close association with outstanding scholars in many different areas. Fields of specialization include:

- Mathematical Economics
- Econometrics
- Money and Finance
- Labor
- Industrial Organization
- Public Finance and Urban Economics
- Monetary Theory and Macroeconomics
- Soviet and Eastern European Studies
- International Trade and Development
- Economic History

Economics graduate students can take elective fields in other departments of the College of Social and Behavioral Sciences or in the Colleges of Business, Agriculture and Home Economics, Engineering, Mathematics, and Physical Sciences when interdisciplinary studies are appropriate.

Fellowships and Assistantships

Because of Ohio State's large undergraduate enrollment and ongoing research programs, there are many part-time teaching and research assistantships that offer financial aid to graduate students. The Department of Economics assists a number of students each year through fellowships and assistantships with stipends ranging from $7,506 to $13,014 per academic year. In addition, teaching, research and administrative assistants, and fellows receive tuition fee waivers. Once a student has been awarded a fellowship or assistantship, financial assistance is possible for as many as five years, provided normal academic progress is maintained.

University Fellowships (stipend $825 per month for 12 months, nonrenewable) are available to well-qualified applicants. In addition, Special University Fellowships (stipend: $825 per month for 12 months, renewable) are available to minority students, primarily blacks of U.S. citizenship.

Additional information about the department may be obtained from the Director of Graduate Studies, Department of Economics, The Ohio State University, 1945 North High Street, Columbus, OH 43210.

ACKNOWLEDGMENTS

Supporting Subscribers

Pittsburgh National Bank

Security Pacific National Bank

State Savings Co.

Referees

Michael Adler
Alberto Alesina
Richard G. Anderson
Herbert L. Baer
Charles R. Bean
Michael Beenstock
Michael T. Belongia
Bruce L. Benson
Allen N. Berger
Ben Bernanke
James M. Boughton
William J. Boyes
Giorgio Canarella
Thomas F. Cargill
Chris Carroll
Nan-Ting Chou
Jeffrey A. Clark
Timothy Q. Cook
Russell W. Cooper
Thomas F. Cosimano
Ramon P. DeGennaro
Ian Domowitz
John B. Donaldson
Michael Dotsey
Bernard Dumas
Eugene Fama
Gary C. Fethke
Shawn M. Forbes
Silverio Foresi
Bruno S. Frey
Jean A. Gauger
Alberto Giovannini
David K. Guilkey
R. W. Hafer
Sangmoon Hahm
Craig S. Hakkio
Thomas E. Hall
Gary D. Hansen
Scott E. Hein
Eric L. Hirschhorn
William (Curt) Hunter
George Kanatas
Gary D. Koppenhaver
G. S. Laumas
Leonardo Leiderman
David J. Longworth
Joyce Manchester
Lucille Mayne
Ronald I. McKinnon
Yash Mehra
David R. Meinster
Arie Melnik
Anne-Marie Meulendyke
Donald J. Mullineaux
John D. Murray
Jonathan Neuberger
James M. O'Brien
Joe Peek
James Pemberton
George G. Pennacchi
Richard H. Pettway
Herakles Polemarchakis
Richard E. Quandt
Assaf Razin
Bradford G. Reid
D. John Roberts
Vance V. Roley
David H. Romer
Nicola Rossi
Mark Rush
Gary J. Santoni
John R. Schroeter
Kathryn Shaw
Richard G. Sheehan
Eugenie D. Short
Pierre L. Siklos
Myron B. Slovin
Richard J. Sweeney
Mark P. Taylor
Daniel L. Thornton
John Thornton
Mark Toma
Bharat Trehan
Haluk Unal
David D. VanHoose
P. V. Viswanath
Paul A. Wachtel
Roy H. Webb
Warren E. Weber
Steven R. Weisbrod
David Wilcox
Thomas F. Willett
David F. Winter
John T. Woolley
Jeffrey M. Wrase

Ohio State
University Press

ISSN 0022-2879

BOOK REVIEWS

(continued from front cover)

Day of Reckoning, by Benjamin M. Friedman

Reviewed by John A. Tatom

JOURNAL OF MONEY, CREDIT AND BANKING

August 1990

ARTICLES

The Macroeconomic Implications of Contract Models with Asymmetric Information *Matthew B. Canzoneri and Anne C. Sibert*

New Results in Support of the Fiscal Policy Ineffectiveness Proposition *Reuven Glick and Michael Hutchison*

Ricardian Equivalence, Rational Expectations, and the Permanent Income Hypothesis *Alfred A. Haug*

The Objectives and Priorities of Monetary Policy under Different Federal Reserve Chairmen *David R. Hakes*

Risk and Parity in Purchasing Power *Roger D. Huang*

Politics and Perceived Country Creditworthiness in International Banking *Thomas L. Brewer and Pietra Rivoli*

The International Debt Crisis and Bank Loan-Loss-Reserve Decisions: The Signaling Content of Partially Anticipated Events *James J. Musumeci and Joseph F. Sinkey, Jr.*

NOTES, COMMENTS, REPLIES

Interest Rate Linkages within the European Monetary System: A Time Series Analysis *Costas J. Karfakis and Demetrios M. Moschos*

Money and Capital in Economic Development: A Test of the McKinnon Hypothesis for Nepal *John Thornton and Sri Ram Poudyal*

Reserve Requirements and the Inflation Tax *L. Dwayne Barney, Jr., Alan Frankle, and Harry White*

(continued on back cover)

JOURNAL OF MONEY, CREDIT AND BANKING

Manuscripts should be submitted in triplicate to the Editors, *Journal of Money, Credit, and Banking*, Department of Economics, Ohio State University, 1945 North High Street, Columbus, Ohio 43210–1172. Carolyn South, Secretary to the Editors. Submission fee: individual subscribers U.S. $30; nonsubscribers U.S. $40. Checks are to be made payable to THE OHIO STATE UNIVERSITY –JMCB and enclosed with submitted manuscripts. Instructions for preparing text and illustrations appear in the February issue.

JOURNAL OF MONEY, CREDIT AND BANKING

VOLUME 22 NUMBER 3 AUGUST 1990

ARTICLES

The Macroeconomic Implications of Contract Models with Asymmetric Information *Matthew B. Canzoneri and Anne C. Sibert* 273

New Results in Support of the Fiscal Policy Ineffectiveness Proposition *Reuven Glick and Michael Hutchison* 288

Ricardian Equivalence, Rational Expectations, and the Permanent Income Hypothesis *Alfred A. Haug* 305

The Objectives and Priorities of Monetary Policy under Different Federal Reserve Chairmen *David R. Hakes* 327

Risk and Parity in Purchasing Power *Roger D. Huang* 338

Politics and Perceived Country Creditworthiness in International Banking *Thomas L. Brewer and Pietra Rivoli* 357

The International Debt Crisis and Bank Loan-Loss-Reserve Decisions: The Signaling Content of Partially Anticipated Events *James J. Musumeci and Joseph F. Sinkey, Jr.* 370

NOTES, COMMENTS, REPLIES

Interest Rate Linkages within the European Monetary System: A Time Series Analysis *Costas J. Karfakis and Demetrios M. Moschos* 388

Money and Capital in Economic Development: A Test of the McKinnon Hypothesis for Nepal *John Thornton and Sri Ram Poudyal* 395

Reserve Requirements and the Inflation Tax *L. Dwayne Barney, Jr., Alan Frankle, and Harry White* 400

BOOK REVIEWS

America in the World Economy: A Strategy for the 1990s, by C. Fred Bergsten *Reviewed by H. W. Arndt* 402

Governing the $5 Trillion Economy, by Herbert Stein *Reviewed by William T. Gavin* 404

JOURNAL OF MONEY, CREDIT, AND BANKING (ISSN 0022-2879). Published quarterly in February, May, August, and November by the Ohio State University Press, 1070 Carmack Road, Columbus, Ohio 43210. Margaret Starbuck, Managing Editor; Peg Carr, Production Editor; Tom Kangas, Subscriptions Manager. Second-class postage paid at Columbus, Ohio, and at additional mailing offices. *Postmaster:* Send address to: *Journal of Money, Credit, and Banking*, Ohio State University Press, 1070 Carmack Road, Columbus, Ohio 43210.

SUBSCRIPTIONS. Individual: U.S. $27.50 per year; library: U.S. $45; student: U.S. $20.00; additional subscriptions to the same address: U.S. $20.00 per subscription. Postage outside the United States: add $5.00 per year. Sponsoring Subscriptions: U.S. $1000 per year. Sustaining Subscriptions: U.S. $500 per year. Supporting Subscriptions: U.S. $100 per year. Claims for missing issues must be made within four months of the date of publication. Allow six weeks for address change. Checks should be made payable to the Ohio State University Press, 1070 Carmack Road, Columbus, Ohio 43210.

BACK ISSUES, REPRINTS, AND MICROFILM. Most back issues from 1983 to the present are available from the Ohio State University press. Microfilms of back volumes and reprints of articles may be obtained from University Microfilms International, 300 North Zeeb Road, Ann Arbor, Michigan 48106. Back volumes from 1969 through 1982 in reprint edition may be obtained from Schmidt Periodicals GmbH, Dettendorf, D-8201 Bad Feilnbach 2, West Germany.

MATTHEW B. CANZONERI
ANNE C. SIBERT

The Macroeconomic Implications of Contract Models with Asymmetric Information

MONETARY MODELS OF THE BUSINESS CYCLE are designed to explain certain stylized facts, such as the positive correlation between monetary innovations and real economic activity, and to explore the nature of employment fluctuations and optimal monetary policy. Two popular paradigms are the islands models of Lucas (1972) and Barro (1976) and the disequilibrium contract models of Gray (1976) and Fischer (1977). Both paradigms have been developed extensively, and their macroeconomic implications are well known.

Lucas (1981) and Barro (1977) criticize the disequilibrium contract models because the wage and employment rules postulated in them are not derived in a welfare-maximizing framework. Lucas (1981, p. 564) concludes that "None of these models offers an explanation as to why people should choose to bind themselves to contracts which seem to be in no one's self interest, and my conjecture is that when reasons for this are found they will reduce to the kind of information difficulties already stressed in my 1972 article."

A new monetary model can be constructed out of the early implicit-contract models of Azariadis (1975), Baily (1974), and Gordon (1974). These contract models are not monetary models because fluctuations in the money supply have no effect on real wages, employment, or output. However, Calvo and Phelps (1977) note that they can be converted into monetary models by the imposition of information asymmetries. The asymmetry Calvo and Phelps suggest is that firms observe

The authors thank Olivier Blanchard, Guillermo A. Calvo, Russell V. Cooper, Edward J. Green, Dale Henderson, Patrick Minford, Preston Miller, Kenneth Rogoff, Neil Wallace, and two anonymous referees for their comments on this work.

MATTHEW B. CANZONERI *is professor of economics at Georgetown University. Anne C. Sibert is assistant professor of economics at the University of Kansas.*

Journal of Money, Credit, and Banking, Vol. 22, No. 3 (August 1990)

productivity shocks while workers do not. If productivity shocks have an aggregate component that is correlated with the price level, then optimal contracts will depend upon prices.[1] This means that price movements caused by monetary shocks will have real effects. The resulting monetary model addresses the criticism of Lucas and Barro; contracts are derived in a welfare-maximizing framework. The conjecture of Lucas is also borne out; the new model rides on the familiar confounding of real and monetary disturbances.

Our purpose here is to draw out the macroeconomic implications of the risk-sharing model of labor contracts.[2] In their pathbreaking paper, Calvo and Phelps (1977) did not actually derive the optimal contract and calculate the resulting equilibrium. If they had, they would have found that their model does not imply a positive correlation between monetary innovations and real activity.[3] Here, we present a model that does produce a positive correlation. We also show that an equilibrium exists and discuss its properties.

In section 1 we derive and analyze the optimal contract under asymmetric information. The framework employed is similar to that of Hart (1983). Firms face a random productivity shock which may take a high or low value. Employment at firms drawing the "good" (high productivity) state is efficient, while employment at firms drawing the "bad" (low productivity) state is inefficiently low. We demonstrate that contractual employment in the bad state is an increasing function of the conditional probability (at the time the contract was written) that the bad state will occur. Contractual employment in the good state is independent of conditional probabilities. These are the properties of optimal contracting with asymmetric information that result in the positive correlation between monetary innovations and real economic activity.

In section 2, we follow Calvo and Phelps in closing the model with a Cambridge money-demand equation. We postulate that each firm's local productivity shock has a serially correlated aggregate component. Equilibrium is established by deriving the probability of the current bad aggregate state (and thus the probability of a firm drawing the bad local state next period), conditional on current prices and other observed variables. From the Cambridge equation, we see that either a bad aggregate productivity shock or a positive monetary innovation will increase the current price level. Thus, it turns out that an unanticipated increase in the price level will increase the conditional probability of the bad aggregate state, increase the conditional probability that an individual firm will draw a bad local state next period, and by our results in section 1, increase employment at firms which actually draw the bad local state next period. A positive correlation between price innovations and real activity (one period later) is established.

In section 3 we discuss other macroeconomic implications of the model. Monetary innovations will cause price innovations, and thus a positive correlation be-

[1]This paper is similar in spirit to Grossman, Hart, and Maskin (1983). Their model, however, is not a monetary one.

[2]There is already an extensive literature discussing the microeconomic implications. See for example Hart (1983) and the references therein.

[3]We demonstrate this in an earlier unpublished paper, Canzoneri and Sibert (1984).

tween monetary innovations and real activity is established. The "employment problem" is described, and implications for monetary policy are drawn out and compared to those of other models.

1. OPTIMAL CONTRACTS WITH ASYMMETRIC INFORMATION

Real and monetary shocks may cause variance in the income streams of risk-averse workers and firms. Thus, they have an incentive to enter into contractual relationships to share risk. If, for example, firms have greater access to financial markets, then it might be optimal for them to offer workers more stable real wage bills in return for a lower average level of income.[4] In this section we describe the optimal labor contract.

The output of the typical firm is

$$y = \hat{x}f(n) \; , \tag{1}$$

where n is hours worked by the representative worker and $\hat{x} \in \{x_1, x_2\}$ is a firm-specific productivity shock.[5] Let $x_1 < x_2$; then state 1 may be called the "bad" state and state 2 the "good" state. Let $U(b - Rn)$ and $V(y - b)$ be the utilities of the representative worker and the firm, respectively, where b is the real wage bill, and R can be interpreted as a reservation wage. The functions $f(\bullet)$, $U(\bullet)$ and $V(\bullet)$ are increasing, strictly concave and twice continuously differentiable. In addition, we assume $f'(0) = \infty$ and $U'(\infty) = V'(\infty) = 0$.

At the end of each period the firm offers its workers a contract, $C = \{n_i, b_i\}$, specifying the period's employment and wage bill as functions of the state, i (= 1,2), that will be drawn next period. If, as we will assume, workers do not observe the productivity shock directly, then the contract must be "incentive compatible." That is, it must not be to the advantage of the firm to lie about which state occurs.[6] The contract may be written in terms of the conditional probability that the bad state will occur,

$$\alpha \equiv \mathrm{Prob}(\hat{x}=x_1|\Omega) \; . \tag{2}$$

The variable Ω denotes the information set; Ω is specified in detail in section 2, where equilibrium is established. It may include any information available to the

[4]See Reagan and Stulz (1986) for a discussion of the impact of capital markets on risk sharing in labor contracts.

[5]An alternative setup was proposed in Azariadis (1975). In his model there is a continuum of workers and each worker is either employed fulltime or laid off. Calvo and Phelps (1977) suggested employing this framework, but Canzoneri and Sibert (1984) demonstrate that it may not yield a positive correlation between monetary disturbances and output.

[6]At first glance, this may appear to be an overly restrictive way of dealing with a potential credibility problem. It might seem that workers may be better off in a contract where the firm is systematically misrepresenting the state. However, Dasgupta, Hammond, and Maskin (1979) and Harris and Townsend (1981) have shown that any allocation resulting from a contract that is not incentive compatible can also be attained from one that is; so there is no loss of generality here.

firm and its workers which will help predict $\hat{x}$. It may, for example, include the price level observed at the time the contract is agreed upon. This price will be seen to be correlated with the local shock that will be drawn during the contract period. Workers are assumed to be mobile between firms, so each firm must offer the same contract.

As a benchmark, we first suppose that information is symmetric in that x is observable by both workers and firms. Then an optimal contract maximizes

$$wE[U(b - Rn)|\Omega] + (1 - w)E[V(y - b)|\Omega] =$$

$$w[\alpha U(b_1 - Rn_1) + (1 - \alpha)U(b_2 - RN_2)] + (1 - w)\,[\alpha V(y_1 - b_1)$$

$$+ (1 - \alpha)V(y_2 - b_2)]\ , \tag{3}$$

where the parameter w picks a particular outcome from the Pareto-optimal set; we take it to be given. The solution, $C^s = \{n_i^s, b_i^s\}$, is characterized by[7]

$$x_i f'(n_i^s) = R\ ; \tag{4a}$$

$$wU'(b_i^s - Rn_i^s) = (1 - w)V'(x_i f(n_i^s) - b_i^s),\ i = 1\ , 2. \tag{4b}$$

The first equation says that the marginal product of labor is equal to the reservation wage in each state. The second equation is the Arrow-Borche condition for efficient allocation of risk.

When workers do not observe $\hat{x}$ directly, the firm may have an incentive to lie about the state that has occurred. If so, the optimal symmetric-information contract, C^s, may not be implementable. This will be the case if $x_2 - x_1$ is sufficiently small.

PROPOSITION 1. *If $x_2 - x_1$ is sufficiently small, then the firm has an incentive to lie in the good state, but not in the bad state.*

PROOF. Suppose $\bar{x}$ is the realized value of $\hat{x}$, and suppose temporarily that $\hat{x}$ is a continuous random variable. If the firm lies and announces a value for productivity that is slightly higher than $\bar{x}$, its change in profits is

$$d[\bar{x}f(n) - b]/dx = \bar{x}f'(n)(dn/dx) - (db/dx)$$

$$= -\ \{(1 - w)V''/[(1 - w)V'' + wU'']\}f < 0\ ,$$

where expressions for dn/dx and db/dx are obtained by differentiating equations (4). Thus, the firm gains by understating productivity. By continuity, these results carry over to the discrete case if x_1 is sufficiently close to x_2.

In the good state the firm can lower its wage bill by reporting that the bad state has occurred, but this also lowers employment and output. Because the firm is risk averse, (4) implies that the wage bill falls more than revenue. In what follows we will assume that x_1 is close enough to x_2 that the symmetric-information contract is not implementable.

[7]The assumptions on $f(\bullet)$, $U(\bullet)$, and $V(\bullet)$ guarantee that a unique solution exists.

Two interrelated facts should be noted before going on to the asymmetric-information case. First, with symmetric information, we do not obtain a monetary model. Equations (4) are independent of the conditional probability α; so fluctuations in money and the price level have no real effects. Second, with symmetric information, there is no conflict between efficiency in the allocation of resources and efficiency in the allocation of risk. Both goals can be accomplished and the result is Pareto optimal ex ante and ex post.

Now consider the case of asymmetric information, where $\hat{x}$ is observed solely by the firm. An optimal contract maximizes (3) subject to the additional constraints

$$x_1 f(n_1) - b_1 \geq x_1 f(n_2) - b_2 \tag{5a}$$

$$x_2 f(n_2) - b_2 \geq x_2 f(n_1) - b_1 \, . \tag{5b}$$

These inequalities are known as "incentive-compatibility" constraints. The first says that the firm cannot increase profits by reporting state 2 when state 1 has occurred, and the second is the analogous condition for state 2.[8] If one of these constraints is binding, it turns out that employment will depend on α and, because α can depend upon the price level, a model where money matters may result. In addition, with these extra constraints, the goals of efficient risk sharing and efficient resource allocation will be in conflict; they can not both be accomplished simultaneously.

Proposition 1 suggests that cheating will only be a problem in the good state, but it does not constitute a proof that only the second constraint in (5) is binding. Here, we are helped by a result due to Hart.

LEMMA 1. *The constraints (5a) and (5b) can be replaced by (5b) and* $n_2 \geq n_1$.

PROOF. This is Hart's (1983) Result 1.

Our strategy is as follows. We maximize (3), assuming that only the second constraint, (5b), is binding. Then, we show that n_2 is greater than n_1, and conclude that the second constraint in Lemma 1 is not binding.

The first-order conditions for this optimization characterize the optimal asymmetric-information contract, $C^a = \{n_i^a, b_i^a\}$. After some rearrangement, they become along with (5b),

$$x_1 f'(n_1^a) = R + \mu(x_2 - x_1) f'(n_1^a)/[w\alpha U'(b_1^a - Rn_1^a)] \, , \tag{6a}$$

$$x_2 f'(n_2^a) = R \, , \tag{6b}$$

$$wU'(b_1^a - Rn_1^a) + \mu/\alpha = (1 - w)V'(x_1^a f(n_1^a) - b_1^a) \, , \tag{6c}$$

$$wU'(b_2^a - Rn_2^a) - \mu/\alpha = (1 - w)V'(x_2^a f(n_2^a) - b_2^a) \, , \tag{6d}$$

[8]We have ruled out intertemporal resolutions of the incentive problem. However, the literature on enduring relations (see Townsend 1982 for example) suggests that it might be difficult for a firm to lie period after period, even if shocks are never observed by workers. This result depends on the firms caring sufficiently about the future.

where μ is the (strictly positive) Lagrange multiplier corresponding to the binding constraint (5b).[9]

Proposition 2 describes the "employment problem" resulting from contracting under asymmetric information. Employment is inefficiently low in the bad state in that the marginal product of labor is greater than the reservation wage, R. R is constant; thus, the level of employment under asymmetric information is also lower than under symmetric information.

PROPOSITION 2.

(i) *In the asymmetric information equilibrium, employment in the good state is efficient, while employment in the bad state is inefficiently low.*
(ii) $n_1^a < n_1^s < n_2^s = n_2^a$.

PROOF. Marginal productivity is equal to the reservation wage in the good state, and greater than the reservation wage in the bad state. This establishes (i). Result (ii) follows from (i), (4a), (6a), and (6b).

With alternative specifications of preferences, it is possible to end up with overemployment in the good state and efficient employment in the bad. Cooper (1983) and Chari (1983) have shown that this will occur if firms are risk neutral and there are positive income effects on leisure. Most macroeconomists would not want to characterize the "employment problem" as too much activity in good times, so we have chosen a specification that gives underemployment in bad times.

By (5b) and (6a)–(6d), it is clear that the optimal contract under asymmetric information will depend only upon α and the realization of $\hat{x}$.[10] The result that is important for the positive correlation between monetary innovations and output is that employment in the bad state is an increasing function of the conditional probability α.[11]

PROPOSITION 3.

(i) $\partial n_1/\partial\alpha > 0$.
(ii) $\partial n_2/\partial\alpha = 0$.

PROOF. Result (ii) follows directly from equation (6b). Result (i) follows from totally differentiating the other first-order conditions and solving for $\partial n_1/\partial\alpha$, a tedious but straightforward task.

The intuition for the above result is as follows. Recall that in the symmetric-information contract, the firm was tempted to lie in the good state. By reporting the bad state, the firm got a lower wage bill, and employment did not fall enough to

[9]The nonlinearity of the constraint raises the possibility of nonuniqueness. However, if new variables $Z_i = f(n_i)$ are defined, then the objective function is concave, and the constraint is linear in the Z_is. So, uniqueness is not a problem.

[10]We have assumed that employment and the wage are determined once the firm reports x. However, it is possible that allowing n_i and b_i to be random (possibly depending on observed prices) might allow the incentive-compatibility constraints to be met at lower cost. Hart (1983) discusses why this may be difficult.

[11]Cantor (1986) and Cantor and Driskill (1988) present models where contracts are less than fully contingent and depend upon prices. In their frameworks a high money shock reduces output. This is because high prices signal low productivity and thus lower employment.

make revenue decrease by as much as the wage bill. The asymmetric-information contract discourages this in two ways. First, it shifts wages out of the good state and into the bad. This is captured in (6c) and (6d) and distorts risk sharing. Second, the asymmetric-information contract lowers employment, and hence revenue, in the bad state. This is captured in (6a), and it leads to inefficiently low employment in that state. The latter approach is only painful if the bad state actually occurs. If the probability of the bad state, α, is small, then it is optimal to make more use of the second approach and have very low employment in the bad state. If, on the other hand, the bad state is likely to occur, then it is better to put more distortion in risk sharing and have more employment in the bad state.

2. GENERAL EQUILIBRIUM AND THE PRICE-OUTPUT CORRELATION

In this section we specify the macroeconomy and compute the equilibrium. We also demonstrate that Proposition 3 leads to a positive price-output correlation.

Let there be a continuum of firms, each producing the same good. The firms can be categorized by the productivity shock they draw in period $t + 1$. Firms of type i draw the local productivity shock x_{i}. There is also an aggregate productivity shock, $\hat{z}_{t+1}$, which is the proportion of the firms that are of type i. The aggregate shock can take two values, z_1 and z_2, where $z_1 > z_2$. Thus we call z_1 the bad aggregate state since more firms are drawing the bad local state. The aggregate shock is assumed to follow a Markov process

$$\pi_k = \mathrm{Prob}(\hat{z}_{t+1} = z_1 | \hat{z}_t = z_k),\ k = 1, 2\ , \qquad (7)$$

where $\pi_1 > \pi_2$. The fact that π_1 is greater that π_2 indicates that the aggregate shock is serially correlated; the bad state is more likely to occur in period $t + 1$ if it occurred in period t.

In order to compute aggregate output we must first describe in more detail the information structure on which contracting is based. Consider the contract for period $t + 1$, which is written at the end of period t. As shown in the last section, this contract will depend upon the realization of the local productivity shock in period $t + 1$ and its conditional probability at the time the contract is written. The information this probability is conditioned upon can include any data known by both the firm and its workers at the end of period t. At the end of period t, the current price level is known, but we assume that other aggregate data becomes available with a one-period lag. In particular, the period-t aggregate productivity shock and the period-t velocity shock are not available until the end of period $t + 1$. Thus, the information available at the end period t includes all current and past prices, all current and past local productivity shocks, and all aggregate shocks dated $t - 1$ and earlier.[12]

[12]Workers do not observe local productivity shocks directly, but the incentive-compatibility constraints ensure that the firms will report them accurately.

This information structure captures the notion, which is central to the islands model, that prices are observed before aggregate output is known. However, it is at odds with the Gray (1976) model in that it does not allow period $t + 1$ contracts to depend on period $t + 1$ prices. We think our assumption is reasonable. Period $t + 1$ prices are a result of period $t + 1$ output, which in turn depends upon the period $t + 1$ contract.

We conjecture (and later show) that the only useful local information is the current productivity shock. An implication of the above conjecture is that all firms which draw x_i at time $t + 1$ and x_j at time t will have the same output. We denote this output by $y_{ij,\ t+1}$ in order to recognize its dependency on the time t and $t + 1$ local shocks, but it will depend upon the realizations of past aggregate shocks as well. Suppose $\hat{z}_{t+1} = z_h$ and $\hat{z}_t = z_k$. Since the zs are the proportion of the firms drawing bad local productivity shocks, the log of aggregate output in period $t + 1$ is

$$q_{hk,t+1} = \log[z_h z_k y_{11,t+1} + z_h(1 - z_k)y_{12,t+1} + (1 - z_h)z_k y_{21,t+1} + (1 - z_h)(1 - z_k)y_{22,t+1}],\ h,k = 1,2\ . \tag{8}$$

Let the conditional probability that the firm will draw x_1 at time $t + 1$ be denoted by

$$\alpha_{j,t+1} = \text{Prob}(\hat{x}_{t+1} = x_1 | \Omega_{j,t})\ , \tag{9}$$

where $\Omega_{j,t} = \{p_t, \hat{x}_t = x_j, D_{t-1}\}$ and D_{t-1} is the set of all aggregate information dated $t - 1$ and earlier. Because the only local information useful in computing the conditional probability is the time t local shock, all firms which draw the local shock x_j at time t will compute the same conditional probability.

Existence of Equilibrium

Let $\hat{z}_t = z_k$ *and* $\hat{z}_{t-1} = z_n$. Following Calvo and Phelps (1977), we close the model with a Cambridge equation

$$m_t + v_t = p_t + q_{kn,t}\ , \tag{10}$$

where m_t is the log of the known part of the money supply, p_t is the log of the price of output, and v_t is either a random velocity disturbance or an unanticipated monetary innovation. It will be assumed that the vs are independent and identically distributed. It might seem that the specification of a Cambridge equation is unnecessarily ad hoc. However, as shall be seen, any specification of money demand which results in a price which is strictly increasing in the money supply and strictly decreasing in output would give similar results.

We assume that agents are rational in the sense that their subjective probability distributions are identical to probability distributions generated by the model. To show that an equilibrium exists, we must make the conditional probabilities (9) consistent with market clearing (10), where output is given by (8). This is done in steps represented by a series of lemmas and, finally, Proposition 4. The proofs of the lemmas are straightforward, but tedious, involving the repeated application of Bayes' formula; they are relegated to an appendix.

The first step is to relate the conditional probability (9) to the probability of the bad aggregate shock in period $t + 1$.

LEMMA 2. $\alpha_{j,t+1} = z_2 + (z_1 - z_2)\text{Prob}(\hat{z}_{t+1} = z_1|\Omega_{j,t})$.

The second step is to relate the probability of the bad state in period $t + 1$ to the probability of the bad state in t.

LEMMA 3. $\text{Prob}(\hat{z}_{t+1} = z_1|\Omega_{j,t}) = \pi_2 + (\pi_1 - \pi_2)\text{Prob}(\hat{z}_t = z_1|\Omega_{j,t})$.

The third step is to relate the probability of the bad aggregate state in period t to the price level in t. Let $\beta_{j,t} \equiv \text{Prob}(\hat{z}_t = z_1|\Omega_{j,t})$. The subscript j recognizes the dependency of this conditional probability on the firm's local productivity shock in period t. However, the probability depends upon realizations of past aggregate shocks as well. Denote the density function of p_t, conditional on $(\hat{x}_t,\hat{z}_t,D_{t-1})$, by $g(p_t|\hat{x}_t,\hat{z}_t,D_{t-1})$. It will be assumed that v_t has a continuous distribution; hence g is a density function rather than a probability.

LEMMA 4. *Suppose that* $\hat{z}_{t-1} = z_n$ $(n = 1,2)$, *then*

$$\beta_{j,t} = \frac{g(p_t|z_1,z_n)}{g(p_t|z_1,z_n) + c_{jn}g(p_t|z_2,z_n)} ,$$

where $c_{1n} \equiv z_2(1 - \pi_n)/(z_1\pi_n)$ *and* $c_{2n} \equiv (1 - z_2)(1 - \pi_n)/[(1 - z_1)\pi_n]$.

By lemmas 2–4, the problem of calculating $\alpha_{j,t+1}$ can be reduced to the problem of calculating two conditional densities of p_t. This confirms our claim that the imposition of a Cambridge money demand function is not overly restrictive. It is only necessary that the price level be monotonic in velocity and output. Calculating the densities can be done using (8) and (10), once the probability distribution of the velocity shock, v_t, is specified. For simplicity, we will assume that the distribution of the velocity shock is normal.[13]

$$v_t \sim N(0,\sigma^2) . \tag{11}$$

[13]The distribution of the velocity shock must be continuous (and have a "large" support) or else the size of price movements will indicate whether they are caused by real or monetary shocks. There must be a confounding of real and monetary disturbances for a monetary model to emerge. The distribution need not be normal, however. If $h(v_t)$ is the density function of the velocity shock, and if h'/h is strictly increasing, then the same results are obtained. This is true of the normal, gamma, and logistic distributions. It is not true of the uniform distribution, but with this distribution prices convey no information about the aggregate productivity shock.

If the time t aggregate shock is $\hat{z}_t = z_k$ and the time $t - 1$ shock is z_n, then

$$p_t = m_t - q_{kn,t} + v_t \,, \tag{12}$$

where $q_{kn,t}$ is given by (8). Thus, given $q_{kn,t}$, the price level also has a normal distribution[14]

$$p_t \sim N(m_t - q_{kn,t}, \sigma^2) \,. \tag{13}$$

Agents do not know the current aggregate productivity shock, but they have enough information to calculate what output would be if $\hat{z}_t = z_1$ or $\hat{z}_t = z_2$ has occurred. Thus, they can calculate $q_{kn,t}$ for $k = 1, 2$.

PROPOSITION 4. *Existence of Equilibrium.*

(i) $\alpha_{j,t+1} = a + b\beta_{j,t}$,

where $a \equiv z_2 + (z_1 - z_2)\pi_2$ *and* $b \equiv (z_1 - z_2)(\pi_1 - \pi_2)$.

(ii) $\beta_{j,t} = \dfrac{n(p_t - m_t + q_{1n,t})}{n(p_t - m_t + q_{1n,t}) + c_{jn}n(p_t - m_t + q_{2n,t})}$,

where c_{jn} *is defined in Lemma* 4, $z_{t-1} = z_n$ *and* $n(\bullet)$ *is the density function associated with the normal distribution with mean* 0 *and variance* σ^2.

PROOF. (i) follows directly from Lemma 2, Lemma 3, and Lemma 4. (ii) follows from Lemma 4, (11), and (12).

By Proposition 4, local information dated prior to t does not help in computing $\alpha_{j,t+1}$. Thus, our earlier conjecture that D_{t-1} does not contain any local information is borne out.

The Price-Output Correlation

Now we can investigate the relationship between price movements in period t and movements in aggregate output in period $t + 1$. Price movements are transmitted to output through the conditional probability of the bad aggregate state in period t, $\beta_{j,t}$. Hence, we need to know how price movements affect this variable.

First, we define a benchmark price level, p_t^*.

$$\begin{aligned} p_t^* &= E(m_t + v_t | D_{t-1}) - .5(q_{1n,t} + q_{2n,t}) \\ &= m_t - .5(q_{1n,t} + q_{2n,t}) \,, \end{aligned} \tag{14}$$

where E is the expectation operator. Note that p_t^* depends on the time $t - 1$ aggregate shock, $\hat{z}_{t-1} = z_n$. Lemma 5 shows that p_t^* is the "uninformative" price in

[14]Note that p_t and its distribution do not depend on $\alpha_{j,t+1}$, the distribution we are trying to find.

the sense that if p_t is equal to p_t^*, the posterior distribution of $\beta_{j,t}$ is equal to its prior distribution:

LEMMA 5. *If $p_t = p_t^*$, then*

$$\beta_{j,t} = \frac{n(p_t - p_t^* - \phi_t)}{n(p_t - p_t^* - \phi_t) + c_{jn}n(p_t - p_t^* + \phi_t)}$$

$$= \text{Prob}(\hat{z}_t = z_1 \mid \hat{x}_t = x_1, D_{t-1}) \; .$$

where $\phi_t \equiv (1/2)(q_{2n,t} - q_{1n,t}) > 0$.

PROOF. This follows from substituting (14) into (ii) of Proposition 4 and utilizing the symmetry of the normal distribution.

The positive correlation between the price level and output is established in Proposition 5:

PROPOSITION 5.

(i) $\partial\alpha_{j,t+1}/\partial p_t = b\partial\beta_{j,t}/\partial p_t$

$$= 2b\beta_{j,t}^2 c_{jn}(\phi_t/\sigma^2)\exp[-2\phi_t(p_t - p_t^*)/\sigma^2] > 0, \; j,n = 1,2$$

(ii) $\partial q_{hk,t+1}/\partial p_t > 0, \; h,k = 1,2.$

PROOF. The first equality in (i) follows from Proposition 4. The second is obtained by differentiating the expression for $\beta_{j,t}$ given in Lemma 5 with respect to p_t. By (i) and Proposition 3, employment and output at firms drawing the bad local productivity shock in period $t + 1$ goes up, while employment and output at firms drawing the good local shock in period $t + 1$ is unaffected; this establishes (ii).

3. FURTHER MACROECONOMIC IMPLICATIONS

In the last section we showed that the imposition of asymmetric information in the optimal contract model is capable of generating a positive correlation between lagged prices and output; this implies a positive correlation between lagged monetary innovations and real economic activity. In this section, we discuss the policy implications and compare them to those of the islands models of Lucas (1972) and Barro (1976) and the disequilibrium contract models of Gray (1976) and Fischer (1977).

The model presented here shares an important policy implication with the islands and disequilibrium contract models. While perfectly anticipated movements in the money supply have no real effects, a benevolent monetary authority may be tempted to create a "surprise" increase.

PROPOSITION 6.

(i) *A change in the value of m_t has no effect on local employment or on aggregate output.*

(ii) *A positive monetary innovation in period t increases employment in period* $t + 1$.

PROOF. (12) implies that $\partial p_t / \partial m_t = 1$. Thus, Proposition 4, (ii) implies that a change in m_t has no effect on $\beta_{j,t}$. This establishes (i). (12) also implies that $\partial p_t / V_t > 0$; so Proposition 5 implies that $\partial \alpha_{j,t+1} / \partial v_t > 0$. (ii) then follows from Propositions 2 and 3.

A benevolent monetary authority might thus conclude that monetary surprises are good. At the expense of some inflation, employment and output can be increased, ameliorating the underemployment problem caused by asymmetric information. The present monetary model rationalizes a loss function for the monetary authority similar to the one posited in Barro and Gordon (1983) and in much of the literature on monetary policy games that followed. Barro and Gordon's rationalization rode on the existence of tax distortions; the new rationalization rides on the existence of private information.[15]

Another implication of our approach is that a monetary policy that made the price level fully revealing of the firms' private information would raise the average level of employment and output. The optimal symmetric-information contract could be implemented. Employment at firms drawing the bad state would increase, while employment at firms drawing the good state would be unaffected. This is a very unusual result. In the islands and disequilibrium-contract models monetary surprises cause employment to fluctuate around the natural rate. If prices became fully revealing, employment would stabilize at this rate, but the natural rate itself would not be affected. It should be noted, however, that no such policy can exist in the particular framework we employ here; at best, monetary policy can make the price level reveal the current aggregate productivity shock (by offsetting velocity shocks).

Consider finally a countercyclical demand policy that (partially) offsets demand disturbances before they pass on to prices and output. In particular, suppose that the monetary authority has an information advantage over the private sector and can therefore predict certain fluctuations in aggregate demand that the private sector cannot. In terms of the simple framework above, we decompose the velocity shock into a prediction (by the monetary authority) and a prediction error, and we let both components be distributed normally; this preserves the normality of the whole shock. The countercyclical policy we have in mind accommodates the predictable part, leaving only the prediction error to pass on to the price level and confound its signal. Clearly, the effect of this demand management policy is to reduce the variance of the velocity shock. The effect of such a policy on agents' decision making is given in Proposition 7.

PROPOSITION 7. *A decrease in the variance of velocity increases the responsiveness of output to prices.*

[15]In the loss function, we would have to replace Barro and Gordon's price prediction error with a money prediction error; the implications for monetary policy games would be unchanged. Of course, the present model does not rationalize the actual inflation term in the loss function.

PROOF. Differentiating the expression for $\beta_{j,t}$ in Lemma 5 with respect to σ^2 yields

$$\partial\beta_{j,t}/\partial\sigma^2 = 2\phi_t\beta_{j,t}^2 c_{jn}\,[(p_t^* - p_t)/\sigma^4]\exp[-2\phi_t(p_t - p_t^*)/\sigma^2]\ ,$$

for $j,n = 1,2$. $q_{hk,t+1}$, is strictly increasing in $\beta_{j,t}$ $(h,k = 1,2)$, thus, $\partial q_{hk,t+1}/\partial\sigma^2 > 0$ if and only if $p^*_t > p_t$.

A demand management policy increases the responsiveness of employment at firms drawing bad (local) shocks to price fluctuations in the preceding period; aggregate output also becomes more responsive to price fluctuations in the preceding period. This is of course a property that is shared with the contract-cum-indexing model of Gray (1976). As the variance of monetary disturbances decreases and the aggregate price level becomes a better signal of productivity shocks, the optimal indexing parameter in her model increases and supply becomes more responsive to price movements. The islands models have a similar property. As the variance of monetary disturbances decreases, local prices become better signals of real shocks, and aggregate supply becomes more responsive to average price movements.

4. CONCLUSION

The task we set out for ourselves when we began this study was to complete the analysis of Calvo and Phelps (1977) and to present their model in a form that would be attractive to macroeconomists. We show that adding information asymmetries to optimal-contract models produces a monetary model. Unanticipated increases in the money supply increase employment and output. The policy implications are largely similar to those of the disequilibrium contract and islands models. Anticipated movements in the money supply have no real effects. A monetary policy that partially offsets monetary disturbances improves the quality of information embodied in the price level and increases employment and output responses to price fluctuations.

However, there are ways in which the model contrasts sharply with the more popular monetary models. The interpretation of the "employment problem" is quite specific, and not closely related to the notions of Keynesian unemployment or neoclassical search: efficiency in the allocation of labor must be traded off with efficiency in the allocation of risk; these goals cannot be achieved simultaneously with asymmetric information. In addition, one policy conclusion stands out: a policy that makes prices fully revealing (if such a policy exists) raises the average level of employment.

APPENDIX

In this appendix, we provide proofs for Lemmas 2, 3, and 4. As stated in the main text, the proofs basically involve repeated use of Bayes' formula.

PROOF OF LEMMA 2

$$\alpha_{j,t+1} \equiv \text{Prob}[\hat{x}_{t+1} = x_1|\Omega_{j,t}]$$
$$= \text{Prob}[\hat{x}_{t+1} = 1, \hat{z}_{t+1} = z_1|\Omega_{j,t}] + \text{Prob}[\hat{x}_{t+1} = x_1, \hat{z}_{t+1} = z_2|\Omega_{j,t}]$$
$$= z_1\text{Prob}[\hat{z}_{t+1} = z_1|\Omega_{j,t}] + z_2\text{Prob}[\hat{z}_{t+1} = z_2|\Omega_{j,t}]$$
$$= z_2 + (z_1 - z_2)\text{Prob}[\hat{z}_{t+1} = z_1|\Omega_{j,t}] .$$

PROOF OF LEMMA 3

$$\text{Prob}[\hat{z}_{t+1} = z_1|\Omega_{j,t}]$$
$$= \text{Prob}[\hat{z}_{t+1} = z_1, \hat{z}_t = z_1|\Omega_{j,t}] + \text{Prob}[\hat{z}_{t+1} = z_1, \hat{z}_t = z_2|\Omega_{j,t}]$$
$$= \pi_1\text{Prob}[\hat{z}_t = z_1|\Omega_{j,t}] + \pi_2\text{Prob}[\hat{z}_t = z_2|\Omega_{j,t}]$$
$$= \pi_2 + (\pi_1 - \pi_2)\text{Prob}[\hat{z}_t = z_1|\Omega_{j,t}] .$$

PROOF OF LEMMA 4.

$$\text{Prob}(\hat{z}_t = z_1|\Omega_{j,t}) = \text{Prob}(\hat{z}_t = z_1|p_t, \hat{x}_t = x_j, D_{t-1})$$
$$= g(z_1, p_t, x_j|D_{t-1})/\Sigma_{s=1}^2 g(z_s, p_t, x_j|D_{t-1})$$
$$= g(p_t|z_1, D_{t-1})\text{Prob}(\hat{x}_t = x_j|z_1, D_{t-1})\text{Prob}(\hat{z}_t = z_1|D_{t-1})/$$
$$\Sigma_{s=1}^2 g(p_t|z_s, D_{t-1})\text{Prob}(\hat{x}_t = x_j|z_s, D_{t-1})\text{Prob}(\hat{z}_t = z_s|D_{t-1}) ,$$

where $g(p_t, x_t, z_t, D_{t-1})$ is the density function of (p_t, x_t, z_t, D_{t-1}). Clearly x_t does not help in predicting p_t once z_t is given.

LITERATURE CITED

Azariadis, Costas. "Implicit Contracts and Underemployment Equilibria." *Journal of Political Economy* 83 (December 1975), 1183–1202.

Baily, Martin N. "Wages and Employment under Uncertain Demand." *Review of Economic Studies* 41 (January 1974), 37–50.

Barro, Robert J. "Rational Expectations and the Role of Monetary Policy." *Journal of Monetary Economics* 2 (January 1976), 1–32.

______. "Long-Term Contracting, Sticky Prices, and Monetary Policy." *Journal of Monetary Economics* 3 (July 1977), 305–16.

Barro, Robert J., and David Gordon. "Rules, Discretion and Reputation in a Model of Monetary Policy." *Journal of Monetary Economics* 12 (July 1983), 101–21.

Calvo, Guillermo, and Edmund Phelps. "Employment and Wage Contingent Contracts." *Journal of Monetary Economics* 5 (supplement 1977), 160–68.

Cantor, Richard. "A Macroeconomic Model with Auction Markets and Nominal Contracts." *American Economic Review* 76 (March 1986), 204–11.

Cantor, Richard, and Robert Driskill. "Open-Economy Macro Policies and the Micro Foundation of Labor Market Arrangements." *Journal of International Economics* 24 (1988) 159–72.

Canzoneri, Matthew, and Anne Sibert. "The Macroeconomic Implications of Labor Contracting with Asymmetric Information." International Finance Discussion Papers: Board of Governors of the Federal Reserve System, No. 248, 1984.

Chari, V. "Involuntary Unemployment and Implicit Contracts." *Quarterly Journal of Economics* 98 (supplement 1983), 107–22.

Cooper, Russell. "A Note on Overemployment/Underemployment in Labor Contracts under Asymmetric Information." *Economic Letters* 12 (1983), 81–87.

Dasgupta, Partha, Peter Hammond, and Eric Maskin. "The Implementation of Social Choice Rules: Some General Results on Incentive Compatibility." *Review of Economic Studies* 46 (April 1979), 185–216.

Fischer, Stanley. "Long-term Contracts, Rational Expectations, and the Optimal Money Supply Rule." *Journal of Political Economy* 85 (February 1977), 191–205.

Gordon, Donald. "A Neoclassical Theory of Keynesian Unemployment." *Economic Inquiry* 12 (December 1974), 431–59.

Gray, Jo Anna. "Wage Indexation: A Macroeconomic Approach." *Journal of Monetary Economics* 2 (April 1976), 221–35.

Grossman, Sanford, Oliver Hart, and Eric Maskin. "Unemployment with Observable Aggregate Shocks." *Journal of Political Economy* 91 (December 1983), 907–28.

Harris, Milton, and Robert Townsend. "Resource Allocation under Asymmetric Information." *Econometrica* 49 (January 1981), 33–64.

Hart, Oliver. "Optimal Labor Contracts under Asymmetric Information." *Review of Economic Studies* 50 (January 1983), 3–35.

Lucas, Robert. "Expectations and the Neutrality of Money." *Journal of Economic Theory* 4 (April 1972), 103–24.

———. "Tobin and Monetarism: A Review Article." *Journal of Economic Literature* 19 (June 1981), 558–67.

Reagan, Patricia B., and Rene M. Stulz. "Risk-Bearing, Labor Contracts and Capital Markets." In *Research in Finance,* vol. 6, edited by Andrew H. Chen, pp. 217–31. Greenwich, Conn.: Jai Press, Inc., 1986.

Townsend, Robert "Optimal Multiperiod Contracts and the Gain from Enduring Relationships under Private Information." *Journal of Political Economy* 90 (December 1982), 1166–86.

REUVEN GLICK
MICHAEL HUTCHISON

New Results in Support of the Fiscal Policy Ineffectiveness Proposition

1. INTRODUCTION

THE "POLICY INEFFECTIVENESS" PROPOSITION of the new classical macroeconomics theory is well known. Under the joint hypotheses of rational expectations and flexible prices, anticipated money and fiscal policy should not influence real output in the short run; only surprises matter.[1]

Recent empirical work has not provided much support for this proposition. Early work by Barro (1977, 1978) appeared to support the proposition that only money surprises affect U.S. real output. However, later research by Mishkin (1982a, b), Gordon (1982), and Makin (1982), among others has cast substantial doubt on these early findings by suggesting that both anticipated and unanticipated changes in money influence output. Several recent studies (McElhattan 1982 and Laumas and McMillin 1984) that have conducted analogous tests of the effects of fiscal policy have found that anticipated and unanticipated fiscal policy changes affect U.S. real output in the short run as well. These independent results concerning the short-term

[1]The new classical theory has its origins in Friedman (1968) and Lucas (1972). Important later statements can be found in Sargent and Wallace (1975) and McCallum and Whitaker (1979). In recent years the theory has found its way into macroeconomic textbooks, for example, Parkin (1984, chapter 24), and Hall and Taylor (1986, chapter 13).

The authors thank Carl Walsh, Dan Friedman, and two anonymous referees for helpful comments on an earlier draft of this paper. Research assistance by Kimberly Luce and John Duffy is gratefully acknowledged. The opinions expressed herein are those of the authors and do not necessarily reflect the views of the Federal Reserve Bank of San Francisco, the Board of Governors of the Federal Reserve System, or the University of California.

REUVEN GLICK *is senior economist at the Federal Reserve Bank of San Francisco.* MICHAEL HUTCHISON *is assistant professor of economics at the University of California at Santa Cruz.*

Journal of Money, Credit, and Banking, Vol. 22, No. 3 (August 1990)

nonneutrality of anticipated monetary policy, on one hand, and of anticipated fiscal policy on the other hand, appear to concur in rejecting the hypothesis of policy ineffectiveness.

There is reason to view this rejection of the policy ineffectiveness proposition with some skepticism, however, because none of these studies investigate the effects of monetary and fiscal policy simultaneously. Real output is affected by a large number of factors, but excluding either monetary or fiscal policy would seem to create the greatest potential shortcoming. Typically, real output is regressed either on anticipated and unanticipated money growth, or on anticipated and unanticipated fiscal stimulus, where the anticipated policy variables are the predicted values from policy equations. To the extent that either anticipated or unanticipated monetary and fiscal policy actions are correlated with each other, previous tests of money neutrality that exclude fiscal variables and tests of fiscal neutrality that exclude monetary variables suffer from an omitted variables problem leading to biased coefficient estimates.

Interactive monetary and fiscal actions create the potential for an omitted variable problem in previous tests of policy neutrality. Sargent and Wallace (1975, 1981) argue on theoretical grounds that government deficits lead to more rapid money growth either contemporaneously or in the future under a fairly general set of circumstances. Empirical support for this relationship using U.S. time series data is reported by Hamburger and Zwick (1981), Levy (1981), Allen and Smith (1983), and Grier and Neiman (1987). Regardless of direct causal linkages, interaction effects may also be induced by monetary and fiscal responses to common shocks. For example, systematic monetary and fiscal responses to unemployment changes through feedback rules may cause covariation in policies. Section 2 briefly discusses the extent of the bias that results from omitting variables when testing policy neutrality in the presence of such interactions.

In the remaining sections of the paper we address the omitted variables problem associated with policy interaction effects by conducting joint tests of the effects of both anticipated and unanticipated monetary and fiscal policy on U.S. real output fluctuations. We reproduce the basic results of previous studies that, when tested separately, anticipated and unanticipated money on one hand and anticipated and unanticipated fiscal policy on the other are significant determinants of real output fluctuations. Our joint tests, however, suggest that fiscal policy is insignificant, while anticipated as well as unanticipated monetary policy remain significant in the short run. The rather surprising support for the fiscal ineffectiveness proposition proves robust to a wide variety of empirical model specifications and estimation procedures. Moreover, our joint tests cannot reject the hypothesis that in the long run all policies, either anticipated or unanticipated, are neutral.

In section 3 money growth and fiscal policy equations are specified using an atheoretical vector autoregression methodology, as in Mishkin (1982a, b) and Laumas and McMillin (1984). The predicted values from these equations serve as our measures of anticipated policy actions and are used to decompose actual policy movements into their unanticipated components. Contemporaneous and lagged values of these anticipated and unanticipated policy components are used as the explanatory variables in an equation for real output changes. These results are discussed in section 4. Several variants of this equation are estimated to test the robustness of earlier studies investigating the effects of anticipated and unanticipated policy actions. Section 5 investigates the robustness of the results to a variety of empirical model specifications and estimation procedures. A brief summary and conclusion follows in section 6.

2. OMITTED VARIABLES BIAS IN TESTS OF THE POLICY INEFFECTIVENESS PROPOSITION

Previous tests of the policy ineffectiveness proposition have typically regressed real output fluctuations either on anticipated and unanticipated money growth or on anticipated and unanticipated fiscal surpluses. As argued above, these output equations are likely to suffer from an omitted variables problem which biases tests of the policy ineffectiveness proposition if monetary and fiscal policies are causally related or covary in response to common factors.

Consider the following "true" reduced-form relation between real output growth (Y) and current and lagged values of anticipated fiscal (AF), unanticipated fiscal (UF), anticipated monetary (AM), and unanticipated monetary (UM) policy, with an orthogonal error term (ϵ):

$$Y_t = \sum_{i=0}^{n} b_{1,i}AF_{t-i} + \sum_{i=0}^{n} b_{2,i}UF_{t-i} + \sum_{i=0}^{n} c_{1,i}AM_{t-i} + \sum_{i=0}^{n} c_{2,i}UM_{t-i} + \epsilon_t \,. \quad (1)$$

If money "matters" and the set of coefficients ($c_{1,0}, \ldots c_{1,n}; c_{2,0} \ldots c_{2,n}$) are not all equal to zero, the estimated coefficients from a regression of Y_t on AF_{t-i} and UF_{t-i} alone will be biased. In the case of the coefficients for, say, anticipated fiscal policy, the extent of this bias can be calculated as

$$\sum_{k=0}^{n} c_{1,k}p_{1,ki} + \sum_{k=0}^{n} c_{2,k}p_{2,ki} \,,\; i = 0 \ldots n$$

and depends on (i) $c_{1,k}$ and $c_{2,k}$, the coefficients of the omitted variables—anticipated and unanticipated monetary policy, and (ii) $p_{1,ki}$ and $p_{2,ki}$, reflecting the correlation between the omitted variables and anticipated fiscal policy.[2]

Previous work indicates that the covariation between money growth and fiscal deficits is likely to be significant, for example, Hamburger and Zwick (1981), Levy

[2]Note the similarity between this issue and that of proper interpretation of "St. Louis" nominal income equations which include contemporaneous and lag money supplies, but exclude other (correlated) fiscal variables. See Sims (1972).

(1981), Allen and Smith (1983), and Grier and Neiman (1987), suggesting a potentially important omitted variables bias. One plausible case is that an anticipated fiscal surplus is negatively related to anticipated money growth ($p_{1,ki} < 0$), and anticipated money growth in turn is positively related to real output growth ($c_{1,k} > 0$). In this circumstance the effect on output of a rise in the fiscal surplus would be subject to a potentially significant downward bias. Thus omitting monetary variables could cause a rise in the budget surplus to appear to have a more contractionary impact than in fact is the case.

In the remainder of this paper we proceed to demonstrate the significance of this bias in prior tests of policy effectiveness.

3. MEASUREMENT OF ANTICIPATED AND UNANTICIPATED POLICY CHANGES

Our basic methodology is the two-step procedure used by Barro (1977, 1978), Makin (1982), and Kormendi and Meguire (1984), among others. In the first step of this procedure, described in this section, anticipated policy equations are specified and estimated. From these equations anticipated and unanticipated policy movements are identified and used as the explanatory variables in the (second step) equation for real output changes. Pagan (1984) has noted that the two-step procedure employed here is biased *against* acceptance of the policy neutrality null hypothesis. Our results failing to reject the null are therefore stronger than the two-step procedure suggests.[3] Nonetheless, in section 5 we discuss the robustness of our results to alternative estimation procedures including the correction for generated regressors bias.

We follow others (Mishkin 1982a, b and Laumas and McMillin 1984) in using an atheoretical statistical technique to specify anticipated policy equations since it is difficult on theoretical grounds to exclude any information available to economic agents. We include variables in our monetary and fiscal policy equations which are of macroeconomic relevance and which are easily available to the public in their attempts to predict future policy stance. As measures of monetary and fiscal policy stimulus we use the percent change in M1, denoted by M_t, and the change in the real middle-expansion trend budget deficit as a percent of potential GNP, denoted by F_t.[4] The explanatory variables included in the equations include lagged values of M_t and F_t; the unemployment rate, U_t; the percent change in the GNP deflator, P_t; the change in the three-month T-bill rate, R_t; as well as a constant, time trend, and seasonal dummies.[5]

[3]Mishkin (1982a, b) argues that joint estimation of the policy prediction equation and the output equation is preferable. Cecchetti (1986) suggests a more general procedure that allows for an incomplete information set in the prediction equation and time-varying coefficients in the output equation. The significance of different estimation techniques is discussed below in footnote 12.

[4]Real middle-expansion trend budget deficit figures were computed by deflating the nominal figures for the difference between expenditures and receipts by the GNP deflator. Potential GNP was obtained from the fitted values of a log-linear regression of GNP on time and a constant, corrected for serial correlation.

[5]Data for all variables was obtained from the Citibank data tapes, except for government expenditure and receipt figures. Nominal statistics for the latter using the middle expansion trend measure were

Theil's $\bar{R}^2$ (minimum standard error) criterion is used to specify the appropriate lag length of the variables in the two equations. We treat the set of variables in each equation in parallel fashion and impose a common lag length. Lag lengths between four and eight were estimated and the equation with the highest $\bar{R}^2$ was chosen for the fiscal and monetary prediction equations, respectively. Throughout this procedure we retain all explanatory variables irrespective of their individual or joint significance.

The choice of a common length lag structure, following Mishkin (1982a, b), has the advantage over sequential procedures designed to exclude lags on particular variables (for example, Laumas and McMillin 1984) in that the results of the latter will in general be dependent on the particular order of variables in the sequence considered. The disadvantage is that sometimes insignificant lags are included in the equations, which gives less efficient estimators. Unbiased estimates of the regressors are obtained, however, and this presumably is the most important criterion for prediction purposes.

The choice of retaining all explanatory variables contrasts with McMillin and Laumas and Mishkin who drop particular sets of variables in their final specifications if they are not jointly significant (at the .05 level). While our approach implies that sometimes insignificant variables are included in the equations with some loss of efficiency, as with the choice of maintaining a common lag length, it lessens some of the arbitrariness in explanatory variable selection. We examine the sensitivity of these results to an alternative procedure for choosing the equation in section 5.

The policy equations are estimated with quarterly data over the 1960:4–1985:4 period.[6] The highest $\bar{R}^2$ is found at seven lags for both the monetary and fiscal anticipated policy equations. The coefficient estimates and summary statistics are presented in Table 1. F-statistics for the null hypothesis that the coefficients of each lagged set of explanatory variables are not significantly different from zero are presented in Table 2.

Similarly to Laumas and McMillin (1984), lagged unemployment is a joint significant predictor of the budget surplus (at the .07 level). In contrast to Laumas and McMillin, we find lagged price inflation is also significant (at .07), while the lagged budget surplus (with a significance level of .55) is not.[7] Similarly to Mishkin, we find lagged money and interest rates play a significant role in predicting money. Unemployment plays a significant role in predicting money as well as the budget surplus, creating the potential for covariation in the two series. The lagged budget surplus

---

obtained from the *Survey of Current Business,* May 1987 (1985:1–1985:4), November 1986 (1984:1–1984:4), March 1985 (1981:1–1983:4), and from unpublished data provided by the Department of Commerce (1959:1–1980:4). All data, except for interest rates, are seasonally adjusted. These data are available upon request.

[6]The start point of the sample was determined by the unavailability of consistent M1 data prior to 1959:1. In addition, data on the budget surplus are available only from 1955 on.

[7]Laumas and McMillin (LM) report on $\bar{R}^2$ of 0.46 in their fiscal policy equation. We obtain an R^2 of 0.48; the corresponding $\bar{R}^2$ is 0.18. Dropping money growth and inflation from the equation "improved" the significance level of lagged budget surpluses to 0.29, still below the results of LM.

TABLE 1

ANTICIPATED FISCAL AND MONETARY POLICY EQUATIONS, 1961:1–1985:4

Explanatory Variable	F_t		M_t	
Constant	−0.34	(−0.91)	2.17	(1.74)†
M_{t-1}	0.05	(1.41)	0.51	(4.14)**
M_{t-2}	0.04	(1.18)	−0.01	(−0.04)
M_{t-3}	−0.01	(−0.19)	−0.02	(−0.13)
M_{t-4}	0.04	(1.09)	−0.12	(−0.91)
M_{t-5}	0.02	(0.60)	0.02	(0.12)
M_{t-6}	−0.02	(−0.42)	0.07	(0.50)
M_{t-7}	0.03	(0.82)	0.04	(0.32)
F_{t-1}	−0.17	(−1.40)	0.14	(0.34)
F_{t-2}	−0.12	(−1.01)	0.05	(0.13)
F_{t-3}	−0.28	(−2.39)**	−0.08	(−0.20)
F_{t-4}	−0.08	(−0.70)	0.16	(0.41)
F_{t-5}	−0.18	(−1.52)	0.01	(0.02)
F_{t-6}	−0.06	(−0.46)	−0.38	(−0.91)
F_{t-7}	−0.16	(−1.39)	−0.64	(−1.68)
U_{t-1}	−0.59	(−2.77)**	−1.49	(−2.10)*
U_{t-2}	1.02	(3.46)**	2.73	(2.75)**
U_{t-3}	−0.66	(−3.00)**	−1.30	(−1.76)†
U_{t-4}	0.08	(0.70)	−0.44	(−1.07)
U_{t-5}	0.56	(2.40)**	1.19	(1.51)
U_{t-6}	−0.93	(−3.12)**	−2.64	(−2.65)**
U_{t-7}	0.52	(2.68)**	1.71	(2.64)*
P_{t-1}	−0.04	(−0.32)	0.16	(1.10)
P_{t-2}	0.03	(0.65)	−0.08	(−0.54)
P_{t-3}	−0.05	(−1.18)	−0.07	(−0.49)
P_{t-4}	0.08	(1.78)†	0.02	(0.16)
P_{t-5}	0.08	(1.82)†	−0.20	(−1.36)
P_{t-6}	−0.07	(−1.68)	−0.13	(−0.90)
P_{t-7}	0.07	(1.59)	0.35	(2.40)*
R_{t-1}	−0.03	(−0.36)	−1.68	(−6.88)**
R_{t-2}	0.05	(0.55)	−0.10	(−0.32)
R_{t-3}	0.07	(0.67)	−0.02	(−0.07)
R_{t-4}	0.05	(0.53)	−0.04	(−0.12)
R_{t-5}	0.12	(1.26)	−0.10	(−0.29)
R_{t-6}	0.07	(0.81)	−0.44	(−1.42)
R_{t-7}	−0.03	(−0.31)	−0.16	(−0.54)
Trend	−0.02	(−2.03)*	0.03	(0.99)
$R/\bar{R}^2$	0.48/0.18		0.77/0.64	
S.E.E.	0.58		1.93	
$Q(30)$	22.1 (0.85)		19.1 (0.94)	

NOTE: F_t = change in the real high employment budget deficit relative to potential GNP, M_t = percent change in M1, U_t = unemployment rate, P_t = percent change in the GNP deflator, R_t = change in 90-day Treasury bill rate. t-statistics are in parentheses after the coefficient estimates. The marginal significance level of the Q-statistic is also in parentheses. Coefficients significant at the .10, .05, and .01 (two-tail) levels are indicated by †, *, and **, respectively.

coeficients, unlike Mishkin's result, are not jointly significant in predicting money.[8] In practical terms, these dissimilarities are not of great significance, since, as shall be seen below, we are able to reproduce the basic second-step regression results of Laumas-McMillin and Mishkin using these prediction equations.

[8]One possible explanation is the Mishkin measures the budget surplus in nominal terms, rather than in real terms as we do. Another is that Mishkin uses a different sample range, 1954:1–1976:4.

TABLE 2

F-STATISTICS FOR EXPLANATORY POWER IN ANTICIPATED POLICY EQUATIONS

Explanatory Variable	F_t		M_t	
M_{t-i}	1.08	(0.39)	3.33	(0.00)**
F_{t-i}	1.53	(0.17)	0.56	(0.78)
U_{t-i}	1.94	(0.08)†	1.95	(0.08)†
P_{t-i}	2.02	(0.07)†	1.23	(0.30)
R_{t-i}	0.50	(0.83)	10.34	(0.00)**

NOTE: See Table 1 for variable definitions. All variables are entered with seven lags. The F-statistics are distributed asymptotically F (7,63) and test the null hypothesis that the coefficients of all seven lagged coefficient values for each variable are equal to zero. The marginal significance levels are in parentheses after the F-statistics.

4. OUTPUT EFFECTS OF POLICY CHANGES

The predicted values from the estimated equations in columns (1) and (2) of Table 1 are used as measures of anticipated fiscal policy (AF_t) and monetary policy (AM_t), respectively. The corresponding residuals represent measures of unanticipated fiscal (UF_t) and monetary (UM_t) policy, respectively. The output effects of these policy changes are determined by estimating equation (1) through the regression of real output growth (Y_t) on both anticipated and unanticipated policy components over the period 1965:1–1985:4. The equation is estimated following Mishkin (1982a, b) using polynomial distributed lags (PDLs), and following Laumas and McMillin, with a fifth-degree polynomial with sixteen lags and a far-end constraint.[9,10] This specification is motivated by the intent to best put our results into perspective with the prior work of these authors.

The estimated results of equation (1) are presented in Table 3. Column (1) of Table 3 presents the coefficient estimation results from regressing real output growth on anticipated and unanticipated fiscal policy only, and may be compared to Laumas and McMillin. The second column presents the results from regressing real output growth on anticipated and unanticipated money, and may be compared to Mishkin. The last column of Table 3 includes both money and fiscal policy, anticipated and unanticipated, in the real output growth equation. Table 4 presents F-statistics and the corresponding marginal significance levels for the null hypothesis that all coefficients for each set of policy variables (AF_{t-i}, UF_{t-i}, AM_{t-i}. UM_{t-i}) are equal to zero.

The first column of Table 3 tells a story very similar to Laumas and McMillin's

[9]In Mishkin's actual specification the log of real GNP is regressed on a constant, current and twenty lagged values of anticipated and unanticipated money, and a time trend, with a correction for fourth-order autocorrelation. The coefficients for the monetary policy variables were constrained to fit along a fourth-order polynomial with the far endpoint constrained. Mishkin employs a nonlinear, least-squares estimation technique that imposes restrictions across the policy and output equations.

[10]The estimation period starts at 1965:4 to accommodate the long lags used for the explanatory variables. With the sample for money supply and budget surplus changes beginning in 1959:1, the sixteen lags on anticipated and unanticipated policy and the additional seven lags in the policy prediction equations used up the first twenty-three observations. This leaves 1965:1 as the start date. Note that while Table 2 of Laumas and McMillin (p. 470) states that their sample range extends from 1961:3 through 1982:4, this range refers to the explanatory policy variables. Given their specification of sixteen lags, the sample range of the dependent variable is 1965:4–1982:4, which is comparable to ours.

(1984, p. 471) basic results: both anticipated and unanticipated fiscal policy matter, and anticipated policy seems to matter more.[11] Both anticipated and unanticipated policy apparently have permanent impacts on real output since the sum of the individual coefficients for anticipated fiscal policy and unanticipated fiscal policy are statistically significant at the .01 and .05 percent levels, respectively. Table 4 indicates that, in addition, the joint hypothesis that anticipated fiscal policy is uncorrelated with output growth ($b_{1,i} = 0$) cannot be rejected at the .05 level.

We also reproduce Mishkin's (1982, p. 122) basic conclusions even though his time interval (1954:1–1976:4) and methodology are somewhat different: both anticipated and unanticipated money matter, but anticipated money seems to play a more important role in influencing output fluctuations.[12] As shown in Table 4, the joint hypothesis that contemporaneous and lagged anticipated money is not associated with real output growth ($c_{1,i} = 0$) is rejected at the .05 level of confidence. The hypothesis that unanticipated money is unrelated to output ($c_{2,i} = 0$) is also rejected. Initial lags on money (shown in Table 3) in both instances are generally positive and significant, and are followed by negative coefficient values at longer lags.[13] Although both sets of variables clearly play an important role in explaining short-run output fluctuations, long-term money neutrality cannot be rejected since the sums of coefficients for both anticipated and unanticipated money are not significantly different from zero.

The final estimation equation—the complete model of equation (1)—is shown in column 3 of Tables 3 and 4. The results are quite different from Laumas and McMillin. None of the individual coefficient values is significant for anticipated and unanticipated fiscal policy at the .05 level. As evidenced by the low t-statistics for the sums of the lags and the low F-statistics, the hypotheses of any short-term or long-term influence of fiscal policy on output growth is rejected. However, the joint hypothesis that either unanticipated monetary policy (UM_{t-i}) or anticipated monetary policy (AM_{t-i}) are uncorrelated with real output growth can be rejected at the .05 level of confidence.[14] Even in this case, however, both unanticipated and anticipated fiscal and monetary policy are apparently neutral in the longer term as the sum of individual coefficients is not significantly different from zero in all cases.

The earlier finding that fiscal policy influences output growth in the absence of

[11]Laumas and McMillin find AF_{t-i} is significant at lags 1–14, while UF_{t-i} is significant at lags 4 through 16.

[12]Mishkin (1982a, b) uses a nonlinear simultaneous estimation procedure for estimating the policy prediction and output equations. Cecchetti (1986) implements a more robust procedure that applies under more general assumptions. Our results conform to theirs, however, indicating that potential shortcomings in the two-step procedure may not be serious in practice. This accords with Mishkin's finding that differences between his and earlier findings by Barro (1977, 1978) and Barro and Rush (1980) are primarily due to the inclusion of lagged policy measures, not estimation techniques.

[13]Mishkin found AM_{t-i} to be significantly positive for lags 0 to 8, and significantly negative for later lags, and UM_{t-i} to be significantly positive only for lag 0.

[14]In other regressions we use unseasonally, rather than seasonally, adjusted money growth in our prediction equations. In the resulting second-stage output regression, anticipated monetary policy was found not to have any significant explanatory power in the short run either. Since we are unable to obtain seasonally adjusted data for all of the other explanatory variables in the prediction equations, we are uncertain of the robustness of this result. The role of seasonal adjustment of the data is an area we are exploring further.

TABLE 3

EFFECTS OF ANTICIPATED AND UNANTICIPATED FISCAL AND MONETARY POLICY ON REAL OUTPUT GROWTH, 1965:1–1985:4

Coefficient	(1)		(2)		(3)	
Constant	1.97	(3.89)**	4.45	(2.26)*	3.82	(1.23)
$b_{1,0}$	2.56	(2.53)*			0.52	(0.42)
$b_{1,1}$	0.18	(0.23)			−1.36	(−0.79)
$b_{1,2}$	−1.41	(−1.79)†			−2.24	(−1.13)
$b_{1,3}$	−2.33	(−3.22)**			−2.33	(−1.17)
$b_{1,4}$	−2.73	(−3.90)**			−1.84	(−0.93)
$b_{1,5}$	−2.74	(−3.74)**			−0.98	(−0.51)
$b_{1,6}$	−2.49	(−3.32)**			0.04	(0.02)
$b_{1,7}$	−2.09	(−2.89)**			1.03	(0.58)
$b_{1,8}$	−1.65	(−2.41)*			1.84	(1.09)
$b_{1,9}$	−1.24	(−1.82)†			2.36	(1.42)
$b_{1,10}$	−0.93	(−1.29)			2.49	(1.49)
$b_{1,11}$	−0.75	(−1.02)			2.23	(1.34)
$b_{1,12}$	−0.71	(−1.01)			1.60	(1.05)
$b_{1,13}$	−0.77	(−1.18)			0.73	(0.57)
$b_{1,14}$	−0.86	(−1.29)			−0.19	(−0.19)
$b_{1,15}$	−0.88	(−1.19)			−0.89	(−1.04)
$b_{1,16}$	−0.66	(−1.04)			−0.99	(−1.43)
$\sum_{i=0}^{16} b_{1,i}$	−19.52	(−3.14)**			2.01	(0.13)
$b_{2,0}$	−1.81	(−1.97)†			−1.43	(−1.66)
$b_{2,1}$	−0.30	(−0.50)			−0.35	(−0.49)
$b_{2,2}$	0.13	(0.20)			−0.16	(−0.17)
$b_{2,3}$	−0.05	(−0.07)			−0.37	(−0.35)
$b_{2,4}$	−0.47	(−0.84)			−0.67	(−0.56)
$b_{2,5}$	−0.90	(−1.64)			−0.83	(−0.66)
$b_{2,6}$	−1.22	(−2.17)*			−0.76	(−0.61)
$b_{2,7}$	−1.34	(−2.42)*			−0.45	(−0.37)
$b_{2,8}$	−1.28	(−2.36)*			0.06	(0.05)
$b_{2,9}$	−1.08	(−2.50)*			0.67	(0.62)
$b_{2,10}$	−0.80	(−1.39)			1.26	(1.18)
$b_{2,11}$	−0.54	(−0.90)			1.72	(1.61)
$b_{2,12}$	−0.35	(−0.59)			1.95	(1.83)†
$b_{2,13}$	−0.28	(−0.47)			1.89	(1.80)†
$b_{2,14}$	−0.32	(−0.50)			1.53	(1.50)
$b_{2,15}$	−0.40	(−0.59)			0.95	(1.01)
$b_{2,16}$	−0.38	(−0.68)			0.34	(0.50)
$\sum_{i=0}^{16} b_{2,i}$	−11.39	(−2.03)*			5.35	(0.47)
$c_{1,0}$			0.17	(1.13)	0.22	(1.10)
$c_{1,1}$			0.13	(1.23)	0.12	(0.78)
$c_{1,2}$			0.15	(1.33)	0.12	(0.81)
$c_{1,3}$			0.17	(1.82)†	0.16	(1.20)
$c_{1,4}$			0.19	(2.30)*	0.21	(1.60)
$c_{1,5}$			0.18	(2.15)*	0.23	(1.75)†
$c_{1,6}$			0.13	(1.56)	0.21	(1.65)
$c_{1,7}$			0.06	(0.74)	0.16	(1.30)
$c_{1,8}$			−0.02	(−0.30)	0.07	(0.64)
$c_{1,9}$			−0.12	(−1.43)	−0.04	(−0.44)
$c_{1,10}$			−0.20	(−2.34)*	−0.15	(−1.66)
$c_{1,11}$			−0.26	(−3.00)**	−0.25	(−2.60)*
$c_{1,12}$			−0.29	(−3.49)**	−0.32	(−3.08)**
$c_{1,13}$			−0.28	(−3.44)**	−0.35	(−2.96)**
$c_{1,14}$			−0.22	(−2.42)*	−0.32	(−2.35)*
$c_{1,15}$			−0.14	(−1.32)	−0.24	(−1.65)
$c_{1,16}$			−0.06	(−0.60)	−0.13	(−1.08)
$\sum_{i=0}^{16} c_{1,i}$			−0.40	(−1.22)	−0.32	(−0.56)
$c_{2,0}$			0.54	(2.21)*	0.55	(2.24)*
$c_{2,1}$			0.38	(2.34)*	0.29	(1.30)

Coefficient	(1)		(2)		(3)	
$c_{2,2}$			0.10	(0.63)	0.07	(0.26)
$c_{2,3}$			−0.18	(−1.29)	−0.10	(−0.35)
$c_{2,4}$			−0.40	(−2.98)**	−0.22	(−0.78)
$c_{2,5}$			−0.50	(−3.40)**	−0.30	(−1.07)
$c_{2,6}$			−0.49	(−3.10)**	−0.34	(−1.28)
$c_{2,7}$			−0.39	(−2.48)*	−0.35	(−1.44)
$c_{2,8}$			−0.22	(−1.51)	0.34	(−1.48)
$c_{2,9}$			−0.04	(−0.26)	−0.31	(−1.27)
$c_{2,10}$			0.12	(0.78)	−0.27	(−0.96)
$c_{2,11}$			0.21	(1.31)	−0.23	(−0.72)
$c_{2,12}$			0.22	(1.35)	−0.19	(−0.56)
$c_{2,13}$			0.13	(0.83)	−0.15	(−0.44)
$c_{2,14}$			−0.02	(−0.09)	−0.12	(−0.35)
$c_{2,15}$			−0.17	(−0.85)	−0.09	(−0.27)
$c_{2,16}$			−0.21	(−1.30)	−0.05	(−0.21)
$\sum_{i=0}^{16} c_{2,i}$			−0.90	(−0.69)	−2.14	(−1.30)
$R^2/\bar{R}^2$	0.30/0.20		0.43/0.35		0.53/0.38	
S.E.E.	3.80		3.42		3.33	
$Q(27)$	12.19 (0.99)		22.74 (0.70)		29.19 (0.35)	

NOTE: $B_{1,i}$, $b_{2,i}$, $c_{1,i}$, and $c_{2,i}$ refer to the coefficients on AF_{t-i}, UF_{t-i}, AM_{t-i} and UM_{t-i}, respectively in equation (1). t-statistics for the coefficient estimates and marginal significance levels for the Q-statistic are in parentheses. Coefficients significant at the .10, .05, and .01 (two-tail) levels are indicated by †, *, and **, respectively.

any consideration for monetary policy is apparently the result of omitted variables bias. A comparison of columns (1) and (3) of Table 3 indicates the extent of this bias. Omitting the role of monetary factors biases the coefficients for AF_{t-i} and UF_{t-i} downward; that is, it results in a seemingly significant negative effect of a rise in the budget surplus on output growth. All of the individually significant coefficients, with the exception of AF_{t-i} at lags 0 and 2, are either less negative or become positive once the monetary variables are included.

We also ran regressions over the shorter sample, 1965:1–1979:4, ending prior to a probable monetary policy regime shift. As with the results reported and discussed above, both anticipated and unanticipated fiscal policy affected GNP growth when considered alone, but not when the unanticipated and anticipated monetary policy variables were included. Interestingly, when considered alone, anticipated, but not unanticipated, monetary policy had a significant impact on output growth. When considered together with the fiscal policy variables, anticipated monetary policy was only marginally significant, while unanticipated monetary policy remained insignificant. The F-statistics, with corresponding marginal significance levels in

TABLE 4

F-STATISTICS FOR EFFECTS OF POLICY MEASURES ON REAL OUTPUT GROWTH

Explanatory Variable	(1)		(2)		(3)	
AF_{t-i}	4.88	(0.00)**			1.35	(0.26)
UF_{t-i}	1.72	(0.14)			1.10	(0.37)
AM_{t-i}			2.93	(0.02)**	2.48	(0.04)*
UM_{t-i}			3.38	(0.01)**	2.52	(0.04)*

NOTE: AF_t = anticipated fiscal policy, UF_t = unanticipated fiscal policy, AM_t = anticipated monetary policy, UM_t = unanticipated monetary policy. The F-statistics test the null hypothesis that the coefficients of contemporaneous and sixteen lagged values of each variable equal zero. The marginal significance levels are in parentheses after the F-statistics. Statistics significant at the .05 and .01 levels are indicated by * and **, respectively.

parentheses, for *AF*, *UF*, *AM*, and *UF* were .95 (.46), .98 (.44), 2.34 (.06), and .43 (.82), respectively.

In order to shed light on the linkages between monetary and fiscal policies which may account for the omitted variables bias, Granger-causality tests of the effects of the anticipated and unanticipated policy measures on anticipated policies were performed. F-statistics for the joint significance of each set of lagged variables and t-statistics for the significance of the sum of each set of lagged variables are presented in Table 5. Interaction effects between anticipated fiscal and monetary policy are clearly evident. Unanticipated money growth leads anticipated fiscal policy, and both anticipated as well as unanticipated fiscal policy lead anticipated money growth. These results indicate that the interaction effects between policies—both anticipated and unanticipated—may be complicated, but are clearly evident and should be accounted for in tests of the policy neutrality hypothesis.

The result that a rise in both the anticipated and unanticipated federal government structural budget deficit (surplus) as a percent of potential GNP leads to a rise (fall) in U.S. money growth is consistent with the predictions of Sargent and Wallace (1975, 1981), and empirical evidence of the U.S. experience offered by Hamburger and Zwick (1981), Levy (1981), Allen and Smith (1983), and Grier and Neiman (1987). Grier and Neiman, in particular, find that the U.S. structural deficit is a major determinant of monetary expansion, and that its effect on money or base money growth between 1957 and 1983 has not varied across political regimes.

The result that unanticipated money growth apparently leads to a systematic or anticipated fiscal policy response has previously been noted as a theoretical possibility by Barro (1979), who presents a model of government behavior where money-based inflation causes deficits because the government acts to keep the quantity of real bonds constant. Moreover, Dwyer (1982) presents vector autoregressive evidence that does not reject this hypothesis. Our result, consistent with Barro's (1979) argument, may be consistent with other explanations as well. For our purposes, however, the important point is that interaction effects between monetary and fiscal policies cannot be rejected.

TABLE 5

GRANGER CAUSALITY TESTS OF POLICY MEASURES, 1962:4–1985:4

Causal Variable		AF_t		AM_t	
AF_{t-i}	F	2.24	(0.04)*	3.07	(0.01)**
	Σ	−0.92	(−2.21)**	−4.34	(−1.98)**
UF_{t-i}	F	4.58	(0.00)**	1.94	(0.08)†
	Σ	−1.28	(4.39)**	−3.15	(−2.06)**
AM_{t-i}	F	1.06	(0.40)	5.21	(0.00)**
	Σ	−0.03	(1.20)	0.65	(4.90)**
UM_{t-i}	F	3.26	(0.01)*	4.92	(0.00)**
	Σ	(0.23)	(2.62)**	−0.26	(0.55)

NOTE: Causality tests are performed for regressions in which all four policy variables are entered with seven lags. The table reports F-statistics which are distributed F (7,64) and test the null hypothesis that the coefficients for each variable are equal to zero. The marginal significance levels are in parentheses. The table also reports the sum of each set of lagged variables (Σ), with the corresponding t-statistic in parentheses. Statistics significant at the .10, .05, and .01 significance levels are indicated by †, *, and **, respectively.

5. ROBUSTNESS OF RESULTS

The specifics of the empirical methodology followed in the previous sections were motivated by an attempt to maintain comparability with previous studies in this area. However, a number of questions arise as to the robustness of the fiscal ineffectiveness proposition to changes in model specification and estimation procedure. In this section, we examine the robustness of this result to (1) employing an alternative method in deriving the proxies for the anticipated and unanticipated policy measures in the first step of our estimation procedure, (2) changes in the endpoint, polynomial degree, and lag-length restrictions associated with PDL specification of the second-step output regression, and (3) correcting for the generated regressors bias associated with the policy measure proxies used in the second-step estimation.

A summary of the results for each of these robustness tests is presented in Table 6. Each panel (A–F) corresponds to a particular model specification, and is described in detail below. Column 1 shows the F-statistics (F) and marginal significance levels (in parentheses) of the null hypothesis test that the contemporaneous and lagged values of anticipated fiscal policy (AF_{t-i}) or unanticipated fiscal policy (UF_{t-i}) are jointly equal to zero when monetary variables (Am_{t-i} and UM_{t-i}) are

TABLE 6

ROBUSTNESS TESTS OF ALTERNATIVE MODEL SPECIFICATIONS FOR EFFECTS OF FISCAL POLICY ON REAL OUTPUT GROWTH

Model Specification	Variable		(1) Without AM_{t-i} and UM_{t-i}		(2) With AM_{t-i} and UM_{t-i}	
A. Policy Measures Derived from FPE Procedure	AF_{t-i}	F	3.33	(0.01)**	1.07	(0.38)
		Σ	−13.72	(−2.10)*	−1.96	(0.15)
	UF_{t-i}	F	1.28	(0.28)	.71	(0.64)
		Σ	−12.43	(−1.74)†	−4.87	(−0.61)
B. Third-Degree PDL	AF_{t-i}	F	6.52	(0.00)**	.22	(0.88)
		Σ	−17.83	(−2.94)**	−6.63	(−0.47)
	UF_{t-i}	F	2.08	(0.11)	1.04	(0.38)
		Σ	−13.14	(−2.42)*	−1.03	(−0.09)
C. No Endpoint Constraint	AF_{t-i}	F	4.34	(0.00)**	.80	(0.56)
		Σ	−18.79	(−2.96)**	1.87	(0.11)
	UF_{t-i}	F	1.29	(0.28)	.79	(0.58)
		Σ	−11.31	(−1.98)*	6.14	(0.52)
D. Unrestricted Lag Structure	AF_{t-i}	F	2.20	(0.02)*	1.13	(0.37)
		Σ	−13.77	(−2.96)**	−6.75	(−0.70)
	UF_{t-i}	F	1.66	(0.09)†	1.65	(0.13)
		Σ	−10.13	(−2.40)*	−6.72	(−1.09)
E. No Anticipated/Unanticipated Policy Distinction	F_{t-i}	F	.96	(0.51)	1.09	(0.39)
		Σ	−11.91	(−2.10)*	−4.41	(−0.79)
F. Generated Regressor Bias Correction	AF_{t-i}	X	2.40	(0.04)*	.45	(0.81)
		Σ	−19.47	(−2.22)*	2.19	(0.08)
	UF_{t-i}	X	.85	(0.51)	.53	(0.75)
		Σ	−11.42	(−1.55)	5.43	(0.32)

NOTES: The F-statistics test the null hypothesis that the coefficients of the contemporaneous and lagged values of noted variable equal zero. The marginal significance levels are in parentheses. The sum of each set of lagged variables (Σ) are also reported, with the corresponding t-statistic in parentheses. Statistics significant at the .10, .05, and .01 levels are denoted by †, *, and **, respectively. Each panel (A–F) represents a different specification of the model or estimation procedure (see text for details). In the case of panel F, chi-statistics (X), rather than F-statistics, are presented.

excluded from the equation. Column 2 reports the results from the "complete" model where monetary variables are included together with the fiscal policy measures.[15] Also reported are the sum of each set of lagged variables (Σ), with the corresponding t-statistics (in parentheses).

Policy Measure Proxies

The method used to drive proxies for policy measures plays an important role in tests of the policy ineffectiveness proposition. Our approach reported in Table 1 is to employ a common lag length structure for all of the variables in the first stage regressions, and to choose an appropriate lag length using the Theil $\bar{R}^2$ (minimum standard error) criteria. Although this provides theoretically unbiased estimation of regressors, the use of some irrelevant variables in the first-step regressions may cause some mismeasurement of anticipated and unanticipated policy and thereby affect the hypothesis tests in the second-step regressions.

To address this issue, we checked the robustness of the fiscal policy ineffectiveness result to an alternative method of first-stage model selection. In particular, we employed Akaike's final prediction error (FPE) method (1973) to pare down the lagged variables in the first-step regressions used to generate the anticipated and unanticipated policy measures. Amemiya (1980) has shown that the FPE procedure may be interpreted as a rule for minimizing the expected (out-of-sample) squared prediction error associated with a forecasting equation.

The FPE criterion indicated that the appropriate lag specification in the money prediction equation is seven lags of money, one lag for the interest rate, and seven lags of unemployment; and in the fiscal prediction equation, one lag of the budget surplus, eight lags of unemployment, six lags of inflation, and two lags of money. This specification of the first-stage regressions accords with the results implied by Table 1 on the basis of those lagged variables with "high" t-statistics.

Using the predicted values from these equations as our proxies for anticipated policies, and the residuals as unanticipated policies, we reestimated the output equation and tested for the fiscal policy ineffectiveness proposition. The summary of results is presented in panel A of Table 6. Consistent with our earlier findings, fiscal policy (anticipated fiscal policy in this instance) appears significant in the restricted model (with monetary variables excluded) shown in column 1, but is insignificant when monetary interactions are taken into account—for either anticipated or unanticipated fiscal policy shifts (column 2).

PDL Restrictions

The second-step estimation results reported in Table 2 embody restrictions on the lag structure for each of the policy measures in order to save degrees of freedom in the estimation and to maintain comparability with previous studies: the restrictions

[15]The complete set of results is quite voluminous, and is therefore summarized in Table 6 for purposes of brevity. Completely detailed results are available from the authors upon request. We find that the basic monetary policy results are generally robust to these tests as well.

included a fifth-order polynomial distributed lag function (PDL) with sixteen lags, and an endpoint constraint. We tested the robustness of our fiscal ineffectiveness result when each of these restrictions is relaxed.

First, the real output equation was estimated with third-degree PDLs. A summary of these results is presented in panel B of Table 6. The original results are not sensitive to this change in model specification. Namely, fiscal policy appears significant when the money measures are excluded from the equation in column 1, but insignificant when the fully specified model is estimated in column 2.

Second, we relaxed the endpoint restriction in the PDL. These results are summarized in panel C of Table 6. The original results are again not sensitive to this change in model specification. With money variables excluded, anticipated fiscal policy is significant and unanticipated fiscal policy is insignificant (in column 1). Both are insignificant in the full model specification when monetary policy variables are included in the estimated equation (column 2).

Third, we estimated the output equation without any PDL restrictions. To ensure adequate degrees of freedom we reduced the number of lags in the estimation from sixteen to twelve. The resulting estimates are reported in panel D of Table 6. Estimated separately, fiscal policy again is significant in the real output equation (column 1)—both anticipated and unanticipated fiscal policy are estimated to have a significant effect on output growth. However, the fiscal ineffectiveness proposition again cannot be rejected for either anticipated or unanticipated fiscal policy when the full model is estimated (column 2).

Generated Regressor Bias

Pagan (1984), Hoffman, Low, and Schlagenhauf (1984), and Murphy and Topel (1985) have demonstrated that the estimates in the output equation will be biased for models in which the regressors for anticipated and unanticipated policy are derived from the two-step procedure that we and others (for example, Barro 1977, 1978, Makin 1982, and Kormendi and McGuire 1984) have employed.

The reason is that the generated regressors themselves are estimated with some error, and not adjusting for this factor will lead to an underestimate of the variance of the coefficients associated with these variables in the output equation. In our case, a downward bias in the estimated standard errors would lead to a *greater* probability of rejecting the null hypothesis that fiscal policy is ineffective in influencing real output growth. That is, the bias in the output equation variance estimates would tend to make it more difficult to reject the ineffectiveness proposition. Hence, our failure to reject the null is a stronger result than the level of statistical confidence indicates.

For completeness, however, we have investigated two alternative approaches for dealing with this issue. Frydman and Rappoport (1987) have shown that the generated regressor bias problem disappears if the anticipated and unanticipated policy measures have the same effects on output growth. In this case consistent estimates of the output effects of the policies are obtainable from normal OLS regressions.

Thus one approach to dealing with the generated regressor bias problem is to jointly test the fiscal policy ineffectiveness proposition together with the null hypothesis that the unanticipated/anticipated distinction is irrelevant.

To test robustness of our results to this change in specification, we estimated an output equation in which only lags of "raw" fiscal policy F_{t-i} $(= AF_{t-i} + UF_{t-i})$ are entered and the effects of anticipated and unanticipated fiscal policy are constrained to be equal. The equation was specified with sixteen lags, but without any additional restrictions on the lag structure (because of the greater degrees of freedom available when no anticipated/unanticipated distinction is drawn). A summary of these results is presented in panel E of Table 6. Without the anticipated/unanticipated distinction, fiscal policy is ineffective when (raw) monetary variables are both excluded or included. Hence, our basic result is robust to relaxation of the maintained hypothesis that a distinction should be drawn between anticipated and unanticipated policies.

Another approach we have investigated is to leave the effects of the anticipated and unanticipated policy measures unconstrained and to correct the variance/covariance estimates for the generated regressor bias implicit in the variance estimates of the model. The summary of these results is reported in panel F or Table 6. The statistical procedure for the correction process follows that of Hoffman, Low, and Schlagenhauf (1984), but is modified to take account of the PDL restrictions. The correction process is described in the appendix to this paper, available from the authors upon request.

Consistent with our earlier finding, fiscal policy appears to have a significant effect on output when monetary interactions are excluded, even when correction is made for the generated regressors bias (column 1). But this result is again reversed when monetary interactions are taken into account: the policy ineffectiveness proposition cannot be rejected in the full model specification (column 2).

6. CONCLUSION

Our paper argues that interactive effects between monetary and fiscal policies are likely to be important, and that ignoring these effects can lead to significant omitted variables bias in tests of the policy ineffectiveness proposition. In contrast to previous research, we jointly test the fiscal and monetary ineffectiveness propositions. Similar to Mishkin (1982a, b), Makin (1982), and others we reject short-run monetary policy ineffectiveness—either anticipated or unanticipated. In contrast to these studies, however, we cannot reject long-term neutrality associated with monetary polices.

It is rather striking that the fiscal policy ineffectiveness proposition, as well as fiscal neutrality generally (that is, both anticipated and unanticipated policy), cannot be rejected in our joint tests for either the short run or long run. Moreover, this result proves robust to a wide variety of empirical model specifications and estimation procedures. This result sheds doubt on Laumas and McMillin's finding that both anticipated and unanticipated fiscal policy have significant output effects. Furthermore, our results suggest that the cause of the omitted variables bias in earlier studies is attributable to interaction effects between monetary and fiscal policies.

It is perhaps most surprising that unanticipated fiscal policy actions do not seem to play a significant role in influencing output in either the short run or long run. It is noteworthy, however, that this result is entirely consistent with theoretical arguments posited by Barro (1974) and others, as well as empirical evidence by Evans (1985), the U.S. Treasury (1984), and others, which suggests that fiscal deficits may be neutral (anticipated or unanticipated) if the tax consequences are appropriately discounted by the market. A cautionary note is in order, however. Fiscal policy may be neutral in its effect on overall economic activity, but may nonetheless have significant effects on the composition of output. Exploring this issue is on our agenda for future research.

LITERATURE CITED

Akaike, H. "Information Theory and an Extension of the Maximum Likelihood Principle." In *Second International Symposium in Information Theory,* edited by B. Petrov and F. Csaki, pp. 267–81. Budapest: Akademia; Kiado, 1973.

Allen, Stuart D., and Murray D. Smith. "Government Borrowing and Monetary Accommodation." *Journal of Monetary Economics* 9 (1983), 605–16.

Amemiya, T. "Selection of Regressors." *International Economic Review* 21 (June 1980), 331–54.

Barro, Robert J. "Are Government Bonds Net Worth?" *Journal of Political Economy* 82 (November 1974), 1095–1117.

______. "Unanticipated Money Growth and Unemployment in the United States." *American Economic Review* 67 (March 1977), 101–15.

______. "Unanticipated Money, Output and the Price Level in the United States." *Journal of Political Economy* 86 (August 1978), 549–80.

______. "On the Determination of the Public Debt." *Journal of Political Economy* 87 (October 1979), 940–71.

Barro, Robert J., and M. Rush. "Unanticipated Money and Economic Activity." In *Rational Expectations and Economic Policy,* edited by S. Fischer. Chicago: The University of Chicago Press, 1980.

Cecchetti, Stephen G. "Testing Short-Run Neutrality." *Journal of Monetary Economics* 17 (May 1986), 409–23.

Dwyer, Gerald P. "Inflation and Government Deficits." *Economic Inquiry* 20 (July 1982), 315–29.

Evans, Paul D. "Do Large Deficits Produce High Interest Rates?" *American Economic Review* 75 (March 1985), 68–87.

Friedman, Milton. "The Role of Monetary Policy." *American Economic Review* 58 (March 1968), 1–17.

Frydman, Roman, and Peter Rappoport. "Is the Distinction between Anticipated and Unanticipated Money Growth Relevant in Explaining Aggregate Output?" *American Economic Review* 77 (September 1987), 693–703.

Gordon, Robert J. "Price Inertia and Policy Ineffectiveness in the United States, 1890–1980." *Journal of Political Economy* 90 (December 1982), 1087–1117.

Grier, K., and H. Neiman. "Deficits, Politics, and Money Growth." *Economic Inquiry* 2 (1987), 201–14.

Hall, Robert E., and John B. Taylor. *Macroeconomics*. New York: W. W. Norton, 1986.

Hamburger, M. J., and Burton Zwick. "Deficits, Money, and Inflation." *Journal of Monetary Economics* 7 (1981), 141–50.

Hoffman, Dennis, L., Stuart A. Low, and Donald E. Schlagenhauf. "Tests of Rationality, Neutrality, and Market Efficiency: A Monte Carlo Analysis of Alternative Test Statistics." *Journal of Monetary Economics* 14 (November 1984), 339–63.

Kormendi, Roger C., and Philip Meguire. "Cross-Regime Evidence of Macroeconomic Rationality." *Journal of Political Economy* 92 (October 1984), 875–908.

Laumas, G. S., and W. Douglas McMillin. "Anticipated Fiscal Policy and Real Output." *Review of Economics and Statistics* 66 (August 1984), 468–71.

Levy, Mickey. "Factors Affecting Monetary Policy in an Era of Inflation." *Journal of Monetary Economics* 7 (1981), 351–73.

Lucas, Robert E. "Expectations and the Neutrality of Money." *Journal of Economic Theory* 4 (1972), 103–24.

McCallum, Bennett J., and J. K. Whitaker. "The Effectiveness of Fiscal Feedback Rules and Automatic Stabilizers under Rational Expectations." *Journal of Monetary Economics* 5 (April 1979), 171–86.

McElhattan, Rose. "On Federal Deficits and Their Economic Impact." Federal Reserve Bank of San Francisco, *Economic Review* (1982), 6–17.

Makin, J. H. "Anticipated Money, Inflation Uncertainty, and Real Economic Activity." *Review of Economics and Statistics* 64 (February 1982), 126–34.

Mishkin, Frederic S. "Does Anticipated Aggregate Demand Policy Matter? An Econometric Investigation." *Journal of Political Economy* 90 (January 1982), 22–51. (a)

______. "Does Anticipated Aggregate Demand Policy Matter? Further Econometric Results." *American Economic Review* 72 (September 1982), 788–802. (b)

Murphy, Kevin M., and Robert H. Topel. "Estimation and Inference in Two-Step Econometric Models." *Journal of Business and Economic Statistics* 3 (October 1985), 370–79.

Pagan, Adrian R. "Econometric Issues in the Analysis of Regressions with Generated Regressors." *International Economic Review* 25 (February 1984), 221–47.

Parkin, Michael. *Macroeconomics*. Englewood Cliffs, N.J.: Prentice-Hall, 1984.

Sargent, Thomas J., and Neil Wallace. "Rational Expectations, the Optimal Monetary Instruments and Optimal Money Supply Rule." *Journal of Political Economy* 83 (April 1975), 241–54.

______. "Some Unpleasant Monetarist Arithmetic." Federal Reserve Bank of Minneapolis, *Quarterly Review* (Fall 1981), 1–17.

Sims, Christopher A. "Money, Income, and Causality." *American Economic Review* 62 (September 1972), 540–52.

U.S. Treasury Department, Office of the Assistant Secretary for Economic Policy. "The Effects of Deficits on Prices of Financial Assets: Theory and Evidence." Monograph, 1984.

ALFRED A. HAUG

Ricardian Equivalence, Rational Expectations, and the Permanent Income Hypothesis

IN CONVENTIONAL KEYNESIAN MACROECONOMIC THEORIES, government bonds were commonly treated as net wealth to the private sector.[1] Assuming that government spending is constant, an increase in government debt would therefore increase consumption. Barro (1974) argues instead that the way government spending is financed has no effect on private sector behavior. According to Barro's Ricardian equivalence proposition, a tax cut today implies increased taxes in the future, as long as the stream of government spending is not reduced. The household sector treats the bonds issued to finance such a tax cut as equivalent to the present value of the implied increase in future tax liabilities. A tax cut does not lead to an increase in consumption or interest rates in the Ricardian case. Instead, the tax cut increases savings in order to pay for the required increase in future taxes. Barro demonstrates that Richardian equivalence holds for a maximizing household in an overlapping generations model that assumes an operative bequest motive, nondistortionary taxes, and perfect capital markets. Barro (1989) surveys Ricardian equivalence.

In theory, wealth effects of government bonds are possible under modified assumptions of the Barro model. Chan (1983), Blanchard (1985), Barsky, Mankiw, and Zeldes (1986), and Feldstein (1988) show how Ricardian equivalence might not hold. However, Barro (1974, 1989) argues that negative as well as positive wealth

An earlier version of this paper was presented at the Econometric Society Winter 1988 Meetings in New York. The author is grateful to Paul Evans, Pok-sang Lam, Stephen McCafferty, J. Huston McCulloch, Gene Mumy, and two anonymous referees of this journal for their helpful comments. Thanks go as well to seminar participants at Claremont McKenna College, the Federal Reserve Bank of St. Louis, the University of Saskatchewan, the University of Southern California (Graduate School of Business), and the University of Texas at Arlington.

[1]See for example Tobin (1980).

ALFRED A. HAUG *is assistant professor of economics at the University of Saskatchewan.*

Journal of Money, Credit, and Banking, Vol. 22, No. 3 (August 1990)

effects may occur. Judd (1987) demonstrates this in a theoretical model with distortionary taxes, finite lives, and adjustment costs. Wealth effects could cancel each other or be altogether negligible. The issue cannot be settled on theoretical grounds. An answer to whether Ricardian equivalence is a good approximation to reality has to come from empirical studies.

The empirical tests of Ricardian equivalence have been carried out in basically two ways. The first way is to determine whether larger deficits are associated with higher interest rates.[2] The second way is to assess whether increases in government bonds lead to increases in household wealth and consequently in consumer spending. In my paper, I will choose the second approach. Seater (1985), Aschauer (1988), and Barro (1989) present surveys of empirical consumption studies. The results of these studies are mixed with respect to Ricardian equivalence. Results are sensitive to the sample period and variables included, and the tests may have low power.[3] Typically, three major problems can be identified in most empirical specifications of Ricardian equivalence tests in a consumption model. First, theoretical equations, which are cast in terms of expected future values, are often approximated in the empirical equations by a distributed lag on realized past values.[4] Second, Evans (1988) points out that the consumption function is ordinarily not derived from a model that nests the Ricardian equivalence hypothesis and an alternative of Ricardian nonequivalence.[5] Third, it is not usually established whether the underlying life cycle or permanent income model is supported by the data. Ricardian equivalence has been extensively tested within consumption models, however.[6]

In this paper, Ricardian equivalence will be tested in a permanent income model with income uncertainty. The empirical model is explicitly derived from intertemporal utility maximization. Rational expectations are postulated along with a representative agent. Specifically, the government budget constraint is incorporated into a type of a consumption model used by Flavin (1981).[7] The model nests Ricardian equivalence and an alternative hypothesis in which households treat government bonds as net wealth.

Flavin (1981, 1985), Hayashi (1982), and others generally specify the permanent income model with variables in levels and then remove a deterministic time trend from the data to achieve stationarity of the variables.[8] Mankiw and Shapiro (1985) criticize this approach. They demonstrate that such detrending can lead to spurious

[2]See Evans (1985, 1987) and Plosser (1987). They find no such association. Dwyer (1982) finds no significant relation between inflation and deficits.

[3]See Barth, Iden, and Russek (1986) and Seater and Mariano (1985).

[4]See Kormendi and Meguire (1986) on this issue. The studies by Aschauer (1985) and Evans (1988) are exceptions.

[5]Evans analyzes empirical effects of tax changes in the Blanchard (1985) model which nests both hypotheses. He finds no support for the alternative to Ricardian equivalence. Leiderman and Razin (1988) use a similar framework and arrive at the same result.

[6]See Seater (1985) and Bernheim (1987) who concludes that the evidence in favor of Ricardian equivalence is weak.

[7]Hayashi (1982), Campbell (1987), and Campbell and Deaton (1987) also use the Flavin model (or a version of it).

[8]Granger and Newbold (1974) show that nonstationary data can produce spuriously large and significant regression coefficients.

excess sensitivity of consumption to income innovations. Flavin (1981, 1985) finds excess sensitivity, that is, consumption is more sensitive to income than predicted by the model.[9] Stock and West (1988) show that the spurious sensitivity is not due to spurious cycles as claimed by Mankiw and Shapiro but rather to the shift in the asymptotic distribution when a deterministic time trend is included. Conventional estimation techniques are valid only if regression coefficients of interest can be rewritten as coefficients on mean-zero stationary variables. In this case, detrending or differencing of the data is not necessary. Stock and West demonstrate that Hall's (1978) regressions can be rewritten in such a form. Flavin's (1981, 1985) and Leiderman and Razin's (1988) consumption regressions cannot be expressed in such a form. The coefficients implied by Leiderman and Razin's alternative to Ricardian equivalence cannot be rewritten for their likelihood ratio tests as coefficients on stationary variables, assuming the data in levels is not stationary. It is also not possible to rewrite the consumption regressions in Evans (1988) in this way. I present evidence that the variables in my model exhibit a stochastic rather than a deterministic time trend, that is, they exhibit a unit root. I explore whether an intertemporal household model incorporating the government budget constraint and specifying variables in first differences might solve the excess sensitivity problem encountered in most consumption studies with aggregate data.[10] Theorems discussed in Stock and West are applied to deal with nonstationary regressors.

The rest of the paper is organized as follows. In section 1, the empirical model will be derived under Ricardian equivalence. Additionally, the alternative hypothesis of incomplete tax discounting is modeled. In section 2, identification, stationarity of variables, and problems with nonstationary regressors are discussed. Excess sensitivity tests of the consumption model are presented. Also, a Keynesian alternative is specified and estimation procedures are suggested. Recently developed cointegration theorems guide statistical inference. The annual U.S. data cover the period from 1929 to 1985. Empirical findings are reported in section 3. Section 4 summarizes the paper.

1. THE INTERTEMPORAL MODEL

In this section, the maximizing problem of a representative household is stated, and the consumption function is derived under both Ricardian equivalence and an alternative of incomplete discounting of future taxes. The utility function is assumed to be time separable over consumption.[11] Labor income is uncertain and labor supply is exogenous. The instantaneous utility function is assumed to be a local

[9]Campbell and Deaton (1987) demonstrate that Flavin's result of excess sensitivity is not inconsistent with their finding of excess smoothness. Campbell and Deaton employ first-differenced data but they do not consider a Ricardian household. Further, they use quarterly data, which raises the question of appropriate seasonal adjustments. See Miron (1986) and English, Miron, and Wilcox (1989).

[10]Hall (1987) surveys various attempts undertaken to solve this problem in the rational expectations approach to aggregate consumption. Also, see Nelson (1987).

[11]See Epstein (1988) for an alternative to time separability.

approximation to the underlying utility function and is specified as a quadratic function.[12] The household maximizes

$$E_t\left[-\frac{1}{2}\sum_{s=0}^{\infty} (1 + \delta)^{-s} (\bar{C}_{t+s} - C_{t+s})^2 \right] \tag{1}$$

subject to the intertemporal budget constraint

$$\sum_{s=1}^{\infty}(1 + r)^{-s} = W_t + \sum_{s=1}^{\infty}(1 + r)^{-s}Y_{t+s} - \sum_{s=1}^{\infty}(1 + r)^{-s}(T_{t+s} - TR_{t+s}) \, . \tag{2}$$

E_t is the expectations operator conditional on information in period t. C_t is real consumption, and Y_t is real before-tax labor earnings. $\bar{C}_t$ denotes the bliss level of consumption. δ is the positive rate of subjective time preference. W_t represents real nonhuman wealth and includes government bonds. Gross tax payments, T_t, and government transfers, TR_t, are lump-sum. Following Barro (1979), monetization of deficits is treated as an inflationary tax. Perfect capital markets are assumed, so that the private and public sectors face the same constant real rate of return r. An infinite horizon is postulated to allow for operative intergenerational transfers, as in Barro (1974).

In order to test for Ricardian equivalence, the government budget constraint is specified so that it can be incorporated into the above maximization problem. In period t, the government sector faces the constraint

$$B_t - (1 + r)B_{t-1} + T_t - TR_t = G_t \, . \tag{3}$$

Real government bonds are denoted by B_t and government spending by G_t. Consecutive forward substitution for bonds in equation (3) leads to the intertemporal constraint

$$\sum_{s=1}^{\infty}(1 + r)^{-s}(T_{t+s} - TR_{t+s}) = B_t + \sum_{s=1}^{\infty}(1 + r)^{-s}G_{t+s} - \lim_{s\to\infty}(1 + r)^{-s}B_{t+s} \, . \tag{4}$$

It is assumed that two types of households exist in the economy. One type forms expectations in such a way that

$$E_t \lim_{s\to\infty}(1 + r)^{-s}B_{t+s} = 0 \, . \tag{5}$$

[12]Flavin (1981, 1985), Aschauer (1985), Bernanke (1985), and Campbell (1987) provide examples of a quadratic utility function in a stochastic consumption model. Hall (1978) demonstrates for the Euler equation that different functional forms are locally approximated by a quadratic form. Further, the quadratic form avoids aggregation problems and allows me to derive a tractable closed-form solution for consumption. A constant relative risk aversion function has no closed-form solution in the stochastic

In order for (5) to be satisfied, government bonds must grow at a rate below r. Equation (5) is a necessary condition for Ricardian equivalence to hold. Since future taxes are completely discounted, government bonds are not perceived as net wealth. Hamilton and Flavin (1986) discuss (4) and (5) in detail. The other type of household is assumed to behave according to the following alternative hypothesis:[13]

$$E_t \lim_{s\to\infty} (1 + r)^{-s} B_{t+s} = B_t \,. \tag{6}$$

(6) implies that bonds grow at the rate r, that is, interest payments for B_t are financed by issuing new debt. If bonds grew at any rate above r, the limit would be infinite. The household in (6) perceives all currently outstanding government bonds as net wealth. Future taxes implied by B_t are not discounted at all.[14]

Equation (6) does not necessarily mean this household presumes that the government will eventually default on its debt. Taxing capacity is assumed to grow with population, for example, real income per capita and taxing capacity increase at the combined rate g. As long as g is equal to or greater than r, debt can grow forever and perpetual debt finance becomes feasible. Barro (1976) discusses whether $r \leq g$ is a tenable steady state. He argues that an altruistic bequest motive would most likely ensure $r > g$ in the steady state. A different bequest motive or a finite household horizon would make a competitive equilibrium possible with $r \leq g$ in the steady state.

Aggregation over the two types of households in the economy or artificially nesting the two hypotheses (5) and (6) leads to

$$\sum_{s=1}^{\infty} (1 + r)^{-s} E_t(T_{t+s} - TR_{t+s}) = (1 - k)B_t + \sum_{s=1}^{\infty} (1 + r)^{-s} E_t G_{t+s} \,. \tag{7}$$

The term k is the fraction of households behaving according to (6) or, in the case of artificial nesting, the weight assigned to (6). Ricardian equivalence requires that k is zero and, therefore, households behaving according to (6) are negligible in number.

In order to get an empirically tractable solution for optimal consumption, I assume that[15]

$$\bar{C}_t = \bar{C} + \left(\frac{1 + \delta}{1 + r}\right) \bar{C}_{t-1} \,.$$

model. However, Hayashi (1982, pp. 898–99) explains why the quadratic form gives a close approximation. Furthermore, I allow for the bliss level of consumption to increase over time.

[13]See Hamilton and Flavin (1986) for a similar approach. They test whether the federal government behaves in such a way that (5) would hold for the government budget constraint. Hamilton and Flavin accept (5).

[14]A special violation of the Golden Rule might make such a fiscal policy feasible. Government debt could have intrinsic value as a medium of exchange for example.

[15]With the assumption of a constant bliss level and $k = 0$, the solution to (1) and (2) is a random walk

This equation may be written as

$$\bar{C}_t = \left(\frac{1 + \delta}{1 + r}\right)^t \bar{C}_0 + \sum_{i=0}^{t-1} \left(\frac{1 + \delta}{1 + r}\right)^i \bar{c} ,$$

where $\bar{C}_0$ is some initial positive value for the bliss level of consumption. Maximizing (1) subject to (2) leads to the Euler equation

$$E_t C_{t+s} = \left(\frac{1 + \delta}{1 + r}\right)^s C_t + \sum_{i=0}^{s-1} \left(\frac{1 + \delta}{1 + r}\right)^i \bar{c} .$$

Multiplying the Euler equation by $(1 + r)^{-s}$ and summing for $s = 1,2, \ldots$ yields

$$\sum_{s=1}^{\infty} (1 + r)^{-s} E_t C_{t+s} = \left(\frac{1 + \delta}{r^2 + 2r - \delta}\right) C_t - \frac{(1 + r)^2}{r(r^2 + 2r - \delta)} \bar{C} ,$$

where I have assumed that $(1 + r)^2 > (1 + \delta)$. Substituting (7) into (2) and the resulting equation into the left-hand side allows me to solve for consumption:

$$C_t = \left\{\frac{(1 + r)^2}{r(1 + \delta)}\right\} \bar{C} + \left(\frac{r^2 + 2r - \delta}{1 + \delta}\right) [W_t - (1 - k)B_t$$

$$+ \sum_{s=1}^{\infty} (1 + r)^{-s} E_t Y_{t+s} - \sum_{s=1}^{\infty} (1 + r)^{-s} E_t G_{t+s}$$

$$+ \alpha \sum_{s=1}^{\infty} (1 + r)^{-s} E_t Tr_{t+s} \Big] \tag{8}$$

I have added the last term involving government transfer payments in order to allow for distributional effects of transfer payments that are not captured by my model. The model assumptions require that $\alpha = 0$. Kormendi (1983) found a significant impact of transfers on consumption. He argues that this is consistent with Ricardian equivalence. On the other hand, Modigliani and Sterling (1986) do not consider distributional effects. Flavin (1981, p. 992) justifies neglecting transitory consump-

---

for consumption with $\left(\frac{1 + \delta}{1 + r}\right)$ as the coefficient of C_{t-1}. I allow here for the bliss level to follow a similar growth process.

tion on an aggregate level. If individual realizations of transitory consumption are independently distributed across the population, aggregate transitory consumption is negligible.

A few qualifications are in order. The approach in my paper is based on Flavin (1981, 1985). However, there are some major differences. She assumes that $r = \delta$, does not include the government budget constraint, and focuses on after-tax labor income. To account for growth, Flavin removes a deterministic exponential time trend from the data. Since I do not follow this procedure, setting $r = \delta$ would imply zero growth for consumption in my model (see Champernowne 1969).

My model also differs from Aschauer's (1985). He assumes that government spending substitutes in part for private consumption in the household's utility function. Only in this case, government spending enters the Euler equation. This permits Aschauer to employ an Euler equation to test Ricardian equivalence. I will allow for government spending to substitute for consumption later in this paper.[16]

Under rational expectations, the consumption function (8) can be rewritten in terms of revisions in the expected streams of future income, government spending, and government transfer payments. These revisions are due to new information that arrives from period $t - 1$ to period t. Substituting the period t household budget constraint

$$W_t = (1 + r)W_{t-1} + Y_t - C_t - (T_t - TR_t) + \epsilon_t \tag{9}$$

into (8) leads, together with (3), to

$$\begin{aligned} C_t = \left\{\frac{(1 + r)^2}{r(1 + \delta)}\right\}\bar{C} + \left(\frac{r^2 + 2r - \delta}{1 + \delta}\right)\{(1 + r)W_{t-1} - (1 + r)B_{t-1} + kB_t + Y_t \\ - C_t - G_t + \sum_{s=1}^{\infty}(1 + r)^{-s}E_tY_{t+s} \\ - \sum_{s=1}^{\infty}(1 + r)^{-s}E_tG_{t+s} + \alpha\sum_{s=1}^{\infty}(1 + r)^{-s}E_tTR_{t+s} + \epsilon_t\Big\} . \end{aligned} \tag{10}$$

The variable ϵ_t reflects measurement errors, is orthogonal to the information set at time $t - 1$, and is serially uncorrelated. The error ϵ_t does not result from stochastic innovations to a time-varying interest rate. The variable TR_t can be expressed as

$$TR_t = (1 + r)\sum_{s=1}^{\infty}(1 + r)^{-s}E_tTR_{t+s-1} - \sum_{s=1}^{\infty}(1 + r)^{-s}E_tTR_{t+s} .$$

[16]Leiderman and Razin (1988) focus on the horizon of consumers and include taxes instead of bonds. They do not deal with nonstationarity in the monthly Israeli data they use. Neither does Evans (1988) deal with nonstationarity. He faces also the difficult task of measuring nonhuman consumer wealth (see Hayashi 1982).

Substituting this equation into (10) and manipulating further leads to

$$C_t = \left\{\frac{(1+r)^2}{r(1+\delta)}\right\}\bar{C} + \left(\frac{r^2+2r-\delta}{1+\delta}\right)\{(1+r)[W_{t-1} - (1-k)B_{t-1}$$

$$+ \sum_{s=1}^{\infty}(1+r)^{-s}E_{t-1}Y_{t+s-1} - \sum_{s=1}^{\infty}(1+r)^{-s}E_{t-1}G_{t+s-1}$$

$$+ \alpha\sum_{s=1}^{\infty}(1+r)^{-s}E_{t-1}TR_{t+s-1}\Big] + k(B_t - (1+r)B_{t-1}) - C_t$$

$$+(1+r)\sum_{s=1}^{\infty}(1+r)^{-s}(E_t - E_{t-1})Y_{t+s-1}$$

$$+(1+r)\sum_{s=1}^{\infty}(1+r)^{-s}(E_t - E_{t-1})G_{t+s-1}$$

$$+\alpha(1+r)\sum_{s=1}^{\infty}(1+r)^{-s}(E_t - E_{t-1})TR_{t+s-1} - \alpha TR_t + \epsilon_t\Big\}\,. \tag{11}$$

$(E_t - E_{t-1})\chi_{t+s-1}$ is the revision of expectations about a variable χ_{t+s} as the consumer moves from period $t-1$ to period t. Rational expectations guarantee that $E_{t-1}(E_t - E_{t-1})\chi_{t+s-1} = 0$. Lagging (8) one period and substituting it into (11) results in

$$C_t = \left(\frac{(r-\delta)(1+r)}{r(1+\delta)}\right)\bar{C} + \left(\frac{1+\delta}{1+r}\right)C_{t-1}$$

$$+ \rho\Big\{k(B_t - (1+r)B_{t-1}) - \alpha TR_t + (1+r)\sum_{s=1}^{\infty}(1+r)^{-s}(E_t - E_{t-1})Y_{t+s-1}$$

$$- (1+r)\sum_{s=1}^{\infty}(1+r)^{-s}(E_t - E_{t-1})G_{t+s-1}$$

$$+\alpha(1+r)\sum_{s=1}^{\infty}(1+r)^{-s}(E_t - E_{t-1})TR_{t+s-1} + \epsilon_t\Big\}\,, \tag{12}$$

where $\rho = (r^2 + 2r - \delta)/(1+r)^2$.

An autoregressive process is specified to quantify the role of current income, government spending, and possibly transfers in signaling changes in permanent income. Government bonds are included because they might have predictive power for future income and government spending (see Aschauer 1985):

$$\begin{bmatrix} \Delta Y_t \\ \Delta G_t \\ \Delta B_t \\ \Delta TR_t \end{bmatrix} = \begin{bmatrix} a_0 \\ d_0 \\ f_0 \\ i_0 \end{bmatrix} + \begin{bmatrix} A(L) & B(L) & D(L) & E(L) \\ F(L) & H(L) & I(L) & K(L) \\ M(L) & N(L) & P(L) & Q(L) \\ R(L) & S(L) & T(L) & U(L) \end{bmatrix} \begin{bmatrix} \Delta Y_t \\ \Delta G_t \\ \Delta B_t \\ \Delta TR_t \end{bmatrix} + \begin{bmatrix} u_t \\ v_t \\ w_t \\ e_t \end{bmatrix} \quad (13)$$

$A(L)$ to $U(L)$ are polynomials in the lag operator L of the form

$$A(L) = a_1 L + a_2 L^2 + \cdots + a_p L^p .$$

$\Delta\chi_t$ is defined as $\Delta\chi_t = \chi_t - \chi_{t-1}$, and a_0, d_0, f_0, and i_0 are constants. The error terms u_t, v_t, w_t, and e_t are serially dependent but may be contemporaneously correlated. Assuming invertibility, equations (13) can be expressed in terms of moving average ($MA(\infty)$). After taking expectations, income is governed by

$$\begin{aligned} E_t \Delta Y_{t+s} = {} & a_0 \sum_{i=0}^{\infty} \lambda_i + \lambda_s u_t + \lambda_{s+1} u_{t-1} + \lambda_{s+2} u_{t-2} + \cdots \\ & + d_0 \sum_{i=0}^{\infty} \phi_i + \phi_s v_t + \phi_{s+1} v_{t-1} + \phi_{s+2} v_{t-2} + \cdots \\ & + f_0 \sum_{i=0}^{\infty} \gamma_i + \gamma_s w_t + \gamma_{s+1} w_{t-1} + \gamma_{s+2} w_{t-2} + \cdots \\ & + i_0 \sum_{i=0}^{\infty} \tau_i + \tau_s e_t + \tau_{s+1} e_{t-1} + \tau_{s+2} e_{t-1} + \cdots \end{aligned}$$

A similar expression is derived for $E_{t-1}\Delta Y_{t+s}$, so that the revision in income differences

$$(E_t - E_{t-1})\Delta Y_{t+s} = \lambda_s u_t + \phi_s v_t + \gamma_s w_t + \tau_s e_t . \quad (14)$$

Equation (12) requires the level of income. I expand (14):

$$E_t Y_{t+s} = Y_{t-1} + E_t(\Delta Y_t + \Delta Y_{t+1} + \ldots + \Delta Y_{t+s})$$

and, in the same way, $E_{t-1}Y_{t+s}$ to arrive at

$$E_tY_{t+s} - E_{t-1}Y_{t+s} = (E_t - E_{t-1})\Delta Y_t + (E_t - E_{t-1})\Delta Y_{t+1} + \ldots$$
$$+ (E_t - E_{t-1})\Delta Y_{t+s} .$$

Substituting in from (14) gives

$$E_tY_{t+s} - E_{t-1}Y_{t+s} = \sum_{i=0}^{s} \lambda_i u_t + \sum_{i=0}^{s} \phi_i v_t + \sum_{i=0}^{s} \gamma_i w_t + \sum_{i=0}^{s} \tau_i e_t .$$

The present value of the revision in the expected path of income, due to information arriving from period $t - 1$ to period t, is

$$\sum_{s=1}^{\infty} (1 + r)^{-s}(E_t - E_{t-1})Y_{t+s-1} = \Psi_Y u_t + \Omega_Y v_t + \Gamma_Y w_t + \Theta_Y e_t ,$$

with $\Psi_Y = \Sigma_{s=1}^{\infty}(1 + r)^{-s} \{\Sigma_{i=0}^{s} \lambda_i\}$, $\Omega_Y = \Sigma_{s=1}^{\infty}(1 + r)^{-s} \{\Sigma_{i=0}^{s} \phi_i\}$, $\Gamma_Y = \Sigma_{s=1}^{\infty}(1 + r)^{-s}\{\Sigma_{i=0}^{s} \gamma_i\}$, and $\Theta_Y = \Sigma_{s=1}^{\infty}(1 + r)^{-s} \{\Sigma_{i=0}^{s} \tau_i\}$. Parallel to the above, I derive for the revisions in government spending

$$\sum_{s=1}^{\infty} (1 + r)^{-s}(E_t - E_{t-1})G_{t+s-1} = \Psi_G u_t + \Omega_G v_t + \Gamma_G w_t + \Theta_G e_t ,$$

where Ψ_G, Ω_G, Γ_G, and Θ_G have the corresponding polynomial parameters from the second row of the inverse matrix above instead of λ_i, ψ_i, γ_i, and τ_i. Ψ_{TR}, Ω_{TR}, Γ_{TR}, and Θ_{TR} are defined in the same way for transfers (being multiplied with α). For equation (12), I obtain

$$C_t = \left(\frac{(r - \delta)(1 + r)}{r(1 + \delta)}\right)\bar{C} + \left(\frac{1 + \delta}{1 + r}\right)C_{t-1} + \rho k\{B_t - (1 + r)B_{t-1}\}$$
$$- \alpha\rho TR_t + \rho(1 + r)\{(\Psi_Y - \Psi_G + \Psi TR)u_t + (\Omega_Y - \Omega_G + \Omega_{TR})v_t$$
$$+ (\Gamma_Y - \Gamma_G + \Gamma_{TR})w_t + (\Theta_Y - \Theta_G + \Theta_{TR})e_t\} + \rho\epsilon_t . \qquad (15)$$

So far, I have assumed that all relevant information is captured by income, government spending, transfers, and bonds. However, consumers might use other available information in addition. As in Flavin (1981), the omission of further information from the set at $t - 1$ will be reflected in the error terms: $u_t = \epsilon_{1t} + \mu_{1t-1}$; $v_t = \epsilon_{2t} + \mu_{2t-1}$; $w_t = \epsilon_{3t} + \mu_{3t-1}$; and $e_t = \epsilon_{4t} + \mu_{4t-1}$. The error terms are made up of two parts: the true innovations, ϵ_{1t}, ϵ_{2t}, ϵ_{3t}, and ϵ_{4t}, using the total information set at $t - 1$; and the portion leading to the discrepancy between the total set and the set employing income, government spending, transfers, and bonds, denoted by μ_{1t-1}, μ_{2t-1}, μ_{3t-1}, and μ_{4t-1}. The latter are assumed to be orthogonal to the total information set and may be serially correlated. The true innovations are not correlated with μ_{1t-1}, μ_{2t-1}, μ_{3t-1}, μ_{4t-1} or the included lagged variables. A similar argument applies to the current period forecast which uses new information arriving in period t. Further information denoted by ζ_t, besides income, government spending, transfers, and bonds, might be relevant. The disturbance term, ζ_t, is serially uncorrelated and uncorrelated with all lagged variables. For equation (15), it follows that

$$\Delta C_t = \left(\frac{(r-\delta)(1+r)}{r(1+\delta)}\right)\bar{C} - \left(\frac{r-\delta}{1+r}\right)C_{t-1} + \rho k\{B_t - (1+r)B_{t-1}\} - \alpha\rho TR_t$$
$$+ \rho(1+r)\{(\Psi_Y - \Psi_G + \Psi_{TR})u_t + (\Omega_Y - \Omega_G + \Omega_{TR})v_t$$
$$+ (\Gamma_Y - \Gamma_G + \Gamma_{TR})w_t + (\Theta_Y - \Theta_G + \Theta_{TR})e_t\} + z_t\,, \tag{16}$$

with

$$z_t = \rho(1+r)\,\{(\Psi_Y - \Psi_G + \Psi_{TR})\mu_{1t-1} - (\Omega_y - \Omega_G + \Omega_{TR})\mu_{2t-1}$$
$$- (\Gamma_Y - \Gamma_G + \Gamma_{TR})\mu_{3t-1} + (\Theta_Y - \Theta_G + \Theta_{TR})\mu_{4t-1}\} + \rho\epsilon_t + \zeta_t\,.$$

The error terms u_t, v_t, w_t, and e_t are contemporaneously correlated with z_t and they are assumed to be serially uncorrelated. The system to be estimated consists of (13) and (16).

The above model is easily altered to allow government spending to substitute for, or complement, private consumption as in Kormendi (1983) or Aschauer (1985). That public consumption may substitute for, or complement, private consumption was first hypothesized by Bailey (1962, 1971). Consumption is assumed to be a linear combination of private consumption C_t and a fraction θ of government spending. After including θG_t, equation (16) becomes

$$\Delta C_t = \left(\frac{(r-\delta)(1+r)}{r(1+\delta)}\right)\bar{C} - \left(\frac{r-\delta}{1+r}\right)C_{t-1} - \theta\left\{G_t - \left(\frac{1+\delta}{1+r}\right)G_{t-1}\right\}$$
$$+ \rho k\{B_t - (1+r)B_{t-1}\} - \alpha\rho TR_t$$
$$+ \rho(1+r)\{(\Psi_Y - (1-\theta)\Psi_G + \Psi_{TR})u_t + (\Omega_Y - (1-\theta)\Omega_G + \Omega_{TR})v_t$$
$$+ (\Gamma_Y - (1-\theta)\Gamma_G + \Gamma_{TR})w_t + (\Theta_Y - (1-\theta)\Theta_G + \Theta_{TR})e_t\} + z_t\,. \tag{17}$$

One would expect to get a negative empirical value for the estimate of θ when government spending is a complement to private consumption.

2. EXCESS SENSITIVITY TESTS, IDENTIFICATION, AND ESTIMATION METHOD

This section is devoted in part to developing a testing methodology for the consumption model in section 1. Besides Ricardian equivalence, the permanent income model is tested. Excess sensitivity is tested by allowing consumption to be more sensitive to income changes than predicted by the permanent income model. Among the alternative hypotheses, a Keynesian-type consumer is considered. It is crucial for tests of Ricardian equivalence to assure that the consumption model used is not rejected itself. Otherwise, the result with respect to Ricardian equivalence may be caused by misspecification of the consumption model.[17] Furthermore, I examine whether the model is identified under the various alternative hypotheses. An estimation method suitable with nonstationary regressors is presented.

The permanent income model is tested by allowing consumption in period t to respond to first differences in income and government spending. Flavin (1981, 1985) follows the same procedure with respect to income. This excess sensitivity test is based on the following argument: once the revision in permanent income due to current period new information is accounted for, current and lagged income and government spending variables should be insignificant if included in the consumption equation. Substituting for ΔY_t from (13) yields

$$\Delta C_t = \left(\frac{(r-\delta)(1+r)}{r(1+\delta)}\right)\bar{C} - \left(\frac{r-\delta}{1+r}\right)C_{t-1} - \theta\Delta G_t + \theta\left(\frac{\delta-r}{1+r}\right)G_{t-1}$$
$$+ \rho k\,\{\Delta B_t - rB_{t-1}\} - \alpha\rho TR_t$$
$$+ \beta_0\,(a_0 + A(L)\Delta Y_t + B(L)\Delta G_t + D(L)\Delta B_t + E(L)\Delta TR_t)$$
$$+ \beta_1\Delta Y_{t-1} + \cdots + \beta_p\Delta Y_{t-p} + \alpha_1\Delta G_{t-1} + \cdots + \alpha_q\Delta G_{t-q} + z_t^* \,, \quad (18)$$

with

$$z_t^* = \rho(1+r)\,\{(\Psi_Y - (1-\theta)\Psi_G + \Psi_{TR})u_t + (\Omega_Y - (1-\theta)\Omega_G +$$
$$\Omega_{TR})v_t + (\Gamma_Y - (1-\theta)\Gamma_G + \Gamma_{TR})w_t + (\Omega_Y - (1-\theta)\Omega_G +$$
$$\Omega_{TR})e_t\} + \beta_0 u_t + z_t \,.$$

The β_i coefficients measure the sensitivity of consumption to income in excess of the response predicted by the model as new information arrives. In the same way, the α_i coefficients measure excess sensitivity of consumption to government spending. β_i and α_i should not be significantly different from zero if the permanent income model is accepted. If government spending substitutes for private consump-

[17] See Altig (1988) and Hayford (1989) for a discussion on fiscal policy and liquidity constraints.

tion, one would expect θ to be positive and significant. Additionally, the Ricardian equivalence hypothesis implies that $B_t - (1 + r)B_{t-1}$ does not enter the consumption function in a significant way.

The five-equation system consisting of (13) and (18) may not be identified. The Flavin test suggests to include as many lags on ΔY and ΔG as are present in the first two equations in (13). In order for the model to be identified, the number of included β_i and α_i parameters cannot exceed the number of lagged variables in these two equations. The parameters r, δ, and $\bar{C}$ are identified in the unrestricted version (18). However, this is not true once k and θ are set equal to zero. In order to assure identification, various values of r will be imposed in the regressions.

A potential problem arises with standard estimation techniques and theorems. In section 3, I will show that C_t, G_t, B_t, TR_t, and Y_t are nonstationary in levels. The variables C_{t-1}, G_{t-1}, B_{t-1}, and TR_t in equation (18) are present in levels. All the other variables appear in stationary form. I apply results derived by Sims, Stock, and Watson (1987) and West (1988) to deal with the nonstationarity problem.

In my model, I hypothesize that C_t, G_t, and B_t are cointegrated of order zero. Engle and Granger (1987) define a vector X_t as cointegrated of order $(d - b)$, if (i) each component of X_t is individually stationary after differencing it d times, and (ii) there exists at least one "cointegrating vector" β (not equal to zero) such that $\beta' X_t$ is stationary after differencing $d - b$ times. The relation of C_{t-1}, G_{t-1}, and B_{t-1} in (18) implies a possible cointegration regression of the form

$$C_t = a + bG_t + dB_t + \varepsilon_{ct} , \tag{19}$$

with a denoting a constant term and ε_{ct} a stationary mean-zero error term. The parameter $b = -\theta$, and $d = -rk \left(\frac{r^2+2r-\delta}{(1+r)(r-\delta)}\right)$. Further, I hypothesize that $\left(1 - \frac{1+\delta}{1+r}L\right)$ is, in the sense of Sims, Stock, and Watson, a generalized cointegrating vector for C_t. Equation (18) has then one nonstationary right-hand-side variable left, TR_t. Results in West may be employed in this case. West shows that instrumental variables estimators, linear in the variables, can be consistent and asymptotically normal for a regression with a single nonstationary right-hand-side variable. The key assumption is that the nonstationary variable has a nonzero unconditional mean for the first difference. Then, the variance-covariance estimates are consistent. I assume that ΔTR_t has a nonzero unconditional mean. In the empirical section of my paper, I will consider the whole sample period and a sample that excludes World War II years. For the sample without the war years, I argue that TR_t, C_{t-1}, and G_{t-1} are cointegrated of order zero. In this case, B_{t-1} is the only nonstationary right-hand-side variable. I assume that ΔB_t has a nonzero unconditional mean.

Engle and Granger propose various tests for cointegration which will be discussed in section 3. Also, they suggest to use the cointegration estimates to form a reduced stationary model. However, Sims, Stock, and Watson prove that such a two-step procedure is asymptotically unnecessary. The estimation can be carried out on the original data. The asymptotic distribution for maximum likelihood estimates is singular normal, and the standard errors are consistent estimates of the true standard errors. If a unit root is present (that is, transfers or bonds), the coefficient on any intercept will have a nonstandard limiting distribution. The limiting distribution of the constant term is irrelevant because the intercept is not subject to statistical inference.

A further problem with standard estimation techniques is that the error term z_t^* might be correlated with ΔB_t, ΔG_t, or TR_t. They are not part of the information set at time $t - 1$. The error z_t^* is only orthogonal to the information set at time $t - 1$. A nonlinear instrumental variables (IV) technique described by Hansen's (1982) general method of moments (GMM) estimators is used in order to achieve consistent and asymptotically normal estimates. My model is linear in the variables but nonlinear in the parameters. ΔB_{t-1} and ΔG_{t-1} will be used as instruments for ΔB_t and ΔG_t. TR_{t-1} will be the instrument for TR_t. Hansen shows that instruments do not need to be exogenous as long as they are predetermined.[18]

The five-equation system will be estimated with the statistical package TSP, version 4.1. The restricted and unrestricted model will be estimated, and the likelihood ratio (LR) statistic will be formed according to Gallant (1987, pp. 457–60). This test statistic is asymptotically distributed χ^2 with degrees of freedom equal to the number of restrictions.

3. EMPIRICAL RESULTS

The estimated consumption model consists of equations (13) and (18). The restrictions implied by the permanent income model and by Ricardian equivalence are tested. Stationarity of the data is analyzed, and the appropriate lag length is determined for the polynomials in (13). The annual data cover the years from 1929 to 1985. Data sources and manipulations are described in the appendix. All data are deflated on a 1982 base. I apply to nondurables and services the corresponding implicit price deflators. All other nominal series are deflated with the price deflator implied by the ratio of nominal nondurables plus nominal services to real nondurables plus real services. The model is estimated over two periods. The first period excludes the World War II years from 1942 to 1949 (allowing for the construction of lags), and the second period includes the war years. A test for structural change is employed to determine whether the war years should be included. Flavin (1985) and Feldstein and Elmendorf (1987) argue that rationing during World War II most likely did not allow consumers to realize their desired levels of consumption. Also, I include a variable to measure the stringency of price controls during World War II. Kormendi (1983, p. 1000, fn. 22) calculated such a variable taking on values of .14

[18]See Tauchen (1986) on the choice of instruments and the small sample properties of the GMM estimates.

for 1943, .28 for 1944, .43 for 1945, .33 for 1946, .14 for 1947, and 0 otherwise. The consumption variable is defined as consumption expenditures on nondurables plus services. The service flow from durables yields utility. Durables expenditure itself does not enter the utility function. It is difficult to construct the service flow from durables. Therefore, I exclude durables. Evans (1988, p. 989, fn. 12) gives the sufficient conditions for deleting durables.

The transfer variable in levels is not stationary over the sample period. Fuller's (1976) and Dickey and Fuller's (1981) tests indicate a unit root. Schwartz's criterion ($SC = -2\ln$ likelihood + $[\ln T]$[# of parameters], where T is sample size) chooses the following autoregression for these tests:

$$TR_t = f + \beta t + \rho TR_{t-1} + \epsilon_{st} .$$

The null hypothesis of a nonstationary unit root ($\rho = 1$) is tested against the alternative of stationarity ($\rho < 1$) by constructing the test statistic $\hat{\tau}_\tau$.[19] Fuller's Table 8.5.2 (p. 373) gives the appropriate critical values. Also, the joint hypothesis $\beta = 0$ and $\rho = 1$ is tested by forming the statistic Φ_3 according to Dickey and Fuller. Table VI in Dickey and Fuller (p. 1063) shows the appropriate critical values. $\hat{\tau}_\tau$ is equal to -1.64 and Φ_3 to 3.53. Excluding the war years leads to $\hat{\tau}_\tau = -1.45$ and $\Phi_3 = 3.27$. The null hypothesis is accepted in all cases at the 5 percent and 10 percent levels of significance. Box-Pierce's Q statistics indicate that the errors are white noise.[20] The results for bonds are $\hat{\tau}_\tau = -2.39$ and $\Phi_3 = 2.86$ ($Q(6) = .38$), and without the war years $\hat{\tau}_\tau = -2.46$ and $\Phi_3 = 3.39$ ($Q(6) = 4.28$). SC selects additionally ΔB_{t-1} for the autoregression. Income produces $\hat{\tau}_\tau = -.65$ and $\Phi_3 = 4.16$($Q(6) = 5.60$), and excluding the war years $\hat{\tau}_\tau = -.35$ and $\Phi_3 = 5.17$ ($Q(6) = 3.86$). No lags on ΔY are included in the autoregression. In all cases, the two null hypotheses are accepted for bonds and income at the 5 percent and 10 percent levels of significance. A unit root is rejected for government spending because $\Phi_3 = 12.05$ ($Q(6) = .66$). Once I include the Kormendi variable for price controls, $\hat{\tau}_\tau = -1.48$ and $\Phi_3 = 1.38$ ($Q(6) = .69$). Without the war years, $\hat{\tau}_\tau = -1.14$ and $\Phi_3 = 4.86$ ($Q(6) = 2.04$). One lag on ΔG is included with the war years and none without the war years. The null hypotheses are again accepted at the 5 percent and 10 percent levels. I will include the price control variable along with government spending in all regressions with the war years.

I apply ordinary least squares estimation to the cointegration equation (19). Engle and Granger (1987) discuss a number of tests for cointegration and recommend the use of the augmented Dickey-Fuller test (ADF; p. 269). The Dickey-Fuller (DF) test is the ADF-test without lags on the first difference of the cointegration residuals. Engle and Granger give the critical values of a 5 percent significance level: -3.37 (for DF) and -3.17 (for ADF). The statistic takes on the following value: $ADF =$

[19]See Fuller (1976).

[20]Q at lag 6 ($Q(6)$) is equal to 4.42 for the full sample, and $Q(6)$ is equal to 3.18 when the war years are excluded.

-3.29 with one lag. The null hypothesis of no cointegration is rejected at the 5 percent level. Excluding the war years changes this result: $DF = -2.41$. The null hypothesis of no cointegration is not rejected. However TR_t, C_{t-1}, and G_{t-1} are cointegrated for this sample period: $DF = -4.67$. Further, I find that $\left(1 - \frac{1+\delta}{1+r}L\right)$ is a generalized cointegrating vector for C_t: $ADF = -7.99$ with one lag. Without the war years, $ADF = -7.45$ with one lag.[21] Therefore, $C_t - \left(\frac{1+\delta}{1+r}\right) C_{t-1}$ is stationary for both sample periods.

The model gives no indication as to the appropriate lag length in the autoregressive processes in (13). Likelihood ratio (LR) tests indicate that the right-hand-side variables included in (20) influence the left-hand-side variables at the 5 percent and 10 percent levels of significance. The SC criterion is employed to determine the lag length for each variable. In contrast to the LR-test, the SC criterion values parsimony, that is, it penalizes for an increasing number of parameters. SC selects the following model:

$$\Delta Y_t = a_0 + a_1 \Delta Y_{t-1} + a_2 \Delta Y_{t-2} + b_1 \Delta G_{t-1} + u_t$$

$$\Delta G_t = d_0 + d_1 \Delta G_{t-1} + e_1 \Delta B_{t-1} + v_t$$

$$\Delta B_t = f_0 + f_1 \Delta Y_{t-1} + g_1 \Delta G_{t-1} + h_1 \Delta B_{t-1} + w_t$$

$$\Delta TR_t = i_0 + i_1 \Delta Y_{t-2} + k_1 \Delta B_{t-2} + l_1 \Delta TR_{t-1} + e_t$$

$$\begin{aligned} \Delta C_t = {} & \left(\frac{(r-\delta)(1+r)}{r(1+\delta)}\right) - \left(\frac{r-\delta}{1+r}\right) C_{t-1} - \theta\left\{G_t - \left(\frac{1+\delta}{1+r}\right) G_{t-1}\right\} \\ & + \left(\frac{r^2 + 2r - \delta}{(1+r)^2}\right) \{k(B_t - (1+r)B_{t-1}) - \alpha TR_t\} \\ & + \beta_0(a_0 + a_1 \Delta Y_{t-1} + a_2 \Delta Y_{t-2} + b_1 \Delta G_{t-1}) \\ & + \beta_1 \Delta Y_{t-1} + \alpha_1 \Delta G_{t-1} + z_t^* , \end{aligned} \tag{20}$$

where a_1, a_2, b_1, d_1, e_1, f_1, g_1, h_1, i_1, k_1, and l_1 are parameters. No additional lags enter the first four equations once the war years are excluded. The model (20) is identified. The autoregression (13) dictates the inclusion of these lags on ΔY and ΔG.

Model (20) is estimated for two samples, the first includes WWII years and the second excludes WWII years. To assure identification of r, δ, and $\overline{C}$, the real interest rate r is imposed on all regressions. I choose three different interest rates to

[21]The SC criterion indicates the reported lag lengths for the ADP tests and the DF tests.

check whether the results are robust. Over the sample period that includes WWII years, the average real Aaa corporate bond rate is 1.47 percent, the average real Baa corporate bond rate is 2.65 percent, and the average real return on common stocks is 8.41 percent. The hypothesis that $\alpha_1 = \beta_0 = \beta_1 = k = \theta = 0$ is not rejected for the sample with the WWII years. The χ^2-statistics for the three rates are 6.12, 5.25, and 3.58 respectively. The statistics are not significant even at the 25 percent level for all three rates.[22] The hypothesis that $\alpha = \alpha_1 = \beta_0 = \beta_1 = k = \theta = 0$ is rejected at the 10 percent level of significance for all three rates ($\chi^2 = 21.29$, 18.70, and 12.26, respectively). This hypothesis is not rejected for the stock rate at the 5 percent level; however, it is rejected for the Aaa and Baa rates at the 5 percent level. In order to test whether the WWII years should be included, I conduct a Hausman-type test for a structural change in the consumption equation parameters. I find a significant change, suggesting to exclude the war years ($\chi^2 = 31.41$).

When I exclude the WWII years, the Aaa corporate bond rate is 2.41 percent, the Baa corporate bond rate is 3.65 percent, and the return on common stocks is 8.32 percent. Table 1 reports IV regression results for model (20) without WWII years. Table 2 shows the results of the restricted version of the model for the three rates. The hypothesis that $\alpha = \alpha_1 = \beta_0 = \beta_1 = 0$ is not rejected for all three rates even at the 25 percent level of significance (χ^2 takes on the values 3.48, 3.53, and 3.85, respectively). However, the hypothesis that $\alpha = \alpha_1 = \beta_0 = \beta_1 = k = 0$ is rejected at the 10 percent and 5 percent levels for the Aaa and Baa rates and is not rejected at the 5 percent and 10 percent levels for the stock rate ($\chi^2 = 15.47$, 13.14, and 7.86, respectively. The hypothesis that $\alpha = \alpha_1 = \beta_0 = \beta_1 = \theta = 0$ is rejected for all rates even at the .5 percent level of significance ($\chi^2 = 47.73$, 47.32, and 47.19, respectively). The parameter estimates of k for the Aaa and Baa rates in Table 2 are positive. However, the values for k are far above one. This seems to suggest that the household sector not only perceives currently outstanding government bonds as net wealth but expects future bond issues to add to its net wealth. The estimates of θ in Table 2 are negative, which implies that government spending complements private consumption. Leiderman and Razin (1988) and Reid (1989) obtained also a negative value for θ; however, Kormendi (1983) estimated a positive value. The parameter estimates in Table 2 fulfill the convergence condition $(1 + r)^2 > (1 + \delta)$. The rate of time preference is positive, $\overline{C}$ takes on a negative value. This does not necessarily imply a negative bliss level (see p. 7).[23]

In order to check the robustness of my results, I derive the real government purchases series and the bond series using the implicit government purchases deflator instead of the nondurables plus services deflator. Also, I include debt interest payments as an additional right-hand-side variable in the consumption regressions. Results are not significantly affected by using the government purchases deflator or including debt interest.

[22]Kormendi (1983) also estimated a significant coefficient for transfers and an insignificant coefficient for government bonds.

[23]See also Lewbel (1987).

TABLE 1

IV—ESTIMATES OF PARAMETERS FOR MODEL (20), WITHOUT WWII YEARS

Parameter	r = 2.41		r = 3.65		r = 8.32	
f_0	54.43	(52.09)	54.38	(52.09)	54.35	(52.09)
f_1	−.34	(.15)	−.34	(.15)	−.34	(.15)
g_1	.38	(.43)	.38	(.43)	.38	(.43)
h_1	.43	(.13)	.43	(.13)	.43	(.14)
a_0	159.87	(55.28)	−.11	(.13)	−.11	(.13)
a_1	−.11	(.13)	−.11	(.13)	−.11	(.13)
a_2	−.07	(.12)	−.07	(.12)	−.08	(.12)
b_1	−.12	(.44)	−.12	(.44)	−.12	(.44)
d_0	59.58	(20.87)	59.53	(20.87)	59.45	(20.87)
d_1	.03	(.16)	.03	(.16)	.03	(.16)
e_1	−.11	(.04)	−.11	(.04)	−.10	(.04)
i_0	23.23	(9.36)	23.27	(9.36)	23.40	(9.36)
i_1	.08	(.02)	.08	(.02)	.08	(.02)
k_1	−.07	(.02)	−.07	(.02)	−.07	(.02)
l_1	.001	(.12)	−.002	(.12)	−.004	(.12)
δ	−.21	(.08)	−.19	(.09)	−.15	(.09)
$\bar{C}$	41.54	(17.10)	62.16	(24.45)	137.42	(50.48)
k	.59	(.42)	.47	(.38)	.17	(.29)
α	−1.37	(.28)	−1.35	(.27)	−1.27	(.23)
θ	−1.25	(.21)	−1.24	(.21)	−1.17	(.23)
β_0	−.19	(1.13)	−.14	(1.04)	−.04	(.88)
β_1	−.03	(.15)	−.30	(.14)	−.04	(.12)
α_1	−.23	(.29)	−.21	(.27)	−.17	(.23)
$Q(6)$	4.19		4.14		3.96	
$\bar{R}^2$	.50		.50		.51	

NOTES: The numbers in parentheses are the standard errors. $\bar{R}^2$ is the adjusted R^2 for the consumption regression. $Q(6)$ is Box-Pierce's Q-statistic (for six lags) for the null hypothesis that the consumption errors are white noise.

TABLE 2

IV—ESTIMATES OF PARAMETERS FOR THE RESTRICTED VERSION OF MODEL (20), WITHOUT WWII YEARS

Parameter	r = 2.41		r = 3.65		r = 8.32	
f_0	60.68	(51.74)	60.46	(51.78)	56.13	(52.06)
f_1	−.34	(.14)	−.34	(.14)	−.34	(.14)
g_1	.24	(.41)	.25	(.41)	.33	(.43)
h_1	.43	(.13)	.43	(.13)	.45	(.14)
a_0	158.02	(52.43)	157.28	(52.40)	152.14	(52.06)
a_1	−.06	(.07)	−.05	(.07)	.007	(.07)
a_2	−.14	(.06)	−.14	(.06)	−.13	(.06)
b_1	−.08	(.28)	−.08	(.28)	−.13	(.27)
d_0	59.56	(20.85)	59.47	(20.85)	58.37	(20.80)
d_1	.04	(.16)	.04	(.16)	.05	(.15)
e_1	−.13	(.04)	−.13	(.04)	−.11	(.04)
i_0	21.07	(9.07)	20.93	(9.06)	21.14	(9.04)
i_1	.07	(.02)	.07	(.02)	.07	(.02)
k_1	−.04	(.02)	−.04	(.02)	−.05	(.02)
l_1	.09	(.11)	.10	(.11)	.09	(.11)
δ	.04	(.01)	.05	(.01)	.09	(.01)
$\bar{C}$	−17.78	(103.07)	−28.63	(146.56)	−179.12	(555.06)
θ	−.59	(.17)	−.59	(.17)	−.42	(.18)
k	14.85	(15.20)	6.16	(3.52)	—	—
$Q(6)$	5.89		6.26		9.73	
$\bar{R}^2$	.33		.33		.31	

NOTES: The numbers in parentheses are the standard errors. $\bar{R}^2$ is the adjusted R^2 for the consumption regression. $Q(6)$ is Box-Pierce's Q-statistic (for six lags) for the null hypothesis that the consumption errors are white noise.

4. CONCLUSION

In this paper, the rational expectations approach to permanent income models of consumption has been extended to incorporate the Ricardian equivalence proposition. The consumption function was explicitly derived from household utility maximization under the null hypothesis of Ricardian equivalence and an alternative of incomplete tax discounting. Both hypotheses were nested within the consumption model. Also, a Keynesian consumption hypothesis was considered. The model was estimated with variables in first differences because the specification with a deterministic time trend was rejected.

The LR-test statistics are too low to reject the permanent income hypothesis, whether or not the World War II years are included. In contrast, Flavin (1981, 1985) and other consumption function studies with aggregate data reject the permanent income model. These studies do not specify a parameter that measures the degree of tax discounting, nor do they investigate whether removing a deterministic time trend from the data is appropriate. The evidence with respect to Ricardian equivalence is mixed. If the World War II years are included in my sample, the joint hypothesis of permanent income and Ricardian equivalence is not rejected. However, I find that the WWII years should be excluded. Then, the joint hypothesis is not rejected only in the case where common stock returns are the measure of r. My data set ends in 1985 because state and local debt values are not available beyond this date. When additional data will become available, the large fiscal deficits experienced by the United States during the 1980s may lead to more decisive test results. Furthermore, the assumption of a constant interest rate might be too strict in an intertemporal consumption model. Future research should therefore consider models with variable interest rates and also address the issue of nonstationary variables.

APPENDIX: DATA SOURCES AND MANIPULATIONS

All variables are defined in per capita terms. The annual U.S. data collected cover the period from 1929 to 1985. The following nominal data are from the *National Income and Product Accounts of the United States, 1929–1982 Statistical Tables,* and for 1983 to 1985 from the July 1986 issue of the *Survey of Current Business:* personal nondurables and services consumption expenditures (Table 1.1); federal, state, and local government purchases of goods and services (Table 1.1); labor income as the sum of "compensation of employees" and "proprietors' income" (Table 1.14); government transfer payments to persons (Table 3.11); and interest payments on governmental debt is line 13 minus lines 16 and 18 in Table 3.1. Implicit price deflators for nondurables, services, and government spending (with 1982 as the base year) are from the same sources (Table 7.4). Population figures are taken from the *Economic Report of the President,* February 1971 and 1986. Population figures are as of July 1.

The market values of privately held federal government debt in December of each year are from Seater (1981, Table 1, Series MVPRIV3) for the period 1929–1941 and from 1942 on from Cox (1985). Cox kindly provided an updated and revised series. I added the market value of state and local debt to the series of federal debt. Seater reports market values for state and local debt from 1929 to 1975 as MVSL in Table 2. Updates are calculated according to Seater's formula. Updates of prices for state and local bonds are reported in various issues of the *Survey of Current Business*. Par values of state and local debt are taken from various issues of the *Statistical Abstract of the United States*. The 1989 issue (109th edition) has figures up to 1986, allowing me to calculate MVSL up to 1985.

The nominal annual interest rate for corporate bonds of the Aaa series and the Baa series (Moody's) are from the *Economic Report of the President:* 1929–1938 data from the 1964 issue and 1939–1985 data from the 1986 issue. Common stock returns are from Ibbotson and Sinquefield (1989).

LITERATURE CITED

Altig, David. "Econometric Analysis of Consumption Behavior and Fiscal Policy: A Review Essay." *Journal of Monetary Economics* 22 (July 1988), 155–64.

Aschauer, David A. "Fiscal Policy and Aggregate Demand." *American Economic Review* 75 (March 1985), 117–27.

______. "The Equilibrium Approach to Fiscal Policy." *Journal of Money, Credit, and Banking* 20 (February 1988), 41–62.

Bailey, Martin. *National Income and the Price Level*. New York: McGraw-Hill, 1962, 1971.

Barro, Robert J. "Are Government Bonds Net Wealth?" *Journal of Political Economy* 82 (November/December 1974), 1095–117.

______. "Reply to Feldstein and Buchanan." *Journal of Political Economy* 84 (April 1976), 343–50.

______. "On the Determination of Public Debt." *Journal of Political Economy* 87 (October 1979), 940–71.

______. "The Ricardian Approach to Budget Deficits." *Journal of Economic Perspectives* 3 (Spring 1989), 37–54.

Barsky, Robert B., N. Gregory Mankiw, and Stephen Zeldes. "Ricardian Consumers with Keynesian Propensities." *American Economic Review* 76 (September 1986), 676–91.

Barth, James, George Iden, and Frank S. Russek. "Government Debt, Government Spending, and Private Sector Behavior: Comment." *American Economic Review* 76 (December 1986), 1158–67.

Bernanke, Ben. "Adjustment Costs, Durables, and Aggregate Consumption." *Journal of Monetary Economics* 15 (January 1985), 41–68.

Bernheim, Douglas B. "Ricardian Equivalence: An Evaluation of Theory and Evidence." Working Paper No. 2330, National Bureau of Economic Research, July 1987.

Blanchard, Olivier J. "Debt, Deficits, and Finite Horizons." *Journal of Political Economy* 93 (April 1985), 223–47.

Campbell, John Y. "Does Saving Anticipate Declining Labor Income? An Alternative Test of the Permanent Income Hypothesis." *Econometrica* 55 (November 1987), 1247–73.

Campbell, John Y., and Angus Deaton. "Is Consumption Too Smooth?" Working Paper No. 2134, National Bureau of Economic Research, January 1987.

Champernowne, David G. *Uncertainty and Estimation in Economics*. San Francisco: Holden-Day, 1969.

Chan, Louis Kuo Chi. "Uncertainty and the Neutrality of Government Financing Policy." *Journal of Monetary Economics* 11 (May 1983), 351–72.

Cox, W. Michael. "The Behavior of Treasury Securities: Monthly, 1942–1984." *Journal of Monetary Economics* 16 (September 1985), 227–50.

Dickey, David A., and Wayne A. Fuller. "Likelihood Ratio Statistics for Autoregressive Time Series with a Unit Root." *Econometrica* 49 (July 1981), 1057–72.

Dwyer, Gerald. "Inflation and Government Deficits." *Economic Inquiry* 20 (July 1982), 315–29.

Engle, Robert F., and Clive W. Granger. "Cointegration and Error Correction: Representation, Estimation and Testing." *Econometrica* 55 (March 1987), 251–76.

English, William B., Jeffrey A. Miron, and David W. Wilcox. "Seasonal Fluctuations and the Life Cycle—Permanent Income Model of Consumption: A Correction." *Journal of Political Economy* 97 (August 1989), 988–91.

Epstein, Larry G. "Risk Aversion and Asset Prices." *Journal of Monetary Economics* 22 (September 1988), 179–92.

Evans, Paul. "Do Large Deficits Produce High Interest Rates?" *American Economic Review* 75 (March 1985), 68–87.

______. "Interest Rates and Expected Future Budget Deficits in the United States." *Journal of Political Economy* 95 (February 1987), 34–58.

______. "Are Consumers Ricardian? Evidence for the United Sates." *Journal of Political Economy* 96 (October 1988), 983–1004.

Feldstein, Martin S. "The Effects of Fiscal Policy When Incomes Are Uncertain: A Contradiction to Ricardian Equivalence." *American Economic Review* 78 (March 1988), 14–23.

Feldstein, Martin S., and Douglas W. Elmendorf. "Taxes, Budget Deficits and Consumer Spending: Some Evidence." Working Paper No. 2355, National Bureau of Economic Research, August 1987.

Flavin, Marjorie A. "The Adjustment of Consumption to Changing Expectations about Future Income." *Journal of Political Economy* 89 (October 1981), 974–1009.

______. "Excess Sensitivity of Consumption to Current Income: Liquidity Constraints or Myopia." *Canadian Journal of Economics* 18 (February 1985), 117–36.

Fuller, Wayne A. *Introduction to Statistical Time Series*. New York: John Wiley & Sons, 1976.

Gallant, Ronald A. *Nonlinear Statistical Models*. New York: John Wiley & Sons, 1987.

Granger, Clive W. J., and Paul Newbold. "Spurious Regressions in Econometrics." *Econometrica* 2 (July 1974), 110–20.

Hall, Robert E. "Stochastic Implications of the Life Cycle-Permanent Income Hypothesis: Theory and Evidence." *Journal of Political Economy* 86 (December 1978), 971–87.

______. "Consumption." Working Paper No. 2265, National Bureau of Economic Research, May 1987.

Hamilton, James, and Marjorie A. Flavin. "On the Limitations of Government Borrowing: A Framework for Empirical Testing." *American Economic Review* 76 (September 1986), 808–19.

Hansen, Lars Peter. "Large Sample Properties of Generalized Method of Moments Estimators." *Econometrica* 50 (July 1982), 1029–54.

Hayashi, Fumio. "The Permanent Income Hypothesis: Estimation and Testing by Instrumental Variables." *Journal of Political Economy* 90 (October 1982), 895–916.

Hayford, Marc. "Liquidity Constraints and the Ricardian Equivalence Theorem." *Journal of Money, Credit, and Banking* 21 (August 1989), 380–87.

Ibbotson, Roger G., and Rex A. Sinquefield. *Stocks, Bonds, Bills, and Inflation: Historical Returns (1926–1987).* Homewood, Ill.: Dow Jones-Irwin, 1989.

Judd, Kenneth. "Debt and Distortionary Taxation in a Simple Perfect Foresight Model." *Journal of Monetary Economics* 20 (July 1987), 51–72.

Kormendi, Roger C. "Government Debt, Government Spending, and Private Sector Behavior." *American Economic Review* 73 (December 1983), 994–1010.

Kormendi, Roger C., and Philip Meguire. "Government Debt, Government Spending, and Private Sector Behavior: Reply." *American Economic Review* 76 (December 1986), 1180–7.

Leiderman, Leonardo, and Assaf Razin. "Testing Ricardian Neutrality with an Intertemporal Stochastic Model." *Journal of Money, Credit, and Banking* 20 (February 1988), 1–21.

Lewbel, Arthur. "Bliss Levels That Aren't." *Journal of Political Economy* 95 (February 1987), 211–15.

Mankiw, N. Gregory, and Matthew Shapiro. "Trends, Random Walks and Tests of the Permanent Income Hypothesis." *Journal of Monetary Economics* 16 (September 1985), 165–74.

Miron, Jeffrey A. "Seasonal Fluctuations and the Life Cycle-Permanent Income Model of Consumption." *Journal of Political Economy* 94 (December 1986), 1258–79.

Modigliani, Franco, and Arlie Sterling. "Government Debt, Government Spending and Private Sector Behavior: Comment." *American Economic Review* 76 (December 1986), 1168–79.

Nelson, Charles. "A Reappraisal of Recent Tests of the Permanent Income Hypothesis." *Journal of Political Economy* 95 (June 1987), 641–46.

Plosser, Charles I. "Fiscal Policy and the Term Structure." *Journal of Monetary Economics* 20 (May 1987), 343–67.

Reid, Bradford G. "Government Budgets and Aggregate Consumption: Cross-Sectional Evidence from Canadian Provincial Data." *Journal of Macroeconomics* 11 (Winter 1989), 121–32.

Seater, John J. "The Market Value of Outstanding Government Debt, 1919–1975." *Journal of Monetary Economics* 8 (July 1981), 85–101.

______. "Does Government Debt Matter: A Review." *Journal of Monetary Economics* 16 (July 1985), 121–31.

Seater, John J., and Roberto S. Mariano. "New Test of the Life Cycle and Tax Discounting Hypotheses." *Journal of Monetary Economics* 15 (March 1985), 195–215.

Sims, Christopher A., James H. Stock, and Mark W. Watson. "Inference in Linear Time Series Models with Some Unit Roots." Working Paper No. E-87-1, Hoover Institution, Stanford University, 1987.

Stock, James H. and Kenneth D. West. "Integrated Regressors and Tests of the Permanent-Income Hypothesis." *Journal of Monetary Economics* 21 (January 1988), 85–95.

Tauchen, George. "Statistical Properties of Generalized Method-of-Moments Estimators of Structural Parameters Obtained from Financial Market Data." *Journal of Business and Economic Statistics* 4 (October 1986), 397–416.

Tobin, James. *Asset Accumulation and Economic Activity*. Oxford: Basil Blackwell, 1980.

West, Kenneth D. "Asymptotic Normality When Regressors Have a Unit Root." *Econometrica* 56 (November 1988), 1397–417.

DAVID R. HAKES

The Objectives and Priorities of Monetary Policy under Different Federal Reserve Chairmen

IN THIS JOURNAL, MILTON FRIEDMAN PRESENTED criticisms and proposed institutional changes for the Federal Reserve in his often cited paper "Monetary Policy: Theory and Practice" (1982). Since Friedman's views on the shortcomings of the institution of the Federal Reserve are so well known, it is unnecessary to repeat them here. However, in his zeal to emphasize the role of bureaucratic inertia in the practice of monetary policy, Friedman stated, "so far as the Federal Reserve System is concerned, the same inability to learn from experience has prevailed under a succession of personalities. Information about the name of the chairman of the Federal Reserve is of little or no use in describing the behavior of the Fed—though the name of the president apparently is" (1982, p. 103).[1] Later, when summarizing this issue, Friedman emphasized that "the issue is not one of particular personalities, but rather of institutional structure" (1982, p. 104). Similar statements by Friedman may be found elsewhere; see Friedman 1985.

Yet, near the time of Volcker's retirement announcement and the nomination of Greenspan as chairman of the Fed, a *Wall Street Journal* editorial suggested that Volcker's approach to monetary policy had been so successful as to earn the nickname "the Volcker Standard" (Kadlec 1987).[2] This suggests that financial markets

The author thanks Tom Wyrick, John Hoftyzer, David Rose, Robert Sorenson, and two anonymous referees for many helpful comments.

[1]This reference to the impact of the president on monetary policy is based on Weintraub (1978); see also Potts and Luckett (1978). The issue of presidential impacts on monetary policy will be addressed separately in section 3.

[2]It should be noted that Kadlec does not view monetary policy as so stable that it deserves the name "the Volcker Standard." He was referring to the opinions of his colleagues in the financial markets. The phrase "Volcker Standard" appears to have been coined by the editors of the *Wall Street Journal* (1983).

DAVID R. HAKES *is assistant professor of economics at the University of Missouri, St. Louis.*

Journal of Money, Credit, and Banking, Vol. 22, No. 3 (August 1990)

perceive a difference in Federal Reserve policy under different Fed chairmen. Further, there has been discussion regarding President Reagan's reappointment of Volcker as chairman in 1983. While the Reagan administration may have had many reasons for removing Volcker as chairman—(1) he was not a Reagan appointee, (2) he carried the political baggage of scapegoat for the early 1980s' recession, (3) he was gaining credit for the current (1983) recovery—they were unwilling to risk destabilizing the financial markets by removing him as chairman.[3] Apparently the financial markets suspect that personalities make a difference in the formulation of monetary policy.

Because there may be disagreement about whether the name of the Fed chairman provides meaningful information about monetary policy, this short paper tests the hypothesis that the objectives and priorities of monetary policy are different under different Fed chairmen. Results of estimates of a standard reaction function strongly suggest that the objectives and priorities of monetary policy do differ under different Fed chairmen. Specifically, tests of structural change of the coefficients in the reaction functions employed in this paper imply that the Burns period may have been a monetary policy aberration. That is, the Martin and Volcker periods are nearly indistinguishable, while the Burns period is significantly different from both the Volcker and Martin periods. In addition, model specifications that allow for an independent influence on monetary policy from different presidential administrations also imply that there are significant differences in monetary policy under different Fed chairmen.

1. METHOD

The monetary policy reaction functions estimated in this paper are of the following form:

$$P_t = b_0 + b_1\hat{IP}_t + b_2\widehat{PPI}_t + b_3\hat{U}_t + b_4\hat{BT}_t + e_{t'} , \tag{1}$$

where

P_t = policy indicator (0 = tight money, 1 = easy money);
$\hat{IP}_t$ = industrial production index (growth objective);
$\widehat{PPI}_t$ = producer price index (inflation objective);
$\hat{U}_t$ = civilian unemployment percentage (unemployment objective);
$\hat{BT}_t$ = balance of trade surplus (international balance objective);
e_t = error term.

[3]There were articles nearly daily in the *Wall Street Journal* from April through June 1983 speculating on whether Volcker would be reappointed. The consensus suggested that while there were many reasons to remove Volcker, there was an overriding reason to keep him—his anti-inflationary stance was reassuring to the financial markets during a period of heavy foreign capital inflow.

The hypothesized signs of the coefficients are

$$b_1, b_2 < 0 \qquad b_3, b_4 > 0.$$[4]

This reaction function has been employed in a previous paper by Hakes (1988), therefore only a brief description of equation (1) will follow.

The dependent and independent variables in the reaction function are the policy indicator and proxies for the objectives of monetary policy, respectively. "Tight money" or "easy money" was employed as the policy indicator for the following reason.[5] The period of concern for this study is the entire post-Accord period. This is to capture the chairmanships of Martin, Burns, and Volcker. Most certainly, there have been changes in operating procedures which could preclude the use of a monetary aggregate or an interest rate (federal funds rate) as the policy indicator. The policy indicator used in this study is independent of the actual operating procedures employed by the Fed, and therefore it is especially useful when analyzing Fed behavior over long periods of time. An additional reason why a monetary aggregate was not employed as the policy indicator is that the money supply (however defined) has not generally been considered a reliable policy indicator with monthly data. As explained by Havrilesky, Sapp, and Schweitzer (1975, p. 841), "monetary aggregates . . . are not yet perceived [by monetary authorities] as instruments, targets, or indicators . . . ". While this was expressed in 1975 (and subsequent Fed announcements suggest that the money supply may intermittently be viewed as a target, but not an indicator of policy), this statement is accurate for the majority of the sample period of this paper. Finally, an additional reason why the federal funds rate was not employed as the policy indicator is that the federal funds rate was not available for a substantial portion of the Martin subperiod.

The independent variables in the reaction function are proxies of the ultimate objectives of monetary policy as established by the Employment Act of 1946. The value of these variables employed in equation (1) are the predicted values from a fifth-order unrestricted vector autoregression containing the objectives of policy and other macroeconomic variables thought to affect the target variables in future periods.[6] By utilizing these "forecasts" of the policy objectives, this reaction function

[4]These expected signs are consistent with previous monetary policy reaction functions (see the survey article by Barth, Sickles, and Weist 1982).

[5]This dichotomous series was generated first by Luckett and Potts (1978). They classified monetary policy *intentions* as "tight" or "easy" from their reading of the Record of Policy Actions of the FOMC for the period 1956–1976. This series was similarly extended by Wallace and Warner (1984) and Hakes (1988) to include the entire 1953–1987 period. For a further explanation of this policy indicator, and some its positive attributes and shortcomings, see Potts and Luckett (1978).

[6]The variables in the VAR model are stationary values of the industrial production index, consumer price index, producer price index, unemployment rate, M1 money supply, personal income, three-month Treasury bill rate, and balance of trade surplus. This unrestricted VAR model contained no dummies for unusual economic events—oil price shocks, changes in financial market regulation, etc. This was done because the policymakers could not have foreseen many of these events. The estimates of equation (1) have not likely been biased by this, however, because estimates utilizing the raw data instead of the VAR forecasts produced similar results. For a more complete description of the forecasting technique, see Hakes (1988). Conceptually similar methods of forecasting have been employed by Abrams, Froyen, and

avoids the coefficient biases associated with using concurrent or lagged policy objectives.[7]

2. RESULTS

To test the hypothesis that the objectives and priorities of monetary policy differ under different Federal Reserve chairmen, equation (1) was estimated with monthly data as a linear probability model and a probit probability model over three subperiods. These three subperiods correspond to the post-Accord chairmanships of Martin (1953.1–1970.1), Burns (1970.2–1978.1), and Volcker (1979.8–1987.8).[8]

Table 1 presents the results of OLS and probit estimates of the reaction function for the Martin years. All coefficients enter with the expected sign, and the coefficients of the producer price index and unemployment are significant at the 1 percent and 5 percent levels, respectively.

TABLE 1

RESULTS OF THE MARTIN YEARS, 1953.1–1970.1

	Probability Model				
	Linear[a]			Probit[b]	
Independent Variable	Estimated Coefficient[c]	t-ratio	Beta Coefficient	Estimated Coefficient	t-ratio
Intercept	0.58	—	—	0.11	—
$\widehat{IP}$	−3.87	−0.54	−0.0250	−9.38	−0.43
$\widehat{PPI}$	−69.34**	−4.70	−0.2491**	−206.06**	−4.41
$\hat{U}$	0.67*	1.96	0.0865*	1.99*	1.91
$\widehat{BT}$	0.001	0.01	0.0004	−0.02	−0.05

[a] $n = 205$, $R^2 = .18$, $F = 11.23$**.
[b] $n = 205$, log likelihood $= -118.79$, $\chi^2 = 40.61$**.
[c] †, *, and ** appearing in Tables 1, 2, 3 and 4 indicate significance at the 10, 5, and 1 percent levels respectively. t-tests are two-tailed while F and χ^2 tests are one-tailed.

Table 2 presents the estimates of the reaction function for the Burns years. There may have occurred radical shifting of policy objectives during Burns' tenure, especially in the face of the first supply shock, causing the results for the Burns period to be strikingly different from the other periods estimated. Neither the F-ratio nor the χ^2 value is significant at the 10 percent level; consequently, the hypothesis that all slope coefficients equal zero cannot be rejected. Only the coefficient of the producer price index is significant and then only at the 10 percent level.

Table 3 presents the results for the Volcker years. As with the Martin period, all

Waud (1980) and Havrilesky (1987). For a discussion of VAR models in general, see Judge et al. (1988, chapter 18).

[7]For a discussion of these biases, see Abrams, Froyen, and Waud (1980).

[8]The Miller period (1978.3–1979.7) was too short to produce reasonable estimates, therefore the Miller period is not considered here.

coefficients enter with the expected sign. The producer price index is significant at the 1 percent level, unemployment and the industrial production index are significant at the 5 percent or 10 percent level, and, as in most other studies, the balance of trade is not significant.

TABLE 2

RESULTS OF THE BURNS YEARS, 1970.2–1978.1

	Probability Model				
	Linear[a]			Probit[b]	
Independent Variable	Estimated Coefficient[c]	t-ratio	Beta Coefficient	Estimated Coefficient	t-ratio
Intercept	0.77	—	—	0.79	—
$\widehat{IP}$	−0.98	−0.08	−0.0063	−5.31	−0.16
$\widehat{PPI}$	−21.66†	−1.66	−0.0778†	−64.86†	−1.75
$\widehat{U}$	0.49	0.90	0.0647	1.63	1.03
$\widehat{BT}$	−0.01	−0.09	0.0043	−0.07	−0.20

[a] $n = 96$, $R^2 = .05$, $F = 1.33$.
[b] $n = 96$, log likelihood $= -58.14$, $\chi^2 = 5.93$.

The similarity between the Martin and Volcker periods is particularly noteworthy and is demonstrated by the estimated beta coefficients. Note that beta coefficients (sometimes called standardized or normalized coefficients) can be used directly to make statements concerning the relative importance of the independent variables in

TABLE 3

RESULTS OF THE VOLCKER YEARS, 1979.8–1987.8

	Probability Model				
	Linear[a]			Probit[b]	
Independent Variable	Estimated Coefficient	t-ratio	Beta Coefficient	Estimated Coefficient	t-ratio
Intercept	0.62	—	—	0.34	—
$\widehat{IP}$	−17.12†	−1.82	−0.1105†	−51.78†	−1.61
$\widehat{PPI}$	−46.15**	−4.01	−0.1658**	−135.69**	−3.63
$\widehat{U}$	0.99†	1.88	0.1304†	3.31*	1.94
$\widehat{BT}$	0.01	0.11	0.0040	0.05	0.14

[a] $n = 97$, $R^2 = .27$, $F = 8.30$**.
[b] $n = 97$, log likelihood $= -52.53$, $\chi^2 = 28.91$**.

a multiple regression model. They are generated by performing an OLS on variables where each variable is normalized by subtracting its mean and dividing by its estimated standard deviation. The beta coefficients reported in this paper suggest that the same ordering of priorities within the policy objectives existed during both Martin's and Volcker's tenure at the helm of the Fed.[9] That is, the reaction function

[9]The beta coefficients reported in this paper should be interpreted with caution because the linear reaction functions may be heteroskedastic. As a result, the linear coefficients are unbiased but may be

for both periods ranked priorities in the following order from first to last: inflation, unemployment, growth, and international balance.

However, the lack of similarity between both the Martin and Burns period, and the Burns and Volcker periods is equally noteworthy. For this reason, tests of structural change were performed on both the linear and probit specifications of the model. Results of Chow tests and log-likelihood tests for each pair of post-Accord chairmanships are reported in Table 4. While the hypothesis that the regression

TABLE 4

RESULTS OF STRUCTURAL CHANGE TESTS

Chairmanships Compared	Chow Test	Log-likelihood Test
Martin/Volcker	$F = 2.09$	$\chi^2 = 8.04$
Martin/Burns	$F = 9.84$**	$\chi^2 = 36.74$**
Burns/Volcker	$F = 5.79$**	$\chi^2 = 21.64$**
Structural change due to Chairmen dummies with Presidential dummies present	$F = 4.76$**	$\chi^2 = 47.18$**

coefficients among periods are the same cannot be rejected for the Martin and Volcker periods at the 5 percent level, this hypothesis is rejected at the 1 percent level for both the Martin and Burns periods, and the Burns and Volcker periods.[10] Clearly, the Burns era stands alone.

3. PRESIDENTIAL EFFECTS

While the preceding analysis strongly suggests that the name of the Fed chairman does provide information about Fed behavior, the methodology may contain a potential shortcoming. Recall that the particular statement by Friedman cited in the introduction of this paper makes reference to a possible independent influence on monetary policy by each presidential administration. (Other papers by Friedman regarding the issue of the influence of the Fed chairman omit this presidential reference.) While there is no clear or direct legislative link between the executive branch and monetary policy other than through the chairman and Board of Governor appointments, recent literature suggests that this issue be addressed (Havrilesky 1988, 1987; Kane 1988; Luckett and Potts 1980; Weintraub 1978).[11]

---

inefficient. Correcting this with generalized least-squares (or similar) would generate efficient but biased coefficients. However, the linear and probit coefficients have shown similar significance. For a discussion, see Ladd (1966).

[10]There is no discontinuity when grouping any two chairmanships because all of the predicted values of the VAR (and therefore the independent variables in the reaction function) are stationary values.

[11]The autocratic nature of the Federal Reserve chairman with regard to the rest of the Board of Governors is documented by Kane (1988). If Kane is correct, the executive may exert little influence over monetary policy by pressuring other members of the Board besides the chairman. However, there is

If the president only exerts influence on monetary policy through the chairman, then further analysis may be unnecessary. That is, the president's impact on monetary policy may already have been captured in the preceding analysis and some chairmen may have been more influenced by presidential considerations than others. Accommodating a president may be at the discretion of the chairman. If this is so, then studies which suggest that presidential administrations make a difference in monetary policy may have simply picked up evidence of some chairmen giving in to presidential desires more than others (Potts and Luckett 1978; Friedlaender 1973).

However, if the president exerts *independent* influence on monetary policy through other appointments to the Board of Governors, the budget deficit (Laney and Willett 1983), or through other means (possibly direct signaling of the macroeconomic objectives of the relevant administration [Havrilesky 1988]) then the variation in monetary policy from different presidential administrations must first be removed before one can analyze the separate impact of the chairman on monetary policy.

For these reasons, equation (1) was reestimated using pooled data with intercept and slope dummies for each of the following presidential periods: Eisenhower, Kennedy/Johnson, Nixon/Ford, Carter, and Reagan.[12] This restricted model was then compared to the full model which employed pooled data (with the presidential dummies) plus the additional variables of intercept and slope dummies for each of the three chairmanships considered. For these estimations, the balance of trade surplus was dropped from the regressions because it was not significant in any of the three individually estimated chairman subperiods. With presidential dummies in both the full and restricted models, Chow tests and log-likelihood tests were executed to determine if the chairmen dummies added significant explanatory power. The results of these tests are reported at the bottom of Table 4. The structural change attributable to the different Fed chairmanships (with variation due to independent presidential influence removed) is significant at the 1 percent level for both the linear and probit specifications of the model.

Tests were performed to determine whether the breakpoints used for each chairman's subperiod were "optimal" in that these breakpoints minimized the sum of squared errors or maximized the value of the log-likelihood function. To this end, all structural change tests were repeated using breakpoints of one year before and one year after the actual breakpoints for each chairman. In each case, the significance of the Chow and log-likelihood tests fell below that of the tests using the actual breakpoints. While not definitive, this exercise implies that moving from one chairmanship to another corresponds with a unique structural change.

---

some evidence to the contrary. Greider (1987) provides a discussion of the impact of the stacking of the Board with "supply-siders" by the Reagan administration and its effects on Volcker's power, and Greider also notes the problems Carter faced due to his choice of appointments to the Board.

[12]This model cannot be estimated with presidential administration dummies for each chairman subperiod separately. Each subperiod would have produced a singular X-matrix because each subperiod would contain a column of zeros for each president not contained in that chairman's subperiod. No cross-multiplied dummies were employed because they also created singularity. This is because there is no period where there is a chairman and no president, or a period with a president and no chairman.

The reader should note that these results do not necessarily provide direct information about the policymaker's utility functions. As pointed out by Abrams, Froyen, and Waud (1980, p. 31), reaction functions "are the output of a constrained maximization, where the constraints are the reduced-form equations that characterize the economy." If the reduced-form equations that characterize the economy are structurally stable (that is, the relationships between the objectives of policy—unemployment, growth, inflation, and balance of trade—are stable), then inferences regarding policymaker's preferences can be drawn directly from the reaction function estimates. Since there is never certainty that these relationships are stable, the results of this paper have suggested only that the objectives and priorities of monetary policy have been different during the three chairmanships analyzed.[13]

Further, the reader should note that the results of this paper are consistent with the notion that presidential administrations have an impact on the formation of monetary policy. That is, the presidential administration dummies as a group were highly significant in the reaction function, as the papers by Friedlaender, Weintraub, Luckett, Kane, Havrilesky, and others would suggest. However, this paper argues that information regarding the president does not exhaust the information set; knowledge of the Fed chairman also contributes to an explanation of monetary policy.

Finally, it should be noted that this paper has argued only that Fed chairmanships have exhibited different policy objectives. This paper has not argued that Fed chairmen have exhibited different policy preferences. That is, when a change in the chairman corresponds to a change in Fed policy, it is not clear whether the new chairman possesses a different set of preferences, or if the new chairman was simply more strongly influenced by presidential desires. Therefore, it is possible that Fed chairmen have significantly different sets of monetary policy preferences, or that all Fed chairmen have similar preferences but that each chairman responds differently to presidential pressures. In either of these two cases, the chairman has a significant impact on monetary policy. Note, however, that the evidence produced in this paper cannot eliminate a third (but somewhat remote) possibility that presidents are expressing a *change* in *their* preferences when they appoint a new chairman. If presidents had *absolute* control over the Fed chairman, then the significance of the chairmen dummies in the reaction function could be interpreted as a change in presidential preferences. However, this possibility is extremely remote as evidenced by the widespread documentation of rifts between the administration and the chairman (see Havrilesky 1988 and Greider 1987).[14]

[13]Recall that the forecasts of the objectives of policy used in this study are actually the predicted values from a fixed-coefficient VAR. Since the quality of the forecasts do not differ significantly across periods analyzed, the reduced-form equations underlying this model are somewhat stable. This, coupled with the fact that the policy indicator is a measure of policy intentions which are directly controllable by the Fed (unlike money market or monetary aggregate indicators which are policy results and therefore subject to nonpolicy shocks), provides an argument that these results might be used to make inferences regarding the policymakers' preferences during the three periods analyzed. Further, if any instability in the underlying reduced-form equations is largely due to political manipulation, then accounting for this with presidential dummies would allow for the reaction function coefficients to be interpreted as providing some direct information regarding policymakers' preferences.

[14]While there is evidence that the administration has some impact on monetary policy, these rifts between the administration and the chairman suggest that the Fed chairman exerts significant indepen-

Considering the two most likely cases discussed above, it is not clear whether Burns possessed different policy preferences than Martin and Volcker, or whether he may have been more easily influenced by presidential pressures. The extent to which the reaction function coefficients may be interpreted as reflecting chairman preferences is positively related to the structural stability of the underlying macroeconomy, and negatively related to the degree of presidential influence that is successfully imposed on the chairman. That is, presidents may influence monetary policy in many ways—directly through an appeal to the chairman, and indirectly through the fiscal deficit, international exchange rate agreements, etc. Those effects that are indirect (not through the chairman) are presumed to be picked up by the presidential administration dummy variables. Those presidential effects that are direct (through the chairman) may be confused with chairman preferences. In any event, the degree to which presidential effects are direct or indirect is untestable. This is because an estimate of a reduced-form reaction function cannot distinguish between a change in a constraint (presidential requests) and a change in preferences. Whether a president can influence policy through the chairman may be an issue of whether presidential requests are *perceived* as binding constraints by the chairman.[15]

4. CONCLUSIONS

This paper examines one issue presented by Friedman in his 1982 paper. That issue is whether information about the name of the Fed chairman provides information about the behavior of the Fed. That there is significant bureaucratic inertia in discretionary monetary policy is not contested in this paper. The results of this paper strongly suggest that the intentions of monetary policy were significantly different among the three chairmanships analyzed. While the Martin and Volcker periods were extremely similar with respect to policy objectives and priorities, the Burns period was statistically distinct from both the Martin and Volcker periods. What is most disturbing is that no form of the reaction function estimated for the Burns period produced a significant F-ratio or χ^2 value.[16] Therefore, it appears that the Fed may have lacked direction or purpose under the Burns chairmanship.

It is largely left to the reader to speculate as to why these chairmanships exhibit different policy objectives and, in particular, why the Burns period was so unusual.

---

dence. In particular, both the Carter administration and the Reagan administration were upset by Volcker's handling of monetary policy from 1979–1984 as measured by their public protest "signals" (Havrilesky 1988). In addition, Kane (1988) suggests that the choice of a chairman by the president is at least partly based on the independence (or lack thereof) of the prospective chairman.

[15]If presidential requests are seen as binding by *all* chairmen, then the results reported in this paper may only suggest that the appointment of a new chairman expresses new policy preferences by the president. This possibility is extremely remote (see footnote 14).

[16]These results are robust with respect to the proxies chosen for policy objectives (CPI instead of PPI, and real personal income instead of the industrial production index). Further, estimates based on the raw data instead of the predicted values of the policy objectives produced similar results. Therefore, if inflation was more difficult to forecast during the 1970s, it has not likely biased these results (see Cullison 1988).

However, Havrilesky, Sapp, and Schweitzer (1975) may provide some insight. Their evidence suggests that Burns accommodated the desires of the presidential administration far more than his predecessor. In fact, estimates of their reaction functions suggest that during the Burns subperiod prior to the 1972 presidential election, monetary policy actions were undertaken with a significant and perverse response to the price level. That is, the Fed under Burns may have "believed that a positive rate of price inflation was desirable in order to reduce unemployment and move leftward along a short-run Phillips curve by validating, rather that resisting, increases in the price level" (1975, p. 847). (They note that when Martin was chairman, even during periods of "easy money," monetary policy retained a significant countercyclical response to movements in the price level.) After the Nixon price freeze, the Fed responded to the price level with its most severe countercyclical actions of the Martin or Burns subperiods. However, by 1973, the Fed abandoned its tight money policy and the money supply grew at twice the average of the 1960s. They conclude "that the Federal Reserve lost much of its anti-inflationary militance when Burns was Chairman" (1975, p. 850), that Burns too easily submitted to pressure for low interest rates, and that monetary policy became more erratic under Burns. There is also evidence that Burns was a very ease-oriented and pliable chairman as late as the early part of the Carter Administration (Greider 1987). This, together with the Miller interregnum (not analyzed in this paper) may have helped fuel the inflation of the late 1970s.

A somewhat related explanation may be derived from the early literature on the political business cycle. The greatest evidence of a monetary induced political business cycle was during the Burns years (Tufte 1978; Luckett and Potts 1980; Wallace and Warner 1984).[17] Note that while this paper provides *no evidence* of a political business cycle (and should not be interpreted as if it did) the results of this paper are *not inconsistent* with the papers suggesting the existence of a political business cycle in the 1970s. That is, if Burns engaged more heavily than other chairmen in a policy of inducing a political business cycle, or if he simply engaged in an erratic policy of repeatedly changing objectives more radically than other chairmen, then reaction function estimates of Burns' entire subperiod would likely generate insignificant coefficients such as those generated in this paper.

LITERATURE CITED

Abrams, Richard K., Richard Froyen, and Roger N. Waud. "Monetary Policy Reaction Functions, Consistent Expectations, and the Burns Era." *Journal of Money, Credit, and Banking* 12 (February 1980), 30–42.

Amemiya, Takeshi. "Qualitative Response Models: A Survey." *Journal of Economic Literature* 19 (December 1981), 1483–1536.

Barth, James, Robin Sickles, and Philip Weist. "Assessing the Impact of Varying Economic

[17]Luckett and Potts (1980) and Wallace and Warner (1984) suggest that the 1972 monetary expansion was somewhat unusual in that they found no overall evidence of a monetary induced political business cycle. Richards (1986) suggests that a monetary induced political business cycle may have existed, but that this monetary cycle had disappeared by the late 1970s suggesting that Volcker did not exhibit a propensity to induce a political business cycle.

Conditions on Federal Reserve Behavior." *Journal of Macroeconomics* 4 (Winter 1982), 47–70.

Cullison, William E. "On Recognizing Inflation." *Federal Reserve Bank of Richmond Economic Review* (July/August 1988), 4–12.

Federal Reserve Bulletin. Board of Governors of the Federal Reserve System, Washington, D.C. various issues.

Friedlaender, Ann F. "Macro Policy Goals in the Post War Period: A Study in Revealed Preference." *Quarterly Journal of Economics* 87 (February 1973), 25–43.

Friedman, Milton. "Monetary Policy: Theory and Practice." *Journal of Money, Credit, and Banking* 14 (February 1982), 98–118.

———. "The Case for Overhauling the Federal Reserve." *Challenge* (July/August 1985), 4–12.

Greider, William. *Secrets of the Temple: How the Federal Reserve Runs the Country*. New York: Simon and Schuster, 1987.

Hakes, David R. "Monetary Policy and Presidential Elections: A Nonpartisan Political Cycle." *Public Choice* 57 (May 1988), 175–82.

Havrilesky, Thomas M. "A Partisanship Theory of Fiscal and Monetary Regimes." *Journal of Money, Credit, and Banking* 19 (August 1987), 308–25.

———. "Monetary Policy Signaling from the Administration to the Federal Reserve." *Journal of Money, Credit, and Banking* 20 (February 1988), 83–101.

Havrilesky, Thomas M., Robert Sapp, and Robert Schweitzer. "Tests of the Federal Reserve's Reaction to the State of the Economy." *Social Science Quarterly* 55 (March 1975), 835–52.

Johnston, J. *Econometric Methods*. New York: McGraw-Hill, 1984.

Judge, George G., R. Carter Hill, William E. Griffiths, Helmut Lutkepohl, and Tsoung-Chao Lee. *Introduction to the Theory and Practice of Econometrics*. New York: John Wiley and Sons, 1988.

Kadlec, Charles W. "The 'Volcker Standard' Isn't One." *Wall Street Journal* (June 17, 1987), p. 26.

Kane, Edward J. "The Impact of a New Federal Reserve Chairman." *Contemporary Policy Issues* 6 (January 1988), 89–97.

Ladd, George W. "Linear Probability Functions and Discriminant Functions." *Econometrica* 34 (October 1966), 873–85.

Laney, Leroy O., and Thomas D. Willett. "Presidential Politics, Budget Deficits, and Monetary Policy in the United States: 1960–1976." *Public Choice* 40 (1983), 53–70.

Luckett, Dudley G., and Glenn T. Potts. "Monetary Policy and Partisan Politics." *Journal of Money, Credit, and Banking* 12 (August 1980), 540–46.

Potts, Glenn T., and Dudley G. Luckett. "Policy Objectives of Federal Reserve System." *Quarterly Journal of Economics* 92 (August 1978), 525–34.

Richards, Daniel J. "Unanticipated Money and the Political Business Cycle." *Journal of Money, Credit, and Banking* 18 (November 1986), 447–57.

Tufte, Edward R. *Political Control of the Economy*. Princeton, N.J.: Princeton University Press, 1978.

United States Department of Commerce. *Business Statistics: 1986*. Washington, D.C.: Government Printing Office.

Wallace, Myles S., and John T. Warner. "Fed Policy and Presidential Elections." *Journal of Macroeconomics* 6 (Winter 1984), 79–88.

Weintraub, Robert E. "Congressional Supervision of Monetary Policy." *Journal of Monetary Economics* 4 (April 1978), 341–62.

ROGER D. HUANG

Risk and Parity in Purchasing Power

1. INTRODUCTION

THE CONCEPT OF PURCHASING POWER PARITY (PPP) has long played a prominent role in theoretical and empirical research. Recently, a number of studies have examined an ex ante representation of (relative) PPP in the context of efficient markets. Often referred to as the ex ante PPP (EPPP) or the martingale model of real exchange rate innovations, it asserts that the expected rate of change in the nominal exchange rates of two countries equals the expected differential in their inflation rates over the same holding period. The model is derived as a consequence of cross-border intertemporal speculation in foreign goods (Roll 1979) or cross-border financial speculation in bonds (Adler and Lehmann 1983). Both the derivations, however, posit that the ex ante real interest rate differential between a pair of countries on nominally riskless bonds is a constant.

An immediate empirical implication of the EPPP is that percentage changes in real exchange rates are serially uncorrelated. A number of studies by Stockman (1978), Roll (1979), Darby (1980), Adler and Lehmann (1983), and others found that the data are consistent with this implication. Additional restrictions of the EPPP were also examined by Cumby and Obstfeld (1984) and Huang (1987). They found that while real exchange rates appear to be mutually uncorrelated at all lags, the additional restrictions are strongly rejected by the data. The evidence therefore

The author is grateful to two anonymous referees, Sebastian Edwards, Jeffrey Frankel, Craig Hakkio, Robert Hodrick, and seminar participants at Vanderbilt University and the National Bureau of Economic Research Conference on the Dynamic Behavior of PPP Deviations for helpful comments.

ROGER D. HUANG *is associate professor of finance in the Owen Graduate School of Management, Vanderbilt University.*

Journal of Money, Credit, and Banking, Vol. 22, No. 3 (August 1990)

indicates substantial departures from EPPP. Holding on to the assumption that expectations are rational, the rejections suggest that the assumption of constant ex ante real rate differentials may have been violated. There are also a number of theoretical asset pricing models, for example, Fama and Farber (1979), Hodrick (1981), and others that deduce the equality between foreign exchange risk premium, defined as the deviation that separates the forward exchange rate from its expected future spot rate, and the expected real interest rate differential. Thus, the deviations from EPPP may be linked to time-varying risk premiums. This interpretation is, however, incomplete.

In contrast to the prevailing interpretation, it can be shown under very general conditions that deviations from EPPP are exactly offset by the difference between a forward exchange risk premium and the expected real interest rate differential. The EPPP model may therefore be deficient in that it attributes all the risk premiums associated with the intertemporal speculative activity by risk-averse economic agents to be incorporated in ex ante real interest rate differentials.

An examination of the current empirical literature also suggests that the movements in foreign exchange risk premiums are unlikely to exactly balance the variations in ex ante real rate differentials. The literature on the equality of expected real interest rates across different countries shows that the hypothesis is rejected [see, for example, Hodrick (1979), Cumby and Obstfeld, (1984), and Mishkin (1984)]. However, the hypothesis that the ex ante differential equals a constant is relatively more robust. The results obtained by Cumby and Obstfeld (1984) are consistent with it and Campbell and Clarida (1987a) also found very low volatility in ex ante real interest rate differentials. This indicates that given the high volatility in departures from EPPP, it is unlikely that they are due solely to the volatility in the expected real interest rate differentials. Furthermore, the work of Fama (1984) and Hodrick and Srivastava (1986) shows that the risk premiums in forward prices are time-varying and are more variable than the expected rate of change in spot exchange rates. Thus, the forward exchange risk premiums may play a potentially more dominant role in accounting for the variations in departures from EPPP.

It is also informative to examine the comovements in forward exchange risk premiums and EPPP deviations. The possibility that they move together is not guaranteed even in the case when the volatilities in risk premiums are big enough to be associated with the variations in deviations from EPPP. Recent studies have examined the joint behavior of risk premiums for different assets. Campbell and Clarida (1987b) examine the term structure of Euromarket interest rates. Giovannini and Jorion (1987, 1988) study excess returns in both the U.S. stock market and foreign exchange market. The literature has also addressed the ability of asset pricing models to explain the variation in risk premiums. Hansen and Hodrick (1983) propose an intertemporal latent variable model to value one-month forward exchange risk premiums. Huang (1989) extends the tests to incorporate forward exchange rates of different maturities. Giovannini and Jorion (1989) use the Sharpe-Lintner CAPM to determine if it can explain movements in foreign exchange rates.

The purpose of this paper is to investigate the behavior of risk premiums associated with forward speculative activity in the context of deviations from EPPP. Two specific sets of issues are investigated. First, I examine the relative importance of forward exchange risk premiums and expected real rate differentials in accounting for departures from EPPP. The null hypothesis of equality between the two variables is rejected if they differ in their contribution to the volatility in deviations from EPPP. Second, I examine the hypothesis that the forward risk premiums and the deviations from EPPP are driven by the same set of common factors. This null hypothesis examines the comovements in the variables to determine if they in fact move together.

In the next section, a general decomposition of ex ante (percentage) change in real exchange rates into a forward exchange risk premium term and an ex ante real interest rate differential is presented. This decomposition is then related to other recent studies of the behavior of real exchange rates.

In section 3, I examine the extent to which the variation in the ex ante change in real exchange rates is linked with the variation in either the forward exchange risk premium or the ex ante real rate differential. For this purpose, the analyses utilize the regression interpretations used by Fama (1984). These interpretations are attractive in that the statistical analysis can be directly conducted in terms of the general decomposition of the change in real exchange rates without additional restrictions on either the forward exchange risk premiums or ex ante real interest rate differentials. All the estimations are performed jointly to account for the interactions in integrated international markets and without positing the second moments to be a constant. In conjunction with the aim of this section, a martingale model of real exchange rates modified for the presence of a forward exchange risk premium is also introduced and analyzed.

The results in section 3 show that the risk premiums investors' demand for speculating in the forward market are more important than their expectations of real interest rate differentials in accounting for deviations from EPPP. This is not to say that the forward exchange risk premiums and the departures from EPPP do in fact move together. Section 4 studies this possibility by investigating if the forward risk premiums and the ex ante change in real exchange rates move together by responding proportionately to the same set of common factors. The specification utilized for this purpose is previously used by Hansen and Hodrick (1983) and Gibbons and Ferson (1985) to test a variant of an intertemporal asset pricing model. The estimations required are nonlinear and are performed with Hansen's (1982) generalized method of moments that allows for conditional heteroskedasticity. The results fail to reject the hypothesis that the risk premiums move in proportion to a single common variable.

Section 5 ends the paper with a summary and a discussion of the implications of the results.

2. EPPP, RISK PREMIUMS, AND EX ANTE REAL RATE DIFFERENTIALS

A general relationship for deviations from EPPP can be obtained from three ingredients. One, invoke the covered interest rate parity condition:

$$F_t^i - S_t^i = R_{t+1} - R_{t+1}^i , \tag{1}$$

where F_t^i is the natural logarithm of the one-period forward exchange rate of U.S. dollar per foreign currency, S_t^i is the natural logarithm of the spot exchange rate of U.S. dollar per foreign currency, and R_{t+1} and R_{t+1}^i are the continuously compounded U.S. and country i nominal returns from t to $t + 1$ on default-free bonds, respectively. The relationship (1) is an arbitrage condition that prevents investors from making unlimited profits. It is also empirically supported [see, for example, Frenkel and Levich (1975, 1977), and Marston (1976)].

Two, define the nominal yields on discount bonds by following Fisher as

$$\begin{aligned} R_{t+1} &= E_t(\delta_{t+1}) + E_t(I_{t+1}) \\ R_{t+1}^i &= E_t(\delta_{t+1}^i) + E_t(I_{t+1}^i) , \end{aligned} \tag{2}$$

where $E_t(.)$ is the rational expectation conditional on all information at time t, δ_{t+1} is the real interest rate over the period t to $t + 1$, I_{t+1} is the U.S. inflation rate over the period t to $t + 1$, and superscript i refers to country i.

Three, decompose the forward exchange rate as

$$F_t^i = E_t(S_{t+1}^i) + E_t(P_{t+1}^i) , \tag{3}$$

where $E_t(P_{t+1}^i)$ is the forward exchange risk premium term. This risk premium is thus the anticipated reward from selling the foreign currency in the forward market. It is now well established that forward exchange rates are biased predictors of subsequent spot rates as stated in (3) [see, for example, Hansen and Hodrick (1980), and Bilson (1981)]. Moreover, the work of Fama (1984) and Hodrick and Srivastava (1986) show that not only is the forward exchange risk premium nonzero but that it is highly variable and exceeds the variability in ex ante change in spot exchange rates.[1]

Combining (1), (2), and (3) then results in the relationship that equates the deviations from ex ante change in real exchange rates to the difference between the ex ante real interest rate differential and the forward exchange risk premium:

$$E_t(S_{t+1}^i - S_t^i) - E_t(I_{t+1} - I_{t+1}^i) = E_t(\delta_{t+1} - \delta_{t+1}^i) - E_t(P_{t+1}^i) . \tag{4}$$

According to (4), when the forward exchange risk premiums are exactly offset by the expected real interest rate differentials, that is,

$$F_t^i - E_t(S_{t+1}^i) = E_t(\delta_{t+1} - \delta_{t+1}^i) , \tag{5}$$

then EPPP holds:

$$E_t(S_{t+1}^i - S_t^i) = E_t(I_{t+1} - I_{t+1}^i) . \tag{6}$$

[1]The study of forward exchange risk premiums was also extended to foreign currency futures markets by Hodrick and Srivastava (1987).

Equation (4) is a highly general relationship; it is valid for any economy characterized by covered interest rate parity and the definitions (2) and (3). It highlights the point that a constant ex ante real interest rate differential is neither sufficient nor necessary to obtain the EPPP model because departures from EPPP can occur due to variations in $E_t(P^i_{t+1})$ and (6) may hold even when both the forward exchange risk premium and $E_t(\delta_{t+1} - \delta^i_{t+1})$ are time-varying as long as their equality is not violated.

The knife-edge case specified by condition (5) when the forward exchange risk premium exactly equals the expected real interest rate differential has received substantial attention in the literature. It was deduced by a number of asset pricing models [for example, Fama and Farber (1979), Hodrick (1981), and Hodrick and Srivastava (1984)]. Since (6) is required in addition to (4) for the equality hypothesis to hold, given the generality of (4), a test of (5) is effectively a test of the EPPP condition (6).

Empirically, numerous studies have examined (6). By focusing only on the serial correlation properties of (6) these analyses, in general, are unable to reject EPPP.[2] In contrast, tests by Cumby and Obstfeld (1984) and Huang (1987) have sufficient power to reject the constraints implied by (6). These rejections are also inconsistent with Korajczyk (1985) who regressed forward exchange risk premiums on ex ante real interest rate differentials and obtained evidence supportive of (5). Since (5) is a special case of (4) only when (6) is valid, a finding that (6) is rejected suggests the need to examine the more general case (4).

Empirical investigations into the contribution of the expected long-run equilibrium real exchange rate and ex ante real interest rate differential to movements in real exchange rates can also be regarded as special cases of (4). For this purpose, the left-hand side of (4) is rewritten in terms of the currently observed and expected future real exchange rates. However, given the generality of the relationship (4), studies have proceeded by imposing additional structure on (4). For example, Shafer and Loopesko (1983) and Sachs (1985) assumed that $E_t(P^i_{t+1}) = 0$. Campbell and Clarida (1987a) allow for the variation in $E_t(P^i_{t+1})$, but posit that the ex post real interest rate differentials follow an ARMA(1,1) process and that $E_t(P^i_{t+1})$ is a constant multiple of $E_t(\delta_{t+1} - \delta^i_{t+1})$. In the following section, a statistical analysis of the roles of $E_t(P^i_{t+1})$ and $E_t(\delta^i_{t+1} - \delta^i_{t+1})$ in the rejection of EPPP is conducted without imposing any additional structure on the difference between $E_t(P^i_{t+1})$ and $E_t(\delta_{t+1} - \delta^i_{t+1})$. This is then followed in section 4 by an investigation of the comovements in the risk premiums and the deviations from EPPP.

3. TIME VARIATIONS IN RISK PREMIUMS AND EX ANTE REAL RATE DIFFERENTIALS

Condition (4) is a highly general specification. Nonetheless, it is possible to examine the volatilities in forward exchange risk premiums, expected real interest rate differentials, and ex ante changes in real exchange rates without the imposition of further structure. This is accomplished by using a regression approach and by

[2]See, for example, the papers by Stockman (1978), Roll (1979), Darby (1980), and Adler and Lehmann (1983).

following Fama's (1984) interpretation of the coefficients in his study of the forward exchange risk premium.[3]

In order to examine the variability in ex ante real rate differentials, consider the following specification:

$$E_t(I_{t+1} - I^i_{t+1}) - E_t(P^i_{t+1}) = E_t(S^i_{t+1} - S^i_t) \ . \tag{7}$$

Condition (7) is identical to (4) except for the absence of $E_t(\delta_{t+1} - \delta^i_{t+1})$. It is thus a forward exchange risk premium-adjusted EPPP that would be violated if expected interest risk differentials are time-varying.

Specification (7) can also be expressed in regression form as

$$(I_{t+1} - I^i_{t+1}) - (F^i_t - S^i_{t+1}) = a^i_1 + b^i_1 E_t(S^i_{t+1} - S^i_t) + v^i_{t+1} \ , \tag{8}$$

where v^i_{t+1} is the error in forecasting the risk-adjusted inflation rate differentials with $E_t(S^i_{t+1} - S^i_t)$. Equation (8) can then be used to test a number of hypotheses. Specifically, consider the following hypotheses:

$H_0(1)$: $(a^i_1, b^i_1) = (0, 1)$.

$H_0(2)$: $b^i_1 = 0$.

$H_0(3)$: $b^i_1 = 1$.

$H_0(4)$: $b^i_1 \geq 0.5$.

$H_0(5)$: $a^i_1 = a^j_1$ and $b^i_1 = b^j_1$, all i,j .

The first hypothesis tests the constraints imposed by the model (7). A rejection of the null is thus a violation of (7). Since the coefficient b^i_1 plays a crucial role in the interpretation of the results, $H_0(2)$ tests the hypothesis that it is insignificantly different from zero. A rejection would indicate that ex ante rate of change in spot exchange rates has power in predicting risk-adjusted expected inflation rate differentials. Hypothesis $H_0(3)$ is a direct test of whether a rejection of (7) is due specifically to time-varying ex ante real rate differentials. This can be seen by noting that under the more general specification (4)

$$b^i_1 = \frac{C[(I_{t+1} - I^i_{t+1}) - (F^i_t - S^i_{t+1}), E_t(S^i_{t+1} - S^i_t)]}{V[E_t(S^i_{t+1} - S^i_t)]}$$

$$= \frac{V[E_t(I_{t+1}-I^i_{t+1})-E_t(P^i_{t+1})]+C[E_t(\delta_{t+1}-\delta^i_{t+1}), E_t(I_{t+1}-I^i_{t+1})-E_t(P^i_{t+1})]}{V[E_t(S^i_{t+1} - S^i_t)]}$$

where $C[.]$ is the covariance operator and $V[.]$ is the variance operator. Since the risk-adjusted EPPP (7) implies that

[3] Volatility tests along the lines suggested by Shiller (1979) and Singleton (1980) can also be utilized for the present purpose.

$$V[E_t(I_{t+1} - I^i_{t+1}) - E_t(P^i_{t+1})] = V[E_t(S^i_{t+1} - S^i_t)] ,$$

a deviation of b^i_1 from one means that $E_t(\delta_{t+1} - \delta^i_{t+1})$ is time-varying. Hypothesis H_0 (4) attempts to further gauge the variability in ex ante real rate differentials by testing to determine if it exceeds the variability in risk-adjusted ex ante inflation rate differentials. This can be seen by noting that, using (4),

$$1 - 2b^i_1 = \frac{V[E_t(\delta_{t+1} - \delta^i_{t+1})] - V[E_t(I_{t+1} - I^i_{t+1}) - E_t(P^i_{t+1})]}{V[E_t(S^i_{t+1} - S^i_t)]} .$$

Thus, a rejection of $H_0(4)$ means that $V[E_t(\delta_{t+1} - \delta^i_{t+1})]$ exceeds the $V[E_t(I_{t+1} - I^i_{t+1}) - E_t(P^i_{t+1})]$. The last hypothesis $H_0(5)$ is to determine the similarities in the violations of (7) across currencies. Therefore, unlike the first four hypotheses that can be scrutinized for a single exchange rate, $H_0(5)$ is a joint test of the null hypothesis that a^i_1 and b^i_1 are the same for all i.

Next, I consider the volatility in departures from the EPPP (6). For this purpose consider the projection of the expected inflation rate differential onto expected change in spot rates:

$$I_{t+1} - I^i_{t+1} = a^i_2 + b^i_2 E_t(S^i_{t+1} - S^i_t) + \epsilon^i_{t+1} , \tag{9}$$

where ϵ^i_{t+1} is the error in predicting the inflation rate differential. The error term ϵ^i_{t+1} also is uncorrelated with all information known at time t. An analogous set of hypotheses corresponding to (8) can be examined here:

$H_0(1)$: Does EPPP hold?
$H_0(2)$: Does the ex ante rate of change in spot exchange rates have power in predicting the ex ante inflation rate differential?
$H_0(3)$: Are deviations from EPPP time-varying?
$H_0(4)$: Does the variability in deviations from EPPP exceed the variability in ex ante inflation rate differentials?
$H_0(5)$: Is there cross-country similarity in deviations from EPPP?

Hypothesis $H_0(1)$ has also been examined by Cumby and Obstfeld (1984) and Huang (1987). It involves testing the constraint, $(a^i_2, b^i_2) = (0, 1)$ imposed by the EPPP formulation on (9). However, the analysis here differs in that a different data set is used and all the bilateral exchange rates are estimated jointly. As in the case for (7), the results for $H_0(1)$ are used to set the stage for an investigation of the $H_0(2)$ to $H_0(5)$.

The analysis for this section is completed by examining the temporal behavior of the forward exchange risk premiums. A regression analysis of the variability of $E_t(P^i_{t+1})$ is an analysis of (3) itself. Therefore, the observations made by Fama (1984) and Hodrick and Srivastava (1986) on the volatility in forward exchange risk premiums is directly relevant here and the tests are not replicated.[4]

[4]The same data source is used here as in Fama (1984).

3A. Estimation Issues

Equations (8) and (9) cannot be estimated directly as the expected exchange rate appreciation is an unobservable variable. To make them operational, $E_t(S^i_{t+1} - S^i_t)$ can be replaced by its ex post realization $(S^i_{t+1} - S^i_t)$ and its forecast error $w^i_{t+1} = (S^i_{t+1} - S^i_t) - E_t(S^i_{t+1} - S^i_t)$. However, since w^i_{t+1} is correlated with the ex post percentage change in real exchange rates, an instrumental variable estimation is needed. Cumby and Obstfeld (1984) found that a constant and one-period lagged inflation rate differentials between all foreign countries examined and the United States are powerful instruments for $E_t(S^i_{t+1} - S^i_t)$. I use the same instruments here. Since a total of nine foreign currencies all in terms of the U.S. dollar are analyzed, this produces a total of nine equations each for (8) and (9) and ten instruments. It is also important to account for the presence of conditional heteroskedasticity of unknown source. This is because the instruments are only predetermined and not exogenous variables. In addition, Cumby and Obstfeld (1984), Hodrick and Srivastava (1984), Domowitz and Hakkio (1985), and others have shown that the conditional distributions of regression disturbances in the foreign exchange equations with predetermined variables are characterized by time-varying covariance matrices. Finally, a joint estimation of different foreign currencies is needed to account for the integration between international commodity and foreign exchange markets. Since all the exchange rates are bilateral dollar rates, it is all the more likely that the innovations in the regressions are contemporaneously correlated. This will yield more efficient estimates and allow for joint tests of the null hypotheses.

All the econometric issues mentioned are addressed by the system-wide application of the generalized method of moment (GMM) of Hansen (1982) or the two-step two-stage least-squares procedure of Cumby, Huizinga, and Obstfeld (1983). The procedure for the current case can be described by considering the simultaneous estimation of (8). Let T be the number of observations, $\mathbf{Y^i}$ be a $(T \times 1)$ vector with typical element $(I_{t+1} - I^i_{t+1}) - (F^i_t - S^i_{t+1})$, $\mathbf{X^i}$ be a $(T \times 2)$ matrix with typical row element $(1, (S^i_{t+1} - S^i_t))$, $\mathbf{b^i} = (a^i_1, b^i_1)'$, and $\mathbf{U^i}$ be a $(T \times 1)$ vector with typical element $U^i_{t+1} = v^i_{t+1} - b^i_1 w^i_{t+1}$. The 9-equation system can then be stacked as

$$\mathbf{Y} = \mathbf{Xb} + \mathbf{U} . \tag{10}$$

$$\begin{bmatrix} \mathbf{Y^1} \\ \mathbf{Y^2} \\ \cdot \\ \cdot \\ \cdot \\ \mathbf{Y^9} \end{bmatrix} = \begin{bmatrix} \mathbf{X^1} & \mathbf{0} & \cdots & \mathbf{0} \\ \mathbf{0} & \mathbf{X^2} & \cdots & \mathbf{0} \\ \cdots & & & \\ & \cdots & \cdots & \cdots \\ \mathbf{0} & & & \\ & \cdots & \cdots & \mathbf{X^9} \end{bmatrix} \begin{bmatrix} \mathbf{b^1} \\ \mathbf{b^2} \\ \cdot \\ \cdot \\ \cdot \\ \mathbf{b^9} \end{bmatrix} + \begin{bmatrix} \mathbf{U^1} \\ \mathbf{U^2} \\ \cdot \\ \cdot \\ \cdot \\ \mathbf{U^9} \end{bmatrix}$$

The GMM is based on the constraint that $\mathbf{U}$ is orthogonal to the instruments used in the estimation. Let $\mathbf{Z}$ be the $(T \times 10)$ matrix of instruments with typical row element $Z_t = (1, Z^1_t, Z^2_t, \ldots, Z^9_t)'$ and $h(U_{t+1})' = (U^1_{t+1}, U^2_{t+1}, U^3_{t+1}, \ldots,$

U^9_{t+1}) be a vector function. The vector of 90 orthogonality conditions can then be expressed as

$$\mathbf{g}(\mathbf{b}) = E[f(U_{t+1}, Z_t)] , \tag{11}$$

where

$$f[(U_{t+1}, Z_t)] = h(U_{t+1}) \otimes Z_t .$$

The sample estimator of (11) is the method of moments estimator

$$\mathbf{g_T}(\mathbf{b}) = (\mathbf{I} \otimes \mathbf{Z})'\mathbf{U}/\mathbf{T} . \tag{12}$$

The estimates for (10) are then chosen by minimizing the criterion

$$J_T(b) = \mathbf{g}_T(\mathbf{b})'\mathbf{W}_T\mathbf{g}_T(\mathbf{b}) , \tag{13}$$

where $\mathbf{W_T}$ is a (90 × 90) symmetric weighting matrix. This yields the estimate

$$\mathbf{b}_T = (\mathbf{X}'(\mathbf{I}\otimes Z)\mathbf{W_T}(\mathbf{I}\otimes\mathbf{Z})'\mathbf{X})^{-1}\mathbf{X}'(\mathbf{I}\otimes\mathbf{Z})\mathbf{W_T}(\mathbf{I}\otimes\mathbf{Z})'\mathbf{Y} , \tag{14}$$

where $\mathbf{I}$ is a (9 × 9) identity matrix. In addition, the asymptotic distribution of $\surd T(\mathbf{b}_T - \mathbf{b}_0)$ is $N(0, (\mathbf{d}_0'\mathbf{W}_0\mathbf{d}_0)^{-1})$, where $\mathbf{d}_0$ and $\mathbf{W}_0$ are estimated by

$$d_T = \frac{1}{T} \Sigma_{t=1}^T \frac{\partial f(U_{t+1}, Z_t)}{\partial \mathbf{b}} , \tag{15}$$

$$(\mathbf{W_T})^{-1} = \frac{1}{T} \Sigma_{t=1}^T f(U_{t+1}, Z_t) f(U_{t+1}, Z_t)' . \tag{16}$$

The optimality of the sample matrix (16) is discussed in Hansen (1982) as case (ii). For the purpose of computing (16), the residuals from estimating (10) with two-stage least squares are used to provide consistent estimates of U_{t+1}.

Various hypotheses across equations and within equations are examined and the Wald test is used to provide the necessary test statistics. A joint hypothesis can be expressed as $\boldsymbol{\theta}(\mathbf{b}_T) = \mathbf{R}\mathbf{b}_T - \mathbf{r} = 0$, where both $\mathbf{r}$ and $\mathbf{R}$ have p rows. The test statistic is then computed as

$$\boldsymbol{\theta}(\mathbf{b}_T)'[(\frac{\partial\boldsymbol{\theta}}{\partial\mathbf{b}'}\bigg|_{\mathbf{b}_T})\mathbf{V}(\mathbf{b}_T)(\frac{\partial\boldsymbol{\theta}}{\partial\mathbf{b}'}\bigg|_{\mathbf{b}_T})']^{-1}\boldsymbol{\theta}(\mathbf{b}_T) , \tag{17}$$

where $\mathbf{V}(\mathbf{b}_T)$ is the asymptotic covariance matrix for $\mathbf{b}_T$ and has an asymptotic chi-square distribution with p degrees of freedom.

3B. Empirical Results

The data used in the study are monthly, beginning in August 1973 and ending in April 1986. The spot and forward exchange rates are for the last Friday of the month from the Weekly Review of the Harris Trust and Savings Bank. The bilateral dollar foreign exchange rates are for Canada (CA), United Kingdom (UK), Belgium (BE), France (FR), Germany (GE), Italy (IT), Netherlands (NE), Switzerland (SW), and Japan (JA). The consumer price indices from the International Financial Statistics are used to compute the inflation rate series.[5]

The evidence acquired from testing (7), the EPPP model with a forward exchange risk premium adjustment, is shown in Tables 1A and 1B. Table 1A shows that hypothesis $H_0(1)$, $(a_1^i, b_1^i) = (0, 1)$, cannot be rejected. Tests of $H_0(2)$ and $H_0(3)$ show that expected changes in spot exchange rates significantly explain movements in expected inflation rate differentials with a risk component and that the b_1^i coefficients are insignificantly different from one. In addition, tests of $H_0(4)$ show that it is consistent with the sample data.

TABLE 1A

JOINT GMM ESTIMATES OF EQUATION (8)

Foreign Currency	Coefficient Estimates a_1^i	Coefficient Estimates b_1^i	Tests of Hypotheses: H_0: $a_1^i = 0$ and $b_1^i = 1$ $X^2(2)$	p-value	H_0: $b_1^i = 1$ t-statistic	H_0: $b_1^i = 0.5$ t-statistic
CA	−.000 (−.130)	1.059 (4.91)	.185	.912	.275	2.59
UK	−.000 (−.234)	.925 (7.75)	.463	.793	−.630	3.56
BE	.001 (.434)	1.146 (9.87)	1.64	.439	1.26	5.57
FR	−.000 (−.171)	.960 (8.58)	.135	.935	−.359	4.11
GE	−.002 (−.889)	1.183 (10.63)	3.76	.152	1.64	6.14
IT	.002 (1.51)	1.201 (9.33)	3.32	.190	1.56	5.45
NE	−.001 (−.679)	1.038 (10.60)	.611	.737	.383	5.47
SW	−.003 (−1.57)	1.050 (7.04)	2.53	.282	.338	3.69
JA	−.003 (−1.64)	1.334 (5.80)	3.34	.188	1.45	3.62

NOTE: The numbers in brackets are t-statistics.

Table 1B displays tests of the cross-equation restrictions for (7). The results show that a joint test of the H_0: $(a_1^i, b_1^i) = (0, 1)$ is powerful enough to reject the null at a very low p-value thus rejecting the specification (7). However, the joint tests of b_1^i coefficients are consistent with those obtained for the single equation tests, indicat-

[5]The data may potentially be misaligned in that the consumer price series more closely reflect mid-month rather than end-of-month observations. Tests using mid-month exchange rate data, however, essentially lead to the same conclusions and are not reported in the paper. An important exception to this is noted in footnote 8.

ing that the rejection of (7) is mainly due to the failure of a_1^i coefficients to equal zero. Further support for this can also be seen from tests of $H_0(5)$, the equality of coefficients across equations. The results show that the intercept terms are highly significantly different from one another, but that the slope coefficients differ significantly only at the 10 percent level. Thus, the results reject the specification (7) but

TABLE 1B

JOINT GMM ESTIMATES OF EQUATION (8), CROSS-EQUATION TESTS

Hypothesis	χ^2-statistic	Degrees of Freedom	p-value
H_O: $a_1^i = 0$ and $b_1^i = 1 \; \forall$ i	53.86	18	0.00
H_O: $b_1^i = 0 \; \forall$ i	219.80	9	0.00
H_O: $b_1^i = 1 \; \forall$ i	13.56	9	0.14
H_O: $b_1^i = 0.5 \; \forall$ i	66.53	9	0.00
H_O: $a_1^1 = a_1^2 = \ldots = a_1^9$	39.69	8	0.00
H_O: $b_1^1 = b_1^2 = \ldots = b_1^9$	13.53	8	0.10

the tests detect very little variation in expected real interest rate differentials at the usual significance levels.

The results from estimating (9) are presented in Table 2A. The constraint $(a_2^i, b_2^i) = (0, 1)$ imposed on (9) by the EPPP is decisively rejected by the sample data at

TABLE 2A

JOINT GMM ESTIMATES OF EQUATION (9)

Foreign Currency	Coefficient Estimates a_2^i	b_2^i	Tests of Hypotheses: H_0: $a_2^i = 0$ and $b_2^i = 1$ X2(2)	p-value	H_0: $b_2^i = 1$ t-statistic	H_0: $b_2^i = 0.5$ t-statistic
CA	−.000 (−1.43)	.188 (2.49)	213.35	0	−10.77	−4.14
UK	−.003 (−7.51)	.041 (.985)	529.87	0	−22.71	−10.86
BE	.000 (.808)	.090 (3.57)	1298.98	0	−36.04	−16.23
FR	−.002 (−10.16)	.117 (7.15)	2990.79	0	−53.72	−23.29
GE	.002 (13.13)	.188 (9.27)	1670.56	0	−40.05	−15.39
IT	−.004 (−14.92)	.213 (7.19)	731.04	0	−26.63	−9.72
NE	.001 (5.13)	.001 (.030)	2140.44	0	−46.09	−23.03
SW	.002 (8.77)	.086 (2.17)	534.29	0	−23.01	−10.42
JA	−.001 (−1.41)	.198 (4.17)	346.37	0	−16.94	−6.38

NOTE: The numbers in brackets are t-statistics.

very low marginal significance levels. These results are consistent with the single-equation estimates obtained by Cumby and Obstfeld (1984) and Huang (1987). An examination of the t-statistics for the b_2^i estimates indicates that for most of the foreign currencies, anticipated changes in exchange rates are capable of predicting the corresponding expected inflation rate differentials. The results for tests of the null hypothesis that $b_2^i = 1$ show that based on the general specification (4), deviations from EPPP are time-varying in nature. In addition, the b_2^i estimates are found to be significantly less than one half so that the volatility in EPPP deviations exceed the volatility in expected inflation rate differentials. These results are in sharp contrast to the lack of variation in expected changes in real exchange rates adjusted for risk premia presented in Table 1.

Table 2B examines the cross-equation restrictions for (9). The results extend all the conclusions reached with single-equation tests to the case of joint tests. In addition, Table 2B reports the results from testing the equality of the coefficients across equations. These hypotheses are also rejected and, thus, support the presence of foreign-currency specific shocks in the market place.

To summarize, the evidence indicates that the EPPP model cum forward exchange risk premium is not compatible with sample data, but that the variation in $E_t(\delta_{t+1} - \delta^i_{t+1})$ is implausibly low to fully account for the systematic failure of the EPPP without the presence of forward exchange risk premium. This result is inconsistent with the equality between ex ante real rate differentials and the forward exchange risk premiums.

TABLE 2B

JOINT GMM ESTIMATES OF EQUATION (9), CROSS-EQUATION TESTS

Hypothesis	χ^2-statistic	Degrees of Freedom	p-value
H_O: $a_2^i = 0$ and $b_2^i = 1 \ \forall\ i$	5831.52	18	0.00
H_O: $b_2^i = 0 \ \forall\ i$	194.65	9	0.00
H_O: $b_2^i = 1 \ \forall\ i$	5072.68	9	0.00
H_O: $b_2^i = 0.5 \ \forall\ i$	997.48	9	0.00
H_O: $a_2^1 = a_2^2 = \ldots = a_2^9$	817.73	8	0.00
H_O: $b_2^1 = b_2^2 = \ldots = b_2^9$	88.54	8	0.00

Given that both the risk premiums and the ex ante change in real exchange rates are time-varying, it is of interest to examine if they in fact move together. Unfortunately, it is difficult, if not impossible, to investigate specific propositions of this at the level of generality expressed in (4). It is, however, important that, given the results of this section, the more specific tests that are employed explicitly acknowledge the time variations in the forward exchange risk premiums and the ex ante change in real exchange rates.

4. COMOVEMENTS IN RISK PREMIUMS AND DEVIATIONS FROM EPPP

This section tests the hypothesis that the movements in forward exchange risk premiums and expected change in real exchange rates are proportional to one another. The particular specification used for this purpose is

$$E_t(r^i_{j,t+1}) = \beta_j E_t(r_{c,t+1}) , \qquad j = 1,2 \tag{18}$$

where $r^i_{1,t+1} = P^i_{t+1}$, the ex post forward exchange risk premium, $r^i_{2,t+1} = (S^i_{t+1} - S^i_t) - (I_{t+1} - I^i_{t+1})$, the realized change in real exchange rates, β_j is the constant proportionality coefficient, and $r_{c,t+1}$ is the unobservable or latent factor common to both $r^i_{1,t+1}$ and $r^i_{2,t+1}$. A similar relationship was first utilized by Hansen and Hodrick (1983) and Gibbons and Ferson (1985) in different contexts. These studies motivate the specification as a specific characterization of the first-order condition deduced by a rational representative investor who maximizes the expected utility of lifetime consumption subject to sequential budget constraints. As such, it is consistent with the intertemporal equilibrium models of Rubinstein (1976), Lucas (1978), Breeden (1979), and Brock (1982).[6] The objective here is to use the specification (18) to provide a convenient, albeit ad hoc, statistical representation that permits tests of the comovements between the two variables of interest.

Instead of specifying the common factor in (18) a priori, I follow Hansen and Hodrick (1983) and Gibbons and Ferson (1985) in considering it to be a latent variable. Since the common factor is formed conditional on all information available at time t, it can be expressed as a function of the information set. Furthermore, by the law of iterated projections, the analysis can be confined to a subset of the information set. Therefore, when the function is assumed to be linear, the expectation on the latent variable can be written as

$$E^*_t(r_{c,t+1}) = \boldsymbol{\alpha}'\boldsymbol{\Gamma}_t , \tag{19}$$

where $E^*_t(.)$ is the mathematical expectation conditional on $\boldsymbol{\Gamma}_t$,$\boldsymbol{\Gamma}_t$ is a $(q + 1)$ vector of variables observed at time t and $\boldsymbol{\alpha}' = (\alpha_0, \alpha_1, \ldots, \alpha_q)$ is the (q + 1) vector of parameters. Thus, the tests conducted are joint tests of (18) and (19).

Additionally, if the tests reject the single latent variable, (18) can easily be extended to multiple factors as shown by Gibbons and Ferson (1985). The estimation procedure here, however, differs from Gibbons and Ferson (1985) in that the conditional covariance matrix of residuals are allowed to be time-varying.

The recent theory of cointegration as developed by Engle and Granger (1987), Stock and Watson (1988), Johansen (1988), and others is also concerned with whether the movements in an n-variable model is driven by common factors. When the expectations in (18) are specified to be nonstationary, a test of (18) is similar to a test of whether the two variables are cointegrated. Generally speaking, when an n-variable model has less than n common stochastic trends, then the model is cointegrated and the variables move together, at least in the long run. However, in generating the expectations in the manner of the latent variable approach, sta-

[6]The authors, however, carefully note that the tests are not those of fully specified equilibrium models.

tionarity of the regressors is required for the conventional asymptotic distribution theory to apply. This requirement is met as the information variables used below are stationary forward premiums. It is also difficult to reconcile the stationarity requirement with nonstationarity predicted values needed for applying cointegration tests.

4A. Estimation Issues

The two equations (18) and (19) can be combined and written as a two-equation system:

$$\mathbf{r}^{\mathbf{i}}_{\mathbf{t+1}} = \Omega\Gamma_{\mathbf{t}} + \mathbf{e}^{\mathbf{i}}_{\mathbf{t+1}} , \tag{20}$$

where $\mathbf{r}^{\mathbf{i}}_{\mathbf{t+1}}$ is a (2×1) vector containing the two returns $r^i_{1,t+1}$ and $r^i_{2,t+1}$, $\mathbf{e}^{\mathbf{i}}_{\mathbf{t+1}}$ is a (2×1) vector of disturbances that are orthogonal to $\mathbf{\Gamma_t}$, $\mathbf{\Omega} = \boldsymbol{\beta\alpha}'$ is a (2×10) matrix, and $\boldsymbol{\beta}' = (\boldsymbol{\beta}_1,\boldsymbol{\beta}_2)$ is the vector of constant coefficients. Since the returns in (20) are restricted to conform to the same latent variable structure in (19), this gives rise to cross-equation constraints. In addition, β_1 is standardized to one because of the nonuniqueness of the latent variable. Thus, there are a total of twenty unrestricted parameters in Ω with a total of eleven parameters to be estimated. This leaves a total of nine overidentifying restrictions in the system.

In order to allow for the presence of conditional heteroskedasticity of unknown origin, a system-wide application of GMM can again be used to estimate (20). The parameter estimates are obtained by minimizing the criterion function (13). However, since the parameters are nonlinear, a two-step procedure suggested by Hansen and Singleton (1982) is adopted to carry out the nonlinear optimization. First, ordinary least squares residuals are used to compute the weighting matrix (16). This weighting matrix is then substituted into (13) and the minimization is carried out to obtain the first set of consistent parameter estimates. In the second step, the residuals obtained in the first minimization process are used to calculate the final weighting matrix which is then used in (13) to obtain the final parameter estimates. Analytic as opposed to numerical differentiations are used to provide the requisite standard errors. Tests of the overidentifying restrictions are then based on a theorem by Hansen (1982) which shows that T times the minimized value of $J_T(b)$ is asymptotically distributed as chi-square with degrees of freedom equal to the number of overidentifying constraints.

4B. Empirical Results

In estimating (20), it is important to choose information variables that have predictive power. The results of section 3 suggest that conditional expectations of risk premiums and changes in real exchange rates vary over time and may, therefore, be predictable. In addition, use of variables that are statistically irrelevant in forecasting the expectational variables can substantially reduce the power of the tests. The information variables chosen here are a constant and the forward premiums for the nine foreign currencies. (Thus, Γ_t is a (10×1) column vector.)

Hodrick and Srivastava (1984) have previously shown that forward premiums are more powerful than lagged forward exchange risk premiums in predicting the forward risk premiums. I found that forward premiums have about the same level of predictive power in forecasting $r^i_{2,t+1}$, the change in real exchange rates.[7]

The results from estimating (20) are reported in Table 3. The starting values for the first step of the estimation procedure are one for β_2 and the α values obtained from estimating the first equation of (20) unconstrained by OLS. The estimates obtained from the first minimization process are then used as the starting values for the second minimization process.

The data appear to be well behaved and the estimations yield relatively precise estimates. The chi-square values in Table 3 show that, with the exception of Belgium, the overidentifying restrictions cannot be rejected.[8] Thus, in general, both the expected change in real exchange rates and the forward exchange risk premiums respond proportionately to the same single latent variable. In addition, the beta estimates in Table 3 are all statistically significant. They are also all negative, indicating that $E_t(P^i_{t+1})$ and $E_t[(S^i_{t+1} - S^i_t) - (I_{t+1} - I^i_{t+1})]$ move in opposite directions as required by (4).

It is, however, possible to extend the analysis to include ex post real interest rate differentials, $r^i_{3,t+1} = (\delta_{t+1} - \delta^i_{t+1})$, as well. As shown by (4), any pairwise combination of $r^i_{1,t+1}$, $r^i_{2,t+1}$, and $r^i_{3,t+1}$ can be examined. With the exception of the one case reported in Table 3, none of the restrictions of a single latent variable specification can be rejected.[9] Therefore, deviations from EPPP respond to the same latent variable that drives either the forward exchange risk premiums or the expected real interest rate differentials.[10]

5. CONCLUSIONS

Deviations from PPP are by now a well-documented empirical regularity. This paper shows that, in general, the deviations of the expected change in the log of real exchange rates from zero in efficient markets or the EPPP can be decomposed into a forward exchange risk premium component and an ex ante real interest rate differential component. The results show that the deviations from EPPP are due to time-varying components that is revealed not only in ex ante real rate differentials but more importantly in forward exchange risk premiums. This is contrary to asset pricing models that predict the equality of forward exchange risk premium and the expected real interest rate differential. Specific tests of the comovements between the forward risk premiums and the ex ante change in real exchange rates also reveal

[7]These results are available from the author upon request.

[8]When mid-month exchange rates are used as discussed in footnote 5, the chi-square value for BE is 10.95 with a p-value of 0.28 so that the overidentifying restrictions are not rejected.

[9]These results are available from the author upon request.

[10]The identification of the state variable that produces the observed results would be an interesting topic for future research.

TABLE 3

LATENT VARIABLE ESTIMATES OF EQUATION (20) WITH $r^i_{t+1} = (r^i_{1,t+1}, r^i_{2,t+1})'$

Foreign Currency	COEFFICIENTS											
	β_2	α_0	α_1	α_2	α_3	α_4	α_5	α_6	α_7	α_8	α_9	χ^2
CA	−0.757	0.007	3.227	0.306	−0.093	−0.011	−2.056	−0.357	0.687	−0.419	0.574	13.064
	0.068	0.003	0.631	0.336	0.265	0.271	0.803	0.166	0.287	0.504	0.147	
	0.000	0.004	0.000	0.182	0.363	0.484	0.006	0.016	0.009	0.204	0.000	0.160
UK	−0.194	0.009	−1.885	5.875	−0.731	0.677	−1.317	−0.945	−0.888	0.913	−0.462	5.769
	0.043	0.009	1.668	1.224	0.966	0.687	2.157	0.569	1.250	1.513	0.544	
	0.000	0.152	0.130	0.000	0.225	0.163	0.271	0.050	0.239	0.274	0.198	0.763
BE	−0.843	0.015	−2.521	3.732	1.610	1.734	−2.488	−0.978	1.823	−1.981	−0.149	22.788
	0.043	0.008	1.504	0.960	0.822	0.776	2.783	0.472	1.023	1.352	0.372	
	0.000	0.036	0.048	0.000	0.026	0.014	0.186	0.020	0.038	0.073	0.345	0.007
FR	−0.783	0.011	−1.645	2.332	−0.544	4.326	−0.884	−0.758	0.282	−0.310	−0.458	5.548
	0.002	0.000	1.271	0.580	0.242	0.891	1.703	0.135	0.427	0.763	0.081	
	0.000	0.019	0.073	0.001	0.135	0.000	0.250	0.020	0.333	0.362	0.055	0.784
GE	−0.855	−0.002	−2.434	2.131	0.192	1.066	2.264	−0.820	0.985	−0.986	0.254	10.509
	0.030	0.007	1.685	0.737	0.668	0.723	2.555	0.526	0.890	1.376	0.438	
	0.000	0.392	0.075	0.002	0.387	0.071	0.189	0.061	0.135	0.237	0.282	0.311
IT	−0.606	0.017	−0.348	1.069	−1.274	0.314	−2.180	2.241	−0.263	0.876	−0.222	5.314
	0.084	0.005	0.875	0.598	0.510	0.323	1.145	0.541	0.543	0.746	0.178	
	0.000	0.001	0.346	0.038	0.007	0.166	0.030	0.000	0.315	0.121	0.107	0.806
NE	−0.831	0.011	−3.340	2.523	−0.095	1.702	−0.460	−0.460	3.996	−2.540	−0.233	9.943
	0.033	0.007	1.654	0.761	0.680	0.654	2.004	0.453	1.076	1.301	0.348	
	0.000	0.068	0.023	0.001	0.445	0.005	0.409	0.156	0.000	0.026	0.252	0.355
SW	−0.563	0.001	−1.376	0.956	0.550	−0.052	0.392	0.011	−0.112	0.858	0.147	11.067
	0.158	0.005	0.987	0.558	0.462	0.439	1.637	0.267	0.470	0.794	0.164	
	0.000	0.389	0.083	0.044	0.118	0.453	0.405	0.483	0.406	0.141	0.186	0.271
JA	−0.722	0.004	−1.497	3.064	−0.506	1.177	−1.744	−0.529	−1.100	1.253	0.613	9.657
	0.128	0.007	1.700	1.030	0.710	0.660	2.083	0.485	0.834	1.381	0.440	
	0.000	0.260	0.190	0.002	0.239	0.038	0.202	0.139	0.095	0.183	0.083	0.379

NOTES: The first number under each coefficient is the coefficient estimate, the second number is the standard error, and the third number is the marginal significance level. The first number under the chi-square column is the chi-square value and the second number is the marginal significance level.

that the two variables move together in that both respond proportionately to a single latent variable.

The evidence suggests that an understanding of the deviations from EPPP is inextricably linked to an understanding of the nature of the risk premiums that characterize forward foreign exchange rates. To the extent that the representation of forward exchange risk premiums in terms of market fundamentals has proven to be an elusive goal, it may be equally difficult to ascertain the determinants of EPPP deviations.

It is important to emphasize that the interpretation of the results in the paper relies on the typical definition of the forward exchange risk premium as provided by (3). The interpretations must also be made in conjunction with the null hypothesis of rational expectations. Recent work of Frankel and Froot (1986), however, suggests an alternative view. Relying on evidence based on survey data, they suggest that the observed bias in the forward discount may instead arise from the failure of the assumption that market participants know the ex ante distribution of exchange rates. Furthermore, all the tests conducted here are based on asymptotic distribution theory and what constitutes a sufficient sample size is unclear. The results obtained may, therefore, suffer from small sample bias.

LITERATURE CITED

Adler, Michael, and Bruce Lehmann. "Deviations from Purchasing Power Parity in the Long Run." *Journal of Finance* 38 (December 1983), 1471–87.

Bilson, John F. O. "The Speculative Efficiency Hypothesis." *Journal of Business* 54 (July 1981), 435–52.

Breeden, Douglas T. "An Intertemporal Asset Pricing Model with Stochastic Consumption and Investment Opportunities." *Journal of Financial Economics* 7 (September 1979), 265–96.

Brock, William A. "Asset Prices in a Production Economy." In *The Economics of Uncertainty,* edited by John J. McCall. University of Chicago Press, 1982.

Campbell, John Y., and Richard H. Clarida. "The Dollar and Real Interest Rates." *Carnegie-Rochester Conference Series on Public Policy* 27 (Autumn 1987), 103–39. (a)

______. "The Term Structure of Euromarket Interest Rates. An Empirical Investigation." *Journal of Monetary Economics* 19 (January 1987), 25–44. (b)

Cumby, Robert E., John Huizinga, and Maurice Obstfeld. "Two-Step Two-Stage Least Squares Estimation in Models with Rational Expectations." *Journal of Econometrics* 21 (April 1983), 333–55.

Cumby, Robert E., and Maurice Obstfeld. "International Interest Rate and Price Level Linkages under Flexible Exchange Rates: A Review of Recent Evidence." In *Exchange Rate Theory and Practice,* edited by John Bilson and Richard Marston, pp. 121–51. Chicago: University of Chicago Press, 1984.

Darby, Michael R. "Does Purchasing Power Parity Work?" National Bureau of Economic Research Working Paper No. 607 (1980).

Domowitz, Ian, and Craig S. Hakkio. "Conditional Variance and the Risk Premium in the Foreign Exchange Market." *Journal of International Economics* 19 (August 1985), 47–66.

Engle, Robert F., and Clive W. J. Granger. "Cointegration and Error Correction: Representation, Estimation and Testing." *Econometrica* 55 (March 1987), 251–76.

Fama, Eugene F. "Forward and Spot Exchange Rates." *Journal of Monetary Economics* 14 (November 1984), 319–38.

Fama, Eugene F., and Andre Farber. "Money, Bonds, and Foreign Exchange." *American Economic Review* 69 (September 1979), 639–49.

Frankel, Jeffrey A., and Kenneth A. Froot. "Interpreting Tests of Forward Discount Bias Using Survey Data on the Exchange Rate Expectations." National Bureau of Economic Research Working Paper No. 1963 (June 1986).

Frenkel, Jacob A., and Richard M. Levich. "Covered Interest Arbitrage: Unexploited Profits?" *Journal of Political Economy* 83 (April 1975), 325–38.

______. "Transaction Costs and Interest Arbitrage: Tranquil versus Turbulent Periods." *Journal of Political Economy* 85 (December 1977), 1209–26.

Gibbons, Michael R., and Wayne Ferson. "Testing Asset Pricing Models with Changing Expectations and an Unobservable Market Portfolio." *Journal of Financial Economics* 14 (1985), 217–36.

Giovannini, Alberto, and Philippe Jorion. "Interest Rates and Risk Premia in the Stock Market and in the Foreign Exchange Market." *Journal of International Money and Finance* 6 (March 1987), 107–23.

______. "Foreign Exchange Risk Premia Once Again." *Journal of International Money and Finance* 7 (March 1988), 111–13.

______. "The Time Variation of Risk and Return in the Foreign Exchange and Stock Markets." *Journal of Finance* 44 (June 1989), 307–25.

Hansen, Lars P. "Large Sample Properties of Generalized Method of Moments Estimators." *Econometrica* 50 (July 1982), 1029–54.

Hansen, Lars P., and Robert J. Hodrick. "Forward Exchange Rates as Optimal Predictors of Future Spot Rates: An Econometric Analysis." *Journal of Political Economy* 88 (October 1980), 829–53.

______. "Risk Averse Speculation in Forward Foreign Exchange Market: An Econometric Analysis of Linear Models." In *Exchange Rates and International Macroeconomics*, edited by Jacob A. Frenkel, pp. 113–42. National Bureau of Economic Research, Cambridge, Mass., 1983.

Hansen, Lars P., and Kenneth J. Singleton. "Generalized Instrumental Variable Estimation of Nonlinear Rational Expectations Models." *Econometrica* 50 (September 1982), 1269–86.

Hodrick, Robert J. "Some Evidence on the Equality of Expected Real Interest Rates across Countries." Manuscript, Carnegie-Mellon University (1979).

______. "International Asset Pricing with Time-Varying Risk Premia." *Journal of International Economics* 11 (November 1981), 573–87.

Hodrick, Robert J., and Sanjay Srivastava. "An Investigation of Risk and Return in Forward Foreign Exchange." *Journal of International Money and Finance* 3 (April 1984), 5–29.

______. "The Covariation of Risk Premiums and Expected Future Spot Exchange Rates." *Journal of International Money and Finance* 5 (March 1986), S5-S21.

______. "Foreign Currency Futures." *Journal of International Economics* 22 (February 1987), 1–24.

Huang, Roger D. "Expectations of Exchange Rates and Differential Inflation Rates: Further Evidence on Purchasing Power Parity in Efficient Markets." *Journal of Finance* 42 (March 1987), 69–79.

______. "An Analysis of Intertemporal Pricing for Forward Foreign Exchange Contracts." *Journal of Finance* 44 (March 1989), 183–94.

Johansen, Søren. "Statistical Analysis of Cointegration Factors." *Journal of Economic Dynamics and Control* 12 (June–September 1988), 231–54.

Korajczyk, Robert A. "The Pricing of Forward Contracts for Foreign Exchange." *Journal of Political Economy* 93 (April 1985), 346–68.

Lucas, Robert E. "Asset Prices in an Exchange Economy." *Econometrica* 46 (November 1978), 1426–46.

Marston, Richard C. "Interest Arbitrage in the Euro-currency Markets." *European Economic Review* 7 (January 1976), 1–13.

Mishkin, Frederic S. "Are Real Interest Rates Equal across Countries? An Empirical Investigation of International Parity Conditions." *Journal of Finance* 39 (December 1984), 1345–57.

Mark, Nelson C. "Time Varying Betas and Risk Premia in the Pricing of Forward Exchange Contracts." *Journal of Financial Economics* 22 (December 1988), 335–54.

Roll, Richard. "Violations of Purchasing Power Parity and Their Implications for Efficient International Commodity Markets." In *International Finance and Trade I,* edited by Marshall Sarnat and G. P. Szego, pp. 133–76. Cambridge, Mass.: Ballinger Publishing Co., 1979.

Rubinstein, Mark. "The Valuation of Uncertain Income Streams and the Pricing of Options." *Bell Journal of Economics* 7 (Autumn 1976), 407–25.

Sachs, Jeffrey D. "The Dollar and the Policy Mix: 1985." *Brookings Papers on Economic Activity* 1 (1986), 117–97.

Shafer, J., and B. Loopesko. "Floating Exchange Rates after Ten Years." *Brookings Papers on Economic Activity* 1 (1983), 1–70.

Shiller, Robert J. "The Volatility of Long-Term Interest Rates and Expectations Models of the Term Structure." *Journal of Political Economy* 87 (December 1979), 1190–1219.

Singleton, Kenneth J. "Expectations Models of the Term Structure and Implied Variance Bounds." *Journal of Political Economy* 88 (December 1980), 1159–76.

Stock, James H., and Mark W. Watson. "Testing for Common Trends." *Journal of American Statistical Association* 83 (December 1988), 1097–1107.

Stockman, Alan C. "Evidence on the Time-Series Behavior of Deviations from Purchasing Power Parity and Implications for Exchange-Rate Theories." U.C.L.A. manuscript (November 1978).

THOMAS L. BREWER
PIETRA RIVOLI

Politics and Perceived Country Creditworthiness in International Banking

THE PURPOSE OF THIS PAPER is to test for the effects of political instability on perceived country creditworthiness. The central questions are (1) Do international bankers and financial markets respond to these political phenomena in their assessments of countries' creditworthiness? and (2) What types of political instability affect creditworthiness perceptions? The determinants of creditworthiness perceptions are of central importance because these perceptions affect both the supply and cost of capital flows to developing countries. The paper represents a departure from most previous studies of country creditworthiness in international banking, such as those by Feder, Just, and Ross (1981) and Shapiro (1981), because it incorporates political as well as economic phenomena. Our results suggest that political variables are at least as important as economic variables in explaining perceived creditworthiness. Therefore, the failure to include measures of political stability in models of country creditworthiness will result in misspecification.

Empirical analyses of the role of political instability in country creditworthiness have been retarded partly because of a failure to recognize that different types of country instability can be quantified. This paper, in contrast, uses systematically generated quantitative indicators of three types of political instability to develop

The authors give special thanks to Dennis Quinn for his assistance and insights. They are also indebted to Dennis Logue, Gunter Dufey, and Johanna Renshaw for discussions about this topic and related research. Finally, they have benefitted from the comments of two anonymous referees and the editor. This research was supported by grants from the Georgetown University School of Business Administration.

THOMAS L. BREWER *and* PIETRA RIVOLI *are associate professors at the Georgetown University School of Business Administration.*

Journal of Money, Credit, and Banking, Vol. 22, No. 3 (August 1990)

models of its relationship with country creditworthiness. We examine the effects of (1) governmental regime change, (2) political legitimacy, and (3) armed conflict.

Section 1 of the paper briefly reviews the empirical literature on country risk and the literature on the effects of country instability on economic conditions. Section 2 explains the theoretical basis of the hypothesized relationship between country creditworthiness and political stability, and distinguishes between types of political instability. In section 3, the empirical results are presented and interpreted. Section 4 summarizes the findings and conclusions and offers suggestions for future research.

1. REVIEW OF THE LITERATURE

The empirical literature on country risk in international banking has focused on explaining actual creditworthiness—that is, rescheduling—and perceived creditworthiness (Frank and Cline 1971; Feder and Just 1977; Feder, Just, and Ross 1981; Feder and Ross 1982; McFadden et al. 1986; Melvin and Schlagenhauf 1986; Morgan 1986). Perceived country creditworthiness has been measured by country risk ratings, secondary market debt prices, and risk premiums charged on sovereign loans. This research has demonstrated that economic variables have predictive power for actual and perceived creditworthiness.

In general, these studies have found that three types of economic variables have predictive power (Morgan 1986). The first is the countries' performance in international trade. A strong performance in trade suggests that the country is better able to generate the hard currency necessary to maintain debt service. Conversely, a large negative trade balance means that either more borrowing or the sale of assets will be required for debt service to be sustained. The second category of important economic variables is related to leverage, either in "stock" terms (the total value of indebtedness) or in "flow" terms (for example, debt service ratios). Third, various measures of liquidity have in some cases been found to be predictors. Although liquidity cannot compensate for poor performance in trade over a sustained period, high liquidity suggests that international reserve assets are available in the event of short-term difficulties.

Many scholars who have addressed these questions emphasize that political as well as economic factors play a role in sovereign lending risk (Shapiro 1985). However, most analyses then proceed to incorporate economic factors only; empirical work in this area is generally devoid of political content. The acknowledgment that "politics matters" is too vague to be helpful to either borrowing countries or international banks. It is likely that the neglect of political factors is due to identification problems—that is, what type of political phenomena matter?—as well as measurement difficulties.

There have been three exceptions to the neglect of political instability in empirical studies of country creditworthiness. Abdullah's (1985) study used a highly judgmental and generalized "political adjustment factor" according to which subjectively assigned points were used to reflect "the change in the underlying political situation." That study therefore did not differentiate among various forms of instability. Citron and Nickelsburg (1987) found political instability to be related to the probability of default in four of the five countries in their longitudinal analysis, but used only an unspecified combination of governmental regime and policy instability as their country instability variable. That study therefore similarly failed to isolate particular dimensions of instability. In their model, Feder and Uy (1985) used "a political turmoil dummy variable," which also encompassed a diverse variety of forms of instability in a single variable.

Numerous papers, however, have examined the relationship between political instability and direct foreign investment (FDI). For instance, Stulz (1983) noted that "political risk must play a significant role as a determinant of net foreign [direct] investment," but did not empirically model the role of political risk in FDI; nor did Braga de Macedo (1983) empirically examine that relationship in a discussion of the Stulz paper. Other papers, however, have tested for the relationship between political instability and FDI. These include studies by Nigh (1985), Levis (1979), and Root and Ahmed (1979). The results have been mixed depending on the time and country as well as the types of instability indicators included.

Other studies have focused on the relationship between political instability and governments' exchange control policies (Brewer 1983), expropriation (Kobrin 1976), and fiscal policies (Brewer 1985; Yu 1987). Weak to moderate associations have been found, depending on the forms of stability.

2. POLITICAL STABILITY AND COUNTRY CREDITWORTHINESS

Political scientists have long known that political institutions and political conditions strongly influence economic growth and development, and that political instability in particular is associated with lower rates of economic growth (Huntington 1968; Moore 1966). Several reasons are usually given for this association. Olson (1982) argues that "instability diverts resources that would otherwise have gone into productive long-term investments into forms of wealth that are more easily protected, or even into capital flight to more stable environments" (p. 165). Olson also argues that unstable societies are characterized by a "markedly disproportionate strength of small groups" which leads to the "perverse policy syndrome," among whose consequences are extremes of income inequality (p. 172). Income inequality is in turn strongly inversely associated with regime stability and economic development (Muller 1988).

As Shapiro (1985) noted, a government's ability to service external debt depends upon the government's ability to extract the necessary resources from its citizens. Stable regimes are more likely to have this ability than are unstable ones. In addition, governmental instability increases investors' uncertainty about economic policies and conditions that directly or indirectly affect the country's creditworthiness, and countries with unstable governments may exercise less fiscal and monetary restraint for fear such restraint would undermine an already fragile regime. We, therefore, expect political instability to be inversely associated with a country's capacity to service its debt and to have a negative impact on perceived creditworthiness.

It is necessary, however, to distinguish among various types of instability, as different forms of instability will have different effects on actual and perceived creditworthiness. At least three different conceptualizations of country instability may be identified in the literature (Hurwitz 1973; Taylor and Jodice 1983).

One conceptualization defines political stability in terms of governmental regime longevity; the frequency of regime change is an (inverse) indicator of country stability. A second approach defines political stability in terms of the "legitimacy" of the government or political system more generally. Legitimacy is based upon the degree to which a country's political system is democratic versus authoritarian, and on the extent to which its citizens therefore enjoy various political rights. It is argued that authoritarian regimes that do not confer basic rights are inherently unstable in the long run, even though they are (by definition) stable in the short run. Finally, a third notion of instability equates it with armed conflict, either internal (civil wars and insurrections) or external.

Prior research has not distinguished across these types of instability in the analysis of country lending. However, they are both conceptually distinct and empirically independent. Therefore, we include measures of all three in our empirical analysis.

3. EMPIRICAL ANALYSIS

The Hypotheses and Data

In the present study, the hypothesis of a negative impact of instability on perceived creditworthiness was tested on data for the thirty most heavily indebted developing countries, as reported in Morgan (1986). Instability cannot be quantified with the same ease as can, for example, trade performance, but it is nevertheless possible to employ proxy measures for the three types of political stability discussed in the preceding section. In addition, for each of the three types of political instability we measure both proximate and chronic instability.

Our measure of governmental regime stability is the frequency of change in political leadership. We examine the frequency of change in (1) the head of government, and (2) the governing group, over a period of time. The governing group refers to a political party, civilian regime, or military government. Both short-term ("proximate") instability scores and longer-term ("chronic") instability scores were computed. The regime instability scores were generated for the period 1967–86 from standard reference sources, including Banks (1987) in particular.

Our proxy for political legitimacy is obtained from the annual reports on human rights reported in Gastil (1987). The reports rank countries on the extent to which the political process is democratic versus authoritarian. Highly ranked countries allow popular participation in government, free and open elections, and political opposition.[1] The proximate political legitimacy scores are those for year-end 1986 and the chronic scores are obtained by averaging scores for the years 1975–1986.

Armed conflict data are also available for both proximate and chronic measures. The proximate armed conflict score is a dichotomous variable which is assigned the value 1 if the country was involved in armed conflict as of year-end 1986. The data are from Goose (1987). The chronic armed conflict score is the number of years the country had been involved in the armed conflict, from the same data source.

A country list and values for all instability scores are presented in the Appendix.

We also expect that economic variables will affect perceived creditworthiness, as reported in prior research. Therefore, we include measures of trade performance and country indebtedness. Our measure of trade performance is the current account balance as a percent of GNP. We expect that this measure will positively influence perceived creditworthiness. Country indebtedness is measured by the ratio of total external debt to GNP. A negative relationship is anticipated. The economic data are from *World Development Report* (World Bank) and *International Financial Statistics* (IMF).

Arguably, additional economic variables should be included in attempting to explain perceived creditworthiness. Our reasons for limiting the economic variables are that the economic relationships have been examined by many authors (as noted above), while we wish to focus attention on the political phenomena. In addition, preliminary empirical tests indicated that the inclusion of other economic variables does not appreciably improve the performance of the model.[2]

Country creditworthiness data were taken from the 1987 *Institutional Investor* and *Euromoney* ratings. Feder and Ross (1982) found a strong positive association between *Institutional Investor* country credit assessments and interest rates in the Euromarket. However, both the *Institutional Investor* and the *Euromoney* ratings are included in the present study because the time period and country coverage differ from those of Feder and Ross. Furthermore, the two indicators appear at slightly different times, and there are time lags between the collection and publication of the scores. The net result is that, in the case of the *Institutional Investor,* there is a lag of only a few weeks after the end of the instability data coverage and about half a year in the case of *Euromoney*. As noted below, the consistent similarity of results for the two sets of creditworthiness indicators suggests that these time lags are not a significant problem.

More importantly, the two indicators are based on different types of data. The *Institutional Investor* scores are survey responses of individual bankers and thus represent to some extent personalized assessments of the countries' creditworthiness. The *Euromoney* scores, on the other hand, reflect actual financial market conditions. The inclusion of the former scores in the study makes it possible to analyze directly and specifically the impact of instability on bankers' expectations

[1]Further information on these and related measures is available in Bollen (1986).

[2]The economic variables included in preliminary tests included the ratio of reserves to imports, the inflation rate, the level of per capita income and the ratio of debt service payments to GNP.

about the countries; the inclusion of the latter scores enables us to analyze more broadly the impact on financial markets.

Both *Euromoney* and *Institutional Investor* scores vary within the range (0–100) and therefore conflict with the normality assumption underlying OLS. However, the scores may be interpreted as probabilities (Feder and Ross 1982), which then allows a logistic transformation of the credit rating, which we employ as the dependent variable.[3]

The Estimation of the Models

The models of the impact of instability on perceived creditworthiness are estimated in two sets of least squares regressions—the first to test for the effects of proximate instability and the second to test for the effects of chronic instability. In each estimation, we include indicators of all three types of political instability as well as the economic variables. The variables are

II = *Institutional Investor* scores.
EM = *Euromoney* scores.
PHI, *CHI* = number of changes in the head of government between respectively, 1982–86 and 1967–86, representing proximate and chronic head instability.
PGI, *CGI* = number of changes in the governing group between, respectively, 1982–86 and 1967–86, representing proximate and chronic group instability.
PPL, *CPL* = political rights scores for 1986 and the mean for 1975–86, respectively, representing proximate and chronic instability.
PAC, *CAC* = armed conflict scores indicating, respectively, armed conflict in progress at the end of 1986 (0,1 variable), and chronic armed conflict (the number of years conflict in progress as of the end of 1986).
CAB = current account balance as percent of GNP in 1986.
TED = total external debt as percent of GNP in 1986.

We estimate equations (1)–(4) to assess the effects of proximate instability. The results are shown in Table 1.

[3]The logistical transformation of credit rating *R* is *LR* where

$$LR = \ln\left(\frac{R/100}{\left(1 - \frac{R}{100}\right)}\right)$$

$$II = \beta_0 + \beta_1 (PHI) + \beta_2 (PPL) + \beta_3(PAC) + \beta_4(CAB) + \beta_5(TED) + e \quad (1)$$

$$II = \beta_0 + \beta_1(PGI) + \beta_2(PPL) + \beta_3(PAC) + \beta_4(CAB) + \beta_5(TED) + e \quad (2)$$

$$EM = \beta_0 + \beta_1(PHI) + \beta_2(PPL) + \beta_3(PAC) + \beta_4(CAB) + \beta_5(TED) + e \quad (3)$$

$$EM = \beta_0 + \beta_1(PGI) + \beta_2(PPL) + \beta_3(PAC) + \beta_4(CAB) + \beta_5(TED) + e \quad (4)$$

The relationships between governmental regime stability and perceived creditworthiness are all significant in the predicted direction. In fact, measured by either the t-statistics or the standardized coefficients, regime stability has a greater impact on credit risk perceptions than do either of the economic variables.[4] This is true for both measures of governmental regime instability: the frequency of change in the head of government (equations 1 and 3) and in the governing group (equations 2 and 4). The other measures of political instability—armed conflict and political legitimacy—bear the anticipated negative sign, but the coefficients are significant only in equation 2.

Equations (5)–(8) were estimated to assess the effects of longer-term, or chronic, instability. On one hand, the significant associations found for regime stability 1982–86 may be limited to the impact of proximate instability in the immediately preceding years. On the other hand, perhaps chronic instability—as indicated by armed conflict or political legitimacy—has an impact as well, despite the findings for proximate instability. The equations are

$$II = \beta_0 + \beta_1(CHI) + \beta_2(CPL) + \beta_3(CAD) + \beta_4(CAB) + \beta_5(TED) + e \quad (5)$$

$$II = \beta_0 + \beta_1(GCI) + \beta_2(CPL) + \beta_3(CAC) + \beta_4(CAB) + \beta_5(TED)\ e \quad (6)$$

$$EM = \beta_0 + \beta_1(CHI) + \beta_2(CPL) + \beta_3(CAC) + \beta_4(CAB) + \beta_5(TED) + e \quad (7)$$

[4]The standardized coefficient B' results in a dimensionless coefficient and is computed by $B' = B(s_x/s_y)$ where s_x and s_y are the standard deviations of the independent and dependent variables, respectively. For the sake of brevity, these coefficients are not included in the table. They are available upon request.

TABLE 1

RESULTS OF ESTIMATION OF EQUATIONS (1)–(4)

Equation	Dependent Variable	Intercept	PHI	PGI	PPL	PAC	CAB	TED	F	R^2
(1)	*II*	.931*	−.347*		−.030	−.314	6.451*	−1.435*	9.071	.654
		(2.637)	(−4.322)		(−.544)	−1.505	(2.374)	(−4.293)		
(2)	*II*	.824*		−.650*	−.073	−.050	4.978	−1.307*	6.055	.581
		(2.062)		(−3.067)	(−1.14)	(−.212)	(1.927)	(−3.450)		
(3)	*EM*	1.293*	−.323*		−.067	−.091	8.695*	−1.295*	6.105	.560
		(2.961)	(−3.253)		(−.992)	(−.355)	(2.586)	(−3.132)		
(4)	*EM*	1.449*		−.973*	−.149*	−.223)	7.136*	−1.127*	10.587	.688
		(3.937)		(−4.979)	(−2.466)	(−1.025)	(2.532)	(−2.232)		

NOTES: *Significant at .05 or less.
t-statistics are in parentheses

TABLE 2

RESULTS OF ESTIMATION OF EQUATIONS (5)–(8)

Equation	Dependent Variable	Intercept	CHI	CGI	CPL	CAC	CAB	TED	F	R^2
(5)	*II*	.792	−.065		−.074	−.006	3.630	−1.374*	4.333	.475
		(1.525)	(−1.880)		(−.887)	(−.523)	(1.605)	(−3.319)		
(6)	*II*	.464		−.032	−.046	−.008	3.795	−1.367*	3.253	.404
		(.851)		(−.542)	(−.512)	(−.671)	(1.460)	(−3.100)		
(7)	*EM*	1.170*	−.063		−.116	−.016	5.50	−1.167*	5.080	.514
		(2.135)	(−1.728)		(−1.319)	(1.402)	(1.53)	(−2.674)		
(8)	*EM*	.855		−.032	−.089	.018	5.659	−1.161*	4.080	.460
		(1.502)		(−.514)	(−.943)	(1.496)	(1.940)	(−2.521)		

NOTES: *Significant at .05 or less.
t-statistics are in parentheses

$$EM = \beta_0 + \beta_1(CGI) + \beta_2(CPL) + \beta_3(CAC) + \beta_4(CAB) + \beta_5(TED) + e \qquad (8)$$

The estimation of equations (5)–(8) are shown in Table 2. The predictive power of equations (5)–(8) is less than that of equations (1)–(4). No significant associations between the chronic instability scores and the creditworthiness scores are evident.

Interpretation of Results

The results show that perceptions of country creditworthiness are more responsive to recent (proximate) evidence of instability in the form of regime change than to long-term (chronic) instability. Country creditworthiness perceptions tend to be based on recent political conditions rather than on a longer-term view of the country's experience.

Perceptions of creditworthiness are also more responsive to evidence of regime change than to evidence of political legitimacy or violent conflict. This finding is consistent with a shorter-term focus on the part of lenders and financial markets. Country creditworthiness assessments that ignore a regime's lack of legitimacy may appropriately be treating it as stable in the short term. Further, an argument can be made that more authoritarian regimes are more creditworthy in the short run. These regimes may be better able to extract resources from the economy, and also better able to institute or maintain austerity programs that lack popular support. Similarly, armed conflict can actually increase regime stability in the short run.

At the same time, however, our results that fail to show a relationship between credit risk perceptions and armed conflict and political legitimacy are counterintuitive. For example, we know that the illegitimacy of the authoritarian regime of Ferdinand Marcos, as well as continued armed conflict in the Philippines, had deleterious effects on the ability to service sovereign debt. Authoritarian regimes increase the chance of violent and revolutionary change, as many recent examples make clear, and therefore we would expect that the risks of country lending would be higher under such regimes.

One explanation for our empirical result is that this intuition is wrong and that lender perceptions are rational—both armed conflict and political legitimacy may be unrelated to debt-servicing ability. A second interpretation, however, is that the lenders' risk assessments are short sighted in their failure to consider a longer-term and more comprehensive view of country stability. Therefore, an important question for future research is whether a relationship exists between actual debt servicing records and measures of legitimacy and armed conflict.

4. CONCLUSIONS

Lender perceptions of credit risk in sovereign lending are of central importance because these perceptions affect both the supply and cost of capital flows to developing countries. The empirical analysis presented in this paper found these conclusions:

1. There was a significant impact of proximate country instability—as indicated by the frequency of governmental regime change—on perceived country creditworthiness. The frequency of regime change appears to be at least as important as economic variables in explaining lenders' risk perceptions. This was true for both instability in the head of government and instability in the governing group. These results were consistent for the two measures of perceived creditworthiness.
2. The results obtained for the other two types of country instability—as indicated by armed conflict and political legitimacy—are less conclusive. Although all of the coefficients for proximate instability bear the anticipated sign, the legitimacy effect is statistically significant in only one estimation. Chronic instability does not appear to have a significant impact.

It is surprising that the presence of armed conflict and political illegitimacy do not provide greater explanatory power for country risk perceptions. Future research should examine whether this finding is consistent with lender rationality—that is, whether these political phenomena are truly unrelated to debt servicing capability, or whether they are instead consistent with the popular view that international banks suffer from shortsightedness.

Our results illustrate the importance of distinguishing among the various types of political phenomena. Political instability is not one phenomenon that can be measured by a single variable, much less a dichotomous variable. It is rather a complex, multidimensional concept requiring multiple indicators. The dimensions of political instability identified in this paper are both conceptually and empirically distinguishable.

We also show that it is feasible to develop quantitative indicators of the various dimensions of political instability which can be included along with economic variables in models of country risk. Such political variables are in effect measures of the performance of different aspects of a country's political system, just as current account balances and debt service ratios are measures of the performance of different aspects of its economic system. Our results show that models of country creditworthiness that rely exclusively on indicators of economic performance will be misspecified.

APPENDIX: COUNTRY LIST AND INSTABILITY SCORES

	CGI	CHI	PGI	PHI	CPL	PPL	PAC	CAC
Algeria	0	1	0	0	6.1	6	0	0
Argentina	3	10	1	3	4.1	2	0	0
Bolivia	5	16	1	3	4.5	2	0	0
Brazil	1	4	1	1	3.6	2	0	0
Cameroon	0	1	0	1	6.1	6	0	0
Chile	2	2	0	0	6.3	6	0	0

(*continued*)

APPENDIX: (*Continued*)

	CGI	CHI	PGI	PHI	CPL	PPL	PAC	CAC
Colombia	1	4	1	1	2.0	2	1	8
Costa Rica	1	5	0	2	1.0	1	0	0
Ecuador	6	6	2	1	3.8	2	1	1
Egypt	0	2	0	0	5.0	5	0	0
Greece	0	1	0	0	1.7	2	0	0
India	2	3	0	0	2.0	2	1	39
Indonesia	0	0	0	0	5.0	5	1	11
Israel	2	6	1	3	2.0	2	1	38
Ivory Coast	0	0	0	0	5.8	6	0	0
Korea	1	1	0	0	4.8	4	0	0
Malaysia	0	3	0	0	3.0	3	1	41
Mexico	0	3	0	1	3.6	4	0	0
Morocco	0	0	0	0	4.1	4	1	11
Nigeria	2	4	1	2	4.8	7	0	0
Peru	4	5	1	2	3.8	2	1	6
Philippines	1	1	1	1	4.8	4	1	16
Portugal	6	9	0	0	2.2	1	0	0
Sudan	2	2	1	1	5.4	4	1	3
Thailand	7	7	0	0	4.4	3	1	21
Tunisia	0	0	0	0	5.7	6	0	0
Turkey	7	7	1	1	2.9	3	0	0
Uruguay	2	7	1	1	4.8	2	0	0
Venezuela	4	4	1	1	1.2	1	0	0
Yugoslavia	0	7	0	5	6.0	6	0	0

LITERATURE CITED

Abdullah, F. A. "Development of an Advanced Warning Indicator of External Debt Servicing Vulnerability." *Journal of International Business Studies* 16 (Fall 1985), 135–41.

Aliber, Robert Z. "A Conceptual Approach to the Analysis of the External Debt of the Developing Countries." World Bank Working Paper No. 421, 1980.

Banks, Arthur S. *Political Handbook of the World.* Binghamton, N.Y.: CSA Publications, 1987.

Bergsten, C. Fred, William R. Cline, and John Williamson. *Bank Lending to Developing Countries: The Policy Alternatives.* Washington, D.C.: Institute for International Economics, 1985.

Bollen, Kenneth A. "Political Rights and Political Liberties in Nations: An Evaluation of Human Rights Measures, 1950 to 1984." *Human Rights Quarterly* 8 (1986), 567–91.

Brewer, Thomas L. "The Instability of Controls on MNEs' Funds Transfers and the Instability of Governments." *Journal of International Business Studies* 14 (Winter 1983), 147–57.

———. "A Comparative Analysis of the Fiscal Policies of Industrial and Developing Countries: Policy Instability and Governmental Regime Instability." *Journal of Comparative Economics* 9 (June 1985), 191–96.

Braga de Macedo, Jorge. "Discussion." *Journal of Finance* 38 (May 1983), 472–75.

Citron, J. T., and G. Nickelsburg. "Country Risk and Political Instability." *Journal of Development Economics* 25 (1987), 385–92.

Cline, William R. *International Debt.* Washington, D.C.: Institute for International Economics, 1984.

______. *International Debt and the Stability of the World Economy*. Washington, D.C.: Institute for International Economics, 1983.

Eaton, Jonathan, and Mark Gersowitz. "Debt with Potential Repudiation: Theoretical and Empirical Analysis." *Review of Economics Studies* 48 (April 1981), 289–309.

Feder, Gershon, and Richard E. Just. "An Analysis of Credit Terms in the Eurodollar Market." *European Economic Review* 9 (1977), 221–43.

______. "A Study of Debt Servicing Capacity Applying Logit Analysis." *Journal of Development Economics* 4 (1977), 25–38.

Feder, Gershon, Richard E. Just, and K. Ross. "Projecting Debt Servicing Capacity of Developing Countries." *Journal of Financial and Quantitative Analysis* 16 (1981), 651–69.

Feder, Gershon, and Knud Ross. "Risk Assessments and Risk Premiums in the Eurodollar Market." *Journal of Finance* 37 (1982), 679–92.

Feder, Gershon, and L. V. Uy. "The Determinants of International Creditworthiness and Their Policy Implications." *Journal of Policy Modelling* 7 (1985), 133–56.

Frank, C. R., and William R. Cline. "Measurement of Debt Servicing Capacity: An Application of Discriminant Analysis." *Journal of International Economics* 1 (August 1971), 327–44.

Gastil, Raymond, *Freedom in the World, 1986*. Westport, Conn.: Greenwood Press, 1987.

Goose, Stephen D. "Armed Conflicts in 1986, and the Iran-Iraq War." In *SIPRI Yearbook 1987*. Oxford: Oxford University Press, 1987, 297–320.

Huntington, Samuel P. *Political Order in Changing Societies*. New Haven: Yale University Press, 1968.

Hurwitz, Leon. "Contemporary Approaches to Political Instability." *Comparative Politics* 5 (1973), 449–63.

Kobrin, Stephen J. "The Environmental Determinants of Foreign Direct Manufacturing Investment: An Ex Post Empirical Analysis." *Journal of International Business Studies* 7 (1976), 29–42.

Lessard, Donald R., and John Williamson. *Financial Intermediation beyond the Debt Crisis*. Washington, D.C.: Institute for International Economics, 1985.

Levis, M. "Does Political Instability in Developing Countries Affect Foreign Investment Flows? An Empirical Examination." *Management International Review* 19 (1979), 59–68.

McFadden, Daniel, Richard Eckaus, Gershon Feder, Vassilis Hajivassiliou, and Stephen O'Connell. "Is There Life after Debt?" In *International Debt and the Developing Countries*. Washington, D.C.: The World Bank, 1986, 179–212.

Melvin, M., and D. Schlagenhauf. "Risk in International Lending: A Dynamic Factor Analysis Applied to France and Mexico." *Journal of International Money and Finance* 5 (1986), 531–48.

Moore, Barrington. *The Social Origins of Dictatorship and Democracy*. Boston: Beacon, 1966.

Morgan, John B. "A New Look at Debt Rescheduling Indicators and Models." *Journal of International Business Studies* 17 (Summer 1986), 37–54.

Muller, Edward N. "Democracy, Economic Development, and Income Inequality." *American Sociological Review* 53 (1988), 50–68.

Nigh, Douglas. "The Effect of Political Events on United States Direct Foreign Investment: A Pooled Time Series Cross-Sectional Analysis." *Journal of International Business Studies* 16 (Spring 1985), 1–17.

Olson, Mancur. *The Rise and Decline of Nations*. New Haven: Yale University Press, 1982.

Paxton, John. *The Stateman's Yearbook*. New York: St. Martin's, 1987.

Root, Franklin R., and Ahmed Ahmed. "Empirical Determinants of Manufacturing Direct Foreign Investment in Developing Countries." *Economic Development and Cultural Change* 12 (July 1979), 751–67.

Saini, Krishan G., and Philip S. Bates. "A Survey of the Quantitative Approaches to Country Risk Analysis." *Journal of Banking and Finance* 7 (1984), 303–16.

Shapiro, Alan C. "Risk in International Banking." *Journal of Financial and Quantitative Analysis* 17 (December 1981), 728–39.

———. "Currency Risk and Country Risk in International Banking." *Journal of Finance* 40 (July 1985), 881–91.

Stulz, Rene M. "On the Determinants of Net Foreign Investment." *Journal of Finance* 38 (May 1983), 459–72.

Taylor, Charles Lewis, and David A. Jodice. "Quantitative Research on Political Instability." In *World Handbook of Political and Social Indicators,* 3rd ed. New Haven and London: Yale University Press, 1983, vol. 2, 1–15.

Yu, Chwo-ming. "A Reconsideration of Measures of Instability." *Journal of Comparative Economics* 11 (March 1987), 116–19.

JAMES J. MUSUMECI
JOSEPH F. SINKEY, JR.

The International Debt Crisis and Bank Loan-Loss-Reserve Decisions: The Signaling Content of Partially Anticipated Events

THE HUGE INCREASES IN LOAN-LOSS PROVISIONS by major bank holding companies (BHCs) in 1987 were a signal of impending asset write-downs of loans to less-developed countries (LDCs).[1] Since loan-loss-reserve decisions, like asset write-downs, are simply bookkeeping adjustments, significant market reactions to such announcements should not be expected. Strong and Meyer (1987), however, found a positive and statistically significant cumulative average residual after the announcement of asset write-downs.[2] Thakor (1987) argues that write-downs have a price effect *not* because they mean much by themselves but because they *signal* events to come. Specifically, he sees write-downs as a signal of "economic value-enhancing corporate restructuring to come in the future" (p. 662).

We use event-study methods to examine security returns for the twenty-five largest U.S. bank holding companies surrounding Citicorp's $3 billion loan-loss-

The authors thank David W. Blackwell, M. Cary Collins, Mary Dehner, Jangsoon Han, Edward J. Kane, Van Son Lai, William L. Megginson, Annette Poulsen, Haluk Unal, and three JMCB referees for their helpful comments and suggestions. A preliminary version of this paper was presented at the 1988 Conference of Bank Structure and Competition sponsored by the Federal Reserve Bank of Chicago and appears in the *Proceedings* of the conference under the title "The International Debt Crisis and Bank Security Returns Surrounding Citicorp's Loan-Loss-Reserve Decision of May 19, 1987." A revised version of the paper was presented at the Emory University-Federal Reserve Bank of Atlanta Workshop on Money, Banking, and Finance. The authors thank the participants in this workshop for their comments.

[1]Write-downs of LDC loans began in 1987 and are likely to continue for several years. See Hill and Truell (1988).

[2]Based on seventy-eight write-down announcements, Strong and Meyer (1987) did not find a statistically significant CAR *before* these announcements.

JAMES J. MUSUMECI *is assistant professor of finance at the University of Georgia.* JOSEPH F. SINKEY, JR., *is professor of finance and The Georgia Bankers Association Chair of Banking at the University of Georgia.*

Journal of Money, Credit, and Banking, Vol. 22, No. 3 (August 1990)

reserve decision of May 19, 1987.[3] We observe positive and significant abnormal returns for Citicorp and other money-center banks when Citicorp announces its reserve allocations. In addition, we find positive abnormal returns for the other money-center banks when they announce their reserve decisions. Thus, although the market anticipated rational follow-the-leader behavior and rewarded it, the event was only partially anticipated (in the sense of Malatesta and Thompson [1985]). We interpret these loan-loss-reserve decisions as foreshadowing the write-down of LDC loans. Such bookkeeping entries affect market prices because they signal economic value-enhancing corporate and strategic restructurings. The specific restructurings include the stepped up disposal of third-world debt, harder-line bargaining with both LDC borrowers and bank regulators, and future equity issues designed to strengthen bank capital adequacy.[4]

1. THE EVENTS

After 4:45 p.m. (EST) on Tuesday, May 19, 1987, Citicorp announced the addition of $3 billion to its reserve for possible credit losses. John S. Reed, Citicorp's chairman, said: "This increase in the reserve is related to the sovereign debt issue and our commitment to play a constructive and continuing role in its resolution."[5] The specific "sovereign debt issue" was Brazil's announcement on Friday evening, February 20, 1987, to suspend interests payments to foreign banks. Following this announcement, the financial press speculated that "the current approach to Latin debt is at a crossroads and that a new order will emerge . . . "[6] Before Citicorp's reserve decision, banks were involved in what Lessard (1987) calls zero-sum negotiating with LDCs. We regard Citicorp's reserve decision as a signal that it was going to adopt harder bargaining positions with both LDC borrowers and bank regulators. For obvious political reasons, Citicorp reported this new negotiating position as "our commitment to play a constructive and continuing role" in the resolution of the international debt crisis.[7]

Citicorp's reserve decision triggered a chain reaction that motivated other money-center banks (see Table 1) and about twenty regional banking companies to "follow the leader." This cartel-like behavior is reminiscent of the price leadership found in

[3]The international debt crisis has spawned numerous event studies of the pricing of bank equities; see Bruner and Simms (1987), Smirlock and Kaufold (1987), Sachs and Huizinga (1987), Strong (1988), Grammatikos and Saunders (1988), Madura and McDaniel (1989), Megginson, Poulson, and Sinkey (1989), and Musumeci and Sinkey (1990).

[4]Although equity announcements generally are associated with declines in share prices, we view them in this case as a necessary part of a practical strategy for dealing with the LDC debt crisis.

[5]News Release, Public Affairs Division, Citicorp/Citibank (May 19, 1987), pp. 1–2.

[6]As reported by Berg (1987) in *The New York Times* (March 3), p. 25.

[7]In its 1987 annual report, Citicorp stated: "we believe that as a result of the reserve decision your Company has been able to respond more effectively to the debt issue" (p. 5). An economist on the House Banking Committee has suggested to us that Citicorp also considered "competitive factors" related to takeover activity among other major U.S. banks in arriving at its reserve decision. In this regard, Citicorp's reserve decision was seen as putting its rivals on the spot, giving it leverage against LDCs, and hurting banks' united front.

the prime-rate convention of the 1950s and 1960s. Unlike the prime-rate convention, however, which was motivated by the desire to keep products similar and maintain market share (much like political parties move to the center to maximize votes), Citicorp's pied-piper parade seems to have been motivated by rational self-interest in a way unrelated to market share. Under this scenario, if Citicorp's price had declined, there would not have been a follow-the-leader effect. When the market reacted positively to Citicorp's reserve decision, the other banks followed suit.[8] An alternative conjecture would be that even if Citicorp's price had declined, other banks eventually would have been forced to follow the leader. Once Citicorp, the bank with the largest stock of Brazilian debt (see Table 3), had recognized the true value of its debt, accountants and regulators could not have permitted other banks to carry the same loans at one hundred cents on the dollar. Since earlier decisions by regional banks to make LDC loan provisions or take write-offs did not have a comparable effect, Citicorp's leadership was important.

2. ACCOUNTING CONSIDERATIONS: THE "NO EVENT" HYPOTHESIS

Under this scenario, the news regarding Citicorp's increase in loan-loss reserves would have little or no effect on bank stock prices. If the market already had a good estimate of Citicorp's (and other BHCs) *real* earnings, then this accounting manipulation or "act of recognition" (of more realistic book values of its outstanding LDC debt) would have no effect on share prices. Specifically, the second quarter accounting earnings that would have been plowed into Citicorp's equity capital as undivided profits were expensed through the provision for loan loss, and reflected on the balance sheet as an addition to the contra-asset account, allowance (or reserve) for loan losses. Other things equal, the decline in net loans was matched by the reduction in undivided profits. Yet the bank's "primary capital," defined for regulatory purposes as equity capital plus loan-loss reserves, did not change, even though second quarter accounting earnings were substantially negative as a result of the "LDC haircut."

3. THE NEW INFORMATION HYPOTHESES

Regarding potential sources of new information for pricing BHC securities, we postulate and discuss four alternative hypotheses. If Citicorp's reserve decision had real economic significance and was a complete or partial surprise to the market, then it would have an effect on bank stock prices.

[8]Of course, banks with little or no LDC exposure had no reason to follow the leader, unless they had energy and farm debt problems which they were "expense hiding" by underallocating to their loan-loss reserves (for example, FirstRepublic in Table 1). At least one bank, BankAmerica, announced on May 19 (and again on May 28) that it would not follow Citicorp's lead; on June 8, however, it reversed its decision and allocated $1.1 billion to its loan-loss reserves.

A. Loan Quality

If the market is strong-form inefficient and the true quality of Citicorp's earnings was "inside information," then the market could react either favorably or unfavorably, depending on how real earnings estimates were revised on the basis of the announcement. Under this hypothesis, Citicorp's announcement provides new or better information on the quality of its LDC loan portfolio and allows the market to more accurately forecast the present value of Citicorp's future cash flows. Because secondary markets for LDC debt existed, however, such news might have already been conveyed to the market. Although the existence of greater disclosure requirements and secondary markets for LDC debt leads us to discount the better-information hypothesis, the timing and amount of the reserve decision could have had important tax consequences.

B. Tax Savings and the Tax Reform Act of 1986

The Tax Reform Act of 1986 changed the treatment of banks' loan-loss reserves beginning in 1987. Specifically, before 1987 all large banks/BHCs used a complicated reserve method designed to meet the needs of accrual accounting (see Wall 1988). The 1986 tax law requires a simpler method of recognizing loan losses when the loan is written off. Could the amount and timing of Citicorp's reserve decision have been calculated to take advantage of the new tax law? A $3 billion addition to loss reserves would certainly be expected to have some tax and cash-flow consequences. If investors focus on real economic earnings after taxes, however, such adjustments already should have been embodied in share prices. In its 1987 annual report, Citicorp recorded income tax expense of $898 million and told investors:

> Income tax expense was recognized in 1987 despite the $3.0 billion addition to the allowance for possible credit losses because only $259 million of tax benefits attributable to the addition to the allowance could be recognized. Unrecognized tax benefits will be used in future years to reduce Federal income tax at the then prevailing rates. (p. 41)

Although the market should have anticipated a future tax break, its timing might still be relevant. Under current tax law, building the loan-loss reserve does not in itself result in a tax benefit; the benefit is realized only when a loan is written off. Nevertheless, the market may have assumed the tax benefit would not come for several years; Citicorp's announcement, therefore, may have signaled more immediate tax savings. Hence, taxes could explain a positive market reaction.[9]

C. Capital Structure

Under 1985 capital guidelines, bank regulators treated one dollar of loan-loss reserve as equal to one dollar of equity capital. After Citicorp's reserve decision,

[9]Citicorp reported income tax expenses of $1 billion in each of 1988 and 1989. In 1988, tax benefits of the 1987 reserve addition were $160 million; no benefits were taken in 1989. During the fourth quarter of 1989, Citicorp added $1 billion to its reserves for LDC debt. Neither the 1987 nor the 1989 reserve additions have forced Citicorp to cut its dividend, which in fact rose from $1.35 per share in 1987 to $1.62 per share as of January 1990.

however, such a policy became suspect, even in the eyes of the regulators. For example, FDIC Chairman Seidman stated: "It (the huge reserve addition) does call into question whether or not reserves should be fully considered as capital."[10] Moreover, based on capital guidelines scheduled for 1992, loan-loss reserves will not be considered part of a bank's core or equity capital but will be counted on a limited basis as part of a bank's total capital.[11]

If loan-loss reserves are not a perfect substitute for equity capital, then additions to reserves increase the riskiness of a bank's capital structure. If the change is material and unanticipated, the market's perception of the bank's insolvency risk would rise along with its cost of funds. On balance, a reserve transfer could adversely affect a bank's stock price. Moreover, if the market expects the bank to attempt to make up the transfer with a future issue of equity, the event is confounded by the trade-off between improved capital structure and potential dilution of earnings.

D. Corporate and Strategic Restructuring

What was the signal Citicorp wanted to send to the marketplace and/or to bank regulators with its loan-loss-reserve decision? Under our corporate and strategic restructuring hypothesis, Citicorp's message is a multidimensional one reflecting future asset write-downs, new equity issues, and a stronger negotiating posture with both LDC borrowers and bank regulators. On balance, we interpret Citicorp's signal as refusal to continue to accept negative net-present-value projects regarding LDC debt. Citicorp began to hint about such a strategic move early in 1987.[12] Overall, our restructuring hypothesis argues for a positive effect on either the present value of Citicorp's future growth opportunities or on the cash flows derived from its assets in place, or both.

Since the LDC crisis became apparent with Mexico's default in 1982, why did it take Citicorp (and other LDC lenders) so long to reach this position? Regulatory pressure is one reason. During the interval between Mexico's default and Citicorp's reserve decision, both Federal Reserve and U.S. Treasury officials attempted to keep the banking cartel of LDC lenders intact by strongly urging them via moral suasion to keep credit flowing to LDCs.[13] The fringe LDC lenders, the regional

[10]As quoted in the *American Banker* (June 15, 1987), pp. 1 and 23.

[11]The new capital guidelines were established in 1987 by the Basle Committee comprised of representatives of the central banks and supervisory authorities of Belgium, Canada, France, Germany, Italy, Japan, Luxembourg, Netherlands, Sweden, Switzerland, United Kingdom, and the United States.

[12]Citicorp began its muscle flexing in early 1987 when it took a firm stance against commercial banks' trend toward concessions on third-world debt; see *The Wall Street Journal* (February 4, 1987), p. 6. Moreover, Citicorp announced on August 19, 1987, plans to raise about $1 billion in equity capital through a worldwide offering of seventeen million shares, an offering successfully completed the following month.

[13]Three examples of such moral suasion are (1) "Volcker Warns against Excessive Caution in International Lending," *American Banker,* (February 3, 1983), pp. 1+; (2) an article in the *Wall Street Journal* (October 22, 1985, p. 7) in which Federal Reserve Chairman Volcker rejected bankers' appeals that federal regulators relax requirements for bank lending to developing countries, even though the government is urging them to step up such lending; and (3) "Volcker: Lack of Foreign Loans Endanger Progress," *Bankers News Weekly* (October 28, 1985), pp. 8+

banking companies, had little to lose and, for the most part, ignored the federal attempts at arm twisting. Until Citicorp's announcement on May 19, 1987, the money-center banks, however, appeared to be dancing to the Fed's music. Nevertheless, earlier recognition of a $3 billion provision would have had a catastrophic effect on Citicorp's equity and would have rendered many of its peers book-value insolvent. Thus, the timing of Citicorp's decision may have been driven by both its own general strategy for dealing with LDC debt and Fed/Treasury preferences.[14]

E. Recapitulation

Since we expect a negative price reaction if the capital-structure hypothesis holds, we can easily distinguish it from the other three new-information hypotheses. Although it is difficult to distinguish empirically among the other three, the existence of secondary markets for LDC debt leads us to discount the loan-quality hypothesis. Moreover, since additions to loan-loss reserves are not necessary for LDC write-downs, we also discount the tax-savings hypothesis. Thus, we view the capital-structure and strategic-restructuring hypotheses as the most plausible ones.

4. LOAN-LOSS LEADERSHIP, RATIONAL FOLLOW-THE-LEADER BEHAVIOR, AND REGULATORY PRESSURE

Our null hypothesis regarding the effect of Citicorp's reserve decision on other BHCs is one of no new information conveyed to the market. Our alternative hypothesis is that of rational follow-the-leader behavior. Under this scenario, rational managers would follow Citicorp's lead if the market rewarded Citicorp for its reserve decision. Since BankAmerica's decline during the 1980s, Citicorp has become the dominant force in the U.S. banking industry. If the market expected other BHCs with heavy LDC exposures to follow Citicorp's reserve/restructuring leadership, then it should reward them similarly. We know after the fact that major BHCs, both money centers and regionals, did follow Citicorp's lead (see Table 1).

Nevertheless, the positive share-price reaction by other money-center BHCs and the observed follow-the-leader behavior could have an alternative explanation.[15] Suppose Citicorp's share price had not risen in response to its reserve decision. Under our scenario, other banks would have had no incentive to follow the leader. It would have been very difficult, however, for accountants, the SEC, and bank regulators to permit other LDC lenders to ignore the implications of Citicorp's decision. Thus, these pressures, rather than our rational follow-the-leader behavior, could be the driving force. A positive market response, however, would seem to rule out the regulatory-pressure argument.

Motivation aside, the important question is: How would the market treat these other BHCs at the time of Citicorp's announcement and would it bid up the share

[14]We thank a *Journal* referee for suggesting the general-strategy argument.
[15]We thank a *Journal* referee for this alternative explanation.

TABLE 1

Chronology of Events Following Citicorp's Announcement of a $3 Billion Addition to its Reserve for Possible Credit Losses, 1987

Announcement Date	Bank	Effective Event Date	Announcement or Addition to Loan-loss Reserves*
May 19	Citicorp	May 20	$3.0 billion
May 19	BankAmerica	May 20	Claims no new reserves
May 26	Norwest Corp.	May 27	$0.2 billion
May 27	Chase Manhattan	May 28	$1.6 billion
May 28	BankAmerica	May 29	Restates no new reserves
June 1	Security Pacific	June 2	$0.5 billion
June 3	Bank of Boston	June 4	$0.3 billion
June 8	BankAmerica	June 9	$1.1 billion
June 11	Chemical	June 12	$1.1 billion
June 11	First Interstate	June 12	$0.75 billion
June 12	First Chicago	June 15	$0.8 billion
June 15	Mellon Bank	June 16	$0.415 billion
June 16	Manufacturers	June 17	$1.7 billion
June 16	Bankers Trust	June 17	$0.7 billion
June 16	National West-minister PLC	June 17	$0.76 billion
June 17	Marine Midland	June 18	$0.4 billion
June 17	Republic, NY	June 18	$0.1 billion
June 18	American Express	June 19	$0.6 billion
June 18	PNC Financial	June 19	$0.11 billion
June 18	Bank of New Eng.	June 19	$0.107 billion
June 22	Continental Ill.	June 23	$0.5 billion
June 23	First Bank System	June 24	$0.16 billion
June 29	Bank of New York	June 30	$0.135 billion
June 29	First Republic, TX	June 30	$0.325 billion
July 7	Midland (London)	July 8	$1.93 billion
July 8	J.P. Morgan	July 9	$0.875 billion
July 21	Wells Fargo	July 22	$0.4 billion
July 21	Irving Trust	July 22	$0.225 billion
August 18	Citicorp	August 19	Plans to issue 17 million shares of common stock or $1B
September 2	Manufacturers	September 3	$0.25B equity issue
September 8	Bankers Trust	September 9	$0.25B equity issue

*The reserve additions for these twenty-five BHCs totaled $18.792 billion. Reserve additions of $100 million or less are excluded from our list. Two of our sample firms had reserve allocations less than $100 million: NBD Corp. $54 million on June 15, 1987 (4:10 p.m.) and First Union $25 million on June 30, 1987. In addition, three of our sample firms, M Corp., NCNB, and SunTrust (see Table 3), made no specific reserve allocation for LDC debt in 1987. Other BHCs announcing reserve allocations greater than $50 but not included in our sample are First Wisconsin ($96 million on June 19), Northern Trust Co. ($85 million on June 16), National City Corp. ($55 million on June 30), and First Wachovia ($50 million on June 19). Equity issues beyond September 8, 1987, have not been researched.
Sources: *The Wall Street Journal* (various issues) and/or the corporate communications offices of the various companies.

prices of BHCs without regard to their LDC exposures and financial strength? To test for differential market responses based on these factors, we regress our abnormal returns against alternative measures of Brazilian exposure, LDC exposure, or BHC financial strength.

5. PARTIALLY ANTICIPATED EVENTS AND THE "FREE-RIDER" PROBLEM

Since the other money-center banks could benefit by Citicorp's reserve decision before they announced their own reserve allocations, a potential "free-rider" problem exists. Specifically, these banks would receive the positive abnormal returns without announcing reserve allocations and would be free riders. Alternatively, in the spirit of Malatesta and Thompson (1985), we can analyze this problem as a partially anticipated event. If a free-rider problem exists or the market fully (100 percent) anticipates that a bank would follow Citicorp's leadership, then it would be rewarded only at the time Citicorp announces. In contrast, if the market only partially anticipates that a bank will make (or is capable of making) a reserve allocation, the bank would receive only a partial reward proportional to the market's expectation of the bank's ability to follow suit. In some cases, the market could deliver negative abnormal returns. BankAmerica, for example, was under pressure because it was thought to be too weak financially to make a reserve allocation. In fact, on May 19 (and again on May 28), 1987, BankAmerica issued a "read-my-lips" statement: "No new reserves." On June 8, it reversed its decision and made a $1.1 billion reserve allocation (see Table 1).

To test our hypothesis of partial anticipation, we estimate and compare abnormal returns for two events: (1) Citicorp's announcement date (May 19, 1987) and (2) each bank's *own* announcement date as shown in Table 1. The sum of these two returns represents a bank's total abnormal return for the two events. If the market perceived that a bank was able to follow Citicorp's lead, the proportion of each BHC's abnormal return on Citicorp's announcement date to the total abnormal return for the two events should be positively related to the bank's likelihood of following suit. If a free-rider problem exists, the proportion should be one with no benefit to any bank on the announcement of its reserve allocation.

Ideally, the proportions could be calculated and interpreted as probabilities of each individual bank's future reserve announcement. The residuals, however, incorporate a large amount of measurement error for any individual bank. Hence, to interpret any bank's ratio of residuals as a good measure of probability is misleading. Portfolio residuals, however, have less measurement error than those for individual banks. If we observe significant residuals, then we interpret the proportions for the portfolios as a probability that a representative bank would follow Citicorp's lead.

We summarize all of our hypotheses for Citicorp's reserve decision in Table 2.

TABLE 2

SUMMARY OF HYPOTHESES FOR CITICORP'S RESERVE DECISION

Null Hypotheses	Alternative Hypotheses
1. No new information for Citicorp	1. New information a. Loan quality b. Tax savings c. Capital structure d. Strategic restructuring
2. No new information for other BHCs	2. Rational follow the leader versus regulatory pressure
3. Full anticipation or free riders	3. Partial anticipation and no free riders

TABLE 3

MAJOR BANKING COMPANIES CROSS-BORDER EXPOSURE TO BRAZIL, DECEMBER 31, 1986

Money-Center Group	$ millions	Percent of Primary Capital and Rank	
Citicorp (22)	4,600	36.0%	22
Bank America (24)	2,741	37.0%	23
Bankers Trust (20)	849	18.5	15
Chase Manhattan (23)	2,740	41.1	24
Chemical (19)	1,446	32.9	20
Continental Illinois (18)	474	19.0	16
First Chicago (17)	733	22.1	17
J.P. Morgan (14)	1,926	30.1	19
Manufacturers Hanover (25)	2,317	42.9	25
Security Pacific (12)	605	14.6	12
Subtotal or average	18,431	26.7%	—
Regional Group			
Bank of Boston (11)	300	13.0%	10
Bank of New England (6)	82	5.9	7
First Bank System (8)	189	9.4	9
First Interstate (13)	504	14.8	13
First Union (1)	*	0.0	1
Irving (21)	398	24.9	18
Marine Midland (16)	621	36.3	21
M Corp (5)	34	2.0	4
Mellon (15)	347	13.9	11
NBD Bancorp (4)	46	3.3	5
NCNB (3)	85	5.0	6
Norwest (10)	**	0.0	2
PNC Financial (7)	141	6.6	8
SunTrust (2)	22	1.2	3
Wells Fargo (9)	594	16.5	14
Subtotal or average	3,510	11.2%	—
Grand total or average	21,941	17.4%	—

NOTES: The rank in the last column is based on "1" as least exposed (safest). The number in parentheses beside the BHC name is its rank (1 = least exposed or safest) for the ratio of total LDC loans to *equity* capital. The single (double) asterisk indicates an exposure of less than 0.5% (0.75%) of total assets. The money-center group of ten BHCs held 82% of Brazil's $22.4 billion in loans from U.S. banks.
SOURCE: "Review of Major Banks' Loan Exposures to Less-Developed Countries." Fixed Income Research, First Boston (June 22, 1987), pp. 10–18.

6. SAMPLE BANKING FIRMS, DATA, AND METHODOLOGY

Our sample banking firms and their outstanding loans to Brazil (as of December 31, 1986) are shown in Table 3. In addition to Citicorp, we analyze nine other money-center or multinational banking companies and fifteen regional banking companies.[16] These twenty-five banking companies are the twenty-five largest U.S. banks/BHCs as listed by the *American Banker* in its report of financial-services stocks on May 19, 1987. As shown in Table 3, the money-center banks had 82 percent of the outstanding U.S. bank loans to Brazil at year-end 1986. Although our sample is relatively small, it consists of the major U.S. lenders to LDCs. We group our stocks into three portfolios: money centers, regionals, and all twenty-five. Stock

[16]We defined our money-center group as the ten largest BHCs based on a relatively large size break between the tenth and eleventh firms.

price and dividend data for these firms were collected from the *Daily Stock Price Record* and used to generate daily returns for our sample BHCs.

We employ the standard event-study framework to generate our empirical findings.[17] We use a 140-day estimation period that runs from Day −143 through Day −4. Our event date is centered on May 20, 1987, with the event period extending from Day −3 to Day +3. Within this event period, we examine one-, three-, five-, and seven-day event windows. Each bank's daily return is regressed against the Value Line Index.[18] Since event-study results may be affected by the method used, we employ alternative return-generating processes (for example, a two-factor model, a market-adjusted model, and CAPM) to calculate abnormal returns (ARs) for each stock, which are then summed to obtain cumulative average returns (CARs).[19] Our portfolio standard deviations were estimated not by aggregating individual deviations, but by looking directly at the distribution of portfolio residuals.[20] As Bruner and Simms (1987) point out, this latter method takes into account the cross-sectional correlation between residuals and reduces any problems arising from the presence of both calendar time and industry clustering.[21]

7. EMPIRICAL FINDINGS

Focusing on the three-day window in Table 4, we find a positive but insignificant abnormal return of 1.40 percent ($t = .99$) for our money-center portfolio. Moreover, Citicorp's abnormal return of 8.26 percent is driving this return. The interesting result, however, is that on Day +1 we find a positive and significant abnormal return for the portfolio of money-center banks, with or without the inclusion of Citicorp. Clearly, the market viewed Citicorp's decision to increase its loan-loss

[17]We employ ordinary least squares (OLS) to estimate our abnormal returns. An alternative approach, considered by some researchers to be "the state of the art," is the seemingly unrelated regression (SUR) technique introduced by Schipper and Thompson (1983) and employed by Smirlock and Kaufold (1987) to test the effect of the 1982 Mexican debt crisis. Binder (1985) presents a survey of event-study methods. Musumeci and Sinkey (1990), who contrast and compare OLS and SUR, conclude that, other things equal, the two techniques should give virtually identical results.

[18]Like the CRSP unweighted index, the Value Line Index is unweighted but it does have two relative disadvantages: (1) it does not include dividends and (2) it is calculated by Value Line as a cross-sectional geometric mean return. If dividends are paid out relatively continuously, then aggregate dividend payout would be a constant, and the first shortcoming would not be a serious problem. The extent to which the second point causes a problem is not known.

[19]We estimated the standard deviation of the CARs using several alternative methods; see Brown and Warner (1980), Ruback (1982), and Jensen and Ruback (1983). Since the estimates were almost identical, we report only those based on the Jensen and Ruback method, which assumes independence of the daily residuals.

[20]Technically, the unbiased estimator of the variance of the sample residuals is a downward-biased estimator of the variance of the forecast errors (for example, see Kmenta [1971]). Although we did not make the appropriate adjustment, the maximum upward bias in our reported t-values is approximately 2 percent.

[21]Using a portfolio of twenty-four banks and a three-day window defined as May 18–20, Sachs and Huizinga (1987) found that "Citicorp's stock went up by 4 percent, while other banks' stocks went down slightly (and without statistical significance)" (p. 587). Our findings for our total portfolio are similar to theirs. Sachs and Huizinga, however, did not analyze money-center and regional banks separately, as we do. Moreover, their three-day window corresponds to our Days −2, −1, and 0 and does not include our Day +1.

TABLE 4

ABNORMAL RETURNS SURROUNDING THE ANNOUNCEMENT OF CITICORP'S LOAN-LOSS-RESERVE DECISION OF MAY 19, 1987

	Day 0		Day +1		3-day window	
Money-Center Group	Res.	*t*-val.	Res.	*t*-val.	CAR	*t*-value
Citicorp	5.47%	3.90	4.71%	3.36	8.26%	3.37
Bank America	−1.62%	−0.72	−0.22%	−0.10	−1.80%	−0.46
Bankers Trust	1.78	1.17	3.31	2.18	2.76	1.05
Chase Manhattan	1.31	0.81	4.23	2.60	4.33	1.54
Chemical	−2.52	−2.16	3.25	2.78	0.39	0.19
Continental Illinois	−2.04	−0.79	−0.09	−0.04	−1.19	−0.27
First Chicago	−0.99	−0.59	0.38	0.22	−2.81	−0.96
J. P. Morgan	2.91	2.08	4.76	3.41	7.00	2.89
Manufacturers Hanover	−3.85	−3.70	2.24	2.15	−4.70	−2.60
Security Pacific	0.46	0.42	0.66	0.60	1.80	0.94
Money-center portfolio	0.09%	0.11	2.32%	2.82*	1.40%	0.99
Top 10 less Citicorp	−0.51%	−0.62	2.06%	2.51*	0.64%	0.45
Regional Group						
Bank of Boston	2.92%	1.55	1.24%	0.66	2.88%	0.88
Bank of New England	−0.74	−0.67	−0.83	−0.75	−2.10	−1.09
First Bank System	−2.02	−1.18	−1.43	−0.84	−3.58	−1.21
First Interstate	0.04	0.03	0.24	0.19	0.44	0.20
First Union	0.06	0.05	0.05	0.04	1.37	0.63
Irving	−3.25	−2.65	−0.32	−0.26	−3.86	−1.82
Marine Midland	−1.11	−1.01	−0.86	−0.78	−1.49	−0.78
M Corp	−0.40	−0.14	−2.79	−0.96	−4.03	−0.80
Mellon	0.04	0.03	0.14	0.08	−4.33	−1.41
NBD Bancorp	3.06	2.01	0.58	0.38	−1.24	−0.47
NCNB	−1.00	−0.54	0.23	0.13	−1.70	−0.57
Norwest	0.59	0.39	−0.28	−0.18	1.41	0.54
PNC Financial	−0.59	−0.58	−2.12	−2.11	−1.55	−0.89
SunTrust	−2.80	−1.75	−0.98	−0.62	−2.74	−0.99
Wells Fargo	−0.71	−0.52	4.33	3.18	0.86	0.37
Regional bank portfolio	−0.30	−0.55	−0.49	−0.89	−1.27	−1.33
Total portfolio (25 BHCs)	−0.14	−0.27	0.63	1.18	−0.20	−0.21

NOTES: Since Citicorp's announcement occurred after markets closed on May 19, Day 0 is defined as May 20. The three-day window extends from Day −1 to Day +1. The market portfolio is proxied by the Value Line Index. For the portfolio returns, an asterisk indicates significance at the 5 percent level. Moving down the table, the estimated portfolio betas are .78, .78, .87, and .83 with corresponding *t*-values of 8.75, 8.80, 14.6, and 14.3. Except for Continental Illinois with an estimated beta of .47 (t=1.69) and Mellon witth an estimated beta of .22 (t=1.14), all of the individual stock betas are statistically significant and range from .62 (t=2.53) for Security Pacific to 1.66 (t=8.90) for NCNB. Jensen and Ruback (1983) *t*-statistics are reported.

reserve as a positive event. Moreover, the Day +1 findings for the other money-center banks suggest they were free riders or the market expected them to follow Citicorp's loan-loss leadership. In either case, investors bid up the share price on the portfolio of yet unannounced money-center banks. Except for the capital-structure hypothesis, all the new-information hypotheses are consistent with a positive market reaction.

Although the abnormal return for the portfolio of regional banking companies was negative, it was not statistically significant. When the money-center and regional banks were combined in one portfolio, the abnormal return was not significantly different from zero.[22] For this total portfolio, the most significant of the returns for the various windows was the one for Day +1 with an abnormal return of 0.63 percent (t = 1.18).

Focusing on the returns for *individual* securities and noting that we attach little importance to the corresponding t-values,[23] some diverse and interesting stories can be told, especially for the money-center portfolio. On Day 0, Citicorp's return was almost 5.5 percent (t = 3.9) after adjustment for market risk. In contrast, the other twenty-four securities show mixed results: fourteen excess returns are negative with three of those having t-values greater than 2.0, and ten excess returns are positive with two of those having t-values greater than two. Within the money-center group, J. P. Morgan, a BHC with widely recognized financial strength, had a positive abnormal return of 2.91 percent (t = 2.1) on Day 0. On Day +1, Citicorp's shareholders continued to benefit from their management's reserve decision with an abnormal return of 4.71 percent (t = 3.4). In addition, on Day +1 seven of the nine other money-center banks had positive abnormal returns. Five of these seven returns had t-values greater than 2.0, led by Morgan with a t-value of 3.41 on an abnormal return of 4.76 percent. As on Day 0, the regionals showed mixed results on Day +1.

A. Survivorship Bias and Tax Considerations

The role of "survivorship bias" in our money-center portfolio needs to be addressed. The two BHCs with negative but insignificant abnormal returns on Day 0, Day +1, and the three-day window are the bailed-out Continental Illinois and the financially troubled BankAmerica. If potential tax savings explain positive abnormal returns, then BHCs with losses would not benefit from an extra deduction. Of the twenty-five firms in our sample, only Continental and BankAmerica had aggregate losses over the period 1984 to 1986. This evidence tends to support the tax-savings hypothesis.

B. Loan-Exposure and Capital-Adequacy Tests

In keeping with our new-information hypotheses, we anticipate a direct relationship between either Brazilian or LDC exposure and the degree of market reward for the build-up of loan-loss reserves. Using Day +1 residuals and with exposure (EX_j) measured as the ratio of Brazilian debt to market value of equity, our estimated relationship for the portfolio of twenty-five BHCs is

$$AR_j = .0009 + \underset{(1.72)}{.0194}(EX_j),\ R^2 = .1144 \text{ and } N = 25.$$

[22]Brown and Warner (1985) observe that direct estimation of the standard deviation of the portfolio residuals leads to less powerful tests than aggregating standard deviations of the individual residuals. Since our test is a less powerful one, we can be more certain of our results when the null is rejected.

[23]Fama [1976, chapter 1] analyzed individual security daily raw returns and found they are not

Although the relationship is positive, it is not statistically significant at the traditional 5 percent level, only at the 10 percent level. Substituting *primary capital* (one of the regulatory definitions of bank capital) for the market value of equity, we find a significant positive relationship with a slope coefficient of .0925 (t = 3.50 and R^2 = .34). Although the market value of equity is, of course, the appropriate deflator for the exposure variable, we believe the stronger relationship using primary capital is a statistical artifact related to the higher market-to-book ratios of the regionals compared to the money-center BHCs. For example, as of December 31, 1986, only two of the money-center BHCs (Morgan and Bankers Trust) had market-to-book ratios greater than one whereas one-half of the regionals had ratios greater than one.

The stronger a bank's capital position is, the more easily it should be able to take an "LDC haircut" via a reserve allocation. Under this scenario, the strength of positive market response should be directly related to the bank's capital position. Using our three-day window, we found a weak positive relationship between the residuals for the total portfolio and the ratio of market value of equity to total assets. The estimated slope coefficient was 0.48 (t = 1.52). Nevertheless, the biggest losers on Day 0 were Manufacturers Hanover (with the largest negative abnormal return at −3.85 percent and a t-value of −3.70), Chemical, and First Chicago. These three BHCs had market-to-book ratios of .49, .67, and .66, respectively. On Day +1 Manufacturers and Chemical rebounded with positive and significant abnormal returns. Together with Continental Illinois and BankAmerica with market-to-book ratios of .27 and .56, respectively, these five BHCs are the weakest members of the money-center group. Excluding Citicorp, the four stronger members of the money-center group, led by Morgan with a market-to-book ratio of 1.42, had average abnormal returns of 1.61 percent on Day 0 and 2.50 on Day +1. In contrast, their five weaker competitors had average abnormal returns of −2.20 percent on Day 0 and only 1.11 percent on Day +1.

Since the correlation between exposure and financial strength was highly negative, our attempts to regress residuals against both of these factors generated insignificant coefficients.

C. Why the One-Day Delay?

Why the market reacted with a one-day delay for the money-center portfolio (less Citicorp) was at first a bit puzzling to us, especially since over the last two hours of trading on May 20 (Day 0) Citicorp's price declined by .75 to close at 53.125. On one hand, the delay suggests that because of the magnitude, importance, and unforeseen nature of Citicorp's decision, it took the market some time to digest how other money-center BHCs would be affected. This explanation is troublesome, however, because it suggests that when really important information arrives the

---

normally distributed, but instead have "fatter tails." Brown and Warner (1985) found this was also true of individual security daily residuals. For these reasons, formal statistical significance cannot be attached to the t-values for individual securities' residuals.

market reacts slowly. On the other hand, the Day +1 responses could reflect the arrival of new information. Based on careful study of information flows on Day +1, however, we found no evidence of any positive news relating to U.S. money-center banks, or negative news relating to regional BHCs. Accordingly, we reject the hypothesis that the Day +1 responses reflect new information. Of course, the obvious new information available at the end of Day 0 was the market's positive response to Citicorp's reserve decision, and the spillover benefit to Morgan. The expected follow-the-leader behavior obviously could not be rewarded until the market reacted to Citicorp's announcement. Why the market might not have been able to do these evaluations simultaneously is discussed next.

D. Discussion: Loan-Loss Reserves and Asset Write-downs

A BHC's provision for loan losses is based, in part, on "management's current evaluation of the anticipated impact of domestic and international economic conditions" (*Citicorp 1987 Report,* p. 50). We interpret the huge increases in loan-loss provisions by major BHCs in 1987 as a signal of impending asset write-downs of LDC loans, write-downs which began later in 1987 and will probably continue for several years. For example, in the fourth quarter of 1989, Citicorp added $1 billion to its LDC loan-loss reserves, a signal of future write-downs. Strong and Meyer (1987) have analyzed the write-down decision and its effect on security prices. Since asset write-downs (or loan-loss reserve decisions) are simply bookkeeping adjustments, significant market reactions to such announcements should not be expected. Strong and Meyer found a statistically insignificant CAR prior to the announcement of a write-down and a statistically significant positive average CAR after the announcement. Thakor (1987) states that this evidence does not contradict semistrong-form market efficiency. He argues that write-downs have a price effect *not* because they mean much by themselves but because they are a *signal* of events to come. He compares write-downs to stock splits, where a split is a signal to the uninformed that high cash flows are expected in the future by *insiders*. Thakor sees write-downs as a signal of "economic value-enhancing corporate restructuring to come in the future" (p. 662).

Couched in terms of "reactive equilibrium," defined by Ofer and Thakor (1987) as situations involving signals related to events linked both in time and in effect, we see Citicorp's reserve decision as a signal of economic value-enhancing corporate and strategic restructuring. Post-event evidence of this restructuring includes Citicorp's $1 billion equity issue in September of 1987, a $2 billion reduction in its portfolio of LDC loans from June 1987 to June 1988, a $1 billion LDC reserve addition during the fourth quarter of 1989, and its continued hard-line negotiating with LDC borrowers and bank regulators. The "effect linkage" of reactive equilibrium is illustrated by other money-center BHCs following Citicorp's restructuring leadership. The market's one-day delay in sorting out these complicated signals and linkages, except for J.P. Morgan, does not suggest to us the failure of semistrong-form market efficiency.

TABLE 5

ABNORMAL RETURNS SURROUNDING CITICORP'S AND OWN BANK ANNOUNCEMENT DATES

	Citicorp Event 3-day window		Own Event 3-day window			
Money-Center Group	CAR	t-value	CAR	t-value	Total Return	Ratio Citi/ Total
Citicorp	8.26%	3.37	8.26%	3.37	8.26%	NM
Bank America	1.80%	−0.46	3.32%	0.85	1.52%	NM
Bankers Trust	2.76	1.05	0.01	0.00	2.77	.996
Chase Manhatttan	4.33	1.54	1.90	0.67	6.23	.695
Chemical	0.39	0.19	3.21	1.59	3.60	.108
Continental Illinois	−1.19	−0.27	−3.49	−0.79	−4.68	NM
First Chicago	−2.81	−0.96	5.49	1.88	2.68	NM
J.P. Morgan	7.00	2.89	1.62	0.67	8.62	.812
Manufacturers Hanover	−4.70	−2.60	3.39	1.87	−1.31	NM
Security Pacific	1.80	0.94	4.24	2.21	6.04	.298
Money-center portfolio	1.40%	0.99	2.80%	3.10*	3.37%	NM
Top 10 less Citicorp	0.64%	0.45	2.19%	2.32*	2.83%	.226
Day +1 only	2.06%	2.51*	1.68%	3.01*	3.74%	.551
Regional Group						
Bank of Boston	2.88%	0.88	−3.40%	−1.04	−0.52%	NM
Bank of New England	−2.10	−1.09	−0.13	−0.07	−2.23	NM
First Bank System	−3.58	−1.21	−0.32	−0.11	−3.90	NM
First Interstate	0.44	0.20	4.26	1.99	4.70	.094
First Union	1.37	0.63	1.07	0.49	2.44	.561
Irving	−3.86	−1.82	−1.57	−0.74	−5.43	NM
Marine Midland	−1.49	−0.78	13.74	7.22	12.25	NM
M Corp	−4.03	−0.80	NA	NA	NA	NA
Mellon	−4.33	−1.41	3.63	1.18	−0.70	NM
NBD Bancorp	−1.24	−0.47	2.13	0.81	0.89	NM
NCNB	−1.70	−0.57	NA	NA	NA	NA
Norwest	1.41	0.54	−0.85	−0.32	0.56	NM
PNC Financial	−1.55	−0.89	0.37	0.21	−1.18	NM
SunTrust	−2.74	−0.99	NA	NA	NA	NA
Wells Fargo	0.86	0.37	3.33	1.42	4.19	NM
Regional bank portfolio	−1.27	−1.33	1.35	1.67	0.92	NM
Total portfolio (25 or 22)	−0.20	−0.21	2.00	3.56*	2.04	NM

NOTES: For Citicorp, Day 0 is defined as May 20. Own announcement dates are shown in Table 1. The three-day window extends from Day −1 to Day +1. The market portfolio is proxied by the Value Line Index. For the portfolio returns, an asterisk indicates significance at the 5 percent level. Jensen and Ruback (1983) t-statistics are reported. NM = not meaningful because one or more of the component returns is negative. NA = not available because no specific reserve allocation was made for LDC debt.

E. Partial Anticipation and the Free-Rider Problem

As shown in Table 5, we find no evidence of a free-rider problem. Focusing on the money-center portfolio less Citicorp, over the three-day window for both events the total abnormal return was 2.83 percent with the returns on Day +1 driving the process. Fifty-five percent of the Day +1 return of 3.74 percent total return occurred at the time of Citicorp's announcement. Thus on average the market perceived about a 50/50 chance that the other money-center banks would follow Citicorp's lead and rewarded them accordingly on the day following Citicorp's announcement. This portfolio received the balance of its abnormal return when it announced, which over the three-day window was 2.19 percent ($t = 2.32$). As with Citicorp's announcement, the bulk of the excess return occurred on Day +1 (1.68 percent with a t-value of 3.01). The returns for the regional and total portfolios shown in Table 5 are driven by Marine Midland, which was an outlier with a return of 13.74 percent over the three-day window for its own announcement.

When we regressed the residuals for own and total returns shown in Table 5 against measures of exposure and financial strength, we found the expected relationships held but they were not statistically significant at the traditional 5 percent level. Another potential explanatory variable is reserve addition/market equity (as a measure of seriousness of anticipated restructuring). The expected relationship holds and is statistically significant. This variable, however, could be a proxy for the ratio of LDC exposure to market equity since the two are highly correlated ($r = .95$).

8. SUMMARY AND CONCLUSIONS

Using standard event-study methods, we have focused on the signaling content of Citicorp's $3 billion reserve decision and the follow-the-leader behavior it generated. As John Reed, Citicorp's chairman, stated on May 19, 1987: "No one asked us to do it, we feel it significantly strengthens the institution."[24] The positive market reaction to the increase in loan-loss reserves is consistent with at least one of our new-information hypotheses, except the capital-structure one. The existence of secondary markets for LDC debt leads us to discount the loan-quality hypothesis. The negative Day +1 response by BankAmerica and Continental Illinois (the only two BHCs in our sample with aggregate losses over the period 1984 to 1986) tends to support the tax-savings hypothesis. Nevertheless, because the write-down of LDC loans does not require a reserve addition, the tax hypothesis is harder to defend analytically. Thus we favor the restructuring explanation.

Given the market's positive reaction to Citicorp's announcement, the managers of other BHCs with heavy exposure to Brazil reacted rationally and eventually followed Citicorp's loan-loss leadership, ignoring John Reed's statement that: "We don't believe everyone in the industry should do this." The market anticipated the pied-piper behavior, however, and bid up on Citicorp's Day +1 the share prices of other banks with major exposures to Brazil, *before* they announced they would follow the leader.

Nevertheless, the follow-the-leader behavior was not fully anticipated as other *money-center* banks were rewarded when they announced reserve allocations, confirming the absence of a free-rider problem. Although most of the regional banks in our sample followed Citicorp's lead, they were not rewarded by the market. Since these companies had little LDC exposure, their reserve allocations were not perceived by the market as important signals. In contrast, we interpret Citicorp's reserve decision, and the subsequent follow-the-leader behavior of the other money-

[24]This quote and the one that follows are from Citicorp's News Release of May 19, 1987; see footnote 4.

center banks, as signals of economic value-enhancing corporate and strategic restructuring.

LITERATURE CITED

Berg, Eric N. "Brazil's Debt: A Key Juncture." *The New York Times* (March 3, 1987), 25, 30.

Binder, John J. "Measuring the Effects of Regulation with Stock Price Data." *Rand Journal of Economics* (September 1985), 167–83.

Brown, Stephen and Jerold Warner. "Measuring Security Price Performance." *Journal of Financial Economics* 8 (September 1980), 205–58.

______. "Using Daily Stock Returns: The Case of Event Studies." *Journal of Financial Economics* 14 (March 1985), 3–32.

Bruner, Robert F., and John M. Simms, Jr. "The International Debt Crisis and Bank Security Returns in 1982." *Journal of Money, Credit, and Banking* 19 (February 1987), 46–55.

Daily Stock Price Record, 1986 and 1987, NYSE and OTC, (Standard and Poor's, New York).

Fama, Eugene F. Foundations of Finance. New York: Basic Books, Inc., 1976.

Greenawalt, Mary Brady, and Joseph F. Sinkey, Jr. "Bank Loan-Loss Provisions and the Income-Smoothing Hypothesis: An Empirical Analysis 1976–1984." *Journal of Financial Services Research* 1 (1988), 301–18.

Grammatikos, Theoharry, and Anthony Saunders. "Additions to Bank Loan-Loss Reserves: Good News or Bad News." (March 1988), revised, New York University.

Hill, G. Christian, and Peter Truell. "Banks Step Up Third World Debt Disposal." *The Wall Street Journal* (June 26, 1988), 6.

Jensen, Michael, and Richard Ruback. "The Market for Corporate Control: The Scientific Evidence." *Journal of Financial Economics* 11 (April 1983), 5–50.

Kane, Edward J. *Economic Statistics and Econometrics.* New York: Harper & Row Publishers, 1968, pp. 341–42.

Kane, Edward J., and Haluk Unal. "Change in Market Assessments of Deposit-Institution Riskiness." *Journal of Financial Services Research* (June 1988), 207–29.

Kmenta, Jan. *Elements of Econometrics.* New York: Macmillan, 1973.

Lessard, Donald R. "Recapitalizing Third-World Debt: Toward a New Vision of Commercial Financing for Less-Developed Countries." *Midland Corporate Finance Journal* (Fall 1987), 6–21.

Madura, Jeff, and William R. McDaniel. "Market Reaction to Increased Loan Loss Reserves at Money-Center Banks." *Journal of Financial Services Research* (December 1989), 359–69.

Malatesta, Paul H., and Rex Thompson. "Partially Anticipated Events: A Model of Stock Price Reactions with an Application to Corporate Acquisitions." *Journal of Financial Economics* 14 (1985), 237–50.

Megginson, William L., Annette B. Poulson, and Joseph F. Sinkey, Jr. "Lending to Developing Countries: How the Stock Market Evaluated the Loans." *Issues in Bank Regulation* (Spring 1989), 27–31.

Musumeci, James J., and Joseph F. Sinkey, Jr. "The International Debt Crisis, Investor Contagion, and Bank Security Returns in 1987: The Brazilian Experience." *Journal of Money, Credit, and Banking* (May 1990), 209–20.

Ofer, Aharon R., and Anjan V. Thakor. "A Theory of Stock Price Responses to Alternative Corporate Cash Disbursement Methods: Stock Repurchases and Dividends." *Journal of Finance* 42 (June 1987), 365–94.

Review of Major Banks' Loan Exposures to Less-Developed Countries. Fixed Income Research, First Boston (June 22, 1987).

Ruback, Richard. "The Effect of Discretionary Price Control Decisions on Equity Values." *Journal of Financial Economics* 10 (March 1982), 83–106.

Sachs, Jeffrey, and Harry Huizinga. "U.S. Commercial Banks and the Developing-Country Debt Crisis." *Brookings Papers on Economic Activity* 2 (1987), 555–601.

Schipper, Katherine, and Rex Thompson. "Evidence on the Capitalized Value of Merger Activity for Acquiring Firms." *Journal of Financial Economics* 11 (April 1983), 85–119.

Smirlock, Michael, and Howard Kaufold. "Bank Foreign Lending, Mandatory Disclosure Rules, and the Reaction of Bank Stock Prices to the Mexican Debt Crisis." *Journal of Business* 60 (1987), 347–64.

Strong, John S. "Signalling and Competitive Valuation: Effects of Citicorp's Foreign Lending Reserve Policy." College of William and Mary (June 1988).

Strong, John S., and John R. Meyer. "Asset Write-Downs: Managerial Incentives and Security Returns." *Journal of Finance* 42 (July 1987), 643–61.

Thakor, Anjan V. "Discussion." *Journal of Finance* 42 (July 1987), 661–63.

Wall, Larry D. "Commercial Bank Profitability: Still Weak in 1987." *Economic Review*, Federal Reserve Bank of Atlanta (July/August 1988), 28–42.

NOTES, COMMENTS, REPLIES

Interest Rate Linkages within the European Monetary System: A Time Series Analysis

A Note by Costas J. Karfakis and Demetrios M. Moschos

The objective behind the foundation of the European Monetary System (EMS) in March 1979 was the creation of a system of monetary stability in Europe. It is generally accepted that the adoption of the EMS has contributed to the reduction of the intra-EMS nominal and real (bilateral and effective) exchange rate volatility relative to the pre-EMS period (Rogoff 1985, Artis 1987, and Taylor and Artis 1988). However, it is not clear how much of this reduction is the result of an increased policy coordination. It has been argued that the maintenance of capital controls by the majority of the countries participating into the EMS has been a crucial element of its functioning.[1] Rogoff (1985) established that the reduction in the variability of real exchange rates in France and Italy over the EMS period was not accompanied by reduced fluctuations in real interest rate differentials, and he attributed this result to the presence of capital controls. The importance of capital controls is also reflected in the increased volatility of the onshore/offshore interest rate differentials (Giavazzi and Giovannini 1987; Taylor and Artis 1988). Nevertheless, it has been argued that due to "leakages," the effectiveness of controls is only temporary (Wyplosz 1988; Steinherr and De Schrevel 1988).

The higher exchange rate stability observed during the EMS period was combined with a reduction in, but not the elimination of, the response of the German mark (DM) cross rates to changes in the effective dollar rate (Giavazzi and Giovannini 1986; Artis 1987). Taylor and Artis (1988), on the other hand, found evidence of nonzero risk premia between DM and the other EMS currencies, but could not reject the zero risk premium hypothesis between dollar and DM. These results which highlight the asymmetric nature of the EMS are consistent with views about the dominant role of Germany in the system ("German leadership" hypothesis).

The authors thank two anonymous referees for helpful comments and suggestions.

[1]Denmark, France, Ireland, and Italy have been using capital controls of various degrees of severity, whereas Belgium has adopted a dual exchange rate as a substitute for controls (Steinherr and De Schrevel 1988).

COSTAS J. KARFAKIS is economist with Olympic Airways, Athens. DEMETRIOS M. MOSCHOS is economist with the Economic Research Department, Bank of Greece, Athens.

Journal of Money, Credit, and Banking, Vol. 22, No. 3 (August 1990)

The present paper addresses the issue of interest rate linkages between Germany and the other EMS countries which participate in the exchange rate mechanism of the system. Firstly, it investigates whether there exist long-run comovements between German and other EMS members' rates by employing integration and cointegration techniques. Then, it examines whether German interest rate changes convey information about future movements of other EMS interest rates.

1. METHODOLOGICAL ISSUES

In a two-country context with highly substitutable assets, international portfolio equilibrium is specified as

$$i_t - i_t^* = E_t s_{t+1} - s_t + v_t \tag{1}$$

where i and i^* denote domestic and foreign interest rates, respectively, E_t refers to expectations at time t, s is the logarithm of the exchange rate (domestic currency per foreign currency unit), and v represents the risk premium. The existence of risk premia implies a departure from uncovered interest parity. If the expected exchange rate change and the risk premium are both stationary, then the interest rate differential is also stationary, in which case there exists a long-run equilibrium relationship between i and i^*.

In a more general context, the existence of a long-run interest rate relationship can be looked at from the viewpoint of cointegration (Engle and Granger 1987) by investigating for stationarity the process

$$i_t - b i_t^* = \omega_t \tag{2}$$

where, in contrast to (1), b is allowed to deviate from unity and the right-hand side of (1) is suppressed into ω_t. The reason for allowing $b \neq 1$ can be clarified by considering interest income taxation and/or the possibility of measurement errors.

The lack of a harmonized tax system within the EMS and the existence of interest income taxation modifies the interest parity condition to

$$i_t(1 - \tau) - i_t^*(1 - \tau^*) = z_t \tag{3}$$

where τ and τ^* are the rates at which interest income is taxed. Equation (3) is equivalent to (2) with $b = (1 - \tau^*)/(1 - \tau)$ and $\omega_t = z_t/(1 - \tau)$. Clearly if $\tau \neq \tau^*$, then $b \neq 1$.

Moreover, in the presence of intercountry differences in the maturity and definition of assets, deviations of b from unity can be attributed to measurement errors in published series. Assume that the interest parity condition (1) holds for some theoretical variables r and r^* which are measured as

$$i_t = \beta + \gamma r_t + u_t \tag{4}$$

$$i_t^* = \beta^* + \gamma^* r_t^* + u_t^* \tag{5}$$

where β, γ, β^* and γ^* capture systematic measurement errors and u_t and u_t^* are stationary random errors. Substituting for r_t and r_t^* into (1), we end up with (2), where $b = \gamma\gamma^{*-1}$, and $\omega_t = \gamma(E_t s_{t+1} - s_t + v_t) + u_t - \gamma\gamma^{*-1}u_t^*$.

In applying the cointegration testing procedure, first the hypothesis that the individual series contain a unit root, that is, they are integrated of order one (I(1)), needs to be tested, since in this case standard statistical inference is invalidated (Phillips 1986). To this end the Dickey-Fuller (DF) and augmented DF (ADF) tests (Fuller 1976; Dickey and Fuller 1981) can be used.[2] Recently Perron (1986), Phillips (1987), Phillips and Perron (1988) proposed nonparametric tests which allow for weakly dependent and heterogenous disturbances. If i_t and i_t^* both contain one unit root, then a test of cointegration can be obtained as the DF (ADF) statistic of the residuals of regression (2) or alternatively as the DW statistic (CIRDW) of (2).

Engle and Granger (1987) have shown that if a set of variables are cointegrated then there exists an error correction (EC) representation and vice versa, in which case there must be Granger-causality (Granger 1969) in at least one direction. It follows that vector autoregressive (VAR) models in differences lead to misspecification if the variables are cointegrated.

2. EMPIRICAL RESULTS

The empirical analysis is carried out using monthly data on short term domestic nominal interest rates for Belgium (B), France (F), Germany (G), Ireland (IRL), Italy (I) and the Netherlands (NL) over the period April 1979 to November 1988.[3]

The DF and Phillips and Perron (1988) test statistics of the null hypothesis of one unit root as well as the joint hypothesis of a unit root and a zero mean for both the levels and the first differences are reported in Table 1. The hypothesis of a unit root in the levels of interest rates can not be rejected for any of the series concerned, regardless of the statistic and the value of the truncation lag (1 = 1,5) used. By contrast, the hypothesis of a unit root in the first differences is rejected in all cases with the exception of Belgium, for which the joint hypothesis is not rejected. The nonrejection of the joint hypothesis is attributed to the presence of a zero mean.[4] These results suggest that all interest rate series are I(1).

[2]The distribution of the DF or ADF test is not invariant with respect to the presence of a constant or a deterministic trend. Dickey, Bell, and Miller (1986) recommend against the inclusion of a trend since this would make a random walk model look stationary. However, they suggest the inclusion of a constant.

[3]The data have been obtained from OECD, *Main Economic Indicators*. These are yields on three-month (B, IRL) or six-month (I) Treasury bills and on three-month loans (F, G, NL). Due to data limitations, the French series cover the period 1981:5–1988:11, and Denmark has not been included in the analysis.

[4]The statistic $\hat{\tau}_{o\mu}$ (Dickey and Fuller 1981) is 0.16 and therefore insignificant, suggesting the presence of a zero mean.

TABLE 1

UNIT ROOT TESTS FOR SHORT-TERM DOMESTIC INTEREST RATES

Statistic	B	F	G	IRL	I	NL
			Country			
			Levels			
			Dickey — Fuller			
$\hat{\tau}_{\mu}$	−1.15	−1.65	−0.87	−1.18	−0.92	−1.14
ϕ_1	0.68	0.93	0.39	0.49	0.43	0.61
			Phillips — Perron			
$l = 1$						
$Z(t_{\alpha}^*)$	−1.46	−1.58	−1.16	−1.71	−0.77	−1.26
$Z(\phi_1)$	1.01	0.07	0.69	1.33	0.30	0.81
$l = 5$						
$Z(t_{\alpha}^*)$	−1.62	−1.91	−1.44	−1.63	−1.16	−1.55
$Z(\phi_1)$	1.36	1.01	1.04	1.19	0.69	1.22
			First Differences			
			Dickey — Fuller			
$\hat{\tau}_{\mu}$	−8.21	−12.87	−7.50	−7.84	−9.15	−9.77
ϕ_1	3.67	82.72	28.11	30.80	75.99	48.01
			Phillips — Perron			
$l = 1$						
$Z(t_{\alpha}^*)$	−8.18	−11.89	−7.56	−7.91	−8.81	−9.76
$Z(\phi_1)$	2.70	79.28	28.60	31.39	73.54	47.88
$l = 5$						
$Z(t_{\alpha}^*)$	−8.22	−12.04	−8.29	−7.66	−10.18	−9.96
$Z(\phi_1)$	4.12	79.58	30.02	29.32	69.18	49.94

NOTE: $\hat{\tau}_{\mu}$ and $Z(t_{\alpha}^*)$ have a critical value of −2.89 (Fuller 1976) and ϕ_1 and $Z(\phi_1)$ a corresponding value of 4.71 (Dickey and Fuller 1981) at the 0.05 level for $T = 100$.

The tests for cointegration between the German and each of the other EMS interest rates, which are reported in Table 2, fail to reject the null hypothesis of noncointegration at the 0.05 significance level in all cases. In view of these results, which indicate that the EMS has not been dominated by stationarities in exchange rate changes and/or in risk premia, the investigation of the hypothesis that German interest rates are indicators of future movements of other EMS members' rates and not vice versa is carried out by means of VAR models in first differences.

The selection of the lag order of the VAR systems is based on two alternative and

TABLE 2

TESTS OF COINTEGRATION BETWEEN GERMAN AND OTHER EMS INTEREST RATES

EMS Country	DF	ADF (4)	CIRDW
Belgium	−2.98	−2.26	0.29
France	−2.72	−1.64	0.21
Ireland	−2.28	−2.86	0.22
Italy	−1.61	−1.93	0.08
Netherlands	−3.03	−2.87	0.28

NOTE: ADF (4) denotes that four lags of the dependent variable are included in the ADF test. The critical values of the DF, ADF (4), and CIRDW tests of cointegration are −3.37, −3.17, and 0.39, respectively, at the 0.05 level for $T = 100$ (Engle and Yoo 1987).

well-established criteria: first, the likelihood ratio test corrected for the degrees of freedom (Sims 1980) and second, Akaike's (1969) information criterion based on the final prediction error (FPE) as implemented by Hsiao (1979). In applying these criteria, the monthly frequency of the data favored the selection of 12 as the maximum lag length.

The lags selected on the basis of each criterion are reported in Table 3. The differences between these lag structures stem from the feature that, contrary to Sims (1980) χ^2-criterion which results in unrestricted VAR systems, FPE does not impose a uniform lag length on all the variables. Efficient estimates of these restricted VAR systems can be obtained by GLS.

TABLE 3

CAUSALITY TESTS OF UNRESTRICTED AND RESTRICTED VAR SYSTEMS

		Unrestricted System (OLS)		Restricted System (GLS)	
System	Dep. Variable	Lags	Marginal Signif. Level of F-test	(m,n)	Marginal Signif. Level of χ^2-test
B, G	B	12	0.000*	(11,12)	0.000*
	G	12	0.478	(3,1)	0.906
F, G	F	1	0.014*	(12,5)	0.046*
	G	1	0.704	(1,5)	0.087
IRL, G	IRL	6	0.294	(8,1)	0.220
	G	6	0.683	(3,1)	0.924
I, G	I	3	0.002*	(11,3)	0.007*
	G	3	0.752	(3,1)	0.810
NL, G	NL	12	0.012*	(9,5)	0.044*
	G	12	0.070	(3,1)	0.177

NOTE: (m,n) denotes the number of lagged dependent and independent variables, respectively. The F and χ^2 tests are calculated for the joint hypothesis that the coefficients of the lags of the independent variable are zero. * indicates significance at 5 percent.

The results of Granger-causality F-tests of the unrestricted VAR systems which are given in Table 3 suggest that the past history of changes in German rates has a predictive power for interest rate changes in other EMS members with the exception of Ireland. On the other hand, German interest rate movements seem to be Granger-exogenous with respect to other EMS members' rates.

In order to check the stability of the equations in which the German interest rate had a significant information content, predictive failure tests over the last six months of the sample were carried out. In all cases the tests did not reject the hypothesis of no predictive failure. Furthermore, to investigate the sensitivity of these equations with respect to exchange rate realignments, predictive failure tests were conducted over the period following the major realignment of 21 March 1983. Again no evidence of predictive failure was found.[5]

The GLS results of the restricted VAR systems in Table 3 replicate the conclu-

[5]The test statistic has an approximate F distribution (Chow 1960). Over the period May–November 1988 the F-values for B, F, I, and NL were $F(6,73) = 0.30$, $F(6,81) = 0.49$, $F(6,100) = 0.28$ and $F(6,73) = 0.73$, respectively. Over the post-March 1983 period the corresponding values were $F(68,11) = 1.68$, $F(68,19) = 0.18$, $F(68,38) = 0.37$, and $F(68,11) = 1.11$.

sions obtained from the unrestricted OLS estimates. This similarity in the findings indicates that the causality results are insensitive to the lag specification.

On the whole, the results suggest that the Belgian, French, Italian, and Dutch interest rate changes can be predicted using information on the past evolution of German interest rate changes, but not conversely. This evidence seems to be consistent with arguments about the pivotal role of Germany in the EMS. It is worth noting that the results are similar across countries with substantial differences in the degree of capital mobility.

To test for instantaneous causality between German and other EMS members' rates, the contemporaneous innovation correlations for each bivariate system has been calculated. The results of Table 4 yield significant correlations with respect to Belgium, Italy, and the Netherlands. In the light of the EMS experience, it seems plausible to interpret the instantaneous causality results on the basis of the arguments pertaining to the German leadership in the EMS. In the case of France, the lack of contemporaneous causality might be possibly attributed to the nature of capital controls.

TABLE 4

Correlation Coefficients of Innovations in VAR Systems

Estimation Method	(G, B)	(G, F)	System (G, IRL)	(G, I)	(G, NL)
OLS	0.36*	0.06	−0.09	0.25*	0.67*
GLS	0.40*	0.03	−0.03	0.36*	0.63*

Note: * indicates significance at 5 percent.

3. CONCLUSIONS

This paper has concentrated on the bivariate analysis of interest rate linkages within the EMS. Cointegration tests have not revealed the existence of systematic interest rate relationships in the long run between Germany and any of the other EMS countries. This finding may be attributed to the nonstationarity of either the expected exchange rate movements or the risk premia. Bivariate vector autoregression analysis has been used to investigate the information content of German interest rates about the future course of other members' rates. An interesting aspect which highlights the dominant role of Germany in the EMS is the evidence of unidirectional interest rate linkages from Germany to other EMS countries, regardless of the nature and degree of restrictions on capital movements.

LITERATURE CITED

Akaike, Hirotugu. "Statistical Predictor Identification." *Annals of the Institute of Statistical Mathematics* 21, (December 1969), 203–17.

Artis, Michael J. "The European Monetary System: An Evaluation." *Journal of Policy Modelling* 9 (Spring 1987), 175–98.

Chow, Gregory C. "Tests of Equality between Sets of Coefficients in Two Linear Regressions." *Econometrica* 28 (July 1960), 591–605.

Dickey, David A., William R. Bell, and Robert B. Miller. "Unit Roots in Time Series Models: Tests and Implications." *The American Statistician* 40 (February 1986), 12–26.

Dickey, David A., and Wayne A. Fuller. "Likelihood Ratio Statistics for Autoregressive Time Series with a Unit Root." *Econometrica* 49 (July 1981), 1057–72.

Engle, Robert F., and Clive W. J. Granger. "Co-integration and Error Correction: Representation, Estimation, and Testing." *Econometrica* 55 (March 1987), 251–76.

Engle, Robert F., and Byung S. Yoo. "Forecasting and Testing in Co-integrated Systems." *Journal of Econometrics* 35 (1987), 143–59.

Fuller, Wayne A. *Introduction to Statistical Time Series,* New York: John Wiley, 1976.

Giavazzi, Francesco, and Alberto Giovannini. "The EMS and the Dollar." *Economic Policy* (April 1986), 456–85.

———. "Models of the EMS: Is Europe a Greater Deutschmark Area?" In *Global Macroeconomics Policy Conflict and Cooperation,* edited by Ralph C. Bryant and Richard Portes, pp. 237–65. London: MacMillan Press, 1987.

Granger, Clive W. J. "Investigating Causal Relations by Econometric Models and Cross-Spectral Methods." *Econometrica* 37 (July 1969), 424–38.

Hsiao, Cheng. "Autoregressive Modelling of Canadian Money and Income Data." *Journal of American Statistical Association* 74 (September 1979), 553–60.

Perron, Pierre. "Tests of Joint Hypotheses for Time Series Regression with a Unit Root." Cahier de Recherche no. 2086, C.R.D.E. University of Montreal, Montreal 1986.

Phillips, Peter C. B. "Understanding Spurious Regressions in Econometrics." *Journal of Econometrics* 33 (1986), 311–40.

———. "Time Series Regression with a Unit Root." *Econometrica* 55 (March 1987), 277–301.

Phillips, Peter C. B., and Pierre Perron. "Testing for a Unit Root in Time Series Regression." *Biometrica* 75 (1988), 335–46.

Rogoff, Kenneth. "Can Exchange Rate Predictability Be Achieved without Monetary Convergence?" *European Economic Review* 28 (June 1985), 93–115.

Sims, Christopher A. "Macroeconomics and Reality." *Econometrica* 48 (January 1980), 1–48.

Steinherr, Alfred, and Geoffroy De Schrevel. "Liberalization of Financial Transactions in the Community with Particular Reference to Belgium, Denmark and the Netherlands." *European Economy* 36 (May 1988), 117–47.

Taylor, Mark P., and Michael J. Artis. "What Has the European Monetary System Achieved." Bank of England Discussion Paper No. 31, (March 1988).

Wyplosz, Charles. "Capital Flow Liberalization and the EMS: A French Perspective." *European Economy* 36 (May 1988), 85–103.

Money and Capital in Economic Development: A Test of the McKinnon Hypothesis for Nepal

A Note by John Thornton and Sri Ram Poudyal

In an important book, McKinnon (1973) offered the hypothesis that in developing countries the demand for money broadly defined is complementary to the demand for physical capital. The hypothesis is derived from an outside money model in which economic units are constrained to self-finance and there are considerable indivisibilities in investment. A much-quoted empirical study by Fry (1978) and published in this journal contrasted the transmission mechanism in McKinnon's model with that of Shaw's (1973) debt-intermediation model. Using pooled data from ten Asian countries, Fry tested the demand for money functions implicit in each model and found that the evidence favored Shaw's approach. Fry conceded that his sample included countries in which financial development had proceeded to such an advanced stage that modern financial assets other than broad money might be used as repositories of funds being accumulated for the purpose of eventual real investment. He concluded that it would be necessary "to look much farther down the development ladder . . . to some of the world's least developed countries in a search for complementarity" (p. 474). Subsequently, Molho (1986) has stressed the intertemporal nature of complementarity to argue that the McKinnon and Shaw approaches need not be considered mutually exclusive. This occurs because most projects are financed in part with own funds and in part from borrowed funds. Thus, there is contemporaneous substitutability between deposits and physical capital but intertemporal complementarity with current deposits intended to finance future investment. While this may be a realistic adaption of the McKinnon model, as Fry (1988) points out, it requires the model to be interpreted as an inside money model in which there are borrowing constraints and indivisibilities that prevent some investors from borrowing all they wish to borrow for lumpy investments, and this is not consistent with McKinnon's own statement of his model. In this note, therefore, we report the results of a test of the complementarity hypothesis on data for Nepal,

The authors are grateful to two anonymous referees for helpful comments and suggestions.

JOHN THORNTON *is National Westminster Bank Lecturer, School of Accounting, Banking, and Economics, University of Wales, and Economist, International Monetary Fund.* SRI RAM POUDYAL *is reader in economics, Tribhuvan University, Kathmandu, Nepal, and economic advisor to the Nepal Rastra Bank.*

Journal of Money, Credit, and Banking, Vol. 22, No. 3 (August 1990)

one of the world's poorest countries and one for which an outside money model may have greater relevance.

McKinnon's work emphasizes the fragmented economic conditions that generally pertain to poor countries. These include the generally small size of private firms, the general lack of finance external to the firm, and the lumpiness of investment. Under these conditions, money is viewed as having a particularly important role to play in improving the quality and increasing the quantity of physical investment since a substantial personal equity is required whenever investment is undertaken. As a result, "average cash balance holdings, therefore, are positively related to the propensity to invest (save) under the formal constraint that all investments are 'self-financed'—as indeed some always are in practice" (p. 58). McKinnon's work thus stresses the nonstatic nature of the demand for money and highlights the accumulation of self-owned money balances as a preparatory measure to the end act of investment. Money, to use his word, is a "conduit" through which the accumulation of an investible sum occurs.

We test for complementarity in the demand for money function and the savings function (to be determined simultaneously with the demand for money) for Nepal over the period 1974/75—1986/87.[1] By many standards the country is close to the bottom of the development ladder. In the World Bank's World Development Report, 1989, Nepal is listed as the joint fifth poorest country in the world in terms of GNP per capita. Over our sample period, the growth of real per capita income fluctuated sharply and averaged just 0.7 percent a year. During this time, there were few financial assets other than money to act as repositories for savings. Treasury bills became a regular part of budget financing after 1975 but the rate of interest offered was never attractive relative to that on bank deposits or to the rate of inflation, so that most issues had to be taken up by the Nepal Rastra Bank (the central bank). The issue of government bonds with interest rates sufficiently high to attract the nonbank public did not begin in earnest until 1984. Furthermore, not until the very end of the sample period were there any issues of bonds by private sector institutions and the ownership structure of the few equity issues that had taken place was highly concentrated.[2] Some notion of the relevance of McKinnon's outside money model for the lowest-income economies is given in Table 1. The table compares the relatively low proportion of broad money and private sector output that is backed by private-sector credit in Nepal and two other of the poorest low-income economies (Ethiopia, Malawi) with that for two other low-income economies somewhat further up the development ladder (India and Pakistan), and three middle-income economies (Thailand, Malaysia, and the Republic of Korea).[3]

The demand for money function is virtually the same as that used by Fry except

[1]The Nepalese fiscal year starts on July 16.

[2]A description of the limited nature of the financial system in Nepal and the associated problems for savings mobilization that is still relevant for much of our sample period is given in Fry (1974), while a review of more recent interest rate liberalization efforts is given in Thornton (1987).

[3]The income classification for countries is taken from the World Bank's World Development Report, 1989.

TABLE 1

MONEY AND FINANCIAL INTERMEDIATION IN SELECTED LOW- AND MIDDLE-INCOME ECONOMIES, 1987

Country	As a Percent of Broad Money			As a Percent of Private Sector Output*
	Government Credit	Net Foreign Assets	Private Sector Credit	Private Sector Credit
Ethiopia	65.2	0.1	7.3	4.4
Malawi	42.2	2.8	32.3	8.6
Nepal	42.8	27.9	39.0	14.9
India	57.4	2.0	56.9	34.7
Pakistan	27.0	5.5	65.0	34.4
Thailand	13.4	15.3	83.3	76.3
Malaysia	0.6	34.1	92.7	77.1
Korea, Rep	3.6	14.8	131.3	58.0

SOURCES: IMF, International Financial Statistics; and World Bank, World Development Report, 1989
NOTES: Private sector output is measured as GNP less government consumption.

that problems in obtaining a consistent and meaningful interest rate series over the full sample period led us to substitute the expected rate of inflation, p^*, for the expected real rate of interest.[4] In Nepal over the sample period there was virtually no change in bank deposit rates so that the expected real rate of interest was essentially determined by variations in p^*. The savings function is also similar to that used by Fry except that ours includes real money balances as an explanatory variable in order to provide a more direct test of complementarity.

The demand for money function estimated is

$$(M/P)_t = \mathrm{m}((\mathrm{S^d/Y})_t, y_t, p^*t, (M/P)_{t-1}) \tag{1}$$

and the savings function is

$$(S^d/Y)_t = s((M/P)_t, g_t, y_t\ (S^f/Y)_t) \; . \tag{2}$$

In these functions, M/P represents real per capita broad money deflated by the GDP deflator, S^d/Y is the domestic savings ratio, y is per capita real GDP and g is its growth rate. S^f/Y is the foreign savings ratio, and t is the time subscript. In the savings function, we would have preferred to focus on private savings ratios but data problems restricted the choice to either the domestic savings ratio or the national savings ratio. In the event, the former was chosen so as to focus on the domestic savings mobilization effort.[5] It was assumed that inflationary expectations were

[4]In McKinnon's study, the change in the wholesale price index is the preferred measure of actual inflation. In the absence of such a series for Nepal, the consumer price index is used here.

[5]Although in Nepal net factor income from abroad, mainly in the form of private remittances from soldiers serving in the Indian and British armies, was an important element in the country's balance of payments over the sample period, we have taken the view that these inflows were largely beyond the influence of domestic financial policy, and that they were in the main inflows to sustain consumption by family members left at home.

formed on the basis of past as well as present rates of inflation and p^* was estimated using the Almon polynomial lag technique. All the variables employed are expressed in local currency (Nepalese rupees) and the variables M/P, y, and g are estimated in natural logarithms.[6]

The two-stage least squares estimate of the demand for money function is

$$\begin{aligned} M/P = & -3.0684 + 0.0708(S^d/Y) + 1.1734(y) - 0.0137(p^*) \\ & (-4.4384) \quad (5.3645) \qquad\quad (5.0467) \quad (-3.1409) \\ & +0.1531(M/P)_{-1} \\ & (0.6422) \end{aligned}$$

$$\bar{R}^2 = 0.9698 \quad \text{D-W} = 1.9074 \quad F = 97.3$$

and for the savings function it is

$$\begin{aligned} S^d/Y = & \ 16.7724 + 7.0880\,(M/P) - 4.0224\,(g) - 5.5175\,(y) \\ & (1.0563) \quad (2.5533) \qquad (-0.8760) \quad (-1.5226) \\ & - 0.3788(S^f/Y) \\ & (-1.7152) \end{aligned}$$

$$\bar{R}^2 = 0.7675 \quad \text{D-W } 1.6300 \quad F = 10.9$$

In both cases, t-values are in parentheses below the estimated coefficients. The coefficients of s^d/Y in the demand for money function, and of M/P in the savings function are both positive and significant. In the demand for money function, the inflation and income variables carry the expected sign and are statistically significant. In contrast, savings mobilization appears to have taken place independently of movements in income variables. This might be accounted for by the fluctuations and absence of any real trend in per capita income and its growth rate over the sample period. However, it is also consistent with a change in the structural composition of savings over the period from traditional forms of saving (typically gold, land, and other property in Nepal) in favor of the accumulation of financial assets. The negative coefficient on the foreign savings ratio is in keeping with the common finding that there is substitutability between foreign and domestic savings. Ordinary least square estimates of the functions provided almost identical results.

These results for Nepal, therefore, show strong support for McKinnon's complementarity hypothesis. They are in sharp contrast to Fry's results obtained from a sample of more developed countries but support his assertion that complementarity is most likely to be a feature of the demand for money in countries close to the bottom of the development ladder.

[6]Data are from the *Quarterly Economic Bulletin,* Nepal Rastra Bank (various issues), and *Economic Survey,* Ministry of Finance, Kathmandu (various issues).

LITERATURE CITED

Fry, Maxwell J. *Resource Mobilization and Financial Development in Nepal*. Kathmandu: Centre for Economic Development and Administration, 1974.

———. "Money and Capital or Financial Deepening in Economic Development?" *Journal of Money, Credit, and Banking* 10 (November 1978), 464–75.

———. *Money, Interest, and Banking in Economic Development*. Baltimore: The Johns Hopkins University Press, 1988.

Mohlo, Lazaros E. "Interest Rates, Savings, and Investment in Developing Countries: A Re-examination of the McKinnon-Shaw Hypotheses." Staff Papers, International Monetary Fund 33 (March 1986), 90–116.

McKinnon, Ronald I. *Money and Capital in Economic Development*. Washington, D.C.: The Brookings Institution, 1973.

Shaw, Edward, *Financial Deepening in Economic Development*. New York: Oxford University Press, 1973.

Thornton, John. "The Short-Run Impact of the May 1986 Interest Rate Liberalization in Nepal." *Journal of Development and Administrative Studies* 9 (December 1987), 13–22.

Reserve Requirements and the Inflation Tax

A Comment by L. Dwayne Barney, Alan Frankle, and Harry White

In a recent article, Brock (1989) considers inflationary finance in an economy where money is demanded because it allows a representative agent to reduce the time spent on "shopping" in the goods market. Brock's model is characterized by an agent with preferences defined over consumption and leisure where currency and demand deposits impact on utility only indirectly through a time constraint. By holding additional money the agent can lower the quantity of time spent on shopping, and thus enjoy more consumption and leisure.

Although Brock's model specifies an endogenous supply of labor in production, the derivations associated with his Figure 1 require the assumption of a fixed supply of labor in production. The purpose of this comment is to generalize some of the expressions obtained by Brock (especially the slope of the iso-welfare curves in Figure 1) to the case of an endogenous supply of labor by applying the envelope theorem to the model.

In Brock's model, the agent's choice variables are functions of the nominal interest rate (i) and the reserve ratio (τ), so that the indirect utility function can be written as follows:

$$V(i,\tau) = U(c^*(i,\tau),\ l^*(i,\tau)) \ .$$

where the superscript * denotes that all variables are at the optimum and all notation used corresponds to the notation used by Brock. The expression for the impact of a change in the interest rate on the agent's utility (Brock's equation A4, p. 120) can then be written as

$$\partial V/\partial i = -\lambda^*(m^* + \tau d^*) \ .$$

A change in the reserve ratio yields (equation A5, p. 120)

$$\partial V/\partial \tau = -\lambda^* i d^* \ .$$

L. DWAYNE BARNEY *is assistant professor,* ALAN FRANKLE *is professor, and* HARRY WHITE *is assistant professor of finance, Boise State University.*

Journal of Money, Credit, and Banking, Vol. 22, No. 3 (August 1990)

Denoting the elasticity of utility with respect to the interest rate by η_{ui} [= $(\partial V/\partial i)(i/V)$] and the elasticity with respect to the required reserve ratio by $\eta_{u\tau}$ [= $(\partial V/\partial \tau)(\tau/V)$], the ratio of elasticities (equation A6, p. 120) is

$$\eta_{ui}/\eta_{u\tau} = [(m^* + \tau d^*)/\tau d^*] > 1 .$$

Thus, the ratio is the monetary base divided by commercial bank reserves. Finally, the slope of the iso-welfare curves (equation A7, p. 120) is

$$di/d\tau = -id^*/(m^* + \tau d^*) .$$

These expressions are substantially simpler than Brock's and, more importantly, generalize his results to the case of an endogenous supply of labor in production.

LITERATURE CITED

Brock, Philip L. "Reserve Requirements and the Inflation Tax." *Journal of Money, Credit, and Banking* 21 (February 1989), 106–21.

BOOK REVIEWS

America in the World Economy: A Strategy for the 1990s, by C. Fred Bergsten. Washington, D.C.: Institute for International Economics, November 1988. xiii + 218 pp.

In this book, Fred Bergsten, the well-known director of the Washington Institute for International Economics, gives a compact account of the huge economic problems facing the United States and outlines a strategy to deal with them. The first chapter, like an extended Executive Summary, gives so lucid a summary of the argument and recommendations that many readers will be tempted to content themselves with it. Even this will be worth their while, but they will benefit from reading on; many points are more fully explained and elaborated.

The first paragraph of the preface, dated October 1988, encapsulates the core problem in six lines: "The international economic and financial position of the United States has undergone dramatic change in the 1980s with the onset of huge external deficits and the corresponding shift from being the world's largest creditor country to the world's largest debtor. The United States has become increasingly dependent on international trade and financial flows, and external economic events in the next few years may have a decisive impact on America's prosperity and even on the success of its foreign policy."

The conclusion sums up what needs to be done to avert a variety of calamities: "An early and effective launch of a strategy of competitive interdependence by the new Administration and Congress could set the stage for a prosperous new decade. . . A failure to address the imbalance successfully could bring forth financial disruption and economic downturn. A dollar collapse and a hard landing for the American economy could occur at any time. Double digit inflation could return. There could be severe and prolonged recession. Protectionist pressures and Third World debt could again assume crisis proportions, jeopardising global stability. The stakes are enormous."

The central objective must be to eliminate the U.S. external deficit by 1992, that is, reducing it at an average annual pace of about $35 billion from the assumed 1988 level of $130–140 billion. Bergsten's strategy to achieve this is three-pronged: First, U.S. macroeconomic policy changes, supported by complementary macroeconomic measures in the surplus countries, designed to raise the U.S. saving rate and reorient the economy toward exports and private investment; second, an activist trade policy; third, mobilization of financial resources to enable Third World debtors to run trade deficits.

The first essential under the first heading is to eliminate the federal government's structural budget deficit (about $150 billion) during the term of the new President by cuts in government programs and tax increases. Bergsten leaves it to others to specify a desirable program of spending cuts, merely suggesting that it would probably include continued leveling of defense spending and further cuts in transfers to higher-income citizens under entitlement programs. Rather than reversal of recent cuts in marginal income tax rates, he favors higher consumption taxes, across-the-board or specific. (He speculates implausibly on falling world oil prices taking the hurt out of higher gasoline tax.) To ensure that the resources released by these cuts in private and public consumption are channelled into exports, Bergsten relies mainly on the exchange rate. "A further depreciation [of U.S. dollars] in 1989 averaging about 15 percent in real terms [from 1987] should be sufficient to eliminate the current account deficit by 1992." But the major surplus countries, especially Japan and Germany, which would have much to lose from a hard landing of the American economy, can assist by policies aimed at rapid and sustained growth of domestic demand and further appreciation of their currencies.

Bergsten's activist trade policy contains nothing very new but he powerfully argues the case for promoting exports rather than restricting imports. The U.S. objective should be trade liberalization in a multilateral framework, to ensure that foreign markets remain open to U.S. exports. "To obtain maximum concessions from both industrialised and developing countries, the United States should offer its own key barriers (including those for agriculture and textiles) on a fully reciprocal basis." He warns against protectionist measures, restrictions on foreign investment in the United States, and pursuit of bilateral free trade areas, and underlines the U.S. stake in successful completion of the GATT Uruguay round.

The third prong is more surprising. Bergsten argues that the Third World debt problem has contributed to the deterioration in the U.S. current account because the fifteen most troubled debtor countries are now paying about $30 billion more in annual debt service than they are receiving in new loans. This "negative financial transfer" requires them to run sizable trade surpluses, in contrast to the deficits that, appropriately for developing countries, they have traditionally experienced. Bergsten proposes a massive program of mobilization of financial resources through the World Bank, the Inter-American Development Bank, and the International Monetary Fund, reinforced by lower interest rates (in the wake of budget deficit reduction), some additional private capital flows, and debt relief for the poorest debtors. Such a program, he thinks, could contribute $10 billion to the required $150 billion reduction in the U.S. external deficit by 1992.

These are the bare bones of Bergsten's strategy. There are many detailed suggestions, the most important perhaps an ambitious proposal for international monetary reform. He proposes a "full target zone system" which would represent a synthesis of the positive elements from the Bretton Woods system, whose fixed rates became far too rigid, and the nonsystem of unmanaged flexibility, with its excessive gyrations and huge misalignments.

> "The key countries would first agree on sustainable and internationally consistent current account outcomes. They would then devise a set of exchange rates thought to be consistent with these outcomes over the medium term, and set a range (extending perhaps plus or minus 10 percent around the targets at the outset) within which their exchange rates would be allowed to fluctuate. The countries would also commit themselves to the adoption of policy changes, as needed, to prevent their currencies from moving outside the ranges."

It takes considerable optimism about the efficacy of international policy coordination to believe that movements outside the range can be contained, so long as freedom of international capital movements remains unrestricted.

A foreign observer can only applaud the general thrust of Bergsten's strategy and admire the ingenuity with which it is worked out and the clarity with which it is presented.

Even one who shares Bergsten's faith in the power of market forces may wonder about his confidence in the capacity of exchange rate changes to shift resources on the required scale. Bergsten claims that "the dollar overvaluation [of the early 1980s] produced the massive trade deficits" and that a sufficient further depreciation can eliminate them. In a section entitled "Can American Compete?" he dismisses the view that lagging productivity growth in the United States has rendered U.S. industry uncompetitive—productivity in manufacturing has been growing at a healthy annual rate of 4 percent, low aggregate productivity growth is distorted by services which are mostly irrelevant to international competitiveness—and has only a little to say about adjustment assistance to endangered industries, among which he lists textiles and apparel, steel, automobiles, and semiconductors.

Apart from slight unease on this score, this reader has reservations about Bergsten's argument at only three points.

The first is minor. One wishes he would not give even momentary currency to the notion that "the United States borrows primarily in its own currency, so it could never 'run out of foreign exchange' and be forced to declare a moratorium on debt service payments." As he points out, "a withdrawal of foreign funds, or even a cessation of new lending . . . could trigger [a sharp fall in the dollar,] a sharp rise in inflation and a recession at almost any time. The mechanisms are different, but the consequences are ultimately the same for any debtor country when its credit runs out." The general overdraft facility which a reserve center enjoys is not unlimited.

The second, painfully noticable to an Australian reader, is Bergsten's reticence in the context of trade policy about agricultural trade, and especially the U.S. policy of trade war with the EEC through export subsidies for wheat and other commodities, at the expense of third countries. A word in support of the Cairns Group's efforts would have been welcome.

Finally, one cannot help but note that nine months after the date of the preface and six months after the inauguration of the new President, there are few signs of the "early and effective launch of a strategy of competitive interdependence by the new Administration and Congress," a strategy to be adopted, launched, and beginning to be implemented "within their first few months in office." Neither the budget deficit nor the external deficit has contracted significantly. On the other hand, none of the predicted calamities is yet in evidence. Indeed the dollar has, perversely, been rising again. Has Bergsten been crying "wolf" too loudly? Or is the wolf at the door?

H. W. ARNDT

Australian National University, Canberra

Governing the $5 Trillion Economy, by Herbert Stein. New York: Oxford University Press, 1989. viii + 145 pp. $17.95.

> At the end of World War II there was agreement—at least among people who think about such things—about what the budget problem was and how to deal with it. The nation's chief problem, and objective, was to maintain high employment. This was a natural priority after the miseries of unemployment in the 1930s and the *blessings of full employment during the war.* (p. 109) (Emphasis added)

Governing the $5 Trillion Economy begins with the proposition that the outcome of recent fiscal policy has been unsatisfactory, and it ends by suggesting how the outcome might be improved. Herbert Stein has devoted much of his life to the study and reform of fiscal policy. With a half century of experience in Washington, he is uniquely qualified to comment on the process of making fiscal policy. Even though Stein is unhappy with the outcome of recent policy, he argues that there is nothing essentially wrong with the current structure of the policy process. Rather, he thinks recent policy outcomes have been unsatisfactory because policymakers lack good information and because the process has been managed badly. He says, "Improving the decision-making process requires better people and better information" (p. 11).

Stein says that we are not allocating national output well. He believes we have too much consumption by the "nonpoor," too much government spending on health care, and too little for defense, for private investment, for education, and for the poor. He quickly reminds us, however, that these are his values; we might have other opinions. How can he be sure, then, that we are not allocating GNP according to the will of the majority? He proposes an answer. He knows we allocate GNP less than optimally because we do not have adequate information to make optimal decisions. The proof, he says, is in the "abundant evidence that the existing compromises are not reached by a reasoned and informed process."

The basic premise of the book—that the structure of the current policy process is satisfactory, but the outcomes are not—is not explained. Stein never clearly distinguishes between the structure of the fiscal policy process and the management within that structure. If policy outcomes are consistently unsatisfactory, then it seems the structure of the policy process must be flawed. Information is not free, and the information set needed to support the current policy process may not be available. The process and the policies should be structured to take account of our ignorance. They should also be structured to protect us as much as possible from the bad managers.

Stein makes three interrelated suggestions for improving fiscal policy without changing the structure of the process. First, government policymakers should think about fiscal policy as a tool for achieving the optimal allocation of national output. Second, they should be more candid about their ultimate and proximate objectives. Finally, they should improve the information available in the policy-making process.

Stein says that what we ultimately should care about is the proper allocation of the national output. This allocation is determined by the values of private individuals as well as by government fiscal and regulatory policies. By looking at the allocation of GNP, Stein argues, we can take the effect of regulations and private decisions into account as we decide how to use the government's resources. Stein gives a brief history of the idea that the budget process should be thought of as a way to allocate the national output. He cites his earlier work with the Committee for Economic Development and the Council of Economic Advisors to show that this idea has been around for some time.

Stein illustrates his proposed method for thinking about and discussing policy in terms of the allocation of national output. He describes a particular baseline budget for 1990 (judged to be the most likely outcome at the time of the publication of this book) and compares it to three alternatives. In each case, Stein shows how he thinks different programs would result in different allocations of GNP. Stein's main innovation is to disaggregate GNP into about fourteen components. He simply illustrates how adding a dollar to one category requires taking a dollar away from another category. Stein also uses this illustration to advocate a particular reallocation of national output according to his own preferences.

Stein (1969) celebrated not only the liberation of monetary and fiscal policy from outmoded thinking about monetary rules and balanced budgets, but also the development and acceptance of a new language for discussing and making policy, the Keynesian macroeconomic tradition. Part of this tradition is the large econometric model organized around the national income accounts. This framework is used both in and out of government as a way to keep track of large amounts of information about the economy.

Stein recommends that political leaders think about how their fiscal actions affect the allocation of GNP. It is a curious recommendation since much of the discussion today already follows this format. Indeed, many private and public evaluations of proposed budgets are directly or indirectly based on forecasts from large econometric models organized around the national income accounts. People using these forecasts typically try to account for other factors, including trends in private spending and regulatory influences.

In this book, and in other writings, Stein continually reminds us that deficits should not be the focus of policy. He stresses the important point that there are many ways to close a deficit, some good policies and others not so good. A similar point might be made about achieving goals for the components of GNP. Measures of output in the GNP accounts are very poor indicators of social welfare. Having a bigger defense budget does not guarantee a more secure society.

Stein's dissatisfaction with actual economic outcomes has been shared by others. Many economists have rejected conventional macroeconomic theories because of these outcomes.[1] In response, economists are now building macro models with microeconomic foundations. These models show how new policies can change the incentives and behavior of individuals as well as how the policies affect macroeconomic outcomes. One of the most important findings to come from this literature is the idea that the long-term effects of fiscal policies can be very different from the short-term impacts.[2] These new developments suggest a need for more micro-information about how policies affect individual behavior, not macro-information about how the policy affects the components of GNP.

There is another way in which Stein's recommendation may not improve the outcome for fiscal policy. The lack of fiscal discipline today may be due in part to politicians who think about their job as allocating GNP, rather than raising and allocating governmental revenues. Following Stein's recommendation encourages politicians to act as if they had a legitimate claim on private output beyond the claims explicitly specified in tax law. Such thinking would naturally encourage politicians to ignore the constraint implied by limited tax revenues.

Stein's second recommendation is that policymakers be more candid about their policy objectives. The most important practical recommendation in this book is that an incoming president should submit a four-year budget. Economists understand there are problems in persuading the government to adopt any policy that has good long-term effects when there are conflicting short-run political objectives. A four-year budget would more clearly show what is sacrificed to achieve a new president's objectives. When the government doesn't commit to a long-term policy, then the long-term outcome is just the accumulation of the short-run actions which are often determined by the procedures. Perhaps Stein is correct that the current procedures would work if there were a precommitment to achieve longer-term objectives.

There is a problem, however. Politicians rationally try to appeal to groups with conflicting goals. The trick for reformers is to find ways to induce political candidates and government agencies to commit to explicit long-term goals. Unfortunately, Stein does not offer any special insight into how we can convince politicians to accept four-year budgets, or how we might convince them to reveal the complete budgetary implications of their priorities before they are elected. Furthermore, Stein is critical of recent proposals that would bind the hands of policymakers when they failed to achieve desired objectives.

Stein criticizes "gimmicks" such as the balanced budget amendment and the Gramm-Rudman-Hollings act (GRH), which impose binding constraints on a subset of the allocation

[1]For a summary of views about the policy implications of recent developments in macroeconomics, see the articles and comments in Gavin and Sniderman (1988).

[2]See the results of policy simulations in Auerbach and Kotlikoff (1987).

problems facing policymakers. He argues that both history and logic show that expenditures do not automatically rise to use up all revenues and that, by analogy, cutting revenues will not automatically limit expenditures.

Stein calls GRH a crude, blunt instrument that prevents the rational allocation of government resources. It results in an outcome that will fit almost nobody's view of an optimal allocation of national output. Nevertheless, given diversity of opinion about objectives and a consensus that government is now too large, it may be the best, most feasible way to reduce the relative growth of government spending. Stein has not suggested an alternative mechanism that would simultaneously achieve consensus, constrain the relative growth of government, and result in better allocation of resources.

The final recommendation is to improve the information used in the policy process. Stein has four suggestions. First, Stein says that information would be improved if policymakers were more explicit about objectives. Stein is probably right about this. Once a political candidate or federal agency is committed to an explicit policy objective, economists begin to examine the assumptions, economic theory, and statistics relating to this objective. For example, when the Federal Reserve adopted explicit targets for the monetary aggregates, everyone began to learn more about the aggregates. Newspapers wrote weekly stories about the release of money supply numbers, and the Federal Reserve devoted more resources to obtaining better information about the level of the nation's money stock. Clearly, being explicit about desired objectives tends to concentrate resources on gathering appropriate information.

Second, Stein says that if the government were to focus clearly on allocating GNP, it would have better information. Focusing more clearly on any objective will improve information. Focusing on GNP implies that the traditional macroeconomic perspective is appropriate. Much of what has been learned about the relation between macro outcomes and individual utility in the last two decades makes this suggestion seem out of date.

Third, Stein argues for a better allocation of the governmental resources used to collect information. No doubt there is a better way to organize the resources used in collecting information. Stein also suggests that more of the government's budget should be dedicated to gathering information. This is an opinion unsupported by analysis. The government already collects an enormous amount of information.

Fourth (and this is implicit throughout the text), Stein hints that one reason for our use of bad information is that we ignore conventional wisdom about the economic effects of fiscal policy. He reminds us that Keynesian ideas about fiscal policy were accepted because they were thought to have provided a way to prevent a recurrence of the Depression. As time passed these ideas came to be accepted as a blueprint for managing aggregate demand in a way that would not only prevent severe downturns, but also prevent, delay, or at least ameliorate, garden-variety recessions.

Many of Stein's recommendations involve going back to conventional ideas and ignoring the policy implications of new developments in macroeconomics. He is critical of ideas associated with the supply-siders as well as ideas associated with Rational Expectations and Ricardian Equivalence theories. In many ways this book is as much a defense of the status quo and the theories that Stein held in 1969 as it is a blueprint for reform.

Consider two distinct views about the role of government economists. The first view might be seen in the Greek root of the word economy, *oikonomos,* the household manager. Government economists who think their job is to help the political leader "manage the household" of the economy will concentrate on economic aggregates such as investment, total employment, total expenditures on health, defense, etc. Their main concern will be to engineer desired outcomes for these aggregates. They will use large econometric and input/output models to organize and monitor the basic information in the national income accounts. They will be able to see full employment during wartime as a "blessing."

On the other hand, there are economists who perceive economics as a way of thinking about how society's rules can be shaped to promote individual utility. These economists will be more interested in how fiscal policies will affect the incentives and opportunities of individuals than in how the policies affect aggregate allocations among the categories in the national income accounts. Many of the economists who worked for the Reagan administration—implicitly criticized throughout this book—were of the second type. They were not so directly interested in government-measured aggregates like budget deficits, net investment, or private savings. Rather, they were more interested in how government rules and expenditures affected incentives and personal opportunities.[3]

While this classification of economic advisors into two groups is somewhat artificial, it may explain the audience reaction to Herbert Stein's new book. This book will not appeal to those who want to reform the fiscal policy process in light of evolving macroeconomic theory. Those who want to reform the government will be put off by the implication that we should accept the large and activist nature of the U.S. government. They will find in this book the elements of a recommendation for large-scale government planning. On the other hand, those who accept conventional macroeconomic theory and who have been called upon to help policymakers manage our $5 trillion economy will praise this book for its wisdom and its practicality.

WILLIAM T. GAVIN
Federal Reserve Bank of Cleveland

LITERATURE CITED

Auerbach, Alan J., and Laurence J. Kotlikoff. *Dynamic Fiscal Policy*. Cambridge: Cambridge University Press, 1987.

Economic Report of the President. Washington: United States Government Printing Office, two issues, 1970 and 1985.

Gavin, William T., and Mark S. Sniderman, eds. *Recent Developments in Macroeconomics*, a special issue of the *Journal of Money, Credit, and Banking*, vol. 20, no. 3, Part II. Columbus: The Ohio State University Press, 1988.

Stein, Herbert. *The Fiscal Revolution in America*. Chicago: University of Chicago Press, 1969.

[3]For an interesting contrast, compare the micro approach to analysis in the *Economic Report of the President* written in 1985 by William Poole and William Niskanen to the macro approach recommended in the *Economic Report of the President* written in 1970 when Stein was a member of the President's Council of Economic Advisors.

An Important Announcement from *Financial Management*

A Special Issue on

"Leveraged Buyouts"

Authors are invited to submit papers on issues related to leveraged buyouts. Topics include (but are not limited to):

- Economic rationale for LBOs
- Stakeholder returns in LBOs
- LBO case histories
- Analytical issues on how to value LBOs
- Effects of the LBO movement on the economy
- Effects of antitakeover defenses on LBOs
- Tax effects of LBOs
- Post-LBO performance
- Post-LBO corporate and financial structure

Dr. Thomas E. Copeland, McKinsey & Company, Inc., has accepted the task of editing the Special Issue. The issue is tentatively scheduled for Winter 1992.

Submissions (6 copies) marked "Leveraged Buyouts Special Issue" should be sent to the Editor of *Financial Management* by December 31, 1990:

James S. Ang
FINANCIAL MANAGEMENT/LEVERAGED BUYOUTS SPECIAL ISSUE
Florida State University
College of Business, R-53G
Tallahassee, FL 32306-1042

Programs of Graduate Study in Finance at The Ohio State University

Ohio State is the largest University in Ohio. It is a major center for graduate education, ranking eighth in the nation in doctoral degrees conferred. There are 350 masters students and 100 Ph.D. students pursuing advanced study in business administration.

Although the Business School is essentially self-contained, the size of its graduate program and the availability of other strong departments such as economics, statistics, and mathematics offer the graduate student considerable flexibility in developing a program of study.

Areas of Specialization. The Finance Faculty of twenty-four full-time professors combines a diversity of talents and interests to offer areas of specialization at the masters and doctoral levels in managerial finance, financial institutions, international finance, financial theory, and investments. Other closely related graduate programs are available in insurance and real estate.

Financial Aid. Four basic sources of financial aid are available: fellowships and teaching, research and administrative assistantships. The fellowships are competitively awarded and the teaching assistantships involve teaching one course per quarter. Continued financial support is normally available if a student is progressing satisfactorily in his graduate program.

Additional information may be obtained from: Director of Graduate Study, Faculty of Finance, The Ohio State University, 1775 College Road, Hagerty Hall, Columbus, Ohio 43210.

Financial Management

The Journal of the Financial Management Association

Vol. 19 Summer 1990 No. 2

9 *Realized Returns and the Default and Prepayment Experience of Financial Leasing Contracts*
Ronald C. Lease, John J. McConnell, and James S. Schallheim

.....

TAXES AND DIVIDENDS

19 *The Impact of Personal Taxes on Corporate Dividend Policy and Capital Structure Decisions*
Rosita P. Chang and S. Ghon Rhee

30 *Taxes and Dividend Policy*
Eli Talmor and Sheridan Titman

.....

INVESTMENT BANKING TOPICS

34 *Pricing the SPIN*
K.C. Chen and R. Stephen Sears

46 *The Valuation of Firm Commitment Underwriting Contracts for Seasoned New Equity Issues: Theory and Evidence*
Sung C. Bae and Haim Levy

.....

REVIEW

58 *Causes, Consequences, and Shareholder Wealth Effects of Management Turnover: A Review of the Empirical Evidence*
Eugene P.H. Furtado and Vijay Karan

.....

APPLICATIONS

74 *A Comparison of Stock Price Predictions Using Court Accepted Formulas, Dividend Discount, and P/E Models*
Glenn H. Petry and Kent Hickman

Membership dues of the Association include a one-year subscription to the journal. Subscription rates are: Regular $40; Sustaining $45. Library subscriptions are $60 per year. Members outside the U.S. add $6 per year to cover overseas postage. All fees must be in U.S. dollars drawn on a U.S. bank. Write Financial Management Association, College of Business Administration, University of South Florida, Tampa, FL 33620.

The Ohio State University Department of Economics Offers Programs of Graduate Study in Economics

The Ohio State University is located in Columbus, capital city of Ohio and a metropolitan area of more than one million people. There are six other institutions of higher education in Columbus as well as the headquarters facility of Battelle Memorial Institute, the largest independent research organization in the world. University students number over fifty thousand, including about eight thousand graduate students. Ohio State is a major center for graduate education, ranking eighth in the nation in degrees conferred. The Ohio State University library system is one of the ten largest library systems in the United States.

Graduate Studies in Economics

The Department of Economics has a faculty of forty members with approximately ninety graduate students in residence at any point in time. The large faculty and relatively small graduate student body make possible in-depth graduate education through close association with outstanding scholars in many different areas. Fields of specialization include:

- Mathematical Economics
- Econometrics
- Money and Finance
- Labor
- Industrial Organization
- Public Finance and Urban Economics
- Monetary Theory and Macroeconomics
- Soviet and Eastern European Studies
- International Trade and Development
- Economic History

Economics graduate students can take elective fields in other departments of the College of Social and Behavioral Sciences or in the Colleges of Business, Agriculture and Home Economics, Engineering, Mathematics, and Physical Sciences when interdisciplinary studies are appropriate.

Fellowships and Assistantships

Because of Ohio State's large undergraduate enrollment and ongoing research programs, there are many part-time teaching and research assistantships that offer financial aid to graduate students. The Department of Economics assists a number of students each year through fellowships and assistantships with stipends ranging from $7,506 to $13,014 per academic year. In addition, teaching, research and administrative assistants, and fellows receive tuition fee waivers. Once a student has been awarded a fellowship or assistantship, financial assistance is possible for as many as five years, provided normal academic progress is maintained.

University Fellowships (stipend $825 per month for 12 months, nonrenewable) are available to well-qualified applicants. In addition, Special University Fellowships (stipend: $825 per month for 12 months, renewable) are available to minority students, primarily blacks of U.S. citizenship.

Additional information about the department may be obtained from the Director of Graduate Studies, Department of Economics, The Ohio State University, 1945 North High Street, Columbus, OH 43210.

ACKNOWLEDGMENTS

Supporting Subscribers

Pittsburgh National Bank

Security Pacific National Bank

State Savings Co.

Referees

Charles F. Adams
Alan J. Auerbach
David Backus
James R. Barth
Christopher Baum
Roland Benabou
Truman F. Bewley
Marcelo Bianconi
James N. Bodurtha, Jr.
Tim Bollerslev
Russell S. Boyer
Michael D. Bradley
Robert F. Bruner
John Bryant
Andrew S. Caplin
Suchan Chae
Winston W. Chang
V. Chari
Robert S. Chirinko
In Choi
Bradford Cornell
N. Edward Coulson
Ramon P. DeGennaro
Michael Denny
Michael Devereux
Robert Eisner
William B. English
Paul D. Evans
Ray C. Fair
Barry L. Falk
Roger E.A. Farmer
Douglas Fisher
Donald R. Fraser
William T. Gavin
Jo Anna Gray
Vittorio U. Grilli
Gikas A. Hardouvelis
David A. Hsieh
Christopher James
John A. James
Douglas H. Joines
David S. Jones
Joseph P. Joyce
Craig S. Hakkio
James D. Hamilton
Peter R. Hartley
Richard C. Hartman
Gregory Hoelscher
Patric H. Hendershot
Timothy D. Hogan
Philip A. Horvath
George Kanatas
James B. Kau
Michael C. Keeley
John Kitchen
Timothy W. Koch
James W. Kolari
Richard W. Kopcke
Peter Kugler
Pamela A. Labadie
Bong-Soo Lee
Christina Y. Liu
Nissan Liviatan
Francis A. Longstaff
James R. Lothian
Gail E. Makinen
Richard C. Marston
Michael Mazzlo
Roger A. McCain
W. Douglas McMillin
Loretta J. Mester
Ross D. Milbourne
Douglas W. Mitchell
James J. Musumeci
James T. Moser
Urs. Muller
Michael Parkin
Hugh T. Patrick
Andrew J. Policano
Stephen Poloz
Hugh T. Rockoff
Jeremy R. Rudin
Martha Schary
Donald E. Schlagenhauf
Apostolos Serletis
Steven A. Sharpe
Gary S. Shea
Joseph F. Sinkey, Jr.
David E. Spencer
Jerome L. Stein
Richard J. Sweeney
James L. Swofford
Richard D. Sylla
Anjan V. Thakor
Carl E. Walsh
Steven B. Webb
William C. Whitesell
James A. Wilcox
G. K. Yarrow
Stephen P. Zeldes

Ohio State
University Press

ISSN 0022-2879

(*continued from front cover*)

BOOK REVIEWS

America in the World Economy: A Strategy for the 1990s,
by C. Fred Bergsten *Reviewed by H. W. Arndt* 00(

Governing the $5 Trillion Economy, by Herbert Stein
Reviewed by William T. Gavin 00(

JOURNAL OF MONEY, CREDIT AND BANKING

November 1990

ARTICLES

Member Bank Borrowing and the Fed's Contractionary Monetary Policy during the Great Depression — *David C. Wheelock*

Targeting Nominal Income in a Dynamic Model — *Vincent Reinhart*

Federal Credit, Private Credit, and Economic Activity — *James S. Fackler*

Analyzing the Stability of Demand-for-Money Equations via Bounded-Influence Estimation Techniques — *Christopher F. Baum and Marilena Furno*

The Term Structure and Time Series Properties of Nominal Interest Rates: Implications from Theory — *Kevin D. Salyer*

Purchasing Power Parity in the Long Run: A Cointegration Approach — *Yoonbai Kim*

An Examination of Cost Subadditivity and Multiproduct Production in Large U.S. Banks — *William C. Hunter, Stephen G. Timme, and Won Keun Yang*

NOTES, COMMENTS, REPLIES

Scottish Banking and the Legal Restrictions Theory: A Closer Look — *Lawrence H. White*

Annual Index

JOURNAL OF MONEY, CREDIT AND BANKING

Manuscripts should be submitted in triplicate to the Editors, *Journal of Money, Credit, and Banking*, Department of Economics, Ohio State University, 1945 North High Street, Columbus, Ohio 43210–1172. Carolyn South, Secretary to the Editors. Submission fee: individual subscribers U.S. $30; nonsubscribers U.S. $40. Checks are to be made payable to THE OHIO STATE UNIVERSITY –JMCB and enclosed with submitted manuscripts. Instructions for preparing text and illustrations appear in the February issue.

JOURNAL OF MONEY, CREDIT AND BANKING

VOLUME 22 NUMBER 4 NOVEMBER 1990

ARTICLES

Member Bank Borrowing and the Fed's Contractionary Monetary Policy during the Great Depression — *David C. Wheelock* 409

Targeting Nominal Income in a Dynamic Model — *Vincent Reinhart* 427

Federal Credit, Private Credit, and Economic Activity — *James S. Fackler* 444

Analyzing the Stability of Demand-for-Money Equations via Bounded-Influence Estimation Techniques — *Christopher F. Baum and Marilena Furno* 465

The Term Structure and Time Series Properties of Nominal Interest Rates: Implications from Theory — *Kevin D. Salyer* 478

Purchasing Power Parity in the Long Run: A Cointegration Approach — *Yoonbai Kim* 491

An Examination of Cost Subadditivity and Multiproduct Production in Large U.S. Banks — *William C. Hunter, Stephen G. Timme, and Won Keun Yang* 504

NOTES, COMMENTS, REPLIES

Scottish Banking and the Legal Restrictions Theory: A Closer Look — *Lawrence H. White* 526

Annual Index 537

JOURNAL OF MONEY, CREDIT, AND BANKING (ISSN 0022-2879). Published quarterly in February, May, August, and November by the Ohio State University Press, 1070 Carmack Road, Columbus, Ohio 43210. Margaret Starbuck, Managing Editor; Peg Carr, Production Editor; Tom Kangas, Subscriptions Manager. Second-class postage paid at Columbus, Ohio, and at additional mailing offices. *Postmaster:* Send address to: *Journal of Money, Credit, and Banking*, Ohio State University Press, 1070 Carmack Road, Columbus, Ohio 43210.

SUBSCRIPTIONS. Individual: U.S. $27.50 per year; library: U.S. $45; student: U.S. $20.00; additional subscriptions to the same address: U.S. $20.00 per subscription. Postage outside the United States: add $5.00 per year. Sponsoring Subscriptions: U.S. $1000 per year. Sustaining Subscriptions: U.S. $500 per year. Supporting Subscriptions: U.S. $100 per year. Claims for missing issues must be made within four months of the date of publication. Allow six weeks for address change. Checks should be made payable to the Ohio State University Press, 1070 Carmack Road, Columbus, Ohio 43210.

BACK ISSUES, REPRINTS, AND MICROFILM. Most back issues from 1983 to the present are available from the Ohio State University press. Microfilms of back volumes and reprints of articles may be obtained from University Microfilms International, 300 North Zeeb Road, Ann Arbor, Michigan 48106. Back volumes from 1969 through 1982 in reprint edition may be obtained from Schmidt Periodicals GmbH, Dettendorf, D-8201 Bad Feilnbach 2, West Germany.

DAVID C. WHEELOCK

Member Bank Borrowing and the Fed's Contractionary Monetary Policy during the Great Depression

> The influence of the reserve banks upon the volume of credit is felt not directly, but indirectly through the member banks. The reserve banks do not "push" credit into use.
>
> Benjamin Strong, U.S. House of Representatives, 1926

INTRODUCTION

THE CONTRIBUTION OF "INEPT" FEDERAL RESERVE monetary policy to the length and severity of the Great Depression is now well understood. In their *Monetary History of the United States,* Friedman and Schwartz (1963) demonstrate the importance of monetary forces in the Depression. And recent studies by Bernanke (1983), Field (1984a,b), and Hamilton (1987) emphasize further the importance of restrictive monetary policy on economic activity from 1929 to 1933. However, the reasons why the Fed failed to respond vigorously to the Depression are not so clear. Were the Fed's failures the product of leadership or other organizational changes? Or, were they caused by the pursuit of a flawed strategy, and thus independent of the System's structure?

Friedman and Schwartz (1963, pp. 407–19) contend that the death of Benjamin Strong, Governor of the Federal Reserve Bank of New York, in 1928, and a subsequent reorganization of the Open Market Committee caused a major change in the Fed's responsiveness to economic conditions. They argue that under Strong's

The comments and suggestions on previous versions from Michael Bordo, Subal Kumbhakar, Huston McCulloch, Larry Neal, Raymond Sauer, Eugene White, Elmus Wicker, and a referee of this journal are gratefully acknowledged.

DAVID C. WHEELOCK *is assistant professor of economics at The University of Texas at Austin.*

Journal of Money, Credit, and Banking, Vol. 22, No. 4 (November 1990)

leadership in the 1920s the Fed had used open-market operations effectively to limit fluctuations in economic activity. But those officials who gained power after Strong's death did not understand the role of monetary policy and permitted widespread bank failures and collapse of the stock of money during the early 1930s.

Two aspects of the Friedman and Schwartz interpretation of Federal Reserve behavior have been challenged. Their view that monetary policy was used effectively during the 1920s has been challenged by Miron (1988), Toma (1989), and Wheelock (1989). Miron shows that output was less stable following the Fed's founding in 1914 than it had been previously. Wheelock finds evidence that the Fed did attempt to stabilize output, but that its operation had no impact on the volume of Federal Reserve credit outstanding. And Toma demonstrates that the Fed's open-market operations had no effect on the supply of money. Since these studies suggest that the Fed's policies were not successful during the 1920s, they imply that the failure of monetary policy to revive the economy during the Depression might not have resulted from a substantial change in Fed behavior.

Wicker (1966) and Brunner and Meltzer (1968) argue that indeed Fed errors during the Depression are traceable to policy during the 1920s. Wicker contends that the Fed had little understanding of how monetary policy should be used to stabilize economic activity. He argues also that the Fed's operations in the 1920s were made in response to international events, not to stabilize the domestic economy (Wicker 1966, pp. 77–94, 106–16). Brunner and Meltzer (1968) and Meltzer (1976) argue that the Fed did not respond vigorously to the Depression because officials believed that low nominal interest rates and little member bank borrowing signaled exceptional monetary ease. Brunner and Meltzer contend that the Fed had been guided similarly by interest rates and bank borrowing during the 1920s and hence that there was no change in Fed behavior.

During the 1920s the Fed developed a reserve position strategy in which it used open-market operations to "target"[1] borrowed reserves. The current Fed procedure of using borrowed reserves as an operating target is quite similar. And, as Thornton (1988, p. 33) describes, "strict adherence to the borrowings procedure will not provide effective money stock control." In this paper I argue that during the 1920s and early 1930s the System's operating tactics caused monetary policy to be ineffective, even destabilizing. The Fed's strategy did not lead to effective money stock control. And the borrowed reserves procedure was particularly inappropriate during the Depression because of instability in borrowed reserve demand induced by financial crises. The Fed failed to account for these shifts, and continued to interpret little borrowing as a sign of exceptional monetary ease. So, despite widespread bank failures and deflation, Fed officials saw little need for vigorous open-market purchases.

The next section describes the Fed's tactics, focusing especially on its theory of borrowed reserve demand. The following sections analyze empirically the demand

[1]I put the word target in quotes since the Fed did not generally specify a quantity target for borrowed reserves. It used the variable more as an indicator of monetary conditions, determining the specific volume of open-market operations needed to achieve its ultimate goals.

for borrowed reserves during the Depression, and illustrate the impacts of the decline in economic activity and the financial crises on that demand. Like Brunner and Meltzer, I conclude that there was no significant change in Fed procedures between the 1920s and early 1930s, and that the Fed's mistakes during the depression can be attributed to its failure to interpret monetary conditions correctly.

THE FED'S STRATEGY AND THEORY OF MEMBER BANK BORROWING

During the early 1920s the Fed observed that when it purchased government securities in the open market the volume of member bank borrowing tended to fall by a like amount. But, despite this apparent inability to change the total volume of Federal Reserve credit outstanding, the Fed observed that market interest rates did seem to respond to its operations. The Fed inferred that

> Various monetary factors—such as gold movements, changes in currency demand, and open-market operations by the [R]eserve [B]anks . . . determine the volume of indebtedness (of member banks to the Federal Reserve) . . . and changes in this indebtedness appear to be the initiating force in corresponding changes in money rates. (Riefler 1930, p. 27)

Thus, largely exogenous flows of nonborrowed reserves were seen as the principal cause of member bank borrowing. And changes in member bank borrowing were thought to produce changes in market interest rates. The Fed inferred that open-market purchases stimulated economic activity by reducing borrowed reserve demand and interest rates. And, similarly, that sales increased member bank borrowing and led to higher rates which would slow economic activity.

Fed publications and statements by System officials during the 1920s make the Fed theory of member bank borrowing clear. The classic statement of the theory was made by Riefler (1930). According to Riefler (1930, p. 28), "member banks are in general reluctant to borrow from the [R]eserve [B]anks, (and) when they do borrow they are in most cases motivated by necessity rather than profit." For an individual bank, deposit outflows produce the necessity. But for the system as a whole, the need for borrowing comes from open-market sales, gold outflows, or any other reduction in nonborrowed reserves.

Although he argued that in general banks do not borrow to exploit profit opportunities, Riefler (1930, p. 34) accepted that bank decisions to borrow were influenced by the differential between the yield on short-term securities and the discount rate:

> [I]t seems highly probable that member banks when they borrow and when they adjust their operations to repay their borrowing are affected to a certain extent by its cost in relation to money rates in the market.

The notion that banks are reluctant to borrow reserves, and do so only when forced to, is fundamental to the Fed's use of borrowed reserves as a policy guide. If this theory is correct, then the level of borrowing will indicate accurately the degree of monetary ease or restraint. Relatively heavy borrowing will reflect pressure on bank reserve positions and tight money, while little borrowing will reflect monetary ease. But, if the Fed's theory is incorrect, and banks do borrow to expand their loans and investments, the level of borrowed reserves will not reflect monetary conditions accurately. Since loan demand increases during economic expansions and declines during recessions, a specific level of borrowed reserves might reflect monetary ease during an expansion and tight money during a recession. Moreover, if the Fed targets a specific level of borrowed reserves, the money supply will tend to increase during expansions and decrease during recessions. For example, during a recession member bank borrowing tends to decline since loan demand falls. If borrowed reserves fall below the Fed's target, the Fed will be tempted to sell securities. The worse a recession, the greater the decline in borrowed reserves, and, paradoxically, the more restrictive the Fed is likely to be. The Fed actually contributes to economic instability by exacerbating procyclical swings in the supply of money.

The Fed did not have an inflexible borrowed reserves target during the 1920s or early 1930s, and it did not sell securities during recessions. However, the Fed did interpret relatively heavy borrowing by banks as a sign of tight money, and little borrowing as a sign of ease. Moreover, from the level of borrowed reserves the Fed determined the appropriate volume of open-market operations necessary to achieve its goals. Benjamin Strong made this clear in a statement to the Governors Conference in 1926 (Chandler 1958, pp. 239–40):

> Should we go into a business recession while the member banks were continuing to borrow directly 500 or 600 million dollars . . . we should consider taking steps to relieve some of the pressure which this borrowing induces by purchasing Government securities and thus enabling member banks to reduce their indebtedness . . . Future changes in our loan account are especially significant as a guide . . .
>
> As a guide to the timing and extent of any purchase which might appear desirable, one of our best guides would be the amount of borrowing by member banks in principal centers . . . .

This statement suggests that Strong would have judged money to be quite easy in 1930–31, since member bank borrowing averaged just $243 million from January 1930 through September 1931 (Board of Governors, 1943, p. 371).[2] It is not evident from Strong's statement that policy would have been more expansionary in 1930–31 had he lived. It suggests also why the Fed made relatively large open-market purchases during minor recessions in 1924 and 1927, but made few purchases in 1930–31. The sharp economic downturn in 1930–31 led to a greater decline in borrowed reserves than in 1924 or 1927. Consequently, the Fed inferred that money was already quite easy, and that few open-market purchases were necessary.[3] Unfor-

[2]Member bank borrowing increased sharply in the final week of September 1931 because of heavy deposit withdrawals brought on by Great Britain's break with the gold standard. However, the Fed did not buy securities in response, supposedly because it lacked sufficient gold reserves to back increased liabilities. Friedman and Schwartz (1963, pp. 399–406) and Wicker (1966, pp. 169–71) dispute this reason, but Epstein and Ferguson (1984, pp. 964–65) argue that the Fed was so constrained.

[3]The Fed bought some $440 million of securities from March through September 1924. Member bank borrowing averaged $620 million in the three months prior to the beginning of these purchases, and did not fall below $250 million during the purchase months. The Fed bought $300 million of securities from March through December 1927. Borrowing averaged $514 in the three months prior to March, and never

tunately, as Friedman and Schwartz (1963, pp. 340–41) show, the Fed's failure to offset the decline in bank borrowing in 1930–31 allowed the stock of money to decline.

Friedman and Schwartz argue that Strong's death and the subsequent reorganization of the Open Market Committee led to the failures of monetary policy during the Depression. Therefore, it is important to know precisely Strong's understanding of the transmission process and of the behavior of borrowed reserves. His statement to the Governors Conference indicates he viewed borrowed reserves as an important guide to monetary conditions. And his testimony that the "Reserve Banks do not 'push' credit into use" (Strong 1926) is significant since it implies a view that expansionary operations are appropriate and effective only if there is an increasing demand for Federal Reserve credit.

Strong's understanding of borrowed reserve demand is less clear. In a speech to the Harvard Graduate Economics Club in 1922 he stated (Chandler 1958, pp. 196–97):

> Practically all borrowing by member banks from the Reserve Banks is *ex post facto*. The condition which gives rise to the need for borrowing had already come into existence before the application to borrow from the Reserve Bank was made, and experience has shown that large borrowings in New York City have in the past usually been explained by the member bank as caused by the borrowing operations of the Treasury, by seasonal demands, but more frequently because of the withdrawal of deposits.

Moreover, Strong said (Chandler 1958, p. 196):

> [I]n the long run, it is my belief that the greatest influence upon the member bank in adjusting its daily position is the influence of profit or loss . . . It may, therefore, be safely stated that as business expands . . . member banks will borrow from the Reserve Banks to make good deficient reserves caused by the expansion of their loans . . . [I]f borrowing at the Reserve Bank is profitable beyond a certain point, there will be strong temptation to use surplus reserves when they arise for the purpose of making additional loans rather than for repaying the Reserve Bank.

And Strong testified before the House Banking Committee in 1926 (United States House of Representatives 1926, p. 345):

> When the country banks borrow of the reserve banks and continue to borrow for a long period, we generally try to find out what the occasion of the borrowing is. It may be that they are borrowing from us just to buy securities . . . It frequently occurs that member banks who have stock exchange loans have to borrow from us for at least one day . . . They frequently borrow for longer periods before calling their stock exchange loans.

Thus, while Riefler's theory recognized that the decision to borrow further or reduce outstanding discounts depended upon the relative cost of doing so, it did not

---

fell below \$400 million during the year. From January 1930 through September 1931 the Fed bought \$290 million of securities. Although borrowed reserves totaled \$500 million in January 1930, they declined sharply and averaged \$243 million through September 1931. Moreover, major banks in New York City were entirely out of debt throughout much of this period, and had accumulated excess reserves. Thus to the Fed, money appeared much easier in 1930–31 than it had in either 1924 or 1927.

recognize that banks would borrow expressly to increase their earning assets. Strong seems to make this link, however. But Brunner and Meltzer (1968) contend that Strong's view of member bank borrowing was consistent with Riefler's.[4] A statement by Strong to the Governors Conference in 1926 supports their contention (Chandler 1958, p. 239):

> Experience in the past has indicated that member banks when indebted to the Federal Reserve Bank of New York . . . constantly endeavor to free themselves from the indebtedness, and as a consequence such pressure as arises is in the direction of curtailing loans.

Although these statements are somewhat contradictory, it does seem that Strong was aware that banks borrowed reserves to extend new loans and to pursue profitable investments. But he also viewed member bank borrowing as an appropriate policy guide and as central to the transmission of monetary policy to credit markets. Apparently Strong did not reject the use of borrowed reserves as a policy guide, despite the implication that if banks do borrow to extend new loans, then the level of borrowing will not reflect monetary conditions accurately.[5]

The Real Bills Doctrine, upon which the Fed's founders intended the System to operate, implies that member bank borrowing should decline during recessions since a lower level of economic activity requires less Federal Reserve credit to sustain it. Most Fed officials believed it was appropriate that Federal Reserve credit contract during recessions. Indeed a minority of these officials argued for open-market sales to hasten the decline.[6] Strong believed that open-market purchases should be made during recessions, but he did not advocate increases in total Federal Reserve credit outstanding.

Was the Fed's theory of the transmission process and its interpretation of member bank borrowing during the depression consistent with that of 1924–29? An answer to this question would provide considerable evidence for the debate over policy consistency.

Wicker (1966) and Brunner and Meltzer (1968) argue that there was no inconsistency in Fed behavior between the 1920s and early 1930s. Referring to open-market policy in 1930, Wicker writes (1966, p. 156):

> [T]he New York (Federal Reserve) Bank did not . . . contemplate substantial purchases of government securities. Its objective was limited in scope and did not go beyond the goal set out by . . . Strong in the nineteen-twenties—that is, to eliminate the indebtedness of the New York and Chicago banks.

However, Schwartz (1981, p. 42) and Epstein and Ferguson (1984, p. 961) contend that officials of the Federal Reserve Bank of New York understood that member bank borrowing was not an appropriate policy guide, but since they do not provide

[4]Brunner and Meltzer refer to this view as the "Riefler-Burgess Doctrine." Meltzer (1976) calls it the "Riefler-Burgess-Strong" analysis.

[5]Of course, I have had to be selective in my quotations. See Strong's testimony in United States House of Representatives (1926), Chandler (1958), Friedman and Schwartz (1963, chapter 6) and Wicker (1966) for more extensive evidence on Strong's views.

[6]See United States Senate (1931) for an interesting compilation of the views of the various Reserve Banks.

direct quotes it is difficult to know precisely the views of these officials. Friedman and Schwartz (1963, p. 370) cite a July 1930 statement by George Harrison, who became Governor of the Federal Reserve Bank of New York after Strong's death, which suggests that he understood this error: "An even small amount of borrowing under present conditions is as effective a restraint as substantially a greater amount was a year ago." But Wicker (1966, pp. 156–57) shows that Harrison ceased to advocate open-market purchases after member bank borrowing by money center banks had been eliminated.

Another official of the Federal Reserve Bank of New York, W. Randolph Burgess, was among the strongest proponents of open-market purchases during the Depression. But in his book, Burgess (1946, p. 250) indicated clearly that there was no change in Fed behavior between the 1920s and early 1930s:

> From 1922 through 1927 the response of the economic organism to relatively small changes in Federal Reserve policy was extraordinary. But in 1928 and 1929 and later in the depression even the most vigorous measures taken by the Reserve System had relatively little effect. Member bank borrowing, interest rates, and the growth of bank credit did indeed respond in a measure but these in turn failed to influence the country's economy.

To Burgess, there was no inconsistency in the use of monetary policy, only in the economy's response to it.

Burgess (1946, pp. 54, 61) also restated Riefler's model of member bank borrowing:

> Banks usually borrow because their reserves have become impaired; that is, they borrow after the event which makes it necessary. Only rarely do they borrow specifically to lend again . . . (but) There were usually some banks, however, which tended to overuse the borrowing privilege . . . .

His (1946, pp. 220–21) explanation of the relationship between member bank borrowing and interest rates was again the classic Fed theory presented by Riefler:

> When the member banks find themselves continuously in debt at the Reserve Banks, they take steps to pay off that indebtedness. They tend to sell securities, call loans, and restrict their purchases of commercial paper and other investments. The consequence is that when a large number of member banks are in debt, money generally becomes firmer . . . and rates increase. Conversely, when most of the member banks are out of debt . . . money rates . . . become easier. This relationship rests largely on the unwillingness of banks to remain in debt at the Reserve Banks.

Moreover, Burgess (1946, p. 195) argued, "interest rates are a sensitive index of changing credit conditions. They are perhaps the best available measure of the adaptation of the credit supply to the country's needs."

Chandler (1971, pp. 133–59) analyzes the policy views of several Fed officials during the Depression. It is clear from his study that during the early 1930s most believed that money was exceptionally easy since market interest rates and borrowed reserves were low.[7] Federal Reserve publications, such as the *Bulletin,* also

[7]In fact, as Chandler and Epstein and Ferguson (1984) show, some Fed officials argued that open-market purchases would have been harmful, interfering with a process of "liquidation," necessary before

indicate that the Fed believed money was easy during 1930 and during the first eight months of 1931. For example, the October 1930 *Bulletin* (p. 613) states:

> Easy credit conditions at the present time are general throughout the county, as indicated by the small volume of indebtedness of member banks to the reserve banks in all Federal Reserve Districts.

The Fed's use of a free reserves strategy in the 1950s and 1960s was an extension of the strategy developed during the 1920s, and it seems unlikely that the Fed abandoned the strategy during the depression.[8] Undoubtedly the Fed would have been more expansionary, particularly in early 1930, had the Federal Reserve Bank of New York retained its role as System leader. But it does seem that the Fed's failures during the Depression were due largely to its flawed strategy. The central flaw in that strategy was the use of borrowed reserves as a policy guide. The following sections illustrate empirically the errors in the Fed model of the demand for borrowed reserves. The results demonstrate the inadequacies of the Fed's theory and suggest further the causes of monetary policy errors during the Great Depression.

AN ALTERNATIVE MODEL OF THE DEMAND FOR MEMBER BANK BORROWING

The first challenge to the theory of member bank borrowing described by Riefler was from Turner (1938). While Riefler concluded that member bank borrowing was generally unresponsive to the discount rate, or to the difference between the discount rate and market interest rates, Turner reached the opposite conclusion, and went on to describe how banks were responsive to the alternative costs of acquiring reserves. Modern theoretical and empirical studies of member bank borrowing, such as Goldfeld and Kane (1966), Dutkowsky (1984), and Dutkowsky and Foote (1985) derive from Turner's pioneering work.

In the Goldfeld-Kane model a bank is faced with an uncertain reserve need, perhaps due to deposit withdrawals or to the bank's own expansionary activities, which is met either by selling a short-term security or by borrowing from the Fed. The reserve need is assumed to be composed of permanent and transitory components. For the empirical analysis, the bank's expected permanent reserve need is measured as a weighted sum of current and past flows of nonborrowed reserves and the intercept, reflecting the bank's desire to expand its earning assets. Given these flows the bank chooses between selling a security and borrowing, depending upon the spread between the yield on the security and the discount rate. Finally, lagged borrowed reserve levels are included in the model to capture stock adjustment. The Goldfeld-Kane model is thus:

---

the start of a business recovery. For example, Governor James McDougal of the Federal Reserve Bank of Chicago argued against open-market purchases in 1930, claiming, "it would be inadvisable to force additional credit into an already oversupplied market." In 1931 McDougal advocated open-market sales, arguing that the Fed's policies had created artificially easy monetary conditions.

[8]Free reserves equal excess reserves less borrowed reserves. See Meigs (1962) for a discussion of the flaws in a free reserves strategy.

$$B_t = a_0 + a_1(r_m - r_d)_t + \Sigma b_i \Delta R^u{}_{t-i} + \Sigma c_j B\text{·} \&ZZ_{wj} + e_t \, . \quad (1)$$

B = the level of borrowed reserves ;

r_m = market interest rate ;

r_d = Federal Reserve Discount Rate ;

R^u = the level of nonborrowed reserves[9] ;

Δ = first difference operator ;

e = random error with zero mean and constant variance.

The principal difference between this model and that of Riefler (1930) is the explicit incorporation of bank desires to expand their asset portfolios, although Goldfeld and Kane do it rather crudely. This paper uses the Goldfeld-Kane model, but, like Goldfeld (1966), I estimate the change in borrowing (ΔB), rather than the level. This equation is derived simply by subtracting B_{t-1} from each side of the Goldfeld-Kane model. Ignoring lagged changes in nonborrowed reserves and those of more than one period in the level of borrowed reserves, the basic model of the flow of borrowed reserves is thus (time subscripts suppressed):

$$\Delta B = a_0 + a_1 \, (r_m - r_d) + b_0 \Delta R^u + (c_0 - 1)B_{-1} + e \, . \quad (2)$$

Dutkowsky (1984) and Dutkowsky and Foote (1985) have recently extended the Goldfeld-Kane model to account for nonlinearity in the relationship between bank borrowing and the market interest rate–discount rate spread. In addition to the discount rate (and transactions costs), Dutkowsky's model incorporates bank reluctance to borrow from the Fed and Fed surveillance of borrowing banks as additional borrowing costs. These latter costs increase with the level of borrowing, and do so at an increasing rate. Dutkowsky derives a switching model of borrowing in which member bank borrowing is zero below some (positive) rate spread. At higher spreads borrowing is positive, but since the implicit cost of borrowing rises as the level of borrowing increases the relationship between borrowing and the rate spread is nonlinear. Finally, at a sufficiently high rate spread, all of the bank's reserve need will be satisfied by borrowing from the Fed and borrowing will be invariant with respect to the rate spread.

Following Dutkowsky, I incorporate switching behavior and nonlinearity in my econometric analysis of borrowed reserve demand for the 1920s and early 1930s. However, the extent to which the Fed discouraged bank borrowing varied consider-

[9]Goldfeld and Kane did not adjust for changes in required reserves until Aigner and Bryan (1968) noted that such an adjustment should be made. From 1924 through 33 there were no changes in required reserve ratios, but because of flows between different bank classes and types of deposit accounts, there were effectively changes in the required reserve ratio. Unfortunately, the data on types of deposits by bank classes do not exist before 1929 which would allow me to correct nonborrowed reserves for these changes.

ably during these years, and hence the applicability of the reluctance/surveillance costs depends on the specific years studied.

During World War I and in the immediate postwar months, the Federal Reserve encouraged member banks to purchase U.S. government obligations by offering a preferential discount rate on borrowings against these securities. Bank borrowing increased substantially in these years, from $134 million in August 1917 (when monthly data are first available) to a peak of $2,780 million in October 1920 (Board of Governors 1943, p. 369).[10] Although the Reserve Banks initiated significant discount rate increases beginning in November 1919, the preferential rate on borrowings secured by government obligations was not eliminated by all Banks until November 1921 (Board of Governors 1943, p. 423). Thus, at least during the war and for some months after, Fed surveillance and bank reluctance to borrow probably had little, if any, effect on borrowing.

By 1920 the Fed's attitude toward member bank borrowing had begun to change. Although the principal reason for discount rate increases in 1919 and 1920 was to limit further declines in the System's reserve position, Fed officials also hoped to control inflation and stock market speculation by curtailing discount loans (Wicker 1966, pp. 32–45). Debate within the Fed centered on how to provide sufficient credit for Treasury financing operations and other "legitimate" needs, without simultaneously encouraging the use of Fed credit for speculation (Chandler 1958, pp. 153–69).

Throughout the 1920s Fed officials became increasingly concerned with limiting the use of Federal Reserve credit to finance stock market speculation. The disagreement within the Reserve System in 1928 and 1929 about how to control this usage is well known (see Friedman and Schwartz 1963, pp. 254–68, and Wicker 1966, pp. 129–43). The Federal Reserve Board called on the Reserve Banks to refuse loans to any bank carrying stock market loans. Although the Reserve Banks generally favored discount rate hikes to limit borrowing, instead of "direct pressure," they did monitor borrowing banks closely.[11] Certainly Fed surveillance was a non-negligible borrowing cost in these years, and it is appropriate to incorporate this cost in the empirical analysis of member bank borrowing.

In contrast to the Fed's theory of member bank borrowing described by Riefler, Goldfeld and Kane argue that banks might borrow reserves to accommodate customer loan demand.[12] During the 1920s and early 1930s the Fed observed that flows of nonborrowed reserves, generated primarily by open-market operations, gold and currency flows, led to opposite changes in borrowed reserves. System officials inferred that the pressure on bank reserve positions generated by these flows was the principal determinant of bank borrowing. But despite the tendency of member bank borrowing to offset changes in nonborrowed reserves, total banking system reserves

[10]For comparison, total member bank reserves equaled $1,141 million in August 1914 and $1,815 million in October 1920.

[11]In response to a Senate Banking Committee survey in 1931, most of the Reserve Banks indicated that they discouraged continuous borrowing by member banks (United States Senate 1931, pp. 790–92).

[12]Earlier, Hodgman (1961) had argued that bank desires to accommodate customer loan demand is a principal determinant of member bank borrowing. And, Goldfeld (1966) found loan demand to be a significant explanatory variable in his member bank borrowing regression.

were not constant in these years. Member bank borrowing declined during the economic downturns in 1924, 1927, and 1929–31, suggesting that as output fell and the demand for loans declined, banks borrowed less from the Federal Reserve. If not offset, total reserves and perhaps the money supply would have fallen.[13]

The substantial decline in borrowed reserves in the early 1930s was likely due in part to decreased loan demand as output and stock market activity declined. I include changes in bank debits (*Debits*) to capture the influence of economic activity on borrowed reserve demand. Suitable monthly data on loan demand are unavailable for the interwar period, as are estimates of national income. Bank debits have often been used as a proxy for income; moreover, they capture financial transactions and other transfers that are sources of loan demand but are not part of current national income. It is expected that increasing debits meant greater loan demand and hence led to increased member bank borrowing from the Federal Reserve.

A second major flaw in the Fed's model was its failure to account for possible instability in borrowed reserve demand induced by financial crises. Friedman and Schwartz (1963) show that banking panics during the Depression produced sharp declines in the deposit-reserve and deposit-currency ratios. Banks became more conservative and were probably less willing to borrow reserves. Describing the failure of borrowing to increase sufficiently to replace outflows of nonborrowed reserves in late 1931, Friedman and Schwartz (1963, pp. 318–19) write:

> The aversion to borrowing by banks, which the Reserve System had tried to strengthen during the twenties, was still greater at a time when depositors were fearful for the safety of every bank and were scrutinizing balance sheets with great care to see which banks were likely to be the next to go . . . .

The Fed seems to have been oblivious to the effects of these crises, and continued to interpret little borrowing as a sign of extreme monetary ease. I include a dummy variable (D) set equal to 1 during the Depression and to 0 before to test the hypothesis that a downward shift occurred in the borrowed reserve demand function. The complete model of borrowed reserve demand estimated here is thus:

$$\Delta B = \alpha_0 + \alpha_1(r_m - r_d) + \alpha_2 \Delta R^u + \alpha_3 B_{-1} + \alpha_4 \Delta Debits + \alpha_5 D + e_1 \tag{3}$$

where $(r_m - r_d) \leq (r_m - r_d)^*$;

$$\Delta B = \beta_0 + \beta_1 \ln(1 + r_m - r_d) + \beta_2 \Delta R^u + \beta_3 B_{-1} + \beta_4 \Delta Debits + \beta_5 D + e_2 \tag{4}$$

where $(r_m - r_d) > (r_m - r_d)^*$.

[13]As noted above, it is probably extreme to argue that Fed officials were unaware of the procyclical nature of borrowed reserves. However, it is clear that they did view borrowing as an appropriate policy guide and, moreover, that there was no reason to offset declines in borrowed reserves during recessions.

The rate differential $(r_m - r_d)^*$ is the spread at which switching occurs. When the spread is less than or equal to $(r_m - r_d)^*$ borrowing will not be the least-cost means of acquiring reserves, and discount loans will be minimal. In this regime borrowing should not be affected by the particular level of the rate spread, or by the bank's desire to accommodate loan demand. Hence the α coefficients should equal zero. Nevertheless, because the model is estimated with aggregate data these variables are included in equation (3). The particular differential at which switching occurs will differ across banks, so in the aggregate borrowing will likely be somewhat responsive to these variables.[14] Equation (4) models borrowing when the rate spread is above the switchpoint. Following Dutkowsky (1984), I assume the relationship between borrowing and the rate spread is log-linear in this region.[15] The coefficients β_1 and β_4 are expected to be positive, while β_2, β_3, and β_5 are expected to be negative.

ECONOMETRIC RESULTS

Tables 1 and 2 report regression estimates of the demand for member bank borrowing for January 1924–February 1933.[16] Separate results are presented for all member banks in the New York Federal Reserve district (Table 1), and for reporting member banks in New York City (Table 2). On average, the New York district accounted for 25 percent of the borrowing of all U.S. member banks during this period. Moreover, only in this district was the discount rate below the market rate of interest, measured here as the commercial paper rate, during the Depression, and then only through May 1932.

Equation (1.1) is an OLS estimate of the basic Goldfeld-Kane model incorporating bank debits and the Depression dummy variable as additional independent variables, but ignoring the possibility of switching or nonlinearity in the rate spread-borrowing relationship.[17] The Depression dummy is set equal to 0 from January 1924 through November 1929, and equal to 1 from December 1929 through February 1933.[18] All of the regression coefficients have the anticipated signs, and those

[14]See Dutkowsky (1984) and Dutkowsky and Foote (1985) for thorough discussions of the problems of estimating a micro-switching regression model with aggregate data. The latter paper considers the consequences of temporal aggregation in which the interest rate differential varies over the course of the month while the monthly average is used in estimation.

[15]Also like Dutkowsky (1984), I do not attempt to estimate the upper switchpoint, that is, the spread at which banks satisfy all of their reserve needs by borrowing and the demand for borrowed reserves is completely inelastic. Dutkowsky argues that the log-linear form captures adequately the leveling out of borrowing at higher rate differentials.

[16]According to Chandler (1958, p. 199) the Fed had begun to use open-market operations to achieve a variety of policy objectives by January 1924, and was inferring the impact of its operations by observing member bank borrowing. Moreover, the Fed had eliminated the preferential discount rate on borrowing secured by government obligations, and had begun to discourage banks from continuous borrowing. Thus it seems appropriate to use this date as the starting point here. I end with February 1933 since the Banking Panic of March 1933 and subsequent institutional changes greatly affected the environment in which banks operated. In addition, there was little bank borrowing after that date.

[17]Seasonal dummy variables also were included in a second set of estimations which are not reported. They had little explanatory power, and in no way altered qualitatively the results presented in Tables 1 and 2.

[18]The initial break in the stock market occurred in late October 1929 but was followed by other significant declines in November. Thus, I chose to set the dummy equal to 0 in November, rather than

TABLE 1

THE DEMAND FOR MEMBER BANK BORROWING, NEW YORK DISTRICT, JANUARY 1924–FEBRUARY 1933

Dependent Variable: ΔB			
Equation	(1.1)	(1.2)	(1.3)
Intercept	14.40	15.93	2.24
	(6.52)*	(8.18)	(8.82)
$(r_m - r_d)$	13.66	6.31	
	(6.52)*	(8.95)	
$\ln(1 + r_m - r_d)$			52.51
			(17.38)**
B_{-1}	−0.11	−0.17	−0.11
	(0.03)**	(0.09)	(0.03)**
ΔR^u	−0.46	−0.06	−0.64
	(0.04)**	(0.03)	(0.04)**
$\Delta Debits$	0.99	1.72	1.12
	(0.53)	(0.62)*	(0.46)*
D	−10.51	−1.60	−18.60
	(5.81)	(7.38)	(5.34)**
ADJ. R^2	.57	.45	.77
S.E.R.	24.93	10.59	19.96
Observations	109	20	89
Switchpoint[a]		0.13	0.13

NOTES: Standard errors in parentheses. Adj. R^2 is the R^2 adjusted for degrees of freedom. S.E.R. is the standard error of the regression. ** indicates statistically significant at the .01 level. * indicates statistically significant at the .05 level.
[a] estimate of $(r_m - r_d)^*$.
Sources and variable definitions: see appendix.

on rate differential, lagged borrowing, and the flow of nonborrowed reserves are statistically significant.

Equations (1.2) and (1.3) incorporate switching behavior and nonlinearity in the relationship between bank borrowing and the rate differential. The rate spread at which switching occurs, $(r_m - r_d)^*$, is estimated using a search procedure to locate that spread that maximizes the value of the log-likelihood function.[19] Once determined, OLS is used to estimate the upper- and lower-regime regressions. The estimate of $(r_m - r_d)^*$ is 0.13, and the null hypothesis of no switching can be rejected at the .01 level.[20] Further, a test of the hypothesis that the switchpoint equals zero also can be rejected (at the .02, but not .01, level).[21] This suggests that

equal to 1. The results reported in Tables 1 and 2 are qualitatively unaffected by setting the dummy equal to 1 beginning in October, November, or December 1929, or in December 1930, at the end of the first major banking crisis.

[19]Specifically, I searched for the value of $(r_m - r_d)$ that maximizes the sum of the log-likelihood values from estimates of equations (3) and (4). See Johnston (1984, pp. 407–409) and Dutkowsky (1984, pp. 417–18) for a further discussion of this procedure.

[20]The specific null hypothesis is a joint hypothesis of no switching and of the presence of a linear relationship between the rate spread and member bank borrowing. That is, it is a test of the equality of all of the coefficients of equation (1.2) with those of (1.3), with a further restriction that the coefficient on $\ln(1 + r_m - r_d)$ in equation (1.3) equals 0. The likelihood ratio statistic equals 73.812; the chi-square statistic with 7 degrees of freedom equals 18.475 at the .01 level.

[21]The null hypothesis is that the switchpoint equals zero, against the alternative that it equals 0.13. The likelihood ratio statistic equals 5.876; the chi-square statistic with 1 degree of freedom equals 6.635 at the .01 level, and 5.412 at the .02 level.

TABLE 2

THE DEMAND FOR MEMBER BANK BORROWING, NEW YORK CITY, JANUARY 1924–FEBRUARY 1933

Dependent Variable: ΔB			
Equation	(2.1)	(2.2)	(2.3)
Intercept	16.36	13.37	5.42
	(6.48)*	(4.36)**	(10.49)
$(r_m - r_d)$	12.27	0.57	
	(7.17)	(5.13)	
$\ln(1 + r_m - r_d)$			44.81
			(21.24)*
B_{-1}	−0.19	−0.20	−0.18
	(0.05)**	(0.07)*	(0.05)**
ΔR^u	−0.41	0.01	−0.60
	(0.05)**	(0.02)	(0.05)**
$\Delta Debits$	1.05	0.52	1.42
	(0.60)	(0.41)	(0.58)*
D	−16.96	−12.97	−22.81
	(7.12)*	(5.87)*	(7.18)**
Ajd. R^2	.45	.24	.64
S.E.R.	27.26	6.83	24.41
Observations	109	20	89
Switchpoint[a]		0.13	0.13

NOTES: See Table 1.

banks were reluctant to borrow from the Fed even at small positive rate differentials, as Dutkowsky's (1984) model predicts.

Equation (1.2) is an estimate of the borrowed reserve demand function when the rate spread is less than or equal to 0.13 [that is, an estimate of equation (3)]. The coefficient estimates from this regression have the anticipated signs, but only that on bank debits is statistically significant. The general lack of significance is not surprising since at rate spreads below the switchpoint borrowing from the Federal Reserve will not be the least-cost means of obtaining reserves. Equation (1.3) is an estimate of borrowed reserve demand when the rate spread is greater than 0.13 [equation (4)]. All the coefficients, except the intercept, have the correct signs and are significant. The results suggest that for rate spreads above 0.13 bank borrowing was responsive to changes in the rate spread, to the lagged level of borrowing, and to flows of nonborrowed reserves. Moreover, they also indicate that member bank borrowing was related positively to economic activity. As economic activity, and hence loan demand, increased, bank borrowing increased. When economic activity declined, as in the early 1930s, member bank borrowing fell.

The coefficient on the Depression dummy variable suggests that there was a significant down-shift in the borrowed reserves demand function following the stock market crash. As the shocks to the financial system worsened, banks probably became even less willing to borrow reserves. Because of the change in bank willingness to borrow from the Federal Reserve, the level of borrowed reserves became an increasingly inaccurate measure of monetary conditions. Nevertheless, Fed officials continued to interpret little borrowing as a sign of exceptional monetary ease.

Table 2 presents regression estimates of the demand for borrowed reserves by weekly reporting member banks in New York City from January 1924 to February 1933. The rate spread at which switching occurs is again estimated to be 0.13, and the null hypothesis of no switching is rejected at the .01 level.[22] Above this spread, the coefficient estimates all have the anticipated signs and are statistically significant [equation (2.3)]. The results suggest further that borrowing was positively related to changes in economic activity, and that a down-shift in the demand for borrowed reserves occurred during the Depression. And they indicate that the failure of Fed officials to interpret the behavior of borrowed reserves correctly contributed to their belief throughout the Depression that monetary conditions were easy.

CONCLUSION

Despite the economic decline which began in mid-1929, and which accelerated following the stock market crash, the Federal Reserve failed to undertake significant expansionary policies until 1932. Friedman and Schwartz (1963) contend that this inaction during the Depression contrasted sharply with the Fed's prompt and vigorous expansionary policies during recessions in 1924 and 1927. However, this paper argues that the apparent change in Fed behavior might actually have resulted from the System's consistent use of member bank borrowing as a policy guide. Fed officials believed that the decline in borrowed reserves following the stock market crash implied that money and credit were plentiful. So, despite the economic contraction, they saw no need for vigorous action. Fed officials believed that their policies were as responsive to changes in economic activity as they had been during the 1920s.

The Fed's borrowed reserves strategy resulted in procyclical monetary policy. Fed officials judged monetary conditions from the level of bank borrowing. They interpreted relatively heavy borrowing as a sign of tight money, and little borrowing as a sign of ease. As a result, the Fed tended to purchase *fewer* securities the *worse* an economic downturn. During mild recessions, as in 1927, member bank borrowing fell little. The Fed responded with relatively heavy purchases of securities, however, interpreting monetary conditions as tight. But during severe downturns, as in 1930–31, member bank borrowing declined substantially. This caused the Fed to interpret monetary conditions as relatively easy, however, and hence to make comparatively few open market purchases.

As Fed officials observed, this study finds that flows of nonborrowed reserves were a principal determinant of changes in borrowed reserves during the 1920s and early 1930s. However, member bank borrowing did not offset these flows precisely.

[22]The likelihood ratio test statistic equals 74.978, while the chi-square statistic with seven degrees of freedom is 18.475 at the .01 level. It was not possible to test the null hypothesis that the switchpoint equals zero because the only month prior to December 1929 when the rate spread was less than or equal to zero also happened to be the only month when New York City banks borrowed from the Fed at an unfavorable rate spread. Thus the lower regime regression could not be estimated in the case where the switchpoint is set equal to zero.

The Fed's theory failed to consider that banks borrow to meet investment and lending opportunities, and hence it did not capture the procyclical nature of borrowed reserve demand. The evidence presented here indicates that economic activity, as measured by changes in bank debits, did have a significant impact on bank borrowing. As economic activity declined during the Depression, loan demand and investment opportunities shrank, and bank reserve demand fell. Because the Fed failed to replace the decline in reserves, the money supply fell.

This study also finds evidence of a downward shift in borrowed reserve demand during the Depression. Financial crises made banks cautious and less willing to borrow reserves. The Fed's failure to recognize this change in bank willingness to borrow contributed to its failure to interpret monetary conditions accurately. Fed officials continued to believe that low levels of bank borrowing signaled easy money. Thus, the failures of monetary policy during the Depression seem attributable largely to flaws in the Fed's strategy, and especially to its use of member bank borrowing as a policy guide. That strategy appeared to work well during the relatively tranquil 1920s, but failed terribly in the environment of crisis and severe contraction of the Depression.

APPENDIX: VARIABLE DEFINITIONS AND DATA SOURCES

Unless noted otherwise, all of the data are from Board of Governors (1943). Page numbers are for that volume. Data are monthly averages of daily figures and are in $ millions, except for bank debits, which are monthly totals and are in $ billions.

B: Member Bank Borrowed Reserves, pp. 169–78 (New York City reporting banks); Federal Reserve Board *Annual Report* (various years) for New York district member banks.

Debits: Debits to Deposit Accounts in New York City, pp. 234–35; Federal Reserve Board *Annual Report* and *Bulletin* (various issues) for New York district.

r_m: Commercial Paper Interest Rate, pp. 450–51.

D: Dummy variable set equal to 0, January 1924–November 1929, and equal to 1, December 1929–February 1933.

r_d: Federal Reserve Bank of New York Discount Rate, pp. 439–41.

R^u: Member bank nonborrowed reserves. Constructed as the difference between total and borrowed reserves, pp. 169–78 (New York City reporting banks); Federal Reserve Board *Annual Report* (various years) for New York district member banks.

LITERATURE CITED

Aigner, Dennis J., and William R. Bryan. "The Determinants of Member Bank Borrowing: A Critique." *Journal of Finance* 23 (December 1968), 832–37.

Bernanke, Ben S. "Nonmonetary Effects of the Financial Crises in the Propagation of the Great Depression." *American Economic Review* 73 (June 1983), 257–76.

Board of Governors of the Federal Reserve System. *Banking and Monetary Statistics*. 1943.

Brunner, Karl, and Allan H. Meltzer. "What Did We Learn from the Monetary Experience of the United States in the Great Depression?" *Canadian Journal of Economics* 1 (May 1968), 334–48.

Burgess, W. Randolph. *The Reserve Banks and the Money Market,* revised ed. New York: Harper and Brothers, 1946.

Chandler, Lester V. *Benjamin Strong, Central Banker*. Washington: Brookings Institution, 1958.

______. *American Monetary Policy 1928–1941*. New York: Harper and Row, 1971.

Dutkowsky, Donald. "The Demand for Borrowed Reserves: A Switching Regression Model." *Journal of Finance* 39 (June 1984), 407–24.

Dutkowsky, Donald, and William Foote. "Switching, Aggregation, and the Demand for Borrowed Reserves." *Review of Economics and Statistics* 67 (May 1985), 331–35.

Epstein, Gerald, and Thomas Ferguson. "Monetary Policy, Loan Liquidation, and Industrial Conflict: The Federal Reserve and the Open-Market Operations of 1932." *Journal of Economic History* 44 (December 1984), 957–83.

Federal Reserve Board. *Annual Report* (various issues).

Federal Reserve Board. *Bulletin* (various issues).

Field, Alexander J. "Asset Exchanges and the Transactions Demand for Money, 1919–1929." *American Economic Review* 74 (March 1984), 43–59.(a)

______. "A New Interpretation of the Onset of the Great Depression." *Journal of Economic History* 44 (June 1984), 489–98.(b)

Friedman, Milton, and Anna J. Schwartz. *A Monetary History of the United States, 1867–1960*. Princeton: Princeton University Press, 1963.

Goldfeld, Stephen M. *Commercial Bank Behavior and Economic Activity*. Amsterdam: North-Holland, 1966.

Goldfeld, Stephen M., and Edward J. Kane. "The Determinants of Member Bank Borrowing: An Econometric Study." *Journal of Finance* 21 (September 1966), 499–514.

Hamilton, James D. "Monetary Factors in the Great Depression." *Journal of Monetary Economics* 19 (March 1987), 145–69.

Hodgman, Donald. "Member Bank Borrowing: A Comment." *Journal of Finance* 16 (March 1961), 90–93.

Johnston, John. *Econometric Methods,* 3rd ed. New York: McGraw Hill Book Company, 1984.

Meigs, A. James. *Free Reserves and the Money Supply*. Chicago: University of Chicago Press, 1962.

Meltzer, Allan H. "Monetary and Other Explanations of the Start of the Great Depression." *Journal of Monetary Economics* 2 (November 1976), 455–71.

Miron, Jeffrey A. "The Founding of the Fed and the Destabilization of the Post-1914 Economy." National Bureau of Economic Research Working Paper no. 2701 (1988).

Riefler, Winfield. *Money Rates and Money Markets in the United States*. New York: Harper and Brothers, 1930.

Schwartz, Anna J. "Understanding 1929–1933." In *The Great Depression Revisited,* edited by Karl Brunner, pp. 5–48. Boston: Martinus-Nijhoff, 1981.

Strong, Benjamin. Testimony in Hearings before the U.S. House of Representatives Committee on Banking and Currency: *Stabilization,* p. 468. 69th Congress, 1st Session, 1926.

Thornton, Daniel L. "The Borrowed-Reserves Operating Procedure: Theory and Evidence." *Review,* Federal Reserve Bank of St. Louis (January/February 1988), 30–54.

Toma, Mark. "The Policy Effectiveness of Open Market Operations in the 1920s." *Explorations in Economic History* 26 (January 1989), 99–116.

Turner, Robert C. *Member Bank Borrowing*. Columbus: Ohio State University, 1938.

United States House of Representatives. *Stabilization*. Hearings before the Committee on Banking and Currency. 69th Congress, 1st Session, 1926, p. 468.

United States Senate. *Operation of the National and Federal Reserve Banking Systems*. Committee on Banking and Currency. 71st Congress, 3rd Session, 1931.

Wheelock, David C. "The Strategy, Effectiveness, and Consistency of Federal Reserve Monetary Policy 1924–1933." *Explorations in Economic History* 26 (October 1989), 453–76.

Wicker, Elmus. *Federal Reserve Monetary Policy 1917–1933*. New York: Random House, 1966.

VINCENT REINHART

Targeting Nominal Income in a Dynamic Model

1. INTRODUCTION

THE PROBLEMS OF MONETARY CONTROL in the 1980s have led to a search for alternative policy rules. Many economists, including Tobin (1983), Hall (1983), Gordon (1985), and McCallum (1988), advocate monitoring the performance of nominal income. While the specifics of their proposals differ, all these theorists emphasize that altering the stock of money in response to changes in nominal income avoids the unpredictable shifts in velocity that play havoc with simple money growth rules.

This paper follows Taylor's (1985) advice and judges a nominal income rule by its effects on the dynamics of the economy, using a perfect-foresight planning model that combines the important contributions of Kimbrough (1986a and b) and Calvo (1983a and b). First, following Kimbrough, money plays an essential role in the economy because real balances help households economize on making transactions.[1] By using explicit functional forms, we derive an exact specification of the desired paths of consumption and real balances. Second, following Calvo, the monetary policymaker plays an essential role because prices are bound by contracts set at staggered and overlapping intervals (as in Taylor 1980). Staggered contracting

The author thanks participants at the December 1989 Monetary Affairs Workshop on "Asset Prices and the Conduct of Monetary Policy," particularly E. S. Phelps. The author has also benefitted from comments from three referees. The views expressed do not necessarily reflect the views of the Federal Reserve Board or any other members of its staff.

[1]Also see the discussion in McCallum (1983) and the work of Romer (1986 and 1987) and Vegh (1989).

VINCENT REINHART *is economist in the Division of Monetary Affairs, Board of Governors of the Federal Reserve System.*

Journal of Money, Credit, and Banking, Vol. 22, No. 4 (November 1990)

imparts inertia to the price level that allows both nominal and real shocks, in the absence of a policy response, to have persistent real effects. We use this model to determine which monetary policy rule—constant growth in the money stock or nominal income—provides the more appropriate response to disturbances.

In a world with sticky prices, a rule that smooths a nominal magnitude, whether money or income, effectively smooths a real magnitude. For certain shocks, such a rule may prolong the transition because it interferes with the private sector's efforts to adjust. We provide a natural pairing:

- Real balances adjust more in response to a financial shock; a nominal-income rule allows the more immediate adjustment because it smooths real income.
- Real income adjusts more in response to a supply shock; a nominal-money rule allows the more immediate adjustment because it smooths real balances.

The following section details the household planning problem and the macroeconomic structure of continuous market clearing under nominal goods-price contracting. The next section compares a fixed-money-growth rule to a fixed nominal-income-growth rule; the steady-state effects are derived explicitly and representative transition dynamics are calculated. Section 4 offers concluding comments.

2. THE MODEL

In this section we specify the household planning problem and detail the macroeconomic background of staggered contracting. Essentially, trade is decentralized so that a consumer carries money to transact with a given firm in the particular market he or she happens to sample; that firm varies its posted price infrequently. At any point in time, there is a well-defined demand for nominal money balances and an overall price level inherited from past contracting decisions. Over time, money balances vary according to an optimal plan and goods prices vary with new contract decisions.

A. Households

We adopt Kimbrough's (1986a and b) strategem to capture why money is essential in an optimizing world: Holding money balances facilitates transactions. Specifically, the cost of transacting at time t, T_t, directly subtracts from potential goods output, y_t. We further simplify Kimbrough's structure by requiring that transactions cost per unit of potential output is quadratic in velocity measured at potential; transactions costs equal,

$$T_t = (k/2) \cdot (y_t/x_t)^2 \cdot y_t \, ; \tag{1}$$

where x is real money balances measured in terms of the prices that this representative agent transacts at and k is a positive constant. Blanchard and Fischer (1989, pp. 58–69) provide a discussion (for the capital stock decision) of optimizing behavior given transactions costs. Equation (1) satisfies the properties of liquidity cost functions required in Feenstra (1986, assumption 1), who also shows that this form is consistent with Barro's (1976) generalized transactions model.

The representative infinitely lived household plans a consumption and real balance path to maximize:

$$\int_0^\infty u(c_s)\, e^{-\rho s} ds \,, \tag{2}$$

subject to a flow budget restraint,

$$Dx = y_t - T_t - c_t - \pi_t x_t - \tau_t \,; \tag{3}$$

where c = consumption per unit time;

π_t = instantaneous inflation rate of the prices of goods this representative agent transacts at;

τ_t = lump-sum transfers or taxes;

ρ = constant rate of time preference;

$u(\cdot)$ is a fully continuous, twice-differentiable function that satisfies the usual conditions; and D defines the time derivative.[2]

Combining (1), (2), and (3) and introducing the costate variable, λ_t, leads to the Hamiltonian,

$$H = u(c_t)\, e^{-\rho t} + \lambda_t[y_t - (k/2) \cdot (y_t/x_t)^2 \cdot y_t - c_t - \pi_t x_t - \tau_t] \,.$$

Necessary conditions for an optimum by the methods of optimal control are[3]

$$\lambda_t = u'\, e^{-\rho t} \text{ ; and}$$

$$D\lambda_t = -\lambda_t[(y_t/x_t)^3 - \pi_t] \,.$$

Any path that satisfies these conditions, the flow constraint (3), and that converges to a steady state fulfills the sufficiency theorem of optimal control and qualifies as a solution to the planning problem.

We can eliminate the costate variable to arrive at the driving equation for consumer choice,

$$Dc = (u'/u'') \cdot [(\rho + \pi_t) - k \cdot (y_t/x_t)^3] \,. \tag{4}$$

[2]See Calvo (1979) for examples of the household's optimization problem in a monetary economy. Calvo (1983a) introduces money in a contracting model through Sidrauski's device of including it in the utility function.

[3]See Kamien and Schwartz (1981, pp. 111–24).

The household varies its consumption spending (thus altering its acquisition of the asset, money) when the opportunity cost of holding real balances, $\rho + \pi$, differs from money's marginal usefulness in lowering the cost of trade.

Independent of the form of $u(\cdot)$, the model produces a steady-state relationship between real balances, income, and the nominal rate reminiscent of the Baumol-Tobin inventory theoretic equation:

$$x_0 = y_0[k/(\rho + \pi_0)]^{1/3} ,$$

where the zero subscript denotes a steady-state value. This long-run "money-demand" relationship exhibits an income elasticity equal to one and an interest elasticity equal to $-1/3$.

The dynamic path of consumption and real balances depends on the complete model, and it will simplify matters to assume a specific form for utility; let instantaneous utility belong to the constant-relative-risk-aversion class,

$$u(c) = \begin{cases} c^{1-\gamma}/(1 - \gamma) , & 0 > \gamma < 1 , \text{ or } \gamma > 1 , \\ \ln(c) , & \gamma = 1 . \end{cases}$$

Equation (4) becomes

$$Dc_t/c_t = [k(y_t/x_t)^3 - (\rho + \pi_t)]/\lambda , \tag{4'}$$

and holds that consumption growth is directly proportional to the spread of the marginal cost of transacting over the nominal interest rate.

B. The Firm Pricing Decision

We follow the Phelps and Taylor assumption that prices are set by contracts negotiated at staggered and overlapping intervals (Phelps 1979, pp. 1–19, and Taylor 1980). The emergence of excess demand requires that all agents raise the prices of the goods that they sell, but they can not all do so at once; agents can only change their prices when they negotiate a new contract. The first contracting parties raise their prices relative to the old price structure. Thus, the marginal price change, π, adjusts freely on impact; since new contracts are only a small part of the total set of goods, the average price level, which is a weighted average of old and new contracts, will move continuously through time. As time elapses, more and more agents respond to the excess demand so that the discrepancy between new price bargains and the existing rate of increase in prices declines. Thus, the logic of the Phelps-Taylor model makes the *change* in inflation a negative function of excess demand.

Calvo has applied this structure to a continuous-time model (Calvo 1983a and 1983b; also see Blanchard and Fischer, 1989 for a discussion). Assume that newly negotiated contracts depend on current excess demand with sensitivity β, and any contract may come up for renewal in a given time interval with an instantaneous "failure rate" equal to δ.[4] The average life of a contract will equal $1/\delta$. Calvo has shown that the inflation rate evolves according to

$$D\pi = -b \cdot (Excess\ demand)\ ; \tag{5}$$

where $b = \delta^2\beta$. Again, as in the Phelps-Taylor discrete-time model, the change in the inflation rate is negatively related to excess demand.

An important micro-mechanism has not yet been specified. In a given interval, households may transact with a firm that prices differently than the overall price index, depending on when that firm last contracted. This suggests that the household may search over a range of price offers. Further, there may be "false trading" in which individual transactions take place at prices which, given an ability to sample more markets, one party would regret. A complete specification would require modeling household search, the firm's potential pricing strategy, and the transfers associated with false trading. The sluggishness of prices introduce enough interesting macroeconomic dimensions to assume these other complications away.

We follow Calvo (1983a) and posit that a "price regulating mechanism" exists that generates lump-sum taxes or transfers which equate the prices individual households pay with the overall price index.[5] Equivalently, we could assume that households enter an actuarially fair price-insurance system that levies fees and pays benefits that have the effect of equalizing prices. This assumption focuses attention on one imperfection implied by the presence of contracts, namely, the rigidity of prices, and allows us to set the price our representative agent transacts at equal to the general price level, p_t.

C. Market Dynamics

Our solution to the planning problem explains a household's desired consumption. We assert that government purchases, g_t, are perfectly wasteful and do not substitute for private consumption. Aggregating over all households in a given time interval, total goods demand equals $c_t + g_t$. Time spent transacting directly deducts from potential output so that the economy faces the capacity constraint,

$$y_t - T_t = [1 - (k/2) \cdot (x_t/y_t)^2] \cdot y_t\ ,$$

leading to the natural definition of excess demand,

$$c_t + g_t - [1 - (k/2) \cdot (x_t/y_t)^2] \cdot y_t\ .$$

[4]Technically, contract life follows a negative-exponential distribution; for a discussion of the underlying assumptions and properties of such a probability process, see Lindgren (1968, pp. 161–67).

[5]Seen in the term τ_t in equation (3).

In what follows, transaction-cost-free potential output, y_t, will be held fixed at y and government purchases will be held fixed at g.

At a point in time, the price level is predetermined so that aggregate demand determines output; over time, the price level adjusts in response to excess demand as specified in the staggered contracting mechanism. The inflation determination equation (5) may be rewritten

$$D\pi_t = b\{[1 - (k/2) \cdot (x_t/y)^2] \cdot y - c_t - g\} , \qquad (6)$$

to arrive at a differential equation in π, c, and x. The next section examines alternative policy rules to close the model.

3. POLICY ALTERNATIVES

A. Controlling Money Growth

The simplest policy rule sets the growth of the nominal stock of money equal to a constant, μ. Real balances evolve over time according to

$$Dx/x = \mu - \pi , \qquad (7)$$

so that, when combined with the planning rule in equation (4′) and the inflation relationship in equation (6), we have a complete dynamic system.[6]

The model can be solved recursively for all steady-state relationships. In the long run, real balances are constant so that

$$\pi_0 = \mu .$$

The level of real balances follows a cube-root law,

$$x_0 = y\ [k/(\rho + \mu)]^{1/3} ,$$

or, in terms of the velocity of money, v,

$$v_0 = [(\rho + \mu)/k]^{1/3} .$$

Given the transactions costs incurred, consumption is determined as

$$c_0 = \{1 - (k/2) \cdot [(\rho + \mu)/k]^{2/3}\} \cdot y - g .$$

This form makes plain the welfare loss associated with inflation (detailed in Kimbrough 1986b, pp. 133–35). Steady-state consumption declines as inflation

[6]Where possible, we suppress time subscripts.

TABLE 1

LONG-TERM MULTIPLIERS

The steady-state effects of a permanent one-unit change:		
in:	on:	
	---x_0---	---c_0---
g	0	-1
y	$1/v_0$	$1 - T_0/y$
k	$x_0/(3\,k)$	$-y\,v_0^2/6$
μ	$-x_0/[3(\rho + \mu)]$	$-x_0/3$

increases because households use resources to economize on real balances. While potential output is fixed, actual spending adjusted for resources used in transacting varies with the long-term inflation rate. Thus, the model suggests that the central bank's choice of μ has steady-state consequences for real variables, including velocity and real income—money is not superneutral. Geweke's (1986) examination of the U.S. data found that velocity does depend on money growth in the long run, supporting this model's prediction, but that money is superneutral with respect to output.

Four types of shocks may disturb this long-term macroeconomic equilibrium: (i) a supply disturbance, dy; (ii) a financial innovation that alters the cost to transacting, dk; (iii) a fiscal change, dg; and (iv) a change in the steady-state inflation goal, $d\mu$. Table 1 summarizes the impacts that these changes would have relative to an initial steady state at (x_0, c_0).

To get to a new long run, however, requires a transition. The policy rule makes nominal money balances continuous and combines with price-setting behavior to make real balances continuous. Any of the disturbances in the first column of Table 1 that makes real balances different from its steady-state value calls forth a dynamic adjustment. Both the initial levels of π, since it is determined by new contract decisions, and c, since it is set at the start of a new planning horizon, are free to jump at the onset of a shock. Thereafter, all three variables must move continuously along a perfect-foresight path.

Linearizing about the steady state, the movement in (c, π, x) can be written

$$\begin{bmatrix} Dc \\ D\pi \\ Dx \end{bmatrix} = \begin{bmatrix} 0 & -1/\gamma & -3(\rho + \mu)/\gamma x_0 \\ -b & 0 & b(\rho + \mu) \\ 0 & -1 & 0 \end{bmatrix} \begin{bmatrix} c - c_0 \\ \pi - \pi_0 \\ x - x_0 \end{bmatrix} . \tag{8}$$

[7]This follows because the determinant equals the product of the characteristic roots and the trace equals the sum of the characteristic roots. For a general discussion, see Hirsch and Smale (1974, pp. 47–55).

[8]Since the characteristic vector **l** is unique only to a scalar multiplication, we normalize by setting $l_3 = 1$.

The dynamics of this system depend on the characteristic roots of the transition matrix; since the determinant, Δ, is negative,

$$\Delta = -3\, b\, (\rho + \mu)/(\gamma\, x_0) < 0 \; ;$$

and the trace is zero, there must be one negative and two positive characteristic roots.[7] Thus, this system exhibits saddlepath stability: For any inherited level of real balances, there is a single (c, π) pair that moves the system to the steady state.

The exact solution to this system depends on the negative characteristic root, say ζ, and its associated three-element characteristic vector, $\mathbf{l} = (l_1, l_2, 1)$.[8] If a disturbance at time $t = 0$ makes x different from x_0 (say x'), the dynamics along a stable transit back to the steady state takes the form

$$\begin{bmatrix} c_t \\ \pi_t \\ x_t \end{bmatrix} = \begin{bmatrix} c_0 \\ \pi_0 \\ x_0 \end{bmatrix} + \begin{bmatrix} l_1 \\ l_2 \\ 1 \end{bmatrix} \cdot [x' - x_0] \cdot e^{\zeta t} \; . \tag{9}$$

Since ζ is negative, the dynamic variables decay back to their steady state. The values of l_1 and l_2 dictate the extent of the jumps in c and π required at the instant of the shock. However, before we describe that transition path more fully, we first examine a much-advocated alternative policy.

B. Controlling Income Growth

Many economists favor a rule that fixes nominal income to a constant growth path. Let us assume that the monetary authority requires the same steady-state inflation target, μ, so that the rule takes the form,

$$\pi_t + Dc_t/c_t + Dg_t/g_t = \mu \; ,$$

along with the initial condition that nominal income cannot move discretely. Since g is held fixed, the policy rule may be expressed in terms of nominal consumption growth.[9] Using our explanation for real consumption growth,

$$\pi + Dc/c = \mu = \pi + [k(y/x)^3 - (\rho + \pi)]/\gamma \; ,$$

this equation defines an implicit relationship for real balances in terms of π and behavioral and policy parameters that must hold at each instant in time. A nominal-income rule shifts some of the burden of adjustment from households to the central bank. The rule imposes smooth aggregate consumption, which must be made con-

[9]As discussed below, an unexpected change in the level of government spending has an impact on initial conditions, not the subsequent movement in variables.

sistent with households' individual desires for an optimal consumption path by central bank action varying asset stocks.

This form highlights the information requirements of a strict nominal-income rule. Rather than the passive fixing of money, central bank action counters contemporaneous disturbances using full knowledge of the structural parameters. We simply assert, within this perfect-foresight setting, that these information requirements are met. The practical application of nominal-income targeting requires a more detailed specification of the rule. For example, McCallum (1988) suggests an explicit feedback form involving reserves and lagged nominal income, while Alogoskoufis (1989) examines the problem of imperfect monetary control.

Real balances at each point in time equal

$$x = y \cdot \{k/[\rho + \pi + \gamma(\mu - \pi)]\}^{1/3} , \tag{10}$$

which shows that a nominal-income rule forces the central bank to offset any systematic effects of inflation on real balances.[10] However, the presence of this inflation effect depends on the degree of relative risk aversion. If, for example, $\gamma = 1$, agents would not vary their holdings of real balances from their steady-state value along an optimal path; the central bank's policy rule would reduce to always maintaining real balances at their long-term level.

In the more likely case of greater risk aversion ($\gamma > 1$), the central bank accommodates a short-term increase in inflation with an increase in real balances, $\partial x/\partial\pi > 0$. Along a transition path, private planners must balance their desires to smooth consumption and economize on cash balances; the more they value consumption smoothing (the higher is γ), the more they vary their real balances. Under nominal-income targeting, the central bank assists the smoothing process by varying the nominal money stock with inflation.

This explanation for real balances can be substituted into the inflation equation,

$$D\pi = b\{[1 - (k/2)\{\gamma\mu + \rho + (1 - \gamma)\pi\}^{2/3}] \cdot y - c - g\} ,$$

which, with the policy rule,

$$Dc/c = \mu - \pi ,$$

gives us a two-variable dynamic system in c and π.

Both μ percent rules arrive at the same steady state, but the dynamics are quite different. Under a nominal-income rule, at the onset of a shock, inflation adjusts (as do, by equation (10), real balances) but the price level does not move; it only adjusts over time when contracts are revised. Thus, smoothing nominal consumption also smooths real consumption, so that any unexpected shock sets off a dynamic adjust-

[10]Dornbusch and Frankel (1988), using a model with ad hoc behavioral relationships, emphasize this point.

ment if it makes consumption different from its steady-state value. The dynamic response to a shock depends on how the initial level of consumption differs from its steady-state level; we must now refer to the second column in Table 1 to describe an initial perturbation.

A linear approximation to dynamics about the steady state takes the form:

$$\begin{bmatrix} Dc \\ D\pi \end{bmatrix} = \begin{bmatrix} 0 & -1 \\ -b & bkx_0(\gamma - 1)/3 \end{bmatrix} \begin{bmatrix} c - c_0 \\ \pi - \pi_0 \end{bmatrix} . \tag{11}$$

Since the determinant of the transition matrix equals $-b$ there must be opposite-signed characteristic roots. Once again, the requirement that the system be stable uniquely determines the jump variable $\pi - \pi_0$, given an inherited value of $c - c_0$. We find that an income rule is well defined. Indeed, both μ percent rules are stable and lead to a unique equilibrium for all values of the behavioral parameters. However, the rules enforce different paths on real as well as nominal magnitudes.

The explicit paths for c and π can be written in terms of the negative characteristic root, ν, and its corresponding two-element characteristic vector, $\mathbf{n}$. If a disturbance at time $t = 0$ makes c different from c_0 (say c'), the dynamic motion will be

$$\begin{bmatrix} c_t \\ \pi_t \end{bmatrix} = \begin{bmatrix} c_0 \\ \pi_0 \end{bmatrix} + \begin{bmatrix} 1 \\ n_2 \end{bmatrix} \cdot [c' - c_0] \cdot e^{\nu t} . \tag{12}$$

The element n_2 determines the extent to which π jumps in response to a shock to c.

C. Comparing Control of Nominal Magnitudes

In our framework, controlling nominal money growth versus nominal income growth differs by

- the real magnitude that is made continuous (x or c);
- the size of the shock that disturbs an initial rest point (measured in the first relative to the second columns of Table 1); and
- the speed of adjustment, governed by the explicit solutions, equations (9) or (12).

This section examines the responses under alternative rules given a permanent change in potential output and a financial innovation.

As Table 1 shows, an increase in potential output requires higher steady-state real balances to support more transactions; the extent of that increase depends on long-term income velocity (which depends only on k, μ, and ρ, independent of the level of income). Steady-state consumption, on the other hand, increases by the rise in potential (less the added transactions costs incurred). Starting from an initial steady state disturbed by an increase in y, the transition under a nominal-money-growth rule depends on how long it takes the initial shock to real balances, Δx_0, to decay at the rate ζ. According to equation (9), consumption moves up discretely by the amount $l_2 \cdot \Delta x_0$ and subsequently moves with x. Under a nominal-income-growth rule, the transition depends on how long it takes the initial shock to consumption, Δc_0, to decay at the rate ν.

Unfortunately, there is no easy analytic form for the negative roots, ζ and ν. If the constant of relative risk aversion equals one, then, as shown in the appendix, the income target allows shocks to decay faster, $|\nu| > |\zeta|$. Table 2 presents calculations of these roots for more general cases, assuming that income velocity equals two when the long-term nominal interest rate is 10 percent. In general, as long as agents are sufficiently risk averse, $\gamma \geq 1$, the nominal-income root is larger (in absolute value). Persistence increases (the roots become smaller in absolute value) for both regimes as contracts become longer and the constant of relative risk aversion increases.

The upper panel of Figure 1 plots out the dynamic path of consumption after a one-unit permanent increase in potential output, when contracts last an average of three years and the risk aversion term equals two. Consumption will have to increase by $1 - (T_0/y)$ overall. If policy constrains nominal income to be continuous, that adjustment must take place as the initial gap decays at the rate ν; the path for c is given by the dashed line in the figure. Along that transition, deficient demand sends inflation below its steady-state level. Since π is below μ, nominal-income rule requires policymakers to contract the nominal-money stock so that x follows the path given in equation (10). Central bank action, restraining real balances, moves away rather than toward the steady state.

If real balances are constrained to be continuous, the level of real balances moves by the μ percent rule, not equation (10), and will be above the level required by the

TABLE 2

Absolute Value of the Negative Characteristic Root

Contract Life (δ)	Fixed Money Growth Coefficient of Relative Risk Aversion (γ)		
	1/2	2	4
3 years	0.33	0.15	0.10
2 years	0.49	0.23	0.14
1 year	0.98	0.45	0.28
1/2 year	1.95	0.90	0.55
Contract Life (δ)	**Fixed Income Growth Coefficient of Relative Risk Aversion (γ)**		
	1/2	2	4
3 years	0.24	0.23	0.22
2 years	0.36	0.34	0.32
1 year	0.73	0.66	0.57
1/2 year	1.52	1.22	0.92

Note: Behavioral and policy parameters are set as follows:

$y = 100$ $\rho = 0.05$
$g = 20$ $\beta = 1/2$
$\mu = 0.05$ $k = 0.0125$

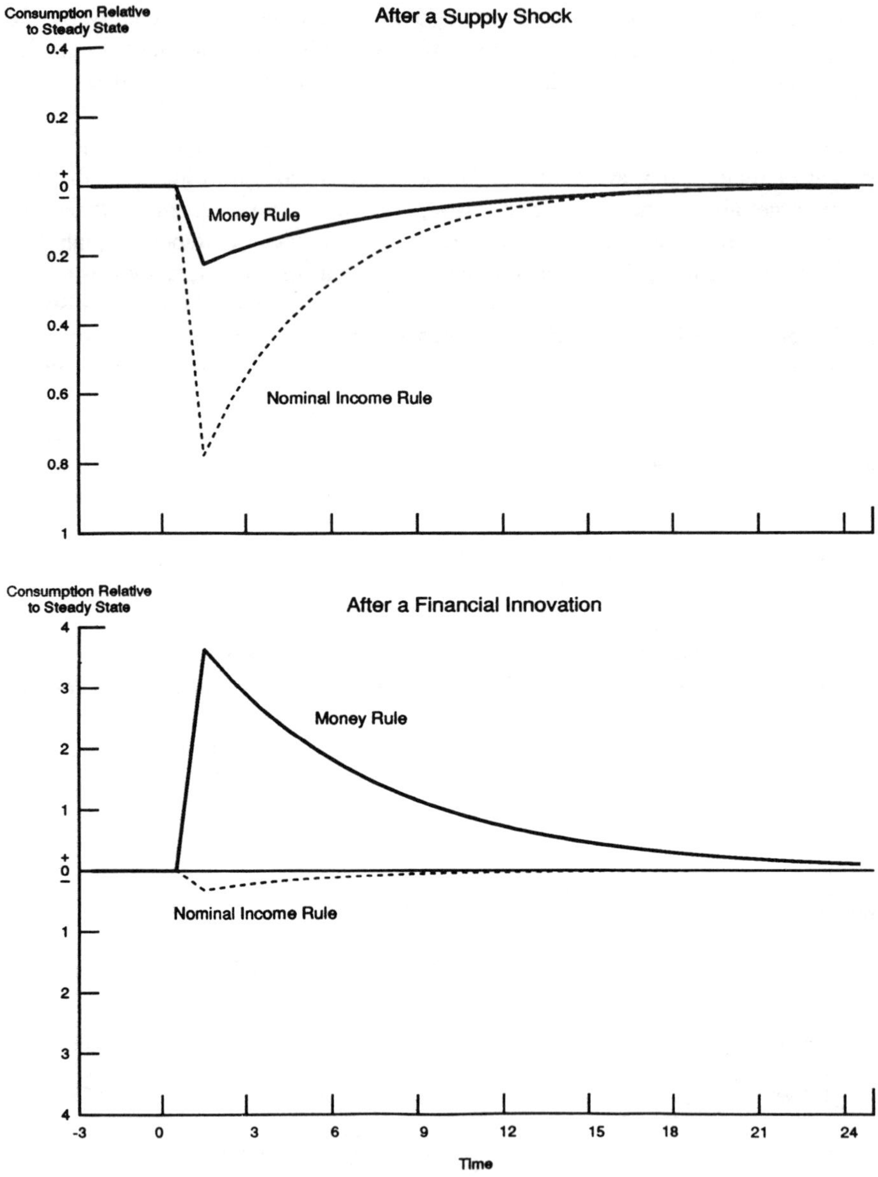

FIG. 1. Response to a Supply Shock and a Financial Innovation.

nominal-income rule; without the restraining action mandated by an income target, on knowledge that y has increased, consumption jumps to reduce the gap relative to the steady-state value $c - c_0$ and subsequently follows the path given by the solid line in Figure 1.[11]

Using the same behavioral parameters, the lower panel of Figure 1 plots out the consequences of a financial innovation that serves to raise the steady-state income velocity from 2 to 2.5.[12] As Table 1 shows, such an innovation lowers steady-state real balances and raises steady-state consumption. Simply, lower transactions costs allow agents to economize more on their holding of real balances and still enjoy higher consumption.

Under a μ percent money growth rule, this financial innovation reduces the long-run relative to the current level of real balances. Central bank action, however, holds the numerator of that variable to a constant growth path. Accordingly, households temporarily increase their consumption spending in an attempt to run down their stock of real balances; this creates excess demand and inflation moves above its steady-state level. Thus, the transition is engineered by private sector action which creates inflation that erodes the too-high stock of real balances; the discrete upward jump in consumption and subsequent transit back to the steady state is given by the solid line in the lower panel of Figure 1. Note that nominal income moves with real consumption, rising discretely with the financial innovation.

Under a μ percent nominal-income rule, the dynamics are driven by the behavior of consumption relative to its steady state, equation (10). Lower transactions costs ultimately promise higher consumption, so that the initial shock to the system is a too-low level of current consumption relative to the long run (the dashed line in the lower panel of the figure). Inflation falls on impact and part of the required adjustment in real balances to their lower long-term level comes immediately as the central bank lowers the nominal money stock.

The paths of the key macro variables in response to a financial shock are markedly different under the two regimes. A money-growth rule communicates a financial shock to the real sector, requiring consumption to adjust asset stocks over time. Our simulations suggest that the results include substantial excess demand and inflation. On the other hand, a nominal-income rule proves the more effective stabilizer because central bank action to smooth consumption delays when households actually take advantage of the higher level of potential output associated with lower transaction costs. Consumption increases only as inflation slows (to keep nominal consumption growing along trend), with the transition lasting until the cumulated below-μ inflation equals the required steady-state gain in real consumption.

Since instantaneous utility only depends on consumption and consumption follows a monotonic path, comparisons of lifetime utility are simple, if not always interesting. After a supply shock, as in the upper panel of Figure 1, consumption falls by more at first and is lower throughout the transition under the nominal-

[11]Clearly then, if $\gamma < 1$, real balances are higher under a nominal-income rule so that c lies above the path implied by a money rule.

[12]k falls 0.0061 to 0.0064.

income rule; appropriately discounted at the rate δ, as in equation (2), lifetime household utility must be lower under the nominal-income rule rather than under a money rule. This result could be quantified to match the calculated roots in Table 2, but another exercise suggests caution.

For a permanent financial innovation, as in the lower panel of Figure 1, consumption moves by more under a money rule than under a nominal-income rule. From a stabilizing perspective, a nominal-income rule dominates; however, since households consume more during the transition under the money rule, that rule generates the higher level of welfare. This highlights the model's chief drawback: The rigidity of prices is imposed (via an assumption about contracting) rather than integrated into the household choice problem. By focusing only on consumption, the model does not capture any welfare loss that may obtain from contract decisions that are inappropriate in an ex post sense. After a financial innovation, a money rule generates the larger consumption response relative to a nominal-income rule because it magnifies private agents' contracting mistake, creating a relatively larger discrepancy between the general price level that obtains after the shock and what contracting parties expected before the shock. For this reason, we have limited the use of welfare comparisons based only on consumption.

Other shocks could be analyzed easily in this framework by referring to Table 1. A change in the secular inflation rate resembles an inflation shock in that it alters the margin between the costs and benefits of holding real balances. Unlike an innovation, a change in μ changes x and c in the same direction; if μ increases, for example, both policy rules result in a transition in which c lies above its new steady-state value. On the other hand, a permanent increase in government spending will not require any prolonged adjustment under either rule. In the long run, an increase in government spending perfectly crowds out consumption and has no effect on real balances. At the announcement of a change in g, an equal and opposite-signed reduction in c will satisfy the new steady state under either rule.

4. CONCLUSION

We have analyzed the choice of monetary policy rule in a Keynesian model in modern dress. Maximizing agents, endowed with perfect foresight, plan their lifetime consumption decisions in the face of two rigidities. First, households need cash balances to aid trade. Second, today's price level is inherited from past contracting decisions so that changes in nominal aggregate demand fall on output in the short run.

With nominal balances necessary to facilitate trade and prices unable to move instantly to clear markets, the central bank can set real balances in the short run. We examine two ways of determining real balances, both μ percent rules. Our theoretical results suggest that the choice between fixed-money growth and fixed-nominal-income growth rules is an empirical assessment that depends on the distribution of shocks to the economy and the specification of consumer choice. As in

Bean (1983) and West (1986), the ranking of regimes under different types of shocks depends on behavioral parameter. Unlike those other analyses, however, this optimizing framework traces this condition to a structural parameter in utility—the coefficient of relative risk aversion. In the likely case of risk-averse households:

- If output variability normally traces to shocks to aggregate supply, then a nominal-money-growth rule more effectively stabilizes real income. This follows because a money growth rule allows private agents more freedom in their current spending decisions. Households, in their desire to smooth consumption over their lifetime, adjust current spending to move more quickly to the steady state.
- If output variability normally traces to financial shocks, then a nominal-income-growth rule more effectively stabilizes real income. This follows because a nominal-income rule mandates that the central bank set real balances to smooth consumption, which reduces the independent role of asset stocks in the private sector's consumption-smoothing decision.

Beyond the choice of policy rule, our model provides an example of the larger issue discussed by Lucas (1987, pp. 20–31), namely the role of consumption variability in the business cycle. Even though this model has distinct Keynesian origins complete with temporary price rigidity, it does incorporate the household planning problem. In response to some shocks, notably shifts in aggregate supply, rational agents desire to alter their spending immediately. A policy attempt to smooth this intention away via a nominal-income rule increases the deviation from the steady state. Thus, discrete shifts in spending do not obviously call for a policy response.

APPENDIX: EVALUATING THE CHARACTERISTIC ROOTS

As discussed in the main text, the dynamic behavior of both system [equation (8) and (11)] depend on their negative characteristic roots. This appendix discusses the properties of those roots [in the manner of Fischer (1979)]. For the nominal-money-growth rule, we are concerned with ζ, the negative root to the characteristic equation:

$$L(\zeta) = \zeta^3 + b[1 - (\rho + \mu)] \cdot \zeta - 3(\rho + \mu)b/\gamma x_0 = 0 \,. \qquad \text{(A.1)}$$

For the nominal-income-growth rule, we are concerned with ν, the negative root to the characteristic equation:

$$N(\nu) = \nu^2 - [bkx_0(\gamma - 1)/3]\,\nu - b = 0 \,. \qquad \text{(A.2)}$$

The function $L(\cdot)$ defines a cubic form in which the risk aversion term only appears in the intercept. A change in γ shifts the $L(\cdot)$ function uniformly and it can be shown that the $L(\cdot)$ function slopes downward along its negative range. Therefore,

(i) *As γ increases, the size of the negative root decreases in absolute value.*

The inflation parameter b enters in the constant term and the coefficients of ζ. As b increases, the intercept becomes more negative and the function becomes flatter along its negative range.[13] Therefore,

(ii) *As b increases, the size of the negative root increases in absolute value.*

Evaluating the $N(\cdot)$ function, it is easy to show that (i) and (ii) follow as long as $\gamma \geq 1$. First, note that the intercept of the $N(\cdot)$ function equals b and the function slopes downward along ν's negative range; as γ increases that slope become steeper. Hence, as γ increases, the $N(\cdot)$ function must cross the negative range of ν further to the left of the origin [proposition (i)]. Second, an increase in the inflation parameter b shifts the $N(\cdot)$ schedule downward and steepens it along the negative range. As long as $\gamma \geq 1$, $\partial N/\partial b$ is guaranteed to be negative; thus, proposition (ii) holds.

Finally, note that if $\gamma = 1$, then $\nu = -b^{1/2}$. Evaluating the money-growth characteristic equation at this point,

$$L(-b^{1/2}) = (\rho + \mu)b^{3/2}[1 - 3\, b^{1/2}/x_0] \; .$$

We can safely assert that

$$b < (x_0/3)^{1/2} \; ,$$

so that $L(-b^{1/2}) < 0$. Since the $L(\cdot)$ function is negatively sloped for negative ζs, it must intersect the horizontal axis to the right of $-b^{1/2}$. Thus,

(iii) *When $\gamma = 1$, the negative root to the nominal-income regime is larger in absolute value than the negative root to the money regime, $|\nu| < |\zeta|$.*

LITERATURE CITED

Alogoskoufis, George S. "Monetary, Nominal Income, and Exchange Rate Targets in a Small Open Economy." *European Economic Review* 33 (April 1989), 687–705.

Barro, Robert J. "Integral Constraints and Aggregation in an Inventory Model of Money Demand." *Journal of Finance* 31 (March 1976), 77–87.

Bean, Charles R. "Targeting Nominal Income: An Appraisal." *Economic Journal* 93 (December 1983), 806–19.

Blanchard, Olivier J., and Stanley Fischer. *Lectures on Macroeconomics*. Cambridge, Mass.: MIT Press, 1989.

Calvo, Guillermo A. "On Models of Money and Perfect Foresight." *International Economic Review* 20 (February 1979), 83–103.

[13]As long as the nominal interest rate is below 100 percent.

———. "Staggered Prices in a Utility-Maximizing Framework." *Journal of Monetary Economics* 12 (September 1983), 383–98.(a)

———. "Staggered Contracts and Exchange Rate Policy." In *Exchange Rates and International Macroeconomics,* edited by Jacob A. Frenkel, pp. 235–52. Chicago: University of Chicago Press for the NBER, 1983.(b)

Feenstra, Robert C. "Functional Equivalence between Liquidity Costs and the Utility of Money." *Journal of Monetary Economics* 17 (March 1986), 271–91.

Fischer, Stanley. "Capital Accumulation on the Transition Path in a Monetary Optimizing Model." *Econometrica* 47 (November 1979), 1433–39.

Geweke, John. "The Superneutrality of Money in the United States: An Interpretation of the Evidence." *Econometrica* 54 (January 1986), 1–21.

Gordon, Robert J. "The Conduct of Domestic Monetary Policy." In *Monetary Policy in Our Times,* edited by Albert A. Ando, Hidekazu Eguchi, Roger Farmer, and Yukio Suzuki, pp. 45–81. Cambridge, Mass.: MIT Press, 1985.

Hall, Robert E. "Macroeconomic Policy under Structural Change." In *Industrial Change and Public Policy,* pp. 85–111. Kansas City, Mo.: Federal Reserve Bank of Kansas City, 1983.

Hirsch, Morris W., and Stephen Smale. *Differential Equations, Dynamical Systems, and Linear Algebra.* New York: Academic Press, 1974.

Kamien, Morton I., and Nancy L. Schwartz. *Dynamic Optimization: The Calculus of Variation and Optimal Control in Economics and Management.* New York: North Holland, Inc., 1981.

Kimbrough, Kent P. "Inflation, Employment, and Welfare in the Presence of Transactions Costs." *Journal of Money, Credit, and Banking* 18 (May 1986), 127–40.(a)

———. "The Optimum Quantity of Money Rule in the Theory of Public Finance." *Journal of Monetary Economics* 18 (November 1986), 277–84.(b)

Lindgren, Bernard W. *Statistical Theory.* New York: Macmillan, Inc., 1968.

Lucas, Robert E., Jr. *Models of Business Cycles.* Oxford, UK: Basil Blackwell, Ltd., 1987.

McCallum, Bennett T. "The role of Overlapping Generations Models in Monetary Economics." *Carnegie-Rochester Series on Public Policy* 18 (Spring 1983), 9–44.

———. "Robustness Properties of a Rule for Monetary Policy." Unpublished. Carnegie-Mellon University, 1988.

Phelps, Edmund S. *Studies in Macroeconomic Theory,* Vol. 1. New York: Academic Press, 1979.

Reinhart, Vincent R. "Interest Rate Smoothing and Staggered Contracting." *Journal of Economics and Business* 42 (February 1990), 1–16.

Romer, David. "A Simple General Equilibrium Version of the Baumol-Tobin Model." *Quarterly Journal of Economics* 101 (November 1986), 663–85.

———. "The Monetary Transmission Mechanism in a General Equilibrium Version of the Baumol-Tobin Model." *Journal of Monetary Economics* 20 (July 1987), 105–22.

Taylor, John B. "Aggregate Dynamics and Staggered Contracts." *Journal of Political Economy* 88 (February 1980), 1–23.

———. "What Would Nominal GNP Targetting Do to the Business Cycle?" *Carnegie-Rochester Conference Series on Public Policy* 22 (Spring 1985), 61–84.

Tobin, James, "Monetary Policy: Rules, Targets, and Shocks." *Journal of Money, Credit, and Banking* 15 (November 1983), 506–18.

Vegh, Carlos A. "The Optimal Inflation Tax in the Presence of Currency Substitution." *Journal of Monetary Economics* 24 (July 1989), 139–46.

West, Kenneth D. "Targeting Nominal Income: A Note." *Economic Journal* 96 (December 1986), 1077–83.

JAMES S. FACKLER

Federal Credit, Private Credit, and Economic Activity

IN 1983, THE FEDERAL RESERVE DECIDED to use a broad credit aggregate, total domestic nonfinancial debt, in the conduct of monetary policy. This aggregate, referred to as "total credit" or "total debt," replaced bank credit as an "associated" policy target. The Federal Open Market Committee (FOMC) stated that it would "monitor total debt flows closely for whatever information they could provide in assessing appropriate responses to developments in the targeted monetary aggregates" (Board of Governors 1983).

The FOMC adopted total credit for at least two reasons. First, financial innovations over the prior decade had lowered the information content of bank credit for monetary policy. Second, the usefulness of traditional monetary aggregates was questioned due to velocity shifts in the early 1980s. These factors implied increased uncertainty about the link between the monetary aggregates and the traditional goals of monetary policy, and stimulated the search for information variables that could help guide monetary policy "in assessing appropriate responses" to the aggregates.

The evidence reported below shows that the federal and nonfederal ("private") components of total credit have significantly different impacts on the economy. Thus, if the FOMC takes seriously the monitoring of total credit in relation to GNP, biases may be introduced into the policy process. If the FOMC has de facto aban-

This paper was completed while the author was a Visiting Scholar at the Federal Reserve Bank of Kansas City. The views expressed are solely those of the author and do not necessarily represent those of the Federal Reserve Bank of Kansas City or the Board of Governors of the Federal Reserve System. Helpful comments and suggestions have been received from M. M. Ali, Dennis Glennon, W. Douglas McMillin, Larry Mote, Don Mullineaux, John Rogers, and the participants in workshops at the University of Kentucky and the Federal Reserve Bank of Kansas City.

JAMES S. FACKLER *is associate professor of economics at the University of Kentucky.*

Journal of Money, Credit, and Banking, Vol. 22, No. 4 (November 1990)

doned total credit as a policy guide, it may be ignoring important information contained in a less aggregated analysis.

This article is organized in the following manner. In the next section, the recent breakdown of the total credit–GNP relationship is documented, along with a discussion of the role that credit aggregates can play in the monetary policy process. In section 2, the methodology to be used and the model to be estimated are presented and discussed. In section 3, the primary results of the investigation are presented. Concluding comments are contained in the last section.

1. CREDIT AGGREGATES AND ECONOMIC ACTIVITY

The relationship between total credit and GNP, which appeared to be stable prior to its adoption as an associated policy target in 1983, has since been unreliable. Between 1960 and 1981, the ratio of total credit to GNP had fluctuated between 1.29 and 1.37, with a standard error of .016. After rising to 1.44 by 1983:1, when total credit was incorporated into the policy process, the ratio climbed to 1.79 by 1987:4. With total credit so far outside its historical range, an investigation is needed of whether this, or any other, credit aggregate can be useful for monetary policy.[1]

Plotted in Figure 1 is the ratio of total credit to GNP. Total credit, the credit aggregate monitored by the Fed, includes funds raised by federal, state, and local governments, corporate bonds, mortgages, consumer credit, and open market paper. Also plotted in Figure 1 are the ratios to GNP of the major components of total credit, federal, and private credit. The federal component represents U.S. government borrowing. The private component, as defined here, includes borrowing by state and local governments as well as by the private sector. As shown in Figure 1, stability in the total credit–GNP relationship until the early 1980s appeared to result from a negative link between its private and federal components.[2]

The instability of total credit relative to GNP appears to be largely the result of a reversal (due primarily to recent large federal deficits) of the downward trend of government debt as a fraction of GNP. Given the shift in the ratio of federal credit to GNP, Figure 1 suggests that total credit is no longer useful for policy purposes. However, given the *relative* stability of the private credit to GNP ratio, dividing credit into its federal and private components (or just using the private part) may yield useful policy information. Of course, evidence from inverse velocities is impressionistic as only ratios of contemporaneous values of the variables are represented. This shortcoming is part of the motivation for the remainder of the paper.

Despite the breakdown of the relationship between total credit and GNP, or perhaps because of it, there is ongoing research about the role of credit aggregates in

[1]Opinions of some on the use of credit aggregates in the monetary policy process has changed substantially in recent years. Friedman (1982), a strong early proponent of using total credit as an information variable, recently has argued (Friedman 1988) against using either money or credit.

[2]Although Friedman (1982) presented hypotheses that can explain the negative relationship, Summers (1986) argued that it was a coincidence.

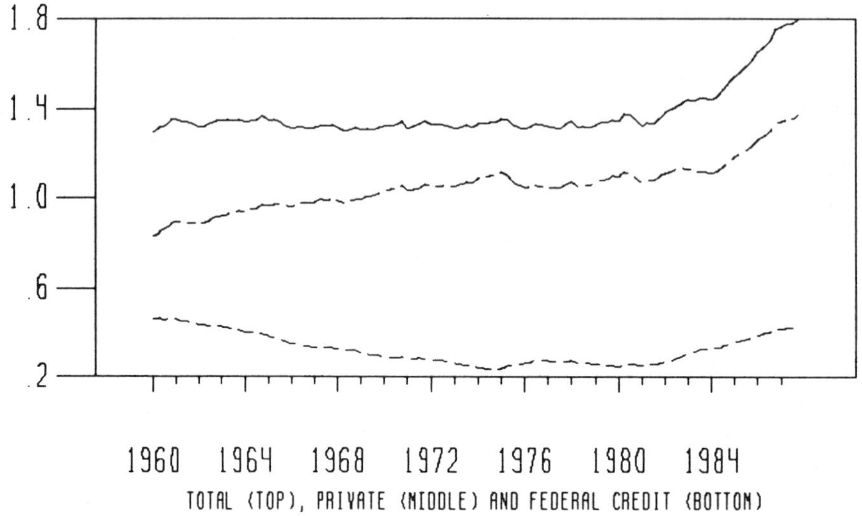

FIG. 1. Ratios of Selected Credit Aggregates to GNP

macroeconomic analysis. One important direction, that of identifying information variables that can serve in the policy process, is discussed below. An information variable is any variable that provides the policymaker with information about the current paths of ultimate goal variables. An information variable need not be controllable. Nor must data on the information variable be available on a regular basis. All that is required is that the information variable provide reliable data on the state of the economy. If an information variable (or variables) indicates that ultimate policy goals will not be met, then the policymaker can alter policy instruments in such a way that achievement of the goals is more likely.

The role of the components of total credit as information variables is examined here for three reasons. First, the apparent intent of the FOMC was to use total credit as an information variable; recall that the FOMC stated that it would "monitor total debt flows for whatever information they could provide in assessing appropriate responses to developments in the targeted monetary aggregates." Second, if the major components of total credit are important for understanding economic activity, they can be quickly incorporated into the policy process since data on these components is already available on a timely basis. Third, private credit dominates other credit aggregates in out-of-sample forecasting of nominal GNP during the 1980s.[3]

The very notion of information variables implies that in practice substantial empirical effort may be needed to identify those variables that contain information

[3]This conclusion follows from the discussion by Fackler (1988), who showed that when private credit was added to a system of macro variables, forecast errors for nominal GNP fell by about 20 percent during the 1980s. Using total credit actually led to a deterioration of GNP forecasts, consistent with the apparent instability of the total credit–GNP relationship.

on the ultimate goals. Thus, while various theoretical models may suggest that "credit" can serve as a good information variable, which credit aggregate best serves this function is an empirical question.

2. ESTIMATING THE ROLE OF CREDIT IN THE ECONOMY

2.1 Methodology

The analysis below employs a vector autoregression (VAR) to estimate the effects of credit on the macroeconomy. Traditional use of this methodology is subject to at least two criticisms. First, the manner in which the objects of interest in VAR analysis, impulse response functions (IRFs) and variance decompositions (VDCs), are constructed is suspect. To obtain easily interpretable IRFs and VDCs, orthogonal innovations from the VAR residuals are constructed. The usual procedure is to use the Choleski decomposition, which imposes recursivity on the structural model describing the residuals from the VAR estimation. Since these decompositions are not unique, each computed IRF and VDC depends on the ordering of the variables. But recursive models are rare in economics, so the "fundamental" shocks to the system under analysis are unlikely to be represented by such a decomposition. Many researchers try to circumvent the nonuniqueness problem by examining IRFs and VDCs for different orderings. Such analyses are nonetheless restricted to the class of recursive models, and are valid only if it is known that the true model is recursive but the causal structure (that is, the ordering) is unknown. Second, even if the decomposition (however chosen) is correct, IRFs and VDCs are seldom reported with confidence bounds. The reader can only wonder whether the reported results have any statistical significance.

Below, attempts are made to avoid each problem. The problem of identifying the fundamental shocks to be used in the construction of IRFs and VDCs is overcome by using the Bernanke's (1986) methodology. The confidence bound problem is avoided by using Sims' (1980) Monte Carlo integration techniques.

Preliminary Data Analysis

The data used in evaluating the role of credit in the macroeconomy are real military spending, the monetary base, M2, Moody's AAA corporate bond rate, the GNP deflator, real GNP, and the federal and private components of total nonfinancial domestic debt. All data are seasonally adjusted except for the interest rate, for which seasonal factors do not exist. Variables such as output, prices, interest rates, M2, and the monetary base are common in small macro models. Real military spending is a proxy for the exogenous elements in fiscal policy. Federal and private debt are included in light of the preliminary evidence presented above that their inverse velocities behave differently than the inverse velocity of total credit.

Each data series used in the analysis is tested for up to two unit roots and deterministic trends using the augmented Dickey-Fuller test. Specifically, the test for a single unit root results from the regression

$$\Delta x_t = \alpha + (\rho - 1)x_{t-1} + \sum_{i=1}^{n} \beta_i \Delta x_{t-i} + \gamma t + \epsilon_t$$

where x_t is the log-level of variable x and where the test is whether the coefficient on x_{t-1} is significantly different from zero. This test is run both including and excluding the time trend, in the latter case constraining $\gamma = 0$. The test statistics are presented in Table 1. The first (second) column presents evidence on the unit root hypothesis for the log-levels of the data in the presence (absence) of a linear time trend. The evidence supports this hypothesis for each series with the possible exception of the monetary base. When the regression is run when x_t represents the first difference of the log-level of x, the test is for the presence of a second unit root, given the first unit root. The third (fourth) column presents the statistics for a test of a second unit root, (that is, for a unit root in the first differences of each series) in the presence (absence) of a linear trend. This hypothesis is rejected in nearly every case using the Dickey-Fuller statistic. Given this evidence, the next-to-last column reports the t-ratio on time in a regression of the difference of each series on a constant, time, and four lags of the dependent variable. With the possible exception of federal credit, there is no evidence supporting a deterministic trend for first differences of the data series. The last column indicates that, with the possible exception of real military spending, each series contains significant drift. As a whole, the results in Table 1 imply that a VAR in first differences including constants may be appropriate. Whether such a VAR is appropriate depends on whether the data is cointegrated.

Engle and Granger (1987) have argued that a VAR expressed in terms of first differences is misspecified if two or more variables are cointegrated. A vector **x** is cointegrated of order (1,1) if each element of **x** is stationary in first differences and a

TABLE 1

TESTS FOR UNIT ROOTS AND TIME TRENDS

Variable	Unit Root Tests				t-statistic for a regression of Δz on:	
	$DF\ \tau_\tau\ [z]$	$DF\ \tau_\mu\ [z]$	$DF\ \tau_\tau\ [\Delta z]$	$DF\ \tau_\mu\ [\Delta z]$	*time*	*constant*
g	−2.01	−1.49	−2.84	−2.78†	0.54	0.81
b	−3.62*	−2.16	−3.41*	−2.97†	1.60	3.21
fc	−1.32	−1.10	−4.01**	−2.74†	2.00	2.00
pc	−2.64	−0.95	−4.29**	−3.95**	1.07	2.83
m	−2.13	−0.37	−3.46*	−3.57**	0.50	3.97
r	−2.71	−1.40	−4.01**	−3.99**	0.53	1.97
p	−2.16	−0.79	−1.44	−1.91	0.47	1.93
y	−3.04	−1.73	−4.82**	−4.60**	1.27	3.64

NOTES: ** = significance at the 1 percent level; * = significance at the 5 percent level; † = significance at the 10 percent level. Critical valves for Dickey-Fuller statistics are in Fuller (1976).

linear combination of the elements in $\mathbf{x}$, $\boldsymbol{\alpha}'\mathbf{x}$, is stationary. For example, y and z are cointegrated if y and z are both $I(1)$ (integrated of order 1) but $y - \alpha z$ is $I(0)$. With several variables there are a variety of possible cointegrating vectors. A test for the number of such vectors has been proposed by Johansen (1988). Specifically, rewrite the k-dimensional VAR $\mathbf{A}(L)\mathbf{X}_t = \boldsymbol{\varepsilon}_t$, with $\mathbf{A}(L) = \mathbf{I} + \mathbf{A}_1 L + \ldots + \mathbf{A}_n L^n$, as

$$\Delta\mathbf{X}_t = \sum_{i=1}^{n-1} \boldsymbol{\Gamma}_i \Delta\mathbf{X}_{t-i} - \boldsymbol{\Pi}\mathbf{X}_{t-k} + \boldsymbol{\varepsilon}_t$$

where $\boldsymbol{\Gamma}_i = -\mathbf{I} + \boldsymbol{\Pi}_1 + \ldots + \boldsymbol{\Pi}_i$, $i = 1, \ldots, k-1$, and $\boldsymbol{\Pi} = -\mathbf{I} - \boldsymbol{\Pi}_1 - \ldots - \boldsymbol{\Pi}_k$. Thus, the matrix $-\boldsymbol{\Pi} = \mathbf{A}(1)$ summarizes the long-term information in the data, and under the null hypothesis of r cointegrating vectors, the rank of $\boldsymbol{\Pi}$ will be r. Johansen shows that a test for the number of cointegrating vectors can be obtained from the eigenvalues of $|\lambda\mathbf{S}_{kk} - \mathbf{S}_{k0}\mathbf{S}_{00}{}^{-1}\mathbf{S}_{0k}|$ where the $\mathbf{S}_{ij}$ for $i,j = 0,k$ are moment matrices formed from regressions of $\Delta\mathbf{X}_t$ and $\mathbf{X}_{t-k}$ on $\Delta\mathbf{X}_{t-1}, \ldots, \Delta\mathbf{X}_{t-k-1}$. Johansen shows that the concentrated likelihood function is formed from the k eigenvalues, and that, with $\lambda_{r+1} > \ldots > \lambda_p$ being the $p - r$ smallest eigenvalues,

$$-2\log(Q) = -T \sum_{i=r+1}^{k} \log(1 - \hat{\lambda}_i)$$

is a test statistic that can be used to test the hypothesis that there are at most r cointegrating vectors. Johansen also reports that an approximation for the distribution of this statistic is $c\chi^2(f)$, where $f = 2(k - r)^2$ and $c = 0.85 - 0.58f^{-1}$. Test results of the hypothesis that there are at most r cointegrating vectors, for $r = 0, \ldots, k - 1$, are reported in Table 2. The results there show that the data do not reject the hypothesis of no cointegrating vectors. Thus, the stationary tests and the cointegration tests suggest that a VAR in first-difference form is appropriate for this data set.

TABLE 2

MULTIVARIATE COINTEGRATION TESTS

r	-2 logQ	p-value
7	.002	.999
6	9.80	.279
5	21.28	.266
4	37.95	.216
3	58.62	.189
2	86.80	.113
1	119.63	.068
0	154.92	.053

Estimation of the VAR

The Bernanke methodology, which represents a blend of structural and reduced-form analysis, is a two-step process. In the first stage, an unconstrained VAR is estimated. In the second stage, a just-identified structural model of the VAR residuals from the first stage is specified and estimated. The residuals from the second stage estimation represent the fundamental shocks to the system. Since these fundamental shocks are uncorrelated and derived from a structural model, theoretically meaningful IRFs and VDCs can be constructed.

Formally, using Bernanke's notation, consider the structural model

$$\mathbf{Y}_t = \sum_{i=0}^{p} \mathbf{B}_i \mathbf{Y}_{t-i} + \mathbf{A}\mathbf{u}_t \quad (1)$$

where $\mathbf{Y}_t$ is a vector of variables, and where $\mathbf{u}_t$ is the vector of fundamental disturbances, with covariance matrix given by $\mathbf{\Sigma}$, a diagonal matrix. The assumption that $\mathbf{\Sigma}$ is diagonal reflects the assumption that the shocks influencing each individual behavioral equation are uncorrelated, that is, fundamental. It is possible, however, for shocks to one market to affect other markets if there are nonzero off-diagonal elements of matrix $\mathbf{A}$.

The reduced form of this model is

$$\mathbf{Y}_t = \sum_{i=1}^{p} \mathbf{C}_i \mathbf{Y}_{t-i} + \mathbf{y}_t \quad (2)$$

with $\mathbf{C}_i = (\mathbf{I} - \mathbf{B}_0)^{-1}\mathbf{B}_i$ and

$$\mathbf{y}_t = \mathbf{B}_0\mathbf{y}_t + \mathbf{A}\mathbf{u}_t \ . \quad (3)$$

Specifying and estimating a model for equation (3) allows estimation of the $\mathbf{u}_t$, the fundamental shocks. Since by construction these $\mathbf{u}_t$ are orthogonal, they can be used to compute conceptually defensible IRFs and VDCs.

Estimation of equation (3) is by the method of moments. Specifically, equation (3) implies

$$\hat{\mathbf{\Sigma}} = \hat{\mathbf{A}}^{-1}(\mathbf{I} - \hat{\mathbf{B}}_0)\mathbf{M}(\mathbf{I} - \hat{\mathbf{B}}_0)'(\hat{\mathbf{A}}^{-1})' \quad (4)$$

where $\mathbf{M} = (\Sigma \mathbf{y}_t \mathbf{y}_t')/T$ is the sample covariance matrix of $\mathbf{y}$. The estimator selects elements of $\mathbf{A}$ and $\mathbf{B}_0$ such that the estimated $\mathbf{\Sigma}$ is diagonal. There are $n(n + 1)/2$ distinct elements of the matrix $\mathbf{M}$. With n equation variances to estimate, in a just-identified system $n(n - 1)/2$ nonzero elements of the $\mathbf{A}$ and $\mathbf{B}$ matrices may be estimated. This is a problem in nonlinear estimation since $\mathbf{\Sigma}$ is a nonlinear combination of the elements of $\mathbf{A}$ and $\mathbf{B}_0$.

The now-standard approach used to generate orthogonal innovations is to use the Choleski decomposition of the estimated covariance matrix, $\mathbf{M}$. This decomposition produces a matrix $\mathbf{G}$, such that $\mathbf{GG}' = \mathbf{M}$, with $\mathbf{G}$ being lower triangular and having positive elements on the diagonal. In the approach used here, the elements of $\mathbf{A}$ and $\mathbf{B}_0$ are chosen such that $\mathbf{\Sigma}$ is diagonal. From equation (4), this implies that the matrix

$$\mathbf{F} = (\mathbf{I} - \mathbf{B}_0)^{-1}\mathbf{A}\mathbf{\Sigma}^{1/2} ,$$

is such that $\mathbf{FF}' = \mathbf{\Sigma}$, where $\mathbf{\Sigma}^{1/2}$ represents a diagonal matrix with diagonal elements that are the square roots of those in the matrix $\mathbf{\Sigma}$. Since $\mathbf{F}$ need not be lower triangular, it provides a decomposition of the covariance matrix based on a structural model that, in general, is not recursive.

Generating Confidence Intervals for IRFs and VDCs

The effects on the macroeconomy of a variable such as credit are investigated by examining impulse response functions and variance decompositions. IRFs, which are analogous to dynamic multipliers, show the predictable response of each variable in the system to a one standard error shock to one of the system's variables. For example, IRFs show the expected responses of real GNP, prices and interest rates to a typical change in private credit. VDCs show the fraction of forecast error variance for each variable that results from its own innovations and from shocks to other variables. For example, in a VAR, the error in an n-period-ahead dynamic forecast of real GNP is partly due to errors in forecasting credit. A VDC for GNP would show the percentages of the forecast error variance of GNP due to shocks to GNP, credit, and each of the other variables in the system.

While use of Bernanke's estimator can produce defensible IRFs and VDCs, their statistical significance is generally unknown. Here, Monte Carlo integration is used to produce confidence bounds for the IRFs and VDCs.[4]

The technique used here is described in detail in, for example, Tiao and Zellner (1964) and Geweke (1988). Briefly, assume a diffuse prior on the parameters on equation (2), the elements of the $\mathbf{C}_i$ and $\mathbf{\Sigma}_\mathbf{y}$ matrices, where $\mathbf{\Sigma}_\mathbf{y}$ is the covariance matrix of the $\mathbf{y}_t$s. Then the posterior distribution of the coefficient and covariance matrices is Normal-inverted Wishart. Random sampling from these distributions can be used to generate confidence bounds with which to evaluate numerically the IRFs and VDCs.[5]

For a particular trial in the random sampling, the decomposition matrix $\mathbf{F}$ was

[4]Another approach to generating the standard errors of the impulse response weights would be to proceed analytically. Baillie (1987) or Lutkepohl (1988) show the derivation of asymptotic standard errors for the moving average representation of a VAR. The shortcoming of such an approach is the lack of knowledge of whether these asymptotic standard errors are good approximations in small samples. (Of course, the shortcoming of the approach employed in the text is the assumption of particular distributions used in the Monte Carlo integrations.) A second problem with the asymptotic approach is the computation of standard errors of the variance decompositions. The VDC is obtained from the covariance matrix of the n-period forecast error: $V(\ell) = \mathbf{A}_0\mathbf{\Sigma}\mathbf{A}_0' + \ldots + \mathbf{A}_{\ell-1}\mathbf{\Sigma}\mathbf{A}_{\ell-1}'$ where the $\mathbf{A}_i$ are the moving average coefficient matrices and $\mathbf{\Sigma}$ is the covariance matrix of the VAR residuals. If the moving average coefficients are normal, then a reasonable conjecture would be that each individual term would be chi-squared. However, the terms in the sum may not be independent, making analytical derivation of the standard errors of the variance decompositions problematical.

[5]An example is in Doan and Litterman (1986). Their example was adjusted for the decomposition matrix derived from the method of moments estimator.

constructed in the following way. The inverse of the sample covariance matrix from the VAR, $\mathbf{\Sigma_y}$, was decomposed using the Choleski decomposition. This matrix was then multiplied by a matrix whose elements were drawn from a population distributed as $N(0,T^{-1/2})$. Multiplying this matrix by its transpose and inverting then yields a covariance matrix drawn from the same population as that presumably generating the data. Using this matrix in place of **M** in equation (4) as an estimate of $\mathbf{\Sigma}$, and recomputing **A** and $\mathbf{B}_0$, yields the decomposition matrix **F** for the particular trial. This matrix is then used in construction of the IRFs and VDCs for that trial.

2.2 *A Model of the Role of Credit in the Macroeconomy*

The estimation technique outlined above requires specification of a structural model to obtain theoretically meaningful IRFs and VDCs. The focus of the modeling effort is on the contemporaneous links among the variables. In terms of equation (1), the aim is to identify and estimate matrices $\mathbf{B}_0$ and **A;** equivalently, the aim is to identify and estimate equation (3), summarizing the relationships for the first-stage VAR residuals.

The model estimated and analyzed below is

$$g = u_1 \tag{5.1}$$

$$b = b_{21}g + b_{23}m + b_{24}r + b_{25}p + b_{26}y + b_{27}fc + b_{28}pc + u_2 \; ; \tag{5.2}$$

$$m = b_{32}b + b_{34}r + b_{35}p + b_{36}y + b_{37}fc + b_{38}pc + u_3 \; ; \tag{5.3}$$

$$r = b_{43}(m - p) + b_{46}y + u_4 \; ; \tag{5.4}$$

$$p = b_{56}y + u_5 \; ; \tag{5.5}$$

$$y = b_{61}g + b_{62}(b - p) + b_{67}(fc - p) + u_6 \; ; \tag{5.6}$$

$$fc = b_{71}g + b_{74}r + b_{75}p + b_{76}y + u_7 \; ; \tag{5.7}$$

$$pc = b_{81}g + b_{84}r + b_{85}p + b_{86}y + b_{87}fc + u_8 \tag{5.8}$$

where lower-case letters represent the first-stage VAR residuals of the corresponding variables. Thus, g is the residual representing real military spending, b is the monetary base, fc is the federal component of total nonfinancial domestic debt, pc is its private component, m is the M2 money supply, r is the corporate bond rate, p is the GNP deflator, and y is real GNP. With eight variables, $8 \times 9/2 = 36$ parameters can be estimated. Of these, eight are equation variances, leaving twenty-eight coefficients to be estimated.

Equation (5.1) reflects the assumption that shocks to real military spending, proxying for exogenous fiscal policy shocks, are unrelated to innovations in the other variables. Equation (5.2) is the Fed's contemporaneous reaction function, with the base responding to innovations in all other variables. The inclusion of some credit variable(s) in the reaction function is consistent with the "information variable" approach to policy: the Fed looks at a wide variety of signals from the economy in formulating policy. The specification used here allows for different responses to federal and private credit. However, the model does not strictly rule out a role for total credit; the model could capture the recent monitoring of total credit if $b_{27} = b_{28}$. This specification is also in the spirit of the prior use of bank credit and the bank credit proxy in the policy process. Of course, the reaction function specified here may not capture the role of bank credit in the reaction function earlier in the period. The approximation implied by equation (5.2) may not be too bad, however, if the credit aggregates are highly correlated with bank credit in the 1960s and 1970s.

Equation (5.3) represents the money supply function in the model, with the money stock responding to the base, credit demands, interest rates, prices and output. The credit aggregates are included since they appear on the asset side of bank balance sheets. As banks construct optimal portfolios of assets in response to various shocks, marginal reallocations among assets (for example, among excess reserves, secondary reserves, and loans to both the private and government sectors) can affect the money supply.

Equation (5.4) represents the money demand function written with the interest rate on the left-hand side of the equation. Equation (5.5) is the aggregate supply function. Equation (5.6) represents aggregate demand, with the demand responding to fiscal policy, wealth as represented by real base money, and real government debt. This latter term represents "Ricardian" effects of government borrowing on aggregate demand.

Equations (5.7) and (5.8) describe the relationships of the credit aggregates to other system variables. These equations can be considered as combinations of interest rates and prices for which the markets for government and private credit are in equilibrium.[6] Specification of equilibrium relationships may be less desirable than separate demand and supply functions for government and private bonds. An expanded system of equations would be needed for such an effort, and attempts along these lines have not succeeded. However, the method used here captures a weighted average excess demand shock in the markets for federal and private debt (see note 7).

The specifications of equations (5.7) and (5.8) suggest that government and private agents respond differently to contemporaneous shocks to the economy. Since these equations represent the distinguishing features of the model, additional discussion of them is necessary.

Equation (5.7) can be arrived at in the following way. Let the supply of, and demand for, federal debt be, respectively,

$$fc^s = c_1 g + c_2 b + c_3 r + c_4 p + c_5 y + v_s \; ; \tag{5.7.1}$$

$$fc^d - p = c_6 r + c_7 (b - p) + c_8 y + v_d \; . \tag{5.7.2}$$

[6]Precedent for such constructions is contained in Patinkin (1965). Equations (5.7) and (5.8) can in principle be aggregated into the empirical analogue of Patinkin's BB curve, which shows the interest rate–price combinations for which the bond market is in equilibrium.

In equation (5.7.1), debt issued by the government in the current period responds to current shocks to spending, interest rates, prices, and output. Inclusion of spending shocks reflects the presumption that spending surprises are financed at least partially through borrowing. Interest rate changes in the contemporaneous period influence government financing, though in a different way than they influence private agents' behavior. First, holding other variables constant for a moment, a decline in bond prices (rise in interest rates) increases the quantity of bonds government must issue to raise a given amount of funding (that is, for a given deficit); the government bond supply function is downward sloping contemporaneously. Second, given a balanced budget, bond price fluctuations do not alter the stock of outstanding government bonds when bonds are only issued (retired) in the event of a deficit (surplus). Third, higher prices imply higher nominal deficits. For a given real deficit, higher nominal deficits increase nominal funding requirements, so that funds raised by the government rise as the price level rises, given real variables. If government bond supplies respond to nominal variables, "money illusion" is implied in government financing decisions. Fourth, inclusion of output in (5.7.1) reflects the fact that government financing needs vary with economic activity. Equation (5.7.2) asserts that real demands for federal debt depend upon interest rates, wealth (as represented by the real base), and income.

Solving equation (5.7.2) for the monetary base, b, and substituting into (5.7.1) yields, after some rearranging,

$$fc = d_1 g + d_2 p + d_3 r + d_4 y + v \, , \tag{5.7.3}$$

with $d_1 = c_7 c_1 / C$, $d_2 = [c_7 c_4 - c_2(1 - c_7)]/C$, $d_3 = [c_7 c_3 - c_2 c_6]/C$, $d_4 = [c_5 c_7 - c_2 c_8]/C$, $v = [c_7 u_s - c_2 u_d]/C$, and with $C = c_7 - c_2$. Equation (5.7.3) is of the same general form as equation (5.7).[7]

Equation (5.8) can be arrived at in an analogous way. Let the supply of, and demand for, private debt be, respectively,

$$pc^s - p = e_1 g + e_2(fc - p) + e_3 r + e_4(b - p) + e_5 y + w_s \, ; \tag{5.8.1}$$

$$pc^d - p = e_6 g + e_7 r + e_8(b - p) + e_8 y + w_d \, . \tag{5.8.2}$$

In equation (5.8.1), the supply of private bonds to the market depends on fiscal factors, interest rates, wealth, income, and current real federal borrowing. The latter term is included to capture "Ricardian equivalence" effects; an increase in government debt may raise private sector savings and hence lower private sector borrow-

[7]The residual in this equation is a weighted average of the demand and supply shocks for federal debt. For an appropriately specified system, this residual should represent "average" shocks observed by market participants since observed shocks are some combination of demand and supply shocks.

There is an interesting special case regarding equation (5.7.3). If there are no wealth effects in the demand function for federal bonds, that is, if $c_7 = 0$, then $v = u_d$ and the shocks to equation (5.7) represent shocks to the federal bond demand function.

ing.[8] In equation (5.8.2), the demand for private debt is postulated to depend on fiscal shocks, interest rates, wealth, and income. Eliminating b from these equations leads to an equation of the form of (5.8), with the coefficient on prices left unconstrained.

Equation system (5) was estimated over 1961:1–1987:4. Given the preliminary analysis of the data, each equation of the first-stage VAR was specified in first differences and included six lags and a constant term.

As the primary emphasis of the paper is to uncover longer-term responses of prices, output, and interest rates to impulses from the financial sector, presentation of the estimates of the parameters in equation system (5) are relegated to the appendix. It should be noted, however, that the parameters appear to be estimated imprecisely, judging from the t-statistics of the coefficients. This is not uncommon for models of the type estimated here,[9] and it is possible to speculate on reasons. First, with quarterly data and in the presence of data collection and processing lags, it is possible that contemporaneous relationships would only show up weakly since evidence on the current quarter available to agents would be largely impressionistic. Second, it is possible that behavioral responses to innovations in variables occur with a lag. Third, the standard errors reported here are computed with a numerical algorithm to differentiate the likelihood function to obtain the information matrix. Various ways exist to undertake these differentiations, and alternative estimates of the standard errors, are possible.[10] Finally, it is always possible that the specified structural model is incorrect.

Prior to presentation of the basic results, a brief discussion of specification tests of equation systems (5) is in order. Several tests have been undertaken that focus on roles of the credit aggregates in equation system (5). Given the nonlinearity of the estimator, it is simplest to use the Wald statistic[11] to test restrictions to (5). These statistics are reported in Table 3. Tests (1) and (2) examine the null hypothesis that

[8] A variety of other explanations for the relationships between private and government indebtedness are contained in Friedman (1982).

[9] Examples include Blanchard and Watson (1986), Bernanke (1986), Walsh (1987), and Rogers (1988). In Bernanke's log-differenced "credit market model," only two of fifteen estimated coefficients have t-ratios in excess of 2.0. In his log-differenced "real business cycle model," again only two of the fifteen coefficient estimates have t-ratios in excess of 2.0. Walsh reports that four of his ten estimated coefficients exceed 1.96. Rogers finds three of his ten coefficient estimates have significant ts.

[10] When equation system (5) was estimated using the FIML subroutine in TSP, many more coefficients were significant, even though the coefficient estimates themselves were virtually unchanged. Specifically, when estimated using the Gauss iterative technique in TSP, nineteen of the coefficients have t-statistics in excess of 1.0, fifteen coefficients have t-statistics in excess of 1.5, and ten coefficients have t-statistics in excess of 1.96. The different t-statistics are likely due to alternative methods for computing the information matrix; see, for example, Judge et al. (1985, p. 179–80). Details on the computed t-statistics from TSP are available on request.

It might also be noted that t-statistics for the coefficients in the standard Choleski decomposition are never reported, despite the wide use that has been made of that decomposition for computing IRFs and VDCs.

[11] The Wald statistic is given by

$$(\mathbf{R}\hat{\boldsymbol{\Theta}} - \mathbf{R}\boldsymbol{\Theta}_0)' \{\mathbf{R}\mathbf{V}(\hat{\boldsymbol{\Theta}})\mathbf{R}\}^{-1}(\mathbf{R}\hat{\boldsymbol{\Theta}} - \mathbf{R}\boldsymbol{\Theta}_0) ,$$

where $\hat{\boldsymbol{\Theta}}$ is the estimate of the parameter vector $\boldsymbol{\Theta}$, $\boldsymbol{\Theta}_0$ is the hypothesized value of $\boldsymbol{\Theta}$, $\mathbf{V}(\boldsymbol{\Theta})$ is the covariance matrix of the estimated $\boldsymbol{\Theta}$, and where $\mathbf{R}$ is a matrix of restrictions. This statistic follows a chi-squared distribution.

TABLE 3

SPECIFICATION TESTS

Hypothesis	Wald Statistic	Marginal Significance Level
(1) $b_{27} = b_{28} = 0$	7.50	.023
(2) $b_{37} = b_{38} = 0$	14.51	.001
(3) $b_{27} = b_{28}$	223.58	.000
(4) $b_{37} = b_{38}$	437.95	.000
(5) $b_{27} = b_{37} = b_{67} = b_{87} = 0$	270.96	.000
(6) $b_{28} = b_{38} = 0$	43.07	.000
(7) $b_{27} = b_{28}$; $b_{37} = b_{38}$; $b_{71} = b_{81}$; $b_{74} = b_{84}$; $b_{75} = b_{85}$; $b_{76} = b_{86}$; $b_{67} = 0$	6818.85	.000

the credit aggregates do not enter the equations for the monetary base and the money supply. Both hypotheses are rejected, so that the aggregates help explain both base and money supply movements. Tests (3) and (4) examine whether the coefficients on private and federal credit are the same in the monetary base and money supply equations. Acceptance of these hypotheses would constitute evidence supporting use of the total credit aggregate, as the FOMC has formally been doing, rather than using the components of the aggregates. Both hypotheses are rejected, so that use of the components of the aggregates appears to be appropriate. Tests (5) and (6) exclude federal and private credit, respectively, as explanatory variables in the system. Both hypotheses are rejected, so that the credit aggregates appear to belong in the system. Finally, test (7) examines the hypothesis that federal and private credit have the same effects on the contemporaneous system. If these two credit aggregates have similar effects on the system, then the effects of the sum of federal and private credit should not differ significantly from allowing them to affect the system separately. This implies that (i) the coefficients on the credit aggregates in the base and money supply equations should be equal; (ii) the reactions of each credit aggregate to other system variables should be equal, implying that the coefficients on g, r, p, and y in equations (5.7) and (5.8) should be equal; and (iii) the coefficients on the credit aggregates in the aggregate demand equation should be equal. With regard to point (iii), this implies restricting the coefficient on federal credit to zero since on the aggregate balance sheet of the private sector, private debt is not wealth. If federal and private credit have identical effects on aggregate demand, then the coefficient on federal credit in the aggregate demand curve should also be zero. Hypothesis test (7) is also rejected by the data. Finally, the entire system, including both contemporaneous and lagged terms, was estimated with the contemporaneous restrictions used in test 7 (and with the other contemporaneous coefficients restricted to the values estimated by the method of moments estimator) and with the further constraint that the sum of the coefficients on lagged federal and private credit in each equation are equal. The unrestricted and restricted systems were estimated using the seemingly unrelated regression technique, and a chi-square statistic for the validity of the restrictions was 328.03, which also rejects the restrictions. As a whole, all these tests suggest that federal and private credit indeed enter the system separately.

3. RESULTS

The paper's basic results are contained in the IRFs and VDCs generated by five hundred Monte Carlo trials. The point estimates and 95 percent confidence bands of the IRFs are shown in Figures 2, 3, and 4. The point estimates and standard errors of the VDCs are reported in Table 4. These results are examined in turn.

Figure 2 shows the impulse responses to a one-standard deviation shock to the monetary base. It is interesting to note that shocks to the base do not have "significant" effects on any of the key variables under discussion here: the AAA interest rate, the GNP deflator, and real GNP. The point estimate of the IRF shows that a rise in the base implies an initial rise in the interest rate, perhaps reflecting policy anticipation effects or rises in inflationary expectations. With a one-quarter lag, the rise in the interest rate is followed by a decline in the growth rate of real GNP. Finally, the point estimate is that positive shocks to the base generate several quarters of rising prices. Although not significant, these point estimates of the IRFs all appear to be largely consistent with traditional explanations of the response of the economy to shocks to the monetary base.

Figures 3 and 4 show that there are significant differences in the ways that federal and private credit shocks affect the economy. Since the shocks in these equations represent linear combinations of underlying demand and supply shocks in the markets for federal and private debt, care must be taken in the interpretation of the response of the economy to these shocks.

In Figure 3, changes in federal debt have no significant effect on the interest rate, prices, or output. In contrast, in Figure 4 an increase in private credit growth significantly lowers the interest rate and inflation in the first year. With a lag of about three and one-half years, a private credit shock also significantly lowers output. One explanation for these results is that the "average" private credit shock represents a net rise in loanable funds to the financial markets. This increase in funds availability lowers interest rates. To the extent that such a net rise in loanable funds represents increased saving, the demand for goods in general would fall, leading to lower levels of aggregate demand and thus lower prices and GNP.

Presented in Table 4 are the results of variance decompositions of the key macro variables for selected horizons out to twenty quarters. Only the twenty-quarter horizon results are explicitly discussed on the assumption that the intermediate horizons represent the continuing dynamic adjustment of the economy to the particular shock. It is assumed that the system has returned to equilibrium by quarter twenty. Reported for the interest rate, inflation and output are point estimates and

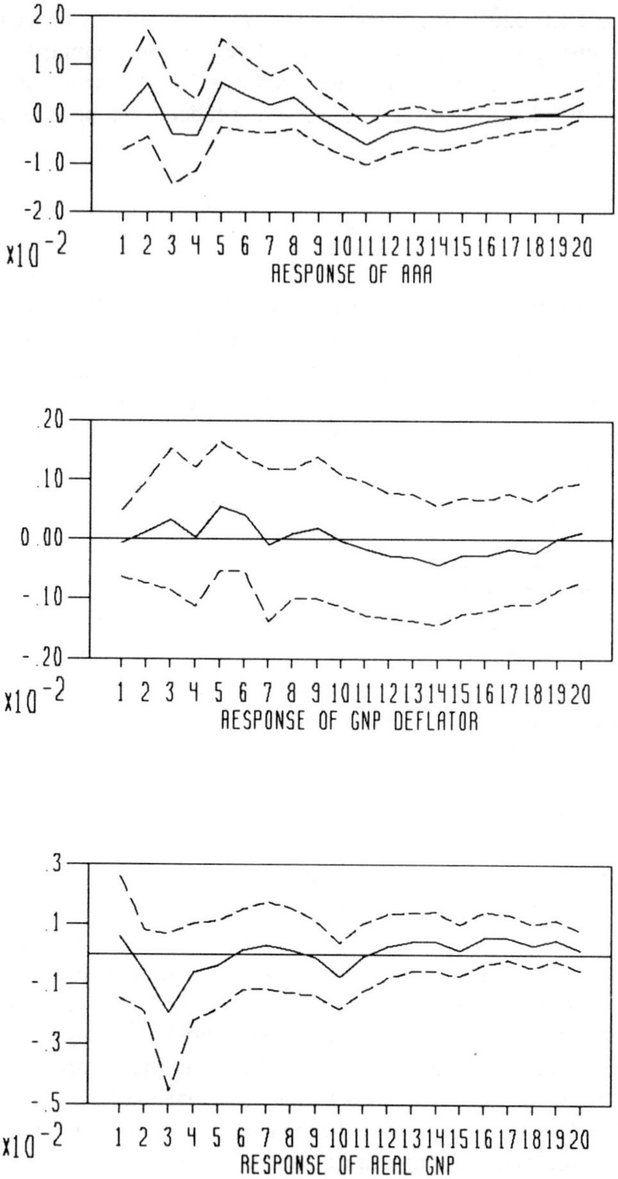

FIG. 2. Responses to Shock to Monetary Base

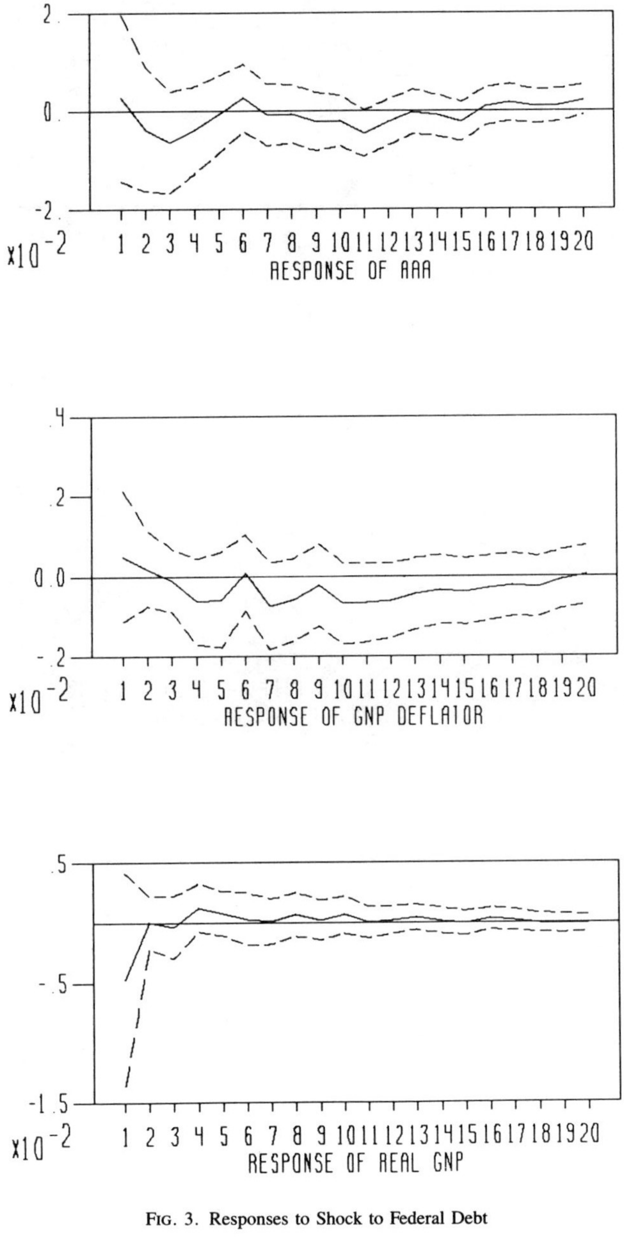

FIG. 3. Responses to Shock to Federal Debt

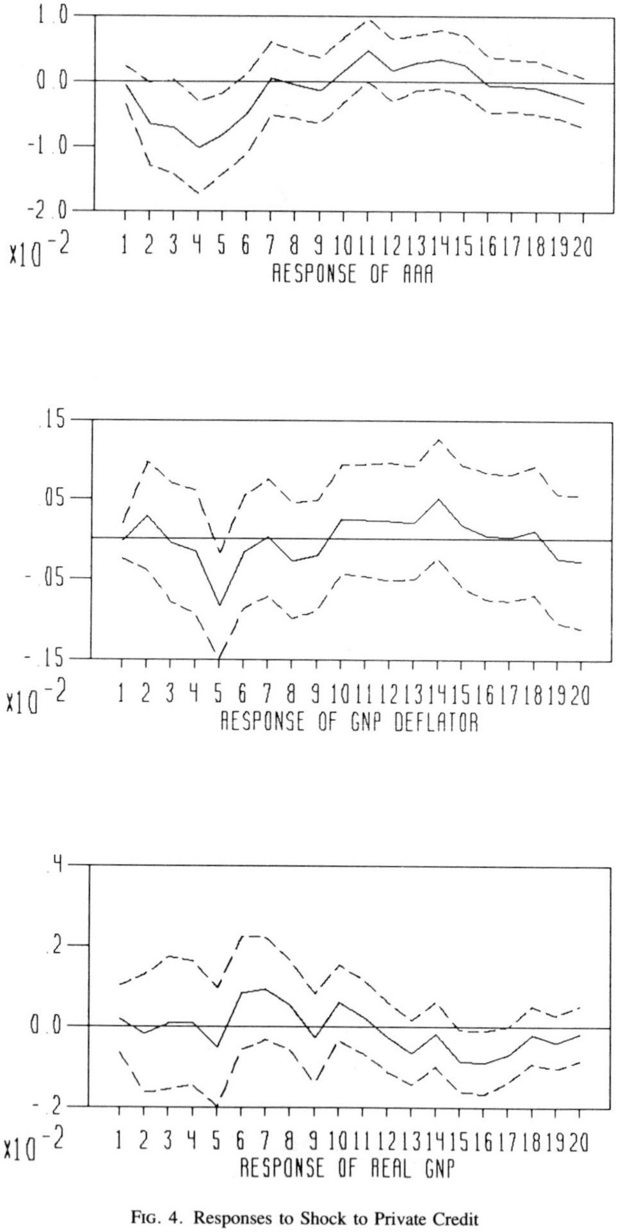

FIG. 4. Responses to Shock to Private Credit

TABLE 4

VARIANCE DECOMPOSITIONS

A. Point estimate (standard deviation) of variance decomposition of Aaa over time:

Variable Shocked	Quarter 4	Quarter 8	Quarter 12	Quarter 20
g	3.2 (3.8)	3.2 (3.8)	3.8 (4.1)	4.8 (4.5)
b	5.5 (3.9)	9.2 (3.7)	11.1 (3.5)	11.6 (3.5)
fc	5.7 (12.4)	5.1 (9.8)	6.4 (9.2)	6.6 (8.7)
pc	14.8 (4.7)	17.5 (4.5)	17.0 (4.4)	17.4 (4.3)
m	6.9 (3.4)	8.2 (3.6)	7.8 (3.6)	7.7 (3.6)
r	61.6 (15.6)	52.9 (12.8)	48.5 (12.0)	42.3 (11.6)
p	1.8 (3.3)	2.0 (3.2)	2.4 (3.3)	2.9 (3.5)
y	0.6 (4.2)	1.9 (4.1)	3.0 (4.0)	3.8 (4.0)

B. Point estimate (standard deviation) of variance decomposition of GNP deflator over time:

Variable Shocked	Quarter 4	Quarter 8	Quarter 12	Quarter 20
g	0.9 (2.3)	5.3 (3.1)	7.4 (5.7)	11.6 (9.2)
b	1.1 (4.9)	3.1 (7.0)	2.7 (8.4)	3.7 (9.1)
fc	5.4 (6.2)	9.1 (5.8)	11.1 (6.3)	10.8 (6.2)
pc	0.9 (2.5)	4.3 (2.6)	3.9 (3.0)	4.6 (3.9)
m	13.9 (5.3)	18.1 (7.1)	23.2 (8.8)	23.8 (9.9)
r	3.7 (4.7)	3.3 (4.3)	4.1 (4.7)	3.6 (5.1)
p	72.0 (12.9)	54.6 (10.2)	45.6 (9.7)	39.8 (9.6)
y	2.1 (4.9)	2.2 (6.0)	1.9 (6.5)	2.1 (6.1)

C. Point estimate (standard deviation) of variance decomposition of real GNP over time:

Variable Shocked	Quarter 4	Quarter 8	Quarter 12	Quarter 20
g	6.8 (4.2)	6.1 (4.0)	6.4 (4.0)	6.5 (4.4)
b	7.8 (3.2)	6.3 (2.9)	6.6 (2.7)	7.4 (2.7)
fc	38.9 (13.8)	31.8 (11.8)	30.2 (11.2)	27.9 (10.5)
pc	0.1 (1.7)	2.8 (1.9)	3.3 (1.9)	5.7 (2.2)
m	2.2 (3.4)	6.2 (3.1)	8.1 (3.1)	8.1 (3.2)
r	5.5 (9.5)	9.2 (8.0)	9.4 (7.6)	10.6 (7.2)
p	9.5 (11.5)	11.9 (10.3)	11.9 (9.7)	11.4 (9.1)
y	29.2 (17.6)	25.6 (15.0)	24.1 (14.2)	22.5 (13.4)

the standard deviations of the variance decompositions of the Monte Carlo simulations.

In panel A of Table 4, it can be seen that, at a twenty-quarter horizon, about 42 percent of the forecast error variance of AAA is accounted by its own innovations. Taking point estimates in excess of twice the computed standard deviation to be "significant," fluctuations in private credit account for a significant portion of nominal interest fluctuations in the "long run" (that is, over the twenty-quarter horizon). The federal credit variable, however, is not significant in explaining interest rate fluctuations. Further, both the monetary base and the money stock have "*t*-ratios" that exceed 2.0. The point estimate of the effect of private credit shocks on the interest rate is as large as the combined effects of the monetary base and the money stock, however. These results suggest both that the private component of total credit is important for interest rate movements (while the federal credit component is not) and that private credit is important relative to traditional monetary aggregates. Important information regarding interest rate changes is lost if the private credit is ignored in the policy process.

Presented in panel B of Table 4 are variance decomposition results for the inflation rate. Other than its own innovations, only money supply shocks have a consistent effect on inflation fluctuations. Note also that neither of the credit aggregates investigated here have roles in explaining inflation fluctuations, although the *t*-ratio on federal credit exceeds 1.7.

Described in panel C of Table 4 is the variance decomposition of output. Its own innovations, along with shocks to the monetary base, the money supply, private credit, and federal credit, are important for output fluctuations. Of special interest for the current discussion is the fact that not only does federal credit account for a significant portion of the output fluctuations, but its impact on output variability is substantially larger than those of the base, the money stock, or private credit. Again, ignoring the separate information contained in the credit measures analyzed here can be costly to policymakers in terms of output variability.

4. SUMMARY AND CONCLUSIONS

A model of credit market activity in relation to key macroeconomic variables has been specified and estimated. Since the estimation procedure used is a blend of structural and reduced-form modeling, an important conceptual shortcoming of the usual VAR methodology has been avoided. In addition, confidence bands for the objects of interest in VAR analysis, impulse response functions and variance decompositions, have been generated using Monte Carlo techniques. Thus, it is possible to assess the statistical importance of the IRFs and VDCs.

The results reported above show that, despite the breakdown in the relationship between total credit and GNP, the federal and private components of total credit individually have important but different effects on economic activity. Inasmuch as the FOMC has been monitoring the total of these two aggregates, and given the apparent erratic behavior of the relationship between total credit and GNP, important information has been lost if the components of the total have not been informally monitored.

LITERATURE CITED

Baillie, Richard T. "Inference in Dynamic Models Containing 'Surprise' Variables." *Journal of Econometrics* 35 (May 1987), 101–17.

Bernanke, Ben S. "Alternative Explanations of the Money-Income Correlation." *Carnegie-Rochester Conference Series on Public Policy* 25 (Autumn 1986), 49–99.

Blanchard, Olivier J., and Mark W. Watson. "Are Business Cycles All Alike?" In *The American Business Cycle,* edited by Robert J. Gordon, pp. 123–79. Chicago: University of Chicago Press, 1986.

Board of Governors of the Federal Reserve System. "Record of Policy Actions of the Federal Open Market Committee." *Federal Reserve Bulletin* 69 (April 1983), 284–91.

Doan, Thomas A., and Robert B. Litterman. *RATS Users Manual,* Version 4.30. Minneapolis: VAR Econometrics, 1986.

Engle, Robert F., and C. W. J. Granger. "Co-integration and Error Correction: Representation, Estimation, and Testing." *Econometrica* 55 (March 1987), 251–76.

Fackler, James S. "Should the Federal Reserve Continue to Monitor Credit?" *Federal Reserve Bank of Kansas City Economic Review* 73 (June 1988), 39–50.

Friedman, Benjamin M. "Debt and Economic Activity in the United States." In *The Changing Roles of Debt and Equity in Financing in U.S. Capital Formation,* edited by Benjamin M. Friedman, pp. 91–110. Chicago, University of Chicago Press, 1982.

______. "Monetary Policy without Quantity Variables." *American Economic Review* 78 (May 1988), 440–45.

Fuller, Wayne A. *Introduction to Statistical Time Series.* New York: John Wiley and Sons, 1976.

Geweke, John. "Antithetic Acceleration of Monte Carlo Integration in Bayesian Inference." *Journal of Econometrics* 38 (May/June 1988), 73–89.

Johansen, Soren. "Statistical Analysis of Cointegration Vectors." *Journal of Economic Dynamics and Control* 12 (June/September 1988), 231–54.

Judge, George C., W. E. Griffiths, R. C. Hill, H. Lutkepohl, and T-C. Lee. *The Theory and Practice of Econometrics,* 2d ed. New York: John Wiley and Sons, 1985.

Lutkepohl, Helmut. "Asymptotic Distribution of the Moving Average Coefficients of an Estimated Vector Autoregressive Process." *Econometric Theory* 4 (April 1988), 77–85.

Patinkin, Don. *Money, Interest, and Prices,* 2d ed. New York: Harper and Row, 1965.

Rogers, John H. "Dollarization in Mexico: A Vector Autoregressive Analysis." Mimeo, University of Kentucky, October 1988.

Sims, Christopher A. "Comparison of Interwar and Postwar Business Cycles: Monetarism Reconsidered." *American Economic Review* 70 (May 1980), 250–57.

Summers, Lawrence H. "Debt Problems and Macroeconomic Policies." In *Debt, Financial Stability and Public Policy,* pp. 165–91. Kansas City: Federal Reserve Bank of Kansas City, 1986.

Tiao, George C., and Arnold Zellner. "On Bayesian Estimation of Multivariate Regression." *Journal of the Royal Statistical Society,* Series B, 26 (1964), 277–85.

Walsh, Carl E. "The Impact of Monetary Targeting in the United States: 1976–1984." Federal Reserve Bank of San Francisco Working Paper 87-04 (April 1987).

APPENDIX

Parameter Estimates of Equation System 5

Parameter	Estimate	t-statistic
b_{21}	.04	2.24
b_{23}	.40	1.26
b_{24}	−.007	.47
b_{25}	−.03	.31
b_{26}	−.12	.92
b_{27}	.04	.34
b_{28}	.33	1.60
b_{32}	−.79	.99
b_{34}	−.02	.60
b_{35}	−.02	.13
b_{36}	.11	1.07
b_{37}	.12	.93
b_{38}	.77	1.78
b_{43}	−.71	.39
b_{46}	−.37	.23
b_{56}	−.11	.65
b_{61}	.06	.38
b_{62}	.66	.25
b_{67}	−.67	.48
b_{71}	−.26	.44
b_{74}	−.13	.32
b_{75}	−1.79	.53
b_{76}	1.72	.34
b_{81}	−.02	1.45
b_{84}	.02	3.14
b_{85}	.17	2.85
b_{86}	.08	2.39
b_{87}	−.17	4.73

Estimated Structural Variances of Equation System 5

Equation	Estimate	t-statistic
1	.00032	7.45
2	.00001	2.21
3	.00002	1.94
4	.00108	5.11
5	.00001	4.39
6	.00010	.42
7	.00037	.31
8	.00001	7.30

CHRISTOPHER F. BAUM
MARILENA FURNO

Analyzing the Stability of Demand-for-Money Equations via Bounded-Influence Estimation Techniques

INTRODUCTION

A SIZABLE FRACTION OF THE APPLIED RESEARCH in monetary economics has been focused on the stability of the U.S. demand-for-money equation in the postwar period. A wide range of econometric techniques has been brought to bear on the issues relating to the apparent instability in this equation's parameters and error variance. In this paper, we approach this issue via bounded-influence estimation of simultaneous equations in the context of an error-correction model. This technique presents unique opportunities for the diagnosis of structural stability and the evaluation of money demand equations' specification.

The plan of the paper is as follows. Section 1 presents a short summary of the bounded-influence estimator for simultaneous equations, and discusses how it may be used to diagnose estimated equations' weaknesses. In section 2, a money demand equation with an error-correction model specification is constructed to illustrate structural change in a single-equation context. In section 3, the equation is reestimated with bounded-influence techniques, and we investigate the degree to which the equation may still lack desirable econometric properties following the introduction of shift dummies. The fourth section presents conclusions and suggestions for further research.

Earlier versions of this paper were presented to the Second International Economic Modelling Conference and the conference of the Society for Economic Dynamics and Control. We acknowledge the comments of conference discussants and participants. The present version of the paper has greatly benefited from the suggestions of an anonymous referee and the editor.

CHRISTOPHER F. BAUM *is associate professor of economics at Boston College.* MARILENA FURNO *is assistant professor at the Universitá di Napoli, Italy.*

Journal of Money, Credit, and Banking, Vol. 22, No. 4 (November 1990)

1. ROBUST ESTIMATION TECHNIQUES IN A SIMULTANEOUS-EQUATION CONTEXT

This section of the paper discusses the rationale for utilizing robust estimation techniques as diagnostic tools in monetary research. Our emphasis in this study is to consider those techniques not as alternative estimation methods to be used in place of the classical least-squares approach, but rather as adjuncts, used to diagnose problems with an estimated money demand equation that might not be so readily visible otherwise. The deviations between least-squares and bounded-influence results may be expected to highlight deficiencies in the specification of the underlying model and its error process; see Krasker, Kuh, and Welsch (1983).

Robust estimation techniques are designed to lessen the dependence of the properties of the estimators on the basic assumptions of the classical regression model. The major goal is to obtain estimates that maintain good properties under small changes of the parametric model and are more stable than least-squares estimates. Stability in this context implies that robust estimates are not critically dependent on the extreme values of the data set (outliers), which tend to attract the fitted line, thus perturbing the least-squares estimates. The derivation of robust estimators involves the definition of a bound on the observations and/or the residuals of the regression, which limits the leverage of particular observations on the final estimated parameters. This restriction on the residuals and/or the so-called "influential outliers" is implemented through a weighting system, so that robust regression can be viewed as a particular kind of weighted least squares. The weighting system allows the researcher to single out observations that have a strong impact in the computation of the estimated parameters, since outliers that turn out to be influential observations are downweighted. The goal is to provide an accurate description of the bulk of data, forcing influential outliers to have large residuals. Furthermore, the extent of downweighting performed by the robust regression highlights the degree of possible misspecification in the equation and/or its error process. If a sizable fraction of the data set is heavily downweighted, the formulation of the equation and its error process should be questioned.

The bounded-influence estimator (BIF), presented by Krasker and Welsch (1982), relies on the concept of qualitative robustness introduced by Hampel (1971). The building block of this estimator is given by the influence function (IF), which measures the impact of each observation on the estimators, and by a statistic that is a transformation of IF, the gross error sensitivity. BIF minimizes the asymptotic variance of the regression while imposing a bound on the gross error sensitivity. The bounded-influence estimator is one of the few robust estimators that have been extended to a simultaneous-equation context. The bounded-influence instrumental variables (BIV) estimator (Krasker and Welsch 1985) is a quite straightforward extension of the single equation approach, with the inclusion of a set of instruments to solve the simultaneity problem. The technical details of these estimators are presented in the appendix, and, in greater detail, in Furno and Baum (1989).

Usage as a Diagnostic Tool

Results generated by the bounded-influence estimator should be useful in evaluating the quality of more conventional econometric estimates. In particular, the BIV point and interval estimates may be compared with their two-stage least-squares or instrumental variables counterparts; sizable discrepancies may be noted as evidence of the equation's misbehavior.[1] The weighting system in BIV points out the location of the downweighted observations in the data set. If the BIV estimates display strong downweighting for some observations and little downweighting for others, attention should be given to the pattern; problems of structural instability and/or heteroskedasticity may be indicated. In the remainder of the paper, we illustrate this use of BIV estimation in the context of a money demand function.

2. AN ERROR-CORRECTION MODEL OF U.S. MONEY DEMAND

Beginning with Stephen Goldfeld's detective work in "The Case of the Missing Money" (1976), numerous researchers have analyzed the behavior of U.S. money demand, attempting to identify the causes of poor forecasting performance of money demand equations over the 1970s. Recent studies of these phenomena have illustrated that weaknesses of predictions are not uniquely American; Patterson (1987) discusses mid-1970s' instability in the British demand for money. In Rose's 1985 study, the instability of the mid-1970s' function is described as "largely taken as a given stylized fact" (p. 439) following the extensive investigations in the literature.

The analysis of time series properties—in particular, the order of integration of economic time series—has become an important aspect of econometric modeling in recent years. This analysis led us to reject a Goldfeld-type log-level specification of the U.S. demand for money, as well as the popular log-difference specification. We found, as have other researchers, that the variables commonly used in money-demand studies are nonstationary stochastic processes—even in log form—and thus may be characterized as $I(1)$. We performed Dickey-Fuller, Augmented Dickey-Fuller, and Phillips-Perron tests on the log of nominal M1 (*LM1NOM*), the log of nominal M2 (*LM2NOM*), the log of real GNP (*LGNP82*), the log of the commercial paper rate (*LCPRATE*), and the log of the implicit GNP deflator (*LPGNP*). The Phillips-Perron test (Phillips and Perron 1988) is perhaps the most general of the tests used, due to its nonparametric nature. The values of the test statistic were, for M1, −0.489; for M2, −2.657; for real GNP, −1.897; for the commercial paper rate, −2.447; and for the implicit deflator, −2.876. These results were achieved

[1]Krasker suggests that the robust and least-squares estimates should be compared via a Hausman specification test. "If all the assumptions are satisfied, we would expect the two estimates to be close, since both are consistent estimators for β. However, if the assumptions are only approximately true, due to a few gross errors or a failure of the linear specification for extreme values of the independent variables, the two estimates might have quite different biases . . . . the MLS (modified least squares) bias will be small, whereas the OLS bias is potentially very large." (1980, p. 1345)

with four lags of the differenced process and a time trend, and should be compared with a 95 percent critical value of −3.45 (Fuller 1976, p. 373). All variables fail to reject the null hypothesis of $I(1)$. Qualitatively similar results were achieved for zero lags in the Phillips-Perron test, as well as for the Dickey-Fuller test with zero or four lags.

The Error-Correction Model

The approach taken toward an appropriate specification of money demand is that popularized by Hendry and Richard (1982) and Hendry, Pagan, and Sargan (1983) in which an equilibrium model (which is a proper cointegrating regression) is first fit to the levels of the variables, and the calculated residuals from that model are used in an error-correction model (ECM) which specifies the dynamic system's trajectory between equilibria. We fit the equilibrium model:

$$LM2NOM_t = \beta_0 + \beta_1 \, LGNP82_t + \beta_2 \, LCPRATE_t + \beta_3 \, LPGNP_t + \epsilon_t \, .$$

This model was estimated via instrumental variables[2] on quarterly data, 1962:1 to 1987:2. The chosen instruments were a constant term and fitted values of *LGNP*82, *LCPRATE*, and *LPGNP*. These fitted values were constructed by regressing each of the variables, in turn, on a constant term and four lags of each of the variables *LGNP*82, *LCPRATE*, and *LPGNP*. These results are presented in the first column of Table 1.

Regression of one $I(1)$ process on several others will be "spurious" unless the set of variables may be shown to be cointegrated—for instance, that the errors of this regression are $I(0)$. In pairwise tests, Engle and Granger (1987, p. 274) found that M1 was not cointegrated with GNP, but M2 and GNP formed a cointegrating vector. In our case, with four stochastic processes in the model, the appropriate critical values are provided by Engle and Yoo (1987, p. 157). For the above model with M1 as the dependent variable, the test statistic is −0.640; for M2 as the dependent variable, the value is −4.21. The Engle-Yoo 90 percent critical value for four variables is −3.89. We thus reject the null of non-cointegration at the 90 percent level of confidence for the model based on M2. The choice of M2 as the relevant aggregate in the money-demand equation is also adopted in the works of Hallman, Porter, and Small (1989) and Small and Porter (1989), who estimate a money-demand equation resulting from an error correction specification in order to model inflation as a discrepancy between the long-run equilibrium price level (p^*) and the actual price level.[3]

[2]A Hausman test was used to establish that estimation via ordinary least squares would involve significant simultaneous bias (at greater than the 99 percent level of confidence). This stands at odds with much of the literature; even those who have used the Hendry methodology (for example, Rose 1985, pp. 449–50) have generally considered OLS to be appropriate. Instruments were constructed from four quarterly lags of each of the right-hand variables.

[3]The set of explanatory variables utilized by Small and Porter (1989) includes a time trend, which is not considered here. The opportunity cost of holding M2 balances—defined as the difference between the three-month Treasury bill rate and the average rate paid on M2 deposits—replaces the commercial

TABLE 1

ESTIMATES OF THE EQUILIBRIUM MODEL

$$LM2NOM_t = \beta_0 + \gamma_0 D_t + \beta_1 LGNP82_t + \gamma_1 (D_t LGNP82_t) + \beta_2 LCPRATE_t + \gamma_2 (D_t LCPRATE_t) + \beta_3 LPGNP_t + \gamma_3 (D_t LPGNP_t) + \epsilon_t$$

Coeff.	IV	IV	BIV $a = \sqrt{k}$	BIV $a = \sqrt{k}$	BIV $a = 1.2\sqrt{k}$	BIV $a = 1.2\sqrt{k}$
β_0	−6.005	−6.119	−5.907	−6.062	−5.893	−6.088
	(0.209)	(0.246)	(0.935)	(0.063)	(0.371)	(0.294)
γ_0		2.048		2.217		2.202
		(0.573)		(0.081)		(0.842)
β_1	1.150	1.181	1.136	1.171	1.133	1.176
	(0.034)	(0.042)	(0.150)	(0.029)	(0.060)	(0.050)
γ_1		−0.359		−0.385		−0.383
		(0.084)		(0.371)		(0.117)
β_2	−0.099	−0.074	−0.098	−0.077	−0.099	−0.076
	(0.007)	(0.009)	(0.018)	(0.014)	(0.011)	(0.011)
γ_2		−0.062		−0.059		−0.060
		(0.014)		(0.047)		(0.022)
β_3	0.976	0.933	0.981	0.938	0.982	0.936
	(0.015)	(0.021)	(0.062)	(0.064)	(0.025)	(0.023)
γ_3		0.222		0.230		0.229
		(0.033)		(0.106)		(0.042)
R^2	0.9992	0.9996	0.9999	0.9997	0.9999	0.9998
S.E.R.	0.0179	0.0133	0.0157	0.0122	0.0149	0.0120
N	102	102	102	102	102	102
Σ BIV Wts.			88.5	75.6	97.4	98.1

NOTE: Estimated standard errors are given in parentheses. The sample is quarterly, 1962:1–1987:2; $D_t = 1$ for $t > 1977{:}4$. Data were taken from the CITIBASE data bank.

The errors from this equilibrium model are then used to specify an error-correction model (ECM) in which the change in the log of nominal M2 is related (via instrumental variables[4]) to its own lag, the lagged error series, and the change in the logs of real GNP and the commercial paper rate:

$$\Delta LM2NOM_t = \delta_0 + \delta_1 e_{t-1} + \delta_2 \Delta LM2NOM_{t-1} + \delta_3 \Delta LGNP82_t + \delta_4 \Delta LCPRATE_t + \nu_t \, .$$

The chosen instruments were a constant term, the lagged errors from the equilibrium equation, the lagged change in M2, and the changes in the fitted values of *LGNP*82 and *LCPRATE*. In this specification, the lagged error series e_{t-1} (the

paper rate variable used in our specification. Small and Porter consider personal consumption expenditures as an activity variable, rather than GNP, and impose a constraint of a unitary long-term elasticity on this variable. Finally, they add four dummy variables to take into account the introduction of credit controls in 1980 and of money market deposit accounts in late 1982. Their sample period is slightly shorter than that we consider.

[4]A Hausman test on the error-correction model established that the instrumental variables technique dominated OLS, with the latter exhibiting simultaneous bias at greater than the 99 percent level of confidence.

error correction term) has the appropriate negative coefficient which is significantly different from zero.

Stability Tests

Although we have avoided one set of pitfalls of time-series modeling with this equilibrium model, we may unquestionably reject the hypothesis of structural stability over the full sample 1962:1–1987:2. For instance, if we posit a structural shift[5] at 1977:4 and conduct a Chow test at that point, we may overwhelmingly reject the hypothesis of no structural change for the equilibrium model; $F(3,94) = 26.3$.[6] All three slope coefficients and the constant term take on significantly different values (*t*s in excess of 3.5) in the post-1977 period, as indicated in the second column of Table 1. The error-correction model, as reported in Table 2, also exhibited significant instability, although of a lesser degree; $F(4,90) = 2.37$. Stability was rejected for the set of all four coefficients (and for the subset of three slope coefficients: $F(3,90) = 3.05$) at the 95 percent level of confidence.

This evidence of structural instability should come as no surprise to anyone familiar with the demand-for-money literature, in which many researchers' estimated equations exhibited structural instability during the late 1970s and early 1980s in response to Fed operating procedure changes, as well as shifts due to the "missing money" and "great velocity decline" phenomena of these periods. Although more sophisticated empirical techniques could be used to search for the point at which the function first exhibited significant instability, we focus below on the additional diagnostic information which bounded-influence estimation techniques may bring to this issue of structural shifts.

3. ANALYSIS VIA BIV ESTIMATES

A significant amount of light might be shed upon the difficulties of this money-demand specification over the 1970s by the application of BIV estimation techniques. By estimating the equation over the entire sample, 1962:1–1987:2, the divergence between IV and BIV estimates may be highlighted. Since we have shown that the IV estimates over the full sample are unstable, we perform this comparison with the equilibrium and error-correction models both with and without shift terms for the 1978:1–1987:2 subsample.[7]

Two sets of BIV estimates of the equilibrium equation are presented in the remaining columns of Table 1. These estimates were constructed using values for the bound a of $\sqrt{k}$ and $1.2\sqrt{k}$, respectively. The first choice corresponds to a very

[5]Inspiration for such a breakpoint was given by Rose's recent article (1985, pp. 449–52). We are not concerned with establishing whether this breakpoint is optimal given the sample, although Rose's evidence strongly suggests that instability occurs in this vicinity.

[6]A test for homoskedasticity between these two subsamples was performed. The error variances could not be distinguished at the 90 percent level of significance.

[7]The shift point of 1978:1 is selected a priori (given Rose's model) and was not data-determined. Its use in this context is purely expository.

TABLE 2

ESTIMATES OF THE ERROR-CORRECTION MODEL

$$\Delta LM2NOM_t = \delta_0 + \lambda_0 \delta_1 e_{t-1} + \delta_2 \Delta LM2NOM_{t-1} + \lambda_2 (D_{t-1} \Delta LM2NOM_{t-1}) + \delta_3 \Delta LGNP82_t + \lambda_3 (D_t \Delta LGNP82_t) + \delta_4 \Delta LCPRATE_t + \lambda_4 (D_t \Delta LCPRATE_t) + v_t$$

Coeff.	IV	IV	BIV $a = \sqrt{k}$	BIV $a = \sqrt{k}$	BIV $a = 1.2\sqrt{k}$	BIV $a = 1.2\sqrt{k}$
δ_0	−0.008	−0.005	−0.007	0.004	−0.007	0.005
	(0.002)	(0.002)	(0.003)	(0.022)	(0.002)	(0.022)
λ_0		0.008		0.007		0.009
		(0.005)		(0.043)		(0.011)
δ_1	−0.278	−0.257	−0.249	−0.204	−0.251	−0.242
	(0.068)	(0.078)	(0.104)	(0.762)	(0.077)	(0.094)
δ_2	0.533	0.761	0.474	0.662	0.475	0.695
	(0.141)	(0.172)	(0.231)	(0.409)	(0.138)	(0.176)
λ_2		−0.404		−0.416		−0.447
		(0.241)		(4.76)		(0.556)
δ_3	0.283	0.046	0.553	0.398	0.536	0.256
	(0.261)	(0.245)	(0.540)	(0.618)	(0.290)	(0.317)
λ_3		0.005		0.011		0.008
		(0.007)		(0.002)		(0.010)
δ_4	−0.052	−0.036	−0.066	−0.042	−0.066	−0.037
	(0.011)	(0.012)	(0.037)	(1.41)	(0.020)	(0.016)
λ_4		−0.026		−0.051		−0.038
		(0.028)		(0.046)		(0.038)
R^2	0.3618	0.3838	0.4364	0.6976	0.2519	0.4663
S.E.R.	0.0064	0.0064	0.0052	0.0044	0.0052	0.0050
N	99	99	99	99	99	99
Σ BIV Wts.			86.9	79.2	93.5	94.1

NOTE: Estimated standard errors are given in parentheses. The sample is quarterly, 1962:4–1987:2; $D_t = 1$ for $t > 1977{:}4$. Data were taken from the CITIBASE data bank.

tight bound, in which many errors' values trigger downweighting of those observations. In this case, the BIV point estimates do not seem to vary far from the classical IV estimates; the largest discrepancy is perhaps that of the intercept-shift coefficient γ_0. The BIV interval estimates are quite distinct from their IV counterparts in several cases, reflecting the effects of applying differential weights to influential observations.

The sets of BIV weights sheds much more light on the estimated equilibrium equation's properties. Figure 1 displays the BIV weights for the "$a = \sqrt{k}$" (tightest-bound) BIV specifications of the equation, fitted with and without a structural shift in 1977:4. The weights "without" the structural shift—the dashed line—are far below one in 1973–74 and 1977–83. Interestingly, however, the weights "with"—generated from the equation with a structural shift in place—are actually much smaller in the post-1977 period. In the period from 1978 on, all but a few of the observations have been downweighted in both these specifications, many substantially (by as much as 80 percent). In the case of a "clean" data set, that is, a data set with no influential outliers, each observation receives a unit weight in a robust regression. A least-squares procedure, on the other hand, always assigns unit weights to each observation, thus assuming that the data set never includes outliers

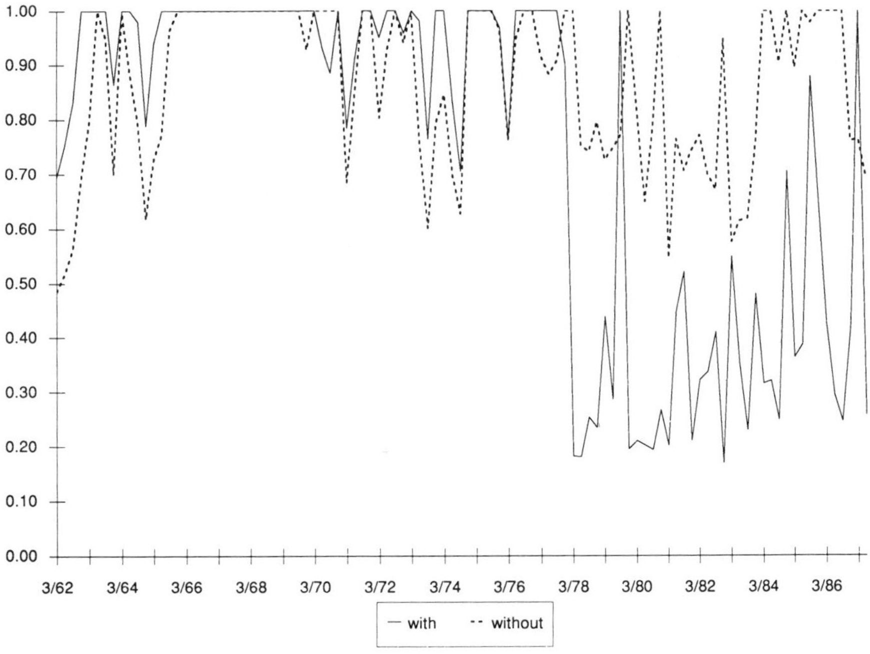

FIG. 1.

or data errors. As a consequence, the sum of weights in a least-squares regression is always equal to the sample size. Thus, in the IV regression considered here, the sum of weights is 102; its reduction to 75.6 in the tightest-bounded specification indicates the degree to which observations' influence in the post-1978 period is being constrained. This might be taken as a reflection of heteroskedasticity caused by the anticipation and implementation of new Fed operating policies in late 1979; however, homoskedasticity cannot be rejected by the data, with $F(59,34) = 1.45$ falling short of a 10 percent level of significance. In this case, we detect more subtle difficulties with the estimates than those that are revealed by many of the standard tests. There is clear evidence of structural instability at the 1977:4 split point in the coefficient vector; there is insufficient evidence to conclude a shift in the error variance at that point. The use of bounded-influence estimation has highlighted the degree to which the introduction of the structural shift has addressed some flaws in the simpler specification while introducing others. Analysis of the BIV weights should cast doubt on the adequacy of the shift parameters' estimates.

Turning to the error-correction equation, we may contrast the IV estimates with two sets of BIV estimates in the remaining columns of Table 2 (constructed with the same bounds). Divergences between the IV and BIV estimates should highlight weaknesses in the IV form of the model. In the point estimates, we may note some variation between IV and BIV estimates of δ_2, but the changes are within the one standard deviation confidence interval. Sizable variations exist for other coefficients, but their point estimates are not significantly different from zero. We note the degree to which the BIV estimates fit the data. The standard error of regression—and in most cases the R^2—of the BIV estimates dominates that of instrumental variables for the equation with shift terms included.

Figure 2 presents the BIV weights for the equation with and without shift parameters. The pattern of weights is indicative of considerable turbulence in 1970–75 and 1977 onward. Once again, the equation including structural shifts exhibits a greater degree of downweighting in the post-1977 period, although the differences are much less marked. Conversely, the equation "without" structural change—the dashed line—contains greater downweighting in the early 1970s.

The BIV weights' message should be carefully interpreted. Most empirical researchers confronted with evidence of structural change have responded by choosing an appropriate point in the sample at which to permit parameter variation. Whether that point's location is known a priori, or whether it is located by search techniques such as CUSUMS tests, Quandt log-likelihood tests, etc., is not at issue here; rather, we are concerned with the modeling of such a change. The information in any sample may not permit any more elaborate modeling of, say, the evolution of key parameters; but it is surely unlikely that a distinct change occurs at one point in time in many financial models. The BIV weights may thus be used to evaluate the degree to which any purported solution to the problem of structural instability has been successful by giving a clear indication of the degree to which data from the vicinity

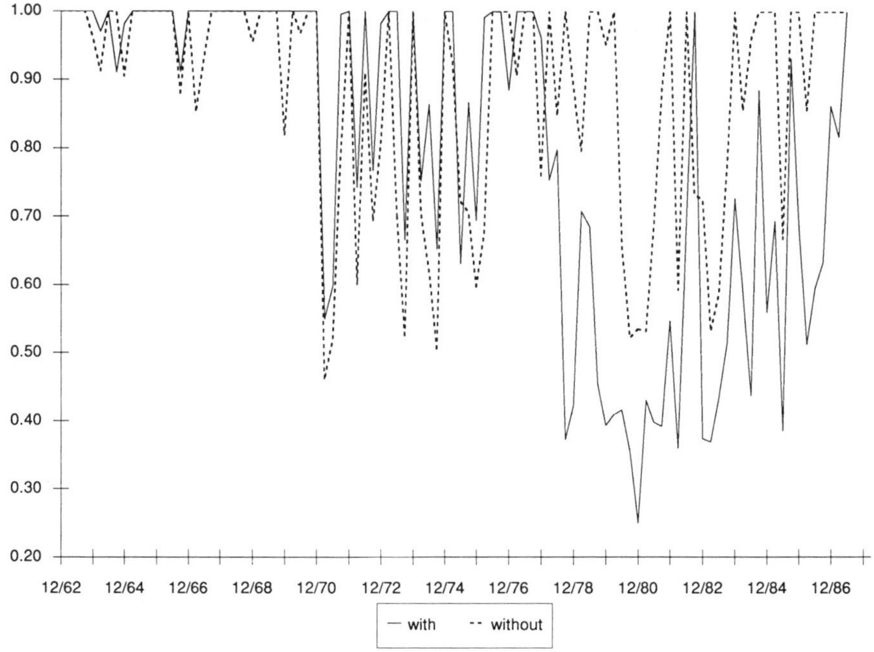

FIG. 2.

of the shift will play an important role in a bounded-influence estimation procedure. If there is very concentrated, severe downweighting of observations in this vicinity, the manner in which the structural change has been modeled should be reevaluated. In the cases of the equilibrium equation and error-correction equation modeled here, it seems evident that the shifts of intercept and slope coefficients have not been sufficient to capture the degree of coefficient turbulence during the era of financial deregulation. Our use of BIV has not provided a solution to the modeling of this turbulence, but it has pointed out weaknesses in the estimates which have not turned up on more conventional diagnostics of structural stability.

4. CONCLUSIONS AND SUGGESTIONS FOR FURTHER RESEARCH

In this paper, we have described an estimation technique—bounded-influence instrumental variables estimation—which may be profitably used to diagnose demand-for-money equations. The application of BIV has served to illustrate the degree to which commonly applied diagnoses of (and remedies for) structural change may not be adequate. Summary statistics and plots based on BIV estimates may have considerable power in such cases to indicate the degree to which classical assumptions are satisfied—even in the absence of a large sample. This may be of particular interest to researchers working with the relatively few time-series data points generated in the aftermath of financial deregulation, Fed policy shifts, and similar institutional changes in the monetary environment. Our application of BIV in this context does not serve to give us a "correctly specified" money-demand equation, but rather to warn the researcher (and his/her readers) of potentially damaging instability in the estimates.

APPENDIX

The objective function of the BIF estimator (Krasker and Welsch 1982) is

$$\Sigma_i w^2(u_i, d(x_i))\ (u_i)^2 \tag{1}$$

where x_i is the ith row of the $\mathbf{X}$ matrix. The partial derivatives of the objective function with respect to the $\boldsymbol{\beta}$-vector yield k normal equations defining the bounded-influence estimator (BIF) for the slope parameters:

$$0 = n^{-1}\ \Sigma_i\ w_i(u, d(x_i))\ (y_i - x_i\beta)\ x_i^T \tag{2}$$

where the weights $w(u, d(x_i))$ are defined as

$$w(u, d(x_i)) = \min\{\ 1,\ a/t\ \}, \qquad t = |u_i/\sigma|\ d(x_i)\ . \tag{3}$$

In equation (3) the constant a is the bound introduced to constrain outliers in both the explanatory variables and the residuals. The weights assume a unit value for $t \leq a$; for large values of t, the weights attached to the corresponding observations are inversely related to the standardized residuals in absolute value, and to $d(x_i)$. The term $d(x_i)$ is the so-called robust distance, and is defined as a quadratic function of the explanatory variables: $d(x_i) = (x_i A^{-1} x_i^T)^{1/2}$. The $(k \times k)$ matrix $\mathbf{A}$ is the robust second moment matrix of the explanatory variables:

$$\mathbf{A} = n^{-1} \Sigma_i \, \omega_i^2(d(x_i)) \, x_i^T x_i \, . \tag{4}$$

Since the $\mathbf{A}$ matrix is only a function of the explanatory variables, these weights are slightly different from those defined in equation (3). They do not include the residuals, and are defined as $\omega(d(x_i)) = \min\,[1, a/d(x_i)]$. The ith weight assumes a unit value if the absolute value of the ith standardized residual times the robust distance of x_i is smaller than the chosen bound a.

Once the weights are defined, the BIF estimator of the variance is analogous to the weighted least-squares estimator for the variance of the equation, but corrected for the downweighting introduced by the robust regression via the tuning constant c:

$$\sigma^2 c = n^{-1} \Sigma_i \, w_i^2(u,d(x_i)) \, (y_i - x_i\beta)^2 \, . \tag{5}$$

The constant c is defined as a function of the average weights: $c = [(n - k)/n]Ew_i^2(d(x_i)) = [(n - k)/n]\, E \min\,(1,a^2/d^2(x_i))$. Thus c represents the square of the average weight due to the explanatory variables times the ratio $(n - k)/n$. The model has a unique solution $(\beta, \sigma, \mathbf{A})$, obtained iteratively, which is asymptotically normal. In the computations required by the BIF estimator, the first step is to iteratively estimate the $\mathbf{A}$ matrix of equation (4), initializing using the robust distances from the familiar projection matrix $X(X^TX)^{-1}X^T$. The next block of computations consists of the joint estimation of the global weighting system $w_i(u_i,d(x_i))$, defined in equation (3), and the regression parameters. These estimates are obtained iteratively, updating at each step the estimates of the slope parameters, as defined in equation (2), the scale parameter σ, defined in equation (5), and the global weights.

The asymptotic covariance matrix of the final estimates is defined as

$$\mathbf{V}_\beta = \sigma^2 \, \mathbf{B}^{-1} \, \mathbf{A} \, \mathbf{B}^{-1} \, , \tag{6}$$

$$\mathbf{B} = E\,[w_i^* \, X^TX] \, , \tag{7}$$

$$\mathbf{A} = E\,\{w_i^2(d(x_i)) \, X^TX\} \, , \tag{8}$$

where $w_i^* = 1$ if $w_i(u,d(x_i)) = 1$, and $w_i^* = 0$ if $w_i(u,d(x_i)) < 1$; that is, the downweighted observations are excluded from the computation of the asymptotic variance of the coefficients.

The bounded-influence instrumental variables (BIV) estimator (Krasker and

Welsch 1985) is a quite straightforward extension of the single equation approach, with the inclusion of a set of instruments Q to solve the simultaneity problem. The assumptions about the instruments are the usual: plim $n^{-1} Q^T X = M$, and plim $n^{-1} Q^T U = 0$. The first-order conditions are the following:

$$0 = \Sigma_i \, w_i(u,q) \, (y_i - x_i\beta) \, q_i^T \, ; \tag{9}$$

$$\sigma^2 \, c = n^{-1} \, \Sigma_i \, w_i^2(u,q) \, (y_i - x_i\beta)^2 \, ; \tag{10}$$

$$\mathbf{A} = \mathrm{n}^{-1} \, \Sigma_i \, w_i^2(q) \, q_i^T q_i \, . \tag{11}$$

Their derivation follows the derivation of the BIF estimator, with q_i as the ith row of the matrix of instrumental variables $\mathbf{Q}$. The weights are $w_i = \min[1, a/\lambda_i]$, where the term λ_i is defined by $|u_i/\sigma| \, (q_i \, A^{-1} q_i^T)^{1/2}$, and the constant c in equation (10) is defined as

$$c = [(n - k)/n] \, E \, \min \, [1, a^2/(qA^{-1}q^T)] \, ; \tag{12}$$

that is, the average weight times the factor $(n - k)/n$. The same iterative method is used to derive a solution for $(\beta, \sigma, \mathbf{A})$.

LITERATURE CITED

Engle, Robert F., and C. W. J. Granger. "Co-Integration and Error Correction: Representation, Estimation, and Testing." *Econometrica* 55 (March 1987), 251–76.

Engle, Robert F., and B. S. Yoo. "Forecasting and Testing in Co-Integrated Systems." *Journal of Econometrics* 35 (1987), 143–59.

Fuller, Wayne. *Introduction to Statistical Time Series*. New York: John Wiley & Sons, 1976.

Furno, Marilena, and Christopher F. Baum. "Computational Aspects of Robust Estimators for Linear Regressions." *Computer Science in Economics and Management* 2 (1989), 221–37.

Goldfeld, Stephen. "The Case of the Missing Money." *Brookings Papers on Economic Activity* (1976) no. 3, 683–730.

Hallman, Jeffrey, Richard Porter, and David H. Small. "M2 per Unit of Potential GNP as an Anchor for the Price Level." *Staff Study 157*, Board of Governors of the Federal Reserve System, April 1989.

Hampel, Frederick. "A General Qualitative Definition of Robustness." *Annals of Mathematical Statistics* 42 (1971), no. 6.

Hendry, David F., Adrian R. Pagan, and J. Denis Sargan. "Dynamic Specification." In *Handbook of Econometrics*, edited by Z. Griliches and M. Intriligator. Amsterdam: North-Holland, 1983.

Hendry, David F., and Jean-Francois Richard. "On the Formulation of Empirical Models in Dynamic Econometrics." *Journal of Econometrics* 20 (1982), 3–33.

Krasker, William. "Estimation in Linear Regression Models with Disparate Data Points." *Econometrica* 48 (1980), 1333–46.

Krasker, William, Edwin Kuh, and Roy Welsch. "Estimation for Dirty Data and Flawed

Models." In *Handbook of Econometrics,* edited by Z. Griliches and M. Intriligator. Amsterdam: North-Holland, 1983.

Krasker, William, and Roy E. Welsch. "Efficient Bounded-Influence Regression Estimation." *Journal of the American Statistical Association* 77 (1982), 595–604.

______. "Resistant Estimation for Simultaneous Equations Models Using Weighted Instrumental Variables." *Econometrica* 53 (November 1985), 1475–88.

Patterson, K. "The Specification and Stability of the Demand for Money in the United Kingdom." *Econometrica* 54 (1987), 41–55.

Phillips, Peter C. B., and Pierre Perron. "Testing for a Unit Root in Time Series Regression." *Biometrika* 75 (1988), 335–46.

Rose, Andrew K. "An Alternative Approach to the American Demand for Money." *Journal of Money, Credit, and Banking* 17 (November 1985), 439–55.

Small, David H., and R. D. Porter. "Understanding the Behavior of M2 and V2." *Federal Reserve Bulletin* (April 1989), 244–54.

KEVIN D. SALYER

The Term Structure and Time Series Properties of Nominal Interest Rates: Implications from Theory

1. INTRODUCTION

There are few relationships in economics and finance that have been studied as often and with such variety of techniques as the term structure of interest rates. Yet, while a host of empirical methods have been employed in these studies, the majority have shared a common theoretical perspective based on the expectations hypothesis. And, as detailed in the survey by Shiller (forthcoming), these tests have also shared the common conclusion of rejecting the empirical implications of the expectations hypothesis. Consequently, there have been renewed efforts to develop an empirically consistent theory of the term structure which, at the same time, maintains the intellectual appeal of the expectation hypothesis (for example, see Campbell's (1986) analysis of the term structure of real interest rates).

The empirical failure of the expectations hypothesis has been interpreted as implying (or, more correctly, defining) the existence of a term premium; more recently, it has also been recognized that the data implies that the term premium varies over time (again, see Shiller (forthcoming)). These observations suggest that a necessary characteristic of any proposed theory of the term structure offered as a replacement for the expectations hypothesis is the potential for generating a time-varying term premium. Since recently developed theories of nominal interest rates based on the representative agent asset pricing paradigm (see Lucas 1982 and LeRoy 1984) do indeed imply a time-varying term premium and, moreover, these

The author is indebted to Alan Stockman, Tom Cooley, Dave Backus, Steve LeRoy, two referees, and the participants in work-shops at Dartmouth College and University of California. Davis, for helpful comments and suggestions.

KEVIN D. SALYER *is assistant professor of economics at University of California, Davis.*

Journal of Money, Credit, and Banking, Vol. 22, No. 4 (November 1990)

models include the expectations hypothesis as a special case, the question is raised whether the restrictions on the nominal term structure implied by these theories are consistent with the data.

In order to address this question, a model of one- and two-period nominal interest rates based on Lucas's (1982) cash-in-advance model is developed in the following section. This analysis generates a set of testable restrictions on the time series behavior of nominal interest rates. Included among these are (1) the volatility of long rates relative to that of short rates, (2) the correlation of the spread between the forward and one-period rates with the subsequent change in the one-period rate, and (3) the sign of the term premium. In section 3, these predictions are compared to the corresponding sample moments using quarterly data on three- and six-month Treasury bills over the period 1959:1–1984:4. This comparison demonstrates that while the model is consistent with restrictions (1) and (2), it predicts the wrong sign of the term premium. Hence, much like the equity premium puzzle studied by Mehra and Prescott (1985) within the barter economy analog of the model employed here, the behavior of the nominal term premium remains unexplained.

2. A MODEL OF ONE- AND TWO-PERIOD INTEREST RATES

In this section, the first-order conditions that describe optimal choices of one- and two-period nominal bonds from Lucas's (1982) cash-in-advance model are studied in order to determine the qualitative equilibrium characteristics of the two interest rates. It is assumed that agents are identical and maximize expected lifetime utility over an infinite horizon. In addition, the utility function is assumed to be time separable with the one-period utility function having the functional form:

$$U(c_t) = \begin{cases} \dfrac{c_t^{1-\gamma} - 1}{1 - \gamma} & \gamma \neq 1 \\ \ln c_t & \gamma = 1 \end{cases} \tag{1}$$

where c_t denotes consumption in period t. Agents' subjective discount rate is denoted by β, $\beta \epsilon (0, 1)$.

Agents face uncertainty due to random growth rates of the endowment (equal to consumption in equilibrium) (g_t), money (μ_t) and the nominal price level (ρ_t). The state of the world is defined to be the realization of the three growth rates; $s_t \equiv (g_t, \mu_t, \rho_t)$. It is assumed that s_t follows a finite state stationary Markov process with transition matrix **Π**. An element of **Π** is denoted $\pi(s, s')$ and is defined by

$$\pi(s, s') = \text{Prob}\,(g_{t+1} = g', \mu_{t+1} = \mu', \rho_{t+1} = \rho' | g_t = g, \mu_t = \mu, \rho_t = \rho) .$$

After the revelation of the state s, agents visit the asset market where returns on previously purchased bonds are received and asset holdings are revised. In particular, new quantities of one- and two-period nominal bonds as well as money are chosen. It is assumed that the purchase price of both bonds is \$1 with one-period bonds returning $\$[n_1(s)]$ in period $t+1$ while two-period bonds return $\$[n_2(s)]^2$ in period $t+2$. Agents then visit the goods market where consumption choices are purchased with money.

At the agent's optimum, the utility foregone from the purchase of an additional bond must, at the margin, be equal to the expected utility the bond's return implies. This intertemporal marginal relation implies the following necessary conditions:

$$\frac{U_t'(s)}{P_t(s)} = [n_1(s)]\ \beta\ E_s\left[\frac{U_{t+1}'}{P_{t+1}}\right] \tag{2}$$

$$\frac{U_t'(s)}{P_t'(s)} = [n_2(s)]^2\ \beta^2\ E_s\left[\frac{U_{t+2}'}{P_{t+2}}\right] \tag{3}$$

where $E_s\,[\cdot]$ denotes expectations conditional on state s and $P_t(s)$ is the nominal price level. I now use the assumptions on preferences and the growth rate processes to simplify equations (2) and (3).

Specifically, these assumptions permit equation (2) to be written as

$$[n_1(s)]^{-1} = \beta E_s\left[\frac{c_{t+1}^{-\gamma}(s')}{c_t^{-\gamma}(s)} \cdot \frac{P_t(s)}{P_{t+1}(s')}\right]. \tag{4}$$

Or, in terms of growth rates

$$[n_1(s)]^{-1} = \beta E_s\,\{[1 + \xi(s')]\} \tag{5}$$

where

$$[1 + \xi(s)] \equiv [1 + g(s)]^{-\gamma}\,[1 + \rho(s)]^{-1}\,. \tag{6}$$

An immediate implication of equation (5) is that the stochastic properties of the function $\xi(s)$ determine the equilibrium behavior of $n_1(s)$. That is, $\xi(s)$ is the relevant state variable for one-period (and, as shown below, two-period) nominal interest rates. Hence, for all that follows, discussion will be in terms of the derived state variable, $\xi(s)$, and its time-series characteristics.

Note that if the cash-in-advance constraint is always binding (which will be the case if $n_1(s) > 0$), then $\rho(s) = \mu(s) - g(s)$. Hence, it would be possible to express $\xi(s)$ directly in terms of the exogenous growth rates of money and the endowment. However, defining $\xi(s)$ in terms of the inflation rate permits a *more* general test of the intertemporal marginal conditions [equations (2) and (3)] associated with one- and two-period nominal interest rates. That is, these expressions and the restrictions they place on the time series properties of nominal interest rates, inflation, and consumption are also consistent with a money-in-the utility model like that studied in LeRoy (1984) as well as a transaction cost model as used in Marshall (1989). By not imposing a theory of price level determination implied by a particular monetary model, the restrictions I derive represent a broader evaluation of the theory of nominal interest rates as captured in equations (2) and (3).

To simplify equation (3), note that the law of iterated expectations implies the following:

$$[n_2(s)]^{-2} = \beta^2 E_s \left\{ \frac{U'_{t+1}}{U'_t} \cdot \frac{P_t}{P_{t+1}} E_{s'} \left[\frac{U'_{t+2}}{U'_{t+1}} \cdot \frac{P_{t+1}}{P_{t+2}} \right] \right\} . \tag{7}$$

Using the assumption on preferences and the definition given in equation (6) results in

$$[n_2(s)]^{-2} = \beta^2 E_s \{[1 + \xi(s')] E_{s'} [1 + \xi(s'')]\} \tag{8}$$

where s'' is used to denote the state in period $t + 2$.

These expressions for equilibrium one- and two-period nominal interest rates imply the following characterization of equilibrium behavior:

PROPOSITION 1 (P1): *If $\xi(s)$ is independently distributed, then $n_1(s) = n_2(s) = n$.*

PROOF: Follows immediately from equations (5) and (8).

To provide some intuition behind (P1), note that using the approximation $\ln(1 + x) = x$ implies

$$\xi(s) = -[\gamma g(s) + \rho(s)] . \tag{9}$$

Suppose γ and/or $g(s) = 0$ for all s implying that either agents are risk-neutral or there is no real risk in the economy. The only uncertainty, therefore, is due to inflation, and with expected inflation equal across all states, all nominal interest rates are constant. At the other extreme, suppose $\rho(s) = 0$ for all s so that there is no inflation. Now nominal interest rates are constant because the expected change in the marginal utility of consumption is constant across all states.

To characterize interest rate behavior when states are serially correlated, assume that $\xi(s)$ follows a two-state Markov process with possible realizations $\xi(h) > \xi(\ell)$. In addition, it is assumed that the transition probability matrix is symmetric with the probability of remaining in the same state denoted

$$\pi = Prob\ (\xi_{t+1} = \xi(i) | \xi_t = \xi(i)] \ ; \ i = (h, \ell) .$$

This characterization implies states are positively or negatively autocorrelated as π is greater than or less than ½. These assumptions permit the following:

PROPOSITION 2 (P2): *$n_1(h) > (<) n_1(\ell)$ and $n_2(h) > (<) n_2(\ell)$ as $\xi(s)$ is negatively (positively) autocorrelated.*

PROOF: The restrictions on the $\xi(s)$ process implies

$$E_h [1 + \xi(s')] > (<) E_\ell [1 + \xi(s')] \text{ as } \pi > (<) 1/2 .$$

This establishes the behavior of $n_1(s)$. Furthermore, it is straightforward to establish that the assumptions imply

$$E_h \{[1 + \xi(s')] E_{s'} [1 + \xi(s'')]\} > (<) E_\ell \{[1 + \xi(s')] E_{s'} [1 + \xi(s'')]\}$$
$$\text{as } \pi > (<) 1/2$$

which establishes the behavior of $n_2(s)$.

To understand these results, assume $\pi > 1/2$ and consider extreme values for γ, $g(s)$, and $\rho(s)$. That is, suppose $\gamma = 0$ and/or $g(s) = 0$ for all s, implying [from equation (6)] the inflation rate is *lower* in the high state and, because of positive autocorrelation, the expected inflation rate is also lower which results in a lower nominal interest rate. If $\rho(s) = 0$ for all s, then the realized and, more importantly, expected consumption growth rate is lower in the high state. The increased demand for savings causes equilibrium nominal interest rates to fall.

An important corollary of (P2) that will be used later in determining the sign of the term premia is that the contemporaneous covariance, $Cov[n_i, \xi]$; $i = 1, 2$ is determined by the pattern of serial correlation for $\xi(s)$. Specifically, $Cov[n_i, \xi] >$ $(<) 0$ as $\pi < (>) 1/2$, that is, $\xi(s)$ is negatively (positively) autocorrelated.

3. THE TIME SERIES PROPERTIES OF NOMINAL INTEREST RATES

The expressions for $n_1(s)$ and $n_2(s)$ are now used to develop a set of restrictions on the time series behavior of the two nominal interest rates. To facilitate this goal, the implied forward rate is defined as

$$f_1(s) \equiv \frac{[n_2(s)]^2}{n_1(s)} \tag{10}$$

so that equation (8) implies

$$[f_1(s)]^{-1} = \beta E_s \left\{ [1 + \xi(s')] \frac{n_1(s)}{n_1(s')} \right\} . \tag{11}$$

This expression, in conjunction with (P1) and (P2), yields the following proposition (again, assuming the two-state process for $\xi(s)$ described earlier):

PROPOSITION 3 (P3): *If $\xi(s)$ is serially uncorrelated, then* $f_1(h) = f_2(\ell) = n$. *If states are positively autocorrelated then*

$$n_1(h) > f_1(h) \; ; f_1(\ell) > n_1(\ell)$$

If states are negatively autocorrelated, then

$$f_1(h) > n_1(h) \; ; \; n_1(\ell) > f_1(\ell).$$

PROOF: The properties of $f_1(s)$ under serial independence are immediately given (P1). For the case of autocorrelation, note that equation (11) implies

$$[f_1(h)]^{-1} = \beta \left\{ \pi[1 + \xi(h)] + (1 - \pi)[1 + \xi(l)] \frac{n_1(h)}{n_1(l)} \right\} ;$$
$$[f_1(l)]^{-1} = \beta \left\{ \pi[1 + \xi(l)] + (1 - \pi)[1 + \xi(h)] \frac{n_1(l)}{n_1(h)} \right\} . \qquad (12)$$

Except for the ratio for one-period interest rates term, these expressions are identical to those for $[n_1 \, (s)]^{-1}$; $s = (h, \ell)$ as given in equation (5). Hence, whether $f_1 \, (s) \gtreqless n_1 \, (s)$ is determined by whether this ratio is greater or less than unity. Since Proposition 2 implies

$$\frac{n_1(h)}{n_1(l)} > (<) \; 1 \text{ as } \pi < (>) \; 1/2 \; ,$$

the stated qualitative relationships between $f_1 \, (s)$ and $n_1 \, (s)$ are obtained.

Two corollaries are generated from (P3). First, the definition of $f_1(s)$ implies that long rates ($n_2(s)$) will be less volatile than $n_1(s)$ regardless of the serial correlation properties of $\xi(s)$. To see this, note that for positive serial correlation the relationship between $f_1(s)$ and $n_1(s)$ can be rewritten (using the definition of $f_1(s)$) as

$$[n_1(h)]^2 < [n_2(h)]^2 < [n_2(\ell)]^2 < [n_1(\ell)]^2$$

where the middle inequality is due to (P2). In the case of negative autocorrelation, (P3) implies

$$[n_1(\ell)]^2 < [n_2(\ell)]^2 < [n_2(h)]^2 < [n_1(h)]^2 \; .$$

Again, (P2) establishes the middle inequality. Hence for both patterns of serial correlation, long rates vary over a smaller interval than short rates. The implication of this result is that the volatility of the conditional term premia generated from this model is not of great enough magnitude to overturn the volatility implications of the expectation hypothesis. That is, in the absence of a time-varying term premium, long rates are a geometric average of current and expected short rates so that the volatility relationship implied by (P3) is predicted. However, for the current model, it is possible for long rates to be more volatile than short rates if the variation in the term premia is great enough; (P3) implies this is not the case.

An additional implication of (P3) is that the unconditional covariance between the forward premium (that is, the spread between $f_1(s)$ and $n_1(s)$) and the subsequent change in one-period rates is always positive. That is, defining

$$fp(s) \equiv f_1(s) - n_1(s) \;, \tag{13}$$

$$\Delta n_1 \; (s, s') \equiv n_1(s') - n_1(s) \;, \tag{14}$$

Proposition 3 implies Cov $[fp(s), \Delta n_1(s, s')] > 0$ for all values of $\pi \neq ½$. Of course, the relationship between the forward premium and the change in the short rates has been extensively studied in empirical tests of the expectations hypothesis of the term structure. According to this hypothesis, the certain return from holding a two-period bond to maturity is equal to the expected return from purchasing a sequence of one-period bonds.[1] That is,

$$[n_2(s)]^2 = [n_1(s)] \; E_s \; [n_1 \; (s')] \tag{15}$$

or

$$f_1(s) = E_s \; [n_1 \; (s')] \; . \tag{16}$$

This relationship can be tested by the regression

$$\Delta n_{1,t+1} = \alpha + \beta fp_t + u_t \tag{17}$$

where $\Delta n_{1,t+1} \equiv \Delta n_1 \; (s, s')$, $fp_t \equiv fp(s)$ and u_t is an error term. Under the expectations hypothesis, the null hypothesis is ($\alpha = 0$, $\beta = 1$). As discussed in Shiller (forthcoming), the overwhelming majority of tests based on this regression reject the null values. On the other hand, the model developed here implies that, while the forward premium should on average predict the direction of movements of one-period rates ($\beta > 0$), it does not imply $\beta = 1$. That is, the forward rate is a biased predictor of the future spot rate with the bias being interpreted as a term premium. Specifically, defining the conditional term premium in terms of the rolling premium (the difference between the return on a two-period nominal bond and the expected return from the purchase of a sequence of one-period nominal bonds)[2] results in

$$tp(s) = [n_2(s)]^2 - [n_1(s)] \; E_s \; [n_1(s')] \tag{18}$$

[1]As discussed in Cox, Ingersoll, and Ross (1981), this is the "return to maturity" version of the expectations hypothesis.

[2]Alternatively, the conditional term premium could be defined as the difference between the expected nominal return from liquidating a two-period bond after one period and the certain nominal return from a one-period bond. The use of this definition, rather than that given in equation (18), does not alter any of the results or conclusions presented in the paper (details of the proof of this statement are available from the author).

or

$$tp(s) = [n_1(s)] \{[f_1(s)] - E_s [n_1(s')]\} . \qquad (19)$$

To determine the sign of the term in brackets [that is, the direction of bias in the regression equation (17)], note that using equation (5) and the definition of the covariance allows equation (11) to be written as

$$[f_1(s)]^{-1} = E_s \{[n_1(s')]^{-1}\} + [n_1(s)] \beta \, Cov_s \{[1 + \xi(s')], [n_1(s')]^{-1}\} \qquad (20)$$

where $Cov_s(\cdot)$ denotes the covariance conditional on state s. Since Jensen's inequality implies $E(x^{-1}) = [E(x)]^{-1} + \delta; \delta > 0$ for any positively valued random variable x, equation (20) can be expressed as

$$[f_1(s)]^{-1} = \{E_s[1 + n_1(s')]\}^{-1} + [n_1(s)] \beta \, Cov_s \{[1 + \xi(s')], [n_1(s')]^{-1}\} + \delta(s) . \qquad (21)$$

Assuming $\delta(s) \simeq 0$ for all s

$$[f_1(s)]^{-1} - \{E_s[n_1(s')]\}^{-1} = [n_1(s)] \beta \, Cov_s \{[1 + \xi(s')], [n_1(s')]^{-1}\} . \qquad (22)$$

Since (P2) implies $Cov_s \{[1 + \xi(s')], [n_1 (s')]^{-1}\} > (<) 0$ for all s as $\pi > (<) ½$ we have

$$[f_1(s)] < (>) E_s [n_1 (s')] \text{ for all } s \text{ as } \pi > (<) ½ . \qquad (23)$$

Or, from (19)

$$tp(s) < (>) 0 \text{ for all } s \text{ as } \pi > (<) ½ .[3] \qquad (24)$$

In other words, if states are positively (negatively) autocorrelated, the expected nominal return from a sequence of one-period bonds will be greater (less) than the certain nominal return from a two-period bond.

Some intuition behind the prediction of the sign of the conditional nominal term premium is developed by considering the determinants of the conditional term premium on real bonds (that is, bonds whose price and return are denominated in units of consumption). As discussed in LeRoy (1982), the sign of the conditional real term premium can be explained by appealing directly to the consumption-based

[3] If $\delta(s) > 0$, the prediction of the sign of the term premia when $\pi > ½$ is true, a fortiori.

CAPM (Breeden 1979). That is, since the conditional real term premium is similar to a risk premium in that it expressed the difference between a certain and expected real return, its sign must reflect the sign of the conditional covariance between the marginal utility of consumption and the return on the risky investment strategy (for example, a rollover of short-term bonds or the liquidation of a long-term bond before maturity). I now demonstrate that, because of the symmetry in the underlying asset pricing equations, an analogous covariance property is reflected in the sign of conditional nominal term premium.

In general, the assumption of time-separable utility implies that the first-order conditions determining optimal choices of assets with a certain return (R) and a risky return (Z) over a two-period horizon are

$$X_t = R_t^2 \, \beta^2 \, E_t(X_{t+2}) \, , \tag{25}$$

$$X_t = \beta^2 \, E_t(Z_{t+2} \, X_{t+2}) \tag{26}$$

where R is expressed as a one-period yield and $E_t(\cdot)$ denotes expectations conditional on the state at date t. For example, if the risky return is due to the purchase of a sequence of one-period bonds then $Z_{t+2} \equiv [1 + i_t]\,[1 + i_{t+1}]$ where i_t is the one-period (either real or nominal) net interest rate. If R_t and Z_t are real returns, then $X_t \equiv U_t'$; if R_t and Z_t are nominal returns, then $X_t \equiv U_t'/P_t$ for the cash-in-advance model studied here. By the definition of conditional covariance (denoted $Cov_t(\cdot)$), the difference between the conditional expected return on the risky asset and the certain return (that is, the conditional risk premium) can be expressed as

$$E_t(Z_{t+2}) - R_t^2 = -\frac{Cov_t(Z_{t+2}, X_{t+2})}{E_t(X_{t+2})} \, . \tag{27}$$

Of course, for real returns this is just the consumption based CAPM. But for nominally denominated assets, (27) implies nominal yields are priced as if agents are concerned about the volatility of U_t'/P_t. An implication of (27) is that while an environment of constant consumption implies a zero real term premium, the nominal term premium will be nonzero if inflation is stochastic.

To see that this property is indeed present in the behavior of the nominal term premium, note equations (22)–(24) imply

$$sign[tp(s)] = sign\,[Cov_s\,\{[1 + \xi(s')],\,[n_1\,(s')]\}] \tag{28}$$

Suppose states are positively autocorrelated so that $tp(s) < 0$ and consider the consequences of a realization of $\xi(h)$ in period $t + 2$. By definition, this implies a high value of U_{t+2}'/P_{t+2}. Furthermore, because of positive serial correlation, the state in period $t + 1$ was, on average, high (that is, $\xi(h)$ prevailed) so that the one-period nominal interest rate in period $t + 1$ was low. Hence, the realized return on the rollover strategy in period $t + 2$ is low, implying a negative covariance between the return and U'_{t+2}/P_{t+2}. From (27), the (nominal) conditional risk premium on the rollover strategy will be positive and the conditional nominal term premium will be negative since $tp(s)$ is defined as the negative of a risk premium.

4. EMPIRICAL TESTS AND RESULTS

As demonstrated in the preceding two sections, the model implies the following restrictions on the data:

$$Var\ (n_1) > Var\ (n_2) \tag{R1}$$

$$Corr\ [fp_t,\ \Delta n_{1,t+1}] > 0 \tag{R2}$$

$$Corr\ [n_{1,t},\ \xi_t] > (<)\ 0 \text{ as } Corr\ (\xi_t,\ \xi_{t-1}) < (>)\ 0 \tag{R3}$$

$$[f_{1,t}] - E\ [n_{1,t+1}] < (>)\ 0 \text{ as } Corr\ (\xi_t,\ \xi_{t-1}) > (<)\ 0\ . \tag{R4}$$

The data used to test these restrictions were obtained from the following sources. The returns on three- and six-month Treasury Bills were used as one- and two-period nominal interest rates respectively. These were obtained from the first month of each quarter as listed in various publications of the *Federal Reserve Bulletin*. Quarterly data on real consumption (excluding durables) and the GNP price deflator were obtained from the National Income and Product Accounts.[4] The sample period was 1959:1 to 1984:4.

Note that (R3) and (R4) depend critically on the serial correlation properties of $\xi(s)$ which, because of the presence of γ (agents' relative risk aversion) in its definition, is an unobservable variable. In order to test the latter two restrictions, artificial series for $\xi(s)$ were generated by combining observations on $(g_t,\ \rho_t)$ with the following assumed values for γ (0.05, 0.25, 0.5, 1.5, 2.0, 3.0, 5.0, 7.0, 10.0)[5] using the approximation in equation (9). The implied sample mean, standard deviation, and first-order serial correlation for the generated series are presented in Table 1. As shown, $\xi(s)$ exhibits positive autocorrelation for all values of γ. Hence the correlation in (R3) should be negative and the forward rate should, on average, be less than the future one-period spot rate.

The values for the relevant sample moments implied by (R1)–(R4) are presented in Table 2. While the model is supported by the data for (R1), (R2), and (R3), the observed behavior of the term premium as reflected in (R4) is dramatically at odds with the prediction of the model. Specifically, the model implies that, on average,

[4]Per capita consumption was not used due to the presence of large outliers in the quarterly population series (published by the Department of Commerce, Bureau of Economic Analysis), as noted by Watson (1986). Since, for the most part, population follows a deterministic trend, the use of actual consumption should at most bias the estimate of the mean of ξ.

[5]This range for γ was chosen since it contains all reasonable estimates for relative risk aversion. See the discussion in Mehra and Prescott (1985).

TABLE 1

MOMENTS OF GENERATED SERIES (ξ)

γ	.05	.25	.50	1.0	1.5	2.0	3.0	5.0	7.0	10.0
E (ξ	−.012	−.014	−.016	−.020	−.020	−.027	−.035	−.051	−.066	.089
sd (ξ)	.007	.007	.006	.007	.008	.010	.015	.025	.035	.051
$Corr$ (ξ_t, ξ_{t-1})	.82	.81	.75	.53	.33	.23	.17	.17	.19	.20

the return from purchasing a sequence of 3-month T-Bills should be *greater* than holding a six-month T-Bill until maturity; over the sample period the sequence strategy generated a *lower* average return than that received on a six-month T-Bill.

As an internal check of the model, an empirical methodology similar to that developed by Mehra and Prescott (1985) in their analysis of the equity premium was employed. Specifically, I combined estimates of the technological paramaters ($\xi(s)$, $\mathbf{\Pi}$) obtained from the data with assumed values for parameters describing preferences (β, γ) in order to generate artificial unconditional expected values for the forward premia using the models in section 2. The test consisted of comparing these artificial moments to the sample moments. In order to obtain estimates of ($\xi(s)$, $\mathbf{\Pi}$), the following two-state representation was used:

$$\xi(h) = \alpha + \delta \ ;$$
$$\xi(\ell) = \alpha - \delta \ .$$

It was assumed $\mathbf{\Pi}$ was a symmetric matrix with elements (π, $(1 - \pi)$) where π is defined by $\pi(h, h) = \pi(\ell, \ell) = \pi$. This restriction implies the ergodic distribution is given by $p(s) = ½$; $s = h, \ell$.

The above two-state representation implies the mean, standard deviation, and first-order serial correlation of ξ are, respectively,

$$E(\xi) = \alpha \ ;$$
$$sd(\xi) = \delta \ ;$$
$$corr(\xi_t, \xi_{t-1}) = (2\pi - 1) \ .$$

TABLE 2

(RI)	$Var(n_1) = 9.38 \times 10^{-4}$; $Var(n_2) = 8.92 \times 10^{-4}$
(R2)	$Corr[fp_t, \Delta n_{1,t+1}] = 0.1269$
(R3)	Contemporaneous Correlation between Three-Month T-Bill Yields (n_1) and ξ

γ	.05	.25	.50	1.0	1.5	2.0	3.0	5.0	7.0	10.0
$Corr(n_1, \xi)$	−.81	−.81	−.80	−.78	−.76	−.74	−.70	−.63	−.57	−.51

(R4)	$E[f_{1,t} - n_{1,t+1}] = .0032$ (standard deviation $= .0011$)

TABLE 3

CONDITIONAL AND UNCONDITIONAL FORWARD BIAS (all values × 10^{-2})

	γ			
	$.05 \leq \gamma \leq 3.0$	5.0	7.0	10.0
$b(h)$	−.02	−.07	−.20	−.53
$b(l)$	−.02	−.08	−.20	−.53
$\bar{B}$	−.02	−.07	−.20	−.54

For a given value of γ, values of (α, δ, π) were chosen so that the moments from the two-state process matched the corresponding entries in Table 1. The remaining parameter describing preferences, β, was held constant at .9925. These values were used as inputs into the previous section's models in order to calculate $[n_1(s), n_2(s)]$ which, in turn, were used to compute the conditional and unconditional bias in the forward rate $[b(s), \bar{B}]$, where these are defined as $b(s) \equiv f_1(s) - E_s\,[n_1(s')]$; $\bar{B} = [\Sigma_s b(s)]/2$.

As shown by the values in Table 3, the positive autocorrelation of ξ does indeed generate a negative rolling premia (both conditional and unconditional) from the model which, as stated earlier, is at odds with the data.

5. CONCLUSION

This paper has examined whether the time series properties of one- and two-period nominal interest rates implied by a simple cash-in-advance model are consistent with that exhibited in the data. While the model is consistent with some broad empirical characterizations, it fails to explain the behavior of the term premium. The failure represents another serious challenge to the representative agent asset pricing paradigm not unlike that of Mehra and Prescott's (1985) discussion of the equity premium puzzle. There, using a standard asset pricing model, they demonstrated that because of the relatively low *variance* of consumption, the model was incapable of generating an equity premium as large as that observed when reasonable values of relative risk aversion were used. Here, it is the *autocorrelation* properties of consumption and inflation that generate predictions for the nominal term premium that are at odds with the data. Perhaps a next step in resolving these equity and term premia puzzles would be the use of more general functional forms in describing agents' preferences; for example a nonseparable utility approach as in Dunn and Singleton (1986) and Constantinides (1989) or a nonexpected utility functional like that discussed in Epstein (1988) and Weil (1989). While these modifications may represent a possibility for salvaging the representative agent asset pricing paradigm with respect to the pricing of real-denominated assets, it is doubtful whether they will help to explain nominal returns and, in particular, the nominal term premia. That is, this paper has demonstrated that positive nominal term premia can be obtained if and only if there is negative autocorrelation in the growth rate of the term U_t'/P_t. As Constantinides (1989) has shown, habit persistence can induce negative autocorrelation in the growth rate of U'_t even though the growth rate of consumption is positively autocorrelated. However, it is my conjecture that this induced negative autocorrelation in the marginal utility of consumption is not, under reasonable parameter specifications, large enough to offset the positive serial correlation of inflation present in the data. Hence, even in light of these alternative preference specifications, the sign of the nominal term premium remains unexplained.

LITERATURE CITED

Breeden, Douglas T. "An Intertemporal Asset Pricing Model with Stochastic Consumption and Investment Opportunities." *Journal of Financial Economics* 7 (1979), 265–96.

Campbell, John. "Bond and Stock Returns in a Simple Exchange Model." *Quarterly Journal of Economics* 101 (November 1986), 785–803.

Constantinides, George. "Habit Formation: A Resolution of the Equity Premium Puzzle." Reproduced, University of Chicago, 1989.

Cox, John C., Jonathan Ingersoll, and Stephen A. Ross. "A Reexamination of Traditional Hypotheses about the Term Structure of Interest Rates." *Journal of Finance* 36 (September 1981), 769–99.

Dunn, Kenneth B., and Kenneth J. Singleton. "Modeling the Term Structure of Interest Rates under Non-separable Utility and Durability of Goods." *Journal of Financial Economics* 17 (1986), 27–55.

Epstein, Larry. G. "Risk Aversion and Asset Prices." *Journal of Monetary Economics* 22 (September 1988), 179–92.

LeRoy, Stephen F. "Expectations Models of Asset Prices: A Survey of Theory." *Journal of Finance* 37 (March 1982), 185–217.

______. "Nominal Prices and Interest Rates in General Equilibrium." *Journal of Business* 57 (April 1984), 177–213.

Lucas, Robert E., Jr. "Interest Rates and Currency Prices in a Two-Country World." *Journal of Monetary Economics* 10 (November 1982), 335–59.

Marshall, David. "Inflation and Asset Returns in a Monetary Economy." Reproduced, Northwestern University Department of Finance, 1989.

Mehra, Rajnish, and Edward C. Prescott. "The Equity Premium: A Puzzle." *Journal of Monetary Economics* 15 (March 1985), 145–61.

Shiller, Robert J. "The Term Structure of Interest Rates." In *Handbook of Monetary Economics,* edited by B. M. Friedman, North Holland, forthcoming.

Watson, Mark W. "Univariate Detrending Methods with Stochastic Trends." *Journal of Monetary Economics* 18 (July 1986), 49–75.

Weil, Philippe. "The Equity Premium Puzzle and the Risk-Free Rate Puzzle." *Journal of Monetary Economics* 24 (1989), 401–22.

YOONBAI KIM

Purchasing Power Parity in the Long Run: A Cointegration Approach

1. INTRODUCTION

PURCHASING POWER PARITY (PPP) is commonly interpreted as the comovement of the exchange rate and the relative price level of two countries. The short-run version of PPP—that is, that this comovement holds in the short run—has been rejected by numerous studies of the recent period of floating exchange rates. (See Frenkel (1981) as a classic example.) Whether such a relationship holds in the longer run still remains controversial and is the subject of this paper.

Propositions concerning long-run relationships have been tested in frequency-domain time series analysis by concentrating on low-frequency comovements of variables. [For instance, see Lucas (1980) and Summers (1983).] Rush and Husted (1985) use this approach to test long-run PPP. The cointegration technique developed by Engle and Granger (1987) offers an alternative in time-domain time series analysis. In this approach, the existence of a long-run relationship among two or more nonstationary processes is tested by examining the stability of deviations from the relationship using the coefficients estimated by fitting static regressions.

Empirical tests of long-run relationships require considerable amounts of data. Although econometric concerns always prefer more observations to less, Hendry (1986) points out that increasing the sample size by simple "time disaggregation" (from years to months, say) is not likely to reveal such long-run relationships. Isard (1983) estimates that two to five years are required for PPP to be reestablished after

The author thanks two anonymous referees for their helpful suggestions on earlier versions of this paper and John Myers for his editorial support. Richard Baillie kindly allowed me to use his program for the Johansen test.

YOONBAI KIM *is assistant professor of economics at Southern Illinois University.*

Journal of Money, Credit, and Banking, Vol. 22, No. 4 (November 1990)

a disturbance, while Frankel (1986) maintains that ten or more years may be required. High-frequency data (for example, monthly data) over a short horizon may not be able to detect convergence that takes this much time. Studies employing high-frequency data of major industrial countries from the recent floating exchange rate period have generally found poor performance of PPP, the existence of a unit root in real exchange rates, or noncointegration of the exchange rate and the price ratio. [For recent additions to this literature, see Adler and Lehman (1983), Baillie and Selover (1987), Corbae and Ouliaris (1988), Enders (1988), and Mark (1990).] On the other hand, PPP seems to hold more closely in the 1920s even in the high-frequency data (Frenkel 1978, 1981; Taylor and McMahon 1988). In this paper, we follow Frankel (1986) who argues that long-run PPP is most accurately tested using annual data over a long period.

Even in studies spanning many years of data, there is conflicting evidence on the long-run performance of PPP. Adler and Lehman's (1983) analysis fails to reject the hypothesis that real exchange rates follow a random walk. Their results therefore suggest that there is little or no tendency for the real exchange rate to return to long-run equilibrium.[1] Frankel (1986), on the other hand, rejects the random walk hypothesis using long annual data for the United States and the United Kingdom.[2]

In this paper, we apply cointegration analysis to examine the long term bilateral exchange rate-price relationship between the United States and each of the following five countries: Canada, France, Italy, Japan, and the United Kingdom. We also test whether the choice of the price index matters by considering two of the most popular price indices in PPP analysis—the wholesale price index (WPI) and the consumer price index (CPI). The exchange rate and WPI data are available for the 1900–87 period and the CPI data for the 1914–87 period.[3]

This paper is organized as follows: the next section reports the results of the cointegration tests. In section 3, a related hypothesis that the real exchange rate follows a random walk is tested. Section 4 reports estimation of error correction mechanism and compares our results with previous tests. In section 5, we test for existence of common trends in the exchange rates and relative prices. Section 6 concludes.

2. THE COINTEGRATION TESTS

PPP implies the following (linear) relationship between the nominal exchange rate and the relative price:

[1]Adler and Lehman interpreted the nonrejection of the random walk hypothesis as evidence for the efficient exchange market hypothesis. PPP holds *ex ante* in relative form, which implies the equality of real interest rates under certain conditions.

[2]We restrict our attention to recent work on PPP. See Officer (1982) and reference therein for traditional studies. Gailliot (1970) showed, albeit informally, that PPP holds in the long-run data set. Johnson (1987) also confirmed PPP using the cointegration technique and long-run U.S.–Canada data.

[3]All data up to 1972 are from Lee (1976). The 1973–87 data are from *International Financial Statistics Yearbook* (IMF, 1988), lines rf, 63 and 64. Lee's data set also covers other countries. They were not included in this study because some observations are missing during the war periods or the marching CPI data are not available. Unfortunately the German case was omitted for this reason.

$$s_t = \theta_0 + \theta_1 p_t + u_t \tag{1}$$

where s_t denotes the nominal exchange rate (the dollar price of foreign currency), p_t is either the ratio of the U.S. WPI to a foreign WPI (w_t) or the corresponding ratio for the CPI (c_t), and u_t is the disturbance term. All variables are in logarithms. Tests of PPP often takes the form of testing $H_o: \theta_1 = 1$.

In this context, the proposition that PPP holds in the long run implies that u_t can be represented by a stationary autoregressive moving-average (ARMA) process. The stationary is assumed to be due to some mean-reverting mechanism in which deviations from PPP disappear with time. The two variables s_t and p_t are said to be cointegrated if (i) the two are nonstationary and integrated of the same order, (that is, the same order of differencing is required to produce stationarity), (ii) there exists a *long-run equilibrium* relationship such as equation (1), and (iii) the error term is stationary. The application of the cointegration technique thus presupposes the nonstationarity of variables under consideration. Then cointegration exists if deviations from the presumed relationship have bounded variability (Banerjee et al. 1986). The relationship such as (1) could then be called the long-run equilibrium.

In order to test whether the exchange rate and the price ratio are cointegrated, we first test for the existence of unit roots in the stochastic process of exchange rates and price ratios. The tests follow Phillips and Perron (1988) and Perron (1988). They are robust to a wide variety of serial correlation and time-dependent heteroskedasticity, which seem very likely in our data set given the length of time-series, the smoothing inherent in the averaging process, and the regime changes that occurred during the time period. The tests therefore have an advantage over the tests proposed by Fuller (1976) and Dickey and Fuller (1979 and 1981).[4]

The tests involve estimating the following OLS equations for a variable y_t:

$$y_t = \hat{\alpha} y_{t-1} + \hat{u}_t \tag{2}$$

$$y_t = \mu^* + \alpha^* y_{t-1} + u_t^* \tag{3}$$

$$y_t = \tilde{\mu} + \tilde{\beta}(t - T/2) + \tilde{\alpha} y_{t-1} + \tilde{u}_t \tag{4}$$

where $\hat{u}_t$, u_t^*, and $\tilde{u}_t$ are residuals and T is the sample size.

Using the regression results, we obtain the following six statistics:

$Z(t_{\hat{\alpha}})$ tests $H_o: \alpha = 1$ in equation (2)

$Z(t_{\alpha^*})$ tests $H_o: \alpha = 1$ in equation (3)

$Z(\Phi_1)$ tests $H_o: (\mu, \alpha) = (0, 1)$ in equation (3)

$Z(t_{\tilde{\alpha}})$ tests $H_o: \alpha = 1$ in equation (4)

$Z(\Phi_2)$ tests $H_o: (\mu, \beta, \alpha) = (0, 0, 1)$ in equation (4)

$Z(\Phi_3)$ tests $H_o: (\beta, \alpha) = (0, 1)$ in equation (4)

In each case, the alternative is that y_t is stationary (for example, $|\alpha| < 1$). Details of obtaining the above six statistics are omitted for space reasons but can be found in

[4]In our case, the Dickey-Fuller tests (not reported) and the Phillips-Perron tests yielded very similar results. See Schwert (1989) for a comparison of the two unit-root tests.

TABLE 1

TESTS FOR UNIT ROOTS IN NOMINAL EXCHANGE RATE AND PRICE RATIOS

		$Z(t_{\alpha*})$	$Z(\Phi_1)$	$Z(t_\alpha)$	$Z(\Phi_3)$	$Z(\Phi_2)$
Canada						
	s_t	−1.17	1.06	−1.92	2.25	1.75
	w_t	−.85	.76	−2.94	5.16	3.68
	c_t	−2.19	2.45	−1.88	3.23	2.15
France						
	s_t	−.83	2.97	−1.67	1.30	2.58
	w_t	−.70	4.88*	−1.23	.50	3.40
	c_t	−1.75	9.06**	−.60	1.36	6.05*
Italy						
	s_t	−.66	2.40	−1.86	1.38	2.38
	w_t	−.61	2.50	−2.00	1.51	2.55
	c_t	−1.18	3.61	−1.63	1.22	2.73
Japan						
	s_t	−.90	1.15	−1.35	.47	.80
	w_t	−.78	1.38	−1.40	.52	1.06
	c_t	−.95	1.63	−1.38	.59	1.18
U.K.						
	s_t	−.25	1.12	−2.72	4.13	3.47
	w_t	.97	2.36	−1.66	3.29	3.43
	c_t	.47	2.51	−1.27	1.55	2.73

NOTES: s_t is the log of the dollar price of the foreign currency. w_t (c_t)(is the log of the U.S.-foreign WPI (CPI) ratio. The period of estimation is 1901–1987 for s_t and w_t, and 1915–1987 for c_t. * and ** denote significance at the 5 and 1 percent levels, respectively. With sample size 50 at the 5 (1) percent significance level, the critical values are −2.93 (−3.58) for Z ($t_{\alpha*}$), −3.50 (−4.15) for Z (t_α), 4.86 (7.06) for Z (Φ_1), 5.13 (7.02) for Z (Φ_2), and 6.73 (9.31) for Z (Φ_3). See Fuller (1976, p. 373) and Dickey and Fuller (1981, p. 1063).

Perron (1988). These $Z(\cdot)$-statistics require the regression of the three first-order autoregressive models only and are free from nuisance parameters such as the order of autoregression in AR processes. As these statistics are asymptotically equivalent to the corresponding Dickey-Fuller tests, critical values from Fuller (1976) and Dickey-Fuller (1981) can be used in testing.

The results of the tests are reported in Table 1 except $Z(t_{\hat{\alpha}})$ as most variables appear to contain a nonzero constant term.[5] None of the simple $Z(t_{\alpha*})$ and $Z(t_{\tilde{\alpha}})$ statistics are significant at the 5 percent level. $Z(\Phi_1)$ and $Z(\Phi_2)$ are significant only for the U.S.–France w_t and c_t ratios; this is probably due to the constant term. Also, tests involving first differences of the series (not reported) reject the presence of unit roots in all cases. Thus, all exchange rate and price series appear to be integrated of order 1.

Table 2 reports the estimation results of the cointegrating equations.[6] In Table 2a the nominal exchange rate is regressed on the price ratio, and Table 2b reports the reverse model. Except for Canada, the coefficients of $w_t(c_t)$ in Table 2a or s_t in Table 2b are close to unity.

[5]Evaluation of $Z(\cdot)$-statistics requires the choice of a truncation lag l corresponding to the maximum order of autocorrelation in the disturbances in the construction of a consistent estimate of variance, $\sigma^2 = \lim T^{-1} E(\Sigma u_t)^2$. In Tables 1 and 3, the results for $l = 3$ are reported. The results are similar for different values of l as long as it is not too large (for example, $l < 10$). A consistent estimate of σ^2 is obtained following a suggestion by Newey and West (1987).

[6]The analysis of PPP conventionally takes the ratio of two price series in regressions. Ahking (1989) used the levels of the price series in an analysis of the dollar-sterling exchange rate in the 1920s and found results that are somewhat contradictory to those obtained by Taylor and McMahon (1988) who used the ratio of the same price data.

TABLE 2a

COINTEGRATING REGRESSIONS: NOMINAL EXCHANGE RATES ON PRICE RATIOS

		const	$w_t(c_t)$	$\bar{R}^2$	σ	$Z(t_{\tilde{\alpha}})$
Canada	A.	−.092	.731	.53	.055	−2.94
	B.	−.051	.551	.11	.078	−1.96
France	A.	−.042	1.015	.99	.150	−4.64**
	B.	.010	.958	.98	.220	−3.59*
Italy	A.	.043	1.029	.99	.230	−3.49*
	B.	−.056	.991	.98	.242	−3.56*
Japan	A.	.015	.959	1.00	.156	−3.38*
	B.	−.085	.953	.98	.328	−1.74
U.K.	A.	−.019	.956	.93	.100	−3.75*
	B.	.039	.996	.85	.143	−2.86

TABLE 2b

COINTEGRATING REGRESSIONS: REVERSE MODEL

		const	$w_t(c_t)$	$\bar{R}^2$	σ	$Z(t_{\tilde{\alpha}})$
Canada	A.	−.087	.728	.53	.054	−2.83
	B.	−.021	.221	.11	.050	−2.74
France	A.	.054	.978	.99	.147	−4.61**
	B.	.017	1.026	.98	.227	−3.51*
Italy	A.	−.020	.961	.99	.223	−3.48*
	B.	.791	.993	.98	.242	−3.53*
Japan	A.	−.004	1.038	1.00	.163	−3.35*
	B.	.132	1.028	.98	.341	−1.67
U.K.	A.	.043	.972	.93	.101	−3.51*
	B.	−.004	.858	.85	.133	−2.60

NOTES: The relative price uses WPI(CPI) for regressions marked with A(B) for the period 1900–1987 (1914–1987). * and ** denote significance at the 5 and 1 percent levels, respectively. The critical value for $Z(t_{\tilde{\alpha}})$ for a sample of size 50 at the 5 (1) percent significance level is −3.29(−4.12). See Engle and Yoo (1987, p. 158).

Table 2 also reports the $Z(t_{\tilde{\alpha}})$ as a test for unit roots in the residual. Note that the estimated residuals of the cointegrating regressions in finite samples will appear more stationary than the true values of the error term. The use of the Dickey-Fuller test will, therefore, reject the null hypothesis of no cointegration too often (Engle and Granger 1987). We use the critical values tabulated in Engle and Yoo (1987, p. 158) as they allow for higher order autocorrelation in error terms.

In most cases, the exchange rate is cointegrated with both the CPI and the WPI ratios at the 5 percent significance level. Exceptions are the Canadian dollar rate with respect to both the WPI and the CPI ratio, and the yen- and pound-exchange rates with respect to the CPI ratio. In general, the hypothesis of noncointegration is more strongly rejected when the WPI ratio is used than when the CPI ratio is used.

Reasons for noncointegration remain to be explored. An examination of the underlying data reveals that noncointegration in the case of the Canadian dollar might be due to the absence of large changes in the exchange rate and the price ratio over the sample period. This is probably the result of similarity in macroeconomic policies of Canada and the United States which have prevented the exchange rate and price ratio from deviating from unity. With relatively little variation in the exchange rate and price ratio, the long-run relationship may have been swamped by short-run dynamics. In the case of the yen-dollar exchange rate and CPI ratio, the noncointegration appears due to nonstationarity combined with slow convergence over the whole period. The case of the U.K.–CPI combination is not clear. Plots of the WPI-based and CPI-based real exchange rates (not shown) do not exhibit much difference in their behavior to warrant the difference in the result of cointegration tests. It might be that the noncointegration result is due to a data problem. Frankel (1986), working with the same combination but with a longer data set, found that the real dollar-pound exchange rate is stationary.

3. DO REAL EXCHANGE RATES FOLLOW A RANDOM WALK?

In this section, we test the hypothesis that the real exchange rate follows a random walk. The hypothesis implies that the tendency for the real exchange rate to return to some long-run equilibrium is very weak or nonexistent. Adler and Lehman (1983) accepted the random walk hypothesis, while Frankel (1986) rejected it. Frankel's test is based on the unit root test by Dickey and Fuller. Adler and Lehman employed a different approach, which will be considered in detail in the next section. Our test is based on the Phillips-Perron tests defined in section 2 and reported in Table 3. $r_t^w(r_t^c)$ is the log of the WPI(CPI)-based real exchange rate.

The results of the unit root tests are that the null hypothesis that the real exchange rate follows a random walk is rejected for all cases except for the CPI-based real Canadian dollar, yen, and pound. An interesting finding is that the WPI-based real yen-dollar rate contains some time trend. Stationarity in that rate is significant only when the time trend is included.

The results are consistent with the cointegration tests reported in the previous

TABLE 3

TESTS FOR UNIT ROOTS IN REAL EXCHANGE RATES

		$Z(t_{\alpha^*})$	$Z(\Phi_1)$	$Z(t_{\tilde{\alpha}})$	$Z(\Phi_3)$	$Z(\Phi_2)$
Canada						
	r_t^w	−3.12*	4.97*	−3.36*	5.85	3.90
	r_t^c	−2.44	3.41	−2.71	3.71	2.71
France						
	r_t^w	−4.56**	10.62**	−4.60**	10.84**	7.23**
	r_t^c	−3.25*	5.42*	−3.54*	6.41	4.28
Italy						
	r_t^w	−3.30*	5.58*	−3.39	5.96	3.97
	r_t^c	−3.52*	6.38*	−3.54*	6.54	4.37
Japan						
	r_t^w	−2.52	3.44	−3.69*	7.08*	4.85
	r_t^c	−1.47	1.31	−2.12	2.77	1.98
U.K.						
	r_t^w	−3.62**	6.69*	−3.53*	6.60	4.41
	r_t^c	−2.84	4.12	−2.88	4.15	2.76

NOTES: r_t^w *and* r_t^c are the log of the real exchange rate, based on the WPI and CPI ratios, respectively. The period of estimation is 1901–1987 for r_t^w and 1915–1987 for r_t^c. See Table 1 for notation and critical values.

section except for the WPI-based real Canadian dollar. The fact that the real exchange rate is a stationary process implies that the cointegrating coefficient between the exchange rate and the price ratio is not too different from unity, as shown already in Table 2.

Overall, both the cointegration tests and the unit root tests indicate that neither Adler and Lehman (1983) nor Frankel (1986) can be generalized. Although our results are more consonant with those of Frankel, they also point out that the choice of price indices matters as seen in the case of Japan. However, the case seems to be more or less unique and probably due to the secular growth in Japan which has been much higher than in the United States during the last three decades or so. PPP is less likely to hold when the two countries differ in their productivity growth and demand patterns and when the price index used gives a significant weight to nontraded goods as does CPI. This is because the price of nontraded goods relative to traded goods tends to rise with productivity growth biased toward traded goods or with a demand shift in favor of nontraded goods (Balassa 1964, Samuelson 1964, and Marston 1987).

4. ESTIMATION OF ERROR CORRECTION MECHANISM

The hypothesis that the real exchange rate follows a random walk was rejected by the finding that the exchange rate and the price are cointegrated, with the cointegrating coefficient close to one. We also showed this by examining the properties of real exchange rates. However, Adler and Lehman (1983) argued that virtually all of the real exchange rates series they considered, using both annual data over a long period and monthly data over a short period, follow a random walk. Their test was based on the martingale model of the change in the real exchange rate. That is, they tested $H_o: \phi_i = 0, i = 1, 2, \ldots, d$, in the following equation:

$$\Delta r_t = \sum_{i=1}^{d} \phi_i \Delta r_{t-i} + u_t \qquad (5)$$

where Δ is the first difference operator and d was set at 6 or 10.

For none of the countries considered in this paper was the hypothesis rejected, either for the period ending in 1972 (as in Adler and Lehman) or for the period ending in 1987. This apparent inconsistency between our results and those of Adler and Lehman can be explained as follows.

The representation theorem by Engle and Granger (1987) suggests that for two cointegrated variables (here s_t and p_t), we can find an error correction mechanism of the following form:

$$\Delta s_t = \delta_0 \Delta p_t + \sum_{i=1}^{d} (\delta_i \Delta p_{t-i} + \eta_i \Delta s_{t-i}) + \gamma E_{t-1} \qquad (6)$$

TABLE 4

SIGNIFICANCE LEVEL OF ADLER-LEHMAN RESTRICTIONS (1907–1987)

	d	H_0^1	H_0^2	H_0^3	H_0^J
Canada	6	.960	.759	.057	.011
	1	.234	.204	.068	.001
France	6	.960	.282	.332	.010
	0	.758	.000	n.a.	.002
Italy	6	.996	.176	.132	.007
	0	.233	.000	n.a.	.000
Japan	6	.908	.849	.014	.000
	1	.990	.012	.629	.001
U.K.	6	.921	.800	.008	.000
	1	.501	.071	.005	.000

NOTES: $H_0^1 : \alpha_0 = 1$; $H_0^2 : \gamma = 0$; $H_0^3 : \alpha_i + \beta_i = 0,\ i = 1, \ldots, n$. H_0^J tests the joint restrictions. The WPI ratios are used.

where E_t is the error correction term and obtained as the residual of the cointegrating equation for the nominal exchange rate. A similar equation can be constructed for Δp_t.[7]

It can then be seen that equation (5) imposed the restrictions:

$$H_o : \delta_o = 1 \; ; \; \delta_i + \eta_i = 0 \; , \; i = 1, 2, \ldots, d \; ; \; \gamma = 0$$

on equation (6). Among the restrictions, $\gamma = 0$ refutes the existence of error correction mechanism and cointegration. Table 4 reports the significance levels of these restrictions, separately and jointly, for the WPI-ratio. Each individual restriction, if tested separately, is rarely rejected at conventional significance levels when six lags are included as in Adler and Lehman. (The case with ten lags is similar.) The joint restrictions are, however, strongly rejected. More interestingly, when insignificant lags are removed from the model, individual restrictions turn out to be much more significant and thus are more likely to be rejected. In the selected model, the restriction on the error correction term (H_o^2) is rejected at the 5 percent level for France, Italy, and Japan, and at the 10 percent level for the United Kingdom; but it is not rejected for Canada. Contrary to their conjecture, the restrictions on coefficients are *less* likely to be significant with *longer* lags. Overall, the results by Adler and Lehman are due to the use of a misspecified model with too many lags.

Table 5 reports the estimated model for the exchange rate and the WPI ratio. (Canada is excluded as the above results indicate noncointegration of the exchange rate and price ratio.) A search was started with a model containing four lagged changes in each variable as well as the constant, the contemporaneous change in Δp_t

[7]Error correction representation usually takes the form of simultaneous equations for Δs_t and Δp_t in which no contemporaneous terms appear on the right-hand side. Efficient estimation requires simultaneous estimation of the two equations. An alternative is to triangularize the system: include the contemporaneous change of the other variable in one equation only. This makes the error terms of the two equations orthogonal to each other. Δp_t is included in equation (6) for this reason. The choice of Δs_t in ECM representation follows an initial investigation showing that the ECM terms are more significant in that equation than in the Δp_t-equation.

TABLE 5

ESTIMATION OF ERROR CORRECTION MODEL (1907–1987)

France:

$$\Delta s_t = 1.094\ \Delta w_t - .372\ E_{t-1}$$
$$(.42) \quad (.10)$$
$$\bar{R}^2 = .61\ \sigma = .122\ DW = 1.98$$
$$Chow(5,74) = 1.06\ \chi^2(5) = 5.66\ Q(25) = 19.93$$
$$LM(2) = 5.18\ \text{ARCH}(1) = 5.92^*\ H(3) = 38.62^{**}$$

Italy:

$$\Delta s_t = -.065 - .488\ E_{t-1}$$
$$(.02) \quad (.08)$$
$$\bar{R}^2 = .27\ \sigma = .185\ DW = 1.64$$
$$Chow(5,74) = .83\ \chi^2(5) = 4.17\ Q(25) = 27.49$$
$$LM(2) = 5.60\ \text{ARCH}(1) = 1.00\ H(2) = 3.42$$

Japan:

$$\Delta s_t = .761\ \Delta w_t - .499\ E_{t-1}$$
$$(.11) \quad (.12)$$
$$\bar{R}^2 = .66\ \sigma = .141\ DW = 1.50$$
$$Chow(5,74) = 1.55\ \chi^2(5) = 7.75\ Q(25) = 25.64$$
$$LM(2) = 7.57\ \text{ARCH}(1) = 4.40\ H(3) = 5.44$$

U.K.:

$$\Delta s_t = .339\ \Delta s_{t-1} + .518\ \Delta w_t - .277\ \Delta\ w_{t-1} - .261\ E_{t-1}$$
$$(.22) \quad (.76) \quad (.15) \quad (.12)$$
$$\bar{R}^2 = .34\ \sigma = .066\ DW = 1.92$$
$$Chow(5,72) = 2.30\ \chi^2(5) = 11.39\ Q(23) = 31.44$$
$$LM(2) = 4.03\ \text{ARCH}(1) = 2.35\ H(10) = 12.25$$

NOTES: Heteroskedasticity-consistent standard errors are in parentheses under coefficient estimates. σ is the standard error of estimate, *DW* is the Durbin-Watson statistic, *Chow* and χ^2 are the Chow and Hendry's tests of predictive accuracy, respectively, *Q* is the Box-Pierce statistic, *LM* is the Lagrange multiplier test of residual serial correlation, ARCH is the Lagrange multiplier test of autoregressive conditional heteroskedasticity, and *H* is the White's test of general heteroskedasticity. All are distributed as χ^2, except *Chow* which has an *F* distribution. Degrees of freedom are inside parentheses. * and ** denote the significance at the 5 and 1 percent levels, respectively.

and the error correction terms.[8] The results show that a parsimonious model of exchange rate movements can be constructed and in such a model the error correction term is invariably significant. The estimated coefficients suggest that about 30 to 50 percent of deviations from PPP are corrected by exchange rate movements within the subsequent year. Various specification tests suggest that the estimated model is quite reasonable given its parsimony. In particular, the Chow and Hendry's prediction tests indicate that the estimated models have impressive predictive power in the last five years of the sample period (1983–1987) which has been characterized as one of the most volatile exchange rate periods.

5. ARE THERE COMMON TRENDS IN THE EXCHANGE RATES AND RELATIVE PRICES?

So far we have discussed the relationship between the exchange rate and the price ratio on a bilateral basis. An implicit assumption is that each of the dollar exchange

[8]Whenever the contemporaneous change in the price ratio (Δw_t) is included, instrumental variable estimation was used in order to avoid biases from simultaneity. Instruments were four lagged values of the own variable and four lagged values of the error correction term.

rates move independently of the others with no long-run relationship. In other words, there are no common trends. Since foreign exchange markets involve simultaneous determination of several exchange rates, one would wonder whether common trends in exchange rates exist as if they are driven by the same fundamentals. If they do, it would affect how one models the joint determination of two or more exchange rates. It would also be interesting to see whether other exchange rates or price ratios share the time trend that seems to exist in the bilateral case of the United States and Japan.

Recently, Stock and Watson (1988) have developed a test for the existence of common trends in a set of nonstationary variables. In the following, we implement the multivariate test for unit roots due to Johansen (1988), which has been applied to an analysis of exchange risk premia by Baillie and Bollerslev (1988). The likelihood-ratio test for the existence of at most r cointegrating factors (or at least $(p - r)$ stochastic trends) in a set of p variables is

$$-2 \ln Q_r = -T \sum_{i=r+1}^{p} \ln (1 - \hat{\lambda}_i) \ . \tag{7}$$

The $\hat{\lambda}_i$s are the squared canonical correlations ($\hat{\lambda}_1 > \hat{\lambda}_2 > \ldots > \hat{\lambda}_p$) between the two sets of residual vectors, $\mathbf{R}_{0t}$ and $\mathbf{R}_{1t}$, obtained in the following two regressions:

$$\Delta \mathbf{X}_t = \sum_{i=1}^{k-1} \Gamma_{0i} \Delta \mathbf{X}_{t-i} + \mathbf{R}_{0t}$$

$$\mathbf{X}_{t-k} = \sum_{i=1}^{k-1} \Gamma_{1i} \Delta \mathbf{X}_{t-i} + \mathbf{R}_{1t}$$

where $\mathbf{X}_t$ is the p-vector of variables and Γ_{ji} are matrices of coefficient estimates. Cointegration holds if r is greater than or equal to 1. Johansen (1988) shows that $-2\ln Q_r$ is distributed as a function of a $(p - r)$-dimensional standard Brownian motion and tabulates the distribution of the test statistic.

Table 6 reports the results along with the 95 percent quantiles. The order of the AR process (k) in x_t is taken as 3. The use of other values makes little difference in the results. We cannot reject the hypothesis that there are five stochastic trends in each set of five exchange rates or relative prices at the 5 percent level. Alternatively, there are no cointegrating factors in the system and the five exchange rates or relative prices share no long-run equilibrium relationship. Our results can be contrasted with Baillie and Bollerslev (1988) who found one common trend among seven *monthly* exchange rates for the recent period of floating exchange rates. It is not easy to explain the difference in results beyond that the present study employs a period and frequency which are different from Baillie and Bollerslev's. But our results are not surprising given that the countries under consideration here have had

TABLE 6

JOHANSEN'S MULTIVARIATE TEST FOR UNIT ROOTS

	$-2\ln Q_r$			
r	s_t	w_t	c_t	95% quantile
4	.045	.135	.754	4.2
3	2.047	1.999	3.963	12.0
2	4.517	4.728	10.664	23.8
1	12.739	13.242	18.456	38.6
0	25.974	30.653	32.200	57.2

NOTE: The 95 percent quantiles are adapted from Johansen (1988, p. 239).

vastly different inflation experience and corresponding movements in the exchange rates. The results support our tests in the previous sections which dealt with bilateral exchange rates separately. They also support our conjecture that the existence of a time trend in the real exchange rate in the U.S.-Japan bilateral case is probably unique among industrial countries.

7. CONCLUDING REMARKS

In this paper, we examined long-run PPP in the bilateral exchange rates of the dollar vis-à-vis five currencies, applying the cointegration technique. The main findings may be summarized as follows: the nominal exchange rate is cointegrated with both the WPI-ratio and the CPI-ratio, except for the Canadian dollar, which is cointegrated with neither. For the yen and the pound, cointegration is found for the WPI-ratio but not for the CPI-ratio. When cointegration is confirmed, the cointegrating coefficient between the exchange rate and the price ratio is close to one. The hypothesis that the real exchange rate follows a random walk is rejected in all cases but the Canadian dollar, yen, and pound in combination with the CPI ratio. The Canadian dollar-WPI combination is interesting in that noncointegration is not rejected but the real exchange rate is stationary. Estimated error correction models suggest that deviations from PPP significantly affect exchange rates in all cases where cointegration is confirmed. Finally, our approach dealing with exchange rates and price ratios on a bilateral basis is supported by the finding that each set of exchange rates or relative prices share no common trends.

Thus PPP seems to hold in general. These results are quite opposite to those obtained using high-frequency data for the recent floating exchange rate period. Testing PPP as a long-run concept would apparently require long-run data. This leads to the question why PPP does not hold for some cases. Our results suggest two probable reasons. One is limited variability in the data. For instance, the U.S.-Canada and U.S.-U.K. relative price ratios have varied much less than the other three pairs. In such cases, it is difficult to strongly reject noncointegration (or accept PPP). Another reason seems to be real shocks and subsequent changers in the price of nontraded goods relative to traded goods. This is first shown as the general finding that the nominal exchange rate is more strongly cointegrated with the WPI-ratio than with the CPI-ratio. In the case of the yen-dollar, the failure to reject noncointegration with the CPI ratio cannot be explained by limited variability since the CPI ratio varied as much as the WPI ratio. It might be due to the secular increase in the relative price of nontraded goods in Japan, which has been higher than in the United States as a result of the long-term differential in economic growth.

LITERATURE CITED

Adler, Michael, and Bruce Lehman. "Deviations from Purchasing Power Parity in the Long Run." *Journal of Finance* 38 (December 1983), 1471–87.

Ahking, Francis W. "Further Results on Long-Run Purchasing Power Parity in the 1920s." *European Economic Review,* forthcoming.

Baillie, Richard T., and Tim Bollerslev. "Common Stochastic Trends in a System of Exchange Rates." *Journal of Finance* 44 (March 1988), 167–81.

Baillie, Richard T., and David D. Selover. "Cointegration and Model of Exchange Rate Determination." *International Journal of Forecasting* 3 (1987), 43–51.

Balassa, Bela. "The Purchasing Power Parity Doctrine: A Reappraisal." *Journal of Political Economy* 72 (December 1964), 584–96.

Banerjee, Anindya, Juan J. Dolado, David F. Hendry, and Gregor W. Smith. "Exploring Equilibrium Relationships in Econometrics through Static Models: Some Monte Carlo Evidence." *Oxford Bulletin of Economics and Statistics* 48 (August 1986), 253–77.

Corbae, Dean, and Sam Ouliaris. "Cointegration and Tests of Purchasing Power Parity." *Review of Economics and Statistics* 70 (August 1988), 508–11.

Dickey, David A., and Wayne A. Fuller. "Distribution of the Estimators for Autoregressive Time Series with a Unit Root." *Journal of the American Statistical Association* 74 (June 1979), 427–31.

______. "Likelihood Ratio Statistics for Autoregressive Time Series with a Unit Root." *Econometrica* 49 (July 1981), 1057–72.

Enders, Walter. "ARIMA and Cointegration Tests of PPP under Fixed and Flexible Exchange Rate Regimes." *Review of Economics and Statistics* 70 (August 1988), 504–508.

Engle, Robert F., and Clive W. J. Granger. "Cointegration and Error Correction: Representation, Estimation, and Testing." *Econometrica* 55 (March 1987), 251–76.

Engle, Robert F., and Byung Sam Yoo. "Forecasting and Testing in Cointegrated Systems." *Journal of Econometrics* 35 (May 1987), 143–59.

Frankel, Jefferey A. "International Capital Mobility and Crowding-out in the U.S. Economy: Imperfect Integration of Financial Markets or of Goods Markets?" In *How Open Is the U.S. Economy?* edited by Ruth W. Hafer, pp. 33–67. Lexington, Mass.: Lexington, 1986.

Frenkel, Jacob A. "Purchasing Power Parity: Doctrinal Perspective and Evidence from the 1920s." *Journal of International Economics* 8 (May 1978), 169–91.

______. "The Collapse of Purchasing Power Parity during the 1970s." *European Economic Review* 16 (November 1981), 145–65.

Fuller, Wayne A. *Introduction to Statistical Time Series.* New York: Wiley, 1976.

Gailliot, Henry J. "Purchasing Power Parity as an Explanation of Long-term Changes in Exchange Rates." *Journal of Money, Credit, and Banking* 2 (August 1970), 348–57.

Hendry, David F. "Econometric Modelling with Cointegrated Variables: An Overview." *Oxford Bulletin of Economics and Statistics* 48 (August 1986), 201–12.

Isard, Peter. "An Accounting Framework and Some Issues in Modeling How Exchange Rates

Respond to News." In *Exchange Rates and International Macroeconomics,* edited by Jacob A. Frenkel, pp. 19–65. Chicago: University of Chicago Press, 1983.

Johansen, Søren. "Statistical Analysis of Cointegrated Vectors." *Journal of Economic Dynamics and Control* 12 (June–September 1988), 231–54.

Johnson, David R. "Cointegration, Error Correction, and Purchasing Power Parity." Department of Economics Research Report no. 87111, Wilfrid Laurier University, June 1987.

Lee, Moon H. *Purchasing Power Parity.* New York: Marcel Dekker, 1976.

Lucas, Robert, Jr. "Two Illustrations of the Quantity Theory of Money." *American Economic Review* 70 (December 1980), 1005–14.

Mark, Nelson. "Real and Nominal Exchange Rates in the Long Run: An Empirical Investigation." *Journal of International Economics* (April 1990), 115–36.

Marston, Richard C. "Real Exchange Rates and Productivity Growth in the United States and Japan." In *Real and Financial Linkages among Open Economies,* edited by S. W. Arndt and J. D. Richardson, pp. 71–96. Cambridge: MIT Press, 1987.

Newey, Whitney K., and Kenneth D. West. "A Simple Positive Semi-Definite Heteroskedasticity and Correlation Consistent Covariance Matrix." *Econometrica* 55 (May 1987), 703–708.

Officer, Lawrence H. *Purchasing Power Parity and Exchange Rates.* Greenwich, Conn.: JAI Press, 1982.

Perron, Pierre. "Trends and Random Walks in Macroeconomic Time Series: Further Evidence from a New Approach." *Journal of Economic Dynamics and Control* 12 (June–September 1988), 297–332.

Phillips, Peter C., and Pierre Perron. "Testing for a Unit Root in Time Series Regression." *Biometrika* 75 (June 1988), 335–46.

Rush, Mark, and Steven Husted. "Purchasing Parity in the Long Run." *Canadian Journal of Economics* 18 (February 1985), 137–45.

Samuelson, Paul A. "Theoretical Notes on Trade Problems." *Review of Economies and Statistics* 46 (May 1964), 145–54.

Schwert, G. William. "Tests for Unit Roots: A Monte Carlo Investigation." *Journal of Business and Economic Statistics* 7 (April 1989), 147–59.

Stock, James H., and Mark W. Watson. "Testing for Common Trends." *Journal of the American Statistical Association* 83 (December 1988), 1097–107.

Summers, Lawrence H. "The Nonadjustment of Nominal Interest Rates: A Study of the Fisher Effects." In *Macroeconomics, Prices, and Quantities,* edited by James Tobin, pp. 201–44. Washington, D.C.: Brookings Institution, 1983.

Taylor, Mark P., and Patrick C. McMahon. "Long-Run Purchasing Power Parity in the 1920s." *European Economic Review* 32 (January 1988), 179–97.

WILLIAM C. HUNTER
STEPHEN G. TIMME
WON KEUN YANG

An Examination of Cost Subadditivity and Multiproduct Production in Large U.S. Banks

1. INTRODUCTION

MUCH PROGRESS HAS BEEN MADE toward understanding the production economics of small banks in the United States. Analysts, employing improved statistical methodologies and measurement techniques, have produced an impressive body of results about which there appears to be a growing consensus.[1] Despite the impressive body of results available concerning production in small banks, it is only recently that studies analyzing the structure of production in large multiproduct banks have appeared. This is somewhat surprising, given the importance of large money center and regional banks in the national and world economies. The recent studies by Hunter and Timme (1986) and Shaffer (1988) find significant economies of scale among the nation's largest banks. Furthermore, it appears that recent technological change in banking exhibited positive scale bias (larger banks benefited more from changes in technology than smaller banks) which

[1]See for example, the studies by Berger, Hanweck, and Humphrey (1986, 1987), Gilligan and Smirlock (1984), and Gilligan, Smirlock and Marshall (1984). Other studies which examine multiproduct cost structures in the financial services industry included those by Kim (1985), Kim (1986), Kolori and Zardkoohi (1987), Lawrence and Shay (1986), LeCompte and Smith (1990), Mester (1987), and Murray and White (1983).

The authors thank George Benston for his helpful comments. Financial support provided by the Georgia State University Research Council is also gratefully acknowledged. The views expressed in this paper are those of the authors and not necessarily those of the Federal Reserve Bank of Atlanta or the Federal Reserve System.

WILLIAM C. HUNTER *is a research officer at the Federal Reserve Bank of Atlanta and a professor at the Emory Business School.* STEPHEN G. TIMME *is associate professor of finance at Georgia State University.* WON KEUN YANG *is a doctoral candidate in finance, Georgia State University.*

Journal of Money, Credit, and Banking, Vol. 22, No. 4 (November 1990)

served to increase the optimal size of the banking firm (see Hunter and Timme 1988). These findings cast serious doubt on attempts to extrapolate the results obtained in studies of production in small banks to the large bank population. These findings also provide a strong rationale for the existence of large banks, but provide little empirical justification for the multiproduct production observed in these banks. Issues related to the multiproduct production and the efficient mix of products in banks requires an analysis of the subadditivity of bank costs.

Using a multiproduct cost function and the intermediation approach to analyzing bank production, this paper thoroughly examines the subadditivity of costs in a sample of 311 of the four hundred largest commercial banks in the United States. This study contributes to the bank production efficiency literature in several ways. First, by analyzing a sample composed of banks of appreciably larger asset size than analyzed in most previous bank cost studies, the production and product mix economies of large banks are revealed. Our sample includes banks with assets ranging from approximately \$1.0 billion to \$78.0 billion, as of the end of 1986, with an average asset size of approximately \$4.0 billion. Almost all previous studies examine banks which average less than \$0.5 billion in assets. Second, in conducting this analysis, we introduce into the bank production literature an extension of the grid approach to examining cost subadditivity developed by Evans and Heckman (1984). The grid approach imposes product mix constraints that are derived directly from the product mixes observed among the sample banks. Thus, the resulting bank output/product mix cost comparisons are more realistic than those previously available in the literature. In addition, the grid approach is more robust than traditional approaches for analyzing subadditivity, since it examines bank cost characteristics for considerably more points along the multiproduct cost manifold. Third, this study, in addition to analyzing ray scale economies, analyzes expansion path scale economies and expansion path subadditivity of costs, two measures recently developed by Berger, Hanweck, and Humphrey (1987) but applied to a sample of small banks. Analysis of the latter two concepts, like the grid approach, allows the efficiency of banks of different sizes and product mixes to be compared.

The translog specification of the bank cost function is the flexible functional form most commonly used to estimate the production characteristics of commercial banks. However, as Barnett and Lee (1985), Christensen and Caves (1980), and Gallant (1981) have demonstrated, estimates using the translog may be inefficient as one moves away from the point of approximation and the approximation region may be small. A fourth contribution of this study is that it derives, for the first time in the banking literature, estimates of banks' cost characteristics using the more flexible minflex Laurent functional form which mitigates the point approximation problem of the translog (see LeCompte and Smith (1990) for an application of the minflex Laurent to the savings and loan industry). For purposes of comparison, we also provide estimates based on the translog specification. The proper definition of output is a problem that continues to plague all bank cost studies. A major theoretical and empirical controversy surrounding the definition of bank outputs relates to the treatment of deposits as outputs or inputs. While it is beyond the scope of the present study to resolve the controversy regarding the definition of bank outputs, we contribute to the debate by providing separate estimates of bank cost characteristics treating deposits first as outputs, and then as inputs.

Our findings are summarized as follows. Holding product mix constant and treating deposits as outputs, we observe returns to scale which are roughly constant for the average sample bank, generally mild diseconomies of scale for the larger banks ($3 billion to $25.0 billion in total assets stated in 1986 dollars), and rather large diseconomies for the largest banks (greater than $25.0 billion in assets) when analyzed on a subgroup basis. Allowing product mix to vary, the results indicate increasing returns in expansion from the smaller output subgroup ($0.8 million in assets) up to about the $2.0 billion output subgroup. Movements from the output class with $2.0 billion in assets to larger classes show either constant or mild diseconomies of scale. With respect to the subadditivity issue, we find that costs are approximately additive for only the smallest sample banks (up to $1.5 billion in assets) and become increasingly superadditive as output is increased above this level. For all results, the estimates derived from the minflex Laurent specification do not differ appreciably from those using the translog specification. In general, when deposits are treated as outputs, our findings for the sample of large banks indicate no evidence of significant scale economies or cost subadditivity.

Holding product mix constant and treating deposits as inputs, we find significantly increasing scale economies for banks up to $5.0 billion in assets and constant scale economies for banks with assets between $5.0 billion and $10.0 billion. Banks with assets between $10.0 billion and $25.0 billion are found to exhibit mild diseconomies, while the largest banks with greater than $25.0 billion in assets exhibit significantly large diseconomies of scale. When product mix is allowed to vary, increasing scale economies are found for banks up to $2.0 billion in assets, and no discernible pattern is displayed for the subgroups composed of larger banks. Regarding cost subadditivity, costs are found to be subadditive for banks up to $5.0 billion in assets and increasingly superadditive for banks with assets in excess of $5.0 billion. Overall, the results derived from treating deposits as inputs suggest that the minimum efficient size bank is larger than that associated with treating deposits as outputs. For the larger banks, that is, those with assets in excess of $10.0 billion, the results are invariant with respect to specifying deposits as outputs or inputs.

Viewed narrowly, these findings imply that cost complementarities are not the *raison d'être* for multiproduct bank production for the largest banks. The results imply that it would pay these banks to break up production into the hands of several smaller firms. On the other hand, it could be argued that the existence of these larger multiproduct banks is consistent with their offering product mixes and branch configurations that minimize both bank costs and the transactions costs incurred by consumers in the acquisition of financial services or with a diversification motive. While these arguments are valid, they represent less than a complete justification for multiproduct production in the absence of subadditive costs. In fact, subadditive costs are sufficient but not necessary for multiproduct production. It is quite possible for multiproduct production to be optimal when outputs are produced independently (Levy and Haber 1986 and Teece 1980, 1982). It is only required that inputs be sharable as opposed to joint. This issue is discussed more thoroughly in section 5 of the paper.

The paper is divided into six sections. In section 2, we define several efficiency measures for the multiproduct banking firm and introduce the grid approach to examining bank costs and outputs. In section 3, the multiproduct cost functions are specified and the data and variable definitions are presented. Section 4 presents the empirical results. The implications of our results for understanding multiproduct bank production are discussed in section 5 along with some commonly overlooked rationales for multiproduct production. A summary and conclusion follow in section 6.

2. COST CHARACTERISTICS OF THE MULTIPRODUCT BANKING FIRM

a. *Traditional Measures and Their Extension*

The cost function of the multiproduct bank is said to be subadditive if for an output vector $\mathbf{Q}^B$ of n products

$$C(\mathbf{Q}^B) < \sum_i C(\mathbf{Q}^i) \tag{1}$$

where

$$\sum_i \mathbf{Q}^i = \mathbf{Q}^B \tag{2}$$

with the constraints that the $\mathbf{Q}^i$ output vectors have nonnegative elements, and nonzero elements for at least two of the $\mathbf{Q}^i$. Knowledge of the degree of subadditivity of bank cost functions is important for regulatory purposes since an industry is a natural monopoly if equation (1) holds for all points along the cost manifold in the relevant range of output.

Using a logarithmic transformation of the bank cost function and holding output mix constant, scale economies along a ray emanating from the origin in output space (ray scale economies) are measured, for a given output bundle $\mathbf{Q}^B$, by

$$RSCE^B = \sum_i \partial \ln C(\mathbf{Q}^B)/\partial \ln Q_i \, . \tag{3}$$

If $RSCE^B$ equals 1.0, production of $\mathbf{Q}^B$ exhibits constant returns to scale, whereas $RSCE^B$ less than (greater than) 1.0, indicates increasing (decreasing) returns to scale.

Economies of scale measures provide useful insights into questions regarding proportional increases in the output vector $\mathbf{Q}^B$ and corresponding percentage changes in total costs (for example, the gains in efficiency from the merger of two local banks with similar output mixes). However, RSCE provides limited insight into cost efficiency questions when product mix is allowed to vary (for example, expansion into retail loans).

Recognizing the limitation of RSCE, Berger, Hanweck and Humphrey (1986, 1987), henceforth BHH, developed a measure, expansion path scale economies (EPSCE), which facilitates the comparison of the efficiency of banks of different sizes and product mixes. BHH contend that as banks grow in size, they move along expansion paths connecting output bundles of increasingly larger size and different product mixes. Expanding from output bundle $\mathbf{Q}^A$ to a larger output bundle with a different output mix, $\mathbf{Q}^B$, EPSCE for $\mathbf{Q}^B$ is measured by

$$EPSCE^B = \sum_i \left[\frac{Q_i^B - Q_i^A}{Q_i^B} \cdot \frac{C(\mathbf{Q}^B)}{C(\mathbf{Q}^B) - C(\mathbf{Q}^A)} \cdot \frac{\partial \ln C(\mathbf{Q}^B)}{\partial \ln Q_i} \right] \tag{4}$$

where Q_i^B and Q_i^A are the ith outputs contained in the output vectors $\mathbf{Q}^B$ and $\mathbf{Q}^A$. An $EPSCE^B$ index less than, equal to, or greater than one indicates, respectively, scale economies, no economies or diseconomies along the expansion path spanning $\mathbf{Q}^A$ and $\mathbf{Q}^B$.

The existence of either increasing RSCE or EPSCE is neither necessary nor sufficient for the existence of multiproduct cost subadditivity. Additional insights into cost subadditivity can be provided by examining RSCE and EPSCE in conjunction with economies of scope, which is a necessary condition for subadditivity. Several banking studies (for example, Gilligan and Smirlock 1984 and Lawrence and Shay 1986) have examined cost subadditivity, using the concept of economies of scope. Overall economies of scope for the output vector $\mathbf{Q}^B$ are measured by

$$SCOPE^B = [C(\mathbf{Q}^B) - \sum_i C(Q_i^B)]/C(\mathbf{Q}^B) \tag{5}$$

where $C(Q_i^B)$ is the cost producing Q_i^B on a stand-alone basis. $SCOPE^B$ measures the percentage change in total cost from single firm versus multifirm production of the output vector $\mathbf{Q}_B$.

Estimates of economies of scope in banking using equation (5) necessitate the extrapolation of estimated cost functions well beyond the range of observed data.[2] BHH recognized this weakness and developed the measure expansion path subadditivity (EPSUB) as an alternative to the traditional measure given in equation (5). EPSUB at $\mathbf{Q}^B$ is measured by

[2]It has also been proposed that insights into scope can be obtained by testing for pairwise output complementarities, $\partial^2 C(\mathbf{Q})/\partial Q_i \partial Q_j \leq 0$ (for example, see Denny and Fuss 1977). There are, however, problems associated with this approach to examining scope economies, especially if the cost function is estimated using the standard translog (for example, see Berger, Hanweck, Humphrey (1987, pp. 505–6), Berger, Hanweck, Humphrey (1986, pp. 48–51), Mester (1987, pp. 440–42), and White (1980).

$$EPSUB^B = [C(\mathbf{Q}^B) - C(\mathbf{Q}^A) - C(\mathbf{Q}^B - \mathbf{Q}^A)]/C(\mathbf{Q}^B) \, , \tag{6}$$

and measures the percentage difference in total costs resulting from a single firm versus a pair of firm producing $\mathbf{Q}^B$. BHH estimate $EPSUB^B$ using observed data for the "representative" firm in the banking subgroups A and B. The motivation behind the development of EPSUB is that a more likely division of $\mathbf{Q}^B$ between two smaller "competing banks" includes the representative bank producing $\mathbf{Q}^A$ along the expansion path connecting $\mathbf{Q}^A$ and $\mathbf{Q}^B$.

Evans and Hickman (1984) also derive an alternative methodology to that given in equation (5) which, under certain restrictions, permits tests of necessary conditions for cost subadditivity. In particular, they utilize a grid approach to test for "quasi-global" cost subadditivity for a two output model of the Bell System. A cost function is quasi-global subadditive if equation (1) holds over an "admissible region" of output combinations consistent with observed data. In determining the division of an observed two-product output bundle between two competing firms within the admissible region, each firm (1) produces some percentage of a minimum observed quantity of both outputs, with the percentages summing to unity, and (2) its final output mix must also be consistent with observed data. For a given observed output bundle, a grid of admissible combinations of competing firms is constructed by varying the percentage of the minimum quantity produced by each competing firm. At each point within the grid, the total cost of producing the combined output bundle is compared on a percentage basis to the sum of the total costs of the competing firms.

B. Grid Subadditivity—An Extension

We extend the Evans and Heckman approach to the analysis of models with five and three bank outputs. In the five-output model the outputs are (1) retail loans, Q_R, (2) wholesale loans, Q_W, (3) transaction accounts (demand deposits and NOW accounts), Q_T, (4) nontransaction accounts (savings and time deposits excluding jumbo CDs and other purchased funds), Q_N, and (5) other bank output proxied by noninterest income excluding service charges on transaction and nontransaction accounts, Q_O. A detailed description of these five outputs is provided in section 3. For a given observed representative output bundle $\mathbf{Q}^B$, defined as the vector of the means of the five outputs for banking subgroup B, two competing firms are constructed such that

$$\mathbf{Q}^B = \mathbf{Q}^1 + \mathbf{Q}^2 \tag{7}$$

where $\mathbf{Q}^1$ and $\mathbf{Q}^2$ are the output bundles of the first and second competing firms, respectively. The elements of $\mathbf{Q}^1$ and $\mathbf{Q}^2$ equal

$$Q_i^f = {}_{min}Q_i + {}_{v}Q_i^f \text{ for } f = 1, 2, \text{ and } i = R,W,T,N,O \tag{8}$$

where Q_i^f is the ith element of firm f's output vector $\mathbf{Q}^f$, ${}_{min}Q_i$ is the minimum quantity of the ith output each competing firm must produce, and ${}_vQ_i^f$ is a non-negative variable quantity of the ith output produced by the competing firm f. In keeping with BHH's notion that banks evolve along expansion paths, the vector of minimum outputs, ${}_{min}\mathbf{Q}$, is given by

$$_{min}\mathbf{Q} = \tfrac{1}{2}\mathbf{Q}^A \, , \tag{9}$$

where $\mathbf{Q}^A$ is the previous smaller representative bank's mean output vector. The minimum quantity is set equal to $\frac{1}{2}\mathbf{Q}^A$ so that the competing banks resemble the representative bank producing the output vector $\mathbf{Q}^A$. This is consistent with the BHH notion that the representative bank producing $\mathbf{Q}^A$ is a most likely source of competition for the larger bank producing $\mathbf{Q}^B$. Establishing the minimum quantity at $\frac{1}{2}\mathbf{Q}^A$ also allows sufficient latitude in creating a grid of bank combinations that might all be likely sources of competition for the representative bank producing $\mathbf{Q}^B$.

For each competing bank the variable quantity of the ith output, ${}_vQ_i^f$ is chosen such that

$$_LR_i \leq ({}_vQ_i^f + {}_{min}Q_i)/\{\Sigma_i({}_vQ_i^f + {}_{min}Q_i)\} \leq {}_uR_i \, , \text{ for } f = 1{,}2 \text{ and } i = R,W,T,N,O \tag{10}$$

where ${}_uR_i$ and ${}_LR_i$ are the upper and lower product mix ratios which are derived from the observed statistical distribution of the output mix for banking subgroup A.

A grid of pairs of competing banks satisfying the conditions in equations (7)–(10) is generated by varying the allowable range of each bank's loans-to-deposits ratio. The loans-to-deposits ratio equals the sum of retail and wholesale loans, Q_R and Q_W, divided by the sum of transaction and nontransaction accounts, Q_T and Q_N. A grid of sixteen pairs of competing firms is formed by dividing the range of the loans-to-deposits ratios for banking subgroup A into quartiles. The grid could be expanded by dividing the range of the loans-to-deposits ratio into smaller segments. The output vectors for the pair of competing firms in row r for firm 1 and column c for firm 2 of the grid, with $r, c = 1, \ldots, 4$, for the four quartiles are derived by imposing the conditions in equations (7)–(10) and the following additional loans-to-deposits condition for firms 1 and 2, respectively,

$$_LLTD_r \leq \{({}_vQ_r^1 + {}_{min}Q_R) + ({}_vQ_W^1 + {}_{min}Q_W)\}/\{({}_vQ_T^1 + {}_{min}Q_T) + ({}_vQ_N^1 + {}_{min}Q\ )\} \leq {}_ULTD_r \, . \tag{11.a}$$

$$_LLTD_c \leq \{({}_vQ_R^2 + {}_{min}Q_R) + ({}_vQ_W^2 + {}_{min}Q_W)\}/\{({}_vQ_T^2 + {}_{min}Q_T) + ({}_vQ_N^2 + {}_{min}Q_N)\} \leq {}_ULTD_C \tag{11.b}$$

where ${}_U LTD_r$ and ${}_U LTD_c$ are the upper limits of the loans-to-deposits ratio over the ranges of r and c and ${}_L LTD_r$ and ${}_L LTD_c$ are the lower limits.

For each cell within the grid for a subgroup, the degree of subadditivity is measured by

$$GRIDSUB^B_{r,c} = [C(\mathbf{Q}^B) - C(\mathbf{Q}^1_{r,c}) - C(\mathbf{Q}^2_{r,c})]/C(\mathbf{Q}^B) ,$$
$$r, c = 1, \ldots, 4 , \tag{12}$$

which measures the percentage difference in total costs associated with a single firm producing the vector of outputs $\mathbf{Q}^B$ compared to a pair of firms producing $\mathbf{Q}^B$, the first producing $\mathbf{Q}^1_{r,c}$ and the second producing $\mathbf{Q}^2_{r,c}$, such that $\mathbf{Q}^1_{r,c} + \mathbf{Q}^2_{r,c} = \mathbf{Q}^B$. Each $GRIDSUB^B_{r,c}$ is tested against the null hypothesis that the cost function is additive, that is, $GRIDSUB^B_{r,c}$ equals zero. Similar to Evans and Heckman, if the maximum estimated value of *GRIDSUB*, $Max(GRIDSUB^B_{r,c})$, is statistically significantly negative, the hypothesis of additive costs for the admissible region for subgroup B is rejected and the hypothesis of cost subadditivity is not contradicted. Evidence against cost subadditivity is provided if either the hypothesis of cost additivity can not be rejected or if $Max(GRIDSUB^B_{r,c})$ is statistically significantly positive, implying superadditive costs. When evaluating $Max(GRIDSUB^B_{r,c})$ over a total of N banking subgroups, if $Max(Max(GRIDSUB^k_{r,c}))$, $k = 1, \ldots, N$, is statistically significantly negative, then the hypothesis of quasi-global subadditivity is not contradicted for the admissible region defined by the N subgroups.

In comparing EPSUB to GRIDSUB, EPSUB will be contained within the admissible region used to estimate GRIDSUB if the competing bank producing ($\mathbf{Q}^B - \mathbf{Q}^A$) satisfies the product-mix ratio constraints in equation (10) and any of the loans to deposits constraints in equation (11).

3. MODEL SPECIFICATION

In this section two models are specified. In the first model, various categories of deposits are specified as bank outputs. In the second model, all deposits are treated as inputs. This treatment of deposits as outputs in one case and inputs in the other is consistent with the theoretical work by Benston and Smith (1976) on one hand, and Sealey and Lindley (1977) on the other. Comparison of the results from the two models should provide insights into the practical significance of the debate concerning the treatment of deposits as output or inputs for the sample banks. In addition, both models are estimated using a translog and a minflex Laurent flexible functional form. As noted above, papers by Barnett and Lee (1985), Christensen and Caves (1980), and Gallant (1981) demonstrate that the error term of the translog may become increasingly heteroskedastic as estimates are derived further away from the point of approximation resulting in inefficient estimates. In addition, the approximation region for the translog may be small. To account for the caveats of the translog, estimates of the cost characteristics using the more flexible minflex Laurent functional form are also derived.

A. *Model 1—Deposits Treated as Outputs*

Translog Approximation

A second-order translog approximation to the multiproduct total cost function is used to derive the cost function characteristics in equations (3), (4), (6), and (12). The second-order approximation is written as

$$\ln TC = \alpha_0 + \Sigma_m \alpha_m \ln P_m + \tfrac{1}{2}\Sigma_m \Sigma_n \alpha_{m,n} \ln P_m \ln P_n + \Sigma_i \beta_i \ln Q_i + \tfrac{1}{2}\Sigma_i \Sigma_j \beta_{i,j} \ln Q_i \ln Q_j + \Sigma_i \Sigma_m \Phi_{i,m} \ln Q_i \ln P_m + \epsilon$$

$$m,n = L, K, I, \text{ and}$$

$$i, j = R, W, T, N, O \qquad (13)$$

where

TC = total costs,
Q_R = dollar volume of retail loans,
Q_W = dollar volume of wholesale loans,
Q_T = dollar volume of transaction accounts,
Q_N = dollar volume of nontransaction accounts,
Q_O = other bank output,
P_L = price of labor,
P_K = price of capital,
P_I = interest rate on purchased funds, and
ϵ = random error term.

In estimating equation (13), the usual symmetry ($\alpha_{m,n} = \alpha_{n,m}$ and $\beta_{i,j} = \beta_{j,i}$) and homogeneity and adding-up ($\Sigma_m \alpha_m = 1$ and $\Sigma_m \alpha_{m,n} = \Sigma_n \alpha_{m,n} = \Sigma_m \Phi_{i,m} = 0$) constraints are imposed.

Difficulties associated with the definition of output, the appropriate level of aggregation of output, and the definition of costs are encountered in all bank costs studies. With regard to the definition of output, we initially use the criterion of value added employed by BHH to determine the composition of the various output categories. Retail loans, Q_R, is comprised of the dollar volume of all residential real estate, agricultural, personal, credit card, and other loans. Q_W is the dollar volume of all commercial real estate, commercial and industrial, and security loans. Securities are excluded from the definition of output since in markets exhibiting low information costs, banks add only negligible if any value to these assets.

Transaction accounts, Q_T, equals the dollar volume of demand deposits, negotiable orders of withdrawal (NOW) accounts, and other interest-bearing checking accounts. Nontransaction accounts, Q_N, equals savings accounts and small time deposits. Q_T and Q_N are defined as bank outputs since, for both categories, banks add value from the provision of services related to, for example, the exchange of goods and record keeping for personal and official purposes (for example, see Benston and Smith 1976 and BHH 1987). Purchased funds are excluded from liability-based outputs since it is a maintained hypothesis that holders of these liabilities receive negligible nonpecuniary benefits or monetary gain other than the receipt of interest.

Other bank output, Q_O, is included in an attempt to capture off-balance sheet activities such as loan sales, letters of credit, and securitization activities which are becoming increasingly important at U.S. commercial banks. The proxy, Q_O, equals annual noninterest income excluding service charges received on transaction and nontransaction accounts and also excludes gains and losses on securities and foreign exchange transactions.

Total costs, *TC,* in equation (13) are defined as total noninterest costs plus allocated interest expense since data limitations require that the output metric be defined in terms of dollars of loans and deposits instead of the number of accounts. Allocated interest equals the product of the ratio of total loans to earning assets times total interest expense. The allocation of interest is necessary since securities are not specified as outputs and, for many banks, a substantial proportion of interest costs are incurred to finance their securities portfolio. The output/cost specification used in this study is consistent with the intermediation approach, discussed in Humphrey (1985), to examining bank costs and is preferable when the issues being examined concern bank economic viability.

Minflex Laurent Approximation

A second-order minflex Laurent approximation is also estimated to provide insights into the sensitivity of the results to the flexible functional form employed in the estimation. Treating deposits as outputs, the second-order minflex Laurent approximation is written as

$$
\begin{aligned}
\ln TC = {} & \alpha_0 + \Sigma_m \alpha_m \ln P_m + \tfrac{1}{2}\Sigma_m (\alpha_{m,m})^2 (\ln P_m)^2 \\
& + \tfrac{1}{2}\Sigma_m \Sigma_{n \neq m} (\alpha_{m,n})^2 (\ln P_m \ln P_n) \\
& + \Sigma_i \beta_i \ln Q_i + \tfrac{1}{2}\Sigma_i (\beta_{i,i})^1 (\ln Q_i)^2 + \tfrac{1}{2}\Sigma_i \Sigma_{j \neq i} (\beta_{i,j})^2 (\ln Q_i \ln Q_j) \\
& + \Sigma_i \Sigma_m (\Phi_{i,m})^2 (\ln Q_i \ln P_m) \\
& - \tfrac{1}{2}\Sigma_m \Sigma_{n \neq m} (\alpha^*_{m,n})^2 (\ln P_m)^{-1} (\ln P_n)^{-1} \\
& - \tfrac{1}{2}\Sigma_i \Sigma_{j \neq \mathrm{i}} (\beta^*_{i,j})^2 (\ln Q_i)^{-1} (\ln Q_j)^{-1} \\
& - \Sigma_i \Sigma_m (\Phi^*_{i,m})^2 (\ln Q_i)^{-1} (\ln P_m)^{-1} + \epsilon \\
& m,n = L,\ K,\ I, \text{ and} \\
& i,j = R,\ W,\ T,\ N,\ O \qquad (14)
\end{aligned}
$$

where all variables are as previously defined and the $\alpha^*_{m,n}$s, and $\beta^*_{i,j}$s and $\Phi^*_{i,m}$s are new parameters.

In addition to the usual symmetry, adding-up and homogeneity constraints, parametric minimality (see Barnett 1985, theorem 2) requires the following restrictions also be imposed on the minflex Laurent approximation in equation (14): $\alpha_{m,n}\alpha^*_{m,n} = \beta_{i,j}\beta^*_{i,j} = \Phi_{i,m}\Phi^*_{i,m} = 0$.

B. Model 2—Deposits Treated as Inputs

Model 2 treats all deposits as inputs. Thus, the output variables Q_T and Q_N are deleted from equations (13) and (14). In addition, the price of interest is redefined as the average interest rate paid on all interest-bearing deposits.

C. Data

Data are primarily from the Federal Reserve end-of-year call reports and report of income and dividends filed by the sample banks for the year 1986. Data for the top four hundred banks ranked by total assets were collected. Forty-seven banks in states with unit banking laws were dropped from the sample since it is believed that analysis of non-unit banking banks will provide more insight into regulatory policies regarding interstate banking and bank mergers. Also, three banks with interstate banking operations, four Puerto Rican banks, and twenty-one banks with credit cards as their major source of business were also dropped. Finally, fourteen banks

TABLE 1

SUMMARY STATISTICS FOR SAMPLE BANKS FOR THE YEAR 1986

		Bank Output in Billions of Dollars Means and Standard Deviations (in Parentheses)					
Asset size $ billions	No. of Banks	Total assets	Q_R Retail loans	Q_W Wholesale loans	Q_T Trans. accounts	Q_N Nontrans. accounts	Q_O Other output
0.8–1.0	45	$ 0.88 (0.06)	$ 0.17 (0.08)	$ 0.38 (0.10)	$ 0.25 (0.07)	$ 0.51 (0.08)	$ 0.01 (0.01)
1.0–1.5	79	1.23 (0.15)	0.25 (0.14)	0.50 (0.14)	0.36 (0.11)	0.66 (0.13)	0.01 (0.01)
1.5–2.0	36	1.73 (0.21)	0.37 (0.17)	0.69 (0.11)	0.52 (0.15)	0.93 (0.13)	0.01 (0.03)
2.0–3.0	48	2.50 (0.28)	0.42 (0.19)	1.07 (0.25)	0.70 (0.20)	1.29 (0.24)	0.02 (0.01)
3.0–5.0	41	3.85 (0.63)	0.70 (0.35)	1.60 (0.47)	1.10 (0.29)	1.82 (0.44)	0.03 (0.02)
5.0–10.0	40	7.11 (1.43)	1.17 (0.63)	3.08 (1.05)	2.04 (0.75)	3.08 (0.83)	0.06 (0.07)
10.0–25.0	13	13.70 (3.18)	1.98 (1.18)	6.11 (2.57)	3.42 (0.81)	5.52 (1.48)	0.11 (0.07)
25.0 plus	9	46.05 (15.86)	5.39 (4.30)	20.09 (7.55)	12.65 (4.15)	16.88 (8.94)	0.89 (0.60)
Overall	311	4.38 (8.25)	0.68 (1.21)	1.88 (3.69)	1.22 (2.25)	1.92 (3.22)	0.05 (0.18)

with either incomplete data or data discrepancies were dropped from the sample. The final sample includes 311 banks. Table 1 presents summary statistics for all banks in the sample and by eight subgroups based on total asset size as reported in the 1986 call reports.

Total cost, TC, equals the sum of salaries, benefits, occupancy, and other expenses, less service charges, plus interest expense allocated to total loans. The price of labor, P_L, equals salaries plus benefits divided by number of employees. The price of capital, P_K, is defined as the ratio of occupancy expanse to net bank premises. When selected categories of deposits are treated as outputs, the interest rate on purchased funds, P_I, is calculated as the interest rate paid on all nonretail deposits (that is, jumbo CDs and Fed funds) divided by the sum of all nonretail deposits outstanding. When all deposits are treated as inputs, the average interest cost for deposits equals the sum of interest paid on all deposits divided by the outstanding amounts of interest-bearing deposits.

4. ESTIMATION AND EMPIRICAL RESULTS

A. Estimation

Full information maximum likelihood (FIML) is used to jointly estimate the models in equations (13) and (14) each with three factor input share equations. Using Shepard's lemma, the share equations are given by $\partial \ln TC / \partial \ln P_m = S_m$, for $m = L, K$, and I where S_m is the mth input's share of total cost. Since the coefficients in the share equations are a subset of those in the cost equations in (13) and (14), joint estimation results in more efficient estimates. However, since $\Sigma_m S_m = 1$, the purchased funds share or average cost of funds equation is dropped from the joint estimation to avoid singularity.

B. Empirical Results—Deposits Treated as Outputs

In the interest of space, the parameter estimates for the translog in equation (13) and minflex Laurent approximation in equation (14) are not reported but are available in Hunter, Timme, and Yang (1989).[3]

Ray Scale Economies (RSCE)

Table 2 reports estimates of ray scale economies (RSCE) for the overall group and the eight subgroups.[4] Using either the translog or minflex Laurent approximation,

[3]Using the $\alpha_{m,m}$s in equation (13) for the translog, Allen own price elasticities, $\sigma_{mm'}$ are computed as $(\alpha_{m,m}/S_m + S_m - 1)$, where S_m is the share of input m (relative to total costs). The estimated elasticities, using average shares for the overall sample are: $\sigma_{K,K} = -0.090, \sigma_{L,L} = -0.660$ and $\sigma_{I,I} = -0.113$ which are all equal to or significantly less than zero. In addition, all partial elasticities, $\delta \ln(TC)/\delta \ln Q_i$ evaluated at the geometric mean of the overall sample are significantly positive. The estimates from equation (13) therefore appear to represent those for a reasonable, concave, cost function. Similar results are found for the minflex Laurent.

[4]The estimated values of RSCE used to compute the derivative in equation (3) are calculated using the estimated parameters of (13) and the mean values of all variables, for example, $\ln P_{W'}$ $\ln Q_R$ and $\ln Q_N$. A similar derivation of RSCE is made using the parameter estimates of the minflex Laurent in equation (14).

TABLE 2

RAY SCALE ECONOMIES (RSCE) AND EXPANSION PATH SCALE ECONOMIES (EPSCE) FOR MODEL 1—DEPOSITS TREATED AS OUTPUTS

Group B Asset Size Class ($ billions)	RSCE Estimated using		Expansion Path from Group A with Assets ($ billions)	EPSCE Estimated using	
	Translog	Minflex		Translog	Minflex
Overall	1.018 (0.016)	1.010 (0.016)	N/A	N/A	N/A
0.8– 1.0	0.988 (0.032)	0.986 (0.028)	0.0	0.988 (0.032)	0.986 (0.028)
1.0– 1.5	1.002 (0.026)	0.997 (0.023)	0.8– 1.0	0.952** (0.019)	0.983 (0.024)
1.5– 2.0	1.019 (0.021)	1.002 (0.019)	1.0– 1.5	0.957* (0.019)	0.970 (0.019)
2.0– 3.0	1.018 (0.017)	1.006 (0.016)	1.5– 2.0	1.060** (0.022)	1.062** (0.020)
3.0– 5.0	1.031* (0.014)	1.024* (0.013)	2.0– 3.0	1.101** (0.015)	1.109** (0.015)
5.0–10.0	1.042* (0.019)	1.032* (0.016)	3.0– 5.0	0.949** (0.015)	0.964** (0.013)
10.0–25.0	1.051 (0.028)	1.040 (0.023)	5.0–10.0	1.042 (0.025)	1.038 (0.024)
25.0 plus	1.118* (0.050)	1.093* (0.039)	10.0–25.0	1.011 (0.041)	1.015 (0.035)

NOTES: RSCE is the elasticity of cost associated with changes in output, holding product mix constant [equation (3)]. EPSCE is the elasticity of cost associated with changes in output at the firm level as measured along the expansion path between Group A and the next largest Group B [equation (4)]. EPSCE is applicable to the analysis of Group B. RSCE and EPSCE are both tested against null hypotheses of one. Asymptotic standard errors in parentheses.
**Significant at the .01 level.
*Significant at the .05 level.

the results for the smallest subgroups by asset size indicate fairly constant returns to scale. The subgroups with assets between $2.0–$25.0 billion appear to have fully exhausted available scale economies and exhibit slight diseconomies of approximately 1 to 5 percent, whereas the largest banks exhibit significantly larger diseconomies. These results differ slightly from those reported in the study by Hunter and Timme (1986) which examined scale economies for a group of large bank holding companies. When interest costs are included in total cost, they reported scale economies of 0.97 and 1.05 for the average sample multibank and one-bank holding company, respectively. Neither scale economies measure was significantly different from 1.0. Shaffer (1988) in an examination of one hundred of the 180 largest commercial banks in the United States found slight scale economies for holding companies with up to $40.0 billion to $60.0 billion in total assets. The differences between the current study's results and those reported by Hunter and Timme (1986) and Shaffer (1988) are believed attributable to differences in methodologies and sample data. Hunter and Timme (1986) use a scalar measure of output instead of a multiproduct specification. See Kim (1985) for a detailed analysis of the output aggregation problem and its impact on scale economies in bank costs studies. Shaffer (1988) used a hedonic cost function instead of the more traditional translog or minflex used in the present study.

Expansion Path Scale Economies (EPSCE)

The estimates of expansion path scale economies, EPSCE, are reported in Table 2 for each subgroup.[5] The results indicate either expansion path economies or diseconomies in the movement from one subgroup to the other. Unlike the RSCE, the EPSCE estimates display no discernible pattern although the larger banks generally exhibit diseconomies. However, the results indicate that most subgroups are within approximately 3 to 5 percent of constant expansion path scale economies. BHH also report no discernible pattern for EPSCE for a sample of much smaller banks than those examined in the present study. The erratic pattern of EPSCE may reflect the dominance of demand factors over the sole concern for minimization of total production cost as banks increase in size, begin to emphasize different markets and, in turn, alter product mix. On the other hand, the pattern observed for ESPCE may simply be an artifact of the violation of the assumptions underlying the derivation of ESPCE in equation (4). In the derivation of ESPCE in equation (4), BHH assume that the representative bank producing the output mix $\mathbf{Q}^A$ is "competitively viable." Competitive viability, for example, requires that for each representative bank, RSCE and ESPCE not differ from 1.0. Unfortunately, the results in Table 2 show these requirements are typically not met and their effect on the estimation of EPSCE for the representative bank producing the output bundle $\mathbf{Q}^B$ is unknown.

Expansion Path Subadditivity (EPSUB)

Table 3 reports estimates of each subgroup's expansion path subadditivity.[6] In the derivation of EPSUB, it is assumed that production of the output bundle $(\mathbf{Q}^B - \mathbf{Q}^A)$ by the residual competing bank is consistent with some market equilibrium. The overall results indicate that costs are slightly superadditive with increasing, though mild, superadditivity for the largest banks up to \$25.0 billion in assets. However, for the largest banks, joint production costs exceed the sum of the total costs of the representative banks producing $\mathbf{Q}^A$ and $(\mathbf{Q}^B - \mathbf{Q}^A)$ by approximately 7.0 percent. The results using the minflex Laurent specification indicate slightly higher superadditivity than those derived using the translog. In addition, the minflex estimates of EPSUB are generally more often statistically significant.

Grid Subadditivity (GRIDSUB)

As stated earlier, increasing RSCE and EPSCE are neither necessary nor sufficient conditions for multiproduct cost subadditivity. In addition, EPSUB may be viewed as depicting one possible division of a representative bank's mean output vector between two competing banks contained within a grid comprised of banks which are most likely to be a source of competition. Additional insights into cost

[5]The estimates of EPSCE are derived using the estimated parameters of equation (13) and the mean values of all the variables for the overall sample. In estimating EPSCE [see equation (4)] the terms $[((Q_i^B - Q_i^A)/Q_i^B)/((C(\mathbf{Q}^B) - C(\mathbf{Q}^A)/C(\mathbf{Q}^B))]$ are treated as constants. Using these mean output values and the geometric mean values for the other variables, the total costs, TC, were estimated using the parameter estimates of the specifications in equations (13) and (14) and exponentiating. The $\partial \ln TC^B / \partial \ln Q_i$ in equation (4) are estimated for equations (13) and (14) treated as variates and the weighted sum in (4) tested against a null hypothesized value of one.

[6]Both *EPSUB* in equation (6) and *GRIDSUB* in equation (12) are estimated using the geometric mean values for the various subgroups and the nonlinear Wald chi-square testing procedure available in the computer program SHAZAM. Both indices are tested against the null hypothesis of zero.

TABLE 3

Expansion Path Scale Subadditivity (EPSUB) and Maximum Grid Subadditivity (GRIDSUB) for Model 1—Deposits Treated as Outputs

Expansion Path		EPSUB Estimated Using		MAX(GRIDSUB) Estimated Using	
from Group A with Assets ($ billion)	to Group B with Assets ($ billion)	Translog (%)	Minflex (%)	Translog (%)	Minflex (%)
0.0	0.8– 1.0	N/A	N/A	N/A	N/A
0.8– 1.0	1.0– 1.5	0.83 (2.22)	1.59 (1.70)	−0.59 (2.41)	−0.29 (2.02)
1.0– 1.5	1.5– 2.0	1.11 (1.74)	1.05 (1.50)	0.39 (1.94)	1.93 (1.66)
1.5– 2.0	2.0– 3.0	−0.30 (1.87)	1.92 (1.29)	0.75 (1.55)	1.38 (1.29)
2.0– 3.0	3.0– 5.0	2.22 (1.79)	3.43** (0.99)	4.02** (1.50)	4.78** (1.20)
3.0– 5.0	5.0–10.0	1.90 (1.07)	2.87** (0.88)	5.59** (1.95)	7.70** (1.15)
5.0–10.0	10.0–25.0	2.49 (1.45)	3.44** (1.12)	8.90** (2.37)	10.61** (1.46)
10.0–25.0	25.0 plus†	6.48** (2.45)	6.69** (1.82)	25.38** (5.94)	30.07** (3.35)

Notes: EPSUB and GRIDSUB measure the percent increase (decrease) in total costs from a single representative bank producing the vector of mean output for Group B, $\mathbf{Q}^B$, versus $\mathbf{Q}^B$ being divided between two competing banks [see eqs. (6) and (12)]. For EPSUB, the first competing bank produces the previous subgroup's (Group A) mean output vector, $\mathbf{Q}^A$, and the second competing bank produces the quantities $(\mathbf{Q}^b - \mathbf{Q}^A)$. For GRIDSUB, the two competing banks produce quantities over a grid of outputs, where the feasible solutions within the grid are determined by the confidence intervals for the centroid of observed product mix ratios for Group $\mathbf{Q}^A$. Asymptotic standard errors in parentheses.
Max(GRIDSUB) is the maximum estimate of GRIDSUB for a given subgroup.
†In estimating GRIDSUB for the greater than $25 billion in assets subgroup, the product ratio constraints [see eq. (10)] for "other" output could not be imposed. At the mean for this subgroup, "other" output as a percentage of total output exceeds the upper limit product ratio constraint [equation (10)] which can be established from the $10.0–$25.0 billion subgroup.
**Significant at the .01 level.
*Significant at the .05 level.

subadditivity may therefore be garnered by examining the more robust GRIDSUB that measures the reduction or gain in costs resulting from other divisions of output within the grid, a representative section of the cost manifold. For each banking subgroup, except for the smallest with $0.8—$1.0 billion in assets, a grid of estimates of GRIDSUB as defined in equation (12) and satisfying the conditions stated in equations (7)–(11) was constructed using the following procedure [see Hunter, Timme, and Yang (1989) for a more detailed description].

Along an expansion path connecting vectors $\mathbf{Q}^A$ and $\mathbf{Q}^B$, the elements of the larger representative bank's output vector, $\mathbf{Q}^B$, are derived from the geometric means of output for subgroup B. Geometric mean values are used to facilitate comparability to the estimates of EPSUB and are consistent with use of the translog. To establish the minimum output vector, ${}_{min}\mathrm{Q} = \frac{1}{2}\mathbf{Q}^A$ in equation (9), the elements in the output vector, $\mathbf{Q}^A$, are derived using the previous (smaller) group's geometric mean output values. The upper and lower product mix ratios in equation (10) and the loans-to-deposits ratios in equation (11) for analysis of cost subadditivity at $\mathbf{Q}^B$ are derived using a three-step process. First, mean product mix and loans-to-deposits ratios are calculated using $\mathbf{Q}^A$. Second, subgroup A's raw output data are used to form distributions of ratios. Assuming normality, the range for a particular ratio is derived from the upper and lower limits of a 99 percent confidence interval from that ratio's distribution. Finally, the upper (lower) limit ratios equal the mean ratios calculated from $\mathbf{Q}^A$ in the first step plus (less) one-half of their respective ranges calculated in the second step.

For each banking subgroup, a set of GRIDSUB estimates are derived by dividing the overall upper and lower loans-to-deposits ratios into quartiles that are then used to specify the upper and lower product mix ratios in equation (11) for each cell within the grid. By varying the loan-to-deposit ratio quartiles, a grid of GRIDSUB indices is estimated. The product mix ratios in equation (10) are held constant and are imposed for each of the competing banks within the grid. For a given output vector to be replicated by the two competing banks and a given cell within the grid, the output vectors for the two competing banks were derived by specifying the conditions in equations (7)–(11) as a linear programming minimization problem.[7] Next, estimates of grid subadditivity for each cell, $GRIDSUB^B_{r,c}$, in equation (12) were calculated using the outputs in $\mathbf{Q}^B$, and the first and second competing firms' output vectors, $\mathbf{Q}^1_{r,c}$ and $\mathbf{Q}^2_{r,c}$ in equation (12), derived from the linear programming model, and the parameter estimate of the cost function in (13).

Table 3 reports estimates of Max(GRIDSUB) for each subgroup. The results indicate costs are either additive or slightly to moderately superadditive over the range of \$.80 to \$5.0 billion in assets. The estimates of Max(GRIDSUB) for banks with \$5.0 to \$25.0 billion in assets suggest an appreciably larger degree of cost superadditivity than do the estimates of EPSUB. The differing results are most likely explained by the fact that EPSUB is derived from a single potential division of an output vector whereas Max(GRIDSUB) is derived from numerous points on the cost manifold, each being consistent with observed output mixes.

The results show that the largest banks, that is, those with greater than \$25.0 billion in assets, exhibit a high degree of superadditivity. For this group, the Max(GRIDSUB) index is approximately 30.0 percent. However, the results for the largest banks need to be interpreted with caution since the product ratio for "other" output, Q_O, can not be imposed for the sample of these largest banks. For the largest banks, the mean percentage production of "other" output exceeds the upper limit of the product ratio derived from the previous group of banks, that is, those with \$10.0 to \$25.0 billion in assets. Despite this, the result for the largest banks is still consistent with the overall results for Max(GRIDSUB). That is, for the admissible region of the output space examined, the null hypothesis of "quasi-global" subadditivity is rejected. In addition, the results suggest that costs tend to become increasingly superadditive as the admissible region of the output space is expanded up to the largest banks.

Overall, when deposits are treated as outputs, the results for RSCE, EPSCE, EPSUB, and Max(GRIDSUB) suggest the absence of increasing scale economies or subadditive costs. These results could be consistent with the sample banks offering product mixes and branch configurations that minimize both bank costs and, viz à

[7]A detailed description of the linear program model used to derive the vector of outputs for the pair of banks whose total output sum to $\mathbf{Q}^B$ is available from the authors.

viz the output of "convenience," transactions costs incurred by consumers in the acquisition of financial services. They may also be attributable to a diversification motive.[8] In an attempt to reduce risks, banks may choose a suboptimal scale of output and product mix when viewed strictly from a production perspective.

C. Empirical Results—Deposits Treated as Inputs

Treating deposits as inputs, the parameters of the respecified translog and minflex Laurent approximations in equation (13) and (14) were also estimated using FIML. In the interest of space, the parameter estimates for translog and minflex Laurent are not reported but are available in Hunter, Timme, and Yang (1989).

Ray Scale Economies (RSCE)

Table 4 reports estimates of ray scale economies (RSCE). Using either the translog or minflex Laurent approximation, the results indicate significantly increasing scale economies for banks with up to $5.0 billion in assets, and constant scale economies for banks with $5.0 to $10.0 billion in assets. These results are in sharp contrast to those reported in Table 2 in which deposits are treated as outputs and banks with up to $10.0 billion in assets exhibit either constant or decreasing scale economies. The ray scale economies measures in Table 4 for banks with $10.0 to $25.0 billion in assets indicate mild diseconomies and significantly large diseconomies for banks with $25.0 billion or more in total assets. These results are similar to those in Table 2 where deposits are treated as outputs.

Expansion Path Scale Economies (EPSCE)

The estimates of expansion path scale economies, EPSCE, are reported in Table 4. The results for EPSCE in Table 4 are similar to those reported in Table 2. Whether deposits are treated as outputs or inputs, EPSCE fluctuates from increasing to diseconomies with the larger sample banks generally exhibiting diseconomies of scale.

Expansion Path Subadditivity (EPSUB)

Table 5 reports estimates of each subgroup's expansion path subadditivity. The results suggest that costs are subadditive for the sample banks with up to $10.0 billion in assets and only slightly superadditive (approximately 1.5 percent) for banks with $10.0 to $25.0 billion in assets. In addition, the estimates derived from the minflex Laurent generally suggest greater sub- or superadditivity than those derived using the translog. These results appear to be appreciably different from those in Table 3 where deposits are treated as outputs. Treating deposits as outputs, the results in Table 3 show that costs, for even the smallest banks, appear to be superadditive with mild superadditivity for banks with $10.0 to $25.0 billion in assets. On the other hand, the results in Table 5 indicate significantly large superadditive costs for the largest banks.

[8]See Benston and Smith (1976) and BHH for a discussion of potential impact of consumer transaction costs and diversification on output decisions at financial intermediaries. The paper by Evanoff (1988) contains an analysis of banking convenience and branching laws.

TABLE 4

RAY SCALE ECONOMIES (RSCE) AND EXPANSION PATH SCALE ECONOMIES (EPSCE) FOR MODEL 2—DEPOSITS TREATED AS INPUTS

Group B Asset Size Class ($ billions)	RSCE Estimated using		Expansion Path from Group A with Assets ($ billions)	EPSCE Estimated using	
	Translog	Minflex		Translog	Minflex
Overall	0.951** (0.016)	0.929** (0.015)	N/A	N/A	N/A
0.8– 1.0	0.904** (0.030)	0.863** (0.027)	0.0	0.904** (0.030)	0.863** (0.027)
1.0– 1.5	0.916** (0.026)	0.881** (0.023)	0.8–$ 1.0	0.941** (0.026)	0.900** (0.024)
1.5– 2.0	0.941** (0.021)	0.915** (0.019)	1.0–$ 1.5	0.942** (0.020)	0.916** (0.019)
2.0– 3.0	0.954** (0.015)	0.932** (0.015)	1.5–$ 2.0	1.058** (0.020)	1.039** (0.020)
3.0– 5.0	0.975* (0.012)	0.963** (0.013)	2.0–$ 3.0	1.096** (0.015)	1.089** (0.015)
5.0–10.0	0.996 (0.018)	0.990 (0.018)	3.0–$ 5.0	0.941** (0.016)	0.935** (0.016)
10.0–25.0	1.027 (0.026)	1.031 (0.025)	5.0–$10.0	1.045 (0.025)	1.043 (0.023)
25.0 plus	1.111* (0.055)	1.144** (0.050)	10.0–$25.0	1.022 (0.044)	1.023 (0.041)

NOTES: RSCE is the elasticity of cost associated with changes in output, holding product mix constant [equation (3)]. EPSCE is the elasticity of cost associated with changes in output at the firm level as measured along the expansion path between Group A and the next largest Group B [equation (4)]. EPSCE is applicable to the analysis of Group B. RSCE and EPSCE are both tested against null hypotheses of one. Asymptotic standard errors in parentheses.
**Significant at the .01 level.
*Significant at the .05 level.

TABLE 5

EXPANSION PATH SCALE SUBADDITIVITY (EPSUB) AND MAXIMUM GRID SUBADDITIVITY (GRIDSUB) FOR MODEL 2—DEPOSITS TREATED AS INPUTS

Expansion Path		EPSUB Estimated Using		MAX(GRIDSUB) Estimated Using	
from Group A with Assets ($ billion)	to Group B with Assets ($ billion)	Translog (%)	Minflex (%)	Translog (%)	Minflex (%)
0.0	0.8– 1.0	N/A	N/A	N/A	N/A
0.8– 1.0	1.0– 1.5	−5.81** (2.18)	−8.24** (2.02)	−7.07** (2.40)	−9.70** (2.22)
1.0– 1.5	1.5– 2.0	−4.82** (1.87)	−6.80** (1.73)	−5.60** (2.01)	−7.04** (1.86)
1.5– 2.0	2.0– 3.0	−3.55* (1.65)	−2.60 (1.56)	−4.26** (1.39)	−5.83** (1.34)
2.0– 3.0	3.0– 5.0	−2.34* (1.06)	−3.42** (1.03)	−1.37 (1.54)	−1.37 (1.32)
3.0– 5.0	5.0–10.0	−0.97 (0.99)	−1.42 (1.00)	1.70 (1.76)	2.62* (1.30)
5.0–10.0	10.0–25.0	1.12 (1.51)	1.53 (1.43)	5.64* (2.44)	7.85** (1.71)
10.0–25.0	25.0 plus†	4.79* (2.44)	9.09** (1.97)	23.59** (6.28)	29.53** (3.82)

NOTES: See Table 3.

Grid Subadditivity (GRIDSUB)

The results from the more stringent test of cost subadditivity using grid subadditivity are reported in Table 5. For banks with up to $5.0 billion in assets, costs appear to be subadditive, with mild superadditivity for sample banks with $5.0 to $10.0 billion in assets. These results are appreciably different from those in Table 3 which suggest that cost for all but the smallest banks are superadditive and banks with $5.0 to $10.0 billion in assets exhibit significantly large superadditive costs. The results in Table 5 also show that banks with assets in excess of $10.0 billion exhibit significantly large superadditive cost which are similar in magnitude to the results which treat deposits as outputs.

5. IMPLICATIONS FOR BANK MULTIPRODUCT PRODUCTION

The results obtained in our empirical analysis do not support the notion that the cost functions of the largest multiproduct banking firms examined are subadditive. The direct implication of this finding is that there are no measurable cost complementarities in multiproduct production among these banks. This finding is in general agreement with the recent results obtained by BHH who examine the smaller banks in the economy. While these findings raise questions concerning the rationale for multiproduct production in banking, they should be interpreted with caution as the results may only apply to our definition of costs and output. The possibility that banks minimize both bank costs and, through the output of convenience, consumers' transactions costs may not be fully reflected in our cost and output measures, as well as factors related to the previously cited diversification motive.[9] While these caveats are clearly relevant, they do not completely reveal the importance of transactions costs and uncertainty as the key determinants of the multiproduct form of production.

As argued by Teece (1980, 1982), market contracting is inferior to production within a multiproduct firm when inputs are transaction-specific and must be exchanged on a recurring basis. Transaction-specific inputs in banking include both indivisible physical capital which is common to two or more products and human capital. The lumpy nature of most bank physical capital means that these inputs are likely to be only incompletely utilized in the production of a single product. Efficiency then dictates the sharing of input services among several outputs. The special nature of these inputs make their exchange through market contracts very risky, since these inputs by their very nature have only a few potential users.

Human capital inputs can be used to produce more than one output but these inputs are also quite costly to transfer between firms. Items such as know-how and

[9]Insights into the potential benefits of product diversification in banking are provided, for example, by Boyd, Graham and Hewitt (1989). Simulating mergers between bank holding companies and other financial firms the authors concluded that the best merger partners appear to be life insurance companies, while the worst partners appear to be securities and real estate firms. Earlier evidence on the potential gains from diversification by bank holding companies was provided by Eisemann (1976).

organizational knowledge are important but elusive.[10] Market contracts for the transfer of these inputs are both difficult to specify and to enforce. As a consequence transfers of these items are more easily accomplished within a multiproduct firm due to more highly developed information networks, auditing capabilities, and internal reward schemes.

One last advantage of the multiproduct form of production is the flexibility it allows in dealing with uncertainty. For example, these firms may reallocate their firm-specific inputs among product lines in response to unanticipated shocks. In addition, the firm has the option of transferring inputs to higher-valued uses in a timely manner. This ability allows the firm to avoid the high transactions costs associated with rapidly accumulating firm-specific capital (for example, see Lucas 1967).

The key factors underlying these advantages of the multiproduct form of production are the ability to revise production plans in response to unanticipated shocks and the prohibitive nature of the transactions costs associated with market contracting for firm and product-specific inputs. These factors imply that it is the shareability of inputs as opposed to any "publicness" of inputs which is necessary for multiproduct production. Public inputs give rise to joint production and hence the notion of economies of scope. Sharable inputs, on the other hand, are transferable between users, but are used in producing only one output at a time. From an *ex ante* perspective, these inputs may be seen as public in the sense that they may be allocated alternatively between products. However, once allocated, the production of different products may be independent. This distinction is key. The shareability of inputs provides an economic justification for multiproduct production even when the production of multiple products is independent. Traditional cost subadditivity is thus seen to be a sufficient but not necessary condition for the multiproduct form of production. Thus, it should pay researchers in future studies of the production economics of the large multiproduct banking firm to explicitly account for such factors as input shareability and flexibility in their analyses. This should help to further improve our understanding of production in there firms.

6. CONCLUSION

This paper presents new tests for cost function subadditivity and hence cost complementarities in banking. Using a grid approach which imposes product mix constraints consistent with those observed among the sample firms, we are able to obtain bank-output/product-mix cost comparisons that are more realistic than those typically found in the literature. By applying the methodology to a sample composed of the larger banks in the U.S. economy, we are able to present novel results on the nature of the cost functions of these large banks. The results imply that the

[10]Prescott and Visscher (1980) cite the following examples of firm-specific human capital: knowledge about the abilities and efforts of personnel, information about the matching of employees with tasks, and technological knowledge specific to the production methods or organizational methods of the firm.

cost functions of these large multiproduct banks are not subadditive, and thus, that there are not measurable cost complementarities in multiproduct production among these types of banks. This does not necessarily mean, however, that these banks would be better off breaking up production into a group of specialty firms. Uncertainty, transactions costs associated with market contracting, and the shareability of inputs, as well as the minimization of consumer-borne transaction costs, may provide sufficient economic justification for multiproduct bank production in the absence of subadditive costs.

LITERATURE CITED

Barnett, William A. "The Minflex Laurent Translog Flexible Functional Form." *Journal of Econometrics* 30 (October 1985), 33–44.

Barnett, William A., and Yul W. Lee. "The Global Properties of the Minflex Laurent, Generalized Leontief, and the Translog Flexible Forms." *Econometrica* 6 (November 1985), 1421–37.

Benston, George J., and Clifford W. Smith. "A Transaction Cost Approach to the Theory of Financial Intermediation." *Journal of Finance* 31 (May 1976), 215–32.

Berger, Allen N., Gerald A. Hanweck, and David B. Humphrey. "Competitive Viability in Banking: Scale, Scope, and Product Mix Economies." Federal Reserve Board: Washington, D.C., 1986.

______. "Competitive Viability in Banking: Scale, Scope and Product Mix Economies." *Journal of Monetary Economics* 20 (December 1987), 501–20.

Boyd, John H., Stanley L. Graham, and R. Shawn Hewitt. "BHC Mergers with Nonbank Financial Firms—An Update." Working paper 431, Federal Reserve Bank of Minneapolis, May 1989.

Christensen, L. R., and D. W. Caves. "Global Properties of Flexible Functional Forms." *American Economic Review* 70 (June 1980), 422–32.

Denny, M., and Melvyn A. Fuss. "The Use of Approximation Analysis to Test for Separability and Existence of Consistent Aggregates." *American Economic Review* 67 (June 1977), 404–18.

Eisemann, Peter C. "Diversification and the Congeneric Bank Holding Company." *Journal of Bank Research* 7 (Spring 1976), 68–77.

Evanoff, Douglas D. "Branch Banking and Service Accessibility." *Journal of Money, Credit, and Banking* 20 (May 1988), 191–202.

Evans, David S., and James J. Heckman. "A Test for Subadditivity of the Cost Function with an Application to the Bell System." *American Economic Review* 74 (September 1984), 615–23.

Gallant, Ronald A. "On the Bias in Flexible Functional Forms and Essentially Unbiased Forms: The Fourier Functional Form." *Journal of Econometrics* 15 (February 1981), 211–45.

Gilligan, Thomas, and Michael Smirlock. "An Empirical Study of the Joint Production and Scale Economies in Commercial Banking." *Journal of Banking and Finance* 8 (March 1984), 67–76.

Gilligan, Thomas, Michael Smirlock, and William Marshall. "Scale and Scope Economies in the Multi-Product Banking Firm." *Journal of Monetary Economies* 13 (March 1984), 393–405.

Humphrey, David B. "Cost and Scale Economies in Bank Intermediation." In *Handbook for Bank Strategy,* edited by R. Aspinwall, and R. Eisenbeis. New York: Wiley & Sons, 1985.

Hunter, William C., and Stephen G. Timme. "Technical Change, Organizational Form, and the Structure of Bank Production." *Journal of Money, Credit, and Banking* 18 (May 1986), 152–66.

______. "Technological Change and Production Economies in Large U.S. Banks." Working paper 88–6, Federal Reserve Bank of Atlanta, 1988.

Hunter, William C., Stephen G. Timme, and Won Keun Yang. "An Examination of Cost Subadditivity and Multiproduct Production in Large U.S. Commercial Banks." Working paper 89–3, Federal Reserve Bank of Atlanta, Revised November 1989.

Kim, Moshe. "Banking Technology and the Existence of a Consistent Output Aggregate." *Journal of Monetary Economics* 8 (September 1985), 181–95.

Kim, H. Youn. "Economies of Scale and Economies of Scope in Multiproduct Financial Institutions: Further Evidence from Credit Unions." *Journal of Money, Credit, and Banking* 18 (May 1986), 220–26.

Kolari, James, and Asghar Zardkoohi. *Bank Costs, Structure, and Performance.* Lexington, Mass.: D. C. Heath, 1987.

Lawrence, Colin, and Robert Shay. "Technology and Financial Intermediation in the Multiproduct Banking Firm: An Econometric Study of U.S. Banks 1979–1982." *Technical Innovation, Regulation and the Monetary Economy,* edited by C. Lawrence and R. Shay. Boston, Mass.: Ballinger, 1986.

LeCompte, Richard, and Stephen Smith. "Changes in the Cost of Intermediation: The Case of Savings and Loans." *Journal of Finance* 45 (September 1990), forthcoming.

Levy, David T., and Lawrence J. Haber. "An Advantage of the Multiproduct Firm: The Transferability of Firm-Specific Capital." *Journal of Economic Behavior and Organization* 7 (1986), 291–302.

Lucas, Robert E., Jr. "Adjustment Costs and the Theory of Supply." *Journal of Political Economy* 75 (August 1967), 321–34.

Mester, Loretta J. "A Multiproduct Cost Study of Savings and Loans." *Journal of Finance* 42 (June 1987), 423–45.

Murray, John, and Robert White. "Economies of Scale and Economies of Scope in Multiproduct Financial Institutions: A Study of British Columbia Credit Unions." *Journal of Finance* 38 (June 1983), 887–902.

Prescott, Edward, and M. Visscher. "Organizational Capital." *Journal of Political Economy* 88 (June 1980), 446–71.

Sealey, C. W., and James T. Lindley. "Inputs, Outputs, and a Theory of Production and Cost at Depository Financial Institutions." *Journal of Finance* (September 1977), 1251–66.

Shaffer, Sherrill. "A Revenue-Restricted Cost Study of 100 Large Banks." Working paper, Federal Reserve Bank of New York, 1988.

Teece, David J. "Economics of Scope and the Scope of the Enterprise." *Journal of Economic Behavior and Organizations* 1 (1980), 223–45.

______. "Towards an Economic Theory of the Multiproduct Firm." *Journal of Economic Behavior and Organization* 3 (1982), 39–63.

White, Halbert. "Using Least Squares to Approximate Unknown Regression Functions." *International Economic Review* 21 (February 1980), 149–64.

NOTES, COMMENTS, REPLIES

Scottish Banking and the Legal Restrictions Theory: A Closer Look

A Comment by Lawrence H. White

The use of Scottish banking experience as counterevidence to the legal restrictions theory of money (White 1987) rests on the view that the Scottish system, before the Bank Charter Act of 1844 closed entry into note-issue,[1] warranted its traditional characterization as "free banking." That is, the regulatory regime approximated laissez-faire closely enough that its institutions, practices, and performance were basically those of an unregulated free-market monetary system.

This interpretation of Scottish banking has been challenged by Tyler Cowen and Randall Kroszner (1989). Wishing to defend the legal restrictions theory, whose vision of a laissez-faire payments system does not coincide with the Scottish experience, they argue that the Scottish regime did not closely enough approximate laissez-faire to provide evidence damaging to the legal restrictions theory. They cite three principal "deviations from laissez-faire" (p. 222): (1) the Act of 1765 "raised impediments to interest-bearing notes and proscribed small denomination notes"; (2) "the prevailing system of liability and incorporation raised barriers to entry into banking"; and (3) "the Bank of England acted as a shadow central bank for Scotland." Cowen and Kroszner [hereafter CK] thus characterize the Scottish system as legally restricted from paying interest on circulating media, as less than competitive, and as dependent upon the Bank of England.

[1]See Gregory (1964) for the text of the 1844 Act (7 & 8 Vict., c. 32). Section X closes entry into bank note issue throughout the United Kingdom. I am not sure why Cowen and Kroszner (1989) choose 1845 as the end date of the Scottish free-banking era. Perhaps they believe that Scotland was not affected until passage of the Scottish Bank Act of 1845.

The author thanks Kurt Schuler, Charles Munn, Randall Kroszner, and Tyler Cowen for useful comments.

LAWRENCE H. WHITE *is associate professor of economics at the University of Georgia.*

Journal of Money, Credit, and Banking, Vol. 22, No. 4 (November 1990)

A closer reading of Scottish banking history, as related in the very sources they rely upon, Checkland (1975) and Munn (1981), undermines these characterizations. The Scottish case does provide relevant evidence against the prediction of the legal restrictions theory that in the absence of relevant legal impediments non-interest-bearing bank notes cannot coexist with interest-bearing assets.[2]

The Act of 1765

The Act of 1765, which banned the option clause and notes smaller than one pound, obviously infringed on laissez-faire, as my 1987 article recognized (White, 1987, p. 451). CK are correct in noting that the ban on the option clause eliminated a useful contractual means of mitigating potential illiquidity problems and associated instability (see Dowd 1988), and that the ban on small notes raised a barrier to entry against very-small-scale issuers (see White 1984, p. 30). They are incorrect, however, in stating that the Act of 1765 "thwarted" the "displacement of non-interest-bearing [banknotes] by interest-bearing instruments."

CK (p. 224) argue that the Act of 1765 accounts for the failure of Scottish banking to deliver the interest-bearing transactions media that the legal restrictions theory predicts for an economy with positive interest rates: "Without the option clause and with the requirement of immediate convertibility, note issuers had no control over the maturity structure of their note liabilities. The legal restrictions theory, however, assumes that there are no obstacles to maturity-matched intermediation. In the absence of maturity matching, risk and liquidity considerations may prevent competetive [sic] forces from equalizing the rates of return on interest-bearing debt and transactions media." Even granting its description of the facts, this argument is insufficient to account for non-interest-bearing bank notes. While liquidity costs due to maturity mismatch imply a (larger) spread between rates of return, they do not imply a *zero* nominal rate of return on banknotes.

More importantly, the premise that "note issuers had no control over the maturity structure of their note liabilities" is factually incorrect. CK apparently assume that postdated bearer instruments were outlawed by the Act of 1765. My article (White 1987, p. 451) speculated that they "may have" been so outlawed. An overlooked passage in Checkland (1975, p. 187) indicates that postdated bearer instruments actually were *not* illegal and were in fact issued. Because of its importance I quote this passage at length:

> By 1810, no less serious for a bank than a run on its notes could be a sudden demand for the repayment of deposits. . . . [T]he traditional form of bank-borrowing from the public, since 1708, had been the Treasurers' or Cashiers' bond. Under this device, the Bank could take in quickly quite large sums, provided by a relatively few large lenders, friends of the bank, at a stated term and at an agreed rate of interest. But with the ending of the optional clause in 1765, it became necessary to become more flexible

[2]The Scottish case also casts doubt on the predictions of CK (pp. 221–22) that under laissez-faire debt-based banking claims would vanish in favor of equity-based payment accounts, and that "transactions media would not bear a fixed relationship with the unit of account." For discussion see White 1989).

> in deposit gathering. This need stimulated the promissory note, also signed by the Treasurer, but more flexible than the bond, easier to issue and *readily passed from hand to hand,* and so, in a sense, almost an extension of the note issue. Such notes were for three or six months, bearing 3% and 4% respectively. It is probable that certain of the provincial banking companies anticipated the Bank of Scotland in this. [Emphasis added.]

The coexistence of non-interest-bearing bank notes with these transferable interest-bearing bank notes is inconsistent with the legal restrictions theory. As CK indicate, the LRT predicts equalization of rates of return between interest-bearing debt and transactions media in the absence of legal barriers to providing equivalent default risk, equivalent transferability, and maturity matching. We can now see that all three of those conditions were met in the Scottish case. A promissory note and an ordinary bank note issued by the same Scottish bank carried identical default risk. Both liabilities "readily passed from hand to hand." A bank issuing three-month and six-month promissory notes could perfectly match the maturities of its assets and liabilities. Yet rates of return on ordinary bank notes and promissory notes differed. Transferable promissory notes did not become the common medium of exchange or otherwise drive non-interest-bearing notes out of circulation.

My explanation (White 1987) for the survival of non-interest-bearing notes as transactions media, even in the face of interest-bearing alternatives, is that the time-and-inconvenience cost of computing the present value of an asset like a promissory note in each transaction exceeds the benefit (at least for denominations below some threshold). The CK explanation, that interest-bearing alternatives were blocked by legal restrictions, is rendered untenable by the existence of transferable bank-issued promissory notes.

A possible strategy for immunizing the LRT prediction from this counterevidence would be to argue that Scottish banking was not sufficiently competitive to compel note-issuers to pay interest on bank notes. This response would beg the question of why issuers paid competitive interest rates on promissory notes and deposits. But CK do emphasize barriers to competition. Accordingly I turn to the question of the competitiveness of Scottish banking.[3]

Small Notes, Charters of Incorporation and Liability Rules

CK (pp. 224–25) point to the 1765 Act's ban on notes below £1 as a barrier to entry. The small note ban did increase the minimum efficient scale of banks (White 1984, p. 30). But it did not rule out effective competition among the numerous larger banks. It remains to be investigated whether competitive pressures in the market for bank liabilities were noticeably reduced.

Following Carr, Glied, and Mathewson (1986) and Carr and Mathewson (1988), CK (pp. 225–27) also point to the restriction of limited-liability charters to three particular banks, which made unlimited liability compulsory for other banks, as a

[3]The following two sections draw heavily from White (1990), which replies to several critics of the free-banking interpretation of the Scottish experience.

barrier to entry. Clearly such restrictions on liability size and on the contractual risk-sharing arrangements firms may adopt are potentially barriers to entry (White 1984, pp. 142–43). Thus CK are correct that entry was not *completely* free. But how much did these barriers inhibit competition in practice?

Following Checkland (1975, p. 480) I had previously suggested (White 1984, p. 41) that the restriction against limited liability banks in Scotland was not binding because "the unchartered banks of Scotland chose to retain unlimited liability in the 1860s and 1870s even after limited liability became available to them" through the Companies Act of 1862. CK (p. 226, n. 12) cite this suggestion, and argue to the contrary, citing Carr, Glied, and Mathewson (1986), that for banks "limited liability was not effectively available until an Act of 1879." Carr et al. point out that while the 1862 Act allowed limited liability for other bank obligations, it retained unlimited liability for note-issues. But this means that the Act of 1862 in fact offered an effective limitation of liability on all but bank notes, which comprised only 7.9 percent of total liabilities for the Scottish banks in 1865 (Checkland 1975, table 44, p. 743), or 6.6 percent of liabilities plus capital (a figure Carr, Glied, and Mathewson themselves cite [p. 10]). If unlimited liability blocked the nonchartered banks from "reaching optimal risk sharing arrangements" as shareholders perceived them, as CK follow Carr and Mathewson (1988) in suggesting, wouldn't those shareholders have found a substantial limitation of liability better than no limitation, and therefore have taken advantage of the 1862 Act?

Carr, Glied, and Mathewson (1986, p. 10) believe that the Scottish joint-stock banks finally adopted limited liability in 1882 because an 1879 Act offered "substantially lessened" liability for notes. On my reading, however, the 1879 Act retained greater shareholder liability for notes than the 1862 Act. Historians of the industry have traditionally attributed the adoption of limited liability not to the change in the law, but to the 1878 failure of the City of Glasgow Bank, which evidently changed the perceptions of shareholders concerning the risks they faced.

We can also assess the bindingness of compulsory unlimited liability before 1844 by contrasting the three limited-liability "public" banks (the Bank of Scotland, Royal Bank of Scotland, and British Linen Company) with the unlimited-liability banks before 1844. CK note that the public banks were larger on average, and (again following Carr and Mathewson) that none of them failed. They regard these facts as evidence that limited liability made it easier for banks to raise capital and that the corporate form was "conducive to survival." These hypotheses are plausible. As contrary evidence, however, several facts about the nonchartered banks as of 1845 (White 1984, table 2.2, p. 37) merit attention: (1) the Commercial Bank of Scotland had more branches than any of the public banks, a greater note circulation than two of the three, and more shareholders than one; (2) the National Bank of Scotland had more branches than two of the three public banks, a note circulation only one percent smaller than that of the second largest public bank, and more shareholders than any of the three; (3) the North of Scotland Banking Company and the Edinburgh and Glasgow Bank each had more shareholders than any of the three public banks; (4) the Union Bank of Scotland had a greater note circulation than two of the three public banks. All told, the public banks ranked first, fourth, and seventh in size of circulation. Banks with unlimited liability apparently did not have great difficulty raising capital on a large scale: five had capitals as large as the Bank of Scotland's £1 million, and eight had capitals as large or larger than the British Linen Company's £500,000. Nor was the survival of unlimited-liability banks obviously impaired once they attained adequate size: none of the five above-named large joint-stock banks failed while they had unlimited liability. (Two of the eight with the largest capitals eventually did fail some time after 1844.)

Still, the banks that made efforts to get legislative charters, and to deny them to other banks, must have wanted them for some reason. CK (p. 226, n. 11) correctly point out that "since resources were expended to fight for and against corporate charters, we can infer that the bankers of the time believed that the privileges associated with charters were valuable." CK cite several possible advantages beyond limited liability, one of which clearly had some value: government customs officers were instructed to accept only the notes of the chartered banks in payment of duties (Checkland 1975, p. 186).

CK also claim that "only they [the public banks] were authorized to 'hold and remit' government revenues." The basis for this claim is unclear, since it is not found in the pages of Munn and Checkland that they cite.[4] Checkland (1975, p. 166) in fact relates that the private bank of Sir William Forbes and Company in the late eighteenth century "had the remittance of the excise duties from Edinburgh to London." He adds: "The Royal Bank had long had the remittance of the customs; the British Linen Company that of the revenue of the Post Office[;] the Bank of Scotland had nothing." Thus a charter was neither necessary nor sufficient to benefit from government patronage.

CK cite two other advantages of charters: "the appearance of official sanction," which is also noted by Checkland (1968, p. 149), and escape from "the uncertain legal identity of unincorporated entities" before 1826. It is not clear how important these really were. But in at least one respect, receivability for duties, the public banks enjoyed politically created rents. The existence of such rents is contrary to strict laissez-faire. Accounts of the Scottish system as free banking have perhaps underemphasized (though they have not ignored) the "preferred position" of the public banks (Checkland 1975, p. 235) in this respect.

Contrary to CK (p. 226), however, the charters did not have the effect of "reducing competitive pressures (hence relaxing the zero-profit condition)" throughout the free banking era. While the public banks may have enjoyed a more-or-less advantaged position before the Commercial Bank of Scotland, the first large joint stock bank, entered in 1810, they clearly faced effective competition between 1810 and 1844. Competition between the public banks and the large joint-stock banks was vigorous in note-issuing, deposit-taking, lending and discounting, inland exchange,

[4]Cowen and Kroszner cite inter alia Checkland (1975, p. 150), a page not relevant to the question. Perhaps they meant to cite Checkland (1968, p. 149), which contains the statement that "A charter was a useful prelude to gaining a share in the holding and remitting of government revenues, a source of trading funds of great value."

and other aspects of the trade.[5] Profit margins for all banks were squeezed as competitive bidding for loans and deposits kept the interest spread between these down to 1 percent (Checkland 1975, pp. 384–88), exactly Neil Wallace's (1983) estimate of the competitive spread in the absence of legal restrictions. Contrary to CK's hypothesis of a "relaxed" zero-excess-profit condition, Munn (1982, p. 118) comments that "the competitive nature of the business" had the result that "profits were reduced and therefore all earning assets had to be managed with fine attention to detail. There was no room for error or even slackness if dividends were to be maintained." Attempts were made in the 1830s and 1840s to limit deposit interest rates and enhance activity charges through cartel agreements, but such agreements proved unsustainable in the face of strong competitive pressures (Checkland 1975, pp. 449–50; Munn 1982, p. 122).

The elimination of excess profits in Scottish banking is evidence of the effectiveness of competition among the banks. CK fail to inquire after this evidence. It appears that they simply assume, incorrectly, that the infringements of laissez-faire to which they point precluded effective competition.

Supposed Dependence upon London and the Bank of England

Cowen and Kroszner (1989, p. 227) claim that "the development and structure of bank obligations [in Scotland] . . . was affected by the existence of a lender of last resort in the Bank of England (BOE)." They go on to state that "the readiness of the BOE to act as a lender of last resort for the Scottish system provided a source of insurance." In their view the Bank, acting as a lender of last resort, extended support at subsidy rates that distorted the banking system: "The support of the BOE effectively socialized the costs of stability and redemption problems."

To act as a "lender of last resort" in the standard sense of that phrase, as described by Humphrey and Keleher (1984, pp. 277–78), is to act as a "backstop or guarantor . . . of a fractional-reserve banking system" or to take on "the responsibility of guaranteeing the liquidity of the entire economy." If this definition is accepted, the Bank of England clearly was *not* a lender of last resort for Scotland before 1844. In a few cases the Bank provided loans to Scottish banks. But in other cases (most importantly the crises of 1825–26 and 1836–37) it refused to lend. In the case of the Ayr Bank in 1772, the Bank of England set such stiff terms that its "support" was declined (Checkland 1975, p. 131). CK give as an example of last-resort lending a long-term credit the Royal Bank negotiated with the Bank of England in 1830. But Checkland (1975, p. 444) adds that "in October 1836 . . . the Bank [of England], as part of a general credit contraction, required the Royal Bank of Scotland to pay off its advance." This withdrawal of credit in a time of stringency was not only much to the consternation of the Royal Bank's general manager, but contrary to the behavior of a lender of last resort.

CK (pp. 227–28) cite a second supposed episode of last-resort lending by the

[5]Generalizations about the Scottish system thus need to be carefully dated. Munn (1982) discusses the structural changes in Scottish banking between 1810 and 1844.

Bank of England to the Scottish banks: "In the crisis of 1792–93, for example, both the Bank of Scotland and Royal Bank of Scotland sought the aid of London and received special large credits to ease their distress (Andreades 1924, p. 188; Checkland 1975, pp. 219–20)." Closer reading of the sources that they cite here shows, however, that the loans in question were granted *not* by the Bank of England, but by the government, and were granted *not* to the banks, but to Scottish business firms. Officials of the Scottish banks had gone to London to plea for general relief measures for Scotland, not for BOE loans to the banks. Thus CK seriously misrepresent this episode when they cite it as an example of how "the [Scottish] public banks depended upon the BOE directly in crisis times."

Fetter (1978, p. 267) makes a relevant distinction between "supporting the market *ex post,* as compared with giving assurance *ex ante* that credit would be available at some price." The second is an essential part of the lender-of-last-resort role of guaranteeing liquidity. Before 1844 (and apparently until the Baring Crisis of 1890) the Bank of England played only the first role, and did not do even that consistently. There is no reason to believe that in making occasional interbank loans the Bank was acting in any way other than to maximize its profits. Contrary to CK, the Bank of England did not extend interbank credit at subsidy rates which "socialized" costs.

Because the Bank of England did not assure its willingness to lend, or even act consistently with such an assurance, it did not act as lender of last resort (in the standard sense) to the Scottish system before 1844. This is not just a terminological point. The substantive point is that the Scottish banks could not have relied or depended *ex ante* on advances from the Bank of England as a backstop source of liquidity. CK (p. 227) recognize that "there was no explicit obligation for the BOE to act as a central bank for the Scottish system." Neither was there any implicit policy of acting in such a manner. Thus CK (p. 228) are incorrect in calling the Bank of England a "shadow central bank" for the Edinburgh banks, and in saying that the Scottish banks faced "incentives to . . . come under the wing of the Bank of England."

In fact the Bank of England explicitly rejected the idea that it had lender-of-last-resort obligations. Fetter (1978, pp. 118–20) describes the Bank's unwillingness to extend credit during the crisis of 1826. In correspondence accompanying the Bank of England's withdrawal in 1836 of its advance to the Royal Bank of Scotland (quoted by Checkland 1975, p. 447), Horsely Palmer of the Bank of England wrote to the Royal Bank that "he deemed it expedient to reduce the Bank's advances to other Banks of issue, thereby making them dependent in such times upon their own respective resources. . . . Every Bank of issue should be prepared to support its own circulation by its own reserve . . . without requiring any issues from the Bank of England."

Cowen and Kroszner (p. 228) are correct in indicating that the Scottish banks relied on the London financial market to meet occasional liquidity needs. The Scottish banks held "secondary reserves" in the form of "good securities, of a kind that could be realised in London without serious loss" (Checkland 1975, p. 1974).

The ability to sell these assets quickly and at low cost for claims on London banks, which the Scottish banks could in many cases use as a redemption medium, or for gold, permitted the Scottish banks to meet their liquidity needs with less specie in their vaults.

Cowen and Kroszner exaggerate the degree of "dependence on London" (CK, p. 228) this arrangement involved. In any specie-based free banking system we should expect to find banks striving to economize on their specie holdings, inter alia by holding liquid securities as secondary reserves. In the Scottish case the market in which these securities could be sold happened to be outside of their banking orbit because London was Britain's financial center, and because the Scottish banks were legally excluded from opening branch offices in London. The Scottish banks did face a binding legal restriction here. But this is presumably not what is at issue when "dependence" on the London financial market is cited. Had they opened London branch offices, the Scottish banks would presumably have made similar use of the London market.

What is at issue is the significance of the Scottish banks' use of the London financial market as a source of liquidity. The Scottish banks relied on the London center in the short-term sense that at any given moment they held securities that they counted on being able to sell there. A surprise "shutting" of the London market would seriously affect them, as it did in the 1797 episode CK cite. But Scottish banks did not rely on London in the long-term sense that access to the London market was essential to the way they economized on specie holdings. Alexander Blair (1826, p. 51), then general manager of the British Linen Company, testified that the Scottish banks might draw gold from Hamburg if it were not available in London. Checkland (1975, p. 194) indicates that they could also draw on Holland to meet occasional liquidity needs.

CK (p. 228, n. 15) quote Checkland's (1975, p. 432) statement that for the Scottish banks "the principal and ultimate source of liquidity lay in London, and, in particular, in the Bank of England." It is true that the Bank of England was the principal source of specie in London. To draw gold from London, the Scottish banks acquired and redeemed Bank of England liabilities. Concentration of London specie reserves in the Bank of England may have distorted the market for specie somewhat. But it probably did not make the constraints on acquiring specie appreciably looser than those the Scottish banks would have faced had there been a plurality of issuing banks serving as specie sources in London. It is not true, as we have seen, that the Bank guaranteed to make reserves available to the market in times of stringency. Interbank loans, such as the Bank of England occasionally made, might have been at least as readily available on similar terms from competitive London issuing banks. An interbank loan market surely would have existed even without a privileged bank in the financial center, and might well have been *more* active.

In the crisis of 1839 the Bank of England turned to the Bank of France for an emergency extension of credit, to meet severe liquidity needs that had brought the BOE close to suspending payments. The Bank also arranged for sizable credits in Hamburg (Fetter 1978, p. 175). Yet no one would say that the London banking system customarily "depended" on the Bank of France, or the Hamburg market, as a lender of last resort. Still less would anyone say that the London banking system was "under the wing" of the Bank of France.

The ability of Scottish banks to borrow reserve money from foreign financial centers is consistent with, and indeed implicit in, the free banking interpretation of Scottish banking according to a model of a small open economy whose base money (specie) is money throughout the world economy.[6] CK (p. 228) argue that "by maintaining a fixed exchange rate between the English and Scots pound, the Scottish bankers permitted London to have a leading role in their monetary activities. BOE policies effectively controlled the Scottish money supply and banking system much as it did in England." But in fact, unlike the English country banks, the Scottish banks did not regularly pay out Bank of England notes as a redemption medium, or regularly hold Bank of England liabilities as an important component of reserves. The Scottish banks did hold working balances with London correspondent banks (which did hold Bank of England liabilities), but not as a major component of their reserves (White 1990). The Scottish money stock was not specifically geared to the quantity of Bank of England liabilities. In the long run, Scotland's money stock was determined by the quantity of money demanded at the given purchasing power of the monetary unit. The purchasing power of the monetary unit was determined by global supply and demand for gold. CK suggest that Scotland played the role of a "small" country to England's "big" country in "a two-country model" of international finance. But surely Britain as whole must be regarded as an open economy during the period of an international specie standard.

In the short run, the Bank of England may well have had the power to disturb the quantity of money in England significantly enough to cause cyclical effects on the price level, interest rates, and real activity, with spill-over effects on the Scottish economy. (The actual transmission mechanism warrants further research.) Far from being inconsistent with the free-banking view of Scotland, this view of the Bank of England's powers was first developed by the Free Banking School in the 1820–44 period. The School argued in defense of Scottish free banking that cyclical disturbances in Scotland had been imported and had not originated with the Scottish banks. The existence of spill-over effects from London to Scotland would imply that the English and Scottish economies were integrated, as the traditional view of Scottish banking has always recognized. It would not imply, contrary to CK (pp. 228–29) that "BOE policies effectively controlled the Scottish . . . banking system," or that "the Scottish system must be considered as a part of the overall British banking system under the aegis of the BOE." A finding of spill-over effects of BOE actions on the United States economy, about which American writers at the time complained, would not led one to deny the distinctness of the English and U.S. banking systems.

[6]White (1984, p. 11) explicitly argues for the applicability of such a model to Scotland.

Conclusion

Cowen and Kroszner's arguments for dismissing Scottish banking before 1844 as counterevidence to the legal restrictions theory of money do not hold up under scrutiny. The Act of 1765 did not outlaw interest-bearing notes. Such notes existed, and did not drive non-interest-bearing notes out of circulation. The Scottish system in its heyday was quite competitive. The privileges of the chartered Scottish banks may have been a source of some small rents worth protecting, but they did not impede competition in intermediation or in the provision of inside money. The Bank of England was not a lender of last resort in the Scottish system before 1844. Nor was the BOE a central bank in the sense of providing a reserve base of high-powered money held by the Scottish banks, except perhaps during the Restriction period. The Scottish banks did use the London financial market to meet occasional liquidity needs, but this did not imply reliance on the good graces of the Bank of England.

At least during the period from 1810 to 1844, then, the free-banking model continues to provide a useful and valid framework for understanding the Scottish banking system. Scottish experience accordingly provides important counterevidence to the prediction of the legal restrictions theory that non-interest-bearing banknotes cannot coexist with interest-bearing assets under laissez-faire.

LITERATURE CITED

Andreades, A. *A History of the Bank of England,* 2nd ed. London: P. S. King, 1924.

Blair, Alexander. Testimony in the *Report from the Select Committee Appointed to Inquire into the State of the Circulation of Promissory Notes under the Value of £5 in Scotland and Ireland . . .* British Sessional Papers, 1826, House of Commons, vol. 3. New York: Readex Microprint, n.d.

Carr, Jack, Sherry Glied, and Frank Mathewson. "Unlimited Liability and Free Banking in Scotland." MS, University of Toronto, 1986.

Carr, Jack L., and G. Frank Mathewson. "Unlimited Liability as a Barrier to Entry." *Journal of Political Economy* 96 (August 1988), 766–84.

Checkland, S. G. "Banking History and Economic Development: Seven Systems." *Scottish Journal of Political Economy* 15 (1968), 144–66.

———. *Scottish Banking: A History, 1695–1973.* Glasgow: Collins, 1975.

Cowen, Tyler, and Randall Kroszner. "Scottish Banking before 1845: A Model for Laissez-Faire?" *Journal of Money, Credit, and Banking* 21 (May 1989), 221–31.

Dowd, Kevin. "Option Clauses and the Stability of a Laissez Faire Monetary System." *Journal of Financial Services Research* 1 (1988), 319–33.

Fetter, Frank Whitson. *Development of British Monetary Orthodoxy, 1797–1875.* Reprint of 1965 ed. Fairfield, N.J.: Augustus M. Kelly, 1978.

Gregory, T. E., ed. *Select Statutes Documents and Reports Relating to British Banking 1832–1928,* vol. 1. London: Frank Cass, 1964.

Humphrey, Thomas H., and Robert E. Keleher. "The Lender of Last Resort: A Historical Perspective." *Cato Journal* 4 (Spring/Summer 1984), 275–318.

Munn, Charles W. *The Scottish Provincial Banking Companies, 1747–1864*. Edinburgh: John Donald, 1981.

______. "The Development of Joint-Stock Banking in Scotland, 1810–1845." In *Business, Banking and Urban History,* edited by Anthony Slaven and Derek H. Aldcroft. Edinburgh: John Donald, 1982.

Wallace, Neil. "A Legal Restrictions theory of the Demand for 'Money' and the Role of Monetary Policy." Federal Reserve Bank of Minneapolis *Quarterly Review* (Winter 1983), 1–7.

White, Lawrence H. *Free Banking in Britain.* Cambridge: Cambridge University Press, 1984.

______. "Accounting for Non-interest-bearing Currency: A Critique of the Legal Restrictions Theory of Money." *Journal of Money, Credit, and Banking* 19 (November 1987), 448–56.

______. "What Kinds of Monetary Institutions Would a Free Market Deliver?" *Cato Journal* 9 (Fall 1989), 367–91.

______. "Banking without a Central Bank: Scotland before 1844 as a 'Free Banking' System." Forthcoming in *Unregulated Banking: Chaos or Order?* edited by Forrest Capie and Geoffrey Wood. London: Macmillan, 1990.

ANNUAL INDEX

Volume 22, 1990
February 1–134
May 35–271
August 273–408
November 409–536

America in the World Economy: A Strategy for the 1990s, C. Fred Bergsten, reviewed, 402–404
Analyzing the Stability of Demand-for-Money Equations via Bounded-Influence Estimation Techniques, Christopher F. Baum and Marilena Furno, 465–77
Arndt, H. W., book review, 402–404

Barney, L. Dwayne, Jr., Alan Frankle, and Harry White, Reserve Requirements and the Inflation Tax, note, 400–401
Basu, Susanto, Miles S. Kimball, N. Gregory Mankiw, and David N. Weil, Optimal Advice for Monetary Policy, 19–36
Baum, Christopher F., and Marilena Furno, Analyzing the Stability of Demand-for-Money Equations via Bounded-Influence Estimation Techniques, 465–77
Bergsten, C. Fred, *America in the World Economy: A Strategy for the 1990s*, reviewed, 402–404
Brewer, Thomas L., and Pietra Rivoli, Politics and Perceived Country Creditworthiness in International Banking, 357–69

Canzoneri, Matthew B., and Anne C. Sibert, The Macroeconomic Implications of Implicit Contract Models with Asymmetric Information, 273–87
Clauretie, Terrence M., and Thomas Herzog, The Effect of State Foreclosure Laws on Loan Losses: Evidence from the Mortgage Insurance Industry, 221–33

Day of Reckoning, Benjamin M. Friedman, reviewed, 268–71
Deaves, Richard, Money Supply Announcements and Market Reactions in an Open Economy, 154–64
Do Liquidity Constraints Vary over Time? Evidence from Survey and Panel Data, Gary S. Fissel and Tullio Jappelli, note, 253–67
Dowd, Kevin, The Value of Time and the Transactions Demand for Money, 51–64
Duca, John V., and David VanHoose, Loan Commitments and Optimal Monetary Policy, 178–94

Economic Forecasts, Rationality, and the Processing of New Information over Time, Steve Swidler and David Ketcher, 65–76
Effect of Import Price Changes on Domestic Inflation, The: An Empirical Test of the Ratchet Effect, Farhad Rassekh and Barry Wilbratte, note, 263–67
Effect of State Foreclosure Laws on Loan Losses, The: Evidence from the Mortgage Insurance Industry, Terrence M. Clauretie and Thomas Herzog, 221–33
Examination of Cost Subadditivity and Multiproduct Production in Large U.S. Banks, An, William C. Hunter, Stephen G. Timme, and Won Keun Yang, 504–25

Fackler, James S., Federal Credit, Private Credit, and Economic Activity, 444–64
Federal Credit, Private Credit, and Economic Activity, James S. Fackler, 444–64
Feltenstein, Andrew, David Lebow, and S. van Wijnbergen, Savings, Commodity Market Rationing, and the Real Rate of Interest in China, 234–52
Fissel, Gary S., and Tullio Jappelli, Do Liquidity Constraints Vary over Time? Evidence from Survey and Panel Data, note, 253–67
Foreign Inflation Transmission under Flexible Exchange Rates and Currency Substitution, John H. Rogers, 195–208
Forerunners of "New Monetary Economics" Proposals, The, Scott Sumner, note, 109–18
Frankle, Alan. *See* Dwayne L. Barney, Jr.
Friedman, Benjamin M., *Day of Reckoning*, reviewed, 268–71
Fry, Maxwell, *Money, Interest, and Banking in Economic Development*, reviewed, 131–34

Gavin, William T., book review, 404–408
Glick, Reuven, and Michael Hutchison, New Results in Support of the Fiscal Ineffectiveness Proposition, 288–304
Gorton, Gary, and Anthony M. Santomero, Market Discipline and Bank Subordinated Debt, note, 119–28
Governing the $5 Trillion Economy, Herbert Stein, reviewed, 404–408
Grossman, Herschel I., Inflation and Reputation with Generic Policy Preferences, 165–77

Hakes, David R., The Objectives and Priorities of Monetary Policy under Different Federal Reserve Chairmen, 327–37

Haug, Alfred A., Ricardian Equivalence, Rational Expectations, and the Permanent Income Hypothesis, 305–26
Havrilesky, Thomas, The Influence of the Federal Advisory Council on Monetary Policy, 37–50
Herzog, Thomas. *See* Terrence M. Clauretie
Huang, Roger D., Risk and Parity in Purchasing Power, 338–56
Hunter, William C., Stephen G. Timme, and Won Keun Yang, An Examination of Cost Subadditivity and Multiproduct Production in Large U.S. Banks, 504–25
Hutchison, Michael M., book review, 129–31
______. *See* Reuven Glick

Inflation and Reputation with Generic Policy Preferences, Herschel I. Grossman, 165–77
Inflation and Taxation with Optimizing Governments, James M. Poterba and Julio J. Rotemberg, 1–18
Influence of the Federal Advisory Council on Monetary Policy, The, Thomas Havrilesky, 37–50
Interest Rate Linkages within the European Monetary System: A Time Series Analysis, Costas J. Karfakis and Demetrios M. Moschos, note, 388–94
International Debt Crisis and Bank Loan-Loss-Reserve Decisions: The Signaling Content of Partially Anticipated Events, James J. Musumeci and Joseph F. Sinkey, Jr., 370–87
International Debt Crisis, Investor Contagion, and Bank Security Returns in 1987, The: The Brazilian Experience, James J. Musimeci, and Joseph F. Sinkey, Jr., 209–20

Jappelli, Tullio. *See* Gary S. Fissel

Karfakis, Costas J., and Demetrios M. Moschos, Interest Rate Linkages within the European Monetary System: A Time Series Analysis, note, 388–94
Ketcher, David. *See* Steve Swidler
Kim, Yoonbai, Purchasing Power Parity in the Long Run: A Cointegration Approach, 491–503
Kimball, Miles S. *See* Susanto Basu
Kormendi, Roger C., and Philip Meguire, A Multicountry Characterization of the Nonstationarity of Aggregate Output, 77–93

Lebow, David. *See* David Feltenstein
Loan Commitments and Optimal Monetary Policy, John V. Duca and David VanHoose, 178–94

Macroeconomic Implications of Implicit Contract Models with Asymmetric Information, The, Matthew B. Canzoneri and Anne C. Sibert, 273–87
Mankiw, N. Gregory. *See* Susanto Basu
Market Discipline and Bank Subordinated Debt, Gary Gorton and Anthony M. Santomero, note, 119–28
Meguire, Philip. *See* Roger C. Kormendi
Member Bank Borrowing and the Fed's Contractionary Monetary Policy during the Great Depression, David C. Wheelock, 409–26
Miller, Stephen M. *See* Athanasios G. Noulas
Money and Capital in Economic Development: A Test of the McKinnon Hypothesis for Nepal, John Thornton and Sri Ram Poudyal, note, 395–99
Money Supply Announcements and Market Reactions in an Open Economy, Richard Deaves, 154–64
Money Supply Announcements and the Market's Perception of Federal Reserve Policy, Steven Strongin and Vefa Tarhan, 135–53
Money, Interest, and Banking in Economic Development, Maxwell Fry, reviewed, 131–34
Moschos, Demetrios M. *See* Costas J. Karfakis
Multicountry Characterization of the Nonstationarity of Aggregate Output, A, Roger C. Kormendi and Philip Meguire, 77–93
Musumeci, James J., and Joseph F. Sinkey, Jr., The International Debt Crisis, Investor Contagion, and Bank Security Returns in 1987: The Brazilian Experience, 209–20
______, International Debt Crisis and Bank Loan-Loss-Reserve Decisions: The Signaling Content of Partially Anticipated Events, 370–87

New Results in Support of the Fiscal Ineffectiveness Proposition, Reuven Glick and Michael Hutchison, 288–304
Noulas, Athanasios G., Subhash C. Ray, and Stephen M. Miller, Returns to Scale and Input Substitution for Large U.S. Banks, 94–108

Objectives and Priorities of Monetary Policy under Different Federal Reserve Chairmen, David R. Hakes, 327–37
Optimal Advice for Monetary Policy, Susanto Basu, Miles S. Kimball, N. Gregory Mankiw, and David N. Weil, 19–36

Politics and Perceived Country Creditworthiness in International Banking, Thomas L. Brewer and Pietra Rivoli, 357–69
Poterba, James M., and Julio J. Rotemberg, Inflation and Taxation with Optimizing Governments, 1–18
Poudyal, Sri Ram. *See* John Thornton
Purchasing Power Parity in the Long Run: A Cointegration Approach, Yoonbai Kim, 491–503

Rassekh, Farhad, and Barry Wilbratte, The Effect of Import Price Changes on Domestic Inflation: An Empirical Test of the Ratchet Effect, note, 263–67
Ray, Subhash C. *See* Athanasios G. Noulas
Reinhart, Vincent, Targeting Nominal Income in a Dynamic Model, 427–43
Reserve Requirements and the Inflation Tax,

Dwayne L. Barney, Jr., Alan Frankle, and Harry White, 400–401
Returns to Scale and Input Substitution for Large U.S. Banks, Athanasios G. Noulas, Subhash C. Ray, and Stephen M. Miller, 94–108
Ricardian Equivalence, Rational Expectations, and the Permanent Income Hypothesis, Alfred A. Haug, 305–26
Risk and Parity in Purchasing Power, Roger D. Huang, 338–56
Rivoli, Pietra. *See* Thomas L. Brewer
Rogers, John H., Foreign Inflation Transmission under Flexible Exchange Rates and Currency Substitution, 195–208
Rotemberg, Julio J. *See* James M. Poterba

Salyer, Kevin D., The Term Structure and Time Series Properties of Nominal Interest Rates: Implications from Theory, 478–90
Santomero, Anthony M. *See* Gary Gorton
Savings, Commodity Market Rationing, and the Real Rate of Interest in China, Andrew Feltenstein, David Lebow, and S. van Wijnbergen, 234–52
Scottish Banking and the Legal Restrictions Theory: A Closer Look, Lawrence H. White, comment, 526–36
Shahin, Wassim, book review, 131–34
Sibert, Anne C. *See* Matthew B. Canzoneri
Sinkey, Joseph F., Jr. *See* James J. Musumeci
Stein, Herbert, *Governing the $5 Trillion Economy*, reviewed, 404–408
Strongin, Steven, and Vefa Tarhan, Money Supply Announcements and the Market's Perception of Federal Reserve Policy, 135–53
Sumner, Scott, The Forerunners of "New Monetary Economics" Proposals, note, 109–18
Suzuki, Yoshio, and Mitsuaki Okabe (eds.), *Toward a World of Economic Stability: Optimal Monetary Framework and Policy*, reviewed, 129–31
Swidler, Steve, and David Ketcher, Economic Forecasts, Rationality, and the Processing of New Information over Time, 65–76

Targeting Nominal Income in a Dynamic Model, Vincent Reinhart, 427–43
Tarhan, Vefa. *See* Steven Strongin
Tatom, John A., book review, 268–71
Term Structure and Time Series Properties of Nominal Interest Rates, The: Implications from Theory, Kevin D. Salyer, 478–90
Thornton, John, and Sri Ram Poudyal, Money and Capital in Economic Development: A Test of the McKinnon Hypothesis for Nepal, note, 395–399
Timme, Stephen G. *See* William C. Hunter
Toward a World of Economic Stability: Optimal Monetary Framework and Policy, Yoshio Suzuki and Mitsuaki Okabe (eds.), reviewed, 129–31

Value of Time and the Transactions Demand for Money, The, Kevin Dowd, 51–64

van Wijnbergen, S. *See* David Feltenstein
VanHoose, David. *See* John V. Duca

Weil, David N. *See* Susanto Basu
Wheelock, David C., Member Bank Borrowing and the Fed's Contractionary Monetary Policy during the Great Depression, 409–26
White, Harry. *See* Dwayne L. Barney, Jr.
White, Lawrence H., Scottish Banking and the Legal Restrictions Theory: A Closer Look, comment, 526–36
Wilbratte, Barry. *See* Farhad Rassekh

Yang, Won Keun. *See* William C. Hunter

The Ohio State University Department of Economics Offers Programs of Graduate Study in Economics

The Ohio State University is located in Columbus, capital city of Ohio and a metropolitan area of more than one million people. There are six other institutions of higher education in Columbus as well as the headquarters facility of Battelle Memorial Institute, the largest independent research organization in the world. University students number over fifty thousand, including about eight thousand graduate students. Ohio State is a major center for graduate education, ranking eighth in the nation in degrees conferred. The Ohio State University library system is one of the ten largest library systems in the United States.

Graduate Studies in Economics

The Department of Economics has a faculty of forty members with approximately ninety graduate students in residence at any point in time. The large faculty and relatively small graduate student body make possible in-depth graduate education through close association with outstanding scholars in many different areas. Fields of specialization include:

- Mathematical Economics
- Econometrics
- Money and Finance
- Labor
- Industrial Organization
- Public Finance and Urban Economics
- Monetary Theory and Macroeconomics
- Soviet and Eastern European Studies
- International Trade and Development
- Economic History

Economics graduate students can take elective fields in other departments of the College of Social and Behavioral Sciences or in the Colleges of Business, Agriculture and Home Economics, Engineering, Mathematics, and Physical Sciences when interdisciplinary studies are appropriate.

Fellowships and Assistantships

Because of Ohio State's large undergraduate enrollment and ongoing research programs, there are many part-time teaching and research assistantships that offer financial aid to graduate students. The Department of Economics assists a number of students each year through fellowships and assistantships with stipends ranging from $7,506 to $13,014 per academic year. In addition, teaching, research and administrative assistants, and fellows receive tuition fee waivers. Once a student has been awarded a fellowship or assistantship, financial assistance is possible for as many as five years, provided normal academic progress is maintained.

University Fellowships (stipend $825 per month for 12 months, nonrenewable) are available to well-qualified applicants. In addition, Special University Fellowships (stipend: $825 per month for 12 months, renewable) are available to minority students, primarily blacks of U.S. citizenship.

Additional information about the department may be obtained from the Director of Graduate Studies, Department of Economics, The Ohio State University, 1945 North High Street, Columbus, OH 43210.

Financial Management

The Journal of the Financial Management Association

Vol. 19 | Autumn 1990 | No. 3

TOPICS IN FINANCING AND FINANCIAL INNOVATIONS

11 Pension Funds and Financial Innovation
Zvi Bodie

23 Participation Financing: A Comparison of the Characteristics of Convertible Debt and Straight Bonds Issued in Conjunction with Warrants
Michael S. Long and Stephan E. Sefcik

35 Averaging Options for Capping Total Costs
Peter Ritchken, L. Sankarasubramanian, and Anand M. Vijh

42 Financing with Preferred Stock
Arthur L. Houston, Jr. and Carol Olson Houston

55 The Use of the Over-Allotment Option in Initial Public Offerings of Equity: Risks and Underwriter Prestige
Richard B. Carter and Frederick H. Dark

.....

CAPITAL BUDGETING

65 Managing Investment Opportunities Under Price Uncertainty: From "Last Chance" to "Wait and See" Strategies
Petter Bjerksund and Steinar Ekern

84 Time-Series Processes of Utility Betas: Implications for Forecasting Systematic Risk
Michael J. Gombola and Douglas R. Kahl

Membership dues of the Association include a one-year subscription to the journal. Subscription rates are: Regular $40; Sustaining $45. Library subscriptions are $60 per year. Members outside the U.S. add $6 per year to cover overseas postage. All fees must be in U.S. dollars drawn on a U.S. bank. Write Financial Management Association, College of Business Administration, University of South Florida, Tampa, FL 33620.

FINANCIAL MANAGEMENT ASSOCIATION
CALL FOR PARTICIPATION IN THE 1991 PROGRAM

DATES: October 9-12, 1991
PLACE: Chicago Hyatt Hotel
Chicago, Illinois

DEADLINE: **January 15, 1991**

The Financial Management Association (FMA) brings together practicing financial managers from industry, financial institutions, and nonprofit and governmental organizations and members of the academic community with interests in financial and investment decision making. The twenty-first annual program, scheduled for October 9-12, 1991 at the Chicago Hyatt Hotel, will stress the interrelationships between theory and practice in financial and investment decision making.

FMA members will receive participation forms and information on preparing abstracts or completed papers in mid-November. Other interested parties may request submission materials by contacting David A. Walker at the address listed below. Finally, please mail the participation forms and abstracts/completed papers so they will arrive by January 15, 1991 to:

David A. Walker
Vice President -- 1991 Program
Financial Management Association
University of South Florida
College of Business Administration
Tampa, Florida 33620
(813) 974-2084

Information on registration, placement and other activities can be obtained from:

Financial Management Association
University of South Florida
College of Business Administration
Tampa, Florida 33620
(813) 974-2084

ACKNOWLEDGMENTS

Supporting Subscribers

PITTSBURGH NATIONAL BANK

SECURITY PACIFIC NATIONAL BANK

STATE SAVINGS CO.

Referees

Shaghil Ahmed
Robert B. Anderson
David A. Aschauer
William A. Barnett
Susan Belden
Michael T. Belongia
Benjamin Bental
Keith Blackburn
Mario I. Blejer
Marshall E. Blume
Henning Bohn
William Bomerger
James A. Brander
Joe Brocato
Jan K. Brueckner
John B. Burbidge
Philippe Callier
Charles W. Calomiris
Victor A. Canto
Winston W. Chang
In Choi
Jeffrey A. Clark
Peter K. Clark
Warren L. Coats, Jr.
Timothy Q. Cook
Ramon DeGennaro
Paul DeGrauwe
Charles D. DeLorme, Jr.
Asli Demirguc-Kunt
Behzad T. Diba
Ian Domowitz
Rudiger Dornbusch
John Driffill
David A. Dubofsky
Gerald P. Dwyer, Jr.
Zvi Eckstein
Robert A. Eisenbeis
Paul Evans
James Fackler
Eugene F. Fama
Jon Faust
Michael J. Fishman
Mark J. Flannery
Maxwell J. Fry
Jordi Gali
C. Alan Garner
William T. Gavin
Cynthia A. Glassman
Michael A. Goldberg
Morris Goldstein
Robert J. Gordon
R. W. Hafer
James D. Hamilton
Timothy Hannan
Scott E. Hein
Robert L. Hetzel
Steven A. Holland
Brian R. Horrigan
James Kahn
Miguel A. Kiguel
H. Youn Kim
Miles S. Kimball
Kent P. Kimbrough
Stephen R. King
Mordechai E. Kreinin
Kenneth Kuttner
Mark L. Ladenson
Pok-Sang Lam
Leonardo Leiderman
Raymond E. Lombra
David J. Longworth
Charles Maling
Catherine L. Mann
Roberto S. Mariano
Joram Mayshar
J. Harold McClure
Bill McDonald
Warwick J. McKibbin
Ronald I. McKinnon
Paul D. McNelis
Yash Mehra
Angelo Melino
Arie Melnik
Douglas W. Mitchell
Jeffrey M. Netter
Phillip Obermiller
Maureen J. O'Hara
Tim C. Opler
Milton Pappas
Douglas K. Pearce
Richard L. Peterson
Pentti J. Pikkarainen
William Roberds
Dani Rodrik
John H. Rogers
V. Vance Roley
David H. Romer
Julio J. Rotemberg
Agnar Sandmo
Sherrill Shaffer
Anne C. Sibert
Daniel E. Sichel
Michael L. Smirlock
David E. Spencer
Erich Spitaeller
Sanjay Srivastava
Richard T. Stasiak
John F. Stewart
Scott Sumner
John A. Tatom
Peter Temin
Merih Uctum
David D. VanHoose
Alan D. Viard
George von Furstenberg
Paul A. Wachtel
Walter Wasserfallen
Warren E. Weber
David W. Wilcox
Stephen D. Williamson
Thomas Woodward
Joseph Zeira

Ohio State
University Press

ISSN 0022-2879